Cases in Marketing Management

Kenneth L. Bernhardt

College of Business Administration
Georgia State University

Thomas C. Kinnear

Graduate School of Business Administration
The University of Michigan

W9-CHM-531

Third Edition ■ 1985

BUSINESS PUBLICATIONS, INC. Plano, Texas 75075

ISBN 0-256-03055-3

Library of Congress Catalog Card No. 84–70994

Printed in the United States of America

1 2 3 4 5 6 7 8 9 0 D 2 1 0 9 8 7 6 5

 This modern text is designed to prepare you for your future professional career. While theories, ideas, techniques, and data are dynamic, the information contained in this volume will provide you a quick and useful reference as well as a guide for future learning for many years to come. Your familiarity with the contents of this book will make it an important volume in your professional library.

EX LIBRIS

Cases in
Marketing
Management

To Kathy and Karen
To Connie, Maggie, and Jamie

Preface

Marketing is an exciting and dynamic discipline. Unfortunately much of the excitement is hidden among the definitions and descriptions of concepts that are a necessary part of basic marketing textbooks. We believe that one way to make the study of marketing exciting and dynamic is to use cases. Cases allow the student to work on real marketing problems, to develop an appreciation for the types of problems that exist in the real world of marketing, and to develop the skills of analysis and decision making so necessary for success in marketing and other areas of business. Cases represent as close an approximation of the realities of actually working in marketing as is possible without taking a job in the field.

Your task as a user of this casebook is to work hard to develop well-reasoned solutions to the problems confronting the decision maker in each of the cases. A framework to assist you in developing solutions is presented in Part 1 of this book. Basically you will be using this, or some other framework suggested by your instructor, to analyze the cases in this book. By applying this framework to each case that you are assigned, you will develop your analytic skills. Like all skills, you will find this difficult at first. However, as you practice, you will get better, until it will become second nature to you. This is exactly the same way one develops athletic or musical skills.

The cases in this book represent a broad range of marketing problems. The book contains consumer and industrial cases, profit and nonprofit cases, social marketing cases, specific marketing area cases, and general cases, plus cases on marketing and public policy. Each case is designed to fit into a specific section of a course in marketing management. The cases are long and complex enough to require good analysis, but not so long and complex to be overly burdensome. Within sections, cases do vary in terms of difficulty and complexity.

Users of the first two editions will note that the fundamental thrust and positioning remains the same in this edition. However, we do note the following changes. First, 15 new cases have been added. Second, a number of cases with greater complexity have been added to allow more in-depth work.

This book contains 42 cases and 2 case-related exercises. Twenty of the cases and both exercises were written by the authors of this book. In some instances we had a coauthor and we have noted the names of the coauthors on the title pages of the cases concerned. We wish to thank these coauthors for their assistance and for allowing us to use the cases: Bruce Bassett, Danny N.

Bellenger, C. Merle Crawford, Jeanne DeAmicis, Tom Ingram, Adrienne L. Kelly, Constance M. Kinnear, Duncan LaBay, Larry Robinson, Sherri McIntyre, Jos Viehoff, and John S. Wright. Also, we owe a special thank you to Cynthia Frey, Bonnie Reece, and Sherri McIntyre for their assistance on a number of cases.

We would also like to thank the executives of the companies who allowed us to develop cases about their problems and who have released these cases for use in this book.

The remaining 22 cases were written by many distinguished marketing casewriters. We appreciate their allowing us to reproduce their cases here. The names of each of these persons are noted on the title pages of the cases concerned: Francis Aguilar, Vincent Blasko, C. Merle Crawford, Cynthia Frey, Christopher Gale, Karl Gustafson, Kenneth Hardy, Robert F. Hartley, Cleon L. Hartzell, Jr., Subhash Jain, Robert Jamieson, C. B. Johnston, Constance Kinnear, Jay E. Klompmaker, Fred W. Kniffin, Charles M. Kummel, Aylin Kunt, Zarrel V. Lambert, Theodore Levitt, Iqbal Mather, Michael Mokwa, David Monieson, Jack Moorman, John H. Murphy, James E. Nelson, Douglass G. Norvell, Charles H. Patti, Michael Pearce, Adrian Ryans, Maria Sannella, Donald Schultz, Donald Scotton, Anne Senansky, Stephen A. Snow, Ralph Sorenson, Hiro Takeuchi, George Taucher, Mark Traxler, Larry Uniac, Jos Viehoff, U. Wiechman, and William R. Woolridge.

In writing some of the cases, we were assisted by graduate student casewriters. We appreciate their efforts. They were: Cheryl Allen on the Samahaiku case, Steven Becker on the Consolidated Bathurst Pulp and Paper case, G. Ludwig Laudisi on the Amtrak case, Terry Murphy and Marty Schwartz on the League of Catholic Women case, and William O. Adcock on the Rich's Department Store case.

We should like to thank our colleagues at Georgia State University, the University of Michigan, and the Case Research Association for their helpful comments on early versions of some of the cases. We would specifically like to thank C. Merle Crawford, Claude Martin, James Taylor, Martin Warshaw, and John S. Wright. We would also like to thank James Scott for his direction on the Dutch Foods (A) case.

The Modern Plastics (A) case is copyright to Danny Bellenger and Kenneth Bernhardt, the Doncaster case to John S. Wright and Kenneth Bernhardt, the Jos. Schlitz Brewing Company case to Constance M. Kinnear and Thomas C. Kinnear, the Litton case to Larry Robinson and Kenneth Bernhardt, the AUTOCAP and Law Offices of Gary Greenwald cases to Kenneth Bernhardt, and the RCA Videodisc and The Note on the Video Game Industry—1983 cases to Thomas C. Kinnear.

Finally, we want to thank Duncan Bauer and the Division of Research, Harvard Business School, for their help and support.

Kenneth L. Bernhardt
Thomas C. Kinnear

Contents

Part 1

An Orientation to the Case Method

Chapter 1

Note to the Student on the Case Method

The case method is different from other methods of teaching, and it requires that students take an active role rather than a passive one. The case method places the student in a simulated business environment and substitutes the student in the place of the business manager required to make a set of decisions. To define it, a case is:

> typically a record of a business issue which actually has been faced by business executives, together with surrounding facts, opinions, and prejudices upon which the executives had to depend. These real and particularized cases are presented to students for considered analysis, open discussion, and final decision as to the type of action which should be taken.[1]

With the case method the process of arriving at an answer is what is important. The instructor's expectation is that the student will develop an ability to make decisions, to support those decisions with appropriate analysis, and to learn to communicate ideas both orally and in writing. The student is required to determine the problem as well as the solution. This method of teaching thus shifts much of the responsibility to the student, and a great deal of time is required on the part of the student.

The case method often causes a great deal of insecurity on the part of students who are required to make decisions often with very little information and limited time. There is no single right answer to any of the cases in this book, an additional source of insecurity. The goal is not to develop a set of right answers, but to learn to reason well with the data available. This process is truly learning by doing.

Studying under the case method will result in the development of skills in critical thinking. The student will learn how to effectively reason when dealing with specific problems. The development of communication skills is also important, and students will learn to present their analysis in a cogent and

---

[1] Charles I. Gragg, "Because Wisdom Can't Be Told," *Harvard Alumni Bulletin*, October 19, 1940.

convincing manner. They must defend their analysis and plan of action against the criticism of others in the class. In the class discussion, individual students may find that the opinions of other members of the class differ from their own. In some cases this will be because the individual has overlooked certain important points or that some factors have been weighted more heavily compared to the weighting used by other students. The process of presenting and defending conflicting points of view causes individual members of the class to reconsider the views they had of the case before the discussion began. This leads to a clearer perception of problems, a recognition of the many and often conflicting interpretations of the facts and events in the case, and a greater awareness of the complexities with which management decisions are reached.

In preparing for class using the case method, the student should first read the case quickly. The goal is to gain a feel for the type of problem presented in the case, the type of organization involved, and so on. Next, the student should read the case thoroughly to learn all the key facts in the case. The student should not blindly accept all the data presented, as not all information is equally reliable or relevant. As part of the process of mastering the facts, it frequently will be desirable to utilize the numerical data presented in the case to make any possible calculations and comparisons that will help analyze the problems involved in the case. The case will have to be read a number of times before the analysis is completed.

The student must add to the facts by making reasonable assumptions regarding many aspects of the situation. Business decision making is rarely based on perfect information. All of the cases in this book are actual business cases and the student is provided with all the information that the executives involved had at their disposal. Often students cannot believe the low level of information available for decision making, but this is often the case. What is required in those situations is the making of reasonable assumptions and learning to make decisions under uncertainty. There is often a strong reluctance on the part of the student to do this, but the ability to make decisions based on well-reasoned assumptions is a skill that must be developed for a manager to be truly effective.

Once the student has mastered the facts in the case, the next step is to identify and specify the issues and problems toward which the executive involved should be directing his or her attention. Often the issues may be very obscure. Learning to separate problems from symptoms is an important skill to learn. Often there will be a number of subissues involved and it will be necessary to break the problem down into component parts.

The next step in the student's case preparation is to identify alternative courses of action. Usually there are a number of possible solutions to the problems in the case, and the student should be careful not to lock in on only one alternative before several possible alternatives have been thoroughly evaluated.

The next step is to evaluate each of the alternative plans of action. It is at this stage of the analysis that the student is required to marshall and analyze all the facts for each alternative program. The assumptions the student is required to make are very important here, and the student must apply all the analytical skills possible, including both qualitative and quantitative.

After all the alternatives have been thoroughly analyzed, the student must make a decision concerning the specific course of action to take. It should be recognized that several of the alternatives may ''work,'' and that there are a number of different ways of resolving the issues in the case. The important consideration is that the plan of action actually decided upon has been thoroughly analyzed from all angles, is internally consistent, and has a high probability of meeting the manager's objectives.

Once an overall strategy has been determined, it is important that consideration be given to the implementation of that strategy. At this stage, the student must determine who is to do what, when, and how. A professor may start out a class by asking the question, ''What should Mr. Jones do tomorrow?'' Unless the students have given some thought to the implementation of the strategy decided upon, they will be unprepared for such a question. Improper implementation of an excellent strategy may doom it to failure, so it is important to follow through with appropriate analysis at this stage.

During the class discussion the instructor will act more as a moderator than a lecturer, guiding the discussion and calling on students for their opinions. A significant amount of learning will take place by participating in the discussion. The goal is for the students to integrate all their ideas, relating them to the goals of the company, the strengths and weaknesses of the company and its competition, the way consumers buy, and the resources available. A suggested framework for the integration of these ideas is presented in the next chapter of this book in the Appendix titled ''Outline for case analysis.''

The student's classroom discussion should avoid the rehashing, without analysis, of case facts. Students should recognize that the professor and all the other students in the class have thoroughly read the case and are familiar with the facts. The objective therefore is to interpret the facts and use them to support the proposed plan of action. The case method obviously requires a great deal of preparation time by the student. The payoff is that after spending this time adequately preparing each of the steps described, the student will have developed the ability to make sound marketing management decisions.

Chapter 2

Introduction to Marketing Decision Making

In Chapter 1, you were introduced to your role in the execution of an effective case course in marketing. In summary, the primary task is to complete a competent analysis of the cases assigned to you. If you have never undertaken the analysis of a marketing case before, you are probably wondering just how you should go about doing this. Is there some framework that is appropriate for this task? Indeed, there are a number of such frameworks. The purpose of this chapter is to present one such framework to you. We think you will find it useful in analyzing the cases in this book.

An Outline for Case Analysis

The Appendix to this chapter is the summary document for the approach we believe that you should use for case analysis. We suggest that you apply the types of questions listed there in your analysis. Figure 2–1 provides an overview of this outline. Basically, we are suggesting that you begin by doing a complete analysis of the *situation* facing the organization in the case. This *situation analysis* includes an assessment of (1) the nature of demand for the product, (2) the extent of demand, (3) the nature of competition, (4) the environmental climate, (5) the stage of the life cycle for the product, (6) the skills of the firm, (7) the financial resources of the firm, and (8) the distribution structure. In some cases legal aspects may also form part of a good situation analysis. The premise here is that one cannot begin to make decisions until a thorough understanding of the situation at hand is obtained.

Once a detailed situation analysis is prepared, one is in a position to summarize the *problems* and *opportunities* that arise out of the situation analysis. These problems and opportunities provide an organized summary of the situation analysis. This in turn should lead to the generation of a set of *alternatives* that are worthy of being considered as solutions to the problems and actualizers of the opportunities.

FIGURE 2-1 Overview of a framework for case analysis

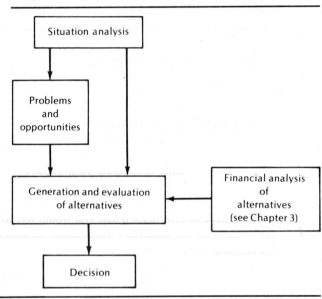

These alternatives are then *evaluated* using arguments generated from (1) the detailed situation analysis, (2) the summary statement of problems and opportunities, and (3) relevant financial analysis (break-even points, market shares, and so on). The use of financial analysis is discussed in Chapter 3. The point here is that we use the situation analysis to generate and evaluate alternative programs. The pros and cons of each alternative are weighed as part of this evaluation and a *decision* is then reached.

A Good Case Analysis

The question naturally arises: In applying the outline in the Appendix to a case, how do I know when I have done a good analysis? The purpose of this section is to raise some points that are often used by instructors to evaluate either an oral or written analysis.

  1. Be complete. It is imperative that the case analysis be complete. There are two dimensions to this issue. First is that each area of the situation analysis must be discussed, problems and opportunities must be identified, alternatives must be presented and evaluated using the situation analysis and relevant financial analysis, and a decision must be made. An analysis that omits parts of the situation analysis, or only recognizes one alternative, is not a good analysis. Second, each area above must be covered in good depth and with insight.

2. Avoid rehashing case facts. Every case has a lot of factual information. A good analysis uses facts that are relevant to the situation at hand to make summary points of analysis. A poor analysis just restates or rehashes these facts without making relevant summary comments. Consider the use of a set of financial facts that might appear in a case:

Rehash: The current ratio is 1.5:1, cash on hand is $15,000, retained earnings are $50,000.

Analysis: Because of a very weak financial position, as demonstrated by a poor cash position and current ratio, the firm will be constrained in the activities it can undertake to ones requiring little immediate cash outlay.

3. Make reasonable assumptions. Every case is incomplete in terms of some piece of information that you would like to have. We would, of course, like to have all the necessary information presented to us in each case. This is not possible for two reasons. First, it would make the cases far too long to be capable of being analyzed in a reasonable period of time. Second, and more important, incomplete information is an accurate reflection of the real world. All marketing decisions are made on the basis of incomplete information. Often, it just costs too much or takes too long to collect the desired information.

A good case analysis must make realistic assumptions to fill in the gaps of information in the case. For example, the case may not describe the purchase decision process for the product of interest. A poor analysis would either omit mentioning this or just state that no information is available. A good analysis would attempt to present this purchase decision process, by classifying the product (a shopping good?), and drawing on the student's real-life experience. Could you not describe the purchase decision process for carpeting, even though you have never read a research report about it?

The reasonableness of your assumptions will be challenged by your fellow students and instructor. This is one of the things that makes case discussions exciting. The point is that it is better to make your assumptions explicit and incorporate them in your analysis than to use them implicitly or not make them at all. If we make explicit assumptions we can later come back and see if our assumptions were correct or not.

4. Don't confuse symptoms with problems. In summarizing a firm's problems a poor analysis confuses the symptoms with real problems. For example, one might list two problems as (1) sales are down and (2) sales force turnover is high. This would not be correct. These are symptoms. The real problem is identified by answering the question: Why are sales down or why is sales force turnover high? For example, sales force turnover may be high due to inadequate sales training. But this may not yet be the root problem. You still need to ask: Why is sales training inadequate? It may be that the sales manager has ignored this area through his or her lack of knowledge of how to train people. What you do is keep asking "why" until you are satisfied that you have identified the root problem.

5. *Don't confuse opportunities with taking action.* One can recognize an opportunity, but not take any action related to it. For example, a large market for a product may exist. This is an opportunity. However, a firm may decide not to compete in this market due to lack of resources or skills or the existence of strong competition. Decisions involve the complex trading-off of many problems and opportunities. Thus, don't make statements that direct action: "target to . . . ; promote as . . . ;" and the like as opportunity statements.

6. *Deal with objectives realistically.* Most cases present a statement from management about their objectives. For example, it might say they want a sales growth rate of 25 percent per year. Good analysis critically evaluates statements of objectives and revises them if necessary. Then it uses these revised objectives as part of the argument about which alternative to select. Poor analysis either ignores the stated objectives or accepts them at face value.

7. *Recognize alternatives.* A good analysis explicitly recognizes and discusses alternative action plans. In some cases, these alternatives are stated in the case. In other cases, the student must develop alternatives beyond those stated in the case. A poor analysis explicitly recognizes only one or two alternatives or only takes the ones explicitly stated in the case.

8. *Don't be assertive.* In some case analyses, the decision that was made is clear to the reader or listener in about the first sentence of the situation analysis. The whole rest of the analysis is then a justification of the desired solution. This type of analysis is very poor. It in effect has asserted an answer before completing a situation analysis. Usually, other alternatives are ignored or treated as all bad, and the desired solution is treated as all good. You must do your situation analysis and recognize alternatives before evaluating them and reaching a decision.

9. *Discuss the pros and cons of each alternative.* Every alternative always has pros and cons. A good analysis explicitly discusses these. In a poor analysis there is no explicit discussion of the pros and cons of each alternative. Problem and opportunity statements serve as the basis of your pro (opportunities) and con (problems) discussion. Different ones relate to specific alternatives.

10. *Make effective use of financial and other quantitative information.* Financial data (break-even points and so on) and information derived from other quantitative analyses can add a great deal to a good case analysis.

Totally ignoring these aspects or handling them improperly results in a poor case analysis. This analysis should be presented in detail in a written appendix or in class if asked for. However, in the body of a paper or in an oral discussion present only the summary conclusions out of the analysis. Say: "The break-even point is 220,000 units," and be prepared to present the detail if asked.

11. Reach a clear decision. You must reach a clear decision. You might like to hedge your bets and say "maybe this, maybe that." However, part of the skill of decision making is to be forced to reach a decision under ambiguous circumstances and then be prepared to defend this decision. This does not mean that you do not recognize limitations of your position or positive aspects of other positions. It just means that despite all that, you have reached a particular decision.

12. Make good use of evidence developed in your situation analysis. In reaching a decision, a good analysis reaches a decision that is logically consistent with the situation analysis that was done. This is the ultimate test of an analysis. Other students may disagree with your situation analysis and thus your resultant conclusion, but they should not be able to fault the logical connection between your situation analysis and decision. If they can, you have a poor case analysis.

The "Outline for case analysis" contained in the Appendix is designed to assist you in doing case analysis. You should keep the points stressed in this section in mind when you apply this outline.

Appendix

Outline for case analysis*

Overview of Analysis Structure

I. Situation analysis
   A. Nature of demand.
   B. Extent of demand.
   C. Nature of competition.
   D. Environmental climate.
   E. Stage of product life cycle.
   F. Cost structure of the industry.
   G. Skills of the firm.
   H. Financial resources of the firm.
   I. Distribution structure.
II. Problems and opportunities
   A. Key problem areas.
   B. Key opportunities.
   C. On balance, the situation is.
III. Generation and evaluation of alternative marketing programs
   A. Objectives defined.
   B. Marketing mix/program decisions.
IV. Decision

Details of Analysis Structure

I. SITUATION ANALYSIS

A. Nature of demand

The purpose of this section is to make *explicit* your beliefs and assumptions regarding the nature of the purchase decision process (consumer or industrial) for the goods or services under investigation. In case analysis we are concerned primarily with developing your *skills* of analysis to identify areas of problems and opportunities and in developing well-supported marketing program recommendations. Conflicting student beliefs and assumptions should lead to interesting and enlightening class discussion regarding the nature of the purchase decision process and its implication for marketing programs. We hope that through this type of class discussion, you will increase your sensitivity to, and understanding of,

---

* This outline is adapted from an unpublished note by Professor James R. Taylor of the University of Michigan. Used with permission.

buyers and their behavior. Again, the value of this type of analysis concerns its application to better *reasoned* and *supported* marketing program decisions. Hopefully, the development of your skills in this area has value in improving your *judgment capabilities* and in increasing your understanding of marketing decision making.

Analysis areas and questions

1. How do buyers (consumer and industrial) currently go about buying existing products or services? Describe the main types of behavior patterns and attitudes.

    a. Number of stores shopped or industrial sources considered.
    b. Degree of overt information seeking.
    c. Degree of brand awareness and loyalty.
    d. Location of product category decision—home or point of sale.
    e. Location of brand decision—home or point of sale.
    f. Sources of product information and current awareness and knowledge levels.
    g. Who makes the purchase decision—male, female, adult, child, purchasing agent, buying committee, so on?
    h. Who influences the decision maker?
    i. Individual or group decision (computers versus candy bar).
    j. Duration of the decision process (repeat, infrequent, or new purchase situation).
    k. Buyer's interest, personal involvement or excitement regarding the purchase (hairpins versus trip to Caribbean).
    l. Risk or uncertainty of negative purchase outcome—high, medium, or low (specialized machinery versus hacksaw blades) (pencil versus hair coloring).
    m. Functional versus psychosocial considerations (electric drill versus new dress).
    n. Time of consumption (gum versus dining room furniture).

    Basically, we are attempting to determine the *who, what, where, when, why,* and *how* of the purchase decision.

    Note: The key to using the above analysis is to ask what are the implications for marketing programs? For example, if the purchase (brand) decision is made in the store and branding is not important to the buyers, what implication does this have for national TV advertising versus in-store display? Do you see how you might *use* this information to support a recommendation for intensive distribution and point-of-purchase promotion and display?

2. Can the market be meaningfully segmented or broken into several homogeneous groups with respect to "what they want" and "how they buy"? Criteria:

    a. Age.

  b. Family life cycle.
  c. Geographic location.
  d. Heavy versus light users.
  e. Nature of the buying process.
  f. Product usage.

Note: For each case situation, you should determine whether a more effective marketing program could be developed for each segment versus having an overall program for all segments. The real issue is whether tailoring your program to a segment will give you a competitive advantage. Of course, there may be negatives to this strategy in terms of volume and cost considerations.

B. Extent of demand

   The purpose of this section is to evaluate demand in an aggregate and quantitative sense. We are basically concerned with the actual or potential size of the overall market and developing sound estimates of company sales potential.

Analysis areas and questions

1. What is the size of the market (units and dollars) now and what will the future hold?
2. What are the current market shares and what are the selective demand trends (units and dollars)?
3. Is it best to analyze the market on an aggregate or on a segmented basis?

  Note: We are basically concerned with making *explicit* assumptions regarding primary and selective demand trends. These estimates are critical to determining the profit (loss) potential of alternative marketing programs.

C. Nature of competition

   The purpose of this section is to evaluate the present and future structure of competition. The key is to understand how the buyer evaluates alternative products or services relative to his or her needs.

Analysis areas and questions

1. What is the present and future structure of competition?
  a. Number of competitors (5 versus 2,000).
  b. Market shares.
  c. Financial resources.
  d. Marketing resources and skills.
  e. Production resources and skills.
2. What are the current marketing programs of established competitors? Why are they successful or unsuccessful?
3. Is there an opportunity for another competitor? Why?
4. What are the anticipated retaliatory moves of competitors? Can they neutralize different marketing programs we might develop?

  Note: Failure to correctly evaluate demand and competition is one common reason for unprofitable marketing programs. Also, Sections A, B, and

C are analysis areas particularly important in making decisions concerning "positioning" your product and developing the marketing program to support your positioning strategy.

D. Environmental climate

It's not hard to identify current marketing programs that have been highly disrupted by a changing environmental climate. The energy crisis together with pollution, safety, and consumerism concerns, can bring many such examples to mind. We are sure you can identify firms who have benefited from the energy crisis. The point is that the environment is constantly changing and those organizations which can adapt to change are the ones which enjoy long-run success.

Analysis areas and questions
1. What are the relevant social, political, economic, and technological trends?
2. How do you evaluate these trends? Do they represent opportunities or problems?

E. Stage of product life cycle

The purpose of this section is to make explicit assumptions about where a product is in its life cycle. This is important because the effectiveness of particular marketing variables may vary by stages of the life cycle.

Analysis areas and questions
1. In what stage of the life cycle is the product category?
    a. What is the chronological age of the product category? (Younger more favorable than older?)
    b. What is the state of the consumers' knowledge of the product category? (More complete the knowledge—more unfavorable?)
2. What market characteristics support your stage of life cycle evaluation?

F. Cost structure of the industry

Here we are concerned with the amount and composition of the marginal or additional cost of supplying increased output. It can be argued that the lower these costs, the easier it may be to cover the costs of developing an effective marketing program (see accompanying table). Basically one is relating the level of fixed cost to variable cost.

	Marginal costs	
	High*	Low†
Selling price per unit	$1.00	$1.00
Variable costs per unit	0.80	0.10
Contribution per unit	$0.20	$0.90

* Such as the garment and auto industries.
† Such as the hotel and telephone industries.

G. Skills of the firm

The purpose of this section is to critically evaluate the organization making the decision. Here, we effectively place limits on what they are capable of accomplishing.

Analysis areas and questions

1. Do we have the skills and experience to perform the functions necessary to be in this business?
    a. Marketing skills.
    b. Production skills.
    c. Management skills.
    d. Financial skills.
    e. R&D skills.
2. How do our skills compare to competitors?
    a. Production fit.
    b. Marketing fit.
    c. Etc.

H. Financial resources of the firm

Analysis areas and questions

1. Do we have the funds to support an effective marketing program?
2. Where are the funds coming from, and when will they be available?

I. Distribution structure

The purpose of this area is to identify and evaluate the availability of channels of distribution.

Analysis areas and questions

1. What channels exist and can we gain access to the channels?
2. Cost versus revenue from different channels?
3. Feasibility of using multiple channels?
4. Nature and degree of within and between channel competition?
5. Trends in channel structure?
6. Requirements of different channels for promotion and margin?
7. Will it be profitable for particular channels to handle my product?

II. PROBLEMS AND OPPORTUNITIES

Here we prepare a definite listing of *key* problems and opportunities identified from the situation analysis which relate to the specific issues or decision questions faced by management.

A. Key problem areas

B. Key opportunities

C. On balance, the situation is:
1. Very favorable.
2. Somewhat favorable.
3. Neutral.

4. Somewhat unfavorable.
5. Very unfavorable.

Note: At this point, the critical issue is whether a profitable marketing program can be formulated or whether a current marketing program needs to be changed in order to overcome the problem areas and/or take advantage of opportunities.

III. EVALUATION OF ALTERNATIVE MARKETING PROGRAMS

A marketing program consists of a series of marketing mix decisions which represent an integrated and consistent "action plan" for achieving predetermined goals. Different marketing programs may be required for various target segments. For a given target segment, alternative programs should be formulated and evaluated as to the effectiveness of each in achieving predetermined goals.

A. Objectives defined
1. Target market segments identified.
2. Volume to be sold (dollars or units).
3. Profit analysis (contribution analysis, break-even analysis, ROI, etc.).

B. Marketing mix/program decisions
1. Product decisions
   a. Develop new product(s).
   b. Change current product(s).
   c. Add or drop product from line.
   d. Product positioning.
   e. Branding (national, private, secondary).
2. Distribution decisions
   a. Intensity of distribution (intensive to exclusive).
   b. Multiple channels.
   c. Types of wholesalers and retailers (discounters, so on).
   d. Degree of channel directness.
3. Promotion decisions
   a. Mix of personal selling, advertising, dealer incentives, and sales promotion.
   b. Branding—family versus individual.
   c. Budget.
   d. Message.
   e. Media.
4. Price decisions
   a. Price level (above, same or below).
   b. Price variation (discount structure, geographic).
   c. Margins.
   d. Administration of price level.
   e. Price leadership.

Note: The above four decision areas involve specific strategy issues which together form a marketing program.

The key to effective marketing decision making is to evaluate alternative marketing programs using information from the situation analysis. The pros and cons for each alternative should be presented and discussed.

IV.   DECISION

The outcome of the evaluation of alternatives is a decision. You must make a decision. Case analysis is designed to develop your skills in making well-supported and reasoned marketing decisions. The quality of your reasoning is much more important than reaching any particular decision. Generally, if your situation analysis is different (you perceive the facts differently and have made different assumptions) from someone else, you should reach different decisions.

Chapter 3

Financial Analysis for Marketing Decision Making

In Chapter 2, we laid out an approach to marketing decision making. The "Outline for case analysis" summarized this approach. There is, however, one more important aspect of a competent case analysis that was not presented in that outline. This is the financial analysis of the alternatives presented in a case.

The ultimate goals of all marketing activities are usually expressed in financial terms. The company has a particular return on investment in mind, or growth in earnings per share. Proposed marketing activities must thus be evaluated for their financial implications. Can you imagine asking your boss for $1 million for a new distribution center or an advertising program without having to present the financial implications of such a request? It does not happen in the real marketing world, nor should it happen in a good case analysis.

Financial analysis can be complex. Our purpose here is to present some simple financial calculations that can be useful in case analysis. More sophisticated financial techniques are left to courses in financial management. Basically, the advanced techniques add little to the understanding of the cases in this book, and take too much time and effort for the reader to implement.

It should clearly be understood that financial considerations are only one aspect in the evaluation of marketing alternatives. Marketing alternatives cannot be reduced to a set of numbers. Qualitative aspects derived from the situation analysis are also relevant. Sometimes the qualitative aspects are consistent in terms of pointing to an alternative to select. In other cases, they may point to different alternatives. The task of the student is to formulate both types of arguments for each alternative, and to select an alternative based upon which arguments the student thinks should carry the most weight.

This chapter assumes that the student is familiar with elementary financial accounting concepts. What we will present here are some useful concepts not usually presented in basic accounting courses.

Contribution

Contribution per unit is defined as the difference between the selling price of an item and the variable costs of producing and selling that item. It is in essence the amount of money per unit available to the marketer to cover fixed production costs, corporate overhead and having done that, to yield a profit. So, if a manufacturer sells an item for $12.00, and the variable costs are $8.40, then

$$SP - VC = C$$

$$
\begin{aligned}
\text{Contribution per unit} &= \text{Selling price} - \text{Variable costs} \\
&= \$12.00 \quad\quad - \$8.40 \\
&= \$ \ 3.60
\end{aligned}
$$

Each unit this company sells gives it $3.60 to cover fixed costs.

Total contribution is the contribution per unit times the number of units sold. So, if this firm sold 20,000 units:

$$
\begin{aligned}
\text{Total contribution} &= \text{Contribution per unit} \times \text{Units sold} \\
&= \$ \ 3.60 \times 20,000 \\
&= \$72,000
\end{aligned}
$$

If the total relevant fixed costs of this product were $42,000, the *profit* earned by this product would be:

$$
\begin{aligned}
\text{Profit} &= \text{Total contribution} - \text{Fixed costs} \\
&= \$72,000 \quad\quad - \$42,000 \\
&= 30,000
\end{aligned}
$$

Costs

$$VC = Fixed\ per\ unit$$

$$FV = Vary\ per\ unit$$

In determining contributions and profit we used the terms variable cost and fixed cost. At this point we want to define them more formally. Variable costs are those costs that are fixed *per unit* and therefore, vary in their total amount depending upon the number of units produced and sold. That is, it takes a certain amount of raw materials and labor to produce a unit of product. The more we produce the more total variable costs are.

Fixed costs are costs that remain constant in *total amount* despite changes in the volume of production or sales. These costs would thus vary per unit depending upon the number of units produced or sold.

Sorting out which costs are variable and fixed is important in good case analysis. The rule to apply is: if it varies in *total* as volume changes, it is a variable cost. Thus, labor, raw materials, packaging, salesperson's commissions would be variable costs. Note that all marketing costs except commissions would be considered fixed costs. Don't be fooled if a marketing cost or other fixed cost is presented in a per unit form. It may look like a variable cost, but it is not. It is only that much per unit at one given volume. For example, if we are told that advertising cost per unit will be $1, what this means is that at the end of the year when we divide total sales into advertising expenditures the result is expected to be $1 per unit. What we must be told is at what volume advertising is expected to be $1 per unit. If the expected volume level is 300,000 units, we then know that the firm intends to spend $300,000 ($1 × 300,000 units) on advertising. This $300,000 is a fixed cost. Note that if they sold less than 300,000 units, the cost per unit would exceed $1 and vice versa. So beware of fixed costs that are allocated to units and presented in a per unit form.

Break Even

A solid perspective on many marketing alternatives can often be obtained by determining the unit or dollar sales necessary to cover all relevant fixed costs. This sales level is called the break-even point. We define

$$1. \quad \text{Break-even point in units} = \frac{\text{Total fixed costs}}{\text{Contribution per unit}}$$

$$2. \quad \text{Break-even point in dollars} = \frac{\text{Total fixed costs}}{1 - \dfrac{\text{Variable cost per unit}}{\text{Selling price per unit}}}$$

or

$$= \text{Break-even point in units} \times \text{Selling price per unit}$$

Let's illustrate these definitions. Suppose that (1) direct labor is $7.50 per unit, (2) raw materials are $2 per unit, (3) selling price is $22 per unit, (4) advertising and sales force costs are $400,000, and (5) other relevant fixed costs are $100,000.

$$
\begin{aligned}
\text{Contribution per unit} &= \text{Selling price} - \text{Variable costs} \\
\text{Contribution per unit} &= \$22.00 - (7.50 + \$2.00) \\
&= \$22.00 - \$9.50 \\
&= \$12.50
\end{aligned}
$$

$$
\begin{aligned}
\text{Break-even point in units} &= \frac{\text{Total fixed costs}}{\text{Contribution per unit}} \\
&= \frac{\$400,000 + \$100,000}{\$12.50} \\
&= 40,000 \text{ units}
\end{aligned}
$$

$$
\begin{aligned}
\text{Break-even point in dollars} &= \frac{\$500,000}{1 - \dfrac{\$9.50}{\$22.00}} \\
&= \frac{\$500,000}{1 - 0.4318181} = \$880,000
\end{aligned}
$$

Alternatively

$$
\begin{aligned}
\text{Break-even point in dollars} &= 40,000 \times \$22.00 \text{ per unit} \\
&= \$880,000
\end{aligned}
$$

Profit Targets

Breaking even is not as much fun as making a profit. Thus, we often want to incorporate a profit target level into our calculations. Basically, we are answering the question: at what volume do we earn $X profits? Covering a profit target is just like covering a fixed cost. So in the previous example, if we set $60,000 as our profit target we would have to sell an additional number of units equal to:

$$\text{Units to cover profit target} = \frac{\text{Profit target}}{\text{Contribution per unit}}$$

$$= \frac{\$60,000}{\$12.50} = 4,800 \text{ units}$$

Total units to reach this target is

$$40,000 + 4,800 = 44,800 \text{ or } \frac{\$500,000 + \$60,000}{\$12.50} = 44,800$$

Break-even analysis is a useful tool for comparing alternative marketing programs. It tells us how many units must be sold, but does not help us with the critical question of how many units will be sold.

Market Share

$$\text{Market share} = \frac{\text{Company sales level}}{\text{Total market sales}}$$

This calculation adds perspective to proposed action plans. Suppose that the total market sales are 290,000 units and our sales level needed to break even is 40,000 units. Thus, the required market share to break even is:

$$\frac{40,000}{290,000} = 13.8\%$$

The question then to ask is whether this market share can be obtained with the proposed marketing program.

Capital Expenditures

Often a particular marketing program proposes expenditures for capital equipment. These would be fixed costs associated with the proposed program. Typically, they should not be all charged to the relevant fixed cost for that proposal. For example, suppose that $5 million are to be expended for equipment that will last 10 years. If we charge all this to the break-even calculation in year one, it will be very high. Further, for years 2 through 10, the break-even point will fall substantially. It is better to allocate this $5 million equally over the 10 years. Thus $500,000 would be a relevant fixed cost in each year associated with the equipment. What one needs to do is to make some reasonable assumption about the useful life of capital assets and divide the total cost over this time period.

Relevant Costs

The issue often arises as to what fixed costs are relevant to a particular proposal. The rule to use is: a fixed cost is relevant if the expenditure varies due to the acceptance of that proposal. Thus, new equipment, new research and development, and so on, are relevant. Last year's advertising or previous research and development dollars, for example, do not vary with the current decision and thus are not a relevant cost of the proposed program. Past expenditures are referred to as *sunk costs*. They should not enter into current decisions. Decisions are future oriented.

Corporate overhead presents a special problem. Generally, it does not vary with a particular decision. We don't fire the president in selecting between marketing programs. However, in some instances, some overhead may be directly attributable to a particular decision. In this instance it would be a relevant cost. We should recognize that to stay in business a firm must cover all its costs in the long run. Also, from a financial accounting point of view all costs are relevant. This type of accounting is concerned with preparing income statements and balance sheets for reporting to investors. In marketing decision making we are interested in managerial, not financial, accounting. Managerial accounting is concerned with providing relevant information for decision making, It, therefore, only presents costs that are relevant to the decision being considered. Such things as allocated overhead or amortized research and development costs only serve to confuse future-oriented decisions.

Margins

Often a case will present us with a retail selling price, when what we really want to know is the manufacturer's selling price. To be able to work back to get the manufacturer's selling price, we must understand how channel margins work.

When firms buy a product at a particular price and attempt to sell it at a higher price, the difference between the cost price and the selling price is called margin or markup or mark-on. Thus,

$$\text{Selling price} = \text{Cost price} + \text{Margin}$$

An example could be:

$$\$1.00 = \$0.80 + \$0.20$$

So a company has bought a product for $0.80, added on a $0.20 margin and is charging $1.00 for the product.

Margins are usually expressed as percentages. This raises the question as to the base on which the margin percentage should be expressed: the cost price or the selling price. Here, if the $0.20 margin is expressed as a percentage of selling price the margin is $0.20/$1.00 = 20 percent. If it were expressed as a percentage of cost price, the margin is $0.20/$0.80 = 25 percent. The most common practice in marketing is to express margins as a percentage of selling price. Margins expressed in this fashion are easier to work with, especially in a multilevel channel situation. Unless explicitly stated otherwise, you may assume that all margins in the cases in this book use selling price as the relevant base.

A number of different types of margin-related problems arise. They include:

1. Determining the selling price, given you know the cost price and the percentage margin on selling price. Suppose that a retailer buys an appliance for $15 and wants to obtain a margin on selling price of 40 percent. What selling price must be charged? The answer $21 is not correct because this margin ($6 = $15 × 0.4) would be on cost price. To answer this question we must remember one fundamental relationship. This is that

$$\text{Selling price} = \text{Cost price} + \text{Margin}$$

Here we are taking selling price as the base equal to 100 percent, so we can write

$$100\% = \$15 + 40\%$$

That is, the cost price plus the margin must add to 100 percent. Clearly the $15 must then be 60 percent of the desired selling price. Thus,

$$\text{Derived selling price} = \$15/60\%$$
$$= \$25$$

The dollar margin is then $10 which is $10/$25 = 40 percent of selling price. The general rule then is to divide one minus the percentage margin expressed as a decimal on selling price, into the cost price. For example, if cost price is $105 and the margin on selling price is 22.5 percent, then the desired selling price is $105/(1 − 0.225) = $105/0.775 = $135.48.

2. Conversion of margin bases. Sometimes a margin is given on a cost price basis, and we wish to convert it to a selling price base or vice versa. How do we make the conversion? Suppose that a product costs $4.50 and sells for $6.00. The margin is $1.50. On a selling price basis the margin is $1.50/$6.00 = 25 percent. On a cost price basis the margin is $1.50/$4.50 = 33.33 percent. The conversion from one percentage margin to the other is easy if we remember that selling price is composed of two parts: margin and cost.

For selling price base.

$$\text{Selling price} = \text{Margin} + \text{Cost}$$
$$\$6.00 = \$1.50 + \$4.50$$

or more important

$$100\% = 25\% + 75\%$$

For cost price base.

$$\text{Selling price} = \text{Margin} + \text{Cost}$$
$$\$6.00 = \$1.50 + \$4.50$$

but here the cost is the 100 percent <u>base,</u> so

$$\$6.00 = \$1.50 + 100\%$$

or

$$133.33\% = 33.33\% + 100\%$$

That is, the selling price should be thought of as 133.33 percent of the cost price.
Conversion from selling price to cost price base.

$$\text{Selling price} = \text{Margin} + \text{Cost}$$
$$100\% = 25\% + 75\%$$

So if we want to convert the 25 percent margin to a cost price basis, the 75 percent that is the cost becomes the relevant base and

$$\text{Margin as a percentage of cost price} = \frac{25\%}{75\%} = 33.33\%$$

Note that this is exactly the same as dividing $1.50 by $4.50.

A simple formula for making this conversion is

$$\text{Percentage margin on cost price} = \frac{\text{Percentage margin on selling price}}{100\% - \text{Percentage margin on selling price}}$$

In our example this is

$$\frac{25\%}{100\% - 25\%} = \frac{25\%}{75\%} = 33.33\%$$

Note that the only piece of information that we need to make this conversion is the margin percentage on selling price.

Conversion from cost price to selling price base.

$$\text{Selling price} = \text{Margin} + \text{Cost}$$
$$133.33\% = 33.33\% + 100\%$$

The margin is 33.33 percent and the relevant selling price base is 133.33 percent, so

$$\text{Margin as a percentage of selling price} = \frac{33.33\%}{133.33\%} = 25\%$$

Note that this is exactly the same as dividing $1.50 by $6.00.

A simple formula for making this conversion is

$$\frac{\text{Percentage margin on selling price}}{} = \frac{\text{Percentage margin on cost price}}{100\% + \text{Percentage margin on cost price}}$$

In our example this is

$$\frac{33.33\%}{100\% + 33.33\%} = \frac{33.33\%}{133.33\%} = 25\%$$

Note that the only piece of information that we need to make this conversion is the margin percentage on cost price.

Multiple Margins

Often a manufacturer gives a suggested retail selling price and suggested retail and wholesale margins. For example, the suggested retail price may be $7.50 with a retail margin of 20 percent and a wholesale margin of 15 percent. To determine the manufacturer's selling price in this situation we simply take the appropriate margins off one at a time. Thus

Retail selling price	$7.50
Less retail margin (20% of $7.50)	1.50
Equals retail cost price or wholesale selling price	6.00
Less wholesale margin (15% of $6.00)	0.90
Equals wholesale cost price or manufacturer's selling price	$5.10

No matter how many levels there are in the channel, the approach is the same. We simply take the margins off one at a time. Note that we cannot just add up the margins and subtract this amount. Here 20% + 15% = 35%, and 35% of $7.50 is $2.63, making the manufacturer's selling price $7.50 − $2.63 = $4.87. This is not correct.

This chapter has outlined some financial concepts that add greatly to our abilities to make sound marketing decisions. These concepts should be applied where needed in the cases in this book.

Chapter 4

A Case with a Student Analysis

The fundamental premise of this book is that one learns by doing. However, it is also recognized that one can learn from example. The purpose of this chapter is to give examples, both good and bad, of case analysis. The framework of analysis presented in the previous two chapters will be used here in order to clarify how one can use the framework.

The case presented in this chapter, "Da-Roche Laboratories, Inc.," is a broad issue marketing case that has no textbook or single "correct" answer. Following the case, a student analysis of the case is presented. In the last section of the chapter we present our commentary on the case analysis.

We suggest the following steps in using this chapter:

1. Read and prepare your analysis of "Da-Roche Laboratories, Inc." This will give you a better perspective on the case analyses presented in this chapter.
2. Read and evaluate the analysis presented here. You may wish to use the points that constitute a good case analysis as presented in Chapter 2.
3. Read our commentary on the case analysis. Compare our view with yours.

Case

Da-Roche Laboratories, Inc.

In December, the officers of Da-Roche Laboratories, Inc., met to discuss the company's sales and advertising plans to re-launch their new product, Dapper-Diaper. The focus of the meeting was the strategy to be used in the marketing of the new product which had recently been approved by the Food and Drug Administration (FDA). They were particularly interested in the possible methods of promoting the product and in the channels of distribution to be used in distributing Dapper-Diaper.

Background

Da-Roche Laboratories, Inc., was established in Jackson, Michigan, to develop and market a new antibiotic baby product, Dapper-Diaper. Dapper-Diaper was composed of an aqueous solution of the antibiotic neomycin sulfate which was placed in a 10-ounce aerosol can. Neomycin inhibited odors in the animal kingdom, and Mr. Roy Crutchfield thought that the antibiotic could be used to eliminate odors from baby diapers. Dapper-Diaper kills bacteria which cause the decomposition of urea and thereby prevents ammonia from forming in diapers.

Da-Roche Laboratories convinced selected doctors to do some initial testing of its new product and the results were very encouraging. Doctors discovered that when sprayed on diapers in the diaper pail, it solved the odor problem. In addition, if sprayed on a clean diaper before it was worn by the baby it appeared to stop or prevent diaper rash on the baby.

Gaining FDA Approval

With a great deal of encouragement from the doctors involved in the initial testing of their new antibiotic product, Mr. D. R. Wiley, then president and general manager of Da-Roche Laboratories, along with Mr. Crutchfield and Dr. John B. Holst, the company's consulting M.D., went to Washington and informed the FDA that they had discovered a new gift to mothers which they wished to begin marketing immediately. The FDA did not agree and told the Da-Roche personnel that they would have to do studies to show that the product actually did what it claimed to do, and at the same time show that there were no harmful side effects from using the antibiotic product.

Thus, while they thought they could go through the Food and Drug Administration (FDA) for approval of a new cosmetic-type product, the Da-Roche executives discovered that they had actually created what was termed a new drug which had to be approved by the New Drug Division of the FDA.

Although the one active ingredient in Dapper-Diaper was neomycin sulfate which had been known and widely used for about 15 years as one of a number of antibiotic products, the ingredient had never been mixed with water and other chemicals and placed in a pressurized spray can for sale over the counter. It appeared that it was due to the packaging and marketing plans for the new product, rather than its active ingredient, that it was declared a new drug, subject to FDA jurisdiction.

Consequently, what started out to be a new cosmetic product which would not have had to prove that it did any good as long as it did not do any harm, ended up being a new drug under FDA regulations. As a result, both the efficacy of the product and the absence of any harmful effects had to be proven to the satisfaction of the FDA committee of doctors. This effort required approximately four years and the expenditure of nearly $500,000 in testing costs alone.

Three basic steps had to be taken to get the required certification by the federal Food and Drug Administration. First, research of all the available literature was undertaken to see what kinds of problems should be researched in experimental situations. Animal testing (toxicity) was next conducted, including autopsy reports of white mice to be sure there were no harmful effects from continued use of the new product. The third step in the testing procedure involved clinical tests on infants using a placebo (the product minus the active ingredient) with double blind and double blind crossover techniques whereby aerosol spray cans labeled X and Y were tested both for safety and for efficacy. The doctors and nurses involved in these clinical observation studies did not know which cans contained the aqueous solution of neomycin sulfate and which contained the placebo, in order to ensure their objectivity throughout the duration of the study. Culture studies of diapers and the babies' skin were made and it was found that the bacteria which produced odor and diaper rash were gradually eradicated in the diaper with no effect on the resident flora (normal balance of bacteria) of the babies' skin.

Finally, at the end of four years, and after 30 visits to Washington and 25 label changes, the FDA approved Dapper-Diaper for over-the-counter sale. Since the machinery for producing the new antibiotic had been purchased and inspected about one and one-half years before the FDA approval had been received, Da-Roche was now able to begin production immediately.

Distribution

The original plan was to obtain distribution in Michigan and then use the capital generated by sales in this area to expand into adjacent markets. This plan was to be repeated until Dapper-Diaper was distributed throughout the United States. To obtain regional distribution as fast as possible, Da-Roche hired a broker's broker. This man had formerly sold to brokers and he was well acquainted with the food and drug brokers in Michigan and knew what it would take to get them to handle the company's product. The brokers, in turn, sold to large wholesale drug companies such as McKesson-Robbins and Hazeltine-Perkins, and to large grocers such as A&P, Kroger, Food Fair, and even to smaller "Mom and Pop" stores in some areas. The brokers also sold to some discount chains such as Kmart. It was felt that established brokers would be much more effective in bargaining with large accounts than salesmen from a new, unfamiliar company.

By March 1, the new product was on the market in many of these retail outlets, and a concerted effort was being made to get every drugstore in Michigan to carry the product as well. This objective was pursued by sending a free sample can of Dapper-Diaper to every major druggist in the state of Michigan. While this plan entailed giving away free more than 2,000 full-size cans of Dapper-Diaper, it also allowed Da-Roche to claim that its product could be found in every major drugstore in the state of Michigan. At the same time, it acquainted all of Michigan's druggists with the new product. By June, brokers had managed to obtain distribution in 80 percent of the stores in eastern Michigan but distribution in the western part of the state was much slower with only about 20 percent of the stores stocking Dapper-Diaper.

Pricing

It was estimated that if the same amount of neomycin as was contained in one 10-ounce can of Dapper-Diaper were to be bought by prescription, it would cost from $5 to $8. After talking with retailers, brokers, and doctors, it was decided that the "suggested retail price" of Dapper-Diaper would be $1.98. The Da-Roche executives, however, expected that it would sell for between $1.60 and $1.70 within four to six weeks after introduction. And, in fact, it was selling for $1.69 in Kroger and other supermarkets as of April 1. The product sold as low as $1.39 in some stores, and the average retail price was about $1.80.

Cost

The average retail price allowed the company enough margin to promote the product properly. The average retail price was about six times the cost of goods sold, which was normal for the drug industry. After discounts and allowances to wholesalers and retailers, the proceeds to the company were about $1 per can. Administrative and overhead costs were $100,000 per year exclusive of marketing costs.

Market Potential

In determining the size of the total market for Dapper-Diaper, Da-Roche executives first found out that there were approximately 8 million babies in diapers in the United States. (There were 350,000 babies in the company's initial marketing area.) A 10-ounce can of Dapper-Diaper was expected to last one month. Da-Roche executives reasoned that they would be able to get 10 percent of the total market to use Dapper-Diaper, resulting in sales of 9.6 million cans per year.

Use of Personal Selling through Ethical Channels to Get Intensive Distribution

The original strategy called for personal selling through five detail men. These men were to call on people in all medical professions to explain the benefits of the new product, how it was used, and where it could be obtained. In addition, small-size free samples were left with the doctor so he could recommend the product to a patient and be able to give her a 10-day supply of Dapper-Diaper as well.

Da-Roche's executives were immediately faced with the problem of how to get the detail men in to see a doctor, especially since they represented a new company with only one product. To solve this problem, the five detail men were each given an hourglass which was timed for three minutes. The detail men then went into the doctor's office and started the sand in motion, asking for three minutes of the doctor's time. Only the essential facts were given to the doctor in the three minutes, after which some free samples were distributed and the detail men attempted to leave. At this point, Da-Roche executives declared 9 out of 10 doctors asked for more information about Dapper-Diaper before the detail man could leave. The following points were made about the new baby product: It is certified by the Federal Food and Drug Administration; it is an antibiotic; its active ingredient is neomycin; it is sold over the counter (no prescription needed); it is safe, because it is made from one of the most nearly perfect drugs known; and it is time saving, economical, easy to use, and it really works.

The use of detail men was selected over consumer advertising for the initial promotional job, because the Da-Roche executives believed that if the product was recommended by doctors, women would surely use Dapper-Diaper and tell their friends about it, too. This would give the new product the most desirable kind of promotion possible—word of mouth.

Another consideration which favored personal selling over consumer advertising was the fact that during the first week of February, when promotion of Dapper-Diaper by the company's detail men was first begun, distribution of the product was just beginning too. If consumer advertising had come in at the same time, the Da-Roche executives believed that much of it would have been wasted because the product was not yet available. It was felt that by April 1, this problem would be remedied and a consumer advertising campaign could be launched at this time. With only a limited amount of money available for advertising, it was important that distribution be achieved before the advertising commenced, in order that the advertising would not be wasted.

Dapper-Diaper consumer advertising campaign

To be consistent with their intensive distribution policy within the introductory selling regions, the Da-Roche executives had planned a consumer advertising campaign which was to begin April 1. They believed that by waiting until April 1, they could be sure that Dapper-Diaper could be readily available to most stores by the time the consumer advertising campaign would begin. Discussion with brokers, people in the trade, and Da-Roche's agency, the La Vanway agency in Jackson, Michigan, resulted in an advertising budget of $50,000 for the first 13 weeks. After that time, advertising would be budgeted at 25 percent of net sales. It was decided that to get maximum reach and frequency, the company should use 30-second and 60-second radio spots, with some 10-second IDs; IDs and 60-second spots on television, with some advertising in trade journals and newspapers.

In anticipation of the FDA's approval of the new use for Dapper-Diaper which was expected in the near future, the company's advertising was based largely on the diaper and not exclusively on the narrower diaper pail use for which the product was currently certified by the FDA. A picture of a baby wearing a top hat, which appeared on the can, became known as "The Happy Baby" and was used in the company's introductory advertising campaign. All advertising carried the line, "Do your baby a favor, ask your baby's doctor."

Protection from Competition

It was hoped that eventually Dapper-Diaper would become almost a generic name, since it would be the first on the market and likely enjoy the status of being the only such product for at least one more year. This protection, it was felt, would be afforded by the patent which was pending on the new product, the trademark and copyrighted Dapper-Diaper name, and the fact that any competitor would have to do extensive testing of the type that took Da-Roche four years, in order to get its product approved by the FDA as a new drug.

Pursuing New Uses

While Da-Roche was still in the process of introducing Dapper-Diaper into its first region which included all of Michigan and part of Ohio and Indiana, it was also engaged in more clinical testing. The product had received FDA approval only as a diaper pail spray. Knowing that it had no harmful effects on babies and that it would inhibit bacteria growth which caused ammonia burn or diaper rash, Da-Roche was seeking FDA approval to promote Dapper-Diaper as a diaper spray as well. For this new purpose the product would be sprayed on a clean diaper before it was to be worn by the baby. Much of the extensive testing which had already been conducted by Da-Roche indicated that when diapers were sprayed in the diaper pail, the diapers became clinically clean prior to washing and helped inhibit the growth of ammonia-producing bacteria, preventing odor and diaper rash.

Dr. J. D. Holst, M.D., Da-Roche's medical liaison with the FDA, explained that with the tests that had already been done, it would only require about six months of tests to return to the FDA requesting permission to use a broader label describing Dapper-Diaper as a diaper spray as well as a diaper pail spray. This additional use for the product could then be promoted by the company's detail men in talking to doctors and in the company's consumer advertising. Thus, while at the time of introduction Dapper-Diaper was only an antibiotic diaper pail spray which would limit the number of bacteria to control odor, its rash-prevention benefit was a by-product which the Da-Roche executives believed might soon become an equally important use for the new product.

Beyond the new use of Dapper-Diaper in controlling ammonia burn, the nature of the product itself and the way in which it worked suggested a variety of entirely new uses for which the new product might be equally well suited. The active ingredient, neomycin, was extremely effective in reducing or completely eliminating bacterial odor, and for this reason it might be used for eliminating all odors caused by organic decomposition. Examples would include a garbage pail or pet spray.

Consideration of a Full Baby-Product Line

Da-Roche executives also considered introducing companion products, such as baby powder and paper diapers, which would help better entrench the company as a producer of a more complete line of baby products and perhaps speed the translation of the brand name Dapper-Diaper into almost a generic concept. Another advantage would be that these companion products, as they were developed, could be promoted along with the Dapper-Diaper spray by the company's detail men as they called on doctors and left free samples and literature.

Results, April–December

The company ran into significant problems as Dapper-Diaper was being introduced. A batch of 180,000 three-ounce cans to be used as samples and distributed to doctors was not approved by the FDA. A change in the can design had resulted in valves which did not fit properly. The company therefore had to use trade cans for samples to distribute to the doctors, and, due to the greater cost of the full-size cans, a smaller number of samples was distributed.

After the product had been distributed to the retailers and had been on the shelf for a short period of time, problems with the full-size can became evident. Some of the ingredients in the product were interacting with the can, causing the can to rust. As the can rusted, the pressure in the aerosol leaked out, making it impossible to get the product out of the aerosol can. The company replaced bad cans, as they were found, with good ones, but then even the good ones turned bad. Finally, the source of the problem was discovered and a change in Dapper-Diaper's formulation had to be developed. Da-Roche then had to get FDA approval on the new formulation and on the new can. In effect, the company had to start all over.

The Present Situation

In December, the company finally received approval from the FDA to again begin marketing Dapper-Diaper. Da-Roche executives were now considering several alternative ways of marketing the product. First, they could follow exactly the same strategy that they followed with the initial launching of the product. This would entail both detail men and consumer advertising with distribution through drugstores, supermarkets, and discount stores.

A second alternative was to take a marketing approach similar to that used for ethical drugs. Thus, the company could use established outlets that do not require the high cost of familiarizing people with the product. Instead, detail men would be used to encourage doctors to recommend the product, and people would therefore become familiar with the product through their doctor's recommendation. This would eliminate the need for a significant amount of consumer advertising required to support a product which is to be distributed through supermarkets and discount stores.

Da-Roche's executives came upon a third alternative after reading an article in *Time* magazine. The article quoted the president of The American Diaper Service Association describing the smell of the diaper pail as diaper services' biggest single problem. The urea content of a new baby's urine is not very heavy, but as the baby gets older, the urea gets heavier. Therefore, after the baby becomes about three months old, the smell in the diaper pail significantly increases. Diaper services supply pails with neoprene bags, and therefore the diapers cannot be soaked. The diapers are usually picked up only once a week so there are 50 to 100 by that time. Mothers, therefore, began to buy diapers and wash them themselves three to four times per week.

The Associated Diaper Services of America and the other trade organization, The National Institute for Diaper Services, have members who make 83 million contacts per year where money changes hands. With the help of these two associations, Dapper-Diaper could be made known to millions of women through diaper service distributors. Da-Roche executives felt that either of the diaper services could sell 2 million cans per year with a minimum of effort. The company executives stated that Da-Roche would be very profitable at that volume.

Da-Roche executives had also made contact with a manufacturer of institutional clothing. This company sold very high quality sleeping garments for babies and mentally retarded children in hospitals and training schools, and other garments for hospitals, penitentiaries, and other institutions. The manufacturer would distribute Dapper-Diaper along with his other products. As the institutions have a large problem with odor, Da-Roche's executives thought that this method of distribution would yield a large market.

Da-Roche executives were also considering one further alternative. A cosmetic broker—the best known in the country—with offices in Dallas, New York, and Chicago, had become interested in Dapper-Diaper. This broker employed over 100 people and distributed products of such well-known companies as Schick, Alberto-Culver, Revlon, and Tampax. The broker told Da-Roche's executives that if they could give him $1 million for advertising, he could guarantee them $3 million in sales with the company's present label (Dapper-Diaper had still not been approved for anything except use as a diaper pail spray).

Example of a Case Analysis of Da-Roche Laboratories, Inc.

After a considerable investment of time, money, and effort, Da-Roche Laboratories is again ready to begin marketing its diaper pail spray, Dapper-Diaper. In the past, the company has operated on pipe dreams, inadequate and incomplete information, and an almost total absence of planning and organization. If the current effort is to prove successful, an in-depth analysis of the opportunities and limitations in terms of product, target market, production facilities, and financial resources must be made. Once these areas have been clearly defined, the company will be in a position to select marketing strategies designed to achieve their objectives.

In reviewing the past performance of Da-Roche, the most evident feature (and most devastating) has been the lack of planning and coordination. For example, advertising was undertaken before the product was available in retail outlets, and distribution was begun before the production process was carefully tested. A PERT type of analysis which indicates the order in which various functions must be completed as well as the time frame involved is necessary to avoid such problems in the future. Had the earlier operation been characterized by systematic, careful planning, money and time could have been saved and possible negative reactions from doctors and consumers could have been avoided.

A second general observation seems relevant in terms of the objectives of the company. Da-Roche executives have rather grandiose ideas of producing a nationally advertised and distributed product, of making Dapper-Diaper a generic concept, and of bringing out a complete line of baby products. They do not have realistic, concise, clearly defined, quantitative objectives or timetables for their accomplishment, however. Rather than pipe dreams about generic names and full product lines, Da-Roche needs to concentrate on specific goals such as achieving a certain percentage of awareness or a given level of sales during each month. A concisely delineated list of objectives and accompanying timetable would assist both planning and evaluation of progress.

In analyzing their current position, Da-Roche must begin with a consideration of their product. It is first of all a unique product providing excellent opportunity for differentiation and possessing real market potential if properly developed and promoted to a viable market. At the present time, however, the product is only a diaper pail spray, not a diaper spray, and marketing strategy must be geared to this limited definition. Although Da-Roche "feels" that the Food and Drug Administration (FDA) will approve their product for more general use within six months, experience has shown the fallacy of seeking to second-guess the FDA's timetable. Instead of six months, final approval may not occur for several years and Da-Roche should direct the current campaign toward the promotion of a diaper pail spray. Contingency long-range plans should also be formulated so that if and when the expanded use is approved, strategic adjustments can be made.

Given the product is a diaper pail spray, the obvious market for Da-Roche is the mothers of young babies. It is unrealistic to define this group as the 8 million babies in diapers throughout the United States as Da-Roche has neither the financial nor production capacity to attempt an immediate nationwide distribution. A more realistic approximation would be the 350,000 babies in the limited area marked for the initial regional introduction. Although this process may result in a slower diffusion and cut overall long-term profits if competition enters the market within a year, a nationwide distribution is not feasible in the current situation.

The initial marketing effort should be aimed at the primary market of mothers with small babies rather than seeking the larger segment of users of odor killing spray. Although it is believed that Dapper-Diaper might be used to eliminate all odor caused by organic decomposition, an attempt to merchandise a multipurpose spray would have several negative effects. First, the market becomes very dispersed and more difficult to identify and reach. Second, the product loses some of its uniqueness and the consumer may have difficulty distinguishing it from other sprays. Further, if the use as a diaper spray is later approved, the mother may have difficulty in accepting the idea that the same spray she uses for the garbage pail and pet should also be sprayed on her baby's diapers! Finally, such a strategy places Da-Roche in direct competition with such industry giants as Lysol. A better approach would be to differentiate the product as specifically designed for diaper treatment and market to the smaller specialized group. Once this segment is saturated and the product reaches maturity, new uses may be introduced to the present user or added markets may be sought to inject new life into the product. The first goal should be to develop the primary product usage, however.

Finally, consideration must be given to production and financial constraints of Da-Roche. Although no details are given as to the source and extent of investments in the firm to date, it is reasonable to assume there are limits to future funds available. By the same token, a beginning operation probably has limited production facilities which would restrict the rate and extent of expansion. Da-Roche is not Johnson & Johnson with almost unlimited facilities and funds to develop and promote new products, and these constraints create important parameters in planning strategies.

The first strategy being considered by Da-Roche is to follow the same plan pursued earlier combining intensive distribution with promotion by detail salespersons and consumer advertising. Intuitively, such an approach would seem both expensive and ineffective. First, Da-Roche is a small unknown company with only one product and will probably have difficulty in persuading doctors to talk with them. Although the hourglass gimmick was successful in the previous promotion, it does not provide a sound basis for long-range relationships between detail salespersons and doctors. With only one product to promote, detail salespeople are also an expense to the operation. In addition, since the product is limited to use as a diaper pail spray at this time, the willingness or pertinence of the doctor's recommendation may be an issue since the busy doctor is more likely to be involved with more vital health issues than diaper pail odor. Finally, the earlier debacle may have created ill will among physicians who were earlier impressed, but later disillusioned by the product's inability to perform satisfactorily.

This intuitive analysis is supported by the figures. Based on a total market in the initial introductory region of 350,000 and Da-Roche's estimate that they could capture 10 percent of the market with 12 purchases each year, annual sales should be 420,000 cans (350,000 × 12 × 10%). First year usage would be lower than this as many consumers would not try until later in the year and would not use 12 cans the first year. With the current cost of goods sold at 30 cents a can (⅙ of average retail price) and the contribution at 70 cents per can ($1.00 manufacturer sales price minus 30 cents variable cost) this would represent a total gross margin of $294,000. The following expenses must then be deducted: *CONTRIBUTION MARGIN*

FIXED.
NOT PART OF COST
OF GOODS SOLD

Administration and overhead	$100,000
Advertising	
Initial	50,000
25% net sales	105,000
Detail/salespeople (5 at 20,000 each)	100,000
Total	$355,000

A loss of $61,000 would be sustained at this level of sales. The break-even point would be 507,143 cans ($355,000 ÷ 70¢) or 12.1 percent of the 4.2 million can market potential. The figures thus support the logical deductions made earlier.

A second strategy being considered involves following the approach employed in marketing ethical drugs using detail salespeople, but saving the cost of direct consumer advertising. The same problems are present in this approach of reaching the doctors, motivating them to recommend the product, and justifying the expense involved with a single item in the product line.

Although some expense is spared by eliminating direct consumer advertising, the potential rate of diffusion is also lessened. It is anticipated that it will be impossible to persuade doctors to push the product enough to acquire a 10 percent usage rate without direct consumer advertising. Indeed a 5 percent acceptance rate is more probable if total reliance is placed on detail salespeople and doctors to disseminate information. This would result in sales of 210,000 cans per year and a contribution of $147,000. Fixed administrative overhead cost ($100,000) and the detail salespeople's salary ($100,000) would result in a loss of $53,000. The break-even level of sales is 285,700 cans ($200,000 ÷ 70¢) or 6.8 percent share of market potential.

Still another strategy offering little intuitive appeal is to hire a cosmetic broker to promote the product. With $1 million for advertising, the broker guarantees $3 million in sales. Even if desirable, it seems questionable that Da-Roche has the funds to invest $1 million in advertising. If funds are available, $3 million in sales would represent a profit of $1 million (administrative costs $100,000, advertising fees $1,000,000, and variable production costs $900,000). It is doubtful that the agency literally "guarantees" the $3 million in sales so that earnings may well be much lower. The break-even sales level would be $1,571,429 ($1.1 million ÷ 70¢) or 1.6 percent of the total market potential.

The final strategy under consideration involves distributing Dapper-Diaper through diaper services and institutional clothing manufacturers. Such an approach seems more realistic in terms of the product and the capabilities of Da-Roche, and offers better profit potential.

As long as Dapper-Diaper is restricted to use as a diaper pail spray, the customers of a diaper service represent an excellent source of heavy users. Diaper pail odor is a significant problem to both the industry and the mother who uses the service. Cooperation by the diaper service is thus very likely.

The financial implications of distribution through a diaper service are as follows:

Cost:	
Fixed administrative cost	$ 100,000
Promotion and advertising	100,000
2 salespersons (to call on diaper service)	50,000
Variable production cost	600,000
(at 2 million cans)	850,000
Earnings (if 2 million cans sold at $1 per can to Da-Roche)	2,000,000
Less cost	850,000
	$1,150,000

Since the fixed costs are relatively low under this strategy, profit can be generated even at a much lower level of sales with a break-even at 357,143 cans ($250,000 ÷ 70¢ contribution per can). Advertising cost will also be lower since close identification of the target market can be made and information distributed directly to this segment.

The objective of the advertising campaign should be to cause the consumer to automatically think of using Dapper-Diaper if they use diaper service. Each customer with the diaper service can be given a free can of Dapper-Diaper when the service is begun. This should be a sample can adequate to last one week until the next delivery date. A leaflet would accompany the sample describing what causes diaper odor and how Dapper-Diaper destroys both odor and bacteria. A form to order another can would be included in case the mother is not at home when the used diapers are picked up. Since distributing exclusively through the diaper company will eliminate brokers, wholesalers, and retailers, it is probable that the cost of marketing Dapper-Diaper will be less under this approach. The diaper service should receive adequate compensation for their bookkeeping and distribution roles and route salesmen should be paid a commission for every can sold. This will help to insure that they adequately "push" the product to the final consumer. If these cost are less than current distribution expenses, the savings could be used to lower the price to the final consumer.

In addition to the free sample, several other promotional activities should be undertaken. First, advertising directly to the consumer should be made using "baby" magazines as the media. Since the sole source of Dapper-Diaper will be through the diaper services, tie-in advertisements with the services should be employed. In addition, attempts should be made to get the service to put Dapper-Diaper's name on their trucks and any promotional literature they distribute.

Concurrent with the use of diaper services, Da-Roche should develop the institutional market. Further investigation is necessary to determine if they should pursue the plan of having the manufacturer of institutional clothing distribute Dapper-Diaper or if Da-Roche's own salespeople should call on hospitals and institutions. Distribution through the clothing manufacturers would minimize fixed cost, but it is possible that Dapper-Diaper would not receive adequate presentation if the manufacturer's salesperson is already handling a large line. Too, certain product changes (such as making larger sizes) may be necessary to attract this market, and Da-Roche should be sure their production facilities are adequate for these additions. Further information is needed to solve these issues, but the institutional market should definitely be investigated and developed if possible. No quantitative calculations are possible since the size of the market is not known, but little additional fixed cost would be involved indicating good profit potential when combined with the diaper service strategy.

The above discussion does not imply that Da-Roche should permanently restrict their market. What the company needs desperately at this point is some base of operations which can produce earnings and sustain the momentum of the company. The diaper service and institutional markets offer this concentrated, easily accessible heavy user segment which can provide an initial earnings base for the company. Such a base is vital at this point and must be established before expansion to larger market segments and more diverse users is undertaken. As the product gains higher awareness levels and the company reaches more balanced financial and production capabilities, strategy revisions can be considered.

Commentary on the Case Analysis

Table 4–1 presents our point-by-point summary evaluation of the case analysis. In our view, it is very well done and our guess is you will agree. We should point out, however, that it is far easier to evaluate an analysis then to do one.

TABLE 4-1 Summary of the evaluation of the case analysis

Criteria	Analysis
1. Completeness	Very complete on all aspects of structure Reasonable depth of analysis
2. Avoids rehash	Good Most points are made with an analysis purpose
3. Makes reasonable assumptions	Excellent
4. Proper problem statements	Excellent; has not confused them with symptoms Somewhat incomplete; e.g., competitors
5. Proper opportunity statements	Good; has not given action statements
6. Deals with objectives realistically	Very good; has questioned this issue Alternatives given and discussed
7. Recognizes alternatives	Excellent; reasonably complete Options are discussed in detail
8. Is not assertive	Generally OK Some actions are implied in situation analysis, but not a big problem here
9. Discusses pros and cons of alternatives	Very good. Leads directly to a conclusion
10. Makes effective use of financial and other quantitative information	Excellent All options are given a good quantitative appraisal
11. Reaches a clear and logical decision	Excellent Decision is consistent with the analysis presented
12. Makes good use of evidence developed in situation analysis	Fair What is given is good but needs to use it more in discussion of pros and cons
13. Overall appraisal	A very good analysis of a tough situation

Part 2

Introduction to Marketing Decision Making

In Part 1 of this book you have studied how marketing decisions should be made. The cases in this section are designed to let you begin to apply this approach in decision making. These cases should be viewed as an opportunity to practice your skills on some broad issue marketing cases before we go to other sections of this book where we study cases that are more specifically tied to product or distribution, and so on.

Case 1

RCA Videodisc Player*

It was December 1981, and it had been nine months since RCA nationally introduced its videodisc player under the SelectaVision label. This introduction was the culmination of $200 million in expenditures, and over a decade-long research and development effort to create a videodisc player which RCA felt would become an established consumer good. See Exhibit 1 for introductory promotional materials.

Sales of videodisc players to retailers had been fewer than expected, and sales to consumers were lower still. This slow start coupled with the high stakes involved was cause for concern at RCA. In fact, RCA's entry into this high risk venture was one of the reasons cited by Standard & Poor's Corporation in June 1981 in lowering the ratings on RCA's commercial paper and preferred stock.[1]

It was unclear which strategy RCA should now pursue, as much of the direction, energy, and momentum behind the introduction of the RCA videodisc player was due to the fact that the videodisc project had been the pet project of RCA Chairman Edgar Griffiths, who retired in June 1981. It was now time, however, to reassess the market and its future, RCA's position in the market, and competitive activity in realigning marketing strategy.

RCA's Videodisc Player Strategy

The unsuccessful introduction by CBS of an electronic video recorder in the 1960s[2] had made RCA actively aware that timing was critical in the introduction of the videodisc player. RCA felt that to be successful, its strategy should simultaneously seek to expand the total videodisc player market, and establish the Capacitance Electronic Disc (CED) technology as the standard in the United States. Equally important to the success of the videodisc player was securing as many rights as possible to software programming. Expansion of the total market

---

* This case was coauthored by Jeanne De Amicis.
[1] *Advertising Age*, June 22, 1981.
[2] *Marketing and Media Decisions*, March 1981, p. 62.

EXHIBIT 1 RCA introductory promotional materials

EXHIBIT 1 *(concluded)*

could be achieved in part by a heavy $20 million advertising campaign for the introductory months of 1981. While competitive advertising campaigns would also assist in expanding the total market, RCA had to insure itself against the possibility of a competitor with incompatible technology walking off with the largest chunk of the market.

Concurrent with consumer market expansion was the hope to develop new uses and markets for the RCA videodisc player. While RCA had targeted the videodisc player to the mass consumer market, it was learned that the player was of potential interest to educational institutions as a teaching aid; to businesses as a training device; or a "memory" source on which to store, and then easily access large amounts of information. Yet, it was clear that for the time being, the success or failure of the videodisc player depended on its acceptance as a durable consumer entertainment good. It was to this market that RCA management was directing its attention.

Several steps were needed to assure that the Capacitance Electronic Disc technology became the standard in the United States. First, the videodisc player must appeal to the mass market, not just the videophile, and it must be readily available. With this in mind, the RCA SelectaVision (CED) videodisc player was positioned as being the easiest to use (fewer features), the cheapest ($499 suggested retail) and having better programming than that of competitors.

Second, RCA sought to gain wide distribution through the use of national retailers. By 1980, Sears, Roebuck & Co. had agreed to include the RCA videodisc player in its Christmas 1981 catalog. However, the system sold through Sears would carry Sears's brand name rather than the RCA label. While RCA would prefer that its label appear on the product, it was more important that the CED technology gain the broad based distribution and mass merchandising afforded through the Sears deal than that RCA build brand name recognition. The situation was one of winner takes all, in terms of establishing the dominant technology. J. C. Penney and Montgomery Ward in late 1981 had also agreed to carry the RCA videodisc player. This represented a major victory for RCA as competitors would have to seek distribution through their own retailer system, a system which would be dwarfed by the combined distribution coverage provided by Sears, J. C. Penney, and Montgomery Ward, as well as RCA's regular distribution channels.

Third, the $20 million RCA planned to spend in the introductory advertising blitz was designed to expand the total videodisc player market, and also help to increase the market share of the RCA player, hence its technology, over those of competitors with incompatible technology.

Development of the RCA Videodisc Player

In the mid-1960s, while still concentrating on competing in the color television market, RCA was concerned over its future direction once the saturation level for color television sets had been reached. It was reasoned that once everyone had a color television, the time would be ripe for the introduction of devices that would supplement the normal function of a color television set. Hence, the ideas of the videocassette recorder and the videodisc player were developed.

The videocassette recorder (VCR) is a tape system that is attached to a television set, and can both record programs and play prerecorded programs. The videodisc player is the visual equivalent of a phonograph; it is a playback-only system that uses prerecorded software and has no recording capabilities. It is attached to a television set and plays discs, prerecorded with television signals just as a phonograph plays prerecorded records.

RCA felt that the videodisc player would have wide appeal as it would be less expensive and less complicated a device than videocassette recorders. Consequently resources and energy were expanded on developing a videodisc system. This paid off, when by the late 1970s RCA had developed the Capacitance Electronic Disc system (CED). This system is a mechanical one that uses a microscopic diamond-tipped stylus that travels through the grooves of a disc, reproducing signals embedded on the surface. This technology features fast forward, and fast reverse, but does not have stereo sound capabilities. Sanyo and Zenith were expected to market CED technology systems.

Two other incompatible technologies had also been developed by competitors. The laser system had been introduced in the U.S. market by Magnavox, under the name MagnaVision in 1978. This laser system is an optical system that uses a small laser to read pits pressed into a disc. It offers stereo sound, fast forward, fast reverse, stop frame, and random access features. Pioneer Electronics also marketed a laser system. See Exhibit 2 for Magnavision and Pioneer ads.

The third incompatible technology, the video high density (VHD) system, has not yet been introduced into the U.S. market (although it has been marketed abroad). In this system, the stylus rides on a grooveless disc, picking up electrical capacitance signals pressed into the disc. The VHD player features: freeze frame, random access, slow motion, and stereo sound, as well as the fast forward and fast reverse capabilities. Matsushita Electric with its JVC brand, Victor of Japan, and General Electric were expected to utilize this technology in their products. Each of these incompatible technologies requires different software. Exhibit 3 summarizes the advantages and disadvantages of the three main current competitors.

Software Programming

Securing software programming and making it readily available to consumers was also of critical importance to the success of RCA's venture. The software issue was further complicated by the fact that the different technologies require different discs. So it was reasoned that the company able to tie-up the majority of software programming, be it by license agreements or some other means, would have a strong competitive advantage. RCA entered into an agreement with CBS whereby CBS, through its CBS Video Enterprises, would press the

EXHIBIT 2 Magnavision and Pioneer advertisements

EXHIBIT 2 *(concluded)*

EXHIBIT 3 A consumer's guide to videodisc players

Features	Philips-MCA (1978)	RCA (early 1981)	JVC (Matsushita) (late 1981)
Retail price	Disadvantage	Advantage	Advantage
No disc or stylus wear	Advantage	Disadvantage	Disadvantage
Stereo sound	Advantage	Advantage	Advantage
Two-hour playback	Advantage	Advantage	Advantage
Freeze frame	Advantage *	Advantage	Advantage
Automatic stop frame	Advantage *	Advantage	Advantage **
Multiple speeds, forward and reverse	Advantage		Advantage
Random frame access	Advantage	Disadvantage	Advantage **
Softwear variety	Advantage	Advantage	Disadvantage

*Available only with 1-hour discs.

**Option.

▨ = Advantage

▧ = Disadvantage

RCA-type disc. RCA spent millions of dollars in royalty guarantees and signed licensing agreements with United Artists, Paramount, 20th Century Fox, Avco-Embassy, Rank Film Distributors, and MGM Film Co. (a subsidiary of CBS) for rights to reproduce 520 films on disc.

The initial RCA disc catalog offered 150 titles including feature movies, Walt Disney movies, sports and music/variety programs, the Best of Television, Drama and Performing Arts programs, programs for children, and programs of special interest. The retail price of the discs ranged from $14.98 to $24.98. Discs would be available through the retail chains, and distribution channels that sold the RCA videodisc player, as well as through the regular CBS record distribution network. Retail margins were about 50 percent. However, complaints had already been received that adequate programming was not available late in 1981 at the retail level. Fixed costs for a disc were about $1 million, while variable costs ran about $2 per pressed disc.

A programming area where RCA chose not to enter was that using X-rated materials. Industry analysis and reports from retail outlets indicated a substantial demand for X-rated programs. RCA felt that any association with X-rated programming, materials, or promotion would severely hurt their corporate image, perhaps causing irreparable damage. Clearly RCA would not exploit this area of programming.

The possibility of establishing a studio to produce programming exclusively for CED videodisc players had been considered by RCA, but company officials felt it was too early a stage in the market development of videodisc players to warrant a heavy investment in such a venture. They felt that for the time being there was ample programming available to satisfy the needs of the videodisc player owners.

RCA was also aware that film producers were considering the possibility of licensing their films to more than one type of disc producer. This was of concern to RCA who had gone to great lengths to secure what it hoped would be exclusive rights to the film reproduction. Some competitors had already entered into joint ventures with studios to produce original programming for the consumer and industrial market needs, as well as to secure licenses.

Market Size

Industry analysis in 1980 predicted that videodisc player purchasers would buy an average of eight discs a year. They estimated that by 1990 the videodisc player market, along with the software market, would be a $7.5 billion business at retail, with prerecorded discs constituting a $200 to $250 million annual retail business. Despite this rosy prediction, there was a shortage of disc manufacturers. Consequently, although RCA had the rights to a substantial amount of software programming, the slow hardware sales coupled with the ensuing low volume of software sales dampened many disc manufacturers' plans to enter the disc market. There were many companies preparing to enter the disc manufacturing business, but choosing to wait until the seemingly inevitable industry shakeout occurred, and product standardization ensued.

Another consideration was the possibility of renting discs. RCA felt disc rental or disc swapping might stimulate the use of, and demand for, videodisc players, but it realized that the film studios would frown upon such activities. The recent film industry legal fight with the videocassette recorder producers concerning royalties, ownership, and production rights in taping programs, was indicative of the battle that might await them if they advocated and participated in disc rental activities. (The film industry suffered a setback in the Supreme Court and the battle has now shifted to the U.S. Congress.)

U.S. demographic changes (such as increasing amounts of leisure time and an increasing emphasis on recreational activities) have helped the growth of the entire video field. RCA felt these trends would carry over to videodisc player sales. RCA also felt that the increased dissatisfaction with broadcast television would aid in the expansion of this market. According to RCA, individuals who own color televisions, who watch a substantial amount of television, and are middle to upper income would most likely be the initial purchasers of videodisc players.

The intent of RCA was to eventually gain as high a level of home penetration as had been achieved with color and black and white televisions.

Anyone who owned a color television was a potential videodisc player purchaser. Analysts predicted that videodisc players would be in 14 percent of the 85 million television homes by 1986 (VCRs are expected to be in 18 percent of the television homes). RCA predicted a 60 percent market share, with Philips having a 30 percent market share, and Matsushita a 10 percent market share. RCA also forecasted that annual videodisc player sales will pass 5 million by 1990. These sales, coupled with disc sales of 200–250 million units would total a $7.5 billion annual business at retail by the end of the decade.

Due to delays in the introduction of the SelectaVision videodisc player and slow initial sales, RCA changed its initial 1981 forecast sales figure of 500,000 units to 200,000 units. By early November 1981, with Christmas sales yet to come, RCA had distributed 100,000 videodisc players to retailers and 1.4 million discs had been sold. Retail sales were about 60,000 to 80,000 players.

Competition

The videocassette recorder (VCR) was the major competitive substitute product for the videodisc player. The major differences between the two products were recording capability and price. A stripped down videocassette recorder had a suggested retail price of about $700, while the RCA Videodisc Player retailed at $499.[3] However, the videocassette recorder had recording capabilities where the videodisc player did not. Further confusing the customer was the incompatible laser technology videodisc player which retailed for as high as $750. RCA felt there was a market for a product without recording capabilities, but with a lower price. In fact, price, ease of use, and abundant programming were the distinguishing features of RCA's videodisc player.

Cable television and movie channels were also possible product substitutes for the videodisc player. Consumers could pay as little as $12–$15/month and see many first run movies on television while a videodisc player calls for an initial $499 outlay and $15–$25 for each disc. For many it may become a question of how often they view movies a second, third, or fourth time. Assuming a new videodisc player purchaser buys eight discs with the initial videodisc player purchase (ignoring the estimated eight discs purchased yearly thereafter), the average total price of $679 would purchase four years of cable television. RCA recognized pay television as a formidable competitor, but the cable industry was still young too, and videodisc players might be able to move in and gain the upper hand.

Philips' North American subsidiary, Magnavox, had been RCA's primary videodisc competitor to date. They were first to market videodisc players, having introduced their laser optical system in 1978. The introduction was a gradual one, going from test market to test market (Atlanta, Dallas, Seattle) before deciding on a city-by-city rollout. By October 1980, Magnavision was available in 30 markets. RCA was aware of some technical difficulties encoun-

---

[3] Retail margins were about 50 percent. RCA's variable costs were estimated at $150 per player on average over the first 200,000 units.

tered in the Magnavox laser system, problems that were not resolved until the summer of 1980. Prior to this time, there had been a significant reliability problem where between 50 percent and 60 percent of the players had to be returned for servicing. This problem appears to have been resolved and Magnavox has continued to be a strong competitor.

North American Philips had changed its strategy by late summer/early fall 1980, and began positioning its videodisc as being the most technically sophisticated player on the market and on the leading edge of laser technology. Its fall 1980 $5 million ad campaign was designed to appeal to the videophile, the video hobbyist, and the innovative individual. It was precisely those individuals who are the first to try something new that Magnavox wanted to attract. However, with a price of $775 Magnavision was significantly more expensive than RCA's SelectaVision videodisc. The Magnavox videodisc player did offer more features than the RCA product, namely: random access, multiple speeds, forward and reverse, automatic stop, freeze frame, and stereo sound. Another attractive feature of the Magnavox videodisc player was the fact that because the system is optical, there is no stylus that could wear down. The laser beam does not wear down the disc either. But RCA felt that a disc would have to be played hundreds of times before the CED system would wear it out.

By December 1980, anticipating RCA's entry into the market, Magnavox sought to change its strategy to appeal to the mass market. Because of its technical sophistication and higher price (Magnavision's price had now come down to $750), Magnavox sought to differentiate its product as being the gourmet video, yet still have mass appeal.

Despite some feeling that two incompatible videodisc technologies could coexist in the marketplace, the general consensus was that only one technology would be the clear winner. North American Philips was just as interested as RCA in gaining a stronghold and eventually dominating this market. Two moves helped to solidify this goal. First, North American Philips bought the Sylvania and Philco television manufacturing operations from GTE. Secondly, North American Philips had bought Magnavox at the outset in preparation and anticipation of entering the videodisc player market. In purchasing Magnavox, North American Philips gained access to the retail and distribution network already in place at Magnavox as well as the well-known name of Magnavox.

Because a color TV screen is needed to display the videodisc player programs, and because of the tendency of many people not to mix components that are not the same brand name, the purchase of the Sylvania and Philco television manufacturing operations by North American Philips was understandable. The reasoning was that a consumer owning a Sylvania TV would be most likely to purchase a Sylvania videodisc player. Undoubtedly this transaction would assist Magnavox's efforts to sell videodisc players, but perhaps more important, it would eliminate a potential ally for RCA in the technology war.

Just as RCA sought to gain the majority of software programming as part of its initial strategy in entering the videodisc market, Magnavox, early on, signed a joint venture agreement with MCA (Universal Studio's parent company), IBM, and Pioneer Electronics. This joint venture established Disco

Vision Associates which will manufacture the discs. Concurrently, Magnavox, Pioneer, and MCA each put up $1 million to create Optical Program Associates to produce original programs and take advantage of the stereo, freeze frame, and other features unique to the laser videodisc system. The association with MCA would also provide Magnavox with the movies and television programs produced by Universal Studios.

The other major competitor on the verge of entering the U.S. market with yet another incompatible technology was Matsushita. Matsushita had had the option of either licensing the RCA CED technology, North American Philips' laser optical technology, or developing its own proprietary technology. Licensing either RCA's or North American Philips' technology would virtually guarantee that Matsushita must compete on something other than price as both RCA and North American Philips would have lower costs by the time Matsushita entered the market. Hence, Matsushita felt the most viable option was to develop its own technology. Consequently the video high density (VHD) technology was developed and Matsushita felt it could sell these VHD videodisc players in the range between RCA's $500 model and Magnavox's $750, probably closer to $500. Furthermore, the Japanese government wanted manufacturers to agree on a single format before entering the Japanese market. Not surprisingly, Japan's Ministry for International Trade and Industry (MITI) announced that Matsushita's VHD technology was the agreed-upon format. If RCA or any other manufacturer wanted to enter the Japanese market, it would have to be done by licensing the VHD technology from Matsushita.

Matsushita, the world's largest consumer electronics company, sells its products in the United States under the brand names National, Panasonic, and Quasar. Victor Co. of Japan, which sells under the JVC label, is also a subsidiary of Matsushita. Matsushita's anticipated late 1981 entry into the U.S. market did not materialize. However, the company had predicted that 30,000 units would be distributed by the end of calendar year 1982.

Zenith Radio Corporation planned to enter the U.S. videodisc market in 1982 with a CED system. Prior to this time, Zenith had agreed to merely market RCA units under its Zenith label. The intent had been to begin in-house videodisc player equipment manufacturing in two to three years. Zenith had purposely kept a low profile and launched no national advertising campaigns. Instead, it left the advertising battlefield open for RCA and Magnavox (and Matsushita when it enters the market), thus forgoing the expense a national advertising campaign necessitates.

Zenith's second quarter 1981 profits fell 50 percent and RCA felt this might interrupt Zenith's ambitious plans to tap the rapidly expanding video market. It was announced that Zenith had already postponed plans to manufacture its own videodisc player. On the other hand, there was some speculation that Zenith intended to change videodisc manufacturers in 1982, presumably to distinguish itself from RCA and to get out of RCA's shadow.

Both Hitachi and Sanyo were planning entry into the U.S. market with the CED system, the Japanese market with the VHD system, and the European market with the laser optical system. All three technologies must be obtained from the respective technology developers. Hitachi will supply Radio Shack with its video players. Neither Hitachi nor Toshiba intended to advertise heavily as RCA was expected to carry the marketing efforts for the CED format.

Pioneer had already entered the U.S. market (and 14 others) with a laser-stylus system that is compatible with Magnavox's laser system, and priced between $750 and $775. Like RCA, in the fall of 1981, Pioneer offered three free discs with the purchase of its videodisc player.

Toshiba plans to enter the U.S. market with a CED player. Neither Sony nor Kenwood have entered the U.S. market yet, but are ready to enter with either/or the CED and VHD systems. They are waiting for the outcome of the initial struggle between RCA, Magnavox, and Matsushita. Both Gold Star and Thomson-C8F were preparing to introduce the laser system.

The International Videodisc Player Market

The international market for videodisc players was quite different from the U.S. market. Often videodisc players filled a void in countries where color television programming was poor, or where television programs and movies were censored by local officials. N.V. Philips (North American Philips' parent company) was based in the Netherlands and already enjoyed a dominant position in the European market with many of its products. Philips might be able to dominate the European videodisc player market with relative ease and establish its laser technology as the standard. Still, RCA felt that there were opportunities to break into this European market.

MITI's announcement that only VHD videodisc players would be sold in Japan put RCA in the disadvantageous position of having to license the VHD technology from Matsushita if it wanted to enter the lucrative Japanese market. VHD technology was not available to all companies, limiting in effect the number of competitors in the Japanese market, as well as giving a boost to Matsushita and other Japanese companies where the VHD technology is proprietary. RCA felt that the reasoning behind the Japanese government's move was to allow Matsushita to become the major manufacturer of videodisc players in Japan, such that it could rapidly develop production cost advantages and lower the price on its product. Then this lower priced product could be marketed in the United States. In this manner Matsushita could become price competitive with RCA, and perhaps gain a stronghold in the marketplace, and even come to dominate the U.S. videodisc market.

Other world markets were not sufficiently developed to support a product such as videodisc players. RCA felt it was not necessary to actively pursue these markets.

First Nine Months' Performance

By late 1981, RCA was clearly disappointed in the first nine months of sales. Not only had the sales forecast of 500,000 units been reduced to 200,000 units, but only 100,000 units had been sold to distributors. One analyst estimated that between 60,000 and 80,000 units had been sold to consumers. Christmas season sales failed to help much. Consequently, RCA began offering a $50 manufacturer's rebate and three free discs with the purchase of a videodisc player, and retailers began cutting prices by $100 to $200 per unit. Concurrently, the $20 million advertising blitz was covering broadcast and print media. Yet RCA had already announced the layoff of 400 of its 4,100 workers at its videodisc and color television manufacturing plant in Bloomington, Indiana. Further action might have to be taken if sales did not pick up.

RCA realized from the beginning that the videodisc player venture was both risky and would require substantial amounts of resources and time before the concept was readily accepted. How much should continue to be invested in the videodisc player business? How might this affect RCA's other businesses? What could RCA do to help boost sales? Unfortunately no consumer studies were available to identify why sales were below expectations.

Case 2

Island Shores*

In February 1982, Tom Smith, vice president and project manager of Enterprise Developers, Inc., was contemplating marketing alternatives available to the firm and the associated risks inherent in real estate development during such turbulent economic times. As Mr. Smith sat in his St. Petersburg, Florida, office trying to organize his thoughts and the market information at his disposal in some meaningful fashion, he was well aware that should the firm act on his recommendation, tens of millions of dollars would be at stake. Within the firm Smith was known for his good insights and solid judgment. While his previous decisions had successful outcomes, there was no guarantee that he was immune from mistakes and in this business mistakes were costly. Corporate expectations to meet a target return on investment of 18 percent added to the pressure that the selected project be more than marginally successful. The final plan to be submitted to the board of directors would have to include consideration of the designated target market, site selection, and architectural design requirements as well as price and promotional strategy.

Company Background

The history of Enterprise Developers was characterized by risk taking and an unusually high rate of success. The firm was founded by three businessmen from New York who had grown up in one of the worst boroughs in the city. They had banded together in the late 1950s to renovate and refurbish a neighborhood tenement building. After buying the burned-out shell from the city for $1,000 they rebuilt it themselves with sweat equity into a model example of low-income housing worth several hundred thousand dollars. The group invested the profits from the sale of this building into other pieces of real estate. Middle-income housing, apartment buildings, and townhouses followed.

---

* This case was written by Cynthia J. Frey, Assistant Professor of Marketing, Boston College and Maria Sannella as a basis for class discussion rather than to illustrate either effective or ineffective handling of an administrative situation.

With each renovation success the profits were reinvested in more property. The group was always alert to a new opportunity.

Encouraged by a friend and the possibility of more lucrative ventures, the trio moved to Miami in 1969. The next five years were spent developing rental units in the central city area. Close to the major business district, these mid-rise style buildings provided convenient access to the city for office workers. The skills that Enterprise acquired in New York City developing high density, urban living units were equally successful in Miami.

During this time period extensive condominium development was occurring along Florida's east coast particularly in the Fort Lauderdale area. Two of the primary groups of buyers were retirees desiring low maintenance home ownership in a warm climate, and investment buyers who might spend three or four weeks a year in their unit and rent the remaining weeks to Florida vacationers looking for an alternative to high price, crowded, hotel accommodations. While this was a time of extraordinary growth for east coast condominium building, with units being sold before construction was even started, little of this development was occurring on the west side of the state.

In an attempt to take advantage of the condominium boom in the early 1970s, Enterprise investigated possible sites throughout the Florida peninsula but found most of the areas best suited to resort or retirement communities vastly overpriced or unavailable. One alternative which caught the trio's interest was a so-called spoil spot in Boca Ciega Bay, 350 miles from Miami between St. Petersburg and Clearwater. From dredging operations by the Army Corps of Engineers, a 320-acre island had been formed. Two bridges connected the island with the northernmost portions of the city of St. Petersburg 25 minutes away by car. The island was comprised of coarse bottom sand from the Bay. Vegetation was sparse and uncultivated giving the area a decidedly remote and desolate atmosphere.

The 320-acre island was offered for sale by a prominent insurance company. Although friends and business associates advised against the acquisition of the parcel for the planned high amenity community, Enterprise purchased the site for $18 million. While clarification of zoning ordinances was the first concern for the developers, taming the wilderness to support human creature comforts would be a time-consuming task.

St. Petersburg Area

St. Petersburg is known for its mild temperatures and beautiful year-round weather. According to the local paper, the *St. Petersburg Independent,* 361 days of sunshine per year are guaranteed. On days when the sun does not appear by 3 P.M., the newspaper distributes the afternoon edition free of charge. Since 1910, only 30 editions have been given away. The record for consecutive days with sunshine is 546.

St. Petersburg, the fourth largest city in Florida, is located on the southern tip of the Pinellas Peninsula. This point of land takes its name from the Spanish

Punta Pinales or Point of the Pine Trees. Tampa Bay is on the east and to the south; the Gulf of Mexico on the west. St. Petersburg Beach, on Long Key, is one of the Holiday Isles, a ribbon of keys separated from the mainland and St. Petersburg by Boca Ciega Bay.

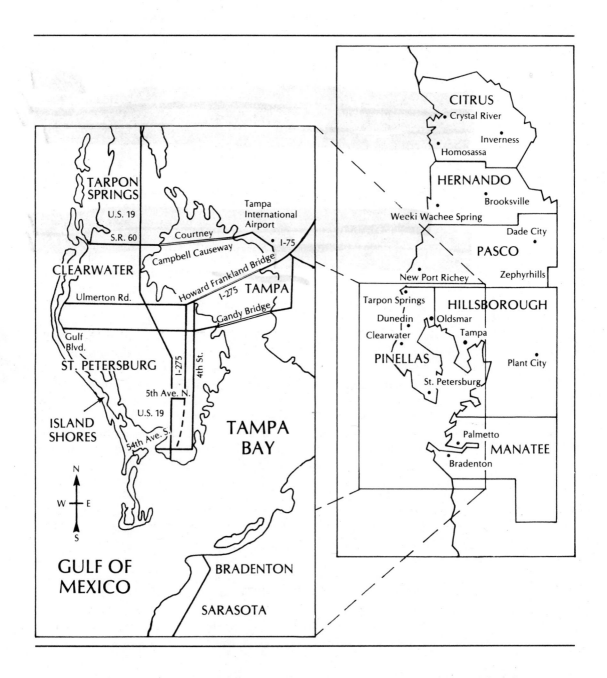

Although the Spanish explorer Narvaez landed on the peninsula in 1528 and marched to Tampa Bay, John C. Williams of Detroit is credited as the city's founder. Williams acquired 1,700 acres of wilderness land in 1876 which later became the nucleus of downtown St. Petersburg. Williams's intention was to establish a resort community to take advantage of the fine weather. However, his remote location had no transportation connection with other Florida population centers. As a result, he agreed to a partnership with Russian exile Piotr Alexeitch Dementieff (a.k.a. Peter Demens) contingent on Demens's completion of a railroad trunk line into the area.

The Orange Belt Line from Lake Monroe near Sanford, Florida was completed in 1888 when Williams's little community had a population of 30. As the story goes, Williams and Demens flipped a coin to decide who would name the new town. Demens won and elected to name the town St. Petersburg after his birthplace. Williams's resort hotel completed around 1890 was fittingly named The Detroit.

As early as 1885 the American Medical Association praised the climate and healthful surroundings as ideal. With its accessibility improved by the Orange Belt Line, the population had climbed to 300 by 1892 when the town was incorporated. Many of the early settlers were British who had emigrated to the Bahamas and Key West. In an effort to expand the resort reputation of St. Petersburg, the Chamber of Commerce established its first promotional budget of $150 in 1902. In 1907 a special tax was levied on year-round residents to support tourist promotion.

Today, thousands of people arrive daily at the Tampa International Airport which also serves St. Petersburg and Clearwater. Considered one of the most modern and efficient airports in the world, Tampa International has shuttle trains from the main terminal to the gates, an assortment of restaurants and boutiques, and a hotel with a revolving penthouse. Fifteen major air carriers fly into the airport, many with international routes to Central and South America and Europe.

St. Petersburg is also known as the Boating Capital of the United States. With boating activity supported by the Municipal Marina downtown and the St. Petersburg Yacht Club, St. Petersburg is home base to some of the most important sailboat and power boat races in the Gulf. The Swift Hurricane Classic, Isla de Mujeres Race, and the Southern Ocean Racing Conference championships represent the highlights of the season.

Fishing is also a favorite pastime in St. Petersburg where people can be seen lining the bridges fishing late into the night. Golf courses are widely available as are tennis courts.

While St. Petersburg has become a preferred retirement community for many, the city has tried to promote business development in the area to balance the population demographics. Since 1970, construction of new plants and plant expansions has totaled 1,196 and 19,005 new jobs have been created. Changes in population demographics in St. Petersburg and the surrounding counties between 1970 and 1979 are presented in Exhibit 1.

EXHIBIT 1 Population and population characteristics change, 1970 to 1979

Metro area

	April 1, 1979 population	Percent of total	Percent change since 1970
Total	1,521,799	100.0%	+39.8%
0–14 years	285,296	18.8	+14.7
15–24 years	217,866	14.3	+43.3
25–44 years	323,700	21.3	+51.2
45–64 years	338,423	22.2	+38.4
65 and over	356,514	23.4	+55.6
18 and over	1,165,496	76.6	+47.9
Median age	40.9 years	—	+2.5 years
White	1,385,288	91.0%	+42.5%
Nonwhite	136,511	9.0	+17.2
Male	716,075	47.1%	+39.1%
Female	805,724	52.9	+40.4

Pinellas

	April 1, 1979 population	Percent of total	Percent change since 1970
Total	725,457	100.0%	+38.9%
0–14 years	112,546	15.5	+14.8
15–24 years	82,771	11.4	+40.1
25–44 years	129,227	17.8	+49.0
45–64 years	171,011	23.6	+37.3
65 and over	229,902	31.7	+49.4
18 and over	584,955	80.6	+45.5
Median age	49.5 years	—	+1.4 years
White	671,331	92.5%	+40.4%
Nonwhite	54,126	7.5	+22.2
Male	334,017	46.0%	+38.9%
Female	391,440	54.0	+38.8

Pasco

	April 1, 1979 population	Percent of total	Percent change since 1970
Total	161,873	100.0%	+113.1%
0–14 years	25,662	15.9	+93.7
15–24 years	17,515	10.8	+111.6
25–44 years	23,962	14.8	+122.1
45–64 years	39,528	24.4	+101.5
65 and over	55,206	34.1	+129.8
18 and over	130,413	80.6	+117.6
Median age	52.0 years	—	−1.4 years
White	157,783	97.5%	+119.4%
Nonwhite	4,090	2.5	+1.5
Male	77,599	47.9%	+110.7%
Female	84,274	52.1	+115.4

Manatee

	April 1, 1979 population	Percent of total	Percent change since 1970
Total	141,188	100.0%	+45.4%
0–14 years	23,837	16.9	+27.2
15–24 years	15,049	10.6	+37.1
25–44 years	24,504	17.4	+58.1
45–64 years	33,874	24.0	+50.1
65 and over	43,924	31.1	+49.8
18 and over	112,346	80.0	+51.3
Median age	49.2 years	—	+.5 years
White	128,068	90.7%	+50.1%
Nonwhite	13,120	9.3	+11.5
Male	66,700	47.2%	+46.7%
Female	74,488	52.8	+44.2

Citrus

	April 1, 1979 population	Percent of total	Percent change since 1970
Total	42,397	100.0%	+120.9%
0–14 years	7,155	16.9	+85.1
15–24 years	3,717	8.8	+81.7
25–44 years	6,215	14.6	+113.4
45–64 years	11,909	28.1	+121.4
65 and over	13,401	31.6	+168.4
18 and over	33,869	79.9	+134.5
Median age	51.9 years	—	+2.8 years
White	40,622	95.8%	+134.3%
Nonwhite	1,775	4.2	−4.4
Male	20,397	48.1%	+119.9%
Female	22,000	51.9	+121.8

Hillsborough

	April 1, 1979 population	Percent of total	Percent change since 1970
Total	634,469	100.0%	+29.4%
0–14 years	147,088	23.2	+7.0
15–24 years	117,580	18.5	+38.8
25–44 years	170,511	26.9	+46.3
45–64 years	127,884	20.2	+27.4
65 and over	71,406	11.2	+39.5
18 and over	450,128	70.9	+38.1
Median age	31.2 years	—	+2.7 years
White	556,174	87.7%	+31.8%
Nonwhite	78,295	12.3	+14.9
Male	304,459	48.0%	+28.1%
Female	330,010	52.0	+30.6

Hernando

	April 1, 1979 population	Percent of total	Percent change since 1970
Total	38,182	100.0%	+124.5%
0–14 years	7,399	19.4	+73.8
15–24 years	4,166	10.9	+93.8
25–44 years	7,104	18.6	+120.7
45–64 years	10,268	26.9	+161.9
65 and over	9,245	24.2	+167.4
18 and over	29,253	76.6	+144.9
Median age	45.8 years	—	+7.6 years
White	35,833	93.8%	+146.1%
Nonwhite	2,349	6.2	−3.9
Male	18,833	49.3%	+125.7%
Female	19,349	50.7	+123.5

Source: University of Florida, Bureau of Economic and Business Research "Age, Race and Sex Components of Florida Population—1979," and 1970 Census. Prepared by: Research Department, St. Petersburg Times and Evening Independent, May 1980.

A survey of newcomers to the St. Petersburg area conducted by Suncoast Opinion Surveys in 1980 reveals some further information. This group of newcomers is considered to represent approximately 19 percent of the adult population in Pinellas County. Survey results are presented in Exhibit 2.

EXHIBIT 2 Demographic profile of Pinellas residents

	Total Pinellas adults	By length of residency		
		Newcomers (2 years or less)	Midterm residents (3–10 years)	Long-term residents (over 10 years)
Total	100%	19%	35%	46%
Sex				
Male	45%	46%	51%	40%
Female	55	54	49	60
Age				
18–24 years	10%	25%	7%	6%
25–34 years	17	20	22	13
35–49 years	21	24	18	22
50–64 years	22	19	23	22
65–74 years	18	10	22	18
75 years and over	12	2	8	19
Median adult age (years)	51.4	38.1	52.0	56.1
Where born*				
Pinellas County	8%	1%	1%	16%
Other Florida	5	7	4	5
Northeast	32	31	37	29
Midwest	31	35	31	29
South	15	17	14	14
West	3	3	4	2
Outside United States	6	6	9	5
Education				
Grammar school	4%	1%	4%	6%
Some high school	11	6	12	12
High school graduate	34	28	32	37
Technical, business school graduate	7	8	8	7
Some college	21	24	21	20
College graduate	23	33	23	18
Employment status				
Employed full time	43%	56%	46%	35%
Employed part time	7	5	7	7
Temporarily out of work	3	6	1	3
Retired	32	19	35	34
Housewife	11	11	7	15
Disabled	2	1	3	3
Other	2	2	1	3

* *Northeast* includes Connecticut, Maine, Massachusetts, New Hampshire, New Jersey, New York, Pennsylvania, Rhode Island, and Vermont.

Midwest includes Illinois, Indiana, Iowa, Kansas, Michigan, Minnesota, Missouri, Nebraska, North Dakota, Ohio, South Dakota, and Wisconsin.

South includes Alabama, Arkansas, Delaware, Washington, D.C., Georgia, Kentucky, Louisiana, Maryland, Mississippi, North Carolina, Oklahoma, South Carolina, Tennessee, Texas, Virginia, and West Virginia.

West includes Alaska, Arizona, California, Colorado, Hawaii, Idaho, Montana, Nevada, New Mexico, Oregon, Utah, Washington, and Wyoming.

EXHIBIT 2 *(continued)*

	Total Pinellas adults	By length of residency		
		Newcomers (2 years or less)	Midterm residents (3–10 years)	Long-term residents (over 10 years)
Women				
Employed outside home	40%	49%	41%	36%
Not employed outside home	60	51	59	64
Household income				
Under $10,000	23%	21%	18%	28%
$10,000–$15,000	18	24	16	17
$15,001–$20,000	19	12	23	19
Over $20,000	40	43	43	36
Median	$17,400	$17,100	$18,500	$16,300
Own/rent residence				
Own, with mortgage	47%	37%	52%	47%
Own, no mortgage	33	19	32	40
Rent	19	42	15	13
Other	1	2	1	†
Type of residence				
Single family	69%	53%	68%	77%
Apartment	11	19	10	7
Condominium	9	11	10	7
Mobile home	9	11	10	7
Other	2	6	2	2
Household size				
1 person	21%	14%	16%	26%
2 persons	41	45	48	35
3 persons	13	15	9	14
4 persons	15	15	15	16
5 or more persons	10	11	12	9
Average	2.5	2.6	2.6	2.5
Children present in household				
No children present	69%	68%	69%	69%
Child(ren) present	31	32	31	31
Race				
White	96%	97%	98%	94%
Nonwhite	4	3	2	6
Household income sources				
Wages/salaries only	40%	53%	39%	36%
Wage/salary and other regular sources‡	25	21	26	26
Other regular sources only	34	26	34	37
No income sources	1	—	1	1
Number of wage earners in household				
None	35%	26%	35%	39%
One wage earner	31	30	33	30
Two wage earners	26	36	19	27
Three wage earners	6	6	11	2
Base	(501)	(93)	(175)	(233)

† Less than one half of 1 percent.

‡ Other regular sources = Other than wages and salaries; includes social security, dividends, interest, alimony, child support, disability, pension, welfare, or other benefits.

EXHIBIT 2 *(continued)*

	Total Pinellas adults	By length of residency		
		Newcomers (2 years or less)	Midterm residents (3–10 years)	Long-term residents (over 10 years)
Four or more	2%	2%	2%	2%
Average	1.1	1.3	1.1	1.0
Residence				
North of Ulmerton Road	43%	55%	44%	37%
South of Ulmerton Road	57	45	56	63
Daily newspapers read regularly				
St. Petersburg Times	83%	83%	82%	84%
Evening Independent	22	15	18	27
Clearwater Sun	23	23	28	20
Tampa Tribune	3	6	4	2
Other	3	4	2	3
None	4	3	3	5
Daily newspapers read yesterday				
St. Petersburg Times	67%	59%	68%	69%
Evening Independent	16	11	8	23
Clearwater Sun	18	18	21	15
Tampa Tribune	2	3	2	2
Other	1	1	—	2
None	15	21	13	14
Sunday newspaper read last Sunday				
St. Petersburg Times	74%	72%	70%	78%
Clearwater Sun	17	16	19	15
Tampa Tribune	1	2	2	—
Broadcast media				
Watched television yesterday:				
6:00–8:59 A.M.	8%	7%	6%	8%
9:00–11:59 A.M.	10	7	10	11
Noon–5:59 P.M.	34	37	27	35
6:00–8:59 P.M.	67	66	70	65
9:00–10:59 P.M.	61	63	63	59
11:00 P.M. or later	30	26	30	31
Don't know when watched	1	—	2	1
Did not watch TV yesterday	11	13	8	13
Subscriber to cable TV	11%	11%	14%	9%
Not cable TV subscriber	89	89	86	91
Listened to radio yesterday:				
6:00–8:59 A.M.	34%	39%	38%	30%
9:00–11:59 A.M.	28	28	29	26
Noon–5:59 P.M.	32	27	37	31
6:00–8:59 P.M.	15	13	14	16
9:00–10:59 P.M.	9	2	11	10
11:00 P.M. or later	7	2	10	8
Don't know when listened	2	2	1	3
Did not listen to radio yesterday	37	38	34	40
Checking account	90%	92%	91%	88%
Base	(501)	(93)	(175)	(233)

EXHIBIT 2 (concluded)

	Total Pinellas adults	By length of residency		
		Newcomers (2 years or less)	Short-term residents (3–10 years)	Long-term residents (over 10 years)
Savings account	89%	82%	92%	90%
At bank	74	76	77	71
At savings and loan	43	34	38	51
At credit union	26	21	30	24
MasterCard or Visa	55%	56	59	52
MasterCard	36	39	41	31
Visa	46	48	46	45
Other credit cards:				
American Express	10%	18%	13%	6%
Diners Club	3	4	4	2
Carte Blanche	2	2	3	2
Passport	18	11	22	18
Base	(501)	(93)	(175)	(233)

Background on Island Shores

Management at Enterprise was convinced that careful planning and gradual development would be critical to the success of the Island Shores project given their previous experience. In order to appeal to both retirees and second-home vacationers, Island Shores had to represent a distinct combination of benefits. While many of the Florida condominium complexes were just places to hang one's hat and residents were dependent on the Ft. Lauderdale or Miami communities for things to do and places to go, the location of Island Shores required that many of these entertainment and recreation options be available on the island. Enterprise's plan called for development of the following amenities: angling, beaches, golf, jogging and bicycle paths, open areas, clubhouse and restaurant, sailing, shopping, sunbathing, swimming pools, tennis and racket-ball courts, and water skiing. In order to attract buyers in the early stages of development at least some of these planned benefits had to be apparent, so the golf course and clubhouse went into construction immediately.

The plan for the island called for high density residential units to be built on the water's edge and a golf course in the center. Since the golf course was considered a major drawing feature, the problems associated with growing grass where none had grown before had to be faced immediately. In 1974 work on the golf course began at the same time as condominium construction. After several false starts and experimentation with many varieties of grass, ground-covers, and shrubs, reasonably well-manicured greens appeared three years later. It became painfully clear that landscaping a "spoil spot" would take perseverance, patience, and a great deal of money. Costs associated with construction of the golf course alone totaled a million dollars.

Michele Perez, an award winning architect from California, was responsible for designing the residential structures in harmony with the island environment. Due to the priority given the 18-hole golf course in the 320-acre parcel and the desire to maximize picturesque views from each condo unit, the residential development plan called for high density construction along the water's edge. The land utilization goal of 14 condominiums per acre was met by Perez's plan for positioning units diagonally to the water rather than lining them up parallel to the beach frontage in traditional fashion. These clusters form miniature neighborhoods while maximizing ocean views. For each cluster a swimming pool and sunbathing deck was constructed which acts as a social gathering spot and provides a recreational area with a relatively large amount of privacy. The large "community pool" concept was considered by Enterprise to be unappealing to many potential residents who were expected to value easy access to the pool's ambience more than its Olympic proportions. Resident parking was designed underneath the buildings to minimize the asphalt perspective so typical of high density living environments.

Four-story and 12-story high-rise units, 2-story townhouses, and free-standing condominium villas were constructed. The units in greatest demand between 1975 and 1980 were villas. Many of them sold before construction was even begun. Two bedroom units in the mid- and high-rise buildings were also very popular. One bedroom high-rise units and townhouses were still available although on a limited basis.

The primary construction materials were stucco and wood which blended with the Spanish architectural influence throughout the St. Petersburg area. As each building was completed, landscaping was carefully undertaken. The landscape architects working for Enterprise were sent to Disney World in Orlando to study plantings. Using similar shrubs which could adapt to conditions at Island Shores, sculptured shrubs and ever-blooming varieties of plants created a garden atmosphere. In 1981 alone, the cost of landscaping approached $1.5 million not counting individual building phases.

In 1975 the condominiums on Island Shores ranged in price from $42,000 to $50,000. The average market value of these units for resale in 1982 is $108,034. Smith's records showed that in December 1981, 70 units had been sold for a total of $7,562,389. Overall, new sales in 1980 were $32 million and sales in 1981 were $34 million. Prices for units still under construction in the Colony Beach portion of the project as of 1982 are shown here.

Villas the least expensive.

	Colony Beach (6 story)	
Model	*Size*	*Price*
Madrid	1 bedroom—1½ bath	$70,000–$ 92,900
Sevilla	2 bedroom—2 bath	$90,900–$125,000
Villa	2 bedroom—2 bath	$86,900–$107,000

	Colony Beach (12 story)	
Model	*Size*	*Price*
Barcelona	2 bedroom—2 bath	$133,000–$162,000
Sevilla	2 bedroom—2 bath	$135,000–$166,000
Villa	2 bedroom—2 bath	$110,000–$117,000

Prices vary for the models depending on what floor they are on in the building and their relative exposure. Each unit has its own balcony, carpeting, a full set of appliances, and assigned parking. Two bedroom–two bath models had been the most in demand with different square footage and floor plans distinguishing Sevilla, Villa, and Barcelona models. Recent prices at Island Shores for villas had been in the range of $79,000 to $112,000, mid-rise units from $70,000 to $250,000, and high-rise units $95,000 to $166,000. Smith was concerned that as costs escalated the project was being priced out of the reach of most people in the market for vacation homes. While the number of one bedroom units could be increased, in the future they did not appear to be the most desirable. He wondered if square footage in the two bedroom–two bath models could be reduced further or if the target market should be narrowed to primary home buyers rather than including vacation home buyers. This would have implications for the physical design of the units and the required storage space. The Colony Beach area with a planned 1,200 units was not scheduled for completion until 1988. Based on previous experience, it was currently estimated that the 340 units, as yet unsold, would be fully occupied by the end of 1984.

Competition

Smith knew from friends in the business and his own observations that competitors' sales had declined in recent months. While he felt Island Shores was more desirable than similar high-rise condominium units located on the Intracoastal Waterway or the Mandalay Channel, he had collected pricing information hoping it would help him develop his marketing plan. In general, unit square footage ranges from 950–1,450 and the selling price from $77–$115 per square foot. Exhibit 3 presents data for projects comparable to the units in Colony Beach.

It was clear that the development firms behind the competition were aggressive and unlikely to give market share to Island Shores without a battle. Smith didn't know for sure how they would respond to the recent market downturn, but he suspected it would be through strengthened promotional efforts. It was likely that the promotion budget for the Colony Beach community would have to be increased just to keep pace with the competition and maintain the build-out schedule for 1984–85.

EXHIBIT 3 Competitive prices

Marina walk

Model	Description	Price range	Units/building
J	2 bedroom—2 bath	$125,000–$150,000	20
K	2 bedroom—den—2 bath	$140,000–$165,000	20
L	2 bedroom—2 bath	$112,500–$142,000	20
M	1 bedroom—1½ bath	$ 90,000–$110,000	20
NE	2 bedroom—2 bath	$155,000–$185,000	20
NW	2 bedroom—2 bath	$167,500–$202,500	20

Sailfish Key

Model	Description	Price range	Units/building
Sunfish	1 bedroom—1 bath	$ 97,900–$ 99,900	6
Yacht	1 bedroom—1½ bath	$110,000–$126,400	10
Corsair	2 bedroom—2 bath	$136,500–$149,500	12
Brigantine	2 bedroom—2 bath	$167,000–$175,000	6
Galleon	2 bedroom—2 bath*	$171,000–$179,500	10
Frigate	2 bedroom—2 bath—den	$215,000	2
Clipper	3 bedroom—2½ bath	$270,000	2

* Corner.

Buyer Profiles

In 1975 the average age of Island Shores condominium buyers was 58. More recently, the average age had decreased to approximately 52 with many buyers in their late 40s. Smith was unsure how to interpret this trend. During the early stages of development, many retirees and investment buyers came from Illinois, Ohio, and Michigan. As economic conditions in these areas worsened, fewer and fewer newcomers seemed to come from the Midwest. To Smith's surprise, an increasing number of European and South Americans were coming to Island Shores over any number of other condominium areas. It seemed that there were growing numbers of buyers from West Germany, France, Venezuela, Argentina, and Mexico. Each nationality tended to cluster together at Island Shores and to maintain close social ties. Whether this pattern would present problems in the long run for the total community was unclear.

A growing concern voiced by condominium residents was the issue of security. The small groupings of units actually facilitated security since neighbors knew each other's comings and goings and watched out for one another. The problem seemed to be caused by transients. When investment buyers rented their condominiums long distance they could exercise very little control over their tenants. Similarly, management at Island Shores had scant information about renters and no power to intervene unless explicit rules and regulations were being violated. Compared to other condominium developments in the St. Petersburg area the relative crime rate at Island Shores was very low. St.

Petersburg itself had little crime compared to other major cities like Miami. Smith began to wonder whether the residents' perceptions of security were more at issue than the occasional burglary. Since one of the objectives of the management was to create an atmosphere of stability in a relaxing environment, any tensions caused by real or imagined security problems would have to be resolved.

Smith wondered if there was some way to encourage more permanent residents and fewer speculative investors to minimize the transient issue. If security personnel were increased it was not clear whether the result would be to alarm or calm the residents and potential buyers. As it had turned out so far, some of the individuals sampling life at Island Shores by renting from absentee owners eventually purchased units on the island although the number of such individuals was small.

Marketing Decisions

Before Smith could recommend a marketing program he needed to establish the basic target market and whether or not to continue building at Island Shores. Secondary data showed that more people leave New York for the South every year than any other state. If this market was to be reached, however, there would be a lengthy process of registering Enterprise with New York state authorities in order to promote land sales to New York residents. Smith estimated this process would take about a year. Enterprise was already registered in Michigan, Illinois, Indiana, Ohio, and Pennsylvania.

Another possible market was comprised of people already in the St. Petersburg area. Considering the escalation of land values in recent years, many individuals could sell their existing property for twice its purchase price. In this event the extensive amenity package at Island Shores, offering both quality golf and boating, might prove very attractive. Promotional efforts would certainly be reduced in reaching this market segment Smith thought.

The international market seemed to be one of growing importance. If this market was actively pursued, the cost and methods of reaching buyers were difficult to determine. The long-run potential of this market was unclear. Smith became even more unsure as he thought about international currency fluctuations and the recent devaluation of the peso.

Expanding on the plan for development at Island Shores was by far the easiest plan of action to adopt in the short run but Smith wondered if perhaps a lower amenity package with a golf course but no ocean access might not recapture the Midwest market. He knew of projects such as The Westside near Tampa Airport which concentrated on patio homes, both attached and detached, with prices from $45,000 to $70,000. The patio home concept was relatively new. There was no yard to speak of with the house, just the fenced patio. In some parts of the country they were known as zero-lot homes. They offered single-family housing with very low maintenance which might prove appealing to retirees and young families. Patio homes had gained acceptance as starter

ALTERNATIVE

7 50?0† over 45 42

homes for young couples and there seemed to be encouragement to expand the target market.

A parcel of 200 acres just east of Bradenton in Manatee County was available for purchase which might prove suitable. With the lower yield per acre of about 6 units compared to 14 units per acre at Island Shores, Smith felt there would be a potential 350–380 units with the remaining land used for a golf course. While the price of the parcel was open to negotiation, the asking figure was $6 million. Smith had 10 days to pick up a 90-day option on this property. This would mean a commitment of $5,000.

If building was continued immediately at Island Shores, the mix of high-rise, mid-rise, and villas needed to be considered as did the two-bedroom and one-bedroom proportion. If prices were to be reduced, something would have to change. Existing plans called for development of the Ocean Watch portion of the project which was a mid-rise building series with 50 two- and three-bedroom condominium units from $175,000 to $260,000. This was a 1982 estimate, but completion was not scheduled until 1985 when prices would certainly be higher. The current plan called for surface preparation of the area beginning in 1983. If the market became highly price sensitive a potential option was to sell the units under a time-sharing arrangement. Smith knew that existing owners in Colony Beach had voiced objection to such a proposal earlier, but then again, Ocean Watch was a different situation. The target market for this type of vacation home would be a totally new one for Enterprise.

Smith realized that forecasting the demand for seasonal vacation homes versus year-round retirement homes was a critical issue that would strongly influence project location and physical design decisions. Until the best target market was identified, little in the way of price or promotional decisions could be resolved. The person interested in a $200,000 condominium would not likely be the same individual considering a $60,000 patio home.

Since the attributes and amenities of the projects would be very different, the promotional messages would also be very different. Smith was responsible for developing the overall marketing strategy for his projects and would make decisions on promotional strategy as well. A local advertising agency would handle the details of implementation such as art, collateral materials, production, and media buying.

Smith felt strongly that when the real estate market picked up, the Tampa–St. Petersburg area would be among the first to lead the upturn. It was difficult to determine, however, which segments of the market represented the best opportunities for Enterprise. As Smith tried to evaluate the different opportunities facing him, he knew that it was going to be a long weekend. Next Wednesday's board meeting would come all too soon.

Case 3

League of Catholic Women

During the summer of 1975 Mary Lynn Landis, the president of the League of Catholic Women, faced a tightening financial situation. In this period of inflation the League's troubles were compounded by the increased number of Detroiters who needed the League's assistance and by the increased administrative complexity of the social service programs established to administer aid. While the League's budget was approaching $1.5 million annually, most support was in the form of federal or foundation grants earmarked for particular social service programs. In the past, membership contributions had been relied upon to defray administrative expenses, but presently membership in the League was on a sharp decline. Mrs. Landis faced the problem of developing a marketing plan to increase membership without appreciably increasing costs by the beginning of the next membership drive in March of 1976.

Founding, Philosophy, History

In 1906 a small group of Catholic women formed the Weinman Center to teach English and religion to foreign-born persons who had settled in Detroit, Michigan. The Weinman Center also functioned as a day nursery and became the first Michigan organization to assist immigrants in establishing themselves. This group of women became the Catholic Settlement Association of Detroit in 1911.

The League of Catholic Women was incorporated out of the Catholic Settlement Association of Detroit in 1915. The League's purpose as originally stated was: "To unite Catholic women for the promotion of religious, intellectual, and charitable work." The charitable work continued the settlement work including family visiting, health care, religious instruction, and maintaining a representative at the juvenile court. The services were directed at women, in particular adolescent and minority adult women, rather than toward families. At the time of incorporation the Weinman Center's program was expanded to include classes in domestic science, sewing, dramatics, dance, manual training, Girl Scouts, athletics, kindergarten, and social clubs. All these classes were taught by volunteers. The Weinman Center program became a model for other League community centers established in 1919 and 1920 in other Detroit neighborhoods.

In the early days of the League's existence there was no ongoing fundraising mechanism. It was then, and remains today, independent of the Catholic Church and as such received no direct aid from the Archdiocese of Detroit. Activities were supported by the personal financing of its members. An example of this financing is the sale of a $30,000 bond issue in 1916 to League members.

The proceeds of that first bond issue established the Watson Street Club House, a residence for homeless girls. In 1925 the League expanded its residence home program by opening the Madeleine Sophie Training Home for Girls. It served primarily delinquent girls and is still operating today as Barat House. The Watson Street Club and the Madeleine Sophie Home created the League's first payroll obligations. While they were staffed primarily by volunteers they had professional social and child care workers on their staffs.

As the League's programs expanded the women began to plan for a headquarters building to house many activities and to provide ample residence rooms for working women and girls living away from their families. The first organized membership drive, held in the early 1920s, netted $11,771.47. This first drive was the kickoff for the Building Fund which resulted in the completion of Casgrain Hall by January of 1928. Casgrain Hall, which still serves as the League's headquarters, was heavily mortgaged and faced foreclosure in its first year. To rescue their building, League members "bought" bricks in the building and avoided foreclosure. The building was paid off by 1940.

In the 1940s the League expanded its services to provide day-care facilities and recreational programs to the black and Latin communities of Detroit. The 1950s and early 1960s saw little change in the League's activities. In the late 1960s the League moved into a new area of rehabilitation programs for women convicts.

Present

Today the League of Catholic Women is the oldest and largest volunteer social service organization operating in Detroit. It is now administered by a 48-member board of trustees, a president (Mrs. Landis), two vice presidents, a secretary, and a treasurer elected annually by the general membership. All officers and board members serve without pay. The League administration is no longer involved in day-to-day operations of social services. In the past 10 years an agency structure (see Exhibit 1) has been created whereby each League agency has responsibility for a particular area of social service (see Exhibit 2). Each agency has a paid professional executive director and staff, responsibility for planning and executing its own budget, and an autonomous board of

EXHIBIT 1 Administrative structure

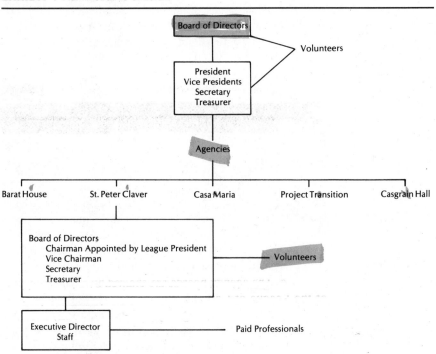

EXHIBIT 2 Synopsis of agency services and funding sources

Barat House

An "open" residence treatment center for up to 20 emotionally disturbed teenage girls, offering psychiatric treatment and educational development. Funded by the United Foundation and the State Department of Social Services.

Casa Maria

Community center in Tiger Stadium area, serving Latinos, blacks, Maltese, and Appalachian whites. It incorporates a nursery school, recreation, crafts, and counseling for youngsters and adult community programs. Funded by Archdiocese Development Fund and federal grants through the Juvenile Facilities Network.

St. Peter Claver

Community center on the lower east side, predominately serving blacks. It incorporates a day-care center, recreation, crafts, and counseling for youngsters and adult community programs. Funded by the United Foundation.

EXHIBIT 2 *(concluded)*

Project Transition

Job training, residence, counseling, and employment assistance for 25 women from the Detroit House of Corrections and other disadvantaged backgrounds. A pilot program initiated by the League in 1971 aimed at offering total rehabilitation for women offenders; it is housed on the fourth floor of Casgrain Hall. Funded by state and federal grants and the Board of Education of the city of Detroit, with some assistance from the League.

Casgrain Hall

Eight-story League building near Wayne State University which provides low-cost residence for women of all ages; offers meeting rooms, ballroom and conference facilities for community activities; and serves as League administration headquarters. Funded by rent receipts; currently carrying a large deficit.

---

directors. The agency boards are chaired by a person appointed by the president of the League of Catholic Women but operate independent of League control. Persons selected to fill agency boards are usually concerned citizens from the neighborhood the agency serves, or professional persons with expertise in social work, health care, or administration. All agency board members serve without pay.

The League is in effect the umbrella administration for the agencies. The agencies operate independently, with supervision from the League board only in areas of general policy and fiscal matters. The League bookkeeping office handles all bookkeeping for the agencies. All federal, state, and foundation grants for agency programs are channeled through the League office and all payables the agencies incur are billed directly to the League.

Casgrain Hall is the one agency that is handled differently. While it has its own board of directors, it is included in the League budget because it does not receive outside aid. In an effort to maintain low-cost housing in the face of rising operating costs, Casgrain Hall has incurred a deficit each of the past four years. This past year it approached $80,000. The problem has been compounded by an environment that has changed drastically since the widespread civil disturbances of 1967. Since then, the 194-room residence hall has experienced an occupancy rate rarely above 60 percent.

The Casgrain Hall deficit consumes more of the League's surplus funds each year. In the past three years the League has been unable to provide any direct financial aid to its other agencies because of the Casgrain drain. The only money that could be applied to the deficit was the unrestricted public support (see Exhibits 3 and 4). The survival of the League seemed to depend on increasing the unrestricted public support.

EXHIBIT 3
LEAGUE OF CATHOLIC WOMEN OF DETROIT, MICHIGAN
Balance Sheets
December 31, 1974,
With Comparative Figures for 1973

	1974	1973
Assets		
Cash	$ 26,020	$ 55,582
Short-term commercial notes	54,945	—
Total	80,965	55,582
Accounts receivable:		
Residence (less allowance for doubtful accounts of		
$1,200 in 1974 and $500 in 1973)	6,199	2,414
Sponsored agencies	9,729	8,222
Related nonprofit corporation	1,544	3,304
Other	117	199
Total	17,589	14,139
Accrued interest receivable	847	151
Prepaid expense	5,255	7,174
Due from restricted fund	8,955	22,693
Total	15,057	30,018
Cash	—	22,340
Grants receivable	216,633	78,629
Total	216,633	100,969
Land, buildings, and equipment fund:		
Land, buildings, and equipment	1,927,586	1,926,413
Less accumulated depreciation	(737,296)	(665,278)
Total assets	$1,520,534	$1,461,843
Liabilities and Fund Balances		
Current funds		
Unrestricted:		
Accounts payable	$ 5,622	$ 6,653
Advance rentals and security	3,098	2,641
Withheld from employees	1,827	2,004
Loan payable	25,000	—
Total liabilities	35,547	11,298
Fund balance	78,064	88,441
Total	113,611	99,739
Restricted:		
Due to unrestricted fund	8,955	22,693
Deferred support	202,629	55,936
Total liabilities and deferred support	211,584	78,629
Fund balance	5,049	22,340
Total	216,633	100,969
Land, buildings, and equipment fund:		
Fund balance	1,190,290	1,261,135
Total liabilities and fund balances	$1,520,534	$1,461,843

EXHIBIT 4

LEAGUE OF CATHOLIC WOMEN OF DETROIT, MICHIGAN
Statement of Support, Revenue, and Expenses,
and Changes in Fund Balances
Year Ended December 31, 1974,
With Comparative Totals for 1973

	1974				
	Current funds		Land, build-ings, and equipment fund	Total all funds	
	Unre-stricted	Re-stricted		1974	1973
Public support and revenue:					
Public support:					
Contributions	$ 16,884	$ 7,220	—	$ 24,104	$ 63,811
Memberships and fund raising	29,749	—	—	29,749	27,781
Grants		91,889	—	91,889	61,674
Total public support	46,633	99,109	—	145,742	153,266
Revenue:					
Residence rents	$171,430	—	—	$171,430	$163,876
Bargain counter sales	56,505	—	—	56,505	49,086
Nursery service fees	96,632	—	—	96,632	96,200
Activities and cafeteria rentals	8,609	—	—	8,609	7,345
Investment income	5,497	—	—	5,497	4,397
Miscellaneous	5,034	—	—	5,034	8,354
Total revenue	343,707	—	—	343,707	329,258
Total public support and revenue	390,340	99,109	—	489,449	482,524
Expenses:					
Program services:					
Residence	255,725	2,697	42,509	300,931	288,067
Nursery	97,426	—	5,409	102,835	112,089
Project transition 1973–1974	171	53,866	2,270	56,307	50,725
Project transition 1974–1975	109	50,019	2,270	52,398	35,993
Contributions to sponsored agencies	10,000	—		10,000	—
Depreciation of facilities used by sponsored agency and related nonprofit corporation	—	—	17,018	17,018	17,018
Total program service	363,431	$106,582	69,476	539,489	503,892
Supporting services:					
Management and general	16,584	—	3,249	19,833	20,740
Membership and communication	6,669	—	168	6,837	8,917
Bargain counters	21,803	—	—	21,803	15,541
Total supporting services	45,056	—	3,417	48,473	45,198
Total expenses	408,487	106,582	72,893	$587,962	$549,090
Excess (deficiency) of public support and revenue over expense	(18,147)	(7,473)	(72,893)		
Other changes in fund balance:					
Current funds used for the purchase of equipment	(1,130)	(918)	2,048		
Transfer—donor release of restriction	8,900	(8,900)	—		
Fund balances, January 1, 1974	88,441	$ 22,340	1,261,135		
Fund balances, December 31, 1974	$ 78,064	$ 5,049	$1,190,290		

Membership

In the early days of the League activity, membership was a loosely defined concept. Any Catholic woman who was in sympathy with League goals and volunteered some of her time to settlement work was considered a member. It wasn't until the early 1920s that membership lists were compiled and an annual dues of $1 was instituted. Early membership rosters indicate that members were drawn primarily from Detroit's upper socioeconomic strata. The lists contain many names from families prominent in the blossoming auto and auto-related industry.

It is evident from records of financial contributions that the early members were not important for their $1 membership dues but for the larger personal resources they could bring to bear on the League's projects. For many years the League operated in a social service sphere in which its programs could be financed almost solely by its members' wealth. This situation changed in the 1930s and 1940s when League programs became more vigorous and the tax laws were changed to place social service more squarely in government hands. Today, large contributions by individual members are rare. The largest component of membership support is now the annual dues.

Today, membership is open to any woman in sympathy with the object of the League. Membership is offered in five classes. Dues are payable annually, charged as follows:

Sustaining	$ 10
Contributing	5
General	2
Life	100
Memorial	100

The bylaws of the League make no distinction between membership classes as to privileges or obligations. Exhibit 5 shows the costs incurred in connection

EXHIBIT 5 Costs associated with membership

Membership:	
Salaries	$1,933.30
FICA taxes	113.04
Employment tax	21.03
Worker's Compensation	16.93
Equipment and maintenance	29.94
Office supplies	965.62
Postage	518.53
Telephone	130.00
Mileage	15.72
Printing	588.00
Administrative expense	1,921.07
	$6,253.18

EXHIBIT 5 *(concluded)*

Communications:	
Salaries	$1,933.30
FICA taxes	113.04
Employment tax	21.03
Worker's Compensation	16.93
Equipment and maintenance	29.93
Office supplies	87.49
Postage	34.95
Printing	95.00
Administrative expense	1,097.76
	$3,429.43

with membership. The League bookkeeping office has always separated these costs into "Membership" and "Communication." Membership consists of those costs incurred in communicating solely with members. Communication costs are primarily the cost of quarterly newsletters.

Membership Drive Structure

Membership drives at the League of Catholic Women are conducted on an annual basis during the designated membership month of March. The drives are coordinated by a central committee consisting of a membership chairwoman and up to 17 membership coordinators (see Exhibit 6). Each coordinator directs the activities in a geographical region called a vicariate. Vicariates are composed of groups of individual churches or parishes in approximately the same geographical area (see Exhibit 7). Vicariates were formed in the Archdiocese of Detroit to foster closer ties and better communication among the member

EXHIBIT 6 Membership drive structure

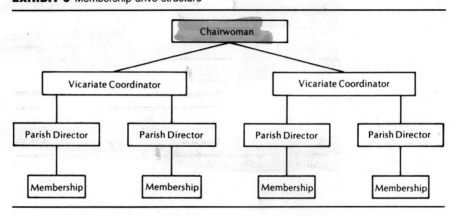

EXHIBIT 7 Map of vicariates

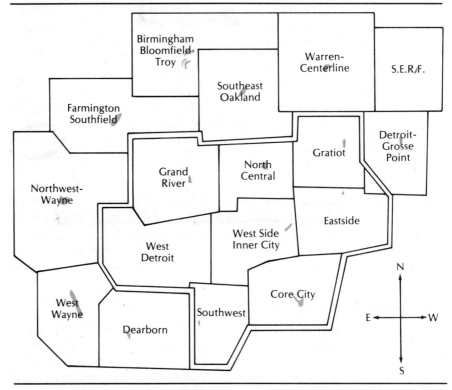

Note: Area enclosed by double line represents city of Detroit limits—outside area: suburbs.

parishes and the central Archdiocese offices. Thus, it became a set of natural regions within which the League could conduct the annual membership drive.

Under each vicariate coordinator in the structure are the parish membership directors (see Exhibit 6). These directors formed the backbone of the general membership structure. It is at this level that much of the major work of the membership drive was conducted. Each parish director had the responsibility for conducting the drive at her own parish in a manner that she deemed appropriate for her parish. Because each parish differed in important characteristics like physical age, and location of the neighborhood, racial and ethnic composition, and accessibility to members, many different methods were employed during the membership drive. The League did not discourage this heterogeneity of technique but in fact encouraged each director to pursue the most appropriate method that the parish director felt would be the most successful during the membership drive.

For the past few years the League has held a luncheon at Casgrain Hall in

February for parish directors as a kickoff for the membership drive. This luncheon has been poorly attended in the past. The League officers believe poor attendance is attributable to the fact that suburban directors fear Casgrain's neighborhood or find the distance prohibitive.

After the kickoff luncheon and during the activities each March the League supplied each parish director with materials to be used to accomplish the membership objectives. These materials included the preprinted membership envelopes containing a blank membership card and a preprinted "Dear Parishioner" letter signed by the respective parish director. These letters detailed the activities of the League and contained other facts and information which would be of interest to prospective League members. In addition to the above, postage paid envelopes addressed to the League and an information brochure suitable for inserting into the parish newspaper were available. These materials are made accessible to the parish directors if they use the convenient order form the League sends to them. Exhibit 8 is an example of League promotional material.

At the beginning of the membership drive each director is issued this publicity information along with a listing of members in her parish from the previous year which are for renewals and a report form used to tabulate the results of the membership drive. Names, addresses, dollar amounts of the donations, and summary totals are the responsibility of each director on the report forms.

Parish directors forward their results and problems to the vicariate coordinators so that the central membership committee is advised of the results. In addition to overseeing the parish directors, the vicariate coordinators are responsible for ensuring that each parish of the vicariate has a director to conduct the membership drive. In the areas of the Archdiocese of Detroit in which the League is active there are 17 vicariates. Contained in these vicariates are 232 parishes of various sizes.

Membership Problem

In the summer of 1975 shortly after the conclusion of the March membership drive the League studied the results comparing them to those of previous campaigns. In June of 1975 the League had 10,145 members that contributed $26,530. But this was a decline of 43 percent from the 1970 total of 17,913 and a decline of 51 percent from the 1965 total of 21,000. Faced with the alarming decline in membership over a 10-year period, a closer examination was conducted. Exhibit 9 presents membership data by vicariates used in examining the problem.

In summary, the results showed that 74 of the 218 parishes did not include at least one member of the League and that the vicariate coordinators had solicited a total of 108 parish directors leaving 124 parishes without directors in 1975. In addition 2,508 members from 1974 did not renew their membership, a total of 25 percent of all the previous year's members.

EXHIBIT 8 Sample promotional materials

Dear Parishioner,

A distraught teenage girl acting out her frustrations; a Chicano pre-schooler learning the alphabet; families being given emergency food supplies; a black grandmother taking sewing lessons; a lonely woman finding a pleasant residence and meals; a woman parolee being counseled in employment skills—these are some of the people you would meet every day in the agencies operated by the League of Catholic Women.

Christ has told us that when we offer food, clothing, refuge, and counseling in His name to His needy ones, we offer it to Him. Since 1906, the League has sought to offer immediate help and a brighter tomorrow to those who have been caught up in the web of poverty, misfortune, or despair—and always in the name of Christ and His Blessed Mother Mary. At the same time it has offered the opportunity for thousands of women across the Archdiocese to unite their hands and prayers in this service.

Yes, membership in the League of Catholic Women makes you a personal participant in these countless daily acts of love and service, as well as a participant in the monthly Mass said for all League members.

The annual drive for memberships is now in progress. Will you join with me and with fellow parishioners in giving your moral and financial support so that the League can continue being a very visible sign of Christian Service and an extension of your hands to the needy?

Most sincerely yours,

Helen Garbo
League Parish Director, St. Johns

DID YOU KNOW THAT . . .

The League is the oldest and largest social service agency in Detroit?

Membership does not require regular meetings or volunteer work?

The League agencies and operations are financed by over $1.5 million annually from memberships, government grants, United Fund giving, private donations, and rental receipts?

Last year, each dollar given through membership was magnified by $50 from the larger funding sources?

The League is dedicated to services to those in need, regardless of race, color, or creed? You don't have to be Catholic to belong or to be served?

EXHIBIT 9 Membership statistics

Vicariate	Number of parishes	Number without members	Number of directors	Number of 1975 members	Percent change during 1970–75	Percent change during 1974–75	Number not re-newed in 1975
Birmingham–Bloomfield–Troy	9	1	7	754	+571%	+10%	178
Warren-Centerline	12	2	4	62	− 50	−15	14
S.E.R.F.	15	10	5	155	− 58	−36	120
Farmington-Southfield	13	2	10	508	− 9	−18	87
Southeast Oakland	11	3	6	555	− 27	−16	217
Northwest Wayne	16	4	6	377	− 44	−24	149
West Wayne	16	10	3	44	n.a.	+25	9
Dearborn	15	3	11	1,091	− 12	+ 4	177
Detroit–Grosse Pointe	11	0	9	2,168	− 29	−12	585
Core City–Downtown	19	6	7	598	− 9	+7	111
East Side	16	10	5	151	− 78	−20	36
Grand River	15	0	7	1,159	− 72	+ 4	260
Gratiot	15	2	9	1,578	− 51	− 8	294
North Central	16	13	2	49	− 82	−49	38
Southwest	13	7	6	210	+ 14	+14	54
West Detroit	12	1	7	445	− 59	+ 4	111
West Side Inner City	8	0	4	241	− 64	−33	68
	232	74	108	10,145			2,508

n.a. = not available.

Executive Reaction

Faced with the data on membership an executive committee consisting of Mary Lynn Landis (president), Marie Mathers (treasurer), and Christine Viceroy (membership chairwoman) discussed the situation in an attempt to rectify it as soon as possible.

During the discussion each executive felt that the major difficulty was finding women to work at the parish level and that the major reason revolved around the notion that these women were mostly employed and unable to devote their energy faithfully to the membership drives. In the same vein the executive committee also hypothesized that the large decline in membership in the last 10 years and especially in the last 5 years has occurred concurrently with the "white flight" from the city to the suburbs. They felt that with the decline of certain inner Detroit neighborhoods along with the threat of court-ordered busing looming in the city, Catholic families had moved to the suburbs where League activity was not well established. They believed that the decline of the once strong city vicariates would be counterbalanced by the increase in the membership roles of the suburban vicariates.

They reasoned that the number of city Catholics had decreased a great deal and that the remaining numbers would be attributed to Catholics in the older age brackets who found it financially impossible to move. (See Exhibit 10.) In

EXHIBIT 10 Total population shifts, 1970–1974

	1970	1974	Percent change
City vicariates:			
Core City—Downtown			
East Side			
Grand River			
Gratiot			
North Central	1,586,383	1,428,250	− 9.9%
Southwest			
West Detroit			
West Side Inner City			
Suburban vicariates:			
Birmingham–Bloomfield–Troy	112,049	127,060	+ 13.4
Dearborn	184,268	173,600	− 5.7
Detroit–Grosse Pointe	68,657	64,710	− 6.0
Farmington-Southfield	128,321	141,000	+ 9.8
Northwest Wayne	213,728	211,575	− 1.0
S.E.R.F.	206,410	201,500	− 2.3
Southeast Oakland	274,580	253,850	− 7.5
Warren-Centerline	189,639	183,800	− 3.0
Western Wayne	213,547	223,600	+ 4.7
Total	1,591,199	1,580,695	− 0.7

Note: Catholic population is estimated at 32 percent of aggregate totals.
Source: Figures obtained from U.S. Census figures, U.S. Department of Commerce, Detroit office.

conjunction with changing neighborhoods, League officers noted that as the neighborhoods in the city changed composition from predominately white to racially mixed and as the crime rate increased in the city much personal contact was lost, personal contact which was extremely necessary for soliciting memberships for the League.

Additionally the three officers cited a continuing problem of handling the membership renewal. Often communication among the parish directors, the vicariate coordinators, and central office was inadequate. Lag time between reports had increased which invariably led to duplication of efforts and burdensome bookkeeping errors. The errors were admittedly disturbing to workers at all levels but caused the greatest consternation at the membership level. This generated a good deal of ill will from the members that was directed toward the central membership office.

Last, Landis, Mathers, and Viceroy felt that the League had become increasingly confused with an organization called the Council of Catholic Women (CCW). The CCW is an umbrella federation which encompasses all women's groups and is funded by the Archdiocese of Detroit. They stated that the League is the oldest and largest participant of the CCW and that many Catholic women were under the mistaken impression that being a member of the CCW automatically included membership in the League. They thought this confusion had hurt the membership drive in the past.

At this point the officers felt that further study of the membership situation was required in order to reshape and restructure their marketing strategy to increase the number of League members. To do this they desired to know more about the population shifts and more about the women who conducted the membership drives at the parish level.

Research Results

Obtaining reliable information on just where the Catholic population was located was a major source of concern since it was vitally important to know where the major market centered. The League discovered that the 1970 census did not include a question on religious preference; therefore, it would have to get reliable estimates from a different source.

Turning to the central offices of the Archdiocese of Detroit, the League hoped that individual parish censuses had been tabulated but it quickly found out that the only centralized population data was collected in 1970 and had been discarded as incomplete and useless.

The director of financial planning at the Archdiocese, Harvey Crane, indicated that the Archdiocese used a reasonably accurate estimate for its financial planning. He told the League that historically the percentage of Catholics within its boundaries was approximately 32 percent of total population in the area. Through sample testing the percentage had been found to change little in recent years and was considered reliable by the financial planners.

So assuming that any population shifts retained the characteristic 32 percent Catholic identity (that is, for every 100 people to move, 32 would be Catholic), the League felt that census data on the changing population might prove helpful to see if the increases and declines in area memberships occurred concurrently and in the same proportion as the changes in population. Exhibit 10 represents this tabulated data. It shows that the vicariates with the greatest shifts in population were Birmingham-Bloomfield-Troy with an increase of 13.4 percent and the city of Detroit with a decrease of 9.9 percent.

In addition to the census information a telephone survey of 47 parish directors was taken in order to study several aspects of the membership drive to determine the importance of their performance on the success of the drive. (The questions and tabulated results are presented in Exhibit 11.)

Close examination of the results reveals several trends. As expected the League learned that the parish directors pursued a wide variety of methods during the membership drive with suitability dependent on the particular parish. But in the area of problems, parish directors indicated largely that lack of response and understanding of the League appeal had become a major difficulty. Many parish directors felt that the market for charitable donations had become increasingly more competitive. More groups were appealing to their parish communities for aid. Directors felt that the number of groups seeking

EXHIBIT 11 Survey of parish directors (47 respondents)

1. What is your method of operation during the drive?
   a. Use church bulletin — 33
   b. Announcements at Mass — 9
   c. Appeal after Mass at church — 10
   d. Use membership envelopes in church — 4
   e. Solicit at Ladies' Clubs — 26
   f. Use personal contact — 11
   g. Go door to door — 9
   h. Corps of helpers used — 14
   i. Send out letters — 18
   j. Phone calls — 20
   k. Invite members to luncheon — 1
   l. Use League speaker — 1
   m. File system of parish women — 1

2. What problems do you encounter during the drive?
   a. No support from parish priest — 10
   b. No response to appeal — 13
   c. Lack of publicity — 9
   d. Lack of knowledge of League activities — 7
   e. Catholics moving out — 13
   f. Young women not interested — 9
   g. Retirement — 3
   h. Competition with other charities — 7
   i. No helpers — 7
   j. Lack of coordination with League office — 5
   k. Director has conflict with other activity — 1
   l. Director no longer wishes to serve — 10
   m. No longer serves as director — 4
   n. Director is no longer a member — 4
   o. Membership implies duties — 6
   p. Membership cards — 2
   q. Cannot go door to door — 5
   r. Unemployment — 7

3. Do you incur personal expenses?
   a. No — 26
   b. Postage — 18
   c. Use of car — 5
   d. Printing — 1
   e. Phone — 4
   f. Luncheon — 1
   g. Pay for some members — 2

4. Do you believe new membership can be increased?
   a. Possible — 24
   b. Impossible — 19
   c. Will only decline — 1
   d. Don't know — 4

5. Do you think you are successful?
   a. Yes — 29
   b. No — 14
   c. Don't know — 4

6. What are the ages of your members?
   a. 20–30 — 0
   b. 30–40 — 6
   c. 40–50 — 13

EXHIBIT 11 (concluded)

d.	50–60	32
e.	60 +	35
f.	Mixed	9

7. What amount of time do you spend on new memberships?

a.	Equal	7
b.	Mostly on new	7
c.	Mostly on old	32
d.	Don't know	7
e.	Neither	2

8. What information are you able to provide?

a.	League pamphlets	37
b.	Personal knowledge	10

9. Is there a best time of day to solicit memberships?

a.	Morning	12
b.	Afternoon	8
c.	Dinner	5
d.	Evening	10
e.	Anytime	8

10. Are you employed?

a.	Yes	7
b.	No	40

Note: Many questions may total more than 47 because multiple responses were recorded to most questions.

help severely restricted their appeal. There was also a tendency on the part of their parish priests to channel charitable dollars to only their own parish projects. In addition many directors noted that it seemed that Catholics were indeed moving out of their parishes. And last the most startling of the tabulations showed that of the 47 directors interviewed, 18 of them no longer served or wished to serve the League as a director while at the same time 29 felt that they were successful as directors.

The League also found through the survey that the membership roles were predominated by members who were over 50 years of age, that it was very possible to increase new membership in future drives, that very little time was in fact delegated to obtaining new members, and that very few of the directors were employed which could have hindered their effect at the parish level. While conducting the phone survey the researchers discovered another critical problem. The most current list of 1975 parish directors contained many inaccuracies. It appeared that the League would have great difficulty in communicating with its parish directors. This was particularly alarming to the officers because parish directors are the only League salespersons who directly contact the membership. Also this list may possibly reflect the present condition of the membership list. Exhibit 12 displays the results of the attempt to contact parish directors by telephone.

EXHIBIT 12 Telephone survey statistics

Parish directors	108
Surveys completed	47
No answer	30
Not home	6
On vacation	5
No longer director	7
Wrong phone number	9
Disconnected phone	5
No phone number listed	8
Director with no members	3

After reviewing this information the League directors were searching for solid solutions to the problems they faced. They wondered how to increase memberships without increasing costs appreciably and what changes in procedure and strategy were needed to accomplish the goal. In effect they pondered what changes in their marketing plan were necessary in light of their present information.

Case 4

Edgewater Marina*

In early January 1978 Captain Nathan Rutledge, proprietor of Edgewater Marina, looked out over the mostly empty docks and remarked to John Burnhart, a graduate student at The Citadel, "I'm starting my second year in this business and I've still got half a mile of empty slips. All I've heard about from Charleston boat owners is that there's a lack of marina space around here, but most of my docks are still empty. I just can't figure out what is wrong with my operation. Any ideas you have, John, would be greatly appreciated."

Background of the Marina

Edgewater Marina, the newest in the Charleston, South Carolina, area, opened for business in February 1977 (see Exhibits 1 and 2). The proprietor, Nathan Rutledge, was a retired Navy captain who had spent the last six years of his navy career in the Charleston area. As he was a sailing enthusiast who had spent the greater part of his adult life near ships and the sea, a marina seemed the ideal business to challenge his managerial talents and provide him the less structured lifestyle he was seeking. The apparent lack of marina space in Charleston (the local Municipal Marina had a long waiting list for slips and the others appeared to be always full) plus his love for the Charleston area provided the incentive for him to construct and operate the Edgewater Marina.

To begin the operation, Rutledge purchased a 10-acre plot of land on the Stono River (see Exhibit 3) with 1,200-foot frontage on the river and began construction in January 1977. The site seemed ideal for a marina as it provided sheltered deep water and was only a quarter mile off the Intracoastal Waterway. The marina is located just off a major two-lane road and is five miles from downtown Charleston. Transit to the ocean could be achieved by either following the Stono River south to its mouth (8 nautical miles) or by following the

---

* This case was prepared by Cleon L. Hartzell, Jr., under the supervision of Professor Douglass G. Norvell of The Citadel as a basis for class discussion rather than to illustrate either effective or ineffective handling of an administrative situation. Used with permission.

EXHIBIT 1 Map of the Charleston area

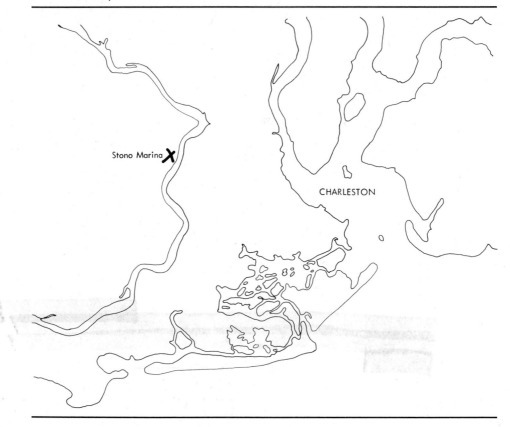

EXHIBIT 2 Charleston area marinas

	Breach Inlet	Mt. Pleasant	Charleston Municipal	Ashley	Ria Scott	Edgewater
Total number berths	6	60	308	92	80*	120
Usually available to transients	0	10	30	12	0	24
Per foot overnight	—	.25	.25	.20	—	.25
Per foot monthly	1.50	1.50	†	2.00	‡	1.75
Gasoline	X	X	X	—	X	—
Diesel	—	X	X	—	—	—
Water	X	X	X	X	X	X
Electricity	X	X	X	X	—	X
Showers	—	—	X	—	—	—
Laundry	—	—	X	—	—	—
Groceries	X	—	X	—	—	—
Restaurant	—	—	X	X	X	—
Snack bar	X	X	X	—	—	X
Ice	X	X	X	X	X	X
Bait	X	X	—	—	—	—
Boat landing	X	X	X	—	—	—

* Dry stack berths limited to boats under 24 feet.

† Monthly charge averaged $35 per month per berth.

‡ Monthly charge of $50 and one year lease required.

EXHIBIT 3 Depths of the river near the marina

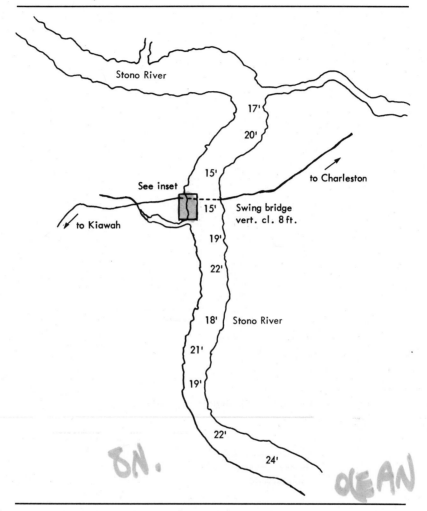

Intracoastal Waterway to Charleston Harbor and exiting there (13 nautical miles). The Stono River inlet was generally used only by knowledgeable local boaters, as the entrance channel was bordered by shifting sandbars. As a result, marker buoys were always being relocated.

The marina was composed of three 660-foot floating docks connected to the shore by a floating access dock and fixed wharf (see Exhibit 4). Utilities provided on the docks included water (marina well), electricity (110/220), and telephone service (hook-up jacks). A public phone was available at the head of the wharf. The docks were lighted at night, and a dockmaster or assistant dockmaster was always present. The one building constructed at the marina

EXHIBIT 4 Docks and facilities at the marina

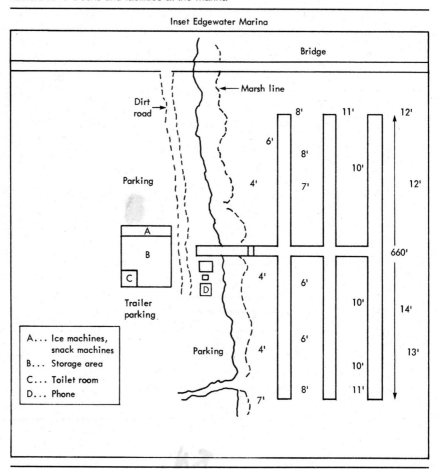

served by partitioning as storage area, toilet facility, and vending machine location. Only one sink and toilet were provided in this building, but facility improvement plans called for the construction of a separate toilet/shower. Captain Rutledge was having problems with the local board of health on this issue and extensive sewage disposal facilities would be required before the additional toilet/shower building could be constructed. Because of the large capital investment required (estimated at $5,000), this project had been indefinitely delayed. The access road was unpaved but well drained. Parking for about 30 cars was provided on an unpaved surface with trees scattered through it. About one fourth of the parking area was unusable after a heavy rain because of the muddy conditions, but this was to be corrected by paving the parking areas within the year. Exhibit 5 shows the financial development plan for the marina.

EXHIBIT 5

EDGEWATER MARINA

Financial Development Plan
Pro Forma Statement of Sources and Application of Funds
For the Year Ending December 31, 1977

Sources of net working capital:

Net income[1]	$ 24,583	
Depreciation	200	
Issuance of long-term debt	100,000	
Owner input	50,000	
Total sources		$174,783

Applications of net working capital:

Procurement of land	81,950	
Land clearing	1,500	
Installation of electricity	1,550	
Storage/toilet building	2,000	
Auto parking area	4,600	
Septic tank	1,180	
Well and pump	300	
Construction of wharf	1,789	
Construction of docks	43,827	
Installation of pilings	18,000	
Installation of water main	1,000	
Toilet/shower building	2,000	
Fuel pumps and storage tanks	7,000	
Total applications		166,696
Increase in net working capital		$ 8,087

Notes:
[1] Owner agreed to not remove any of the net income from the business during the first year of operation.

Captain Rutledge hoped that the marina would be a family business. His eldest son was to act as dockmaster and live aboard a houseboat at the marina. Also, a second son and a daughter acted as assistants during the peak boating season. All were to be paid wages for their services, and these were deducted from operating revenue as expenses. Because of his independent retirement income from the Navy, Captain Rutledge was to leave the first operating year's income from the marina in the business to build up the net working capital. The dock rental rate structure was based on the prevailing rates at the other local marinas. Charges were $1.75 per foot per month of the boat length plus 10 percent of the boat's length for maneuvering room. Rents were due monthly in advance and no leases were required. The rate for transient boats was set at 25 cents per foot per day with no surcharge for utilities (except telephone). Exhibits 6, 7, and 8 show the projected financial statements of the Edgewater Marina for 1977.

EXHIBIT 6

EDGEWATER MARINA

Pro Forma Cash Budget
January 1–December 31, 1977

	January	February	March	April
Cash receipts:				
Collection of dock rents[1]	$ 0	$ 1,848	$ 3,696	$ 5,544
Boat care service	0	0	0	0
Fuel, oil, and parts	0	0	0	0
Total cash receipts	0	1,848	3,696	5,544
Cash disbursements:				
Procurement of land	80,000	0	0	0
Administrative services	2,000	50	75	100
Supplies	100	50	50	50
Utilities	50	110	120	170
Loan payments	0	1,170	1,170	1,170
Land improvements	2,100	600	600	0
Facilities				
Wharfs and docks[2]	1,200	35,026	14,195	14,195
Building/equipment	3,830	0	0	0
Insurance	800	0	0	0
Wages[3]	0	0	0	0
Taxes	0	0	0	0
Miscellaneous	0	100	100	100
Total cash disbursements ...	90,080	37,106	16,310	15,785
Net cash gain (loss)	($ 90,080)	($ 35,258)	($ 12,614)	($ 10,241)
Cumulative net cash flow	(90,080)	(125,338)	(137,952)	(148,193)
Analysis of cash flow				
Beginning cash balance[4]	150,000	59,920	24,662	12,048
Net cash gain (loss)	(90,080)	(35,258)	(12,614)	(10,241)
Ending cash balance	59,920	24,662	12,048	1,807

Notes:

[1] Dock rent based on $1.75/foot of dock space at 80 percent usage rate.

[2] Total of 3,960 linear feet of dock space available by April 30.

[3] Wages are for the assistants to owner/manager. Initially these positions are not filled.

[4] Initial cash provided by owner's investment and bank loans.

EXHIBIT 6 *(continued)*

EDGEWATER MARINA

Pro Forma Cash Budget

January 1–December 31, 1977

	May	June	July	August
Cash receipts:				
Collection of dock rents	$ 5,544	$ 5,544	$ 5,544	$ 5,544
Boat care service	700	700	700	700
Fuel, oil, and parts	0	0	0	0
Total cash receipts	6,244	6,244	6,244	6,244
Cash disbursements:				
Administrative services	100	150	150	150
Supplies	50	50	100	100
Utilities	270	380	430	430
Taxes	150	150	200	200
Insurance	150	200	200	200
Wages	1,000	1,000	1,000	1,000
Facilities				
Buildings[5]	2,000	0	0	0
Equipment[6]	0	0	2,700	900
Payment on loans	1,170	1,170	1,170	1,170
Fuel...........................	0	0	0	4,000
Land improvements[7]	0	0	0	1,400
Miscellaneous	200	200	200	200
Total cash disbursements ...	5,090	3,300	6,150	9,950
Net cash gain (loss)	$ 1,154	$ 2,944	$ 94	($ 3,706)
Cumulative net cash flow	(147,039)	(144,095)	(144,001)	(147,607)
Analysis of cash flow				
Beginning cash balance	1,807	2,961	5,905	5,999
Net cash gain (loss)	1,154	2,944	94	(3,706)
Ending cash balance	2,961	5,905	5,999	2,293

Notes:

[5] Additional toilet building to be built in May.

[6] Fuel pumps and storage tanks installed starting in July and ending in November.

[7] Improvements to automobile parking area.

EXHIBIT 6 *(concluded)*

EDGEWATER MARINA

Pro Forma Cash Budget

January 1–December 31, 1977

	September	October	November	December
Cash receipts:				
Collection of dock rents	$ 5,544	$ 5,544	$ 5,544	$ 5,544
Boat care service	700	700	700	700
Fuel, oil, and parts	300	300	400	450
Total cash receipts	6,544	6,544	6,644	6,694
Cash disbursements:				
Administrative services	150	150	150	150
Supplies	100	100	100	100
Utilities	455	455	530	530
Taxes	200	200	250	250
Insurance	200	200	300	300
Wages	1,500	1,500	1,800	1,800
Facilities				
Buildings	0	0	0	0
Equipment	1,500	1,500	500	0
Payment on loans	1,170	1,170	1,170	1,170
Fuel	0	0	0	4,000
Land improvements	700	700	0	0
Repairs	0	100	100	350
Income tax	0	0	0	200
Miscellaneous	200	200	300	300
Total cash disbursements ...	6,175	6,275	5,200	9,150
Net cash gain (loss)	$ 369	$ 269	$ 1,444	($ 2,456)
Cumulative net cash flow	(147,238)	(146,969)	(145,525)	(147,981)
Analysis of cash flow				
Beginning cash balance	2,393	2,762	3,031	4,475
Net cash gain (loss)	369	269	1,444	(2,456)
Ending cash balance	2,762	3,031	4,475	2,019

EXHIBIT 7

EDGEWATER MARINA

Pro Forma Income Statement
For Year Ending December 31, 1977

	Actual	*Pro forma*
Revenues:		
Dock rent	$18,480	$55,440
Boat care service	3,800	5,600
Sales of fuel, oil, and parts	0	1,450
Total revenue	22,280	62,490
Expenses:		
Administrative	1,200	1,425
Utilities	3,100	3,930
Wages	5,000	10,800
Interest	5,534	5,534
Sales tax	600	1,600
Cost of goods sold	0	1,368
Depreciation	200	200
Repairs	400	550
Miscellaneous	1,000	2,100
Insurance	2,550	2,550
Supplies	850	950
Total expenses	20,434	31,007
Earnings before income taxes	1,846	31,483
Income taxes	0	7,100
Net earnings	$ 1,846	$24,383

EXHIBIT 8

EDGEWATER MARINA

Pro Forma Balance Sheet
As of December 31, 1977

			Actual		*Pro forma*
Assets					
Current assets:					
Cash			$ 6,885		$ 2,019
Accounts receivable			1,200		0
Fuel/supplies			700		6,632
Prepaid expenses			315		0
Total current assets			9,100		8,651
Fixed assets:					
Land			84,400		88,050
Buildings	$ 3,830			$ 5,830	
Equipment	0			7,000	
Wharfs and docks	81,400			64,616	
Less accumulated depreciation	2,130[1]			200	
Net buildings/equipment/wharfs and docks			83,100		77,246
Total fixed assets			167,500		165,296
Other assets:					
Intangible assets			300		300
Total assets			$176,900		$174,247
Liabilities and Net Worth					
Current liabilities:					
Accounts payable			$ 1,390		$ 0
Accrued taxes			0		7,100
Expenses payable			1,000		0
Total current liabilities			2,390		7,100
Long-term liabilities:					
Notes payable			92,664		92,664
Total liabilities			95,054		99,764
Net worth:					
Rutledge, capital			40,923		74,483
Jones, capital[2]			40,923		0
Total capital			81,846		74,483
Total capital and net worth			$176,900		$174,247

Notes:

[1] Depreciation calculated on straight-line basis over 40-year period.

[2] In May 1977 Edgewater Marina was changed from a sole proprietorship to a partnership between Captain Nathan Rutledge and Captain Alan Jones. The owners' equity in the marina was recapitalized as follows:

Rutledge, capital $40,000
Jones, capital $40,000

Captain Jones is to be a silent partner. All profits will be equally divided between Captain Rutledge and Captain Jones. As of January 1, 1978 Captain Rutledge will receive a salary of $15,000 per year for managing the marina.

The First Operating Year

By May of 1977 all dock construction was complete and utilities installed. Costs for materials and labor used in building the docks ended up being 26 percent higher than was originally planned. As occupancy rate for dock space was only 15 percent, the marina was experiencing a severe cash flow problem. Captain Rutledge contacted an old friend from his Navy days, Captain Alan Jones, and convinced him to invest in the marina. The details of this arrangement are shown in note 2 to Exhibit 8. This provided a fresh infusion of $30,000 into the business and figuratively allowed Rutledge to keep his head above water. All additional facility improvements were deferred until revenues picked up and costs were closely monitored to conserve cash.

It was obvious by July that the marina would not come close to the 80 percent occupancy rate that had been envisioned. While the docks were now half full, many of the boat owners indicated that they would be either moving their boats to warmer climates in the fall or removing them from the water altogether. Up until this time Captain Rutledge had relied on word-of-mouth advertising to make the public aware of his marina. The Mid-Atlantic edition of the Waterway Guide made no mention of the Edgewater Marina and only hinted that a marina might be constructed along the Stono River in 1977. The swing bridge just north of the marina blocked its view from the Intracoastal Waterway, and the few transients that managed to find it were usually boats that had been turned away from the full Municipal Marina. Exhibit 9 shows the breakdown of the boats at the Edgewater Marina in July.

The rest of 1977 showed no improvement, and many boat owners left the marina that fall. The occupancy rate for 1977 averaged out to 27 percent instead of the hoped for 80 percent. No additional facility improvements were accom-

EXHIBIT 9 Edgewater Marina list of boats present (July 1977)

Trailer boats	
14 feet–20 feet	4
20 feet–28 feet	11
Sailboats	
20 feet–30 feet	12
30 feet	5
Pleasure cruisers	
26 feet–34 feet	10
34 feet–44 feet	4
Sport fishermen	
20 feet–30 feet	6
30 feet	3
Yachts	
45 feet	1
Houseboats	3
Total	59

plished, and this left the marina without a toilet/shower building, paved parking, or fueling equipment. One bright spot had been the demand for boat care service (hull painting, minor mechanical repairs) that had come from the boats that had utilized the marina. If the same demand percentage had occurred from an 80 percent full marina, income from this source would have been twice that predicted. With the arrival of 1978 and the start of the boating season only two months away Captain Rutledge was indeed anxious for any ideas to improve marina operations and occupancy rate.

The Market

John Burnhart's interest in boating and a course he was presently taking in marketing at The Citadel motivated him to undertake an analysis of the market for marinas in the Charleston area. He first talked to some of the boat owners who were still present at the marina and asked them how they had come to choose the Edgewater Marina. All were local boat owners and 30 percent indicated lack of space at other marinas caused them to pick Edgewater. Another 40 percent chose Edgewater because it was the most convenient for their needs. The remaining 30 percent were either dissatisfied with something at other marinas (long leases, lack of dredging, lack of personal service) or said they just like the friendly relaxed atmosphere at Edgewater. Many indicated that the lack of fueling facilities was a bother and could cause them to switch marinas at a later date. While this told Burnhart why the present occupants of Edgewater Marina were there, it didn't explain all those empty spots.

A survey of the other area marinas revealed that all of their occupancy rates were at least 75 percent and that the 308-slip Municipal Marina was completely full. A comparison of marinas (see Exhibit 2) showed that Edgewater offered fewer facilities than most other marinas its size. Data from the boating registrations office showed 27,244 powered boats registered in the Charleston area. While most of these boats were not candidates for marina berths, they did use marine supplies. The number of boat registrations had been growing at an average rate of 8 percent over the past five years, and it was anticipated that this trend would continue.

While Burnhart knew that transient boat traffic on the Intracoastal Waterway was seasonal, he learned that both the boating season and the total number of boats traveling was on the increase. In an attempt to gauge this traffic, he examined the records of a bridge across the Waterway near Charleston which had a low vertical clearance. The bridge operator was required to record the name, type, and state of registration of all boats for which the bridge was opened. Results of this examination are shown in Exhibit 10. If the seven busiest months are averaged (April–October) and it is assumed that the bridge acts as a gate for 80 percent of the traffic, then approximately 565 transient boats pass through Charleston per month during the boating season. This does not take into account any boats not using the Intracoastal Waterway by making the outside passage (assumed less than 5 percent). The only marinas presently

EXHIBIT 10 John F. Limehouse swing bridge
(vertical elevation 12 feet)

Bridge openings for the year 1977. Bridge operator
records name of boat, type, and state of registry.

	Yachts	Sailboats	Monthly total
January	45	32	77
February	24	14	38
March	116	42	158
April	309	167	476
May	511	185	696
June	230	74	304
July	141	66	207
August	244	81	325
September	498	192	690
October	312	152	464
November	101	51	152
December	32	20	52

Note: It is estimated that 80 percent of all transient boats
passing under the bridge require its opening.

catering to these boaters were the Charleston Municipal and the Ashley. Only
the Charleston Municipal offered showers, laundry facilities, and marine supplies. In the peak months many transients were rafted against one another or
were turned away completely at the Municipal Marina because of lack of space.

Advertising by the local marinas was almost nonexistent. Of the local
marinas only the Municipal and the Ashley had paid advertisements in the
Waterway Guide. Edgewater was now running a daily ad in the classified
section of the local paper, and Mt. Pleasant Marina had its fishing supply store
advertised in a small local distribution fishing magazine. The Municipal received indirect advertising through yacht brokers and repair facilities who were
located near it. No organization existed to represent the interests of Charleston
area marinas although there had been talk of organizing one when the city
proposed the building of a new city supported marina. The proposed marina
would have 400 slips and be located at a naval museum across the harbor from
downtown Charleston. Local private marina operators expressed concern that
this constituted unfair competition in that the proposed marina would be
subsidized by the city. No action had been taken since the proposal was made,
and if such an undertaking was authorized, it would not go into operation for at
least three years.

The Analysis

It was now early February and John Burnhart knew Captain Rutledge was
eagerly looking forward to his comments and recommendations. As John
looked through the data collected (including Exhibit 11) he realized the problems the Edgewater Marina was experiencing could only be solved by a

EXHIBIT 11 Boating registrations in Charleston County during 1977

Boat length	Number of boats	Open	Cabin	House	Other	Outboard	Inboard	In/out	Auxiliary	Other
Less than 14 feet	4,920	4,651	0	0	269	4,127	12	0	13	768
14 feet to less than 18 feet	10,887	10,435	62	1	389	9,601	211	327	35	813
18 feet to less than 22 feet	882	656	179	4	43	506	84	206	29	57
22 feet to less than 26 feet	414	179	200	13	22	141	123	114	7	30
Greater than 26 feet	338	111	173	29	25	21	246	52	10	9
Total	17,441	16,032	614	47	748	14,396	676	699	94	1,677

complete marketing analysis and program. Who were the Marina's intended customers, how numerous were they, and what products and services were they seeking? How do you reach and influence this market segment? What would the boating population want in the future and should preparations be made now to meet these needs? These were just a few of the questions that required answering.

Case 5

Exercise on Financial Analysis for Marketing Decision Making

An important part of the analysis of alternatives facing marketing decision makers is the financial analysis of these alternatives. This exercise is designed to give students experience in handling the types of financial calculations that arise in marketing cases. If you can do the calculations in this exercise, you should be able to handle the financial calculations necessary to properly do the cases in this book.

1. You have just been appointed the product manager for the "Flexo" brand of electric razors in a large consumer products company. As part of your new job, you want to develop an understanding of the financial situation for your product. Your brand assistant has provided you with the following facts:

a.	Retail selling price	$30 per unit
b.	Retailer's margin	20%
c.	Jobber's margin	20%
d.	Wholesaler's* margin	15%
e.	Direct factory labor	$2 per unit
f.	Raw materials	$1 per unit
g.	All factory and administrative overheads	$1 per unit (at a 100,000 unit volume level)
h.	Salesperson's commissions	10% of manufacturer's selling price
i.	Sales force travel costs	$200,000
j.	Advertising	$500,000
k.	Total market for razors	1 million units
l.	Current yearly sales of Flexo	210,000 units

* An agent who sells to the jobbers, who in turn sell to the retailers.

Questions

1. What is the contribution per unit for the Flexo brand?
2. What is the break-even volume in units and in dollars?
3. What market share does the Flexo brand need to break even?

4. What is the current total contribution?
5. What is the current before tax profit of the Flexo brand?
6. What market share must Flexo obtain to contribute a before tax profit of $2 million?

2. One of the first decisions you have to make as the brand manager for Flexo is whether or not to add a new line of razors, the "Super Flexo" line. This line would be marketed in addition to the original Flexo line. Your brand assistant has provided you with the following facts:

a.	Retail selling price	$40 per unit
b.	All margins the same as before	
c.	Direct factory labor	$ 3 per unit
d.	Raw materials	$ 2 per unit
e.	All factory and administrative overheads 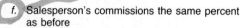	$ 2 per unit (at a 50,000 unit volume level) $100,000
f.	Salesperson's commissions the same percent as before	
g.	Incremental sales force travel cost	$ 50,000
h.	Advertising for Super Flexo	$600,000
i.	New equipment needed	$500,000 (to be depreciated over 10 years)
j.	Research and development spent up to now	$200,000
k.	Research and development to be spent this year to commercialize the product	$500,000 (to be amortized over five years)

Questions

1. What is the contribution per unit for the Super Flexo brand?
2. What is the break-even volume in units and in dollars?
3. What is the sales volume in units necessary for Super Flexo to yield, in the first year, a 20 percent return on the equipment to be invested in the project?

3. The $40 per unit selling price for Super Flexo seems high to you. You thought you might lower the price to $37 per unit and raise retail margin to 25 percent.

Question

What is the break-even volume in units?

Part 3

Marketing Research and Forecasting

The need for good information is pervasive of all marketing decision making. Most cases in this book present some information provided by marketing research. However, they also leave many points of uncertainty. The skill of marketing decision making is the use of the information that is available, along with explicit assumptions about uncertain points to make good decisions. The suggestion that we do marketing research has usually not been allowed in other parts of this text. In this section we turn to the undertaking of marketing research activity.

First, let us define marketing research. It is the systematic gathering, recording, and analyzing of data about problems relating to the marketing of goods and services. There are three kinds of marketing research: (1) exploratory, (2) conclusive, and (3) performance monitoring. Exploratory research is useful for identifying situations calling for a decision and for identifying alternative courses of action. Conclusive research is useful for evaluating alternative courses of action and selecting a course of action. Performance monitoring research is designed to provide the control function over marketing programs.

The marketing research process may be thought of as being composed of the following steps:

1. Establish the need for information.
2. Specify the research objectives and information needs.
3. Determine the sources of data.
4. Develop data collection forms.

5. Design a sample.
6. Collect the data.
7. Process the data.
8. Analyze the data.
9. Present research findings.

The responsibility for the execution of these stages is shared by the marketing manager and the marketing researcher. They both must be sure that the problem has been defined properly, that the objectives make sense, and so on. The researcher holds primary responsibility for the technical details of the study. However, he or she must always be prepared to explain these aspects to the manager in nontechnical terms.

Marketing research costs money. Before it is undertaken, it must be ascertained that the value of the information provided justifies the cost. Also, before research is undertaken, the use to which that research will be made should be clearly understood. A specific decision should be the target of the research and the way the new information will be used in helping make the decision should be clearly understood.

This note and the cases in this section focus on the managerial aspects of marketing research. The technical details are mostly left for more advanced texts.

Case 6

Bay-Madison, Inc.*

survey

In January 1980, Mr. George Roberts, research director of Bay-Madison, Inc., a large advertising agency, was faced with the problem of how best to conduct a study on Rill, a product of the Ellis Company, one of the agency's clients.

Rill, a powdered cleanser, was first introduced by the Ellis Company in 1923. Its original use was as a heavy-duty cleansing agent for removing dirt and stains from porcelain, metal, and ceramic tile surfaces. A unique bleaching property of the product eliminated the necessity for scrubbing and it contained no abrasive material. In 1936, the company's research department developed and added to the product an ingredient which imparted a light, fluffy texture to textile products washed in a mild solution of Rill. Recognizing the problem of keeping such articles as baby clothes, towels, and blankets soft through repeated washings, the company had promoted Rill both as a cleanser and as a laundry wash water additive since 1937. Over the years, about 50 percent of the company's advertising had featured the product solely as a cleanser, 30 percent as a laundry additive and 20 percent as a dual-purpose product.

Rill was nationally distributed in a concentrated form in three can sizes—4 ounces, 8 ounces, and 1 pound. Six other nationally distributed cleansers and two nationally distributed laundry additives posed formidable competition.

The product had sold well during the earlier years, but during the past five years unit sales had declined considerably apparently because of competition, although dollar volume over this period had remained fairly constant.

Company and agency personnel were in basic disagreement as to whether the product should be promoted as a cleanser, a laundry additive or a dual-purpose product. In order to formulate marketing and advertising strategy for the coming year, the agency personnel believed it was necessary to supplement the quantitative information they had on unit sales, outlets, margins, and distribution with information of a more qualitative nature on consumer attitudes

---

* This case was written by C. B. Johnston, Dean and Professor of Marketing, University of Western Ontario. Used with permission.

qualitative info.

toward the product, usage patterns, and opinions on different product charac-teristics such as strength or concentration, odor, and package size.

In November 1979, Mr. Roberts and his staff had drawn up a research proposal which they had forwarded to six marketing research firms for detailed information regarding the following:

1. An appraisal of the proposal and suggestions for any changes.
2. A price quotation on the project (*a*) as outlined and (*b*) including any suggested changes.
3. A brief description of the staff who would handle the project.
4. Time required for preparation, implementation, tabulation, and final pre-sentation.
5. Pilot testing suggested.
6. Detailed explanation of suggested sample size.
7. Information on the firm's executive personnel, interviewing staff, and the projects handled over the preceding two years.

The research proposal contained a description of the product's marketing problems, the objectives of the proposed research, broad suggestions regarding research methodology, and a proposed questionnaire.

In his proposal, Mr. Roberts outlined the major marketing problems as follows:

1. We really want to know how many people would buy Rill because (*a*) it is a cleanser, (*b*) it is a laundry additive, or (*c*) it is a dual-purpose product.
2. How do people buy products like Rill? Is it better to have a strong product or a weaker one? What size package should we have? Should it smell like soap or like perfume? At what price should it be retailing?
3. Do people see Rill as being a good, average, or poor product? What do they like about it? What don't they like about it?
4. Do people want a one-use product or a multi-use product?

By early in January, Mr. Roberts had received the submissions of all six marketing research firms requested to bid on the job.

Three of these firms were eliminated after preliminary consideration of their submissions revealed either inadequate staffs, superficial recommenda-tions, or excessively high costs.

In considering the three remaining firms, Mr. Roberts felt he was ham-pered by his lack of knowledge of the techniques proposed by two of the firms and his inability to decide whether it was reasonable to expect that a detailed plan could be drawn up from the information he had provided in his proposal.

Two of the firms under consideration, National Research Associates and The Progressive Research Group, had outlined quite comprehensive plans for the research. The third, H. J. Clifford Research, had merely stated that they would not attempt to formulate any research plans from what they considered inadequate information. They believed the only way a detailed plan could be formulated was "through a continuing cooperation, based on mutual confidence, between the research firm, the advertising agency and the client."

Mr. Roberts knew that many marketing research executives considered the third firm to be the outstanding marketing research company in the country and because of this, he did not believe they could be overlooked.

SUBMISSION OF NATIONAL
RESEARCH ASSOCIATES

information over/will.

Introduction

The present research proposal is based upon the assumption that it is crucial to obtain answers to the following marketing problems:

1. Is it advisable to continue to promote Rill as a multipurpose product?
2. If it is, should its various uses be promoted simultaneously or separately and what are the promotional approaches which would be most effective?
3. If it is not advisable to continue its promotion as a multipurpose product, for what uses could Rill be most successfully promoted?
4. What would be the most effective promotional approaches for the uses decided upon?
5. Would it be advisable to launch another product, or possibly the same product under a different name, for either of its uses?
6. What are the ways in which Rill distribution, packaging, pricing, and merchandising could be improved?

20-50 in depth interview more than enough.

Research Objectives

To be able to plan a sound and effective marketing policy for Rill it will be essential to know:

1. The present market position of Rill in relation to its competitors in each of the fields in which it is used.
2. The reasons why Rill is in its present position in each of these markets.

I. Consumer Habits and Practices   *Do small test*

The study will provide as complete a description as possible of the cleanser and laundry additive markets. Data will be provided in regard to (1) users and nonusers, (2) brand usage, (3) purchasing habits, and (4) usage habits.

This information will be cross-analyzed by age, socioeconomic status, community size, and level of education of the respondent.

II. Consumer Attitudes, Opinions, and Motivations

The study will thoroughly explore the underlying reasons for the market strengths and weaknesses of Rill in each of the usage categories as completely as possible under the broad headings of:

1. The underlying attractions or resistances to using any product for each of the purposes with which Rill is concerned.
2. The comparative strength of attractions to using Rill and to using competing brands for each of these purposes.
3. The comparative strength of resistances to using Rill relative to competing brands.

Some of the specific topics which will be investigated under these general headings are discussed below:

1. The perceived uses of Rill and its major competitors.
2. Factors affecting the perception of Rill; i.e., confusion regarding usage, incompatibility of uses, one use more efficient than the other, and where the attitudes toward the product originated.
3. Attributes of the most desirable product for each of the uses.
4. Common knowledge of the attributes of various brands now on the market.
5. Associations evoked by the brand name Rill and the brand names of competing products.

III. Consumer Knowledge of, and Attitudes toward, Relevant Advertising

1. How far the terms and phrases currently used in promoting Rill and competing brands are seen as (*a*) meaningful, and (*b*) appropriate to the product and its uses?
2. What copy points and adjectives might be most effective for the promotion of each use?

IV. An Evaluation of the Advertising Themes and Approaches Used by Rill

The research will attempt to determine whether the themes and approaches used in past and present Rill advertising are likely to operate toward overcoming resistances to Rill and capitalizing on sources of attraction.

V. An Assessment of the Rill Packages

The Rill package will be tested to determine:

1. Its visual effectiveness as evidenced by its attention-getting ability, its legibility, its memorability, its apparent size.
2. Its psychological effect on the consumer's perception of the brand.

Methodology

Market survey. Face-to-face interviews will be conducted with 2,275 home-makers who will be asked to give factual information about the products they use for each purpose. This survey will show the competitive position of Rill, but will not attempt to provide "reasons why."

Intensive interview study. The "reasons why" Rill is in its present position will be explored in 200 one-and-one-half to two-hour depth interviews which will attempt to discover attitudes, perceptions, and feelings toward the product and its uses.

The depth interview is designed to prompt the revelation of true attitudes and reasons for them by employing projective techniques which, instead of emphasizing personal behavior, invite comment on the behavior of others.

In-depth interviewing takes place in a relaxed, informal atmosphere. Interviews are usually conducted in the respondent's home and her verbatim responses to questions are noted.

The interview schedule contains a large number of open-ended and close-ended queries.

In addition, it employs a variety of techniques, most of which are taken from, or patterned after, standard psychological tests. A description of some of these techniques is given below.

1. The Personification Test. This is essentially an extension of the projective technique employed in psychological testing. It involves an attempt on the part of the respondent to describe certain products in human terms. Such an approach provides an opportunity for the expression of attitudes and opinions not otherwise easily obtainable.

2. The Thematic Apperception Test (TAT). Like the Personification Test, this test is similar to the TAT in psychological projective testing. It consists of presenting to the respondent an unstructured drawing of a particular situation and asking him to "make up a story" of what is happening.

3. Word Association Tests. Respondents are asked to relate what comes to mind when a given word or phrase is read to them. This technique aids in throwing light on areas which may warrant fuller investigation.

4. The Semantic Differential Test. This method, developed by us, has been designed to provide insights and information in regard to the perception of company and product attributes.

Fundamentally, the test consists of having the respondent rate a series of products on specially designed scales. The scales are so designed as to provide an extremely sensitive measure in regard to many dimensions as applied to the various products.

The manner in which these data (along with the data obtained through the use of other techniques) are analyzed makes it possible to determine:

A. The extent to which a given product's image is correlated with the perceived "ideal" product.
B. The desirable direction of change in the perceived product attributes, if such change is found necessary.

Other techniques which may be employed include: (*a*) rank-ordering tests, (*b*) sentence completion tests, (*c*) forced choice tests, (*d*) paired comparison tests, and (*e*) true-false tests.

Laboratory study. Our visual laboratory is equipped to evaluate the relative effectiveness of various merchandising and advertising stimuli. By means of specially designed instruments it will be possible to evaluate the relative effectiveness of the Rill package and label in comparison with those of major competitors.

The various tests which will be conducted include:

1. Attention-getting tests.
2. Product recognition tests.
3. Brand identification tests.
4. Visibility and legibility tests.
5. Memorability tests.
6. Apparent size tests.
7. Color preference and association tests.

Sample

Market survey. For the purposes of economy it is suggested that a quota-controlled, weighted, national sample of 2,275 housewives be employed. The accompanying table presents an unweighted sample in proportion to household figures and the proposed weighted sample.

The unweighted sample exceeds the number of interviews necessary to ensure reasonable reliability.

However, to allow for a cross analysis of white and black and urban and rural respondents, a total of 3,113 interviews would be required. The weighted sample cuts by 50 percent the number of interviews in the Midwest and the West. The data from these areas will be mathematically converted to representative proportions in the final tabulation.

Intensive study. Quota-controlled samples of 450 white and 150 black homemakers will be used.

Laboratory study. The number of respondents varies from test to test, but the samples will be designed to ensure statistical reliability.

Field Staff

Market survey. Our field staff of 455 interviewers located across the country will conduct the interviews and will be specially briefed and trained for this survey.

Intensive study. Our staff of 88 university-trained depth interviewers will conduct an average of seven interviews each.

Brief Description of Firm

National Research Associates has conducted almost 400 separate and varied research projects since its establishment in 1954. The success of the organization is portrayed by its rapid growth from a small unknown company to a recognized leader in the field in the United States. Further attestation has been the establishment of ''continuing relationships'' with many clients. The company is an ''official training ground'' for graduate students in the Department of Social Psychology at a prominent university.

The following individuals will be involved in this project:

R. J. Morrison, Ph.D., research coordinator and major client and agency contact; academic training—B.Sc., M.Sc., and Ph.D., 1944 to 1959, major universities; research experience—wide experience in research as study director, consultant and research associate in four U.S. universities from 1944 to 1956; teaching experience—seven years of lecturing in psychology at two American universities.

A. Milton, study director; graduate in economics with 10 years' experience in the research field including 3 years with a prominent United Kingdom research firm and a number of years with other English companies.

H. W. Rolland, associate study director; senior staff psychologist who will coordinate the intensive study phases of the research. M.Sc. working on Ph.D.

R. W. Brown, associate study director; university graduate in sociology and statistics—10 years' experience in research—will handle tabulation and statistical analysis.

(Four additional staff members were listed, all of whom were university graduates.)

| | Rural | | | | Urban | | Total | |
| | Farm | | Nonfarm | | | | | |
	Unweighted	Weighted	Unweighted	Weighted	Unweighted	Weighted	Unweighted	Weighted
Southeast	44	44	76	76	132	132	252	252
Northeast	101	101	110	110	614	614	825	825
Midwest	126	63	139	70	837	436	1,102	569
West	179	90	107	53	324	162	610	305
South Central	22	22	60	60	242	242	324	324
Total	472	320	492	369	2,149	1,586	3,113	2,275

Time and Cost Estimates

The research can be completed in 12 weeks after finalization of the research design. The cost is estimated at $62,000, 50 percent payable upon initiation of the study and 50 percent upon completion.

SUBMISSION OF THE PROGRESSIVE RESEARCH GROUP

Nature of the Problem

It is possible that the two major uses of Rill may, in combination, affect the market negatively. Women may think of it primarily in one sense or the other and those who regard it as a cleanser may not be willing to use it as a laundry additive, or vice versa.

In addition to this possible overall problem, there are certain marketing specifics which may also be important.

1. Is the product right?
2. What about its physical characteristics (strength or concentration, odor, physical form)?
3. What about its psychological connotations?
4. What about the packaging (size of package, nature of package, labeling, and package)?

We propose a consumer study covering the major areas of behavior and attitude including:

1. Brand personality and image for each of several cleansers (including Rill).
2. Brand personality and image for each of several laundry additive products (including Rill).
3. Habit pattern on home cleaning (including products used).
4. Habit pattern on laundry additives (including products used).

Scope of the Study

We see this as a national study as it is entirely possible that varying areas may display differing habits and attitudes.

The section of this proposal dealing with the sample will show the reasons underlying our recommendations. We suggest a total of 750 interviews in this consumer study and the sample will be of a "tight" nature.

The Sample

Type of sample. The sample will be of such a nature that it properly represents the homemaker population in terms of region, socioeconomic group, urban-rural, and the like.

The sample design will be a known probability sample. Primary sampling units will be selected proportionately across the country, and randomly selected starting points will be chosen from which a predetermined path of interviewing will be followed.

Size of sample. We recommend a total sample of 750 housewives.

There are several reasons. The first concerns our belief that no sub-sample on which results are based should have fewer than 150 cases.

The other reason concerns overall accuracy with a sample of 750 cases. Better than 9 times out of 10, results based on this total sample should be accurate within some 2.4 percent; this level of sampling accuracy on an overall basis seems highly acceptable for the purposes of this particular study.

Numerical distribution of interviews is indicated in the accompanying table.

	Natural proportional distribution of sample	Proposed sample distribution	Weighting factor	Weighted cases
Southeast	77	125	2	250
Northeast	211	211	3	633
Midwest	265	177	5	885
West	130	130	3	390
South Central	67	107	2	214
	750	750		2,372

Fieldwork

Our field staff is of highest quality. It has been built over a 10-year period, and we spend a sizable amount of money each year on maintenance and development of this staff.

The field staff totals 723 workers, and all states and community sizes are represented.

Supervision

We maintain a staff of 20 salaried regional supervisors across the country. With the exception of a few small remote areas, this means that every interviewer works under the direct control of a regional supervisor.

Qualifications of Interviewers

The average interviewer on our staff has been working for the firm for approximately four years. For our consumer work, we make use of women who, on the average, have the following characteristics: (1) they fall between the upper middle and lower middle socioeconomic group, (2) they have completed some or all of high school, (3) they are extroverted, and (4) they are above the average in intelligence.

The Questionnaire

It is difficult to evaluate your questionnaire without considerable field testing. In the present case, there has been no effort at all to do so. We would save our "criticism" for (a) detailed discussion with the agency, and (b) considerable field testing.

We have conducted a group interview with the subject matter pretty much in its present sequence, though the questions asked were more of an open-minded variety than contained in the questionnaire draft submitted with your specifications.

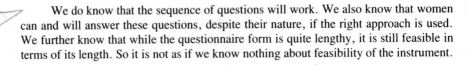

We do know that the sequence of questions will work. We also know that women can and will answer these questions, despite their nature, if the right approach is used. We further know that while the questionnaire form is quite lengthy, it is still feasible in terms of its length. So it is not as if we know nothing about feasibility of the instrument.

Field Testing

As a result of the group interview, it will be possible—though we have not taken the time to utilize it in such a manner—to study the consumer response to the interview so carefully as to make sure that the phrasings used in the questionnaire follow the words and phrases used in the consumer's actual thinking. The group interview thus means that we are that much further ahead in the phrasings of this questionnaire, even though it so far has not been utilized for such a purpose.

We plan a field test—or perhaps several—with a total of 100 homemakers distributed among people of varying socioeconomic groups, largely concentrated (for efficiency of handling) in the Chicago Metropolitan Area to make sure that the sequence and phrasing are of such a nature as to be understandable, to get cooperation, and to obtain unbiased replies.

Description of the Firm

The Progressive Research Group began operations in 1948 and, as such, is one of the oldest marketing research companies. Over the years the company has handled a large number of projects and has among its clients many of the largest consumer goods manufacturers.

The company possesses the most advanced computer equipment in the country and constant improvements are being adopted to speed up and make more economical, complete, and detailed client reports.

The following persons will direct the project:

A. W. Willis, B.A., overall project coordinator; president of The Progressive Research Group and a graduate in economics from a large university.

B. K. Walker, M.B.A., project director and client contact; vice-president and a graduate in business administration from a major university.

R. C. Moffatt, Ph.D., project adviser; major in sociology—five years' research experience as project director with large U.S. advertising agency before joining The Progressive Research Group in 1957. Three years spent as lecturer and consultant at two large American universities.

Time and Cost

Our report should be available 12 weeks after the finalizing of the project details. Our estimate of the cost of this project is $38,900 plus or minus 10 percent. It is our practice to bill one half of the estimated cost at the time of authorization with the final half billed on delivery of the report.

In discussing these proposals with his assistant, Mr. Jacks, Mr. Roberts wondered whether his own staff could not answer some of the questions if a thorough study of past Consumer Panel reports were conducted. For some ten years Bay-Madison had received full reports from an independent research company which ran a consumer panel, but these had only been used for day-to-day planning. Never, for instance, had a long-term, thorough study of the trends in Rill sales been compared with the various advertising and promotional campaigns the company had used or to the various price levels that had existed from time to time. Mr. Jacks was particularly enthusiastic about the idea as he had long maintained that the agency was not getting full value from the panel data. He said that he would personally like to work on such a project.

Mr. Roberts, in considering the idea further, estimated that such an analysis could be done for approximately $9,000. He had checked with the research company and found that all past reports were kept on automatic data processing cards. The company was most interested in the idea as an experiment and estimated that all the data required by the agency could be compiled for about $2,500. Mr. Roberts thought he could release Mr. Jacks from his other duties for a period of two months and that the cost of Mr. Jacks' salary, statistical and secretarial help, and other expenses would not exceed $5,500.

It was at this point that Mr. Roberts found himself in January 1976. He knew a decision had to be made quickly as the client was very anxious to get the Rill situation straightened away.

Use whats available
is data relevant
is data accurate
#1500
constructed to
people who
use prod.

The Atlanta Journal and Constitution (A)

Mr. Ferguson Rood, research and marketing director for *The Atlanta Journal* and the *Atlanta Constitution,* was still perspiring from the three-block walk in the hot August sun back to his office from the meeting he had just been to at Rich's Department Store. At the meeting, he had been told that Rich's, the newspaper's largest advertiser, wanted to test the effectiveness of TV and radio advertising versus newspaper advertising for its upcoming Harvest Sale. He had promised to make his suggestions for the research plan in 48 hours, and felt he had much work to do in that short time. He wondered what recommendations he should make for the study, and was concerned that the research design and questionnaire be developed so that the study would represent fairly the effectiveness of *The Atlanta Journal* and the *Atlanta Constitution.* As he began to review his notes from the meeting, he picked up the phone to call his wife and tell her he would be home very late that evening.

Background

The Atlanta Journal and the *Atlanta Constitution* are a union of two of the largest circulation newspapers in the South. The *Atlanta Constitution,* winner of four Pulitzer Prizes for its efforts in the area of social reform, was founded June 16, 1868. *The Atlanta Journal,* founded February 24, 1883, became the largest daily newspaper in Georgia by 1889. Also a winner of the Pulitzer Prize, *The Journal* is the Southeast's largest afternoon newspaper.

In 1950, *The Atlanta Journal* and the *Atlanta Constitution* were combined into Atlanta Newspapers, Inc., a privately held company. The two newspapers maintained independent editorial staffs, and there was very little overlap of readers. Exhibits 1 through 4 present data concerning the adult readership of the newspapers, the gross reader impressions, reach and frequency, and readership over five weekdays and four Sundays.

To provide the advertisers and potential advertisers with information necessary to help them make their advertising media decisions, the newspaper does a considerable amount of research, often approaching $25,000 in a year.

EXHIBIT 1 Gross readership impressions, reach, and frequency of *The Atlanta Journal* and *Constitution*

Gross reader impressions

The Atlanta Journal and *Constitution* in 15-county metro Atlanta:

During any five weekdays, 864,500 adults read *The Atlanta Journal* or *Constitution* an average of 3.5 times for a total of 3,025,800 weekday gross reader impressions.

During any four Sundays, 907,600 adults read *The Atlanta Journal* and *Constitution* for an average of 3.4 times for a total of 3,085,800 Sunday gross reader impressions.

These newspapers deliver 3,933,400 adult gross reader impressions when one Sunday is added to five weekdays.

Reach and frequency of newspaper reading

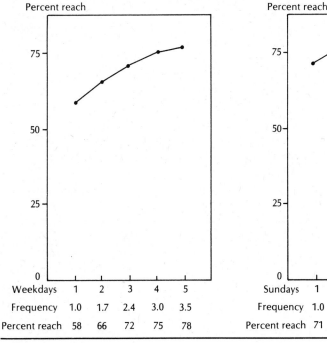

Weekdays	1	2	3	4	5
Frequency	1.0	1.7	2.4	3.0	3.5
Percent reach	58	66	72	75	78

Sundays	1	2	3	4
Frequency	1.0	1.8	2.6	3.4
Percent reach	71	77	81	82

EXHIBIT 2 *The Atlanta Journal* and *Constitution* readership information

78 percent of all daily circulation and 66 percent of all Sunday circulation is within 15-county metro Atlanta.

Of all metro Atlanta adults, 644,400 read *The Atlanta Journal* or *Constitution* on the average weekday. Of this total, 412,700 read *The Journal* and 366,100 read the *Constitution*. 134,400 adults read both. On the average Sunday 782,200 metro Atlanta adults read *The Atlanta Journal* and *Constitution*.

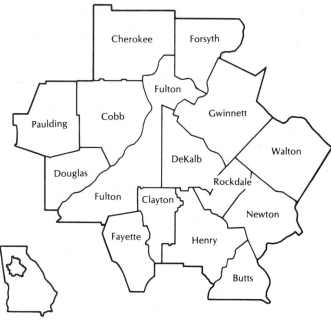

15-county metro Atlanta

Adult readers of *The Atlanta Journal* and *Constitution* in 15-county metro Atlanta

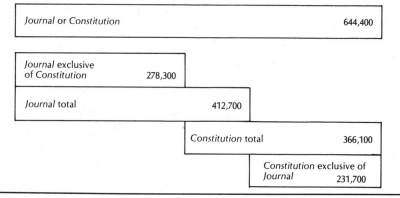

Journal or *Constitution*	644,400
Journal exclusive of *Constitution*	278,300
Journal total	412,700
Constitution total	366,100
Constitution exclusive of *Journal*	231,700

EXHIBIT 3 Readership of *The Atlanta Journal* and *Constitution* over five weekdays

644,400, or 58 percent, of all metro Atlanta adults read *The Atlanta Journal* or *Constitution* on the average weekday. Over five weekdays these newspapers deliver 864,900, or 78 percent, of all metro-area adults with an average frequency of 3.5 days.

	Total metro area adults	Average 1-day readership		Cumulative 5-weekday readership		
		Number	Percent	Number	Percent	Frequency
Total adults	1,105,500	644,400	58	864,900	78	3.5
Sex						
Female	588,500	331,700	56	447,600	76	3.5
Male	517,000	312,700	61	416,800	81	3.5
Household income						
$25,000 and over	104,200	85,900	82	102,700	99	4.2
$15,000–24,999	195,300	146,400	75	181,900	93	4.0
$10,000–14,999	241,900	152,800	63	203,900	84	3.7
$5,000–9,999	334,200	170,600	51	241,800	72	3.5
Under $5,000	229,900	88,500	39	133,000	58	3.3
Age						
18–34	470,500	234,500	50	345,200	73	3.4
35–49	305,600	197,200	65	250,300	82	3.9
50–64	211,900	145,800	69	184,600	87	3.9
65 and over	116,500	66,700	57	84,700	73	3.9
Race						
White	872,800	528,800	61	685,100	78	3.9
Nonwhite	232,700	115,600	50	180,100	77	3.2
Education						
College graduate	173,500	138,000	80	172,600	99	4.0
Part college	194,700	137,600	71	174,100	89	4.0
High school graduate	360,500	225,000	62	302,900	84	3.7
Part high school or less	365,600	137,000	38	202,200	55	3.4

EXHIBIT 4 Readership of *The Atlanta Journal* and *Constitution* over four Sundays

782,200, or 71 percent, of all metro Atlanta adults read *The Atlanta Journal* and *Constitution* on the average Sunday. Over four Sundays these newspapers deliver 907,300, or 82 percent, of all metro-area adults with an average frequency of 3.4 Sundays.

	Total metro area adults	Average 1-Sunday readership	Cumulative 4-Sunday readership	Number of Sundays frequency
Total adults	1,105,500	782,200	907,300	3.4
Sex				
Female	588,500	418,800	477,800	3.5
Male	517,000	363,400	429,500	3.4
Household income				
$25,000 and over	104,200	89,100	97,200	3.7
$15,000–24,999	195,300	168,800	180,700	3.7
$10,000–14,999	241,900	190,100	216,400	3.5
$5,000–9,999	334,400	215,600	267,300	3.2
Under $5,000	229,900	118,500	145,600	3.3

EXHIBIT 4 *(concluded)*

	Total metro area adults	Average 1-Sunday readership	Cumulative 4-Sunday readership	Number of Sundays frequency
Age				
18–34	470,500	313,000	390,000	3.2
35–49	305,600	221,300	248,500	3.6
50–64	211,900	167,000	179,900	3.7
65 and over	116,500	80,600	88,500	3.6
Race				
White	872,800	633,100	727,900	3.5
Nonwhite	232,700	149,100	179,100	3.3
Education				
College graduate	173,500	150,200	163,700	3.7
Part college	194,700	157,300	180,200	3.5
High school graduate	360,500	273,900	313,500	3.5
Part high school or less	365,600	192,300	240,000	3.2

Most of the research is designed to be used in selling advertising to a wide range of advertisers, and includes data on retail trading areas, shopping patterns, product usage, and newspaper coverage patterns. In addition to Mr. Rood, the research department had two other trained market researchers and one secretary.

Although there are nine daily newspapers in the Atlanta trading area, all but *The Journal* and the *Constitution* have very small circulations. The principal competition for large advertisers is with radio and TV stations. Exhibit 5 presents information on the circulation of the print media in the Atlanta area. Exhibit 6 contains information on the broadcast media in Atlanta. Although there were 40 radio stations, 28 AM and 12 FM, and 6 TV stations, WSB Radio and TV dominated the market. WSB Radio, for example, was consistently rated among the top six stations in the nation, and had a greater Atlanta audience than the next four stations combined. WSB-TV and WSB Radio, both affiliated with the NBC Network, were owned by Cox Broadcasting Corporation, which also owns television stations in Charlotte, Dayton, Pittsburgh, and San Francisco and radio stations in Charlotte, Dayton, and Miami. Cox Broadcasting and WSB-TV and Radio stations shared corporate headquarters in Atlanta.

EXHIBIT 5 Circulation of print media in Atlanta

Metro Atlanta newspapers	Edition	Total circulation
Dailies		
Atlanta Constitution	Morning	216,624
Atlanta Journal	Evening	259,721
Journal-Constitution	Sunday	585,532
Gwinnett Daily News	Evening (except Sat.)	10,111
Gwinnett Daily News	Sunday	10,100
Marietta Daily Journal	Evening (except Sat.)	24,750
Marietta Daily Journal	Sunday	25,456

EXHIBIT 5 (continued)

Metro Atlanta newspapers	Edition	Total circulation
Fulton County Daily Report	Evening (Mon.–Fri.)	1,600
Atlanta Daily World	Morning	19,000
Atlanta Daily World	Sunday	22,000
Wall Street Journal	Morning (Mon.–Fri.)	16,180
Jonesboro News Daily	Evening (Mon.–Fri.)	9,100
North Fulton Today	Evening (Mon.–Fri.)	2,300
South Cobb Today	Evening (Mon.–Fri.)	2,400
New York Times	Morning (Mon.–Sat.)	500
New York Times	Sunday	3,100
Weekly newspapers		
Atlanta Inquirer		30,000
Atlanta Voice		37,500
DeKalb New Era		16,400
Atlanta's Suburban Reporter		3,900
Lithonia Observer		2,765
Northside News		8,000
Georgia Business News		4,900
Southern Israelite		4,300
Decatur-DeKalb News		73,000
Southside Sun (East Point)		37,700
Tucker Star		10,000
Alpharetta, Roswell Neighbor		6,800
Austell, Mableton, Powder Springs Neighbor		12,123
Acworth, Kennesaw-Woodstock Neighbor		3,242
Northside, Sandy Springs, Vinings Neighbor		20,836
Smyrna Neighbor		6,872
College Park, East Point, Hapeville, South Side, West End Neighbor		18,813
Chamblee, Doraville, Dunwoody, North Atlanta Neighbor		14,963
Clarkston, Stone Mountain, Tucker Neighbor		15,074
The Journal of Labor (Atlanta)		17,500
Austell Enterprise		1,911
The Cherokee Tribune (Canton)		7,100
Rockdale Citizen		6,031
The Covington News		6,000
The Forsyth County News		4,800
Dallas New Era		4,075
Douglas County Sentinel		7,350
South Fulton Recorder (Fairburn)		4,000
Fayette County News		4,500
Jackson Progress Argus		2,635
The Weekly Advertiser (McDonough)		5,650
The Walton Tribune (Monroe)		5,102
Lilburn Recorder		5,000
Lawrenceville Home Weekly		2,000
The Great Speckled Bird (Atlanta)		7,925
The Georgia Bulletin		14,000
The Covington News (Tues. & Thurs.)		6,200
Creative Loafing in Atlanta		30,000
Atlanta area newspapers*		
Cobb		28,000
North Fulton		36,000
North DeKalb-Gwinnett		45,000
South DeKalb		44,000
South Fulton-Clayton		53,000

* These are supplements to *The Atlanta Journal,* and circulation is to *The Atlanta Journal* subscribers only.

EXHIBIT 5 *(concluded)*

	Total circulation
Major magazines in Georgia	
American Home	70,485
Better Homes and Gardens	145,962
Good Housekeeping	114,045
McCall's	139,728
Ladies' Home Journal	128,331
Family Circle	106,245
Woman's Day	100,566
Redbook	86,354
National Geographic	103,941
Reader's Digest	331,240
Newsweek	41,070
Time	60,438
U.S. News & World Report	40,417
TV Guide	345,871
Playboy	98,389
Sports Illustrated	38,263
Outdoor Life	25,918
True	18,244
Southern Living	95,000
Progressive Farmer	70,000
Cosmopolitan	25,075
Calendar Atlanta	50,000

Source: WSB Research Department.

WSB Radio was founded in 1922 by *The Atlanta Journal* newspaper. In 1939, former Democratic presidential nominee and Governor of Ohio James M. Cox acquired the newspaper-radio combine. In 1948, WSB-TV was founded, and two years later the newspapers and broadcast media were separated when Atlanta Newspapers, Inc., was established. Today, there is no relationship between the newspapers and WSB Radio and TV.

Rich's Department Store was the largest advertiser for *The Journal* and the *Constitution,* accounting for almost 5 percent of their advertising revenue, and was WSB's largest local advertiser. Founded in 1867, Rich's by 1970 had grown to a company with seven stores distributed throughout Atlanta as shown in Exhibit 7. Sales were approximately $200 million per year with earnings after taxes of almost 5 percent of sales. The company was classified as a general merchandise retailer, and carried a very wide line of products including clothing, furniture, appliances, housewares, and items for the home. Rich's dominated the Atlanta market, with close to 40 percent of department store sales and approximately 25 percent of all the sales of general merchandise. The merchandising highlight of the year was the annual Harvest Sale, first held in October 1925. The sale typically ran for two weeks, and had become a yearly tradition at Rich's.

EXHIBIT 6 Broadcast media in Atlanta

Location	Station/ network	Established	Frequency	Power	Channel	Network
Metro Atlanta AM radio stations						
Atlanta	WSB (NBC)	1922	750 khz	50 kw		
	WAOK	1954	1380 khz	5 kw		
	WGKA (ABC)	1955	1190 khz	1 kw day		
	WGST (ABC-E)	1922	920 khz	5 kw day 1 kw night		
	WIGO (ABC-C)	1946	1340 khz	1 kw day 250 w night		
	WIIN (MBS)	1949	970 khz	5 kw day		
	WPLO	1937	590 khz	5 kw		
	WQXI	1948	790 khz	5 kw day 1 kw night		
	WXAP	1948	860 khz	1 kw		
	WYZE (MBS)	1956	1480 khz	5 kw day		
Decatur	WAVO	1958	1420 khz	1 kw day		
	WGUN	1947	1010 khz	50 kw day		
	WQAK	1964	1310 khz	500 w		
N. Atlanta	WRNG (CBS)	1967	680 khz	25 kw day		
Morrow	WSSA	1959	1570 khz	1 kw day		
East Point	WTJH	1949	1260 khz	5 kw day		
Smyrna	WYNX	1962	1550 khz	10 kw day		
Buford	WDYX	1956	1460 khz	5 kw day		
Austell	WACX	1968	1600 khz	1 kw		
Lawrenceville	WLAW	1959	1360 khz	1 kw		
Marietta	WCOB	1955	1080 khz	10 kw day		
	WFOM	1946	1230 khz	1 kw day 250 w night		
Canton	WCHK (GA)	1957	1290 khz	1 kw day		
Covington	WGFS	1953	1430 khz	1 kw day		
Cumming	WSNE	1961	1170 khz	1 kw		
Douglasville	WDGL	1964	1527 khz	1 kw		
Jackson	WJGA	1967	1540 khz	1 kw day		
Monroe	WMRE	1954	1490 khz	1 kw		
Metro Atlanta FM radio stations						
	WSB-FM	1934	98.5 mhz	100 kw		
	WPLO-FM	1948	103.3 mhz	50 kw		
	WZGC-FM	1955	92.9 mhz	100 kw		
	WKLS-FM	1960	96.1 mhz	100 kw		
	WQXI-FM	1962	94.1 mhz	100 kw		
	WBIE-FM	1959	101.5 mhz	100 kw		
	WLTA-FM	1963	99.7 mhz	100 kw		
	WJGA-FM	1968	92.1 mhz	3 kw		
	WCHK-FM	1964	105.5 mhz	3 kw		
	WGCO-FM	1969	102.3 mhz	100 kw		
	WABE-FM	1948	90.0 mhz	10.5 kw		
	WREK-FM	1968	91.1 mhz	40 kw		
Metro Atlanta television stations						
	WSB-TV	9/29/48			2	NBC
	WAGA-TV	3/8/49			5	CBS
	WXIA-TV	9/30/51			11	ABC
	WTCG-TV	9/1/67			17	IND
	WETV	1958			30	NET
	WGTV	1960			8	NET

Source: WSB Research Department.

EXHIBIT 7 Map of Atlanta and seven Rich's stores

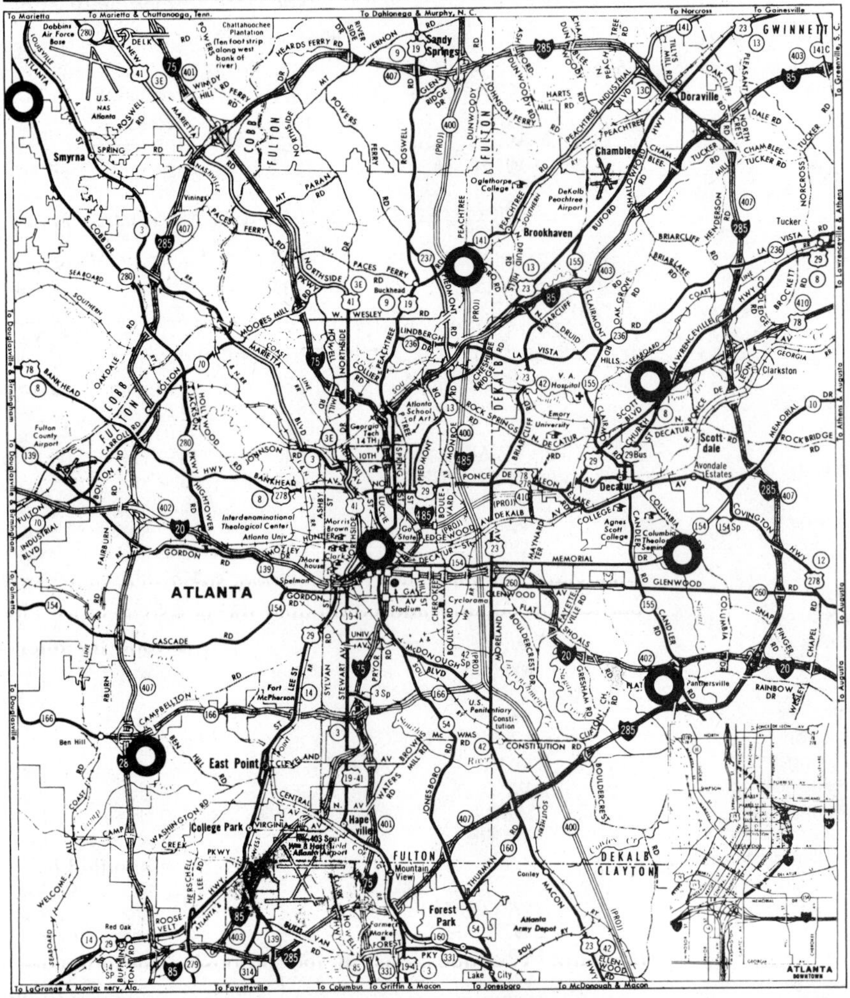

Background on the Media Effectiveness Study

Before preparing his proposal to Rich's for the media effectiveness study, Mr. Rood reflected upon the events of the past 24 hours. The day before, he had received a phone call from the vice president and sales promotion director from Rich's, inviting him to the meeting at Rich's the next day. Having been told that Rich's research director and the research director of WSB-TV and Radio would also be there, Mr. Rood had been a little apprehensive before going. At the start of the meeting he was asked if the Atlanta newspapers would be interested in participating in a cooperative research study aimed at measuring the effectiveness of various advertising media during Rich's September Harvest Sale, their largest annual sales event. It became immediately apparent that the research director from WSB, Jim Landon, had met with the Rich's people the week before, and was undoubtedly the source of the idea to conduct the study. A document was then passed out that had been prepared by WSB and was entitled "Suggestions for Rich's Media Research." This document is included in the Appendix, and outlines the objectives of the study, a suggested methodology, together with a questionnaire.

The suggested objectives for the project were: (1) to measure the ability of TV, radio, and newspapers to sell specific items of merchandise in Rich's seven Atlanta stores; (2) to determine how each advertising medium complements the others in terms of additional units sold to various segments of the customer population (age, sex, charge account ownership, and so on); (3) to determine what each advertising medium contributed in regard to additional store traffic. Mr. Rood's broadcasting counterpart stated at the meeting that "If Rich's is interested in conducting research to measure the effectiveness of various advertising media, WSB-TV and WSB Radio will be happy to assist." Rood had no choice, so he volunteered the support of the newspapers to the study.

The Rich's research manager then asked if the media would participate financially in the study. Mr. Rood suggested that each of the three media participate equally and committed the newspapers to $500 for a study that he figured should cost between $2,500 and $3,000 for interviewing. Mr. Landon indicated that Cox Broadcasting would be willing to put in $500 each for TV and radio.

They then discussed how the research could be conducted. The WSB proposal suggested in-store surveys, with a separate survey conducted for each item of merchandise tested. The survey would be conducted by Rich's employees working overtime in appropriate store locations during the peak shopping hours. The tabulation of the results could be handled by the broadcast station's computer. Care was to be taken to ensure that the TV, radio, or newspaper advertising for the individual items not be "stacked" in favor of one particular medium. The questions in the proposed questionnaire (see the Appendix) included questions on how the respondents happened to buy the merchandise at Rich's, if they recalled seeing TV, newspaper or radio advertising, and if they bought anything else. Questions were also asked concerning age and ownership of a Rich's charge account.

Mr. Landon stated that WSB was not trying to take business away from the newspapers, and that Rood had nothing to fear. His recommendation was that Rich's not take anything away from the newspaper advertising budget. He suggested that the amount of space purchased in the newspapers be the same as the previous year, with additional monies being committed to the broadcast media. The Rich's sales promotion director then discussed some of his thoughts concerning the study. He indicated that Rich's had been sending 400,000 direct mail pieces to announce the Harvest Sale; this year they would send 200,000, diverting the other money to broadcast. This would make $7,600 available for broadcast, and another $12,000 to $15,000 would be made available to purchase broadcast time.

The Harvest Sale was to open with courtesy days on Monday and Tuesday, September 21–22, with the sale beginning the evening of the 22nd and running for 13 days. While decisions concerning which sales items were to be included in the study and the media schedules to be used were not yet available, some progress had been made. Approximately 10 items were to be researched, and the newspaper ads on Sunday, September 20, would include all or most of the 10 items. Newspaper ads for the items would be repeated Monday and Tuesday with emphasis on *The Journal*. The interviews were to be conducted Monday through Wednesday.

On Sunday and Monday, with a possible spillover to Tuesday due to availability, Rich's would run 120, 30-second TV commercials on all commercial stations except Channel 17. During the same time they would run 120 radio 30-second commercials on a list of stations which had not yet been determined. With both TV and radio, WSB was to get the lion's share if availability could be arranged. Mr. Rood felt certain in view of the client and the research that WSB would manage to come up with several prime-time commercial openings even if it meant bumping some high paying national advertisers.

Eleven items were mentioned as possible subjects for the research. The 10 final items selected would come mostly from this list, although 1 or 2 other items might be chosen. The items mentioned included (1) color TV console at $499; (2) custom-made draperies; (3) Sterns & Foster mattress at $44; (4) carpeting at $6.99 per square yard; (5) Gant shirts at $5; (6) Van Heusen shirts and Arrow shirts at two for $11; (7) women's handbags at $9.99; (8) Johannsen's shoes; (9) pants suits; (10) Hoover upright vacuum cleaner; and (11) GE refrigerator.

Mr. Rood, who had not said very much at the meeting, then asked for 48 hours to review the proposal. Everyone agreed to this, and Mr. Rood promised to present a counterproposal at that time.

Even though it had been rather obvious who initiated the idea for the study and that he at first felt that newspapers were being "set up" by WSB, it had been basically a friendly and relaxed meeting among friends. Mr. Landon and Mr. Rood had worked together in the Atlanta Chapter of the American Marketing Association and had a great deal of mutual respect. Mr. Rood thought Landon was a tough competitor, and understood that he had been successful using awareness type studies in Cox Broadcastings' other markets to gain additional advertising for broadcast.

When he returned to his office, Rood pulled out some of his files on Rich's. He noticed that the amount of advertising had been fairly constant, approximately 40 pages over the two-week period, during the past three Harvest Sales, and that basically the same products had been promoted. A typical Harvest Sale ad is included in Exhibit 8. He also pulled from the files rate schedules for *The Atlanta Journal* and *Constitution* and WSB (see Exhibits 9

EXHIBIT 8 Typical Rich's Harvest ad

EXHIBIT 9 *The Atlanta Journal* and the *Atlanta Constitution* retail display rates

Open rate per column inch:*

Constitution	$8.15
Journal	$11.27
Combination	$14.83
Sunday	$15.56

Yearly bulk space rates:

Inches per year	Cost per inch			
	Constitution	Journal	Combined	Sunday
100	$6.21	$8.43	$11.09	$11.65
250	6.16	8.35	11.00	11.55
500	6.10	8.28	10.90	11.45
1,000	6.05	8.21	10.81	11.35
2,500	5.99	8.13	10.70	11.24
5,000	5.93	8.05	10.59	11.12
7,500	5.90	8.01	10.54	11.07
10,000	5.87	7.97	10.48	11.01
12,500	5.85	7.93	10.43	10.96
15,000	5.82	7.89	10.38	10.90
25,000	5.70	7.73	10.17	10.68
50,000	5.61	7.69	10.05	10.61
75,000	5.51	7.65	9.93	10.53
100,000	5.41	7.61	9.81	10.46
150,000	5.21	7.51	9.56	10.31
200,000	5.01	7.41	9.32	10.15
250,000	4.81	7.31	9.08	9.99

* There are 8 columns by 21 inches or 168 column inches on a full page.

EXHIBIT 10 WSB radio and TV advertising rates

	One minute	20/30 seconds	10 seconds
WSB-AM radio: Spot announcements— package plans*			
12 per week	$40.00	$34.00	$24.00
18 per week	38.00	30.00	21.00
24 per week	32.00	26.00	19.00
30 per week	28.00	24.00	17.00
48 per week	26.00	20.00	15.00
WSB-FM radio: Package plan—52 weeks†	16.00	14.00	

WSB-TV
  Daytime rates
    60 seconds $ 75–235 depending on program
    30 seconds   40–140 depending on program
  Prime-time rates
    60 seconds‡ $540–660 depending on program
    30 seconds   390–725 depending on program

* Available 5:00–6:00 A.M., 10:00 A.M.–3:30 P.M., and 7:30 P.M.–midnight, Monday–Saturday; and 5:00 A.M.–midnight, Sunday. Best available positions in applicable times—no guaranteed placement.
† Quantity discounts available. For example, 18 times per week for 52 weeks is one half the above rates.
‡ Very few available.

and 10), even though he realized that the exact media schedule would be developed by Rich's advertising agency. Approximately $100,000 would be spent promoting the Harvest Sale, with perhaps a third of this amount being devoted to the sale items.

Mr. Rood decided that he would have to assume confidence in the effectiveness of the newspapers. He felt if the study were done right he would get his share of media exposure and influence. The other decision he quickly made was that in preparing his comments on the proposed research, he would take Rich's point of view rather than that of *The Atlanta Journal* and *Constitution*. He then began to review the events of the day and the WSB proposal in light of what he felt Rich's needed to know. He also knew that whatever he proposed would have to be acceptable to Mr. Landon. Noting the lateness in the day, he began work on the counterproposal.

Appendix   Suggestions for Rich's Media Research

Objectives

If Rich's is interested in conducting research to measure the effectiveness of various advertising media, WSB-TV and WSB-Radio will be happy to assist. As a basis for discussion, here are suggested objectives for this project:

1. Measure the ability of TV, radio, and newspapers to sell specific items of merchandise in Rich's seven Atlanta metro stores.
2. Determine how each advertising medium complements the others in terms of additional units sold to various segments of the customer population (age, sex, charge account ownership, etc.).
3. Determine what each advertising medium contributes in regard to additional store traffic.

How the Research Could Be Conducted

The project could consist of a series of in-store surveys. A separate survey would be conducted for each item of merchandise tested. The more items tested, the more reliable the results of the overall research project.

If possible, all seven Rich's stores in the Atlanta metro area should participate in the research.

Each survey could be conducted by placing interviewers (Rich's personnel working overtime) in appropriate store locations during "peak" shopping hours with instructions to complete *brief* questionnaires with customers purchasing the item being tested. (See accompanying questionnaire.)

The interview could cover how the customer got the idea to buy the item, other planned purchases in the store during the same visit, charge account ownership, and any other pertinent data. Each interview would last less than a minute and would not bother the customers.

The sample size would vary, depending upon the number of stores participating, the type of merchandise and the sales volume. Interviewers would strive to include all customers purchasing the items during peak hours. Tabulation of the results could be handled by the WSB computer.

Careful Attention to Items and Media Schedules

In order to make the research valid and meaningful, the items to be tested must be selected carefully. In addition, care should be taken to ensure that the TV, radio, or newspaper advertising for these items is not "stacked" in favor of one particular medium. Close attention to the items being tested and the media schedule for each is necessary.

Questionnaire

The proposed questionnaire follows:

(All customers purchasing the item advertised are interviewed.)

1. *How* did you happen to buy this merchandise at Rich's?

   Saw on TV ( )
   Heard on radio ( )
   Saw in newspaper ( )
   TV and radio ( )
   TV and newspaper ( )
   TV, radio, and newspaper ( )
   Saw on display ( )
   Other: _____ ( )

ASKED OF CUSTOMERS NOT MENTIONING A MEDIUM: (2, 3, 4)

2. Do you recall seeing this merchandise advertised on the TV?
   Yes ( )
   No ( )

3. Do you recall seeing this merchandise advertised in the newspaper?
   Yes ( )
   No ( )

4. Do you recall hearing this merchandise advertised on the radio?
   Yes ( )
   No ( )

5. Are you buying *anything* else at Rich's today?
   Yes ( )
   No ( )
   Maybe ( )
   Don't know ( )

6. Do you have a charge account at *Rich's*?
   Yes ( )
   No ( )

7. In which group does your age fall?
   Under 25 ( )
   25–34 ( )
   35–49 ( )
   50 and over ( )

Store _____

Time of Interview _____

Case 8

Wyler Unsweetened
Soft Drink Mixes*

As Kenneth Otte sat in his office in Northbrook, Illinois, in early October 1977, he felt a bit like Jack in the children's story "Jack and the Beanstalk." He was facing a major challenge against a dominant foe, General Foods' Kool-Aid powdered soft drink mix, the giant of the unsweetened drink mix category.

The question Otte was considering was whether or not to recommend a major national introduction of Wyler's Unsweetened Soft Drink Mix against Kool-Aid in 1978. He knew RJR Foods' Hawaiian Punch was considering such a move and because of Kool-Aid's dominant position in the market, a 92 percent share and virtually unchallenged in its 50-year existence, he questioned whether there was room for more than one additional brand in the market. If he waited another year, it might be too late. If, however, he introduced in 1978 and Hawaiian Punch did, too, perhaps neither would achieve their goals. The question was more complex than just whether or not to introduce the product. Wyler's Unsweetened Soft Drink Mix had just completed the second year of testing under Otte's direction with somewhat mixed results. There was certainly time to make changes and adjustments to the program, but the question was, what changes should he investigate or recommend prior to a January meeting with the Wyler sales and broker force?

Management had requested a review of the situation and Otte's recommendations by November 1, 1977. Since a national introduction in 1978 would require substantial investment spending, Otte had several questions facing him. Should he recommend a national program for 1978? If not, what recommendation should be made? More test markets or fine-tuning of his present program?

If he did recommend a national program, what, if any, changes should be made in the recently completed test program? He wondered about such questions as advertising, promotion, distribution, and others. He still had time to investigate and test new ideas, but exactly what did the results of the test

---

* This case was prepared by Professor Don E. Schultz and Mark Traxler of Northwestern University. Reproduced by permission.

markets mean? As Otte prepared to develop his recommendation, he reviewed the entire situation of the category, the product, competition, and test market results. Did he have enough ammunition to challenge the Kool-Aid giant?

Company History

Wyler Foods is a Chicago-based company manufacturing several products. Their line includes instant soups, boullion powders and cubes, and powdered soft drink mixes. The original company was organized in the late 1920s and in 1930 introduced Cold Kup soft drink, a presweetened mix in a pouch. It was available in four flavors. About the same time, Peskin Company introduced Kool-Aid, an unsweetened soft drink mix. Peskin was later acquired by General Foods and Wyler was purchased by Borden. Wyler continued to concentrate on the presweetened soft drink mix market. In 1954, a powdered lemonade mix was introduced very successfully. By 1977, lemonade flavor accounted for approximately 40 percent of all Wyler soft drink mix sales.

Wyler and Kool-Aid continue to battle in the soft drink mix market with Wyler dominant in the presweetened market and Kool-Aid in the unsweetened area. In the early 1960s, Kool-Aid entered the presweetened market with an artificially sweetened product using cyclamates. This sweetener was banned by the federal government in 1969 and Wyler, with its sugar sweetening, rapidly gained ground in the mix market. As a result of the ban Wyler moved up to a 20 percent share of the presweetened market. In 1972, Wyler introduced an industry "first" by packaging presweetened soft drink mixes in cannisters of 10 to 15 quarts. With this innovation, Wyler's share of the presweetened market increased to over 40 percent. Shares have declined slightly from this level as increased competitive pressures have segmented the market. Wyler did not have an unsweetened entry until initiating a test in 1976.

Soft Drink Market

The liquid refreshment market, composed of hot, cold, and alcoholic beverages, is limited in growth by the "Share of Belly" concept which suggests that human beings can consume just so much liquid in a given year. All entries in the soft drink mix market are competing with all other potable refreshments for some space in an unexpandable belly. The level of per capita liquid consumption, under this concept, is tied to the U.S. population growth rate and changing consumer preferences.

In 1977, soft drink mix quart sales increased 9 percent over the previous year. During that same period, single strength drinks remained unchanged while carbonated beverage sales increased 7 percent. Otte predicts that soft drink mix tonnage will increase by 5 percent in 1978. Carbonated soft drinks will continue to grow, but less dramatically; canned fruit drinks will decline by 10 to 15 percent; and iced tea mixes will grow between 5 and 7 percent.

Powdered Soft Drink Mixes

The soft drink mix business, the 12th largest dry grocery product category, accounts for about 10 percent of all soft drink sales. It has increased in both quart and dollar sales each year since 1970. This growth is due to a greater demand for more product convenience, a wider assortment of flavors, and a more economical cold beverage alternative to carbonated drinks and single-strength canned drinks. In 1977 the segment is expected to produce sales of $503 million. Otte predicts that with a 5 percent growth in 1978, soft drink mixes will generate $565 million in sales.

The division of the powdered drink mix market is somewhat confusing. In terms of quart equivalent tonnage, the market is divided into 52.4 percent presweetened and 47.6 percent unsweetened. In terms of dollar sales, the split is 74.6 percent presweetened and 25.4 percent unsweetened. The major difference is the cost per quart of the sweetened product versus the unsweetened. More families purchase presweetened soft drink mixes than unsweetened; however, the unsweetened buyer appears to be a much heavier consumer (or purchaser at least). The presweetened buyer purchases the product an average of every 56.5 days compared to the more frequent purchase pattern of the unsweetened buyer who purchases every 46.7 days. Consumer panel data shows that both unsweetened and presweetened purchasers pick up an average of six pouches on each shopping occasion.

In comparison with other beverage categories, soft drink mixes are inexpensive, with unsweetened drink mixes the least expensive of all. Mixes are less than half the cost of carbonated beverages and single-strength canned drinks. Unsweetened mixes are least expensive due to the economy of adding one's own sugar. Exhibit 1 compares beverage costs per 4-ounce serving.

EXHIBIT 1 Beverage cost per 4-ounce serving

Beverage	Price
Unsweetened powdered mix	3.0¢
Presweetened powdered mix	4.7
Iced tea mix	5.0
Frozen orange juice	10.2
Single-strength drinks	10.4
Carbonated soft drinks	11.7
Chilled orange juice	11.7

higher profit margin.

Source: *A. C. Nielsen Food Index*, May 1977.

The buyer profile for powdered soft drink mix users shows that about two thirds of all U.S. households purchase the product. The primary buyer is the female homemaker between the ages of 18 and 44, with the heaviest concentration in the 25 to 34 age range. She is unemployed and has a high school education. Husband's occupation is blue collar, clerk, or salesman with an annual household income between $10,000 and $20,000. The typical family has three or more individuals including children under age 18. Users who consume at least five glasses per day are concentrated in the north central and southern United States (Exhibit 2).

EXHIBIT 2 Soft drink mix usage by area

	All users				Heavy users			
Area	Number of people who use product (000)	Percentage of users in each area	Percentage of people in each area who are users	Relative index	Number of people who use product (000)	Percentage of users in each area	Percentage of people in each area who are users	Relative index
Northeast	5976	18.8	40.5	81	2206	21.7	15.0	94
North central	10484	33.0	59.5	119	3220	31.7	18.3	114
South	10128	31.9	49.4	99	3353	33.0	16.3	102
West	5209	16.4	48.0	96	1393	13.7	12.8	80
Total	31797	100.1			10172	100.1		

Source: Target Group Index, 1977.

Soft drink mix sales are highly seasonal. Sales peak during the summer months and drop off entirely during the winter. Many grocers, particularly in the northern climates, do not stock powdered soft drink mixes during the winter months after the summer inventory is sold. An attempt to overcome this extreme seasonality was initiated in 1976 by Wyler's. Their "second season" promotion strategy, which promotes to both the consumer and the trade, was designed to encourage year-round product usage.

Unsweetened Powdered Soft Drink Mixes

The basic ingredients of a powdered soft drink mix consist of citric acid, artificial flavors, ascorbic acid (vitamin C), artificial color, and, depending on whether sweetened or unsweetened, some sugar. Kool-Aid and Wyler's are packaged in 2-quart foil pouches. Hawaiian Punch is expected to follow that format. Directions for mixing a single package are as follows: Empty contents into a large plastic or glass pitcher. Add one cup of sugar and quantity of ice water to make 2 quarts. Stir.

A comparison of the available and most popular flavors shows that the "red" flavors and grape are by far the fastest selling. Exhibit 3 lists the available flavors for Wyler's and, in the case of Kool-Aid, the 6 out of 16 flavors that constitute 73 percent of their unsweetened volume. The flavors listed for Hawaiian Punch are those that they have offered in their presweetened line. The unsweetened market is dominated by Kool-Aid with a 92 percent share, 4 percent is private label (A&P Cheri-Aid and Kroger's Flavor Aid), and 4 percent goes to others including Wyler's test market.

EXHIBIT 3 Unsweetened mix flavors

Kool-Aid	Wyler's	Hawaiian Punch
Strawberry	Strawberry	Strawberry
Cherry	Cherry	Cherry
Fruit Punch	Fruit Punch	Red Punch
Grape	Grape	Grape
Orange	Orange	Orange
Lemonade	Lemonade	Lemonade
		Raspberry

The unit cost to the retailer for the major competitors is 9.4 cents per pouch. The wholesale selling price for Wyler's and Kool-Aid is $26.95 per case. Although the store price per pouch ranges from 10 to 13 cents, suggested retail is 12 cents. This provides a 21.7 percent profit margin. The following figures show the retail profit margin for the common out-of-store prices.

Price	Retail profit margin
10 cents	6.0 percent
11	14.5
12	21.7
13	27.7

In the grocery aisle, the unsweetened category is normally placed next to the presweetened powdered soft drink mix section. The product is displayed on trays containing 72 pouches with three shelf facings. Wyler's and Kool-Aid cases contain four 72-pouch trays. Hawaiian Punch has announced that they will offer trays containing 36 pouches with two shelf facings, two trays per case.

Wyler's has instructed their food broker salespeople to position Wyler's unsweetened next to the same Kool-Aid flavor, to stack no more than two trays high, and to avoid stacking one flavor on top of another. Floor display racks are offered by both Wyler's and Kool-Aid to increase brand awareness and stimulate trial. The Wyler's rack holds 15 cases and provides secondary distribution. However, store managers are reluctant to use racks because the aisles are becoming too cluttered.

Introducing Wyler's Unsweetened

In 1977, Wyler's Unsweetened was introduced into 33 broker areas representing 28 percent of the U.S. population and 40 percent of total unsweetened category sales. Only 25 of the 33 areas had achieved adequate distribution by mid-1977. The successful 25 areas comprised 17.2 percent of the U.S. population and 33.7 percent of the total unsweetened category volume. The unsweetened case volume achieved a 6 percent share during the peak months of

June and July 1977 and declined to 5 percent in October. Projected for the whole nation, the share was 3.2 percent in the peak and 2.5 percent on a continuing basis.

According to 1977 Target Group Index figures, Kool-Aid's strongest concentration both presweetened and unsweetened was in the south and north central regions. Wyler's strength, primarily based on presweetened sales, was centered in the north central region. Possible reasons for this difference are that powdered soft drink mixes started and have remained popular in the north central region and that Kool-Aid has many more users in each region than Wyler's, with only 33 measured broker areas. Exhibit 4 shows the regional concentration.

The target market selected for Wyler's introduction differed slightly from the one selected by Kool-Aid. The notable differences were household head's occupation and the market size. Exhibit 5 summarizes Wyler's target market demographics. The prime users were children 2 to 12 who were thought to have little influence on the purchase decision. The female homemaker bought the products she thought best for her family. Hence, most Wyler's advertising was directed at mothers.

Wyler's entered the market with two main advertising copy themes. "Double Economy" stressed Wyler's as an unsweetened drink for the entire family which was economical because you add your own sugar and the entire family enjoyed. The second advertising theme claimed that Wyler's unique flavor boosters (salt and other flavor enhancers) made Wyler's taste better. Both

EXHIBIT 4 Kool-Aid soft drink mix usage by area

	All users				Heavy users			
Area	Number of people who use product (000)	Percentage of users in each area	Percentage of people in each area who are users	Relative index	Number of people who use product (000)	Percentage of users in each area	Percentage of people in each area who are users	Relative index
Northeast	4109	17.0	27.8	73	2441	23.2	16.5	100
North central	7660	31.6	43.4	114	4298	40.9	24.4	148
South	8372	34.6	40.8	107	2490	23.7	12.1	74
West	4073	16.8	37.5	99	1288	12.2	11.9	72
Total	24214	100.0			10517	100.0		

EXHIBIT 5 Wyler's target market demographics

Demographic variable	Wyler's	Kool-Aid
Income	$15,000–$19,999	$15,000–$19,999
Household size	3 or more	3 or more
Age of female head	Under 45	Under 45
Age of children	12 and under	Any under 18
Occupation of household head	White collar	Blue collar
Market size	500,000–2,500,000	Non-SMSA

executions emphasized the red flavors and vitamin C content and soft-pedaled lemonade. While the two campaigns were used in the test, they were both considered interim efforts. On the basis of the test, a new claim based even more on flavors was being considered. This involved the use of Roy Clark, the television personality, as spokesperson, who would stress the good taste of Wyler's. Spot television was the major medium used in the market tests but was backed by print as coupon carriers.

Kool-Aid's advertising came in three varieties with separate messages for general brand awareness, economy of use, and children. The general brand awareness execution was a nostalgia appeal to mothers which said, ''You loved it as a kid. You trust it as a mother.'' The economy of use execution showed children's preferences for Kool-Aid's flavor over single-strength beverages and the economy of adding one's own sugar. The execution with children showed the Kool-Aid ''Smiling Pitcher'' saving the day by foiling some dastardly deeds. Most advertising was placed in television; 70 percent network and 30 percent spot, evenly divided between day and night. It is anticipated that Hawaiian Punch would take advantage of their character ''Punchy'' to introduce the new unsweetened powdered mix since he has been used extensively before.

For the 1977 test, Wyler had divided the media budget into a peak and second season push. A total of $1,010,000 was to be invested in spot television in the 33 broker areas that made up the test. From mid-April to mid-August, Wyler had purchased spot TV in prime, day, and early fringe time. For the second season, the schedule was to be composed of day, early, and late fringe time from September until Christmas and from late January into late March. Otte had received a suggestion from the agency that if the tests were continued in 1978, media weight tests should probably be undertaken since a level pattern had been used in the 1977 test markets.

Compared to Wyler's test program, Kool-Aid was spending approximately $18 million in measured media in 1977. Six million was being spent for presweetened, 6 million for unsweetened, and 6 million for the Kool-Aid brand. Two thirds of the network budget was being used for weekdays and was directed toward women. The remainder was being spent on a Saturday/Sunday rotation directed at kids. Spot TV funds were being allocated almost evenly between day (36%), night/late night (34%), and early fringe (30%). During the peak season, Kool-Aid planned on spending $13,405,000 divided into $6.580 million in the second quarter and $6.825 million in the third quarter. The second season expenditure was $4.59 million divided into $2.57 million in the first quarter and $2.025 million in the fourth quarter. It was expected that Kool-Aid would probably spend about $20 million in 1978 for consumer advertising.

Otte anticipates that Hawaiian Punch, if they introduce, would spend $4.7 million in a 1978 introduction. Two thirds would probably be used in network (33.5% each for day and prime) and 33 percent for spot. Advance information indicated that this budget would break down to $3.2 million for network ($1.6 million in prime and daytime) and $1.5 million for spot.

In addition to the heavy consumer advertising, Wyler's spent $827,670 on consumer promotions during the tests to generate trial and awareness. These included samples and various coupon drops. Several print media were being used to deliver both coupons and samples, such as Sunday supplements and best food day newspaper sections. It was still too early to determine the results of these promotions for 1977.

Trade promotions in 1977 were budgeted at $292,330. All were in case allowances to encourage retailers to stock Wyler's unsweetened. No matter how much money Wyler's spent on consumer advertising and promotion it appeared from tests the trade would not stock another powdered soft drink mix without sizable case allowances to sweeten the deal since most of the powdered drink mix inventory traditionally had been sold to retailers on trade deals. Whether entering additional tests or going national in 1978, Otte felt to ensure successful distribution a case allowance of $3.60 between the end of February and the end of April 1978 would be needed if Wyler's continued the test market or went national. The case allowance would be the highest ever offered in the unsweetened drink mix category.

Otte had conducted research testing consumer reactions to both the product and the advertising. In terms of product quality, the difference between Kool-Aid and Wyler's unsweetened was essentially parity. However, in-depth taste tests revealed that the grape and strawberry flavors of Kool-Aid rated higher than Wyler's. This was a matter of substantial concern since these two flavors were the two most popular in the unsweetened category.

Wyler's ''Double Economy'' commercial was evaluated by Burke Research in 1977 and by the McCollum/Spielman research organization in July–August 1977. By Burke norms, Wyler's did very well. For the target market of women 25 to 34, 35 percent recalled the commercial in ''day after'' testing. The norm was 27 percent. The McCollum/Spielman study indicated strong awareness of the brand name, but specific recall of Wyler's unsweetened was low.

The situation, as Otte sees it, is that heavy advertising and consumer promotion are necessary to combat the consumer's neutral attitude toward unsweetened powdered soft drink mixes. Awareness of unsweetened brands is much lower than that of presweetened mixes. However, Kool-Aid has extremely high brand awareness. Otte feels that the Wyler's name is associated with powdered soft drink mixes in the consumer's mind, though there is no consumer research to back this up. Also heavy trade promotion is necessary to get the product on the shelves.

If he decided on another test plan in 1978, Otte estimated that he would need a minimum investment of $4 million for Wyler's unsweetened. The plan would involve $2.2 million in media advertising and $1.8 million in consumer promotions. If he decided to introduce nationally, he would need a substantially larger budget than that. What to do? Should he risk another test and perhaps lose the opportunity to go national to Hawaiian Punch or should he develop a plan to invade Kool-Aid's territory in 1978 on a national basis? The risks and the rewards were great either way.

Case 9

Modern Plastics (A)*

Institutional sales manager Jim Clayton had spent most of Monday morning planning for the rest of the month. It was early July and Jim knew that an extremely busy time was coming with the preparation of the following year's sales plan.

Since starting his current job less than a month ago, Jim had been involved in learning the requirements of the job and making his initial territory visits. Now that he was getting settled, Jim was trying to plan his activities according to priorities. The need for planning had been instilled in him during his college days. As a result of his three years' field sales experience and development of time management skills, he felt prepared for the challenge of the sales manager's job.

While sitting at his desk, Jim recalled a conversation that he had a week ago with Bill Hanson, the former manager, who had been promoted to another division. Bill told him that the sales forecast (annual and monthly) for plastic trash bags in the Southeast region would be due soon as an initial step toward developing the sales plan for the next year. Bill had laughed as he told Jim, "Boy, you ought to have a ball doing the forecast being a rookie sales manager!"

When Jim had asked what Bill meant, he explained by saying that the forecast was often "winged" because the headquarters in New York already knew what they wanted and would change the forecast to meet their figures, particularly if the forecast was for an increase of less than 10 percent. The experienced sales manager could throw numbers together in a short time that would pass as a serious forecast and ultimately be adjusted to fit the plans of headquarters. However, an inexperienced manager would have a difficult time "winging" a credible forecast.

Bill had also told Jim that the other alternative meant gathering mountains of data and putting together a forecast that could be sold to the various levels of

---

* This case was coauthored by Professor Tom Ingram, University of Kentucky, and Professor Danny N. Bellenger, Texas Tech University.

Modern Plastics management. This alternative would prove to be time-consuming and could still be changed anywhere along the chain of command before final approval.

Clayton started reviewing pricing and sales volume history (see Exhibit 1). He also looked at the key account performance for the past two and a half years (see Exhibit 2). During the past month Clayton had visited many of the

EXHIBIT 1 Plastic trashbags—sales and pricing history, 1975–1977

	Pricing dollars per case			Sales volume in cases			Sales volume in dollars		
	1975	1976	1977	1975	1976	1977	1975	1976	1977
January	$6.88	$ 7.70	$15.40	33,000	46,500	36,500	$ 227,000	$ 358,000	$ 562,000
February	6.82	7.70	14.30	32,500	52,500	23,000	221,500	404,000	329,000
March	6.90	8.39	13.48	32,000	42,000	22,000	221,000	353,000	296,500
April	6.88	10.18	12.24	45,500	42,500	46,500	313,000	432,500	569,000
May	6.85	12.38	11.58	49,000	41,500	45,500	335,500	514,000	527,000
June	6.85	12.65	10.31	47,500	47,000	42,000	325,500	594,500	433,000
July	7.42	13.48	9.90*	40,000	43,500	47,500*	297,000	586,500	470,000*
August	6.90	13.48	10.18	48,500	63,500	43,500	334,500	856,000	443,000
September	7.70	14.30	10.31	43,000	49,000	47,500	331,000	700,500	489,500
October	7.56	15.12	10.31	52,500	50,000	51,000	397,000	756,000	526,000
November	7.15	15.68	10.72	62,000	61,500	47,500	443,500	964,500	509,000
December	7.42	15.43	10.59	49,000	29,000	51,000	363,500	447,500	540,000
Total	$7.13	$12.25	$11.30	534,500	568,500	503,500	$3,810,000	$6,967,000	$5,694,000

* July–December 1977 figures are forecast of sales manager J. A. Clayton and other data comes from historical sales information.

EXHIBIT 2 1977 key account sales history (in cases)

Customer	1975	1976	First six months 1977	1975 monthly average	1976 monthly average	First half 1977 monthly average	First quarter 1977 monthly average
Transco Paper Company	125,774	134,217	44,970	10,481	11,185	7,495	5,823
Callaway Paper	44,509	46,049	12,114	3,709	3,837	2,019	472
Florida Janitorial Supply	34,746	36,609	20,076	2,896	3,051	3,346	2,359
Jefferson	30,698	34,692	25,044	2,558	2,891	4,174	1,919
Cobb Paper	13,259	23,343	6,414	1,105	1,945	1,069	611
Miami Paper	10,779	22,287	10,938	900	1,857	1,823	745
Milne Surgical Company	23,399	21,930	—	1,950	1,828	—	—
Graham	8,792	15,331	1,691	733	1,278	281	267
Crawford Paper	7,776	14,132	6,102	648	1,178	1,017	1,322
John Steele	8,634	13,277	6,663	720	1,106	1,110	1,517
Henderson Paper	9,185	8,850	2,574	765	738	429	275
Durant Surgical	—	7,766	4,356	—	647	726	953
Master Paper	4,221	5,634	600	352	470	100	—
D.T.A.	—	—	2,895	—	—	482	—
Crane Paper	4,520	5,524	3,400	377	460	566	565
Janitorial Service	3,292	5,361	2,722	274	447	453	117
Georgia Paper	5,466	5,053	2,917	456	421	486	297
Paper Supplies, Inc.	5,117	5,119	1,509	426	427	251	97
Southern Supply	1,649	3,932	531	137	328	88	78
Horizon Hospital Supply	4,181	4,101	618	348	342	103	206
Total cases	346,007	413,217	156,134	28,835	34,436	26,018	17,623

key accounts, and on the average they had indicated that their purchases from Modern would probably increase about 15–20 percent in the coming year.

Schedule for Preparing the Forecast

Jim had received a memo recently from Robert Baxter, the regional marketing manager, detailing the plans for completing the 1978 forecast. The key dates in the memo began in only three weeks:

August 1	Presentation of forecast to regional marketing manager.
August 10	Joint presentation with marketing manager to regional general manager.
September 1	Regional general manager presents forecast to division vice president.
September 1–September 30	Review of forecast by staff of division vice president.
October 1	Review forecast with corporate staff.
October 1–October 15	Revision as necessary.
October 15	Final forecast forwarded to division vice president from regional general manager.

Company Background

The plastics division of Modern Chemical Company was founded in 1965 when Modern Chemical purchased Cordco, a small plastics manufacturer with national sales of $15 million. At that time the key products of the plastics division were sandwich bags, plastic tablecloths, trash cans, and plastic-coated clothesline.

Since 1965 the plastics division has grown to a sales level exceeding $200 million with five regional profit centers covering the United States. Each regional center has manufacturing facilities and a regional sales force. There are four product groups in each region:

1. Food packaging: Styrofoam meat and produce trays; plastic bags for various food products.
2. Egg cartons: Styrofoam egg cartons sold to egg packers and supermarket chains.
3. Institutional: Plastic trash bags and disposable tableware (plates, bowls, and so on).
4. Industrial: Plastic packaging for the laundry and dry cleaning market; plastic film for use in pallet overwrap systems.

Each product group is supervised jointly by a product manager and a district sales manager, both of whom report to the regional marketing manager. The sales representatives report directly to the district sales manager but also work closely with the product manager on matters concerning pricing and product specifications.

The five regional general managers report to J. R. Hughes, vice president of the plastics division. Hughes is located in New York. Although Modern Chemical is owned by a multinational oil company, the plastics division has been able to operate in a virtually independent manner since its establishment in 1965. The reasons for this include:

1. Limited knowledge of the plastic industry on the part of the oil company management.
2. Excellent growth by the plastics division has been possible without management supervision from the oil company.
3. Profitability of the plastics division has consistently been higher than that of other divisions of the chemical company.

The Institutional Trash Bag Market

The institutional trash bag is a polyethylene bag used to collect and transfer refuse to its final disposition point. There are different sizes and colors available to fit the various uses of the bag. For example, a small bag for desk wastebaskets is available as well as a heavier bag for large containers such as a 55-gallon drum. There are 25 sizes in the Modern line with 13 of those sizes being available in 3 colors—white, buff, and clear. Customers typically buy several different items on an order to cover all their needs.

The institutional trash bag is a separate product from the consumer grade trash bag which is typically sold to homeowners through retail outlets. The institutional trash bag is sold primarily through paper wholesalers, hospital supply companies, and janitorial supply companies to a variety of end users. Since trash bags are used on such a wide scale, the list of end users could include almost any business or institution. The segments include hospitals, hotels, schools, office buildings, transportation facilities, and restaurants.

Based on historical data and a current survey of key wholesalers and end users in the Southeast, the annual market of institutional trash bags in the region was estimated to be 55 million pounds. Translated into cases, the market potential was close to 2 million cases. During the past five years, the market for trash bags has grown at an average rate of 89 percent per year. Now a mature product, future market growth is expected to parallel overall growth in the economy. The 1978 real growth in GNP is forecast to be 4.5 percent.

General Market Conditions

The current market is characterized by a distressing trend. The market is in a position of oversupply with approximately 20 manufacturers competing for the business in the Southeast. Prices have been on the decline for several months but are expected to level out during the last 6 months of the year.

This problem arose after a record year in 1976 for Modern Plastics. During 1976, supply was very tight due to raw material shortages. Unlike many of its competitors, Modern had only minor problems securing adequate raw material supplies. As a result the competitors were few in 1976, and all who remained in business were prosperous. By early 1977 raw materials were plentiful, and prices began to drop as new competitors tried to buy their way into the market. During the first quarter of 1977 Modern Plastics learned the hard way that a competitive price was a necessity in the current market. Volume fell off drastically in February and March as customers shifted orders to new suppliers when Modern chose to maintain a slightly higher than market price on trash bags.

With the market becoming extremely price competitive and profits declining, the overall quality has dropped to a point of minimum standard. Most suppliers now make a bag "barely good enough to get the job done." This quality level is acceptable to most buyers who do not demand high quality for this type of product.

Modern Plastics versus Competition

A recent study of Modern versus competition had been conducted by an outside consultant to see how well Modern measured up in several key areas. Each area was weighted according to its importance in the purchase decision, and Modern compared to its key competitors in each area and on an overall basis. The key factors and their weights are shown below:

		Weight
1.	Pricing	.50
2.	Quality	.15
3.	Breadth of line	.10
4.	Sales coverage	.10
5.	Packaging	.05
6.	Service	.10
Total		1.00

As shown in Exhibit 3, Modern compared favorably with its key competitors on an overall basis. None of the other suppliers were as strong as Modern in breadth of line nor did any competitor offer as good sales coverage as that provided by Modern. Clayton knew that sales coverage would be even better next year since the Florida and North Carolina territories had grown enough to add two salespeople to the institutional group by January 1, 1978.

Pricing, quality, and packaging seemed to be neither an advantage nor a disadvantage. However, service was a problem area. The main cause for this, Clayton was told, was temporary out-of-stock situations which occurred occasionally primarily due to the wide variety of trash bags offered by Modern.

During the past two years, Modern Plastics had maintained its market share at approximately 27 percent of the market. Some new competitors had entered the market since 1975 while others had left the market (see Exhibit 4).

EXHIBIT 3 Competitive factors ratings (by competitor*)

Weight	Factor	Modern	National Film	Bonanza	South-eastern	PBI	BAGCO	South-west Bag	Sun Plastics	East Coast Bag Co.
.50	Price	2	3	2	2	2	2	2	2	3
.15	Quality	3	2	3	4	3	2	3	3	4
.10	Breadth	1	2	2	3	3	3	3	3	3
.10	Sales coverage	1	3	3	3	4	3	3	4	3
.05	Packaging	3	2	2	3	3	1	3	3	3
.10	Service	4	3	3	2	2	2	3	4	3

Overall weighted ranking†

1.	BAGCO	2.15	6. Southeastern	2.55
2.	Modern	2.20	7. Florida Plastics	2.60
3.	Bonanza	2.25	8. National Film	2.65
4.	Southwest Bag (Tie)	2.50	9. East Coast Bag Co.	3.15
5.	PBI (Tie)	2.50		

* Ratings on a 1 to 5 scale with 1 being the best rating and 5 the worst.

† The weighted ranking is the sum of each rank times its weight. The lower the number, the better the overall rating.

EXHIBIT 4 Market share by supplier, 1975 and 1977

Supplier	Percent of market 1975	Percent of market 1977
National Film	11	12
Bertram	16	0*
Bonanza	11	12
Southeastern	5	6
Bay	9	0*
Johnson Graham	8	0*
PBI	2	5
Lewis	2	0*
BAGCO	—	6
Southwest Bag	—	2
Florida Plastics	—	4
East Coast Bag Co.	—	4
Miscellaneous and unknown	8	22
Modern	28	27
	100	100

* Out of business in 1977.
Source: This information was developed from a field survey conducted by Modern Plastics.

The previous district sales manager, Bill Hanson, had left Clayton some comments regarding the major competitors. These are reproduced in Exhibit 5.

EXHIBIT 5 Characteristics of competitors

National Film	Broadest product line in the industry. Quality a definite advantage. Good service. Sales coverage adequate, but not an advantage. Not as aggressive as most suppliers on price. Strong competitor.
Bonanza	Well-established tough competitor. Very aggressive on pricing. Good packaging, quality okay.
Southeastern	Extremely price competitive in southern Florida. Dominates Miami market. Limited product line. Not a threat outside of Florida.
PBI	Extremely aggressive on price. Have made inroads into Transco Paper Company during 1977. Good service but poor sales coverage.
BAGCO	New competitor in 1977. Very impressive with a high-quality product, excellent service, and strong sales coverage. A real threat, particularly in Florida.
Southwest Bag	A factor in Louisiana and Mississippi. Their strategy is simple—an acceptable product at a rock bottom price.

EXHIBIT 5 *(concluded)*

Sun Plastics	Active when market is at a profitable level with price cutting. When market declines to a low profit range, Sun manufactures other types of plastic packaging and stays out of the trash bag market. Poor reputation as a reliable supplier, but can still "spot-sell" at low prices.
East Coast Bag Co.	Most of their business is from a state bid which began in January 1976 for a two-year period. Not much of a threat to Modern's business in the Southeast as most of their volume is north of Washington, D.C.

Developing the Sales Forecast

After a careful study of trade journals, government statistics, and surveys conducted by Modern marketing research personnel, projections for growth potential were formulated by segment and are shown in Exhibit 6. This data was compiled by Bill Hanson just before he had been promoted.

EXHIBIT 6 1978 Real growth projections by segment

Total industry	+ 5.0%
Commercial	+ 5.4%
Restaurant	+ 6.8%
Hotel/motel	+ 2.0%
Transportation	+ 1.9%
Office users	+ 5.0%
Other	+ 4.2%
Noncommercial	+ 4.1%
Hospitals	+ 3.9%
Nursing homes	+ 4.8%
Colleges/universities	+ 2.4%
Schools	+ 7.8%
Employee feeding	+ 4.3%
Other	+ 3.9%

Source: Developed from several trade journals.

Jim looked back at Baxter's memo giving the time schedule for the forecast and knew he had to get started. As he left the office at 7:15, he wrote himself a large note and pinned it on his wall—"Get Started on the Sales Forecast!"

Part 4

Product and Brand Management Decisions

The six cases concerned with product strategy decisions in this section involve a number of different kinds of decisions. Many marketers believe that product decisions are the most critical of the marketing mix variables because of their importance to consumers in their decision-making process, and because product decisions, once made, are not quickly or easily reversed or changed. Promotion and pricing changes, for example, can be made much more quickly and with greater ease. Furthermore, most product changes usually require changes in the rest of the marketing strategy—changes in promotion, pricing, and sometimes distribution.

Before examining the various issues in the product strategy area, the concept of what a product is should first be understood. A product is "anything that can be offered to a market for attention, acquisition, or consumption; it includes physical objects, services, personalities, places, organizations, and ideas."[1] A product is thus much more than its physical properties and is everything a consumer buys when he or she makes a purchase. It is a set of want-satisfying attributes. It is important to understand this definition because what the consumer is buying is not necessarily what the company thought it was marketing. So marketers must be aware of consumer attitudes, values, needs, and wants with respect to their products.

The major decisions related to product strategy are:

---

[1] Philip Kotler, *Marketing Management: Analysis, Planning and Control,* 3d ed. (Englewood Cliffs, N.J.: Prentice-Hall, 1976), p. 183.

1. What new products should be developed?
2. What changes are needed in current products?
3. What products should be added or dropped?
4. What positioning should the product occupy?
5. What should the branding strategy be?

A brief discussion of some of the concepts related to each of these decisions follows.

New Product Development

The sales and profits of a product category tend to change over time. The pattern a product category typically follows is called the product life cycle. It is defined to have the introductory, growth, maturity, and decline stages. Because most products reach the maturity and decline stages eventually, a marketer must continually seek out new products which can go through the introductory and growth stages in order to maintain and increase the total profits of the firm. But what new products should be introduced?

To answer this question, a marketer must consider the objectives of the firm, the resources available, the target markets the firm is trying to satisfy, and how the new product would fit in with other products offered by the company and the competition.

To successfully develop new products, the organization will have to set up formalized strategies for generating new product ideas, means for screening these ideas, product and market testing procedures, and finally commercialization. The objective is to obtain products which are differentiated from those of its competitors and which meet the needs of a large enough segment of the market to be profitable.

Changes in Current Products

The needs, wants, attitudes, and behavior of consumers change over time, and a company must change its products also or risk losing these consumers to a competitor who more quickly responds to these changes in the marketplace.

Should new features be added to the product? Should the warranty be extended? Should the packaging be changed? Should new services be offered? The marketer must continually monitor its target market and the competition to be able to answer such questions.

What Products Should Be Added or Dropped

A marketer must make decisions concerning the product mix or composite of products the firm will offer for sale. This requires decisions concerning the width and depth of products. Width refers to the number of product lines marketed by the firm. For example, General Electric has many lines while

Kellogg's has concentrated on breakfast foods. The depth of the product mix is the number of items offered for sale within each product line. Kellogg's, for example, would have a very deep product line with many different alternatives offered for sale.

Whether a product line should be extended or reduced depends on a number of factors, including financial criteria, market factors, production considerations, and organizational factors. The marketer in making these decisions must examine the potential profit contributions, return on investment, impact on market share, fit with consumers' needs, fit with the needs of the channels of distribution, and the expected reactions of competitors. The production and organizational considerations include impact on capacity for other products, and on the goals and objectives of the firm, both in the short and long run.

Product Positioning

Product positioning is defined as that idea that is put into the consumers' minds by telling them how our product differs from its competitors. The position we strive to occupy will depend on the different market segments available, the attributes of our product compared to the needs of each segment, and the positions occupied by our competitors against each market segment.

Branding Strategy

The basic decisions here are whether or not to put brand names on the organization's products, whether the brands should be manufacturers' or distributors' brands, and whether individual or family brands should be used.

These decisions depend on the company's resources, objectives, the competition, and consumer choice behavior. For example, a small firm with little resources and much competition in a product category where consumers perceived small differences in the brands available, would probably choose to market its product using private distributors' brands. Family brands such as General Electric and Campbell's are used when the marketer wants the consumer to generalize to the new products all those attributes he associates with the family brand name. The time and money required to establish the brand's name is much lower with this strategy but it does not allow the marketer to establish a separate image for the new product.

Case 10

Amtrak

In late 1975, the management of Amtrak faced a number of major decisions concerning their Detroit-Chicago route. They were considering purchasing a number of new Amfleet trains to put on this run. There were also questions about what services to offer on these trains if they were purchased.

History of Amtrak

Amtrak was established through federal legislation on April 30, 1971, as a last-ditch attempt to revitalize intercity rail service in the United States. Railroads, during the previous 10 years, had found it difficult to compete with other modes of transportation—in particular, the private automobile (and the new interstate highway system it used), and the jet aircraft in domestic service. Travel by rail in the United States had declined from 70 percent of all intercity travel in 1947, to less than 5 percent in 1971.

Amtrak, a single nationwide passenger rail system, was designed to lure travelers back to the rails. In an era of increasing awareness of energy limitations, and of ever-growing numbers of people utilizing modes of transport other than the auto, revitalization of American rail service was viewed as a necessity. Amtrak's goal was increased ridership through refurbished equipment, modernization of terminal facilities, speed increases, and greater overall convenience.

At the time of the Amtrak takeover, no intercity passenger rail cars had been built in 10 years, and no passenger technology existed in the country to design and build modern cars. Stations were antiquated and without modern facilities of any kind in many cases. Equipment was in an almost constant state of malfunction, and was seldom cleaned. Connections were often impossible, or highly inconvenient. Rail service held little attraction for anyone except fearful flyers and train buffs. The National Railroad Passenger Corporation (Amtrak's official name) had its hands full.

For the purpose of service development, the various railroad lines and routes were divided into two categories: long-haul services and short- and medium-distance corridors. Long hauls were generally those routes of 700 or more miles, serviced by overnight or two day trains (e.g., The Broadway Limited, 900 miles, 17 hours, overnight between Chicago and New York). Corridors were lines over which several trains a day in each direction were operated. In particular, the corridors of less than 300 miles were thought to be ideally suited for high-quality, high-speed service, which could compete with the airlines. This style service if implemented, it was reasoned, could attract business travelers and others for whom travel time was of great importance. Amtrak had a good reason to believe this would work too: the New York-Washington corridor had offered such service since 1969—the Metroliners—and was very successful.

The Detroit-Chicago Corridor

In the case of the Detroit-Chicago corridor (279 miles), Amtrak saw an opportunity to duplicate the fine operation between New York and Washington. As late as the early 1960s, the New York Central Railroad (which originally operated Amtrak's Detroit-Chicago line) had offered high-quality rail service on the route. Running times between the two cities were as fast as four and a half hours, and luxurious meal and parlor car service was offered. With the completion of Interstate 94 through to Detroit from Chicago, and the introduction of the 727 jet on ''short-hop'' flights, much of the market for this type of service disappeared. The train was no longer fast enough. As travel volume dwindled, services were cut.

First the parlor cars (first-class service aimed toward business travelers) came off, then the diners with their sitdown meal service. Coaches and snack bars remained. When Penn Central was formed in 1967 (via the merger of the Pennsylvania and New York Central Railroads), high losses were viewed as reason to further cut service quality. Car cleaning was minimized; maintenance became irregular. In 1969, running times were lengthened to five and a half hours. The Penn Central in its annual report served notice it wanted as few passenger trains as possible. Just prior to Amtrak's takeover of the route, Penn Central offered three trains in each direction a day over the route, one without food service at all, the other two with limited snack service. On-time performance was poor. Rats were once reported in the coaches. The service offered was as poor as it could possibly be.

On May 1, 1971, Amtrak took over this corridor. And as with many routes throughout the country, its first major step was to cut the frequency of service. Thereafter, two trains a day in each direction operated between the two cities. It was, according to Amtrak, a temporary economy move to limit the deficit. Further, said Amtrak in newspaper advertising, the remaining trains would be vastly improved.

Improvement was first accomplished by running the trains (the *Wolverine* and the *Saint Clair*) with cars from the C&O Railroad. Its equipment was in far better shape than the Penn Central's, which was immediately withdrawn from service to be rebuilt. The replacement equipment was more comfortable and better maintained, but meal service was still very limited. The schedule remained five and a half hours from endpoint to endpoint. Amtrak also began an advertising program in Detroit, basically just to tell people that the trains were there (many had forgotten or didn't know rail service existed to Chicago). As with other areas of the country, Amtrak promised refurbished cars within a year. The result was a stop in the decline of ridership, and a gradual turnaround by the end of the first year of operation. Unlike the original plans, refurbished cars began to arrive piecemeal—a car here or there, mixed in with older, untouched equipment. But this nonetheless showed good intentions. Schedules were adhered to better as well, and connections at Chicago were improved. This was aided by Amtrak's consolidation of all operations to one Chicago terminal—Union Station—and the elimination of across-town transfers.

But there were many problems with the initial effort as well. Amtrak operated its trains by contractual arrangement with the railroads—in this case, Penn Central. Because of this, they had only indirect control over on-board staff, and the dispatching and running of trains. Problems en route were handled by the railroad in the old manner—which often meant not handling them at all. Amtrak couldn't instruct attendants as to the way to deal with passengers, because the attendants still worked for the railroads. Amtrak, because of the situation, could say little about service quality or uniformity.

Equipment was also maintained by the railroad. Often, after individual cars had been rebuilt (at very high cost), they fell into disrepair because of continued poor maintenance. The age of the equipment was also a problem. The average car was 20 years old. While pleasant inside and comfortable to travel in, they were too old to be completely reliable. Air-conditioning failed or heating gave out while trains were en route. Since no passenger railroad cars had been built in the United States for almost 10 years, no technology was immediately available to construct new equipment.

Stations along the route presented many problems. Without exception, they were run-down, dirty, and without modern facilities. The Detroit station, once a busy rail center, was a decaying edifice, vast and frightening. Serving only four trains a day when Amtrak first took over, it was far too large for its task. Located on the west side of Detroit, it was inconvenient for persons from the east and north suburbs to get to it. The Niles, Michigan station had no heat, and in Battle Creek the main body of the station had been closed for several years. Conditions were so bad, several of Amtrak's advisory board recommended that three of the stations be ripped down rather than trying to fix them up, and new ones be built in their place.

The Energy Crisis

In 1973, after two years of operation, refurbished equipment ran on the corridor exclusively, stations were painted at last, and on-time operation (on the same slow schedule) became a reality. Then, in the fall of that year, the energy crunch descended on the nation. Gasoline prices and air fares went up substantially, and millions of Americans were forced onto public transportation. Suddenly, Amtrak had its hands full. Trains that were never more than half full were carrying three times their normal load. Overcrowding became commonplace. On the corridor, trains were unreserved (meaning that there was no limit on the number of tickets sold per train). Trains that could comfortably seat 300 people were carrying about 600. Food would run out almost before the trains left their originating stations. Passengers, due to the crowding, sometimes stood for four or five hours, or sat on suitcases in the aisles. Personnel became rude and discourteous. Fistfights broke out on occasion between conductors and irate passengers. The refurbished equipment in many cases couldn't take the abuse and wear it received from carrying this many people. The interiors became damaged and weren't repaired. Heating and air-conditioning were as erratic as ever. Malfunctioning equipment was allowed out on the line for the first time in Amtrak history, so that more cars were available to seat more people.

Amtrak received a ghastly black eye during the energy crunch. It was not able to adequately meet the hordes of people who suddenly came back to the rails. The Detroit-Chicago corridor in particular fared dismally in terms of service, with equipment, food service, and personnel getting more complaints than almost anywhere else in the system. But in two areas, things were positive. On-time performance remained good despite the crowds (which often slowed things down elsewhere) and ridership remained high into the summer of 1974.

The Turboliners

Based on these final two factors, Amtrak made a firm commitment to upgrade service on the route. In late 1973, the corporation leased two French Turboliner trains for experimental use on the St. Louis–Chicago corridor. Since no modern passenger equipment was yet available in the United States, Amtrak went to Europe where new trains could be acquired almost immediately. The Turbos' better schedules, improved food service, and high on-time reliability resulted in greatly improved ridership to and from St. Louis. Amtrak decided to purchase these two and four more sets of Turbo equipment, and to place some of them in service between Detroit and Chicago. In April of 1975, the Detroit-Chicago corridor became all turbo. As part of the service improvement program, an additional midday train was added, bringing the number of trains on the route to six daily; that is, in each direction, a morning, noon, and evening train. The new equipment was extremely sleek and modern. Its exterior was reminiscent of the Japanese "Bullet" train, and its interiors were plush, quiet, and featured giant windows and automatic sliding glass doors between each car. Food service was provided cafeteria-style, with an area adjacent to the galley for eating and lounging, and fold-down trays available at each coach seat.

Because of the new technology that the equipment utilized, it was maintained at a special service facility in Chicago constructed specifically for this purpose. Service personnel were specially trained to work on board the new trains and thus the quality level of individual service was vastly improved. The introduction of the new service was accompanied by an innovative and clever advertising campaign on Detroit and Chicago television stations, and on local radio stations along the route. Perhaps because of the new trains themselves, or the extensive advertising, or the added service, or the coordination of the entire promotion, ridership on the corridor increased 72 percent the first month, and over 150 percent within three months. The trains ran regularly at their 300-passenger capacity. They were so successful, in fact, that a whole new set of problems arose.

Foremost among them was a problem related to their new technology. Because the equipment was foreign, it was constructed in a manner quite different from traditional American railway design. Hence, the maintenance people "out on the line" (that is, anywhere but at the service facility) didn't know how to work on the new trains. The troubleshooting manuals on board each train were no help to them either—they were in French. As a result, if air-conditioning failed on a trip, it probably remained broken until the train returned to its Chicago maintenance facility. Sometimes that meant several trips if loads were heavy, and 300 . . . , 600 . . . , 900 uncomfortable passengers. More than once public address announcements were made asking anyone who could read French to come to the cockpit and translate the manual for the English-only maintenance personnel.

The popularity of these trains led to another problem—overcrowding. Unlike conventional American equipment, cars couldn't be added or removed from the Turbos. They had a fixed number (five) and a standard carrying capacity of 300 people. They ran as unreserved trains, however, meaning that Amtrak would sell tickets to as many people as wanted to ride, and often that was over 300. On weekends, some passengers stood for five and a half hours, all the way to Detroit, or Chicago. Even when there were no technical or capacity difficulties, the sleek, new Turbos still serviced stations in Michigan that were at least 50 years old, and which for the most part hadn't been renovated. Ann Arbor was the single exception, but its refurbished station was far too small for the growing number of passengers using the facility. These difficulties marred the generally good impression the turbotrains gave in advertising, and on the many good trips they made. The public failure resulted in a somewhat negative reputation. This was by no means pervasive though, and the trains continued to do well on the route. On subsequent routes where Turbos were assigned, ridership increased as well, seemingly justifying the argument that if modern services were provided, the American public would travel by rail.

The success of this equipment also occurred, it should be pointed out, without great schedule improvement. Due to track conditions, the high-speed capabilities of the new trains could not initially be used, so it was the trains themselves, rather than their speed, that accounted for their popularity. With track improvement, it was reasoned, they would be even more attractive to intercity travelers.

Research data indicated that the average age of Detroit-Chicago train riders was 35 years old, with about 65 percent traveling on vacations, 25 percent on business, and 10 percent for other reasons.

The Decisions to Be Made

In late 1975, the management of Amtrak faced a number of decisions with respect to the Detroit-Chicago route.

1. The first decision concerned the possibility of purchasing a number of Amfleet trains for the route. These trains were being built by the Budd Company of Philadelphia for use on a number of Amtrak routes. Amfleet trains combined the modern aspects of the European Turboliners (speed, new interiors, standardized seating and food service) with the flexibility of old-style conventional equipment. On an Amfleet train, cars could be added or removed as load factors changed. Since they were American built, the difficulty of foreign technology was eliminated. In addition, Amfleet trains offered the possibility of first-class, daytime accommodations featuring reserved seats and at-seat meal service.

In order to run three trains a day in each direction, Amtrak would have to purchase four locomotives and 24 Amfleet cars. The average Amfleet train on this run was thus expected to have one locomotive and six cars. Each locomotive would cost about $540,000. The price of cars varied depending on whether the car was a coach, first-class, parlor, dinette, and so on. On average the cars would cost Amtrak $425,000 each. A car would hold up to 84 passengers, with 60 in some cars. The useful life of this equipment was expected to be 20 years.

2. The second decision related to whether or not first-class accommodations should be available on the Detroit-Chicago Amfleet trains, if these trains were purchased. This service would include reserved seating and meal service at that seat. Reserved seats were spaced two together and a seat by itself, giving three seats across the car. About 10 percent of the seating capacity of an average six-car train could be available for first-class service. The incremental cost of meals and personnel to Amtrak of each first-class seat sold was estimated to be about $5.

3. A related decision here concerned the price of a first-class ticket, if such service were made available. The price of a coach ticket was $17.50 one way. This compared to $19.50 for the five-hour bus ride, and $39 for a coach seat, and $58 for a first-class seat for the one-hour plane ride.

4. At first, the Amfleet trains would continue to take five and a half hours to travel from downtown Detroit to downtown Chicago. They were capable of traveling much faster, but track conditions would not allow this. Amtrak was considering spending $3 million on track and signal improvements in the next year. This money and a great deal more to be put up by Conrail (the regional freight railway of the northeast) could improve the tracks such that travel could be cut to under four hours within a few years. The Amtrak funded improvements were expected to have about a 10 year useful life. The management of

Amtrak was wondering whether or not they should spend this money, and aim for shorter run times.

5. There were five major stations on the Detroit-Chicago run. Amtrak was considering upgrading them. The cost to Amtrak would be $150,000 per station. The rest of the cost would be covered by the state of Michigan, and local cities. A 20-year useful life was expected on each improved station.

6. Amtrak's advertising agency was Needham, Harper, and Steers. They had developed an advertising campaign for the Amfleet trains in general, and the Detroit-Chicago corridor more specifically. They planned to use a mix of television, radio, and newspapers. The media costs to Amtrak for the Detroit-Chicago run were proposed to be $300,000 per year.

The management of Amtrak wondered what decisions should be made with respect to the Detroit-Chicago corridor.

Case 11

Videoshop— Mark-Tele, Inc.*

Cable television began to spread rapidly across the United States during the late 1970s. It was promoted to subscribers predominantly as an entertainment medium that would provide an expanded choice of high quality television programming.

Some advertising and marketing experts perceived cable television differently. They saw it as opening a revolutionary new dimension in commercial communications. In the short run, cable television would generate new advertising and direct marketing opportunities. As telecommunication technology improved in the long run, cable television could become a direct threat to conventional shopping systems. Most experts, however, forecasted that significant changes in consumer shopping patterns were at least a decade or two away. Mr. Richard Johnson disagreed. He was the managing director of Mark-Tele, Inc., one of the most innovative and aggressive cable television companies.

During the fall of 1981, Mr. Johnson began to prepare a proposal for presentation to his board of directors at their forthcoming winter meeting. The proposal would suggest that Mark-Tele develop several new television channels. These channels would be unconventional. Most cable channels involved either an entertainment, educational or public information format. The proposed new channels would involve innovative commercial formats using telecommunications technology that would allow organizations to market and sell directly to consumers in their own homes. A new marketplace would be created. Mr. Johnson named this concept, "VideoShop."

The New Venture

Several months earlier, Mr. Johnson had created a new ventures task force. The mission of this task force was to generate and study novel programming formats that could be 'developed into new cable channels in the near term, and possibly

* This case was prepared by Professor Michael P. Mokwa and Mr. Karl Gustafson, MBA 1981, of the Arizona State University as a basis for class discussion rather than to illustrate either effective or ineffective handling of a managerial situation. Copyright © 1982 by the authors.

into new networks in the long run. These new channels would be used by Mark-Tele to generate additional revenues, to increase its subscription base, and to allocate operating costs more effectively.

The current capacity of the Mark-Tele cable system was 52 different channels, but only 31 werre in use. When Mark-Tele began operations, they had only 12 channels but had grown steadily. Costs had been relatively constant regardless of the number of channels that Mark-Tele operated. Thus, Mr. Johnson perceived Mark-Tele's cost structure as highly fixed, and he foresaw the development of new channels as a means of distributing these costs. Mr. Johnson expected that new channels would draw new subscribers, that subscription rates could be raised as more channels were added, and that subscription revenue could grow faster than corresponding operating costs.

The new ventures task force was carefully selected. It included the operations and sales managers from Mark-Tele, two product development specialists from Mark-Tele's parent company, and a consultant from the communications industry. An excerpt of their report to Mr. Johnson is presented in the Appendix.

The task force recommended that Mark-Tele should develop several new cable channels using the television as the medium for shopping. Each Mark-Tele subscriber could "tune into" these shopping channels. The subscriber could control and execute an entire shopping experience in the home. Products and services could be purchased directly, or the subscriber could gather specific information about a particular product or service and competitive offerings before making an important buying decision. The task force report indicated that 11 different product or service lines appeared viable for the new shopping concept.

Mr. Johnson was thrilled with the new venture idea and the task force report. He wanted to develop and implement the concept quickly. First, he selected a distinctive name for the venture, identifying it as VideoShop. Next, he met informally with some prospective salespeople, distributors, and retailers from different product and service fields. Most of these meetings were casual lunches or dinners. Mr. Johnson sensed some strong, but very cautious interest and support from some prospective suppliers. Then, he carefully reviewed and screened the list of product and service lines that had been proposed in the task force report.

Mr. Johnson felt that each of the proposed lines was feasible, but he wanted to focus his efforts on those products and services (*a*) that appeared to be easiest and most profitable to implement in the near term and (*b*) that appeared to have the strongest interest among the prospective suppliers with whom he had met. Five lines were selected for development:

1. Catalog sales by regional and national retailers.
2. Ticket reservations for concerts, plays, and sporting events, as well as reservations at local restaurants.
3. Airline ticket reservations and vacation planning.

4. A multiple listing service for real estate companies to display homes and commercial property that were for sale in the area or possibly from areas across the country.
5. Grocery products.

Mr. Johnson expected that he could find outstanding firms from each product or service field to participate in the VideoShop venture under terms that Mark-Tele would set forth. He thought the costs to each firm would be small when compared to the benefits of newly accessible markets.

Mark-Tele's Background

Mark-Tele was founded in 1977, as a wholly owned subsidiary of Intertronics, Inc., a large corporation based in New York City. Intertronics was founded in 1973 as a joint venture among three well-respected, multinational firms. One firm was primarily in the information processing industry. Another was a publishing and broadcasting conglomerate, and the third was a high-technology producer in electronics. The mission of Intertronics was to design, develop, and implement innovative, applied telecommunications systems for domestic consumer markets. Intertronics received financial support and full technological cooperation from its parent companies, but was operated as an autonomous venture. Intertronics managed each of its subsidiaries using the same orientation.

During 1978, Mark-Tele bid to install cable television systems in several large metropolitan areas in the United States. Late that year, Mark-Tele was granted the right to install a cable television system in a large growing southwestern metropolitan area. Mark-Tele's management was excited to begin operations and to enter this particular area.

The area had more than a sufficient number of households to profitably support a cable television company according to industry standards. More important, the population was growing rapidly. National and international companies were locating headquarters or building large manufacturing facilities in the area. The growth of industry meant a tremendous increase in the number of families relocating into the area. This growth was projected to continue for at least the next 15 years, thus representing a very attractive cable market for Mark-Tele. Intertronics would use Mark-Tele's location as the test site for a new type of cable television technology. The traditional type of cable used in cable television systems was a "one-way" cable because a "signal" could be directed only from the cable television company *to* the individual households attached to the service.

Recently, Intertronics had developed a "two-way" cable that was capable of transmitting and receiving signals both from the cable television company and from individual households connected to the system. As such, a home could send signals *back* to the cable television company. Two-way cable communication processes were used in a few other areas of the country, but these cable systems required the use of a telephone line along with the one-way cable. The cost of the new two-way cable was nearly four times the cost of the one-way cable. Because Mark-Tele was a test site, they and their subscribers received the cable system at a substantially reduced cost.

To implement the two-way cable, Mark-Tele installed an interactive device to the television set of each of its subscribers. These devices facilitated communication between the Mark-Tele building and individual homes. The interactive devices resembled a small desk-top electronic calculator. These devices were expensive to install, but Intertronics absorbed most of the installation cost. The remaining cost was reflected in slightly-higher-than-average monthly subscription charges paid by subscribers. The subscription charge for basic cable services from Mark-Tele was $11 per month. The comparable rate that Mark-Tele would charge for one-way cable would be $8.50 per month.

Mark-Tele's first year of operations concluded with 5,000 subscribers and a small negative net operating profit. In the following year, Mark-Tele subscriptions increased to 38,000 generating a net profit of almost $1.4 million. In 1980, Mark-Tele continued to aggressively attract more subscribers reaching 50,000 total. Net profit increased to exceed $2 million. Financial statements for 1979 and 1980 are presented in Exhibit 1.

Research by Mark-Tele suggested that the potential number of homes for the cable network in their market area exceeded 400,000 over the next five

EXHIBIT 1

VIDEOSHOP—MARK-TELE, INC.

Income Statement Fiscal Years
Ending December 31, 1979, and 1980

	1979*	1980†
Revenues:		
Subscription revenue	$4,560,000	$6,600,000
Pay service revenue	4,104,000	5,400,000
Total revenues	8,664,000	12,000,000
Expenses:		
Operation expense (includes salaries)	3,852,000	5,248,000
Sales expense	1,913,400	2,610,300
Interest expense	136,200	136,200
Depreciation expense	74,800	74,800
Rent expense	46,000	46,000
Equipment maintenance expense	32,500	34,700
Total expenses	6,054,900	8,150,000
Gross profit	2,609,100	3,850,000
Taxes at 47%	1,226,277	1,848,000
Net profit	$1,382,823	$2,002,000

* Based upon subscriptions of 38,000 homes with a subscription rate of $10 per month per home, and average home "pay service" of $9 per month per home.
† Based upon total subscriptions of 50,000 homes with a subscription rate of $11 per month per home, and average home "pay service" of $9 per month per home.

EXHIBIT 2 1980 demographic analysis of Mark-Tele subscribers*

Family size	Percent	Age of paying subscriber	Percent
1	17.6%	18–25	22.4%
2	22.8	26–35	19.2
3	10.8	36–45	19.6
4	19.3	46–55	17.7
5	15.1	56–65	7.1
6	5.8	66–75	8.3
7 or more	8.6	76 and over	5.7

Family income	Percent	Residency	Percent
$ 8,000 or less	1.3%	Homeowners	71.6%
$ 9,000–$18,000	15.7	Renters	28.4
$19,000–$28,000	18.3		
$29,000–$35,000	17.5		
$36,000–$45,000	19.6		
$46,000–$59,000	12.7		
$60,000 or more	14.9		

Number of hours home television active per week	Percent	Number of years of education of paying subscribers	Percent
0– 7	2.5%	0– 8	1.4%
8–14	15.1	9–11	22.5
15–21	17.2	12	21.8
22–28	40.7	13–15	26.3
29–35	20.8	16 or more	28.0
36 or more	3.7		

* Based upon 50,000 subscribers.

years. In 10 years, the market potential was forecast to be nearly 750,000 homes. A demographic profile of current subscribers is presented in Exhibit 2.

Mark-Tele offered many different channel formats. These channels provided a wide variety of programming for virtually any type of viewer. Several of the channels were "pay television." For these, a household would pay an additional charge beyond the basic monthly rate. Pay television services were very successful. The revenue from pay services nearly matched basic subscription revenue for Mark-Tele in 1980. A schedule for the allocation of Mark-Tele's 52-channel capacity is presented in Exhibit 3. Both current and prospective channels are listed.

EXHIBIT 3 Channel allocation schedule

Cable channel number	Designated programming/service
1	Mark-Tele channel listing*
2	Program guide*
3	Local transit schedule*
4	Classified ads and yard sales*
5	Weather radar and time*
6	Dow Jones cable news*
7	Reserved for future use

* Active channel.

EXHIBIT 3 *(concluded)*

Cable channel number	Designated programming/service
8†	Home Box Office*
9†	Showtime*
10†	The Movie Channel*
11†	Golden Oldies channel*
12	Reserved for future use
13	Reserved for future use
14	Cable News Network*
15	Reserved for future use
16	UPI News Scan*
17	Government access*
18	Music Television*
19†	Stereo rock concert*
20	Educational access*
21	Educational access: New York University*
22	Proposed educational access
23	Proposed interactive channel for lease
24	Proposed interactive channel for lease
25	Proposed interactive channel for lease
26	VideoShop: *Retail sales channel*
27	VideoShop: *Entertainment tickets and restaurants*
28	VideoShop: *Grocery products*
29	VideoShop: Reserved
30	VideoShop: Reserved
31	USA Network*
32	WTBS, Atlanta, Channel 17*
33	WOR, New York, Channel 9*
34	K/ / /, Local ABC affiliate
35	Christian Broadcasting Network*
36	ESPN (sports) network*
37	K/ / /, local station, Channel 15*
38	K/ / /, local NBC affiliate, Channel 8*
39	K/ / /, local CBS affiliate, Channel 11*
40	Proposed channel for lease
41	Concert connection*
42	WGN, Chicago, Channel 9*
43	Public access: Cultural bulletin board*
44†	Proposed games channel
45	Public access: Library information*
46	Proposed public access
47	Public Broadcasting System
48	Reserved for future banking transactions
49	VideoShop: *Airline Tickets and Travel*
50	VideoShop: Real Estate Showcase
51	Reserved for future use
52	Reserved for future use

* Active channel.

† Optional pay service.

Cable Television Technology

Cable television became increasingly popular during the 1970s. This can be attributed largely to significant advances in computer and communications technologies, as well as regulatory and legal changes, in the telecommunications industry.

The Mark-Tele cable television system was controlled by a sophisticated configuration of minicomputers with high speed communications between each processor. Three computers, each used for a different task, insured that viewers would have access to the cable network at all times.

The main computer transmitted cable signals to each individual home using the two-way cable lines. The second computer's function was to back up the main computer in the event that a system failure might occur. The second computer would be a vital element of the VideoShop system because it could be used as an update system for suppliers to amend information regarding their products or services. This computer also could be used to transmit the orders or reservations placed by "shopping" subscribers directly to prospective suppliers. The third computer functioned as another backup, if system failures would occur simultaneously to the main computers. A very sophisticated software application integrating the communication network and operating system had been developed to assure 99 percent uptime for the cable system. A diagram sketching the Mark-Tele cable system is presented in Exhibit 4.

The cable system incorporated two different types of storage devices. The first type of storage disk (a magnetic disk) was used to store data, such as billing information about a particular subscriber. The second type of disk involved an innovative technology that could be used extensively by the VideoShop system. The disk, called a *videodisc unit,* was capable of storing images or pictures like a movie camera. VideoShop suppliers could store images of their products and services on these disks so that subscribers to the cable system could access the images at any time. Only through the use of the new two-way cable developed by Intertronics would it be possible to incorporate the videodisc units (VDU) into a cable network. The two-way cable allowed signals to travel from the main computer to an individual television, and from the television back to the main computer.

Two-way communication was possible through the use of the interactive indexing device attached to each subscriber's television. This indexing device was a small box, about the size of a cigar box. It contained special electronics allowing the device to transmit data back to the main computer. On top of the indexing device, there were 12 keys simply called the keypad. An individual subscriber would use the keypad to call up "menus," sort through a menu, and send data back to the main computer. A *menu* is a computer term used to describe listings of general categories from which additional information can be drawn.

Using a prospective VideoShop example, a menu for a channel containing airline information could first indicate to a viewer the different airlines from

EXHIBIT 4 Mark-Tele two-way cable system

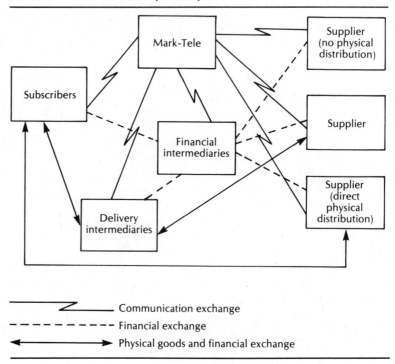

—————————⚡—————— Communication exchange

– – – – – – – – – – Financial exchange

◄—————————► Physical goods and financial exchange

which to choose. The viewer could then push the key on the keypad that corresponds to the airline that he or she was interested in using. The next menu could show all the different cities to which the chosen airline flies. The viewer then could push the key on the keypad that corresponds to the city to which he or she wishes to travel. The following screen could provide the flight numbers and times during which flights are available. From the information on that screen, the user could make a reservation which would be transmitted to the airline's computer through the Mark-Tele computer. Finally, the reservation would be logged, confirmed, and ticket(s) mailed to the viewer. The entire transaction would take only a few minutes to execute. The shopper would control the entire experience in the home environment. It would be simple and efficient.

VideoShop Channels

Mr. Johnson believed that the most significant factors that would affect the successful acceptance of VideoShop by consumers were: (1) the quality of the picture viewed by the subscribers; (2) the accuracy of the information provided by suppliers to shoppers; (3) the convenience and ease of using the system to shop: (4) the technical reliability of the system; and (5) the delivery, billing, and return policies of suppliers. Mr. Johnson felt strongly that control over suppliers would be vital to assure the success of VideoShop. He thought that Mark-Tele should form a small consumer satisfaction department to conduct VideoShop consumer studies, to review the VideoShop policies and operations of all involved suppliers, and to resolve all consumer problems and complaints.

Mr. Johnson felt that the five shopping channels that he had selected from the list generated by the task force would work well given the nature of the success factors that he perceived to be important. He prepared a brief description for each of the prospective shopping channels and a pro forma income statement. He would use these to build his presentation for the forthcoming board meeting and to develop a prospectus to sell the VideoShop concept to suppliers. The pro forma statement is presented in Exhibit 5.

EXHIBIT 5

VIDEOSHOP—MARK-TELE, INC.

Pro Forma Income Statement
VideoShop Operation*

Revenue:
Catalog purchase channel	$300,000
Airline reservation channel	400,000
Ticket sales and restaurant channel	150,000
Multiple listing service channel	36,000
Total revenues	886,000

Expenses:
Salaries	240,000
Administrative expense	52,000
Communication expense (telephone lines)	19,200
Depreciation expense	15,700
Interest expense	13,820
Equipment maintenance	4,200
Total expenses	344,920
Contribution	$541,080

* Based upon 50,000 subscription base and task force projections.

The Catalog Sales Channel(s)

National and regional retailers could use the VideoShop system to sell and promote their entire merchandise lines including their most current items and prices. Shoppers would have the opportunity to view merchandise on the television screen in their own home, avoiding the inconvenience of a shopping trip or the boredom of thumbing through a catalog book. Information about products and prices could be presented in a format similar to catalog books, or innovative action formats could be developed to simulate a store environment or create some novel context.

Retailers would be responsible for developing appropriate videodisc units and keeping information current. Mark-Tele could provide a consulting service to help suppliers produce effective videodiscs. Mark-Tele could also reserve the right to reject any material that was felt to be inappropriate. However, Mark-Tele would attempt to be open-minded. For example, products that consumers find embarrassing to purchase at a store could be considered a prime prospect for VideoShop, if presentations were tasteful.

A shopper could use the interactive indexing device to direct and control an entire shopping experience. This could involve viewing information about product features and prices from one retailer, and then quickly switching to another retailer's presentation for comparative information. In addition, a shopper desiring more extensive information could access a brief demonstration or informative advertisement about a product. After selecting a product, the interactive device could transmit the order through Mark-Tele's computing system directly to the retailer's processing system. The retailer could present alternative payment programs and specific delivery schedules or instructions. The shopper could charge purchases using national or store credit cards, and could pick-up the merchandise directly (but conveniently) or could have it delivered.

Mark-Tele could charge each retailer a service fee based upon a fixed percentage of shoppers' invoice values (before taxes). Individual retailers could be billed monthly and various payment programs could be formulated. The new ventures task force estimated that an average home would purchase a minimum of $300 worth of retail merchandise annually through VideoShop. They proposed a service charge rate of 2 percent. Mark-Tele could also generate revenue by selling video consulting services to the suppliers.

This shopping and marketing scenario could be the prototype for all the VideoShop channels. Adaptations for different product or service lines and shopping patterns would be relatively easy to implement.

Ticket Sales and Restaurant Reservation Channel

VideoShop could provide detailed information concerning local entertainment alternatives to subscribers. Entertainment organizations could present exciting promotional spots using the videodisc technology and sell tickets directly to VideoShop subscribers.

Entertainment shoppers could use video menus to select a particular entertainment form such as movies, theater, or sporting events. On another menu, they could view all the relevant alternative events, and then access specific promotional spots about events which interested them. These spots could blend information about performance schedules and locations with features about, or highlights of, the event. The shopper could select an event and a specific performance, then purchase tickets. Tickets could be sold using conventional diagrams of seating arrangements, innovative graphic formats, or the shopper could actually be presented with the view from a specific seat or area of seating using the videodisc technology. When tickets were purchased, these could be paid for using credit cards at the time of purchase, or payment could be mailed or made at the time of the event. Likewise, tickets could be mailed or picked up.

Another dimension of this channel could be a restaurant promotion and reservation feature. Restaurant menus and promotional spots could be made accessible for diners. Once diners have chosen a particular restaurant using the menu and spots, they could make a reservation and even select a specific table (if the restaurant developed, as part of its VideoShop system, a seating arrangement routine similar to that of the entertainment organizations).

All VideoShop ticket purchases and reservations could be transmitted directly from the shopper's home through Mark-Tele computers to the restaurant or ticket outlet. Most restaurants and small entertainment organizations would have to purchase or lease a small *intelligence* computing terminal to receive reservations or ticket orders and to keep information updated. Intertronics could supply these.

The task force felt that this channel could generate at least $150,000 revenue per year given the current subscriber base. They recommended a $25 per month minimum charge to restaurants and a 50 cent service fee per ticket reservation. They were unsure of a fee schedule for entertainment organizations that would only promote events and would not be selling tickets directly through VideoShop. However, they thought that rates similar to commercial advertising rates would be appropriate.

Airline Ticket Sales and Travel Accommodations Channel

Discussions with the task force concluded that an airline ticket sales channel could be the easiest for Mark-Tele to implement and operate in the short run, and also could be most lucrative financially. Projected revenue for the first years of operating this channel was $400,000 based upon a very conservative usage rate and an extremely competitive pricing policy.

This channel could allow subscribers to make airline reservations, purchase their tickets, and select travel accommodations using the same fundamental interactive shopping procedures as other VideoShop channels. Shoppers could avoid the aggravating inconveniences of current airline reservation systems, and could quickly do comparative shopping which current systems have inhibited. Research has shown that comparative shopping for airline fares often can save hundreds of dollars. Once a flight has been selected, the subscriber also could make hotel or motel reservations. VideoShop could allow hotels and motels to visually present rooms and surroundings and to promote themselves to *all* travelers.

Perhaps the most important characteristic of this channel could be the potential ease of implementation, once cooperation was secured from the airlines. The format and basic system used within the airlines industry to transmit, display and process schedules, fares, and ticket information appeared to be compatible with the Mark-Tele system. Mark-Tele computers and cable lines could be used to link shoppers directly with airline ticket reservation systems bypassing reservationists and travel agents. Subscribers could select itineraries, then secure reservations and pay using major credit cards. Tickets could be mailed or picked up at airport ticket counters or other service locations.

Mark-Tele could record each ticket purchase and charge the appropriate airline a fixed fee of $4 per ticket. This rate was half of the $8 rate charged by most travel agents. The task force believed that a minimum average of two tickets would be purchased by each subscribing household per year. Revenue estimates were not made for the travel accommodations feature of this channel.

Multiple Listing Service Channel

A few large local REALTORS®[1] expressed strong interest in the VideoShop concept. Traditional promotional tools used to stimulate buyers' interest and help them make decisions about what properties to see in person included classified newspaper ads, newspaper supplements, brochures, ''for sale'' signs, the multiple listing catalog, and photographs of properties posted on an agency's wall. Most REALTORS and buyers found these boring. More important, they simply did not present most properties effectively. A frequent complaint among Realtors and buyers was the high cost in time and dollars wasted traveling to, and viewing personally, properties that were not represented well in a promotion or informational item. VideoShop could provide an exciting and effective method for presenting real estate.

While this VideoShop channel could be accessed by any subscriber, the channel would open a new commercial consumer market for Mark-Tele cable subscriptions—the realty agencies. Many agencies had a television on the premises to entertain clients and their children or to provide a means ''to catch the news'' when business was slow. Some agencies already had purchased cable service from Mark-Tele.

A general issue was raised by the task force whether to charge a commercial subscriber different fees than a residential subscriber. A more specific issue regarding this channel was whether to limit access to realty agencies and others willing to pay an additional fee for it, or to open it for public access. The task force recommended open access and suggested that a minimum of 30 realty agencies would need to participate. Each could be charged a monthly fee of $100 or an annual fee of $1,000. The REALTOR would be responsible for producing and maintaining high quality videodiscs with accurate and updated information. Mark-Tele could provide technical assistance and would monitor this channel carefully.

---

[1] REALTOR® refers to a member of the National Association of REALTORS® who subscribes to its Code of Ethics.

Grocery Products Channel

One of the most exciting prospects for VideoShop could be a grocery products channel. It was the most interesting but difficult channel for which to design a format.

Grocery products are purchased very frequently, and everyone must buy. Consumers have tended to develop relatively consistent grocery shopping patterns. Expenditures on grocery items have been swelling. Many consumers find going shopping to be tedious, laborious, and inconvenient. Others, such as people with handicaps or shut-in, simply cannot get to stores or cannot shop freely and comfortably in modern superstores. Likewise, groceries producers, wholesalers and retailers have been threatened by escalating cost structures that reduce their margins substantially.

A VideoShop grocery channel, thus, could provide consumers with convenience, comfort, low shopping risks, and potential savings. For suppliers, it could generate increased control over operations and costs and higher profits. However, this VideoShop channel would directly attack an expensive, firmly established distribution network and basic, traditional patterns of shopping. Strong resistance from many consumers could be anticipated, and suppliers not involved in the venture could be expected to retaliate competitively. Also, there could be critical barriers to providing shoppers a total assortment of grocery products including frozen and "fresh" items and to implementing a cost-effective delivery service or pickup procedure. Undoubtedly, these "bugs" could be worked out. The recommendation for this channel was to maintain its high priority as a channel to develop in the near term, but initially and quickly to invest funds in more design and research before contacting any specific prospective suppliers.

Conclusion—A Time for Reflection and/or Action

One more time, Mr. Johnson critically reviewed the task force report and his brief descriptions of prospective VideoShop channels. He felt simultaneously excitement, enthusiasm and some frustration. He and the task force had worked hard and creatively to formulate the idea of VideoShop. They thought that most technological barriers could be overcome, and they projected a very favorable cost structure. Definitely, VideoShop was a concept whose time had arrived! Mark-Tele's board, composed largely of Intertronics personnel, would have to be convinced.

Mark-Tele was a small company with only a few people and tight resources. It already was a high investment and high risk experimental venture receiving considerable financial support and subsidy from Intertronics. Would Intertronics feel that VideoShop was an extension of the Mark-Tele experiment or a contamination of it? Could the board be convinced to provide more resources and assistance, and what would they expect in return?

If VideoShop received approval and support from the board, Mr. Johnson was not exactly sure in which direction to proceed. While he had identified the primary prospective channels, which specific channel or channels should be developed first? What would be the operational design for a channel, and what type of marketing program would be needed to maximize market awareness and shopper adoption?

Mr. Johnson was also concerned that some of his assumptions and some of those of the task force might be too optimistic, particularly those concerning the costs to suppliers. The task force had recommended that prospective suppliers should incur most of the start-up and maintenance expenses, and the risks. Yet, it appeared that Mark-Tele would skim the VideoShop revenues without much direct cost or risk. Would suppliers accept Mark-Tele's conditions for operations? The entire supply issue would require significant attention. Which specific suppliers would contribute most to VideoShop? Which suppliers would work best with Mark-Tele, and what type of relationships would evolve? How would a marketing program be formulated to reach prospective suppliers?

Suddenly, Mr. Johnson realized that he was vacillating. If Mark-Tele didn't implement VideoShop soon, someone would. VideoShop was a great idea. Mr. Johnson simply lacked the strategic plan that he could use to convince the board and to market VideoShop to suppliers and shoppers.

Appendix

New Venture Task Force Report Proposing a Telecommunications Shopping System*

We recommend that Mark-Tele design and implement a telecommunication shopping (TCS) system immediately. This proposed new venture appears to be a natural extension of Mark-Tele's experimental mission and an excellent application of Mark-Tele's distinctive technological capabilities in the telecommunications field.

A TCS system would allow a Mark-Tele subscriber to become an active shopper and buyer in the privacy of the home using only the television. Facilitated by Mark-Tele's sophisticated communications and computing technologies, a TCS system subscriber would be able to view and buy a large variety of products and services that conventionally would have required the shopper to leave the home and travel to view and purchase. A TCS system would also serve the suppliers of many different products and services with an opportunity to break away from costly traditional market channels and to inexpensively expand their market coverage and increase sales substantially.

For Mark-Tele, a TCS system would increase revenues, diversify its revenue base, and distribute its high fixed costs efficiently. A TCS system could be used as a promotional tool to build and maintain Mark-Tele's local subscrip-

---

* This is an abridged version of the committee's report. The authors thank Ms. Sherri Katz for her contribution to this report.

tion base. Current subscription rates could be raised with the addition of the TCS system, or an additional fee could be charged to subscribers who desire to participate in the TCS system. Suppliers and shopping subscribers would also be charged for services that Mark-Tele would provide in the development and operation of the TCS system. In the longer run, Mark-Tele could potentially develop TCS networks that could be sold to other cable systems. Clearly, early entry into the TCS field would be lucrative financially for Mark-Tele.

In the remainder of this report, we will discuss: (1) significant environmental factors that influence the TCS market; (2) a general strategy for targeting the TCS system; (3) prospective product and service offerings; and (4) developmental issues for promoting the TCS system.

The Environment of TCS

Economic, technological, legal and regulatory, and social trends are emerging in support of a TCS system.

Increased consumer spending is predicted to continue, but gains for retailers will be restricted by inflationary pressures. There will be a slower pace of store expansion during the 1980s. Many of the major metropolitan areas are overbuilt with retail space, and developers often are experiencing difficulty obtaining sites and financing. Retailers similarly are experiencing rising rents. Sales growth at many shopping centers has fallen due to slow growth of suburban communities and shrinking distances that consumers are willing to travel to shop as gasoline prices continue to advance.

Retailers are attempting to boost productivity, consolidate store space, and cut costs to improve returns. Inflation has increased operating costs more rapidly than sales during the last 10 years. Many retailers have been attracted to discount pricing policies. The catalog showroom has become one of the fastest-growing segments of discount merchandising featuring national-brand products at discount prices while operating on lower overhead than department stores.

Considering sociocultural trends, women are continuing to enter the work force, thus having less time to engage in shopping for staples, as well as for discretionary purchases. Greater emphasis on recreational activities continues, and individuals are reluctant to sacrifice leisure time to shop in stores. Convenience is emerging as a high priority.

Consumers are emphasizing their self-identity. As such, consumers are demanding more individuality in goods and services, often desiring distinctive products that individual stores may not be able to afford to inventory and display. Definitely, there has been more intense consumer preference for specialty items and services difficult to find in the Mark-Tele market area.

An increase in the number of single-parent and single-person households has led to increased in-home shopping. Nonstore innovations such as pay-by-phone, specialty mail-order catalogs, and toll-free phone ordering have become increasingly popular. Catalog shopping currently offers a full line of merchandise together with prices and features that permit a consumer to comparison shop at home without having to spend time inefficiently searching for products in crowded stores, waiting for sales help, or at times being annoyed by overzealous clerks.

In addition, the increasing age of the population, proliferation of retirement communities, and declining mobility of individuals in their later years make catalog shopping very attractive.

There are significant technological advances that will influence the TCS system. In the past, alphanumerics and graphics, but not still or moving "pictures," could be retrieved from a data bank and displayed on a television screen; however, Intertronics' innovative technologies have advanced moving picture capabilities. This new technology has permitted the consumer to control the timing, sequence, and content of information through the use of the keypad. As such, the convenience of purchasing on impulse without need for either a telephone or advance credit arrangements is viable. Purchases can be charged automatically to a bank or credit card account.

Development of videodiscs and video cassettes, which to date have been used by viewers to record television programs, has significant promise for advertising and catalog media. Potential exists for suppliers to mail lower-cost video catalogs on a complimentary basis or in lieu of printed direct-mail offerings.

Consumers are being exposed to, and are accepting, complex, technical items such as videotape recorders, home computers, and debit cards for use with automatic teller machines. Home computers and the development of *videotex,* the generic term for home information-retrieval systems, will provide functions compatible with those of the TCS system. Many consumers will easily develop the technical skills and sophistication needed to actively participate in the TCS system.

The political-legal context is confusing. The Federal Communications Commission has decided that cable franchising is mainly the province of local jurisdictions. All cable companies must interact with local governments to obtain and maintain authority to operate. While Mark-Tele has secured exclusive rights in their metropolitan area, changes in federal and local policy must be monitored, and good rapport with local leaders should be cultivated continuously.

The TCS venture raises questions concerning supplier and financial contractual arrangements. The antitrust implications of arrangements with some large institutions should be studied in more detail on a case-by-case basis. Moreover, movement into the retail sector by Mark-Tele through the TCS system will mean closer scrutiny by federal and local consumer protection agencies such as the Federal Trade Commission and Consumer Product Safety Commission. Finally, Mark-Tele will need to carefully consider protection of the privacy of personal, financial, and transactional data about subscribers to the TCS system. Controls must be established to prevent unauthorized access to information in the system data banks and to guard against unauthorized purchasing.

The General Competitive Context

Industry observers clearly are divided when projecting the evolution of electronic shopping and its acceptance by both consumers and the industry. Consumers appear interested in the potential convenience, extended selections, fuel economies, discount prices and time savings offered by the concept of shopping at home. Furthermore, at least 10,000 firms have expressed interest in the concept of electronic shopping. Currently, all forms of nonstore retailing are growing rapidly, and continued growth is forecast. Major developments in nonstore retailing will be reviewed.

Mail-Order Catalogs

General department store merchandisers, catalog showrooms and specialty houses periodically mail catalogs to targeted groups of consumers. An average mail-order house distributes from 6 to 20 catalog issues yearly at a cost often approaching two dollars each. Circulations range from about 100,000 to over a million for each mailing. The results have been outstanding. Over $26 billion was spent by consumers on mail-order items in 1978—an increase of $12 billion in three years. By comparison, in-store retailing sales grew at a rate less than half of the mail-order rate. Mail-order firms' aftertax profits averaged 7 percent during this period.

Specialty firms such as L. L. Bean, Dallas's Horchow Collection, Talbot's of Massachusetts, and Hammacher-Schlemmer of New York have become more prominent in the field. Specialty-oriented catalogs are accounting for 75 percent of total mail-order sales, and mail-order catalogs currently contribute 15 percent of the total volume of Christmas season sales.

Telephone and mail-generated orders received by traditional store retailers such as Bloomingdales, Penneys, and Sears are increasing three to five times faster than in-store sales. Sears found that 9.1 percent of its sales came from outside catalogs in 1977 and an additional 11.4 percent from catalog counters in the stores. Montgomery Ward derived 13 percent of its sales from catalogs.

In-flight shopping catalogs used by major airlines are additional evidence of the increasing popularity of nonstore shopping. MasterCard, American Express, and Visa have increased their direct mail offerings to their credit card holders and are expanding their assortment of merchandise.

The Catalog Showrooms

The catalog showroom is one of the fastest growing fields of retailing. Catalogs are used to promote and feature jewelry, housewares, appliances, sporting goods, and toys at discount prices. Customers visit the showroom to inspect merchandise and to make purchases. Analysts suggest that 85 percent of sales are generated by the catalogs and the remainder by test selling products promoted on the showroom floor. Sales for 1980 are estimated to be $7.8 billion, an increase of 11 percent from 1979. Forecasts for 1981 suggest a 20 percent gain in sales revenue. The number of showrooms across the country is nearly 2,000.

Noninteractive Shopping Using the Cable

Comp-U-Card of Stamford, Connecticut is a seven-year-old telephone merchandising firm. For an annual fee of $18, it offers members a discount on a broad line of durable goods. Members shop around familiarizing themselves with products and prices. Then, they call Comp-U-Card toll-free for specific information about an item's availability and price. If a purchase decision is made, the consumer provides membership and credit card numbers to an operator, and the merchandise is prepared for delivery. An experimental project has been proposed in which Comp-U-Card would use cable systems and satellite transmission to present product and price information to its subscribers. A transmitted schedule would alert subscribers to the time when particular product information would be presented. Subscribers would continue to use the telephone when ordering. In October 1980, Federated Department Stores acquired a substantial interest in Comp-U-Card.

Telephone purchasing systems using cable presentations are currently operating in Europe. In March 1979, the British Post Office, which runs Britain's telephone system, opened a ''viewdata'' service called ''Prestel.'' Viewers are presented listings of games, restaurants, and consumer product evaluations. Products and services can be purchased on credit by phone. France launched a similar service called ''Antiope'' in 1979.

A few U.S. companies are testing similar systems. Viewdata Corp., a subsidiary of the Knight-Ridder newspaper chain, proposed to install a permanent system in southern Florida by 1983. First Bank System of Minneapolis will be testing a videotex system in North Dakota similar to the Antiope system of France.

Interactive Cable Systems and Videotex

Since December 1977, Warner Communications and American Express have been involved with a $70 million joint venture testing the QUBE two-way system of Warner Amex Cable in Columbus, Ohio. Currently, the system serves 30,000 of the 105,000 homes in its service area. American Express and Warner Communications propose to build other QUBE systems in such metropolitan areas as Houston, Pittsburgh, and Cincinnati. Both Sears and Penneys currently are testing the QUBE system.

In May 1981, American Telephone & Telegraph (AT&T) endorsed a videotex concept in which a home computer terminal must be purchased. AT&T has set out to develop its own system. AT&T would be a formidable opponent to anyone in the market, considering the firm's capabilities and financial strength. Thus, there are a number of legal actions being undertaken to prevent AT&T's direct entry into the videotex market, for fear it could become a monopoly power. However, strong deregulation sentiments may overcome the opposition and facilitate AT&T's entry into the market.

In summary, the TCS market is embryonic. Growth in nonstore retailing is providing a solid foundation upon which TCS systems can build. Over $100 million already has been invested by U.S. firms to design and test various TCS systems, and at least 83 experimental projects are being conducted around the world. As a result, Mark-Tele must be prepared to match formidable competition, and we feel confident that Mark-Tele can.

Target Market Considerations

The TCS system must be carefully tailored and targeted to meet market demands and expectations. There are two different markets that must be considered when developing this venture: (1) the suppliers and (2) the shoppers.

We propose that the TCS system be targeted to the ultimate *user*—the subscribing shopper. A TCS system that is designed well will sell itself to suppliers. Suppliers, therefore, should be considered as a dimension of the "total product" that will be offered to target shoppers. This approach will allow Mark-Tele to retain maximum control and autonomy in the design and implementation of this venture.

The Target Market—Shoppers

A careful review of the size and characteristics of the current and potential Mark-Tele subscription base indicates substantial market potential and buying power. However, critical analysis of shopping and buying behavior is necessary to isolate the most lucrative prospective customer segments and to understand their prospective TCS behavior. Three buying factors appear to be very important: (1) risk perceptions, (2) convenience orientations, and (3) buyer satisfaction.

Risk. Buying is a complex experience filled with uncertainty and related risks of unfavorable consequences. Fundamentally, consumers confront the uncertainty of achieving their buying goals and risks such as embarrassment or wasting time, money, or effort in a disappointing buying or shopping experience. Consumers usually are not highly conscious of these until they face new, different, or very important buying decisions or situations. In general, shopping is used to reduce uncertainty, risk, and potential disappointment. More specifically, consumers shop to help refine their buying goals, to search for and evaluate specific products and items, to execute transactions, and to favorably reinforce past purchase behaviors.

When consumers consider TCS experiences, they must feel comfortable and in control. All shopping and buying uncertainties, risks, and potenial negative consequences must be minimized throughout the total TCS experience. Initially, the consumer must learn how to operate/interface with the TCS system. One positive experience should build into others.

During the TCS experience, some traditional risk-reduction tactics such as personal inspection of merchandise or interaction with salespeople will not be available to the shopper. However, there are significant risk-reduction tactics that will be accessible. These include:

> Visual and audio comparison of a wide assortment and range of products and services.
>
> Information access and collection controlled by the shopper.
>
> Information availability regarding many product features and all terms of sale and delivery.
>
> Promotional messages that present products and services in attractive, exciting, and believable formats.
>
> Past experiences with the product, service, brand, or supplier.
>
> Personal experiences shared by significant friends, relatives, or peers.
>
> Testimonials from respected celebrities, peers, or experts.
>
> Continuous building of positive shopping experiences with the TCS system.

These risk-reduction tactics should be incorporated into the TCS system design and promoted during operations.

In short, we suggest (*a*) that uncertainty and risk can be significantly reduced by presenting TCS and its products and services as personal and uncomplicated and (*b*) that shopping confidence can be built by involving shoppers in positive TCS experiences. For example, some exploratory studies have indicated that shoppers feel confident ordering merchandise by television when: (1) the product or service is easily recognizable and clearly identified by brand, retail, size, color, and/or other relevant properties; (2) consumers could access the information when they felt ready to actually make the purchase; and (3) consumers had purchased the product or service previously.

Convenience. Shopping is a problem-solving activity. The TCS system offers solutions to many nagging problems encountered when shopping conventionally. Consider the following common aggravations: having to carry merchandise; adapting to limited store hours; poor and confusing displays of merchandise; difficulty finding desired items; dealing directly with salespeople; spending time and money traveling to the store; crowds of shoppers; and the boredom and fatigue of going from department to department and store to store. These are some of the inconveniences of conventional shopping systems that TCS can overcome.

A strong need or orientation for convenience is an appropriate base for identifying and understanding the primary target market for the TCS system. The following customer characteristics should be used to identify target market boundaries and to isolate specific segments within the primary target market. In the future, these could be cross-tabulated with other demographic, behavioral, and media characteristics to further refine target segment definitions and to tailor market programs.

Primary target customers for the TCS system are those Mark-Tele subscribers:

With greater than average need or desire for convenience.

With restricted mobility because children are at home.

With appropriate buying power and media (credit cards).

Who compile shopping lists regularly.

Who are frequent catalog shoppers.

Who rely extensively on newspaper, magazine, or television advertising.

Who are loyal to specific brands or suppliers.

Who do not like to travel or find it very difficult to travel.

Who do not like to deal with crowds.

Who are handicapped physically.

Who are actively engaged in time-consuming leisure activities.

Who are senior citizens.

Satisfaction. A consumer must have a satisfying experience each time that the TCS system is used. Otherwise, it is very likely that the consumer will not use TCS again and may discuss the bad experience with other shoppers and discourage their future use of the system. Thus, Mark-Tele must maintain tight control over suppliers. A consumer satisfaction department should be formed within Mark-Tele. This group should monitor all TCS activities, conduct market research, investigate all consumer complaints, and make certain that all consumers are fully informed and satisfied with TCS.

Supplier Market Implications

After selecting general product and service categories and designing a general format for each TCS channel, Mark-Tele should direct attention to the supplier market. At that time, Mark-Tele should evaluate prospective suppliers regarding the relevance of their product or service assortment, their delivery and financial capabilities, the quality of their promotional strategies, and their desire to enter into this unconventional market. We feel that Mark-Tele's technical competence and captive subscription base will provide substantial leverage in all negotiations with suppliers. The actual marketing effort should involve personal selling programs custom designed for each prospective target supplier.

Prospective Products and Services

Preliminary research on TCS systems has uncovered a number of product and service lines that are appropriate for our target market and appear to be financially and technically feasible. As this innovative approach to shopping evolves and consumer acceptance and involvement grow, many other products and services could be incorporated. However, the most feasible products and services currently are:

1. Standard catalog items.
2. Staple grocery items.
3. Gifts and specialty items.
4. Appliances and home entertainment equipment.
5. Toys, electronic games and equipment, basic sporting goods.
6. Banking and financial services.
7. Classified ads.
8. Multiple listing service of local properties.
9. Ticket, restaurant, and accommodations reservations.
10. Educational classes.
11. Automobiles.

We cannot stress too strongly that TCS will involve a high degree of risk perceived by consumers. This must be reduced by offering products and services with which consumers are familiar and comfortable and that involve a minimum number of simple shopping decisions for consumers.

The consumer must *learn* to use the TCS system. Mark-Tele must guide this learning experience and make sure that consumers have consistent, positive shopping experiences that become reinforcing. The following services/features should be incorporated into the TCS system to reduce shopping risks and facilitate consumer satisfaction:

Easy-to-use indexing devices.

Top quality visual and audio representation.

Professional promotions.

Up-to-date information on specials.

Competitive pricing policies and convenient payment methods.

TCS availability 24 hours per day, seven days per week.

Maintenance service availability 24 hours per day, seven days per week.

Accurate order-taking and order-filling.

Prompt delivery or pickup services.

Quick and equitable handling and resolution of customer complaints.

Exceptional reliability.

Eventually, the TCS product and service assortment could be broadened and channel features changed. However, the products and service lines outlined in this report appear to involve minimal consumer risks, high potential for competitive advantage and target consumer satisfaction, and substantial returns for Mark-Tele.

The Competitive Advantage and TCS Promotion

A competitive advantage over conventional suppliers can be achieved by Mark-Tele if the TCS system is designed to serve the needs and expectations of the identified target market by actively considering their prepurchase deliberations, by guiding their purchase activities, and by reinforcing their postpurchase satisfaction. This must be complemented with accurate and reliable order processing and with prompt, efficient logistical support. Above all, Mark-Tele must communicate and promote its distinctive capabilities. We believe that the following distinctive features of the TCS system should be emphasized:

1. The extensive variety and depth of product and service assortments.
2. The vast amount of relevant information that is easily accessible and allows consumers to make better choices.
3. The excitement, involvement, convenience, and satisfaction of shopping in the privacy of one's home using space-age technology and the simplicity of the television.
4. The insignificant, negligible, and indirect costs to consumers particularly when compared to the opportunities and benefits.

We feel that the best medium for promotion of the TCS system will be the television itself. Promotional information should be presented on all television channels other than pay channels. The TCS system initially should be portrayed as a new, exciting service available to all Mark-Tele subscribers. After this campaign, the theme should be changed to focus on *how* the TCS system works *for* and *with* the subscriber/consumer. A final campaign should be developed to reinforce and to encourage extended usage of the TCS system.

Enclosures and brochures in billing statements should be used extensively in support of the television campaigns to alert subscribers to the availability of the TCS system, to detail operational dimensions, and to discuss changes and additions to the system before these occur. Demonstration projects probably can be executed using the television rather than personal contact.

Mailing, print media, and personal selling appear to be appropriate means for reaching prospective subscribers as the cable system expands, as well as a means to retrack and increase penetration of cable services in areas in which these already are available. However, the TCS system should be promoted as only one dimension of the total Mark-Tele cable package to prospective subscribers.

Finally, ''word of mouth'' will be a vital factor underlying acceptance and use of TCS. Active stimulation and encouragement of this free, highly effective form of promotion should be implemented and maintained using both creative advertising strategies and other promotional tactics such as special cable rates to subscribers who get friends or relatives to sign up and use the system.

Conclusion

The recommendation of our committee is that Mark-Tele design and implement the proposed new venture concept—a telecommunication shopping system. We have identified the target customer and viable products and services to satisfy their needs and Mark-Tele's objectives. Development of the supplier market and control over suppliers also has been discussed.

Overall, the distinct advantages of the TCS concept would include: (1) the wide variety of products and services that would be available to consumers; (2) the unique and novel process of shopping; (3) the ease, convenience, and privacy of shopping and buying; and (4) the special buying incentives such as comparative sales prices and controlled access to extensive amounts of information regarding products and services.

We recommend immediate action on this proposal to ensure and enact a competitive advantage in this revolutionary marketplace.

Case 12

The Gillette Company*

In July 1978, Mike Edwards, brand manager for TRAC II®,[1] is beginning to prepare his marketing plans for the following year. In preparing for the marketing plan approval process, he has to wrestle with some major funding questions. The most recent sales figures show that TRAC II has continued to maintain its share of the blade and razor market. This has occurred even though the Safety Razor Division (SRD) has introduced a new product to its line, Atra. The company believes that Atra will be the shaving system of the future and, therefore, is devoting increasing amounts of marketing support to this brand. Atra was launched in 1977 with a $7 million advertising campaign and over 50 million $2 rebate coupons. In less than a year, the brand achieved a 7 percent share of the blade market and about one third of the dollar-razor market. Thus, the company will be spending heavily on Atra, possibly at the expense of TRAC II, still the number one shaving system in America.

Edwards is faced with a difficult situation, for he believes that TRAC II still can make substantial profits for the division if the company continues to support it. In preparing for 1979, the division is faced with two major issues:

1. What are TRAC II's and Atra's future potentials?
2. Most important, can SRD afford to heavily support two brands? Even if they can, is it sound marketing policy to do so?

Company Background

The Gillette Company was founded in 1903 by King C. Gillette, a 40-year-old inventor, utopian writer, and bottle-cap salesman in Boston, Massachusetts. Since marketing its first safety razor and blades, the Gillette Company, the parent of the Safety Razor Division, has been the leader in the shaving industry.

---

* This case was written by Charles M. Kummel under the direction of Professor Jay E. Klompmaker of the University of North Carolina. Copyright © 1982 by Jay E. Klompmaker, reproduced by permission.
[1] TRAC II® is a registered trademark of The Gillette Company.

The Gillette safety razor was the first system to provide a disposable blade that could be replaced at low cost and that provided a good inexpensive shave. The early ads focused on a shave-yourself theme: "If the time, money, energy, and brainpower which are wasted (shaving) in the barbershops of America were applied in direct effort, the Panama Canal could be dug in four hours."

The Pre-World War Years

With the benefit of a 17-year patent, Gillette was in a very advantageous position. However, it was not until the First World War that the safety razor began to gain wide consumer acceptance. One day in 1917 King Gillette came into the office with a visionary idea: to present a Gillette razor to every soldier, sailor, and marine. Other executives modified this idea so that the government would do the presenting. In this way, millions just entering the shaving age would give the nation the self-shaving habit. In World War I, the government bought 4,180,000 Gillette razors as well as smaller quantities of competitive models.

Daily Shaving Development

Although World War I gave impetus to self-shaving, World War II popularized frequent shaving—12 million American servicemen shaved daily. This produced two results: (1) Gillette was able to gain consumer acceptance of personal shaving and (2) the company was able to develop an important market to build for the future.

Postwar Years

After 1948, the company began to diversify through the acquisition of three companies which gave Gillette entry into new markets. In 1948, the acquisition of the Toni Company extended the company into the women's grooming aid market. Paper Mate, a leading maker of writing instruments, was bought in 1954, and the Sterilon Corporation, a manufacturer of disposable supplies for hospitals, was acquired in 1962.

Diversification also occurred through internal product development propelled by a detailed marketing survey conducted in the late 1950s. The survey found that the public associated the company as much or more with personal grooming as with cutlery and related products. Gillette's response was to broaden its personal care line. As a result, Gillette now markets such well-known brands as Adorn hair spray, Tame cream rinse, Right Guard antiperspirant, Dry Look hair spray for men, Foamy shaving cream, Earth Borne and Ultra Max shampoos, Cricket lighter, Pro Max hair dryers as well as Paper Mate, Eraser Mate, and Flair pens.

Gillette Today

Gillette is divided into four principal operating groups (North America, International, Braun AG, Diversified Companies) and five product lines. As Exhibit 1 indicates, the importance of blades and razors to company profits is immense. In nearly all the 200 countries in which its blade and razors are sold, Gillette remains the industry leader.

In 1977, Gillette reported increased worldwide sales of $1,587.2 million with income after taxes of $79.7 million (see Exhibit 2). Of total sales, $720.9 million were domestic and $866.3 million were international, with profit contributions of $109 million and $105.6 million, respectively. The company employs 31,700 people worldwide with 8,600 employees in the United States.

72% of employees outside the U.S.A. 27% in U.S.A

EXHIBIT 1 Gillette sales and contributions to profits by business segments

| | Blades and razors | | Toiletries and grooming aids | | Writing instruments | | Braun electric razors | | Other | |
Year	Net sales	Contributions to profits	Net sales	Contributions to profits	Net sales	Contributions to profits	Net sales	Contributions to profits	Net sales	Contributions to profits
1977	31%	75%	26%	13%	8%	6%	23%	13%	12%	(7)%
1976	29	71	28	15	7	6	21	10	15	(2)
1975	30	73	30	15	7	5	20	8	13	(1)
1974	30	69	31	17	7	6	20	5	12	3
1973	31	64	32	20	7	5	22	10	8	1

Source: *Gillette Annual Report for 1977, p. 28.*

EXHIBIT 2 The Gillette Company annual income statements, 1963–1977 ($000)

Year	Net sales	Gross profit	Profit from operations	Income before taxes	Federal and foreign income taxes	Net income
1977	$1,587,209	$834,786	$202,911	$158,820	$79,100	$79,720
1976	1,491,506	782,510	190,939	149,257	71,700	77,557
1975	1,406,906	737,310	184,368	146,954	67,000	79,954
1974	1,246,422	667,395	171,179	147,295	62,300	84,995
1973	1,064,427	600,805	155,949	154,365	63,300	91,065
1972	870,532	505,297	140,283	134,618	59,600	75,018
1971	729,687	436,756	121,532	110,699	48,300	62,399
1970	672,669	417,575	120,966	117,475	51,400	66,075
1969	609,557	390,858	122,416	119,632	54,100	65,532
1968	553,174	358,322	126,016	124,478	62,200	62,278
1967	428,357	291,916	101,153	103,815	47,200	56,615
1966	396,190	264,674	90,967	91,666	41,800	49,866
1965	339,064	224,995	75,010	75,330	33,000	42,330
1964	298,956	205,884	72,594	73,173	35,500	37,673
1963	295,700	207,552	85,316	85,945	44,400	41,545

Statement of Corporate Objectives and Goals

At a recent stockholders' meeting, the chairman of the board outlined the company's strategy for the future:

> The goal of The Gillette Company is sustained growth. To achieve this, the company concentrates on two major objectives: to maintain the strength of existing product lines and to develop at least two new significant businesses or product lines that can make important contributions to the growth of the company in the early 1980s.
>
> In existing product lines, the company broadens its opportunities for growth by utilizing corporate technology to create new products. In other areas, growth is accomplished through either internal development or the acquisition of new businesses.
>
> The company uses a number of guidelines to evaluate growth opportunities. Potential products or services must fulfill a useful function and provide value for the price paid; offer distinct advantages easily perceived by consumers; be based on technology available within, or readily accessible outside the company; meet established quality and safety standards; and offer an acceptable level of profitability and attractive growth potential.

The Safety Razor Division

The Safety Razor Division has long been regarded as the leader in shaving technology. Building on King Gillette's principle of using razors as a vehicle for blade sales and of associating the name ''Gillette'' with premium shaving, the division has been able to maintain its number-one position in the U.S. market.

Share of Market

Market share is important in the shaving industry. The standard is that each share point is equivalent to approximately $1 million in pretax profits. Over recent history, Gillette has held approximately 60 percent of the total dollar market. However, the division has put more emphasis on increasing its share from its static level.

Product Line

During the course of its existence, Gillette has introduced many new blades and razors. In the last 15 years, the shaving market has evolved from a double-edged emphasis to twin-bladed systems (see Exhibit 3). Besides Atra and TRAC II, Gillette markets Good News! disposables, Daisy for women, double-edge, injector, carbon, and Techmatic band systems (see Exhibit 4). Within their individual markets, Gillette sells 65 percent of all premium double-edged blades, 12 percent of injector sales, and almost all of the carbon and band sales.

EXHIBIT 3 Gillette percentage of U.S. blade sales (estimated market share)

Key
- Carbon
- Premium double edge
- Techmatic
- Injector
- TRAC II
- Daisy
- Good News!
- Atra

Techmatic introduced ↓ (1967)
First injector ↓ (1968)
TRAC II introduced ↓ (1971)
Daisy for women (1973)
Good News! for men ↓ (1976)
Atra introduced ↓ (1977)

Total values by year:
Year	Total
1964	58
1965	56
1966	56
1967	59
1968	60
1969	59
1970	60
1971	58
1972	57
1973	57
1974	57
1975	57
1976	56
1977	54
1978	54

Segment values (Carbon / Premium double edge / Techmatic / Injector / TRAC II / Daisy / Good News! / Atra):

Year	Carbon	Premium double edge	Techmatic	Injector	TRAC II	Daisy	Good News!	Atra
1964	46	12						
1965	40	16						
1966	34	20	2					
1967	31	22	6					
1968	27	23	8	2				
1969	23	23	10	3				
1970	20	26	11	3				
1971	17	26	11	4				
1972	16	24	10	3	4			
1973	13	21	8	3	12			
1974	12	19	6	4	16			
1975	10	18	5	3	20	1		
1976	9	16	4	2	21	1	3	
1977	8	13	3	2	20	1	6	1
1978	8	12	2	2	19		7	3

EXHIBIT 4 Safety Razor Division product line, June 1978

Product line	Package sizes	Manufacturer's suggested retail price
Blades:		
TRAC II	5,9,14,Adjustable 4	$1.60, 2.80, 3.89, 1.50
Atra	5,10	$1.70, 3.40
Good News!	2	$.60
Daisy	2	$1.00
Techmatic	5,10,15	$1.50, 2.80, 3.50
Double-edged		
Platinum Plus	5,10,15	$1.40, 2.69, 3.50
Super-Stainless	5,10,15	$1.20, 2.30, 3.10
Carbon:		
Super Blue	10,15	$1.50, 2.15
Regular Blue	5,10	$.70, 1.25
Injector:		
Regular	7,11	$1.95, 2.60
Twin Injector	5,8	$1.40, 2.20

9

EXHIBIT 4 *(concluded)*

Product line	Package sizes	Manufacturer's suggested retail price
Razors:		
TRAC II	Regular	$3.50
	Lady	$3.50
	Adjustable	$3.50
	Deluxe	$3.50
Atra		$4.95
Double-edged:		
Super Adjustable		$3.50
Lady Gillette		$3.50
Super Speed		$1.95
Twin Injector		$2.95
Techmatic	Regular	$3.50
	Deluxe	$3.95
Three-Piece		$4.50
Knack		$1.95
Cricket Lighters	Regular	$1.49
	Super	$1.98
	Keeper	$4.49

Marketing Approach and Past Traditions

During 1977, the Gillette Company spent $207.9 million to promote all its products throughout the world, of which $133.1 million was spent for advertising, including couponing and sampling, and $74.8 million for sales promotion. In terms of the domestic operation, the Safety Razor Division uses an eight-cycle promotional schedule whereby every six weeks a new program is initiated. During any one cycle, some but not all the products and their packages are sold on promotion. Usually one of the TRAC II packages is sold on promotion during each of these cycles.

> Gillette advertising is designed to provide information to consumers and motivate them to buy the company's products. Sales promotion ensures that these products are readily available, well located, and attractively displayed in retail stores. Special promotion at the point of purchase offers consumers an extra incentive to buy Gillette products.[2]

In the past the company has concentrated its advertising and promotion on its newest shaving product, reducing support for its other established lines. The theory is that growth must come at the expense of other brands. When TRAC II was introduced, for example, the advertising budget for other brands was cut, with the double-edged portion being decreased from 47 percent in 1971 to 11 percent in 1972 and TRAC II receiving 61 percent of the division budget (see Exhibit 5).

---

[2] *1977 Gillette Company Annual Report*, p. 14.

EXHIBIT 5 Gillette advertising expenditures, 1965–1978 (percentage of total market)

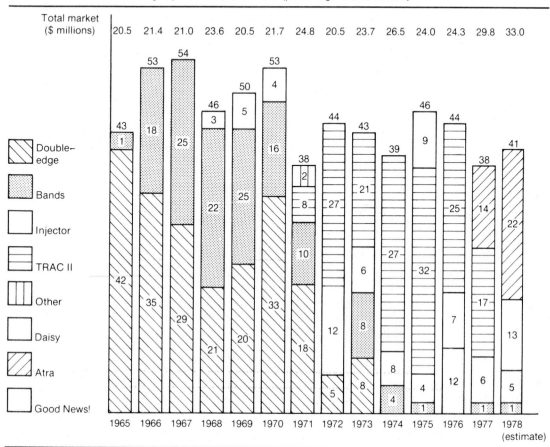

A long-standing tradition has been that razors are used as a means for selling blades. Thus, with razors, the emphasis is on inducing the consumer to try the product by offering coupon discounts, mail samples, and heavy informational advertising. Blade strategy has been to emphasize a variety of sales devices—such as discounts, displays, and sweepstakes at pharmacies, convenience stores, and supermarkets—to encourage point-of-purchase sales. In spite of this tradition, razor sales are a very significant portion of division sales and profits.

At the center of this marketing strategy has been the company's identification with sports. The Gillette "Cavalcade of Sports" began with Gillette's radio sponsorship of the 1939 World Series and continues today with sponsorship of the World Series, Super Bowl, professional and NCAA basketball, as well as boxing. During the 1950s and 1960s, Gillette spent 60 percent of its ad dollars on sports programming. Influenced by research showing that prime-time entertainment offered superior audience potential, the company switched to a prime-time emphasis in the early 1970s. However, Gillette has recently returned in the last two years to its sports formula.

Marketing Research

Research has been a cornerstone to the success of the company, for it has been its means of remaining superior to its competitors. For example, Gillette was faced in 1917 with the expiration of its basic patents and the eventual flood of competitive models. Six months before the impending expiration, the company came out with new razor models including one for a dollar. As a result, the company made more money than ever before. In fact, throughout the history of shaving, Gillette has introduced most of the improvements in shaving technology. The major exceptions are the injector which was introduced by Schick, and the stainless-steel double-edged blade introduced by Wilkinson.

The company spends $37 million annually on research and development for new products, product improvements, and consumer testing. In addition to Atra, a recent development is a new sharpening process called "Microsmooth" which improves the closeness of the shave and the consistency of the blade. This improvement was to be introduced on all of the company's twin blades by early 1979. Mike Edwards believes that this will help to ensure TRAC II's retention of its market.

At the time of Atra's introduction, Gillette research found that users would come from users of TRAC II and nontwin-blade systems. This projected loss was estimated to be 60 percent of TRAC II users. Recent research indicates that with heavy marketing support in 1978, TRAC II's loss will be held to 40 percent.

The Shaving Market

The shaving market is divided into two segments: wet and electric shavers. Today, the wet shavers account for 75 percent of the market. In the United States alone, 1.9 billion blades and 23 million razors are sold annually. Gillette participates in the electric market through sales of electric razors by its Braun subsidiary.

Market Factors

There are a number of factors at work within the market: (1) the adult shaving population has increased in the past 15 years to 74.6 million men and 68.2 million women, (2) technological improvements have improved the quality of the shave as well as increased the life of the razor blade, and (3) the volume of blades and razors has begun to level off after a period of declining and then increasing sales (see Exhibit 6). Although the shaving market has increased

EXHIBIT 6 Razor and blade sales volume, 1963–1979

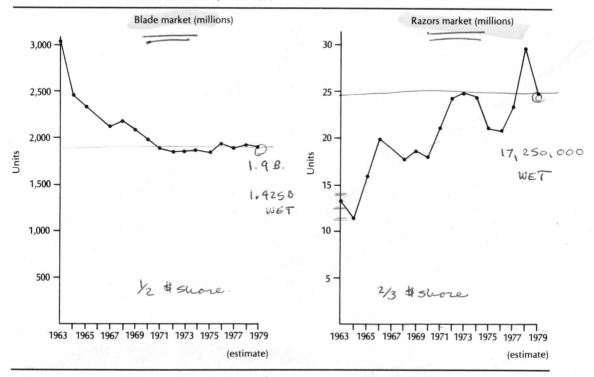

Blade market (millions)

1.9 B.
1,425B
WET

½ # share.

Razors market (millions)

17,250,000
WET

2/3 # share

1963 1965 1967 1969 1971 1973 1975 1977 1979
(estimate)

slightly, there are more competitors. Yet Gillette has been able to maintain its share of the market—approximately two thirds of the dollar-razor market and a little over half of the dollar-blade market.

2.5
.83
3.33

Market Categories

The market is segmented into seven components: new systems, disposables, injector, premium double-edged, carbon double-edged, continuous bands, and single-edged systems. In the early 1900s the shaving market consisted primarily of straight-edges. During the past 70 years, the market has evolved away from its single- and then double-edged emphasis to the present market of 60 percent bonded systems (all systems in which the blade is encased in plastic). Exhibit 7 shows the recent trends within the market categories.

Competitors

Gillette's major competitors are Warner-Lambert's Schick, Colgate-Palmolive's Wilkinson, American Safety Razor's Personna, and BIC. Each has its own strongholds. Schick, which introduced the injector system, now controls 80 per-

EXHIBIT 7 Recent share trends (percent)

Volume	1972	1973	1974	1975	1976	1977	1978, 1st half
Units:							
New systems	8.8%	20.6%	28.8%	36.2%	39.9%	40.8%	43.8%
Injector	20.2	17.6	17.1	16.3	15.7	14.2	12.8
Double-edged:							
Premium	39.4	34.9	30.8	27.4	24.5	21.1	19.0
Carbon	12.0	10.6	9.4	8.1	7.3	7.6	6.6
Bands	13.1	10.3	8.0	6.4	4.7	3.7	2.7
Disposables	—	—	—	—	2.5	6.9	9.7
Single-edged	6.5	6.0	5.9	5.6	5.4	5.7	5.4
Total market	100.0%	100.0%	100.0%	100.0%	100.0%	100.0%	100.0%
Dollars:							
New systems	11.8%	26.9%	36.9%	46.0%	50.1%	50.1%	52.1%
Injector	21.8	18.6	17.8	16.4	15.0	13.8	12.5
Double-edged:							
Premium	41.5	34.2	28.7	24.0	20.8	18.1	16.1
Carbon	6.1	5.4	4.7	4.2	4.0	4.1	3.5
Bands	15.4	11.8	8.7	6.5	4.8	3.6	2.8
Disposables	—	—	—	—	2.8	7.5	10.5
Single-edged	3.4	3.1	3.2	2.9	2.5	2.8	2.5
Total market	100.0%	100.0%	100.0%	100.0%	100.0%	100.0%	100.0%

cent of that market. ASR's Personna sells almost all of the single-edged blades on the market. Wilkinson's strength is its bonded system which appeals to an older, wealthier market. BIC has developed a strong product in its inexpensive disposable system.

Competitive pricing structure is comparable to Gillette within the different system categories. Although all the companies have similar suggested retail prices, the differences found on the racks in the market are a function of the companies' off-invoice rates to the trade and their promotional allowances. It is not much of a factor at this time; private label covers the range of systems and continues to grow.

Market Segmentation

The success of Gillette's technological innovation can be seen in its effect on the total shaving market. Although there are other factors at play in the market, new product introductions have contributed significantly to market expansion as Exhibit 8 indicates.

EXHIBIT 8 New product introductions and their effects on the market, 1959–1977

Year	Product segment	Sales blade/razor market ($ millions)	Change (percent)
1959	Carbon	122.4	Base
1960	Super blue	144.1	+ 17.7 over 1959
1963	Stainless	189.3	+ 31.3 over 1960
1965	Super stainless	201.2	+ 6.3 over 1963

EXHIBIT 8 (concluded)

Year	Product segment	Sales blade/razor market ($ millions)	Change (percent)
1966	Banded system	212.1	+ 5.4 over 1965
1969	Injector	246.8	+ 16.3 over 1966
1972	Twin blades	326.5	+ 32.2 over 1969
1975	Disposable	384.0	+ 17.6 over 1972
1977	Pivoting head	444.9	+ 15.9 over 1975

Sales increase.

Twin-Blade Market

Research played a key role in the development of twin blades. Gillette had two variations—the current type in which the blades are in tandem; the other type in which the blades, edges faced each other and required an up-and-down scrubbing motion. From a marketing standpoint, and because the Atra swivel system had problems in testing development, TRAC II was launched first. The research department played a major role in the positioning of the product when it discovered hysteresis, the phenomenon of whiskers being lifted out and after a time receding into the follicle. Thus, the TRAC II effect was that the second blade cut the whisker before it receded.

Since its introduction in 1971, the twin-blade market has grown to account for almost 60 percent of all blade sales. The twin-blade market is defined as all bonded razors and blades (e.g., new systems: Atra and TRAC II; disposables: Good News! and BIC). Exhibit 9 shows the trends in the twin-blade market.

During this period many products have been introduced. These include the Sure Touch in 1971, the Deluxe TRAC II and Schick Super II in 1972, the Lady TRAC II, Personna Double II, and Wilkinson Bonded in 1973, the Personna Flicker, Good News!, and BIC Disposable in 1974, the Personna Lady Double II in 1975, and the Adjustable TRAC II and Schick Super II in 1976.

EXHIBIT 9 The twin–blade market,1972–1978 ($ millions)

	1972	1973	1974	1975	1976	1977	1978, estimate	1979, estimate
Razors	$ 29.5	$ 32.1	$ 31.4	$ 31.3	$ 31.5	$ 39.7	$ 53.8	
Disposables	—	—	—	—	14.5	41.5	64.9	
Blades	31.6	72.0	105.7	147.5	176.3	183.7	209.2	
Total twin	61.1	104.1	137.1	176.2	222.3	264.9	327.9	
Total market	$326.5	$332.6	$342.5	$384.0	$422.2	$444.9	$491.0	$500.0

Advertising

In the race for market share, the role of advertising is extremely important in the shaving industry. Of all the media expenditures, television is the primary vehicle in the twin-blade market. For Gillette, this means an emphasis on

C

maximum exposure and sponsorship of sports events. The company's policy for the use of television is based on the concept that TV is essentially a family medium and programs should therefore be suitable for family viewing. Gillette tries to avoid programs that unduly emphasize sex or violence.

As the industry leader, TRAC II receives a great deal of competitive pressure in the form of aggressive advertising from competitors and other Gillette twin-blade brands (see Exhibit 10). For example, the theme of recent Schick commercials was the "Schick challenge," and BIC emphasized its lower cost and cleaner shave in relation to those of other twin-blade brands. However, competitive media expenditures are such that their cost per share point is substantially higher than TRAC II's.

EXHIBIT 10 Estimated media expenditures ($000)

	1976	1977, 1st half	1977, 2nd half	Total 1977	1978, 1st half	Total 1978 estimate
Companies:						
Gillette	$10,800	$ 4,800	$ 6,400	$11,200	$ 8,100	$13,800
Schick	7,600	3,700	4,300	8,000	4,300	8,900
Wilkinson	2,700	1,400	2,200	3,600	1,400	2,200
ASR	2,600	700	200	900	200	800
BIC	600*	4,300	1,800	6,100	4,000	7,300
Total market	$24,300	$14,900	$14,900	$29,800	$18,000	$33,000
Brands:						
TRAC II	$ 6,000	$ 3,300	$ 1,700	$ 5,000	$ 2,400	$ 4,000
Atra	—	—	4,000	4,000	4,500	7,500
Good News!	1,900	1,200	600	1,800	700	1,600
Super II	2,600	1,400	2,600	4,000	3,000	4,600

* Product introduction.

Despite competitive pressures, TRAC II is aggressively advertised too. As a premium product, it does not respond directly to competitive challenges or shifts in its own media; rather, the advertising follows a standard principle of emphasizing TRAC II's strengths. As Exhibits 11 and 12 indicate, the TRAC II media plan emphasizes diversity with a heavy emphasis on advertising on prime-time television and on sports programs. In addition, TRAC II is continually promoted to retain its market share.

For 1978, the division budgeted $18 million for advertising, with Atra and TRAC II receiving the major portion of the budget (see Exhibit 13). The traditional Gillette approach is for the newest brand to receive the bulk of the advertising dollars (see Exhibit 5). Therefore, it is certain that Atra will receive a substantial increase in advertising for 1979. Whether the division will increase or decrease TRAC II's budget as well as whether it will increase the total ad budget for 1979 is unknown at this time.

EXHIBIT 11 TRAC II media plan, 1976, 1977 ($000)

	Quarter				
	1	2	3	4	Total
1976					
Prime	935	575	1,200	550	3,160
Sports	545	305	450	1,040	2,440
Network total	1,480	880	1,650	1,590	5,650
Other	80	85	70	165	400
Total	1,560	965	1,720	1,755	6,000
1977					
Prime	1,300	900	300	—	2,500
Sports	500	400	400	400	1,700
Network total	1,800	1,300	700	400	4,200
Print	—	—	200	200	400
Black	75	75	75	75	300
Military, miscellaneous	25	25	25	25	100
Total	1,900	1,400	1,000	700	5,000

EXHIBIT 12 TRAC II media plan, 1978

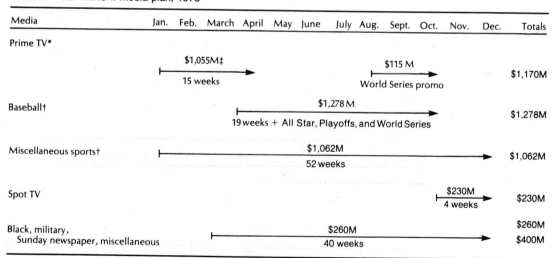

Media	Jan.	Feb.	March	April	May	June	July	Aug.	Sept.	Oct.	Nov.	Dec.	Totals
Prime TV*			$1,055M‡ 15 weeks						$115 M World Series promo				$1,170M
Baseball†					$1,278 M 19 weeks + All Star, Playoffs, and World Series								$1,278M
Miscellaneous sports†		$1,062M 52 weeks											$1,062M
Spot TV											$230M 4 weeks		$230M
Black, military, Sunday newspaper, miscellaneous				$260M 40 weeks									$260M $400M

Note: M = $1,000.

* Prime-time TV advertising:

KAZ	Love Boat
ABC Friday Movie	Different Strokes
Tuesday Big Event	Real People
ABC Sunday Movie	Duke
Roots Two	Rockford Files

† Sports TV advertising:

Wide World of Sports, Saturday	NBA Basketball
College Basketball	History of Baseball
NBA All Star Game	Game of the Week Day
International Teen Boxing	This Week Baseball
Wide World of Sports, Sunday	

EXHIBIT 13 Razor Division marketing budget, 1978

	Atra line	TRAC II line	Good News!	Double-edged blades	Double-edged razors	Techmatic line	Daisy	Injector line	Twin injector	Total blade/razor
Marketing expenses:										
Promotion*	42.3	69.4	65.2	92.2	75.4	52.7	58.4	77.5	48.3	60.7
Advertising†	55.6	28.8	31.2	4.6	—	—	39.0	—	26.3	36.5
Other	2.1	1.8	3.6	3.2	24.6	47.3	2.6	22.5	25.4	2.8
Total marketing	100.0	100.0	100.0	100.0	100.0	100.0	100.0	100.0	100.0	100.0
Percentage line/total direct marketing	34.1	38.4	14.9	7.6	.4	.3	3.4	.2	.7	100.0
Percentage line/total full revenue sales	20.5	41.8	13.4	16.8	1.4	2.1	2.2	.6	1.2	100.0

* Defined as off-invoice allowances, wholesale push money, cooperative advertising, excess cost, premiums, contests, and prizes.
† Defined as media, sampling, couponing, production, and costs.

TRAC II

The 1971 introduction of TRAC II was the largest in shaving history. Influenced by the discovery of the hysteresis process, by the development of a clog-free dual-blade cartridge, and by consumer-testing data which showed a nine to one preference for TRAC II over the panelists' current razors, Gillette raced to get the product to market. Because the introduction involved so many people and was so critical to reversing a leveling of corporate profits (see Exhibit 2), the division president personally assumed the role of product development manager and lived with the project day and night through its development and introduction.[3]

Launched during the 1971 World Series promotion, TRAC II was the most frequently advertised shaving system in America during its introductory period. Supported by $10 million in advertising and promotion, TRAC II results were impressive: 1.7 million razors and 5 million cartridges were sold in October; and during the first year, the introductory campaign made 2 billion impressions and reached 80 percent of all homes an average of 4.7 times a week. In addition, a multimillion-unit sampling campaign was implemented in 1972 which was the largest of its kind.

For five years TRAC II was clearly the fastest growing product on the market, and it helped to shape the switch to twin blades. Its users are predominantly young, college-educated, metropolitan, suburban, and upper-income men. The brand reached its peak in 1976 when it sold 485 million blades and 7 million razors. In comparison, projected TRAC II sales for 1978 are 433 million blades and 4.2 million razors. During this period, TRAC II brand contribution decreased 10 percent (see Exhibit 14). Competitors' responsive strategies seem to be effective. The growth of Super II during the last two years is attributed to certain advantages it has over TRAC II. Super II has higher trade allowances (20% versus 15%), improved distribution, an increased media expenditure, and generally lower everyday prices.

In preparing the 1979 marketing plans, the objective for TRAC II was to retain its consumer franchise despite strong competitive challenges through consumer-oriented promotions and to market the brand aggressively year round. Specifically, TRAC II was

1. To obtain a 20 percent share of the cartridge and razor market.
2. To deliver 43 percent of the division's profit.
3. To retain its valuable pegboard space at the checkout counters in convenience, food, and drug stores as well as supermarkets.

In 1978, Mike Edwards launched a new economy-size blade package (14 blades) and a heavy spending campaign to retain TRAC II's market share. He employed strong trade and consumer promotion incentives supported by (1) new improved product claims of a "microsmooth" shave, (2) new graphics,

---

[3] For an excellent account of the TRAC II introduction, by the president of Gillette North America, see William G. Salatich, "Gillette's TRAC II: The Steps to Success," *Market Communications,* January 1972.

EXHIBIT 14 TRAC II line income statement, 1972–1978

	1972*	1973	1974	1975	Base 1976	1977	Estimated 1978
Full revenue sales (FRS):							
Promotional	28	41	71	100	100	110	112
Nonpromotional	38	91	89	83	100	80	65
Total	32	60	78	93	100	99	95
Direct cost of sales:							
Manufacturing	63	77	93	111	100	88	83
Freight	51	80	91	106	100	82	80
Total	62	77	93	111	100	88	83
Standard profit contribution	26	56	75	89	100	101	97
Marketing expenses							
Promotional expenses:							
Lost revenue	26	39	72	100	100	114	126
Wholesale push money	455	631	572	565	100	562	331
Cooperative advertising	27	36	58	71	100	115	133
Excess cost	25	50	59	83	100	63	92
Premiums	3	29	16	28	100	78	217
Contests and prizes	7	21	110	115	100	215	109
Total	26	40	67	90	100	112	129
Advertising:							
Media	90	83	110	119	100	96	75
Production	96	128	130	104	100	196	162
Couponing and sampling	470	344	177	112	100	166	131
Other	19	120	68	78	100	54	54
Total	124	110	108	117	100	96	78
Other marketing expenses	108	120	847	617	100	242	86
Market research	122	65	47	34	100	134	91
Total assignable marketing expenses	67	69	87	102	100	106	108
Net contribution:	14	53	81	85	100	100	94
Percentage of promotional FRS/total FRS	56	43	58	76	63	70	74
Percentage of promotional expense/promo FRS	15	16	16	15	11	17	20
Percentage of promotional expenses/total FRS	9	7	9	10	11	12	15
Percentage of advertising expenses/total FRS	28	13	10	9	7	7	6
Percentage of Media expenses/total FRS	17	8	8	8	6	6	5

* Each year's data are shown as a percentage of 1976's line item. For example, 1972 sales were 32 percent of 1976 sales.

and (3) a revised version of the highly successful "Sold Out" advertising campaign (see Exhibit 15). Midyear results indicated that TRAC II's performance had exceeded division expectations as it retained 21.6 percent of the blade market and its contribution exceeded the budget by $2 million.

Atra (Automatic Tracking Razor Action)

Origin

Research for the product began in Gillette's United Kingdom Research and Development Laboratory in 1970. The purpose was to improve the high standards of performance of twin-blade shaving and, specifically, to enhance the TRAC II effect. The company's scientists discovered that a better shave could be produced if, instead of the shaver moving the hand and face to produce the

EXHIBIT 15

Gillette TRAC II®

THE GILLETTE COMPANY
SAFETY RAZOR DIVISION

LENGTH: 30 SECONDS

"SOLD OUT"
(MICROSMOOTH-GIRL) SUPER II

BBDO

COMM'L NO.: GSRD 8033

IRVING: Sold out again!???
(SFX: DING!)

CUSTOMER 1: The new improved
Gillette TRAC II, please.

IRVING: Er . . . say . . . who needs
improved when these twin blades'll do.

CUSTOMER 1: TRAC II has micro-
smooth edges . . . makes the blades
smoother than ever.

IRVING: Shave better than these?

CUSTOMER 1: Better, safer, smoother
. . . and comfortable.

IRVING: Comfort . . . schmomfort . . .
you don't have . . . But . . . but . . . b-b . . .

CUSTOMER 2: Do you have the new
improved Gillette TRAC II?

IRVING: Improved TRAC II??
(INNOCENTLY) Improved TRAC II?

ANNCR: The new improved Gillette
TRAC II. Micro-smooth edges make
it a better shave.

3

best shaving angle for the blade, the razor head could pivot in such a way as to maintain the most effective twin-blade shaving angle. Once the pivoting head was shown to produce a better shave, test after test, research continued in the Boston headquarters on product design, redesigning, and consumer testing.

The name "Atra" came from two years of intensive consumer testing of the various names which could be identified with this advanced razor. The choice was based on how easy it was to remember the name, how well it communicated the technology, its uniqueness, and the feeling of the future it conveyed. Atra stands for *Automatic Tracking Razor Action.*

Introduction

Atra was first introduced in mid-1977. The introduction stressed the new shaving system supplemented by heavy advertising coupled with $2 razor rebate coupons to induce trial and 50-cent coupons toward Atra blades to induce brand loyalty. An example of Atra advertising is shown in Exhibit 16. During its first year on the national market, Atra was expected to sell 9 million razors although 85 percent of all sales were sold on a discount basis. Early results showed that Atra sold at a faster level than Gillette's previously most successful product, TRAC II. The Atra razor retails for $4.95. Blades are sold in packages of 5 and 10. TRAC II and Atra blades are not interchangeable. Because of Gillette's excellent distribution system, it has not had much problem gaining valuable pegboard space.

Current Trends and Competitive Responses in the Twin-Blade Market

There was quite a bit of activity in the shaving market during the first half of 1978. Atra has increased the total Gillette share in the razor and blade market. During the June period, Atra razors continued to exceed TRAC II as the leading selling razor whereas Atra blades share was approximately 8 percent, accounting for most of Gillette's 4 percent share growth since June 1977. Thus, the growth of Atra has put more competitive pressure on TRAC II. In addition, the disposable segment due to BIC and Good News! has increased by five share points to a hefty 12 percent dollar share of the blade market. Combined with TRAC II's resiliency in maintaining share, competitive brands have lost share: Schick Super II, ASR, and Wilkinson were all down two points since June 1977.

In response to these recent trends, the TRAC II team expected competition to institute some changes. In an effort to recover its sagging share, Edwards expected the Schick Muscular Dystrophy promotion in October 1977 to help bolster Super II with its special offer. The pressure may already be appearing with Schick's highly successful introduction of Personal Touch for women in this year, currently about 10 percent of the razor market, which has to draw TRAC II female shavers. In addition, it appears inevitable that Schick will bring out an Atra-type razor. This will remove Atra's competitive advantage but

EXHIBIT 16

Gillette Atra

:30 second commercial   GSRS7013 "Impossible, Yes"   August, 1977

ANNCR (VO): Could Gillette make a razor that does the impossible?

Yes.

Could it shave closer with even more comfort?

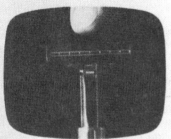

Yes.

Gillette introduces Atra . . .

the first razor with a pivoting head . . .

that safely follows every contour of your face.

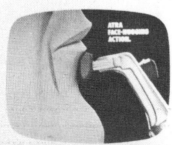

This Atra face-hugging action keeps the twin-blades at the perfect angle.

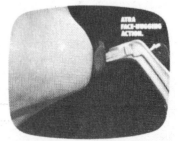

You've never shaved this close with this much comfort.

MAN: Impossible!

*ANNCR: The New Gillette Atra Razor.

Yes, it's the impossible shave.

increase pressure on TRAC II with the addition of a second pivoting head competitor.

Continuing its recent trends, it appears that the disposable segment of the market will continue to expand. The first sign of this is the BIC ads offering 12 BIC disposables for $1. Good News! received additional advertising support in the latter half of the year as well as the introduction of a new package size. One of Edwards's major objectives is to emphasize the importance of TRAC II to upper management. Besides the introduction of the microsmooth concept, a price increase on TRAC II products will be implemented soon. It is unclear whether the price change will have an adverse effect on brand sales.

In preparing the 1979 TRAC II marketing plan, Edwards realized that Atra would be given a larger share of the advertising dollars following a strong year, and the disposable market would continue to grow. TRAC II share remained questionable, depending on the level of marketing support it received. Whether TRAC II will be able to continue its heavy spending program and generate large revenues for the division remains to be seen. These factors, as well as the company's support of Atra, made 1979 a potentially tough year for Mike Edwards and TRAC II.

1979 Marketing Plan Preparation

Edwards recently received the following memorandum from the vice president of marketing:

Memo to: Brand Group

From: P. Meyers

Date: July 7, 1978

Subject: 1979 Marketing Plans

In preparation for the marketing plan approval process and in developing the division strategy for 1979, I would like a preliminary plan from each brand group by the end of the month. Please submit statements of objective, corresponding strategy and levels of dollar support requested for the following:

1. Overall brand strategy[4]—target market.
2. Blade and razor volume and share goals.
3. Sales promotion.
4. Advertising.
5. Couponing and sampling.
6. Miscellaneous—new packaging, additional marketing research, marketing cost saving ideas, etc.

See you at the weekly meeting on Wednesday.

---

[4] Brand strategy means positioning the brand in such a way that it appeals to a distinguishable target market.

In developing the TRAC II marketing plan, Edwards had to wrestle with some strategy decisions. To get significant funding, how should he position TRAC II in relation to Atra and the disposables? Also, how does he convince the vice president that dollars spent for TRAC II are more effective than expenditures on Good News! or Gillette's electric razors?

Case 13

Northern Telecom (A)*

In early 1975, a three-person task force, with representatives from Northern Telecom Limited, Bell-Northern Research Limited and Bell Canada, was asked to develop a strategy for Northern Telecom in the central office switching market. Central office switching equipment is the telephone exchange equipment owned by telephone companies that connects a user with the telephone at the number he/she has dialed. This equipment includes both local telephone exchanges and toll or long distances exchanges that connect all the local exchanges together. The decisions about Northern Telecom's central office switching strategy were viewed as crucial ones, since research and development expenditures in excess of $50 million and revenues of hundreds of millions of dollars were at stake.

Northern Telecom's major entry in the central office switching market, the SP-1, was experiencing rapid growth, but competitors were aggressively introducing new products which threatened to cut into future sales of the SP-1.

The task force was faced with two major alternatives:

1. Introduce all or part of a new digital central office switching line as soon as possible, with the first major elements of the product line being available in 1979, the exact timing depending on how quickly R&D and human resources were built up in the program. The technical and business risks associated with such a strategy were viewed as being very large. If the decision to proceed with an early introduction of one or more digital central office switches was made, decisions also had to be made about the relative priority to be given to the various digital switches under development and their associated software packages. Furthermore, the timing of any announcement of one or more of the digital switches competitive with Northern Telecom's existing product line might have an adverse effect on new sales of the existing line, leaving only extension sales for existing SP-1 offices.

---

* This case was prepared by Professor Adrian B. Ryans as a basis for class discussion rather than to illustrate either effective or ineffective handling of an administrative situation. Copyright © 1982. The School of Business Administration, The University of Western Ontario.

2. Delay the introduction of the digital switching line until 1981 or later. This would alleviate Northern Telecom's short-run cash flow problems, and would probably extend the product life cycle of the SP-1 switch. Since the SP-1 switch was under increasing competitive pressure, one possibility was to introduce an updated enhanced version of the SP-1 switch (perhaps called the SP-2. Depending on the number and type of enhancements selected, this upgraded switch could be announced within a few months and could be available to customers by 1977.

The Company

Prior to 1956, Northern Electric Company Limited (as Northern Telecom was formerly called) was 40 percent owed by Western Electric, the manufacturing arm of American Telephone and Telegraph (AT&T), and in the words of a Northern Telecom executive, "operated very much like a branch plant." Its prime mandate was to manufacture Western Electric products for Bell Canada, and its product line generally lagged Western Electric's by two to three years. During this period Northern Electric had only a very small R&D staff.

In 1956, Western Electric signed a consent decree with the U.S. Department of Justice in which it agreed, among other things, that it would relinquish any ownership of Northern Electric. Northern Electric then became a wholly owned subsidiary of Bell Canada. Having no product line of its own, Northern Electric agreed to license many Western Electric products on the same basis as several other independent companies. The close working relationship between Northern Electric executives and engineers and their Western Electric counterparts soon began to weaken. Northern Electric, at this point, was essentially a company with no product line of its own and no R&D expertise in key technology areas, but with a firmly established business base in Canada and excellent engineering and manufacturing skills.

The Development of a Central Office Switching Product Line

In 1958, Northern Electric Laboratories was established in Belleville, Ontario with a staff of 30 to 40 people. This operation was moved to new facilities in Ottawa, Ontario in 1960 and a priority task became the acquisition of expertise in switching and transmission, and the development of a product line that would meet Canadian needs. One of the first switching products developed by the Laboratories was the SA-1, a 1,000-line crossbar system using Western Electric-type components.[1] Introduced in the early 1960s, over 1,000 SA-1 switches were sold, mostly in Canada. Two other switches, the N5-1 and N5-2, were the result of modifications to a Western Electric product to reduce its live capacity to meet the Canadian market's needs.

---

[1] An overview of central office switching technology is contained in a later section.

In the early 60s, it became apparent to Northern Electric management that the next generation of products would make extensive use of electronics to replace electromechanical components. Bell Canada had continued to have a working relationship with AT&T through a service contract. Before this relationship ended, Bell Canada was anxious to get access to the latest technology AT&T had to offer. AT&T had announced an electronic central office switch (the #1 ESS) in the early 1960s, with the first installation to occur in 1965 in New Jersey. Bell Canada was able to negotiate an arrangement whereby Northern Electric would manufacture under license a #1 ESS switch for the World's Fair in Montreal (Expo '67). This provided a world showcase for AT&T's technology. This contract resulted in Northern Electric becoming involved both with Bell Laboratories (the R&D arm of AT&T) and Western Electric as part of the development team. A switch was manufactured and installed for the World's Fair site by Northern Electric. Ultimately, a total of 11 of these #1 ESS switches were built under license from Western Electric for Bell Canada. The switch was a large local switch able to handle from 10,000 to 60,000 lines. It was designed for major metropolitan areas such as Toronto and Montreal, and was expensive to manufacture on Northern Electric's scale. The product was phased out of the Northern Electric product line in the early 1970s.

Northern Electric's experience with the #1 ESS switch reinforced management's desire to develop a product line attuned to the needs of the Canadian market—particularly products that would be economical at low line sizes and would continue to be economical over a wide range of line sizes. By 1964, the basic architecture of such a product had been outlined. The SP-1 (Stored Program 1st System) had stored-program-control and an electromechanical network using a miniature crossbar (MINIBAR[2] switch) designed by Northern Electric. This promised to be a robust system; for example, if there were problems with the computer system, connections would be maintained during the problem (i.e., telephone conversations would not be cut off because of the computer problem). In 1965, a commitment was made to proceed with the SP-1, and the product development team grew from half a dozen people in 1965 to well over a hundred by the end of the decade. The first trial office (a switch installed in a telephone company exchange) was installed near Ottawa in November 1969, and based on this trial the product details were finalized. Detailed manufacturing engineering was then begun, manufacturing capacity installed, and the first commercial office was placed in service in November 1971. During this period, the introductory marketing campaign for the SP-1 began. Seminars were held across Canada for telephone company executives. The first sale outside Bell Canada was to Alberta Government Telephones.

By 1975, versions of the SP-1 switch were available that could handle local exchanges from about 3,000 to 25,000 telephone lines, medium-sized toll exchanges, and a combination of both. In the toll exchanges, operator positions

---

[2] Registered trademark of Northern Telecom.

were tied directly into the exchanges allowing small telephone companies to play a bigger role in handling their own profitable toll business. This was an important selling point to independent telephone companies in the U.S. who were always in conflict with AT&T Long Lines over toll revenues. By 1975, every major telephone company in Canada bought the switch and the SP-1 achieved about a 90 percent market share of the addressed segments of the switching market in Canada. Sales through 1975 were much higher than expected, with 25 percent of 1974 sales being made in the United States, and the SP-1 was viewed by non-AT&T companies in North America as the premium stored program switch. Some sales were also made in the Caribbean. The sales history and some sales forecasts for the product, by customer type, are shown in Exhibit 1. The expected flattening of sales in 1975 in the United States was due largely to the 1974–75 recession, which was having a significant impact on capital expenditure programs in the telephone industry.

EXHIBIT 1 Sales history and sales forecasts for SP-1 central office switches ($ millions)

Year	Canada	United States	Other exports	Total
1971	6	0	0	6
1972	15	0	0	15
1973	33	2	0	35
1974	76	26	0	102
1975 (estimated)	148	27	0	175
1976 forecast	137	12*	0	149
1977 forecast	171	8*	8	186
1978 forecast	183	9*	7	198
1979 forecast	192	10*	12	214
1980 forecast	202	12*	15	229

* Northern Telecom was to begin manufacturing some SP-1 switches in the United States beginning in 1976. These forecasts only include exports from Canada to the United States. Forecasts of shipments from the U.S. plant were not available.

Source: Company records.

Bell-Northern Research

By 1970, Northern Electric Laboratories had become a major research and development organization, employing about 2,000 people. At that time the decision was made to incorporate it as a separate entity. On January 1, 1971, Bell-Northern Research Limited (BNR) came into being and the employees of Northern Electric Laboratories became employees of the "new" company. BNR did research and development work for both Northern Telecom and Bell Canada with about 70 percent of its funding coming from the former and the remaining 30 percent from the latter. A very close working relationship continued among the three organizations.

The Telephone Industry

At the end of 1974, 357 million telephones were in service around the world, and that number had been growing by about 8 percent per year. About 44 percent of the world's telephones were located in the United States and Canada, with a further 27 percent and 12 percent in Western Europe and Japan, respectively. The total investment in telecommunications plant and equipment to support the North American telecommunications network alone exceeded $110 billion in 1975. Construction expenditures by telephone companies in North America, which included expenditures on switching equipment, had grown (in nominal dollars) at over 15 percent in Canada and 9.5 percent in the United States during the period 1965 to 1975. Expenditure growth rates were even higher outside North America.

Canada

Bell Canada, its subsidiaries, and its affiliated companies (New Brunswick Telephone Co., Maritime Telegraph and Telephone Co., Newfoundland Telephone Co., and Island Telephone Co.) provided most of the telephone services in Ontario, Quebec, the Atlantic Provinces, and the Northwest Territories. Together, these companies operated about 8.4 million telephones and were expected to spend approximately $225 million on central office switching equipment in 1975.

There were four major non-Bell telephone companies operating in Canada. British Columbia Telephone Company, a subsidiary of the U.S.-based General Telephone and Electronics (GTE), had about 1.5 million telephones in service. Alberta Government Telephones, Saskatchewan Telecommunications, and Manitoba Telephone System together had about 2.0 million telephones in service. Several hundred smaller telephone companies served about 300,000 telephones. Between them, the non-Bell companies were expected to spend about $150 million on central office switching products.

All the major Canadian telephone companies were members of the Trans-Canada Telephone System (TCTS), which coordinated transcontinental telephone service, data communications, and television network facilities. In 1973, TCTS members had put into operation the world's first commercial national digital data transmission facility called Dataroute, demonstrating the Canadian telephone companies' leadership in, and belief in, digital technology.

United States

About 144 million telephones were in service in the United States in early 1975. AT&T (Bell System), which included 24 Bell System and associated operating companies, provided service to about 82 percent of the telephones in the United States. Western Electric was wholly owned by AT&T and, as a matter of policy after the 1956 consent decree with the U.S. Justice Department, with very few exceptions sold its products exclusively to Bell System operating companies and to the U.S. government. The operating companies were accustomed to purchasing their equipment from Western Electric. Western Electric's total sales in 1974 were $7.4 billion, and it had a net income of $310 million. AT&T was expected to spend $1,650 million on switching equipment in 1975.

The remaining 18 percent of the telephones in the United States were served by about 1,600 independent telephone companies. While many of these companies were tiny, some were very large companies. General Telephone and Electronics (GTE) serviced about 45 percent of all telephones served by the independent telephone companies and had telephone-related revenues of almost $2 billion. The major independent telephone companies, the number of telephones they served, and their estimated 1975 expenditures on switching equipment are shown in Exhibit 2. The large independent telephone companies provided a full range of telephone services. Smaller independent telephone companies typically relied on others, particularly AT&T Long Lines, for the provision of toll services. The two largest of the independent telephone companies, GTE and United Telecommunications, had their own major manufacturing companies, GTE Automatic Electric and North Electric, respectively, which supplied much of the central office switching equipment to their owners.

The independent telephone companies generally served the more rural areas of the United States, not the major concentrations of population (although a GTE operating company did serve much of Los Angeles). This resulted in a higher proportion of their central offices being in the smaller line sizes relative to the Bell System. The Bell System, through AT&T Long Lines, serviced the long distance and international markets which required a large number of large toll central offices. In fact, while only 23 percent of AT&T's central offices had less than 1,000 lines, 64 percent of the independent's central offices were this size. Conversely, 43 percent of AT&T's central offices had over 5,000 lines, whereas only 8 percent of the independent's central offices were this large.

EXHIBIT 2 Major U.S. independent telephone companies in 1975

Company	Number of telephones served (000)	Estimated expenditure on central office switches in 1975 (millions)
General Telephone Company	11,800	$218
United Telecommunications	3,236	70
Continental Telephone	2,246	⎫
Central Telephone	1,222	⎬ 240
Other independent telephone companies	7,500	⎭

Europe

The European market for central office switching equipment was growing rapidly, with total expenditures on central office switching equipment in 1974 amounting to $3 billion. The European market was more fragmented than the North American market, since each country had its own government postal telegraph and telephone company (PTTs). Most of the PTTs had restrictive technical standards and took other steps to protect their domestic telecommunications equipment manufacturers. Furthermore, Europe had quite different technical standards for telephone switching equipment than North America and Japan, which meant that a manufacturer had to extensively modify his switching equipment if he wanted to sell in both markets. The development cost of these general modifications for the overseas market was estimated by Northern Telecom to be up to $20 million for a particular type of central office switch, with at least an additional $1 million to meet the idiosyncrasies of each individual PTT. Nevertheless, despite these barriers, the European market was an attractive market with a lot of future potential. Telephone service penetration was typically only one third to one half of the U.S. penetration of 60 telephones per hundred people. Much of the European telephone plant and equipment was obsolete and was ripe for replacement. In much of the rest of the world the situation was similar except that telephone penetration levels were even lower in most countries.

Northern Telecom's View of the 1975 Market

Northern Telecom executives generally viewed their North American customers as falling into three major segments: (1) Bell Canada, its subsidiaries and affiliated companies; (2) system telephone companies (the other telephone companies in TCTS, the Bell System operating companies in the United States, and the major independent telephone companies in the United States); and (3) the smaller independent telephone companies in the United States and Canada. The first two of these segments operated full telephone systems, including local and major toll (long distance) switching systems.

Northern Telecom's close relationship with Bell Canada gave it access to operating company information which was very useful in setting product specifications and planning production. These two companies also shared the same knowledge base with Bell-Northern Research. Many executives viewed this close working relationship as providing a major advantage to both corporations. Bell typically identified its approximate requirements for switching equipment from Northern Telecom about two to three years in advance and provided detailed specifications of its needs about one year in advance. Northern Telecom provided firm price quotations at this point and such prices were required to be as low or lower than those provided to any other customer.

Alberta Government Telephones (AGT), Manitoba Telephone, and Saskatchewan Telecommunications used a more competitive buying procedure, with AGT being the most extreme on this dimension. AGT typically developed tender documents with a detailed set of specifications, and Northern Telecom and other interested manufacturers would be asked to submit bids. B.C. Telephone and Quebec Telephone were special cases in the Canadian market, reflecting their status as subsidiaries of GTE. Since GTE had its own manufacturing subsidiary, GTE Automatic Electric, B.C. Telephone and, to a lesser extent, Quebec Telephone bought most of their switching equipment from GTE Automatic Electric. B.C. Telephone only bought switching equipment from Northern Telecom when Automatic Electric didn't manufacture the required type of switch, or when Automatic Electric couldn't meet its delivery requirements. Overall, Northern Telecom's share of the Canadian central office switching market, excluding British Columbia and the market for add-on extensions to non-Northern products, was about 90 percent. Most of the remaining 10 percent went to GTE Automatic Electric.

In the United States, the major independent telephone companies, except the GTE and United Telecommunications operating companies, generally used competitive tenders to buy equipment. This left about 8 percent of the U.S. market being awarded on a competitive tender basis. Their needs and buying criteria were generally similar to the major Canadian telephone companies and, hence, they were usually seeking similar benefits from the switching products. These customers typically bought switching equipment from more than one supplier.

Many of the smaller independent telephone companies used low interest loans from the Rural Electrification Authority (REA) to buy switching equipment. The REA set specifications for switching equipment, and telephone companies using REA money to purchase switches had to use a competitive tender against specifications, with the business being awarded to the lowest bidder who met the specifications. However, a 6 percent penalty was applied to the bids of suppliers with insufficient U.S.-manufactured equipment in their proposals. In total in the United States, about 80 percent of Northern Telecom's switching equipment sales were the result of competitive tenders, with the remainder being directed orders. Many of the smaller independent telephone companies did not have a sophisticated engineering capability within their organizations. Thus, in making major decisions about what equipment to buy, they often relied on what the respected larger telephone companies were doing, particularly those that seemed to be in a position to make an "unbiased" choice.

The Bell System operating companies and the GTE operating companies generally bought almost all their central office switching equipment from Western Electric and GTE Automatic Electric, respectively. Only in rare circumstances when these manufacturing subsidiaries were unable to supply required equipment in a timely manner did they go to outside vendors.

In dealing with all segments of the market, Northern Telecom executives believed customers preferred to deal with a supplier who could offer a full line of switching equipment to meet their needs. For large telephone companies, this would include everything from small local exchanges to large local and toll exchanges.

The sales of central office switching systems was comprised of two parts: (1) the sale of the initial switch and (2) the extension sales which allowed the basic switch to be expanded to meet the growth in the market served by the exchange. In the case of the SP-1 switch, the average initial installation was approximately 8,000 lines, and the average ultimate capacity of each exchange sold was expected to be 20,000 lines. In other words, for every $1.00 spent on an SP-1 initial office, another $1.50 or more in extension sales would occur in subsequent years. Once a customer purchased an initial office from Northern Telecom or another vendor, they were committed to purchasing the extension equipment from the same vendor. Thus, the product life cycle for a central office switch such as the SP-1 was made up of two subcycles, the first being initial sales and the second being extension sales. With respect to the SP-1 sales in Canada (shown in Exhibit 1) 100 percent of the sales in the period 1970 to 1973 had been initial sales, with this percentage declining to 90 and 82 in 1974 and 1975, respectively.

The importance of extension sales to the customer also made it difficult for new suppliers, particularly foreign suppliers without local manufacturing and support facilities, to break into the central office switching market. Telephone companies had to be convinced that a supplier was in the market for the long term so that the telephone companies would be able to expand their switches and obtain spare parts many years into the future.

Central Office Switching Systems Technology

A central office switching system is the equipment that connects a telephone user's telephone with the telephone number dialed. Sometimes, as in the case of a long distance call, connections might have to be made through several central offices (local or toll exchanges) before the two telephones are connected (see Exhibit 3a). Essentially, a central office switching system has two major components: the switching network and the central control systems. The switching network is the electromechanical or electronic equipment that connects two telephone lines together and provides the dial tone, ringing, and busy signals. The control system activates the switching functions.

Digital Transmission of Speech and Data

Human speech shows up on an oscilloscope as an analog wave (see Exhibit 3b). The height of the wave is directly proportional to the level of the signal transmitted. The number of waves in a given time period is a representation of the pitch or frequency of the signal. Thus, the analog wave is a direct electrical representation of the sound waves used to generate it, and is readily converted back to sound waves at the earpiece of the receiving handset.

In a digital system, the analog wave from the transmitting source is sampled at constant intervals, represented by the dots on the wave in Exhibit 3c. A digital signal is then generated to describe the position of the dot on the wave. The digital signal takes the form of a binary word of eight bits (which can describe 256 different positions of the dot). A sample signal is shown in Exhibit 3d. In order to get an accurate representation of the original analog wave, it must be sampled several thousand times every second by a codec (*co*der and

EXHIBIT 3 Digital technology

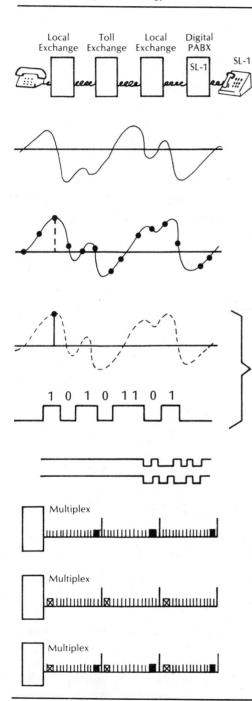

Exhibit 3a

To connect two telephones, connections might have to be made through local and toll exchanges (collectively called central office switching equipment), and perhaps through a private automatic branch exchange (PABX).

Exhibit 3b

Human speech as it shows up on an oscilloscope.

Exhibit 3c

In a digital system, the analog wave from the transmitting source is sampled at constant intervals. If the location of just the dots is transmitted, the analog wave can be accurately reconstructed at the receiving end.

Exhibit 3d

Each sampled point on the wave is converted into an 8-bit binary word.

Exhibit 3e

A digitized conversation is transmitted in this form.

Exhibit 3f

Multiplexing can be used to transmit several conversations over one pair of wires. Each conversation is assigned to its own time slots. Here, one conversation occupies one time slot, and a second conversation (marked "x") occupies a second time slot. Thus, both conversations can share the same transmission path without any interference.

Source: Company records.

*dec*oder)—a specialized electronic circuit. Technically, this process is called pulse code modulation (PCM).

After a conversation has been digitized, it looks like Exhibit 3e, with one path for transmission in each direction. This compares to only one path required to transmit analog signals. At first glance, this might seem uneconomical, but digital communication can utilize multiplexing to dramatically cut transmission costs. Multiplexing simply involves the interleaving of several conversations on a single communication path (2 wires). A sample is taken from the first conversation, then one from the second conversation, and so on, forming a frame of a predetermined number of samples. Each succeeding frame contains samples of the same conversations in the same sequence. At the receiving end, the samples are removed from the frames by a demultiplexer and the multiple analog signals reconstructed by a codec. Thus, all the conversations share the same two wire transmission path, but are separated by time (see Exhibit 3f). Technically, this approach to signal transmission was called time division multiplexing (TDM).

Switching Systems

Space division switching (SDM), with different conversations being transmitted over separate wires, was the method the telephone industry had used prior to the mid-1970s to switch its analog signals. The earliest SDM switches were electromechanical step-by-step systems (S X S systems). While these systems were cheap, relatively simple in design, and had large line capacity, they required large amounts of space, had few features, had high labour and maintenance costs, and were "noisy," making them satisfactory for voice communications but not "clean" enough for data communication.

The next generation of SDM switches, first introduced by L. M. Ericsson of Sweden and later by AT&T in the 1930s, were electromechanical crossbar switches. These crossbar switches had several advantages over S X S switches, including more features, a more compact size, and lower labour and maintenance costs. However, these systems were difficult and expensive to extend. An evolutionary improvement over the basic crossbar system was one using reed relays rather than regular relay connections for connection points in the crossbar system. The reed relays operated more rapidly, consumed less power, and were easier to control than the earlier electromechanical switches.

A major advance in switching was the development of electronic switches, the first commercial model of which was the #1 ESS switch developed by AT&T and introduced commercially in 1965. The #1 ESS switch again used SDM signal path technology.

Modern exchanges, such as the SP-1 switch, used stored program control systems. Here, the software program controlling the system is stored in the alterable memory. This allows changes in the control system to be readily made. The availability of stored-program-control systems meant that a switch could be given a variety of features by making changes in the software. The computer could be readily programmed to handle maintenance, traffic analysis, and a host of other tasks that have to be done by a telephone company.

Northern Telecom and other industry executives believed that a successful all-digital system would provide significant benefits to users and telephone companies beyond those of state of the art stored-program-control analog systems. Being able to move many times as many signals over one transmission line would lead to better utilization of communication lines. Being digital, the information being sent was always uniform; that is, it was a bit of information, either a pulse or no pulse (again, see Exhibit 3e). When a signal of this type became degraded through line loss, etc., it could readily be regenerated through the use of a digital repeater. These repeaters were tuned to look for bits and didn't blindly reproduce all signals in their inputs. Thus bits having lost their square shape could be regenerated to their original format resulting in a clean, interference-free signal. This was particularly important when transmitting data.

Northern Telecom first made use of the TDM–PCM technology in the T1 carrier which was commercially demonstrated in 1963. The T1 carrier was used for inter-exchange transmission of signals, but it was expensive to manufacture and was only economically practical on heavily used portions of a telephone company's network.

By 1972, the first laboratory samples of large-scale integrated (LSI) circuits were becoming available. This allowed very complex circuits of hundreds or thousands of individual components to be put on a tiny electronic chip. By 1975, Northern Telecom had been able, with the assistance of LSI technology, to incorpoate time division multiplexing, pulse code modulation, and stored-program-control into a private automatic branch exchange (PABX), the SL-1. A PABX is essentially a small switching system that controls the private telephone system within a company or other organization's office or factory facility.

Northern Telecom executives and engineers could envision fully digital switching and transmission systems in the future with digital switches, transmission systems, and digital PABXs all linked together. In this environment, a subscriber set generates an analog signal which travels to a line interface at the local exchange containing the codecs and multiplexers. The conversation, now in a digital format, travels through one or more toll offices to a local digital exchange. Here it could be converted to analog for a local line, or it could be forwarded in digital form to a digital PABX, where it is finally converted to analog form for the subscriber.

Competition

The market for central office switching products was intensely competitive, with North American, European, and Japanese companies competing for shares of it. The major manufacturers and their estimated sales of telecommunications equipment (including central office switching equipment) are shown in Exhibit 4.

EXHIBIT 4 Major manufacturers of telecommunications equipment and worldwide 1974 sales and net incomes

Company	Sales	Net income
Western Electric (U.S.A.)	$7,400 million	$311 million
ITT (U.S.A.)—telecommunications equipment only	3,000 million	176 million
Siemens A.G. (West Germany)—telecommunications equipment only	1,600 million	—*
L. M. Ericsson (Sweden)	1,500 million	79 million
Nippon Electric Company (Japan)	1,500 million	18 million
Northern Electric (Canada)	958 million	54 million
GTE Automatic Electric (U.S.A.)	700 million	42 million
—Canadian subsidiary	117 million	6 million
North Electric (U.S.A.)—subsidiary of United Telecommunications	290 million	7 million
Stromberg-Carlson (U.S.A.)—subsidiary of General Dynamics	234 million	10 million

* Income on total sales of $6,600 million was $92 million.

Source: *Telecommunications Market: Operating Telephone Company and Manufacturers Statistics,* Northern Electric Company Limited, 1975.

Western Electric was the largest manufacturer of central office switching equipment in the world. As a result of the 1956 consent decree, it was not generally a factor in non-AT&T markets. A high proportion of its 1975 switching equipment sales were stored-program-control ESS switches of different sizes (#1 ESS, #2 ESS and #3 ESS). In the mid-1970s, AT&T had announced a very large digital toll switch, the #4 ESS, which was for sale to non-AT&T companies in the U.S. and Canada. This was a specialized toll switch for use in the largest metropolitan areas (e.g., Toronto, Montreal and Vancouver in Canada) and had a fairly limited market. The product was expected to be available in 1976 or 1977.

Both GTE Automatic Electric and North Electric (the United Telecommunications manufacturing subsidiary) also had large captive markets in their own companies. GTE Automatic Electric's sales of its #1 EAX stored-program-control analog switch were growing, even though Northern Telecom executives believed that the SP-1 switch had better architecture and features that allowed it to be used in a wider range of applications. The announced #2 EAX switch, which was expected to be commercially available in 1978, was expected to be a very formidable competitor to the SP-1. Automatic Electric had also announced a digital medium size toll switch, the #3 EAX. This switch was scheduled for introduction in late 1978. This switch was expected to have some impact on sales of the SP-1 in toll applications. In many ways, the first serious competition for the SP-1 in 1973 and 1974 had been provided by North Electric's NX-1E stored-program-control analog switch. Several versions of the switch were available, including local and toll switches.

International Telephone & Telegraph (ITT) was the largest European-based supplier of telephone equipment. It had market shares of about 15 percent, 32 percent, 25 percent, and 42 percent of the switching market in Italy,

West Germany, United Kingdom, and France, respectively. In 1974, ITT had introduced its Metaconta-L line of stored-program-control analog switches into the North American market, and this line was beginning to provide new competition for Northern Telecom.

In 1974, Ericsson was developing and promoting its AXE stored-program-control analog switch in Europe, and some industry observers believed that this product's architecture had benefited from knowledge of the strengths and weaknesses of the SP-1 architecture, and was superior to it. Ericsson was believed to be developing digital switches that would be integrated into the AXE line.

NEC America, a subsidiary of Nippon Electric Company, manufactured a stored-program-control analog switch, the D-10. In 1974 and early 1975, NEC had been very aggressive in its pricing on some bids in North America.

A brief description of the major competitive stored-program-control analog switches that were available or had been announced for the North American market are included in Exhibit 5. While these switches had a nominal size range, they were usually most competitive within a more limited range of line sizes. These switches generally cost between $150 and $300 per line depending on the size of the switches, its features, and so forth. Exhibit 6 contains the particular switches Northern Telecom executives viewed as being most competitive in each of the major market segments. They did not view the SP-1 as being competitive in really large local and toll applications due to its maximum line size capacity. Furthermore, Stromberg-Carlson had a stranglehold on the small switch segment of the independent market with their old technology X-Y step-by-step equipment. SP-1 and other stored-program-control switches could not compete at the smaller line sizes with the X-Y system.

EXHIBIT 5 Competitive stored-program-control analog switches—available and announced

Company	Product	Nominal size range (in lines)	Comments
Northern Telecom	SP-1	3,000–25,000	
GTE Automatic Electric	#1 EAX	4,000–40,000	Competitive with SP-1 in large line sizes. Northern Telecom felt architecture inferior to SP-1. Doesn't have all the features of SP-1.
	#2 EAX	4,000–40,000	Introduction expected in 1978. Viewed as a very serious threat to SP-1.
ITT (Europe)	Metaconta-L	5,000–60,000	Introduced in 1974. Active bidding for orders in the U.S. and Canadian markets.
North Electric	NX-1E	1,000–20,000	Significant sales to U.S. independents.
Stromberg-Carlson	ESC-1	2,000–20,000	Significant sales to U.S. independents.
Siemens (West Germany)	ESK	500– 3,000	Field trial underway in North America.
Philips(Netherlands)	PRX	5,000–25,000	No sales to date in North America.
Nippon Electric	D-10	2,000–40,000	Introduced in Japan in 1971. First North American installation expected in early 1977.

Source: Company records.

EXHIBIT 6 Competition—by size and type of exchange and market segment—available and announced

	Small	Medium	Large	
			Local	Toll
Bell Canada and subsidiaries and affiliates	None*	None	None	Automatic Electric #3 EAX† Western Electric #4 ESS‡
Other Canada	Automatic Electric #1 EAX	Automatic Electric #1 EAX Automatic Electric #2 EAX	Automatic Electric #1 EAX ITT Metaconta-L	Automatic Electric #3 EAX†
United States	Automatic Electric #2 EAX North Electric NX1E Stromberg-Carlson ESC1	Automatic Electric #2 EAX Automatic Electric #1 EAX North Electric NX1E ITT Metaconta-L		

* Bell Canada would likely buy only Northern Telecom products in these sizes and types of switches.
† The Automatic Electric #3 EAX was an announced digital toll switch and was expected to be able to handle 10,000 to 20,000 trunks.
‡ The Western Electric #4 ESS was a huge digital toll switch which could handle 25,000–100,000 trunks (i.e., it was only suitable for very large metropolitan areas such as Toronto, Montreal, Vancouver, and major U.S. cities). Western Electric had begun to market this product to non-AT&T companies, including companies in Canada.

Source: Company records.

Digital Switch Development Efforts at Northern Telecom

Prior to 1969, digital switching had been regarded by the telecommunications industry as possible, but too expensive to be practical. The rapid advances in electronics in the late 1960s led Bell-Northern Research (BNR) Systems Engineering to reexamine the status of digital switching in 1968. In early 1969, they reported:

> The feasibility of integrated (TDM–PCM) switching has been demonstrated in many countries and the successful results show, without a shadow of a doubt, that such a system is technically viable. Digital switching in the present situation can hardly compete with conventional switching systems. . . . However, the near availability of large scale integrated circuits will probably change the competitive position in favour of digital switching within 5 years, and definitely within 10 years. In addition, the development of the pulse code modulation transmission system, which is now well underway in most industrialized countries, will eliminate the need for interface equipment, and, therefore, will give integrated switching a decisive advantage over conventional systems, both from economic and technical viewpoints.

They recommended that Northern Electric consider very seriously the development of an integrated digital switching system to be available for domestic sales within 7 to 10 years.

The report and its recommendations were not accepted by all managers in Bell Canada and Northern Electric. A great deal of money and manpower was then being used to bring the SP-1 stored-program-control analog switch to market. Since it incorporated the latest technology, many managers were convinced that this switch would meet the telephone companies' switching needs for the next 15 years and they were not convinced that there was a need to spend money on the exploratory development of a digital switch.

In early 1971, Bell Northern's Systems Engineering Group notified selected individuals in Bell Canada, BNR, and Northern Electric that technological advances in memories, logic, crosspoints, and so forth, now convinced them that the SP-1 system would be obsolete for new local and toll installations by 1980. Exploratory development work on digital switching had been under way in other countries for as long as 12 years. In late 1971, work began at BNR to build a laboratory "test bed" to demonstrate the technical feasibility of digital switching, and to demonstrate solid state digital switching and circuit design techniques. The test bed would also assist in providing estimates as to the costs of developing a digital switch. In 1972, an initial budget for digital research was proposed by the switching division to the Board of Northern Electric calling for expenditures of $22 million over 7 years with $1.5 million firm for 1974.

In 1972, BNR demonstrated a Large Scale Integration (LSI) codec that would be a key element in any digital switching product. This codec was a key element in the SL-1 PABX, which was to be available by late 1975. By 1973, BNR concluded that its exploratory development program had successfully demonstrated the technical feasibility of digital switching, and that the SP-1 program was providing a solid base of experience in stored-program-control techniques, much of which would be applicable to a digital switch. In late 1973, market research on the non-Bell North American market began. At the same time, a detailed economic analysis of the impact of using digital switching in Bell Canada's Montreal switching network suggested by projection that Bell Canada might be able to reduce its capital expenditures in the metropolitan areas in its service area by $100 million in the period 1982–92, if it moved to digital switching. BNR Systems Engineering was now convinced that a digital switch had good potential.

In November 1974, the Digital Switching Division was formed in Northern Telecom Canada to begin developing a product plan for the digital line. A similar organizational change occurred within BNR Development. In December 1974, the realization began to spread that development of a line of digital switches was going to require huge expenditures on research and development (much more than the $22 million envisioned in 1972), and that these expenditures might have a major negative impact on Northern Telecom's earnings. Some executives pointed out that delaying development of the digital switches for 2 or 3 years would relieve Northern Telecom's tightening cash flow situation. Selected financial data for Northern Telecom is shown in Exhibit 7.

EXHIBIT 7 Northern Telecom Limited selected financial data 1971–1974

	1974	1973	1972	1971
Earnings and related data ($ millions)				
Revenues	957.7	608.1	531.3	573.8
Revenues of company manufactured products	799.8	512.9	448.5	473.4
Research and development expenses	44.0	32.7	28.0	29.7
Provision for income taxes	49.6	30.5	21.0	14.5
Net earnings	53.8	32.0	20.1	12.6
Financial position at December 31				
Assets				
Cash and equivalent	14.1	69.4	52.3	27.4
Accounts receivable	144.9	100.1	85.5	104.5
Inventories	255.0	177.3	112.5	112.2
Current assets	433.7	360.1	260.1	253.6
Gross plant	278.2	261.5	237.5	230.0
Accumulated depreciation	158.2	142.5	128.4	124.4
Net plant	120.0	119.0	109.1	105.7
Investments in affiliates	9.0	6.5	5.5	5.0
Other assets	5.1	6.7	1.7	1.3
Total assets	567.8	492.3	376.4	365.6
Liabilities				
Current liabilities	150.6	149.7	84.9	83.3
Long-term debt	104.5	69.6	73.5	77.1
Owner liabilities	27.5	28.0	25.9	21.4
Shareholder's equity	285.2	245.0	192.1	183.8
Total liabilities	567.8	492.3	376.4	365.6

Source: Company records.

These financial concerns precipitated a major review of Northern Telecom's whole digital switching strategy. Three people were appointed to develop a marketing strategy for central office switches. A presentation was to be made to the Tricorporate Policy Coordinating Committee (which includes top executives from BNR, Northern Telecom, and Bell Canada). The task force was composed of Dr. Donald Chisholm from BNR, Mr. Lloyd Webster from product line management at Northern Telecom, and Mr. Bill Anderson from Engineering at Bell Canada.

The Situation in March 1975

While the telephone industry was still strongly feeling the effects of the 1974–75 recession, economists were beginning to forecast robust growth in the Canadian and U.S. economies in 1976 and 1977. Most Northern Telecom executives, in early 1975, believed that the degree of competition in the central office switching market would increase markedly during this same period of time. GTE's #2 EAX, and other similar second generation stored-program-control analog switches as well as late market entrants such as ITT's Metaconta-L, were expected to have a negative impact on new initial orders for the SP-1. Executives also believed that one or more of several competitors might introduce digital switches in North America in the 1978–82 time frame. Stromberg-Carlson, IBM, North Electric, Philips, ITT, Ericsson, and Nippon Electric Company were all believed to be doing some development work on digital switches, and might be able to introduce such a product in the North American market by 1980. Something had to be done to maintain and improve Northern Telecom's position in the central office switching market. Two major alternatives were open to Northern Telecom.

Alternative 1: Delay Introduction of the Digital Switching Line

To make no firm commitment to a major research and development effort on a digital switching line yet, and to merely continue with exploratory research on digital switching. Given the increasing competitive pressure on SP-1, the SP-1 could be upgraded or enhanced to make it more competitive with the second generation stored-program-control analog switches that were becoming increasingly available. Several enhancements were possible including increasing the line capacity of the switch with a new processor, improved memories, and replacing the MINIBAR electromechanical network used on the SP-1 with a sealed reed network. Northern Telecom's own tests suggested that their MINIBAR switch was cheap to manufacture and outlasted and outperformed reed networks, but many customers viewed sealed reed systems as the newer and better technology. Development costs for an enhanced version of the SP-1 (perhaps called the SP-2) might vary from $5 million to $20 million or even more depending on the particular enhancements incorporated. The risks associated with this alternative would depend on the particular enhancements selected, but were in all cases significantly less than those associated with a digital product line, since no major new advances in technology or manufacturing capability were required to bring it to market.

Alternative 2: Move Rapidly to Introduce the Digital Switching Line

To commit immediately to a heavy research and development program to introduce some or all of the digital switching products as rapidly as possible. As of March 1975, exploratory or development work was either being considered or was underway on five separate digital products:

1. D256—this was a digital switcher-concentrator which would be used in a small community to switch calls in that community and to concentrate the outgoing/incoming calls for digital transmission to/from the central office serving the community. The product was designed to serve from 24 to 256 lines. The earliest this product could be available was 1976.
2. SL-1—development work was well advanced on Northern Telecom's SL-1 PABX, which was to be available to customers in late 1975. It was considered possible to develop a small central office switch from this product by 1979.
3. DMS (no number assigned)—this was another digital switch designed to serve small local offices with 1,500 + lines. It could be available in 1979.
4. DMS (no number assigned)—this was a large digital toll switch handling up to 50,000 trunks. It could be available in 1980.
5. DMS (no number assigned)—this was a large digital local switch with the capacity to handle up to 100,000 lines. It could be available in 1981.

The work to date on the last three of these products had only been very exploratory and no firm commitment to develop them in any time frame had been made.

This line of digital products, when fully available, would greatly improve Northern Telecom's coverage of the central office switching market. Executives expected the line to provide major benefits to telephone companies in terms of low space requirements, substantial reductions in outside plant, particularly cable (given that many digital signals could be handled on one transmission line), and lower maintenance and operating costs. The proposed digital line could accommodate growth from a very small number of lines to very large line sizes, would allow telephone companies to service small communities cost effectively through the satellite switchers-concentrators and, in general, would provide the customer with a very flexible system.

While most observers of the telephone industry expected that the industry would eventually move to all digital systems, the conventional wisdom was that such a change would not really begin to occur until the early- to mid-1980s. Bell Laboratories and AT&T executives, who met frequently with the executives of independent telephone companies to set equipment standards, etc., regularly voiced this view. AT&T was heavily committed to stored-program-control analog switches (and was, in the mid-1970s, installing almost one #1 ESS office every working day, somewhere in the U.S.). Since digital transmission of signals between exchanges was increasingly prevalent in North America, Bell Labs and Western Electric people claimed that the logical point of entry for digital switches was in large toll switches, since the digital machines could be directly tied into the digital transmission network without the need for any analog to digital interfacing. This was where Western Electric's #4 ESS and Automatic Electric's #3 EAX switches would fit. Thus, it was generally believed that, at that time, digital switching provided few advantages at the local exchange level.

Within Northern Telecom's digital alternatives there were options. Work on parts of the line could be accelerated by increasing expenditures on R&D, or cash could be conserved in the period 1975–78 by initially focusing development on the small local offices (products 1 to 3). Two of the possible plans under consideration were:

Plan A—Focus major development efforts on the small local office switch only. With this option, R&D expenditures on the digital line would be $32 million. The small local office would be available in 1979.

Plan B—Develop the architectural concepts for the total line initially with a phased introduction of the digital line (small local office in 1979, large toll office in 1980, and a large local office in 1981). Under this plan, R&D expenditures were expected to total $66 million.

Some managers were also concerned that a major acceleration of the digital line could have a negative impact on its future competitiveness. In one internal memorandum to members of the task force, it was pointed out that "the timing of the digital switch affects the technology/manufacturing plateau on which the design will be based—too soon may result in noncompetitive costs after initial introduction. Too advanced a technology base may result in a high risk design, delays, and subsequent field problems." In the same memorandum, the vice president of marketing pointed out that the realization of the full potential of a digital switch would only be realized in a digital transmission environment. The greater the amount of digital transmission equipment in place, the less interfacing needed between analog and digital switches, and the more economical the digital switch would be. However, the vice president of marketing stated that he felt that even in early 1975 the mix of digital/analog transmission circuits was such as to make the cost savings significant for most telephone companies.

If the decision was made to proceed rapidly with the digital switching line, top management realized that an integral part of their decision was when and how to time announcements of the various products. Sales of the SP-1 were growing rapidly, and management wanted to sell as many initial offices as possible in order to generate the largest volume of subsequent extension business. This extension business was captive business and was typically more profitable than the initial orders, since competitive pressures were less and costs were lower. Furthermore, announcement of a digital switch competitive with the SP-1 would probably have a negative impact on the sales of this product and its product life cycle.

Preparing for the Presentation

As the members of this task force began putting together their presentation for the Tricorporate Policy Coordinating Committee meeting on March 6, 1975, they realized that this was perhaps the most critical decision Northern Telecom would make in the 1970s. The R&D costs involved in developing the digital switching line were very large compared to other projects Northern Telecom had been involved in in the past. The technological problems associated with the digital switches were huge—one executive, who was familiar with the technical problems involved, suggested that the development of the digital toll switch alone was about eight times as complex as the problems of developing the SP-1. But the market potential for central office switches was huge. One study done by Northern Telecom market researchers suggested that the market available to Northern Telecom in North America alone would be about $1.5 billion between 1980 and 1984 (see Exhibit 8). This excluded any extension sales and possible sales to the telephone operating companies of AT&T, GTE (including B.C. Telephone in Canada), and United Telecommunications. In one confidential internal memorandum that the task force had just received from a member of their staff, the manager stated:

> Can Northern afford the program? Central office switching is the real strength of the industry. It is the most difficult to get into because of the high investment needed and the depth of experience to reduce (customer risk). It also represents essentially a captive long-term business once the initial offices are sold. *Northern Telecom cannot really afford not to be in digital switching*—it is a matter of minimizing investment and selecting the right time. If it comes to a choice of priorities, there are many other product investments that should be cancelled before Northern's position in the central office switching business is jeopardized.

The week before the March 6 meeting, Mr. Lloyd Webster, the Northern Telecom representative on the task force was to meet with the top management group of Northern Telecom to hammer out their position with respect to digital switching for the Policy Coordinating Committee meeting. As he reviewed all the inputs provided by a large number of Northern Telecom managers, he wondered what position he should take in the meeting with Northern Telecom top management. As he thought about the decision, he kept coming back to the risks involved for Northern Telecom. "Are we sure we can build a digital line? Are we right that this is the time to go digital, when Bell Laboratories and others think it is premature? Are we willing to bet $70 million of Northern Telecom's money that this is the right time to go digital? What is the probability, if we do choose a digital option, that all we do is kill a successful profitable product line?"

EXHIBIT 8 Estimated size of available North American market ($ millions)

Year	Canada* Local	Toll	U.S.A.† Local	Toll	Total	Number of equivalent lines (000's)‡
1980	73	17	86	4	180	630
1981	82	18	196	5	300	1,100
1982	93	19	205	5	322	1,240
1983	105	20	210	5	340	1,290
1984	112	21	220	5	358	1,365
Total	465	95	917	23	1,500	5,640

* Canadian available market excludes B.C. Telephone requirement, SP-1 extension sales, and all crossbar and step-by-step extension sales.

† U.S.A. available market excludes AT&T, GTE, and United Telecommunications markets, and the SP-1 extension market. The toll market includes only the one U.S. independent telephone company, that had previously bought a medium-sized toll switch from Northern Telecom. This was believed to be a conservative estimate of the available toll market in the United States.

‡ Equivalent lines were calculated by adding the number of local lines to five times the number of toll trunks.

Source: Company records.

Case 14

Southgate Shopping Center*

In April 1976, Mr. Dale Schlesinger, manager of Southgate Shopping Center in southeast suburban Cleveland, Ohio, pondered a formidable new competitor destined to open a bare eight tenths of a mile away by the following August. The new competitor was a gigantic shopping mall, Randall Park Mall, billed as the largest in the world. It had been under construction for well over a year. In April, one of the department store sites had been finished, and the Penney store at Southgate closed its doors and moved to the new shopping center. In so doing, the J. C. Penney Co. enlarged its store from 65,000 square feet to 200,000 square feet. The new mall when completely opened in August would have five other major department stores in addition to hundreds of smaller stores.

Southgate

Origin and Facilities

The center is located on major traffic interceptors near an interstate highway. Southgate is presently the largest shopping center in Ohio and one of the largest in the United States. However, it is nothing like the behemoth soon to open. It consists of 135 stores and 1,350,000 square feet of building area; parking is available for 9,000 cars. However, it is old. It was opened in 1955 with 36 stores. Penney's was the first department store to come into Southgate, doing so in 1956 with the same 65,000 square foot store that it was leaving in 1976. Over the next several decades, Southgate experienced several expansions that brought it to its present sales of $150 million a year.

Southgate is not an enclosed mall for the all-weather comfort that is the mark of most new shopping centers constructed in the last decade. Furthermore, Southgate is not even a mall. (A mall center is the prototype for virtually all

---

* This case was written by Robert F. Hartley, Professor of Marketing, and Donald W. Scotton, Professor and Chairperson, Department of Marketing, Cleveland State University. Used with permission.

large centers today. Two or more department stores typically are placed at either end, with smaller specialty stores between. The major feature of a mall is a pedestrian walkway in the center. The entire complex can be enclosed or roofed to create all-weather shopping. Benches, trees, fountains, and "outdoor" restaurants are often placed in the mall. Parking typically is on all sides. The larger malls may have several floors of stores, each opening to the mall.) Rather, Southgate is a strip center that has grown in separate phases to accommodate the increase in consumer demand. Exhibit 1 shows the layout of Southgate.

EXHIBIT 1 Physical layout of Southgate

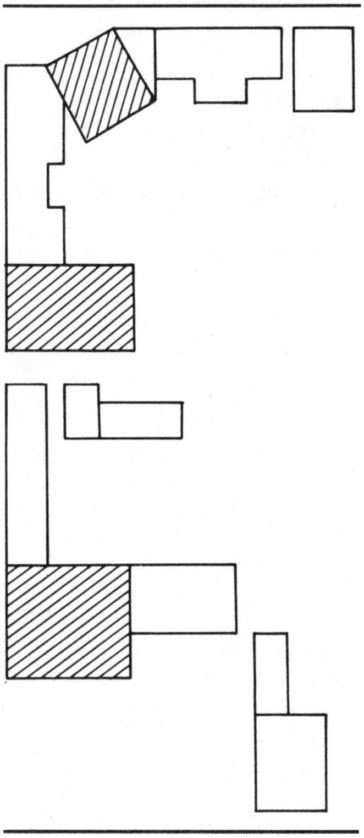

The Stores

There were three department stores: the Penney store of 65,000 square feet, and the May Company and Sears Roebuck stores, each having approximately 200,000 square feet. These stores are known as generator stores. That is, they pull people to them, sometimes from a considerable distance, and thereby contribute greatly to the traffic flow in their vicinity. Typically, in most shopping centers the greatest customer traffic is near the major department stores; these then become vital to the overall success of a shopping center. With the imminent opening of Randall Park Mall, Southgate is facing an erosion of its generator stores. As noted before, Penney's has already left, and as of June 1976, the 65,000 square foot former Penney store was standing vacant. Sears will be leaving Southgate in March; the May Company store intends to remain there, but May Company and Sears are both opening new units in the new mall, only eight tenths of a mile away. Exhibit 2 shows the directory of stores in the Southgate Center prior to development of the Randall Park Mall.

EXHIBIT 2 Southgate store directory

Department stores, general merchandise, and variety stores
F. W. Woolworth
J. C. Penney
May Company
Sears, Roebuck

Apparel stores (men's)
Bond Clothes
Calvin's Specialty Shop
Cleveland Tux Shop
Diamond's Men's Shop
Harry's Clothing
Jerry Mills Clothes
Lyon Tailors
Parker's
Richman Brothers
Southgate Custom Tailor
Tie Rack

Apparel stores (women's)
Bride & Formal
Klothes Line
Lane Bryant
Lerner Shop
Life Uniform
Motherhood Maternity Shop
Parklane Hosiery
Red Robin
Town & Country Shop

Ups & Downs
Winkelman's

Shoe stores
Dr. Scholl's Foot Comfort Shoes
Faflik Shoes
Flagg Shoes
Hahn Shoes
Miles Shoes
Nobil Shoes
Thom McAn Shoes
The In Step

Food Stores and restaurants
A&P
Arby's Beef House
American Harvest Health Food
Blue Grass Restaurant
Butcher Shop, The
Euclid Fish
Famous Recipe Restaurant
Fanny Farmer Candies
Fisher Fazio-Costa
Hough Bakery
International House of Pancakes
Lombardo's Pizza & Spaghetti
Maxson's Restaurant
New York Bakery
Oriental Terrace Restaurant
Pick-N-Pay

Teddi's Restaurant
York Steak House

Service establishments
Allied Wigs
Andre Duval
Central National Bank
Cleveland Automobile Club
Cleveland Trust Company
Continental Bank
Cuyahoga Savings
D. O. Summers
Midland Guardian Loans
Mr. Angelo Wigs
National City Bank
Southgate Key & Shoe Repair
Southgate Laundromat
Southgate Patio Barbers
Southgate Village Barber Shop
Southgate Village Beauty Salon
Sun Finance
The Hair Dresser
Third Federal Savings & Loan Association
Travel Agent Tours
Union Commerce Bank
Union Savings & Loan
Universal CIT Credit Corporation

EXHIBIT 2 *(concluded)*

U.S. Life Credit
United States Post
 Office

Miscellaneous
Agency Rent-A-Car
Alexander Flowers
A. M. Rose Tile
Bandstand Records
Bedrooms Unlimited
Big Auto Center
Blonder's
Burrow's
Candle Barn
Cleveland Typewriter
Fun City
Goodyear Service
 Center
Great Phone Company
Immerman's Craft
 Center
Industrial Electric

J. B. Robinson
 Jewelers
Jo Ann Fabrics
Kronheim's
Laurel Camera
Leader Personnel
Lemon Tree Cards &
 Gifts
Marlen Jewelers
Mr. Magic Car Wash
Olan Mills Studios
One-Hour Martinizing
Owl Optical
Pearl Carpet
Pet Kingdom
Pompelli Organs
Putt-Putt Golf Course
Radio Shack
Rayco Seat Covers
Regal Carpeting
R.H.P. Auto Centers
Sample House

Sherwin Williams Paint
 Store
Singer Sewing Center
Southgate Beverages
Southgate Cinema
Southgate Jewelry
Southgate Lanes
Southgate Music
 Center
State Liquor Store
Sun Optical
Uniroyal Home &
 Tire Center
Furniture Land
Vision Center
Weight Watchers

Drug stores
Cunningham Drug
Gray Drug
Southgate Medical
 Pharmacy

Draw of Southgate

The major newspaper of Cleveland, *The Plain Dealer,* has for many years served its advertisers by conducting research as to the "draw" of the major shopping centers in the Cleveland metropolitan area. In this research, license plates of cars in the parking lots of their respective shopping centers are recorded and then traced to their home address. In 1975, a study was made about the Southgate shopping center: 6,631 cars were thus observed and their home locations geographically plotted. This study was done long before Randall Park Mall had opened, although it was under construction at the time.

It was found that 42.9 percent of the cars in attendance at Southgate came from more than five miles away. The survey also found that 48.9 percent of the cars were from the suburban communities of Maple Heights, Garfield Heights, and Bedford—these being located either contiguous to Southgate or south and southwest of it. The next highest percentage of cars was from east Cleveland, with 21.5 percent. An analysis of traffic by economic areas showed that 77.1 percent of the cars were from census tracts with median incomes of more than $11,000.[1]

---

[1] *Analysis of Customer Attendance, Southgate, 1975,* Marketing and Research Department, *The Plain Dealer,* Cleveland, Ohio.

Randall Park Mall

Randall Park Mall is located almost straight north of Southgate. It will have six major department stores for generators, and 260 other stores, altogether some 2.2 million square feet all under one roof. Exhibit 3 shows a physical diagram of the complex. Sales have been estimated "conservatively" at $200 million for the first year.

EXHIBIT 3 Physical layout of Randall Park Mall

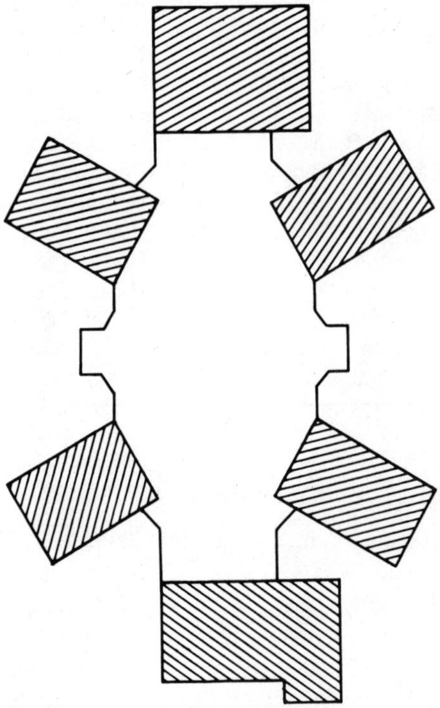

In typical mall fashion, parking in profusion will be on all sides of the complex. The enclosed mall will permit an array of amenities upon which one can only speculate before the grand opening. Two interstate highways are in close proximity to the new center.

Trends in Shopping Center Development

Mr. Dale Schlesinger, manager of Southgate, indicated that the trend in shopping centers is toward giantism. But as shopping centers become larger, it seems reasonable to expect that there must be an ultimate limit to size. How far is the average customer willing to walk? How many levels of stores can be piled up without confusing the customer? How many cars can be accommodated in a parking lot before the logistics of parking, finding one's car, and hiking to it will become too burdensome? And how about traffic congestion near a huge shopping center?

Despite these nagging worries, developers are building ever-bigger shopping complexes, and seemingly doing so successfully:

> Billed at the time as the world's largest enclosed multilevel shopping center, Woodfield opened 25 miles northwest of Chicago. It cost $90 million to construct, has 2 million square feet of space, 215 shops and services, and three major department stores, including the largest stores Sears and Penney have ever built and the largest suburban store that Marshall Field has ever put up.[2]

Along with these huge retail centers, often other commercial, recreational, and cultural facilities are developed nearby, such as hotels, apartment houses, office buildings, cultural centers, churches, and theaters. The result is that more and more the newer giant shopping centers are becoming miniature downtowns. A. Alfred Taubman, developer of Woodfield, says: "We are not competing against other centers or suburban business districts. We are competing against downtown Chicago. So we must come as close as we can to the strength and depth of selection you find in Chicago's core area. And if that kind of philosophy means building gigantic centers, then that's what we'll build."[3]

Edward J. DeBartolo, the nation's largest shopping center developer (who is building the Randall Park Mall), has built over 30 large ones in 10 years. He has never had a failure and he knows of few. DeBartolo says, "the national failure rate [of large shopping centers] over 25 years has been a fraction of 1 percent."[4]

What kind of a drawing power can a large center generate? Gene A. Robens, general manager of a southern California 1.2 million square foot mall, says: "When you talk about a shopping center as large as ours, you have to be sure you can draw from a 10- to 15-mile radius."[5] For the 2.2 million square foot facility of Randall Park Mall, conjecture is that it will draw from Akron 30 miles to the south, from Youngstown 50 miles to the southeast, and even from western Pennsylvania 70 miles to the east.

Reactions of Southgate

Mall Manager

Despite the looming threat of unknown magnitude, and the actual or imminent departure of two of his major tenants, Penney's and Sears, Dale Schlesinger

---

[2] "Shopping Centers Grow into Shopping Cities," *Business Week,* September 4, 1971, p. 34.

[3] Ibid., p. 38.

[4] As quoted in *Forbes,* "Why Shopping Centers Rode Out the Storm," June 1, 1976, p. 35.

[5] "Shopping Centers Grow into Shopping Cities," p. 38.

was not unduly worried. While he expected to lose some business initially, he thought this would be soon regained. He admitted that for the first three months of the Randall Park opening, it would be impossible to compete. The sheer volume of grand opening advertising—both on the part of the mall itself, and that of individual tenants—and the natural curiosity that the general public would have to visit this huge agglomeration of stores, would defeat any defensive efforts Southgate might take at this time. Schlesinger conceded that he was projecting a 10 percent loss of sales the first year after the Randall opening. He expected sales to be back to normal in the second year. "We think Southgate will remain viable, and will even have long-term growth," Schlesinger stated.

While the loss of two of his major traffic generators might seem like a major blow to the center, Schlesinger was negotiating with both K mart and Wards to replace Penneys and Sears. In the spring of 1976, there was still a waiting list of prospective tenants for the smaller stores and shops.

Strengths of Southgate Relative to Randall Park Mall

In defense of his optimistic attitude regarding the new competition, Schlesinger noted a number of natural advantages that should accrue to Southgate.

First, he thought Southgate would benefit from a "spillover effect." By this, he expected that the sheer size and resulting volume of traffic drawn to the Randall Park Mall would result in such congestion, confusion, and shopping inconvenience that a goodly portion of shoppers would look around for a nearby and more convenient center to fill at least some of their shopping needs. Because Southgate was less than a mile away, it would be the primary beneficiary of this spillover business.

Southgate presents its tenants with a definite rent advantage over the new mall. The range of rents per square foot are $2 to $8 at Southgate, versus $8 to $18 at Randall Park Mall. The difference in rents—which reflects the older center constructed at a time of much lower costs—could provide a major deterrent for any Southgate tenant contemplating a move to the new mall. More profit could be achieved at considerably less sales volume than would be the case at Randall. The lower cost structure also means that most tenants should be able to ride out the several lean months associated with the grand opening at the competing mall.

Southgate presumably offers its customers more ease and convenience of shopping. Being smaller and an attenuated strip type of center, customers can park close to the doors of those stores they want to visit; and they can get in and out faster than would be possible in a large mall. Furthermore, Southgate has three large supermarkets and these are big generators of customer traffic on a continuous basis. It is not expected that Randall Park Mall will have any supermarkets, and indeed an enclosed mall is not the ideal setting for such a store due to the inconvenience of handling bulky purchases. Therefore, Southgate is assured of considerable customer traffic regardless of Randall Park Mall.

Schlesinger also cited the probability that customer loyalty built up over 20 years with the "friendly merchants" of Southgate would not be quickly lost. "While customers may initially go to Randall Park Mall out of curiosity, many of them will come back here to buy, back to where they're known and appreciated."

Perhaps Southgate has another potential advantage vis-à-vis Randall. A major part of its customers come from the south. And the new Randall Mall is north of Southgate. This puts Southgate in the position of being an "interceptor." It is sited between a major source of customers and the new shopping mall. Many people may evince reluctance to pass by a shopping center—such as Southgate—to get exactly the same product at a greater distance. Of course, Randall Park Mall will act as an interceptor for customers coming from the north, and Southgate may get few of these customers. But according to the shopping center study of customer attendance conducted by the Cleveland *Plain Dealer*, Southgate was not getting much of this business before the opening of the Randall Park Mall.

Southgate Merchant Attitudes

The attitudes of the mall management at Southgate are optimistic. But how about the attitudes of the individual store operators? Are they as optimistic, or are they running scared? In a research study conducted by students at Cleveland State University, 30 merchants at Southgate were interviewed. While parts of the interviews are unstructured, one aspect was completely structured. The merchants were asked to check their attitudes and intentions to react on a series of scales numbered from 1 to 7, as shown in Exhibit 4.

While the range of responses, particularly to questions 1 and 2, was wide, reflecting those who thought the new mall would affect Southgate and their

EXHIBIT 4

1. What do you think will be the effect of Randall Park Mall on your shopping center?

Will affect severely		Will affect slightly		Will not affect		Will affect favorably
1	2	3	4	5	6	7

Results: median of 30 responses, 3.5.

2. What do you think will be the effect of Randall Park Mall on your store here?

Will affect severely		Will affect slightly		Will not affect		Will affect favorably
1	2	3	4	5	6	7

Results: median of 30 responses, 3.9.

EXHIBIT 4 *(concluded)*

3. What changes, if any, do you think you will make due to Randall Park Mall?

(a)	Much more advertising		Somewhat more advertising			No change in advertising	
1	2	3	4	5		6	7

Results: median of 30 responses, 5.3.

(b)	Much lower prices		Somewhat lower prices			No change in prices	
1	2	3	4	5		6	7

Results: median of 30 responses, 6.0.

(c)	Much more merchandise assortment		Somewhat more merchandise assortment			No change in merchandise assortment	
1	2	3	4	5		6	7

Results: median of 30 responses, 6.1.

(d)	Substantial remodeling		Some remodeling			No change in facilities	
1	2	3	4	5		6	7

Results: median of 30 responses, 6.5.

business severely to those who thought the effect would be favorable, the median and the concentration of attitudes was that there would be no more than a slight effect. And the planned reactions to the new mall were generally "do nothing different." Thus the general optimism of Dale Schlesinger regarding the impact of Randall Park Mall on Southgate was supported by a majority of the merchants.

Planned Centerwide Promotions and Marketing Strategy

The management of Southgate Center conceded that nothing could be done to combat or defend against the expected massive promotional thrust of the grand opening of Randall Park Mall. "Any advertising or other promoting we do for the first three months of the grand opening push of Randall would be simply money down the drain." But promotional efforts are being expanded, both for the period before this grand opening and for the time after the initial excitement of a grand opening has ebbed.

Starting April 12, 1976, more than three months before the scheduled opening of Randall, TV commercials (which are new for the shopping center industry in Cleveland) are planned for the three major TV channels. These will be narrated by Ted Knight of the "Mary Tyler Moore Show" and will stress the convenience and variety of stores and services available at Southgate. These TV commercials will be run over a two-year period, but with time out during the three months of the Randall grand opening.

Radio has been used regularly in the past 20 years to promote the entire shopping center, informing about special events, and in particular playing up the convenience of shopping at Southgate. It will continue to be used with newspapers, the traditional medium for retail advertising.

Southgate has had annual major shopping center promotions that have always attracted large crowds. A Christmas Parade and a Sidewalk Fair have been two of the most successful. It should be recognized, however, that an extended strip center such as Southgate has more difficulty in running overall shopping center promotions than mall-type shopping centers. Malls are more compact, less strung out, and the new enclosed center malls are adaptable to a variety of promotions. Auto shows, art exhibits, minicircuses, special exhibits of all kinds, and many types of entertainers such as rock 'n' roll bands and magician acts can readily be accommodated in the mall. These pull considerable customer traffic which benefits all tenants.

The Southgate management does not plan to permit the center to run down or deteriorate. Mr. Schlesinger responded that external repairs will be made as needed: "We certainly are not running scared." At the same time, there is no need to do extensive remodeling to make Southgate "more competitive." Eventually there may be some remodeling, especially in the area of lighting, but not until after Randall opens and the initial impact becomes more muted.

Admittedly the huge new mall cannot be entirely countered by Southgate. There is no way for it to remake itself into another colossal mall to match Randall. Its physical structure does not permit some of the "extra touches" that developers can throw into a mall, such as fountains and waterfalls; two- and three-story sculptures; trees, shrubs, and flowers; and colorful birds in huge cages. Nor can Southgate match the greatest amenity of all: an enclosed, climate-controlled mall for comfortable all-weather shopping, impervious to rain, sleet, snow, and summer heat.

But Dale Schlesinger is betting that Randall Park Mall is too big for its own good. "After all, a customer needs only so much variety of goods; after that, the additional variety simply becomes redundant." Southgate stands ready and conveniently nearby to catch the spillover of customers satiated with the sheer size of Randall.

Case 15

The Clorox Company*

As a part of his regular procedure for reviewing the health of the company's marketing operation, John S. Hanson, group vice president, The Clorox Company, decided to take a look at the brand management system through the eyes of an impartial outsider. How, in other words, would a nonmarketing, consumer product observer see the Clorox system? How would the observations be interpreted and what were the implications of these observations in respect to the selection of new brand managers?

To this end an engineering manager enrolled in the Stanford Sloan Program was given permission during the spring of 1977 to interview throughout the company and to write up his impressions.

History of the Company

The Electro-Alkaline Company of Oakland, California, began commercial production of liquid chlorine bleach in 1913. The initial markets for this new product were limited to laundries, breweries, walnut wood bleachers, and municipal water companies. These companies used the product for bleaching, stain removing, deodorizing, and disinfecting. The original form of the product was a much more concentrated solution than is currently available on the retail market. In 1914 the Clorox brand name was registered, the company's diamond trademark was registered the following year, and in 1922 the firm changed its name to Clorox Chemical Corporation. During its first eight years of business the company achieved distribution in the Pacific Coast states and Nevada and initiated eastern U.S. distribution with the appointment of a distributor in Philadelphia. Advertising was begun in 1925 in 20 western newspapers and four farm journals. In 1928 the company was reorganized as Clorox Chemical Company, and common stock was issued for the first time. By 1939 the

* This case was written by Jack Moorman and Stephen A. Snow.

Reprinted from *Stanford Business Cases 1978* with permission of the publishers, Stanford University Graduate School of Business, © 1978 by the Board of Trustees of the Leland Stanford Junior University.

company operated production facilities in Oakland, Chicago, and Jersey City. By 1955, 10 additional plants were in operation around the country. In 1953 the Clorox Company initiated spot television advertising.

In 1957 the Procter & Gamble Company acquired Clorox Chemical Company, but within three months the FTC charged Procter & Gamble with attempting to lessen competition among household bleach manufacturers. Shortly thereafter the FTC ruled that Procter & Gamble had to divest itself of Clorox. Litigation continued until 1968 when the Supreme Court upheld the FTC ruling. Directly after the Supreme Court ruling the Purex Corporation, manufacturers of the principal competitor of Clorox liquid bleach, filed suit against Procter & Gamble, charging that the company's acquisition of Clorox violated antitrust laws.

During 1968 Procter & Gamble divested itself of Clorox by offering for sale 15 percent of Clorox stock and subsequently offering the remaining 85 percent to Procter & Gamble shareholders on the basis of 3.85 shares of Clorox stock for each share of Procter & Gamble stock. The stock was listed on the New York Stock Exchange in August, and in January 1969 Clorox began operation as an independent company. (See Exhibit 1 for relevant data regarding Clorox's operations during the period 1968 to 1977.)

EXHIBIT 1 Clorox Company performance, 1968–1977

Year ending June 30	1977	1976	1975	1974	1973
Net sales*	$872,817	$822,101	$721,505	$537,601	$412,631
Net income*	32,265	27,262	21,150	19,656	26,922
Earnings per share (primary)	1.44	1.22	.95	.88	1.23†

Year ending June 30	1972	1971	1970	1969	1968
Net sales*	$188,203	$145,866	$ 98,212	$ 85,365	$ 85,854
Net income*	19,252	15,031	12,010	11,173	11,411
Earnings per share (primary)	2.15	1.68	1.48	1.40	1.43

* In thousands of dollars.
† Reflects two-for-one stock split effective November 1972.

Product Expansion

Until 1969 the Clorox Company made and sold only one product, Clorox liquid bleach. With the exception of one unsuccessful introduction of a general purpose household cleaning solution, Boon, in 1946, the company's new product introductions consisted of minor variations[1] of its basic brand of liquid bleach or of package modifications.

After the divestiture by Procter & Gamble, however, Clorox management

---

[1] The basic product was never changed, although changes in the strength of the bleach solution were attempted.

began to implement a previously adopted program of growth which called for the development of: (1) a line of nonfood household products; (2) a line of specialty food products; (3) a line of food and nonfood products for the food service industry.

The company planned to seek acquisitions to accelerate its sales and earnings growth. At the same time it would strengthen existing brands and over the long term expand its business through internal development of new products.

The first step toward a broadened line of retail consumer products was the acquisition of Jiffee Chemical Corporation, manufacturer of Liquid-plumr drain opener. This was closely followed by the acquisition of Formula 409 Spray Cleaner from Harrell International. Exhibit 2 presents the proliferation of Clorox-owned brands which are marketed by Clorox.

The expansion into the food service line began several years later. In 1972 Clorox acquired the Martin-Brower Company, a distributor of disposable packaging items, food and nonfood products, and restaurant supplies to fast-food restaurants and institutions. The Clorox Company also established the Clorox food service products division to market institutional versions of its retail brands. (See Exhibit 3 for Clorox performance on the three basic groups.)

EXHIBIT 2 Product expansion, Clorox Company 1969–1977

Brand name	Description	Source of development	Year acquired or marketed
Liquid-plumr	Drain opener	Acquisition	1969
Clorox 2	Nonchlorine, dry oxygen bleach	Internally developed	1969
Formula 409	General purpose household cleaner	Acquisition	1970
Formula 409	Disinfectant bathroom cleaner	Acquisition	1970
Litter Green	Cat box filler	Acquisition*	1971
BinB Mushrooms	Canned mushrooms, broiled in butter	Acquisition	1971
Kitchen Bouquet	Flavoring sauce	Acquisition	1971
Cream of Rice	Hot cereal	Acquisition	1971
Hidden Valley Ranch	Salad dressing mixes	Acquisition	1972
Kingsford	Charcoal briquets and barbecue products	Acquisition	1973
Prime Choice	Steak sauce	Internally developed	1973
Mr. Mushroom	Mushrooms in natural cooking juices	Internally developed	1973
Cooking Ease	Natural vegetable cooking spray	Acquisition	1974
Salad Crispins	Seasoned croutons	Acquisition	1974
Soft Scrub	Mild-abrasive liquid cleaner	Internally developed	1977

* Patents and concepts for institutional products were purchased, and these were subsequently developed into consumer products.

EXHIBIT 3 Clorox performance 1972–1977 by basic lines of business ($ millions)

Year ending June 30	1977	1976	1975	1974	1973	1972
Net sales						
Retail consumer products						
Nonfood products	$342.5	$308.7	$268.1	$223.8	$225.8	$167.6
Specialty food products	63.7	59.7	56.7	44.0	25.8	20.6
Subtotal	406.2	368.4	324.8	267.8	251.6	188.2
Food service industries	466.6	453.7	396.7	269.8	161.0	—
Total	$872.8	$822.1	$721.5	$537.6	$412.6	$188.2
Income*						
Retail consumer products	$ 74.6	$ 55.0	$ 43.4	$ 32.8	$ 46.9	$ 41.5
Food service industries	3.6	5.8	7.5	7.2	5.5	—
Total	$78.2	$ 60.8	$ 50.9	$ 40.0†	$ 52.4	$ 41.5

* Income before taxes on income and before allocation of corporate expenses not directly attributable to a specific line of business.
† Does not reflect one-time loss from discontinued operations.

As new companies were acquired, they often maintained their organizational integrity within the Clorox corporate structure. Indeed, in several instances newly acquired companies were treated as separate profit centers. The corporate organization underwent various revisions during the first few years after the Clorox divestiture from Procter & Gamble. (See Exhibit 4 for the current organization of the Clorox Company.)

In the 1973 annual report, Clorox President Robert Shetterly informed stockholders that he was deemphasizing acquisitions as a means of further product expansion during the short term and that emphasis would be placed on utilizing internal resources for new product development. As a step toward this objective, the company moved to supplement its R&D capabilities by signing a 10-year agreement with Henkel KGaA of West Germany in 1974. Henkel is the second largest European producer of detergents, cleaners, and related products. It subsequently acquired a minority equity position in Clorox by purchasing 20 percent of the company's outstanding shares. Under the terms of the agreement Clorox is licensed to market Henkel-developed products on a royalty basis in the United States, Canada, and Puerto Rico and has access to Henkel technology for developing new products. Clorox agreed to pay Henkel minimum royalties of $1 million per year beginning in 1976. These payments will be credited against future royalties earned by Henkel on products marketed by Clorox.

In the 1977 annual report, Shetterly announced that Clorox once again was looking for suitable acquisitions to build the company's business. At the time, he said, Clorox would seek opportunities to expand its liquid bleach market internationally.

Clorox ventured into the international sphere in 1973 when it set up a Canadian marketing operation that eventually would sell most of the company's

EXHIBIT 4 The Clorox Company organizational diagram

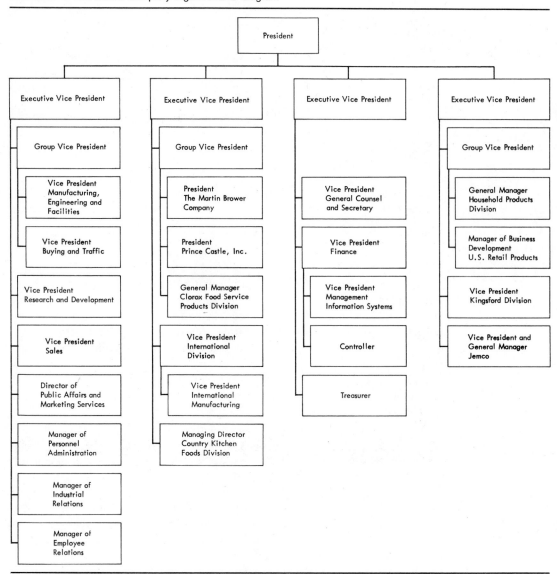

retail products as well as a line of household cleaners and personal products marketed in Canada under the French Maid brand name. That same year Clorox acquired Country Kitchen Foods, England's leading mushroom growing and marketing company. In 1975 the company began bleach production in its first offshore plant in Puerto Rico. In addition, in the period between divestiture from P&G and 1975, the company had developed export markets for liquid bleach in about 30 countries and had licenses that produced Clorox in Latin America and the Middle East.

The Brand Management System

Clorox has been a strong supporter of brand management. In 1977 the marketing operation in the household products division was organized as shown in Exhibit 5.

EXHIBIT 5

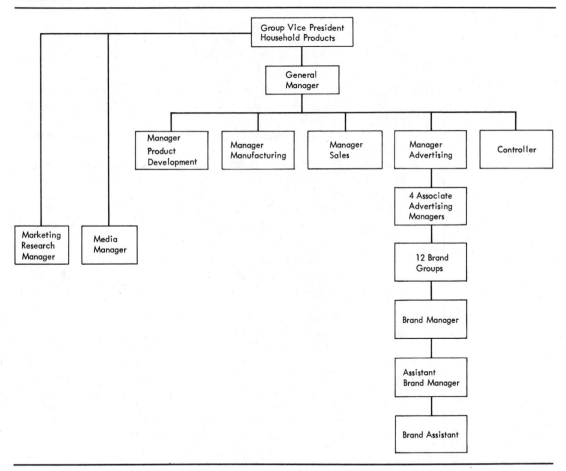

Although a bit unusual from an orthodox organization point of view, it is useful for the reader to think in terms of two subdivisions below General Manager: (1) Brand and (2) all other. The significance of this dichotomy will be explained shortly and underlies the heart of the Clorox system.

There were five job levels in the brand system: brand assistant (BA), assistant brand manager (ABM), brand manager (BM), associate advertising manager (AAM), and advertising manager (AM). The focus of this case is on the brand manager and lower levels, that is, assistant brand manager and brand assistant. (See Exhibits 6, 7, and 8 for relevant job descriptions.)

EXHIBIT 6

Job description
Clorox brand manager

Function: To contribute to the overall growth of Clorox through development, recommendation, and implementation of effective marketing programs capable of building brand volume, share, and profit for assigned brands. The brand manager is charged to:

a. Provide management with relevant data regarding the state of the business, serving as management's antennae in the category to identify problems and opportunities.
b. Develop recommendations which are designed to stimulate brand growth.
c. See that all programs are coordinated and run properly, serving as the focal point for all brand related activity.
d. Insure that brand personnel learn the skills to handle multifaceted responsibilities of the job.

The brand manager's specific marketing responsibilities are as follows:
1. *Product*—Insure that the product and package are superior to competition within cost constraints demanded by the marketplace and profit considerations. Requires consumer usage/attitude and product research, establishment of product improvement objectives, and periodic review of progress toward these objectives.
2. *Positioning*—Position the product to maximize volume within the existing consumer and competitive environments. Periodically review marketing strategy in light of changing consumer needs, wants, and attitudes, and competitive product positionings and sales. Develop and test alternative copy and promotion strategies attuned to the marketing strategy to improve the brand's overall positioning.
3. *Copy*—Insure that the copy provides the optimum selling power. Demands an ongoing effort in development and testing of new copy pools, different executional formats, and alternative copy strategies.
4. *Media*—Insure that media plans are designed to deliver advertising in the most effective and efficient manner against the brand's target audience. Requires periodic review of target audience criterion and testing of alternative mixes of media vehicles within budget constraints, as well as testing of different media weights.
5. *Promotion*—Plan, execute, and evaluate with the assistance of the sales department consumer and trade promotions which are cost-effective in increasing brand volume. Demands testing of a variety of promotions each

EXHIBIT 6 *(concluded)*

> fiscal year and testing, on a periodic basis, alternative annual promotion levels and/or alternative consumer/trade promotion splits within existing budgets.
>
> 6. *Volume control*—Make adjustments as necessary in fiscal year plans to deliver volume base.
>
> *The brand manager's specific management information responsibilities are as follows:*
>
> 1. *Volume*—If fiscal year overshipment or undershipment seems obvious, inform management and recommend action.
> 2. *Competitive developments*—Report significant competitive activity and recommend defensive action.
> 3. *Product problems*—Analyze and recommend action on any product or package problems which threaten volume.
> 4. *Problem markets*—Identify, analyze, and propose remedial action.
> 5. *Schedule changes*—Advise promptly when delays from expected test market or expansion dates are encountered and explain reason for delay.
> 6. *Costs/P&A*—Report significant shifts and recommend action, (e.g., price increase).
> 7. *Governmental actions*—Report on any legislative or regulatory activities that could affect the business and recommend action.

Although this case does not deal extensively with the AM and AAM levels of management, it is useful to know the overall roles these managers play. The AM manages all aspects of marketing, except sales execution, for the division. This manager's key objectives are not only achievement of short-term volume and profit goals but also development, testing, and expansion of new products, improved products, and line extensions. These latter goals are heavily emphasized by top management because they insure continued corporate growth. The AAMs largely serve coordinating, controlling, training, and strategic overview roles between the AM and BMs. They also have final decision-making authority on promotion activities within existing budgets and handle many of the administrative jobs in the advertising department.

The entry level job was that of BA. The BA was primarily responsible for monitoring the product budget, developing sales promotion, and analyzing market information (e.g., sales data from the company's management information system, consumption data from the A. C. Nielsen Company, and additional data from other outside market research services). New projects were added as competence was gained until the BA was sent out for "sales training," a 12-week field sales assignment.

Promotion to ABM followed this selling experience. Emphasis was placed upon learning advertising copy and media, developing long-term business-building programs, assisting and helping train the BA in the area of sales pro-

EXHIBIT 7

Job description
Clorox assistant brand manager

Marketing responsibilities:

1. *Business building plans*—Develop, recommend, and execute those key projects which, long term, will have a major effect on the shipments/consumption of the brand. Examples of these are the introduction of new sizes/ products, major distribution building programs, or major trial generating promotions.
2. *Copy*—Work with the brand manager in providing direction to the advertising agency in the development of new executional formats (based on current strategy) and the testing of new copy strategies/executions. Also, work with technical and legal departments on copy clearance/claim support.
3. *Media*—In conjunction with the brand manager provide the agency with direction on new ways to reach more efficiently the brand's target audience. This may take the form of media mix tests or testing of different media levels.
4. *Product*—Insure that a product which fulfills consumer needs and wants is marketed within cost constraints.
5. *Market research planning and analysis*—Initiate and analyze those market research projects which will yield information upon which the brand may act to improve current market position or correct an ongoing problem.
6. *Package design*—Insure that the package in the marketplace is appealing, eye-catching, and connotes those attributes of the product most important to consumers.

Management information:

1. *Market research*—Analyzes research and recommends next steps to correct any problems or capitalize on any opportunities.
2. *Media*—Analyze results of media testing and recommend action to be taken.
3. *Schedule changes*—Inform brand manager of delays in the progress of key projects in order that management may be apprised of the delay and the reason why.

---

motion. ABM was a transition job which could last from one to two and a half years, depending on the capabilities of the ABM and the needs of the company.

When the ABM was promoted to BM, he[2] was given overall marketing responsibility for one or more products, including planning, forecasting, and controlling volume and spending for these products. He also supervised ABMs and BAs. Due to rotation and normal turnover, not all brand groups were fully staffed with a BA and ABM.

---

[2] Although we use the masculine gender throughout this text rather than both masculine and feminine (e.g., he/she) to improve readability, the reader should assume this refers to both female and male brand personnel.

EXHIBIT 8

Job description
Clorox brand assistant

Marketing responsibilities:
1. *Sales promotion*—Plans, in consultation with other brand group members and the sales department, national and test promotions. Writes promotion recommendations and issues related feasibility requests and production orders. Implements consumer-oriented portions of promotions (e.g., coupon copy and media, sample drops, and the like) and oversees and/or cooperates with sales department in implementing trade-oriented portions of promotions (e.g., preparation of organizers, selection of salesman's incentives, and so on). Controls all budgeting for promotions. Evaluates promotions.
2. *Budget administration and control*—Reviews and codes invoices. Reconciles the budget with accounting on quarterly basis. Closes out budget with accounting at the end of the fiscal year.
3. *Market analysis*—Analyzes Nielsen data and writes bimonthly Nielsen reports. Audits other sources of market information (monthly shipment reports, SAMI's, and the like) and writes analytical reports as necessary.
4. *Shipment estimates*—In consultation with assistant brand manager and/or brand manager prepares monthly shipment estimate which forecasts next three months' shipments with supporting rationale.
5. *Competitive activity*—Monitors competitive activity reported by sales (promotion and pricing activity), agency (competitive media spending) and other sources (periodicals, and so on). Writes reports on significant developments.
6. *Public relations*—Cooperates with consumer services in handling special consumer-oriented problems which fall outside normal consumer service activities. Works with research services (home economists) and public affairs on brand related consumer information projects.

Other areas where brand assistants may contribute, depending upon individual brand assignments, are as follows:
1. *Package design*—Development of design objectives. Interface with package designers, marketing services, and technical staff on development, consumer testing, and feasibility determination on design. Recommendation, implementation, and evaluation of any test market.
2. *Business-building tests*—Work with assistant brand manager and/or brand manager on one or more of the following aspects of business-building tests—planning, recommendation, implementation, and evaluation.

Management information: Reports to brand manager on:
1. *Competitive activity*—Significant competitive developments.
2. *Budget variance*—Any variations from budget forecasts.
3. *Promotion problems*—Any problems with implementation of promotions.
4. *Consumer relations*—Any product problems which threaten volume.

In terms of day-by-day operations, the brand management group considered the other Clorox functions as "staff" to them. Hence, the earlier reference to *brand* and *all other*. Nonetheless, it must be recognized that brand had no direct authority over sales, manufacturing, market research, and product development. But it did have the responsibility to obtain from staff the inputs necessary to successful marketing. Each functional group, for this purpose, had a representative designated to deal with the brand manager. An integral part of this system of "responsibility without direct authority" was the fact that brand controlled budgets for areas such as market research and package design and represented staff's channel to top management. For example, a departmental request for information or specific action was typically directed to the brand manager, who not only had to concur but was the interface with top management. Communication to top management, in other words, was generally through the brand groups.

Perhaps the best summary of the brand manager's role is contained in Exhibit 9.

EXHIBIT 9 Interface matrix

Brand manager responsibilities	Work with these departments		Brand role
1. Product or package improvement	Sales, R&D, market research, manufacturing, and controller	1. *a.*	Develop objectives for product or package development.
		b.	Approve aesthetics.
		c.	Develop consumer research objectives, fund research and summarize results.
		d.	Determine unit profit potential and return on investment.
		e.	Recommend test market to management.
		f.	Write manufacturing production orders for test market production of product.
		g.	Analyze test market results and recommend national expansion.
2. Positioning	Advertising agency, market research, and legal	2. *a.*	Develop alternative positionings.
		b.	Develop consumer research objectives and fund research.
		c.	Analyze research results and recommend test market.
		d.	Analyze test market results and recommend national expansion.

EXHIBIT 9 *(concluded)*

Brand manager responsibilities	*Work with these departments*		*Brand role*
3. Copy	Advertising agency, market research, and legal	3. *a.*	Review agency copy submissions and select copy to be presented to management.
		b.	Approve final production for on-air copy testing.
		c.	Analyze copy test results.
		d.	Recommend national airing of copy.
4. Media	Advertising agency and media services	4. *a.*	Review agency media objectives and strategies and recommend alternatives.
		b.	Review and modify agency media plans with help of media services.
		c.	Forward agency media plan to management.
		d.	With help of media services monitor implementation of media plan.
5. Sales promotion	Sales, manufacturing, promotion development, and legal	5. *a.*	Develop national promotion plan with help of sales department.
		b.	Recommend plan to management.
		c.	Write manufacturing production order for production of sales promotion product.
		d.	Implement consumer portion of promotion (i.e., coupons, samples, and so on) and fund all trade allowances and consumer promotions.
6. Volume control	Sales	6. *a.*	Monitor shipments.
		b.	If undershipment of objectives seems possible, recommend remedial marketing efforts.

Climate

Clorox had been a Procter & Gamble subsidiary from 1957 until separated by government order in 1969. The "P&G" influence pervaded Clorox. A number of top and middle management people had either stayed with Clorox after divestiture or had joined Clorox from Procter & Gamble. The P&G style of memo writing, job titles, and organization continued.

The brand management system had been very strong at P&G and continued to be strong at Clorox. The brand managers played a ''line management'' role within the marketing function at Clorox. The reasoning for this was that the BM had direct responsibility for the most critical marketing factor—advertising—and had the broadest exposure to the operations of the company and the best overall perspective on his product and markets.

The BM was able to accomplish his goals through other people by using his control over the product budget, his position as the coordinator of all information, and his interpersonal skills. He had to be successful ''at getting others to do the job.''

But there was even more to the essential nature of the brand manager's job, a perspective that can only be expressed by senior management. These men looked upon brand managers as people who could be expected to ask the type of questions a top manager might ask, gather the facts necessary to make a decision, and then recommend a course of action in a very succinct memo. The net effect was that top management's job of managing the marketing of a large number of diverse brands in diverse categories became easier and more effective. The system assured that all brands, even those with small sales, were given attention and that a variety of marketing approaches designed to stimulate growth would at least be explored and recommended.

The power of the brand manager rested largely in his authority to ask questions anywhere in the company and demand carefully thought out, responsible answers, as long as the questions and answers were limited to matters which either directly affected the consumer of his product or affected his brand's contribution margin (revenue less manufacturing and shipping costs and brokerage commission). In addition, the successful brand manager had informal authority arising from his superior knowledge vis-à-vis any functional specialist in the company of all consumer aspects of his product, and he had the power to discuss his recommendations (in writing, usually) with top management.

Selection and Screening

Typically, brand assistants were recent MBAs from such schools as Stanford, Berkeley, Columbia, Northwestern, and Wharton with minimum work experience, particularly in brand management. In recent years Clorox had hired some graduates with advertising experience as well as some transferees from other Clorox departments, but these were exceptions. Brand managers were almost always promoted from within.

During the initial hiring process, Clorox had been seeking individuals who were intelligent, trainable, competitive, aggressive, and hard-workng. Ideal candidate qualities were generalized as: analytical ability; communication skills; the ability to plan, organize, and follow through; the ability to work well with others; leadership; resourcefulness and ingenuity; decision-making skill; drive and determination; and maturity.

Training

The introduction of the new brand assistant was strenuous. Although the initial jobs might range from planning promotions to writing market research summaries (see Exhibit 8), there was a lot of arduous "number crunching." Hours were long, often including weekends. There were no shortcuts or special courses and readings that could by-pass this breaking-in period. Nor was there much sympathy for the neophyte. Everyone in brand had been through the same experience, recognized its necessity, and knew the work could be done. "Help" was mainly in the form of providing initial direction, pointing out errors, and the suggestion of new projects as competence increased. The newer projects were invariably more interesting and challenging, which provided additional incentive to master the earlier tasks. And as the new BAs were hired, the more mundane jobs could be passed down.

The purpose of this training was to internalize certain "first principles" which were considered necessary to maintain the brand management system:

I. *All information can be derived from numerical data.*
   Brand people have minimal contact with either customers or suppliers. Customers are normally represented by market research findings and sales results. Suppliers are represented by specific liaison people. Thus it follows that there must always be an analytic justification for a project or program. The results need to be reduced to cases of product and P&A (revenue minus all costs except advertising).

II. *Concern for mistakes.*
   Brand people are trained to be detail-oriented and are concerned about not making errors. No mistake, particularly in a memo, was too small to be noticed. The feedback was intensive since memos were commented on in writing as they were passed up and down the distribution chain. If anyone found a mistake, then everyone who missed it was embarrassed.

III. *The budget is a critical device by which the brand manager exercises some basic control.*
   This first principle is a bit deceptive, however. It is true that some staff groups—market research, sales merchandising, and package design—are dependent upon brand for funding of projects, but it would be erroneous to conclude that brand uses the budget as a club. The range of interrelationships between brand and staff is too involved to be reduced to the single lever of money control.

IV. *Career success requires "The Clorox Style."*
   The Clorox Style contributes to the climate and mystique which makes brand management successful. This style includes dress, memo format, job concept, and attitude. Memos conform to a particular writing style and format and are not supposed to exceed two pages without an attached summary. Brand people must be the resident experts on everything affecting their products. The BM thinks of himself as the general manager

of a very small company. Nonetheless, brand people must maintain their aggressive, competitive attitude without hurting their relations with staff. The BA may achieve a basic competence in one to two years. This competence is recognized by the addition of more complex assignments. As his credibility and influence with the staff increase, the BA conforms more and more to the brand "image." BMs estimate that they spend as much as 25 percent of their time training BAs and ABMs. In fact, the entire brand management system is a training program. There is no such thing as an old BM; there is no place for the person who doesn't want to be promoted.

Management Information Systems

The BM used current data almost exclusively, even though comprehensive historical files were maintained. Meetings were usually frequent and short with only a few people present. Telephone calls were also frequent and short. Memos were passed through for comment and review by the BM. Magazines might be scanned for ideas, but they were seldom read. For many BMs, only the Nielsen chart books, the product fact book, and project folders were kept within easy reach.

Tests were used extensively to determine the accuracy of the information routinely received so that results could be optimized and problems avoided. Brand people went out into the field infrequently, yet they had a strong perception about what was happening through their tests and the management information system.

Emphasis had to be placed on the management information system because the BM changed products about every eighteen months to two years and thus lost all of his personal contacts in the agency and staff groups who tended to remain with the products.

Relationship with the "Big Five"

The five groups which brand dealt with regularly were the advertising agency, sales, market research, manufacturing, and product development. With each group there were conflicts which the BM had to resolve. These conflicts might include work priorities, differences of opinion about strategy or objectives, or disagreements over project timing. Brand argued that they had the responsibility for volume and spending without explicit authority to force staff compliance. These other departments, however, saw brand as more in control due to their final authority to make recommendations to top management as well as their role in setting initial objectives. The other departments would have preferred a better understanding (by brand) of their role and problems, yet essentially believed in the brand system as the best way to run Clorox.

Rotation and Promotion

Brand people were expected to shift products about every two years. Due to attrition, new hires, and promotions, the time could vary but seldom exceeded two and a half years. It took a BM several months to become familiar with a new assignment and perhaps a year to implement a major strategy. Thus, the typical BM was working on his predecessor's strategy for much of his tenure.

Performance was judged on a number of bases:

1. How well did he train?
2. Did he prepare a sound annual marketing plan and was he able to sell it to management?
3. How well did his product perform against volume objective in the marketplace (regardless of who prepared the budget)?
4. What sort of major improvements or line extensions were proposed (though not necessarily implemented)?
5. How well did he master the "Clorox Style"?

This last criterion referred to the fact that Clorox used an evaluation sheet which included such factors as: communication, analysis, thoroughness, prioritization, productivity, organization, leadership, work with others, responsibility, ability to accept criticism, motivation, maturity, capacity, judgment and attitude.

Summary

Brand management at Clorox was a total system. The climate, selection, training, and promotion all tended to encourage the "best and brightest" people to dedicate themselves to making a product successful.

The people were supported by a management information system and organizational structure that allowed them to be trained on the job and rotate from product to product at frequent intervals. The products were all marketed in a similar enough way, i.e., advertising, sales promotions, grocery store outlets, and so on, that the system and organization were the same for each.

The strength of the system lay in the fact that each product had a "champion" who attempted to achieve volume and share objectives as predicted in an annual plan. The short term was not sacrificed for the long term since the long term generally represented the incumbent's proposed strategy and ongoing business-building tests, and the short term represented his predecessor's strategy. In addition, a pool of potential general management talent was being established and utilized as managers moved up.

The Interviews

Although the general outline of the system was essentially as depicted, individual managers saw reality in slightly different ways. Therefore, it may be insightful to add depth to the description by noting a number of remarks gathered by the interviewer. Needless to say, these remarks are personal interpretations—meant to put some meat on the bones. The danger, of course, is that the reader might accept each at its face value or fail to recognize that they may appear out of context. In the writer's view, however, they are consistent with his interpretation of the "true environment." The remarks are presented in "question and answer" format.

Question 1: You typically hire MBAs with a small amount of work experience. What do you look for and how would you describe their jobs as BAs?

Brand Manager 1: I find it takes several months for a BA to become acclimated. He is usually too theoretically oriented; at this level, pragmatic application of judgment to problems is more important.

The most important thing for a BA to learn is to pay attention to details. Even "typos" have a dollar impact. The BA should learn to think things through comprehensively.

The BA begins working about 10 hours per day plus homework, but the time goes down as he learns his job.

All marketers are pretty much alike—aggressive, detail-minded—and that's what we look for.

BM 2: The biggest problem a new BA has is to learn how to juggle projects and determine priorities. Business schools teach sequential problem solving but "brand" requires juggling 15 trivial things and 1 major one. The BA's initial problem is establishing credibility. Brand requires a mixture of talents but no one specific personality is appropriate. Brand people do consider themselves "prima donnas."

BM 3: The BA's problem is simply a lack of experience with the Clorox system. The system relies on numbers, and the numbers come from the BA. The BA is constantly calculating and must think in analytic terms.

The BA must work very hard, develop rapidly, and learn what brand is all about. It takes two to six months for the BA to have a good grasp of the job and become acclimated to the system. All training is on-the-job.

The BA is responsible for sales promotions and the budget. It is important for the BA to develop creative ways to solve problems.

The BA must determine what motivates people and use it.

Question 2: What is the relationship between *brand* and the *other departments*?

BM 1: *Brand* is considered with respect by the advertising agency, but *brand* is committed to the agency because the BM can't fire them.

Most of the people in other departments do not want to move as fast as brand. It is a problem conveying the urgency and importance of timing.

The BM is responsible for planning, and the other departments for advice and/or execution.

Knowledge is power and the BM is the resident expert on his products.

BM 2: Brand is more a line than a staff function.

Brand has a responsibility for achieving volume objectives and keeping profit/case close to target level, but brand has no direct authority over many other departments which impact his ability to achieve objectives. Management recognizes that sometimes performance is beyond the control of brand.

Brand doesn't have to be nice to suppliers and sometimes becomes a tyrant due to the pressure.

BM 3: Brand controls the money. Many other departments must rely upon brand for direction and project funding.

The advertising agency has account executives who deal with brand and the agency's creative and media departments. The agency presents a national media plan once a year. Since the budget is mainly advertising, brand and the agency write the request.

Sales promotions are originated by brand and proposed to sales.

Brand recommends and analyzes market research and test markets. The purpose of these is to avoid "national blunders" although the risk is relatively small with ongoing products.

Question 3: What common characteristics do brand managers have?

BM 1: The important attributes are aggressiveness and attention to detail.

BM 2: The BM must have an aggressive outlook toward life, be competitive, like to win, and be action-oriented.

It's important to learn to do a thorough analysis of all inputs.

Question 4: How does a brand manager spend his time?

BM 1: Daily activities are coordination, short questions and answers on the telephone, and commenting on memos passing through. Wide variation exists, but a day might have one hour for thinking and strategy, one hour for standard reports, one hour for the "in/out basket," two hours on the phone, one hour with subordinates, and two hours in meetings.

Dealings are mainly with the "Big Five": the account executives at the advertising agency; sales; manufacturing coordinator; market research; and the product development specialists.

On the average the BM flies to the field once every three months.

Brand's job is to study the product, determine what is needed, and prioritize projects. The budget for this is set once a year.

BM 2: The most important job of brand is the budget request and appropriation. Once each year, a two-to-three hour meeting is held which lays out how and why money is to be spent for the next year. During the period preceding this meeting, much of a BM's time may be spent with the agency. During the remainder of the year the time falls off with the time spent in once-a-week meetings and telephone calls.

The second major job is the brand improvement objectives meeting which is also held once a year. Brand works with R&D to develop both short-term and long-term product development plans.

Brand strategies require one and a half to two years to implement. Long-range planning is important because few changes can be made in the short term due to long lead times in production and media planning.

Most of the BM's time is spent on specific projects.

Heavy use is made of the telephone and many short meetings are held, usually with six people or less.

Brand has a meeting with the product development center every two weeks.

Question 5: How often does a brand manager change brands?

BM 1: All brand people are interchangeable, although it takes about two to four months to become the most knowledgeable. You spend one to two years on a brand.

BM 2: Rotation is caused by promotions and departures and occurs every one and a half to two years. Continuity is provided by the staggered rotation of BAs, ABMs, and BMs. Once you rotate, you usually don't have time to find out how your old product is doing.

Part 5

Distribution Decisions

Marketers must make decisions on how to present the products they produce to their ultimate purchasers. Most producers do not present their products to end consumers themselves. They tend to make use of wholesalers and retailers.

The marketing decision maker has a number of decisions to make with respect to the distribution of a product. These include:

1. The types of wholesale and retail intermediaries to use.
2. The number of wholesale and retail intermediaries to use of each type.
3. The number of levels in the channel (degree of directness).
4. The ways to motivate existing channel members to perform effectively.

The first cases in this section deal with these issues. Beyond these decisions are a series of decisions concerning the physical distribution of the product. These include: customer service level, inventory size, order quantities, reorder points, warehouse locations, and tranportation.

The next section of this note is a short reminder of some of the concepts related to each of these decision points.

Types of Intermediaries

There are many different types of wholesale and retail intermediaries. They vary on the types of products they carry and the services that they are able to perform. The decision on which types of intermediaries to utilize is related to the services that a firm desires to have performed. This is in turn related to the resources and skills of the firm and the needs and behavior of the ultimate consumer.

The Number of Intermediaries

The firm must decide whether to have intensive, selective, or exclusive distribution at the wholesale and retail levels. This decision is related to the quality of support these intermediaries will give in each situation, the ability of the firm to service the intermediaries and the behavior of the ultimate consumer. For example, a wholesaler whom you want may only be willing to carry your products on an exclusive basis, or you may not be able to afford to contact all the retailers of a particular type. Alternatively, consumers may demand that your product be available at all outlets. This may force you into an intensive distribution situation.

Number of Channel Levels

The decision on how direct a channel from producer to ultimate consumer should be related to the cost of alternative channels, the service and control provided, the characteristics of the end consumer in terms of their numbers and geographic location, the perishability and bulkiness of the product, plus the characteristics of the firm, and competitive activity.

Motivation

Once a channel is selected, motivating its members to perform effectively is an important activity. Motivating vehicles include monetary things such as margins, allowances, and cooperative programs; service activities such as training and technical advice, inventory taking, and display management; and provision of physical items such as racks. Also important here are the interpersonal relationships among the people in the intermediaries and in your firm.

Physical Distribution Management

Physical distribution management is a complex area where management science techniques have become important. In simple terms, the decision maker sets a customer service level (for example, deliver 95 percent of all orders within seven days) and then makes inventory, warehousing, and transportation decisions to reach this service level at minimum cost. The customer service level is set by considering costs, consumer behavior, and competitive activity.

Case 16

Samahaiku Electronics

In May 1976, Mr. J. Akanu, overseas sales manager for Samahaiku Electronics of Japan, was attempting to define the best way to enter the U.S. market with the company's line of solid-state color and black and white televisions.

Samahaiku began in 1930 as a manufacturer of radios and sound equipment marketed in the Far East. In 1958, they expanded into television. Samahaiku distributed a full line of equipment to independent retail outlets who supplied their own service on warranties. Samahaiku equipment was noted for its reliability and high-quality amplification characteristics. Styling was not of major importance to the company. They relied mainly on their reputation for quality and in-store promotion by salespersons who could explain the finer features of the products in order to attract customers.

The European Entry

In early 1958, Samahaiku was considering widening its distribution of radios and audio equipment to either Europe or the United States. At that time, they were a strong marketer in Japan, Taiwan, Australia, New Zealand, and scattered areas of Southeast Asia. In May 1958, the decision was made to enter into full distribution in Europe rather than the United States. This decision was based on two factors. First, many of their present customers had European ties (Australia and New Zealand to England; Vietnam to France, and so on) which they hoped to be able to use. Second, the U.S. market seemed flooded with the full range of radio and sound equipment from the high-priced, high-quality type to the mass distributed, low-quality type. All segments had heavy U.S. and foreign competition.

By September 1958, Samahaiku was distributing their radio line in all the Western European and Scandinavian countries with the exception of Ireland and Finland. This rapid distribution had been achieved through the use of Janssen Imports, Ltd., a leading European importer-exporter headquartered in Denmark. Janssen had been able to obtain anywhere from 1 to 10 outlets in each country, usually in the largest city or cities, and usually in the relatively new (for Europe) "department stores."

At the end of 1958, Samahaiku was distributing through 37 independent outlets. Only 28 of these were able to service units under the Samahaiku warranty, and the company was searching for service outlets which could supplement these distributors. In the nine nonservice stores, there was a replacement policy in effect.

Sales to European markets in the last four months of 1958 were 13,500 radios, totaling approximately $190,000 (in U.S. equivalents) at retail. Orders were running well above the sales figures, as Samahaiku was not able to supply the unexpectedly large increased volume demanded.

Black and White Television

The officers of Samahaiku had, for some time, thought that expansion was necessary if they were to reach the growth objectives of 15 percent per year that they had set for the company. With this expansion in mind, they had allocated money to the development of a black and white television set in 1954. By late 1958, the consensus was that they had a very marketable product which met the company's high standards of quality. Production and marketing had worked together in forecasting projected sales for the next three years for Samahaiku's primary markets. Based on production of three models at an average retail price of $460, sales for the last seven months of 1959 were estimated at 17,000 units and 1960 sales at 35,000 units. The 1961 sales of 42,000 units were based on an average retail price of $450. With the European market estimates added in, the sales figures were forecast at 25,000, 80,000, and 95,000 units, respectively. The European market was felt to have much greater potential than the primary markets.

Samahaiku management then gave the go-ahead for the long-planned plant expansion which would give the company's two plants total capacity to produce 1 million radios and 850,000 television sets per year, in addition to approximately 50,000 other units of sound equipment. This construction was completed in May, giving seven months of full production in 1958.

Throughout the 1960s Samahaiku's sales increased steadily in all markets. In 1965, Samahaiku dropped Janssen as its distributor in Europe, in favor of a direct selling method in which Samahaiku maintained its own warehouses and sales force.

Situation in 1970

In 1970, Samahaiku was using full capacity at the two plants. Television sales were better than expected as were sales of sound equipment units. Radio sales were down in units sold, but had increased in revenue, due to increased sales of the more expensive AM/FM and shortwave units. Comparative sales are shown in Exhibit 1.

By 1970, the R&D department had developed and tested their own solid-state technology and applied it to black and white and color television sets. The firm had actually produced a few hundred color sets in 1969 for test markets.

EXHIBIT 1

A. Samahaiku sales 1961 and 1969

	1961	1969
Radio units	675,000	890,000
Revenue from radio sales*	$ 6,075,000	$12,460,000
Television units	120,000	250,000
Revenue from TV sales*	$13,200,000	$26,250,000
Other sound equipment units	24,000	37,000
Revenue from sound equipment sales*	$ 1,200,000	$ 2,590,000

B. Breakdown of sales geographically (percent)

	Far East	Europe
Radio units	70%	30%
Revenue	55	45
Television units	33	67
Revenue	30	70
Sound equipment units	28	72
Revenue	20	80

* U.S. dollars.

These models were quickly accepted and the dealers were anxious to be able to sell in quantity. Again, the question of expansion and distribution arose. It was decided that if the firm was to be a successful full-line competitor in color television, a new, modern facility should be built. A new plant costing $2.4 million was scheduled to be completed in late 1973. This plant would be able to produce approximately 1.6 million color sets per year, depending on the product mix. Samahaiku estimated they could produce about 400,000 color sets using the old facilities between May 1970 and late 1972. Samahaiku management had been contemplating expanding their markets as well. They agreed that if acceptance of the new line in European markets met their expectations, their next step would be serious consideration of entering the U.S. market.

Situation in 1975

The new Samahaiku plant was completed in January 1973. Production figures for 1970–74 are shown in the accompanying table. Sales were made in all markets, but the European market accounted for 75 percent of the units sold.

	Television sets	
	Black and white	Color
1970	780,000*	60,000
1971	820,000*	130,000
1972	800,000	140,000
1973	600,000	400,000
1974	570,000	615,000

* Excess over production capacity purchased from other Japanese television companies.

The Samahaiku line consisted of four black and white models: 9-inch, 13-inch, 19-inch, and 21-inch portables. The color line had 13-inch, 19-inch, and 21-inch portables plus a 25-inch console model. The average factory price to retail accounts of a black and white portable (excluding freight) was $86. The average costs were direct materials $36, direct labor $8, factory overhead $2, and advertising $2.[1] Color sets were factory priced to retail accounts at $152 (average) for the portables and $300 for the console model. Costs were $68 for direct materials and $9.50 direct labor, plus $2.50 for factory overhead and $3 advertising.[2] Direct materials costs were $80 more for the console model. About 15 percent of the factory overhead and advertising costs were applicable to the U.S. market.

The U.S. Market

The black and white market in the United States was highly price sensitive at this time, and Samahaiku was considering several options including cutting price, selling at a discount to large-volume dealers, paying freight on all orders over a certain amount, or offering special prices on certain models if ordered in quantity. The color market was not as price sensitive. Quality and reliability were of much greater concern.

The U.S. market was a completely different one than the European or Far East markets. While Samahaiku had only two to five competitors in their Far East and European markets, there were over 25 in the United States. Data on the top five manufacturers are shown in Exhibit 2.

EXHIBIT 2 Estimated market shares of television brands (percent)*

	First set	Second set
Zenith	20.0%	7.3%
RCA Victor	18.9	6.8
General Electric	7.4	5.1
Admiral	7.1	3.1
Sears (Silvertone)	6.8	3.3

* The five next largest manufacturers had a 21.5 percent share of first sets and 7.37 percent of second sets.

In 1974, portables had 98 percent of the black and white market and 67.8 percent of the color market. Console and combination models accounted for the balance. The 1975 estimates for portables were 98.5 percent and 66 percent, respectively (Exhibit 3).

---

[1] Based on a standard production volume of 600,000 units.
[2] Based on a standard production volume of 700,000 units.

EXHIBIT 3 Estimated U.S. television market (units and retail dollars)

	Unit sales	
	1974	1975*
Black and white	5,544,000	6,868,000
Color	7,337,000	8,411,300
	12,881,000	15,279,300

	1975 dollar sales*	
Size (inches)	Black and white	Color
Under 12	$ 128,072,000	$ 821,800
12–15	289,943,000	237,946,500
16–17	47,232,000	302,280,000
18		49,920,000
19	163,903,500	1,179,920,000
21		44,000,000
23	20,630,500	391,500,000
25		1,201,785,000
Total	$ 649,781,000	$3,408,173,300
Total black and white and color sets	$4,057,954,300	

* These are estimates.

Distribution outlets in the United States handling televisions were: furniture stores (38,732), household appliance stores (20,262), radio and TV stores (29,890), department stores (11,240), catalog showroom/mail-order houses (7,671), discount stores (17,887), and other types (9,874). Sales by outlet type are shown in Exhibit 4.

EXHIBIT 4 Television sales by outlet type (percent)

	1974		1975*	
	Color	Black and white	Color	Black and white
Furniture stores	17%	5%	18%	5%
Department stores	20	18	20	18
Appliance/TV/radio	30	30	32	28
Catalog/mail-order	5	4	5	4
Discount chains	28	25	25	25
Others	—	18	—	20

* Estimate.

The furniture stores usually handled larger models, especially consoles. The salespersons were well-informed about cabinetry and styling, but usually not too knowledgeable about electronics. The furniture stores usually sold at suggested retail price, yielding about a 55 percent margin on retail selling price, and offered no in-store service facilities.

Department stores were a large source of sales for both black and white and color sets. The salespersons were quite knowledgeable, and engaged in a fair amount of trying to get the customer to "trade up." Prices were sometimes discounted, particularly in larger chains. The department stores usually got about a 42 percent margin. In addition, they were eager to seek "deals" on quantity buys, closeouts, and so on. Most of the large stores had their own service facilities, and carried their own private brands.

Appliance/radio/TV outlets consisted of two types: the discount appliance stores and the regular "retail" stores. The discount houses were high volume, low-price operations which, to obtain low overhead, often had no service facilities for TV. The salespersons were usually paid on commission and were aggressive in selling their higher margin models. Price-cutting was a necessity and dealers often bought in large quantity lots, watching for deals, damaged-model sales, and other ways to cut costs. The typical margin on both black and white and color sets was only about 22 percent in this type of outlet. Regular retail appliance/radio/TV outlets usually had knowledgeable salespersons and large service departments. Margins averaged about 35 percent.

Catalog showroom/mail-order sales were usually limited to a few smaller brands. Little selling at point-of-purchase could be done and no service was offered.

Discount chains, such as K mart stores, were a growing force in retailing televisions. Discounters had only lately begun handling TV and large appliances. They bought in large quantity at lowest possible cost. The manufacturers were usually willing to cut prices in order to obtain large volume orders. Some of the larger chains were beginning to engage in private branding, as well, from which they were able to gain very favorable terms from manufacturers. For example, a U.S. manufacturer who engaged in private branding for one of the large chains usually obtained a margin (average) of 19 percent versus 34 percent for national brand sales. Chains usually required the customer to contact the company or independent service facility for warranty service. Some stores supported "service centers" which would simply accept the set and send it on to the manufacturer for repairs. Selling at point of sale was almost nonexistent at the chains. With low overhead and low margins (20 percent), the salespersons were usually few in number and rarely informed about electronics or the differences in major lines. These stores also carried very small lines of a few manufacturers concentrating for the most part on the low end of the model line. All the different outlets paid freight, as a rule, with the exception of the discount chains, who, if billed for freight, would simply deduct it from the invoice.

Exhibit 5 gives representative average retail prices of black and white, and color television sets by type of retail outlet. These prices are for the size of models that Samahaiku markets. Mr. Akanu wondered how many and what type of accounts Samahaiku should try to obtain.

EXHIBIT 5 Representative average retail price by type of television outlet for the size of television sold by Samahaiku

Type of television	Furniture stores	Department stores	Appliance/ radio/TV discount stores	Appliance/ radio/TV regular stores	Discount chains
Black and white portable	—	$150*	$115*	$130*	$115*
	—	120†	—	—	89†
Color portable	—	270*	200*	240*	195*
	—	220†	—	—	160†
Color consoles	$700*	600*	—	—	—

* Manufacturers' brands.
† Private brand.

Distribution Alternatives

In selling to the U.S. retail accounts they obtained, Samahaiku was considering two basic alternatives. The first alternative was to sell through import/export-electronics wholesalers. These wholesalers would obtain and maintain retail accounts, plus provide warehousing services. Under this alternative, Samahaiku would have to provide its own service facilities. It was felt that two centers, one on the East Coast, and one on the West Coast would have to be established. These centers were designed to supplement retail account service departments. Rental on suitable property was estimated at $48,000 per year for each center. Margins for the import/export-electronics wholesalers would be 11 percent of the factory price to retail accounts. This margin was given by Samahaiku lowering its factory price 11 percent below the standard factory price to retail accounts. It was expected that the wholesalers would sell to retail accounts at approximately the Samahaiku factory price to retail accounts.

The other distribution alternative that Samahaiku was considering was to sell direct to retail accounts using their own company salespersons. On the average a salesperson could handle approximately 200 retail accounts. Their function was to obtain accounts, provide promotional displays, technical assistance, and serve as a liaison between retailers and the factory. They would be paid a straight salary ($14,000), plus expenses ($6,000). This alternative would require Samahaiku to obtain their own warehouse space in four locations in the United States. It was estimated that suitable facilities could be obtained at a total cost of $250,000 per year. Inventory carrying costs were expected to be about 15 percent of annual warehouse costs. Service facilities costs would be the same as under the distribution alternative.

Mr. Akanu wanted to begin shipping to the U.S. market as quickly as possible. He was anxious to select the appropriate retail selling structure for his product, and to select the best distribution alternative for his situation.

Case 17

Thompson Respiration Products, Inc.*

Victor Higgins, executives vice president for Thompson Respiration Products, Inc. (TRP), sat thinking at his desk late one Friday in April 1982. "We're making progress," he said to himself. "Getting Metro to sign finally gets us into the Chicago Market . . . and with a good dealer at that." *Metro,* of course, was Metropolitan Medical Products, a large Chicago retailer of medical equipment and supplies for home use. "Now, if we could just do the same in Minneapolis and Atlanta," he continued.

However, getting at least one dealer in each of these cities to sign a TRP Dealer Agreement seemed remote right now. One reason was the sizeable groundwork required—Higgins simply lacked the time to review operations at the well over 100 dealers currently operating in the two cities. Another was TRP's lack of dealer-oriented sales information that went beyond the technical specification sheet for each product and the company's price list. Still another concerned two conditions in the Dealer Agreement itself—prospective dealers sometimes balked at agreeing to sell no products manufactured by TRP's competitors and differed with TRP in interpretations of the "best efforts" clause. (The clause required the dealer to maintain adequate inventories of TRP products, contact four prospective new customers or physicians or respiration therapists per month, respond promptly to sales inquiries, and represent TRP at appropriate conventions where it exhibited.)

"Still," Higgins concluded, "we signed Metro in spite of these reasons, and 21 others across the country. That's about all anyone could expect—after all, we've only been trying to develop a dealer network for a year or so."

The Portable Respirator Industry

The portable respirator industry began in the early 1950s when polio stricken patients who lacked control of muscles necessary for breathing began to leave

---

* This case was written by Professor James E. Nelson and DBA Candidate William R. Woolridge, the University of Colorado. This case illustrates neither effective nor ineffective administrative decision making. Some data are disguised. © 1983 by the Business Research Division, College of Business and Administration and the Graduate School of Business Administration, University of Colorado.

treatment centers. They returned home with hospital-style iron lungs or fiber glass chest shells, both being large chambers that regularly introduced a vacuum about the patient's chest. The vacuum caused the chest to expand and, thus, the lungs to fill with air. However, both devices confined patients to a prone or semiprone position in a bed.

By the late 1950s, TRP had developed a portable turbine blower powered by an electric motor and battery. When connected to a mouthpiece via plastic tubing, the blower would inflate a patient's lungs on demand. Patients could now leave their beds for several hours at a time and realize limited mobility in a wheelchair. By the early 1970s, TRP had developed a line of more sophisticated turbine respirators in terms of monitoring and capability for adjustment to individual patient needs.

At about the same time, applications began to shift from polio patients to victims of other diseases or of spinal cord injuries, the latter group existing primarily as a result of automobile accidents. Better emergency medical service, quicker evacuation to spinal cord injury centers, and more proficient treatment meant that people who formerly would have died now lived and went on to lead meaningful lives. Because of patients' frequently younger ages, they strongly desired wheelchair mobility. Respiration therapists obliged by recommending a Thompson respirator for home use or, if unaware of Thompson, recommending a Puritan-Bennett or other machine.

Instead of a turbine, Puritan-Bennett machines used a bellows design to force air into the patient's lungs. The machines were widely used in hospitals but seemed poorly suited for home use. For one thing, Puritan-Bennett machines used a compressor pump or pressurized air to drive the bellows, much more cumbersome than Thompson's electric motor. Puritan-Bennett machines also cost approximately 50 percent more than a comparable Thompson unit and were relatively large and immobile. On the other hand, Puritan-Bennett machines were viewed by physicians and respiration therapists as industry standards.

By the middle 1970s, TRP had developed a piston and cylinder design (similar in principle to the bellows) and placed it on the market. The product lacked the sophistication of the Puritan-Bennett machines but was reliable, portable, and much simpler to adjust and operate. It also maintained TRP's traditional cost advantage. Another firm, Life Products, began its operations in 1976 by producing a similar design. A third competitor, Lifecare Services, had begun operations somewhat earlier.

Puritan-Bennett

Puritan-Bennett was a large, growing, and financially sound manufacturer of respiration equipment for medical and aviation applications. Its headquarters were located in Kansas City, Missouri. However, the firm staffed over 40 sales, service, and warehouse operations in the United States, Canada, United Kingdom, and France. Sales for 1981 exceeded $100 million while employment was just over 2,000 people. Sales for its Medical Equipment Group (respirators, related equipment, and accessories, service and parts) likely exceeded $40 million for 1981; however, Higgins could obtain data only for the period 1977–1980 (see Exhibit 1). Puritan-Bennett usually sold its respirators through a system of independent, durable medical equipment dealers. However, its sales offices did sell directly to identified "house accounts" and often competed with dealers by selling slower moving products to all accounts. According to industry sources, Puritan-Bennett sales were slightly more than three fourths of all respirator sales to hospitals in 1981.

EXHIBIT 1 Puritan-Bennett Medical Equipment Group sales

	1977	1978	1979	1980
Domestic sales:				
Model MA-1:				
Units	1,460	875	600	500
Amount ($ millions)	8.5	4.9	3.5	3.1
Model MA-2:				
Units	—	935	900	1,100
Amount ($ millions)	—	6.0	6.1	7.8
Foreign sales:				
Units	250	300	500	565
Amount ($ millions)	1.5	1.8	3.1	3.6
IPPB equipment ($ millions)	6.0	6.5	6.7	7.0
Parts, service, accessories				
($ millions)	10.0	11.7	13.1	13.5
Overhaul ($ millions)	2.0	3.0	2.5	2.5
Total ($ millions)	28.0	34.0	35.0	37.5

Source: *The Wall Street Transcript.*

However, these same sources expected Puritan-Bennett's share to diminish during the 1980s because of the aggressive marketing efforts of three other manufacturers of hospital-style respirators: Bear Medical Systems, Inc., J. H. Emerson; and Siemens-Elema. The latter firm was expected to grow the most rapidly, despite its quite recent entry into the U.S. market (its headquarters were in Sweden) and a list price of over $16,000 for its basic model.

Life Products

Life Products directly competed with TRP for the portable respirator market. Life Products had begun operations in 1976 when David Smith, a TRP employee, left to start his own business. Smith had located his plant in Boulder, Colorado, less than a mile from TRP headquarters.

He began almost immediately to set up a dealer network and by early 1982 had secured over 40 independent dealers located in large metropolitan areas. Smith had made a strong effort to sign only large, well-managed durable medical equipment dealers. Dealer representatives were required to complete Life Product's service training school, held each month in Boulder. Life Products sold its products to dealers (in contrast to TRP, which both sold and rented products to consumers and to dealers). Dealers received a 20 to 25 percent discount off suggested retail price on most products.

As of April 1982, Life Products offered two respirator models (the LP3 and LP4) and a limited number of accessories (such as mouthpieces and plastic tubing) to its dealers. Suggested retail prices for the two respirator models were approximately $3,900 and $4,800. Suggested rental rates were approximately $400 and $500 per month. Life Products also allowed Lifecare Services to manufacture a respirator similar to the LP3 under license.

At the end of 1981, Smith was quite pleased with his firm's performance. During Life Products' brief history, it had passed TRP in sales and now ceased to see the firm as a serious threat, at least according to one company executive:

> We really aren't in competition with Thompson. They're after the stagnant market and we're after a growing market. We see new applications and ultimately the hospital market as our niche. I doubt if Thompson will even be around in a few years. As for Lifecare, their prices are much lower than ours but you don't get the service. With them you get the basic product, but nothing else. With us, you get a complete medical care service. That's the big difference.

Lifecare Services, Inc.

In contrast to the preceding firms, Lifecare Services, Inc. earned much less of its revenues from medical equipment manufacturing and much more from medical equipment distributing. The firm primarily resold products purchased from other manufacturers, operating out of its headquarters in Boulder as well as from its 16 field offices (Exhibit 2). All offices were stocked with backup parts and an inventory of respirators. All were staffed with trained service technicians under Lifecare's employ.

EXHIBIT 2 Lifecare Services, Inc., field offices

Augusta, Ga.	Houston, Tex.
Baltimore, Md.	Los Angeles, Calif.
Boston, Mass.	New York, N.Y.
Chicago, Ill.	Oakland, Calif.
Cleveland, Ohio	Omaha, Nebr.
Denver, Colo.	Phoenix, Ariz.
Detroit, Mich.	Seattle, Wash.
Grand Rapids, Mich.*	St. Paul, Minn.

* Suboffice.
Source: Trade literature.

Lifecare did manufacture a few accessories not readily available from other manufacturers. These items complemented the purchased products and in the company's words, served to "give the customer a complete respiratory service." Under a licensing agreement between Lifecare and Life Products, the firm manufactured a respirator similar to the LP3 and marketed it under the Lifecare name. The unit rented for approximately $175 per month. While Lifecare continued to service the few remaining Thompson units it still had in the field, it no longer carried the Thompson line.

Lifecare rented rather than sold its equipment. The firm maintained that this gave patients more flexibility in the event of recovery or death and lowered patients' monthly costs.

Thompson Respiration Products, Inc.

TRP currently employed 13 people, 9 in production and 4 in management. It conducted operations in a modern, attractive building (leased) in an industrial park. The building contained about 6,000 square feet of space, split 75/25 for production/management purposes. Production operations were essentially job shop in nature: skilled technicians assembled each unit by hand on work benches, making frequent quality control tests and subsequent adjustments. Production lots usually ranged from 10 to 75 units per model and probably averaged around 40. Normal production capacity was about 600 units per year.

Product Line

TRP currently sold seven respirator models plus a large number of accessories. All respirator models were portable but differed considerably in terms of style, design, performance specifications, and attendant features (see Exhibit 3). Four models were styled as metal boxes with an impressive array of knobs, dials, indicator lights, and switches. Three were styled as less imposing, "overnighter" suitcases with less prominently displayed controls and indicators. (Exhibit 4 reproduces part of the specification sheet for the M3000, as illustrative of the metal box design.)

Four of the models were designed as *pressure machines,* using a turbine pump that provided a constant, usually positive, pressure. Patients were provided intermittent access to this pressure as breaths per minute. However, one model, the MV Multivent, could provide either a constant positive or a constant negative pressure (i.e., a vacuum, necessary to operate chest shells, iron lungs, and body wraps). No other portable respirator on the market could produce a negative pressure. Three of the models were designed as *volume machines,* using a piston pump that produced intermittent, constant volumes of pressurized air as breaths per minute. Actual volumes were prescribed by each patient's physician based on lung capacity. Pressures depended on the breathing method used (mouthpiece, trach, chest shell, and others) and on the patient's activity level. Breaths per minute also depended on the patient's activity level.

Models came with several features. The newest was an assist feature (currently available on the Minilung M25 but soon to be offered also on the M3000) that allowed the patient alone to "command" additional breaths without having

EXHIBIT 3 TRP respirators

Model*	Style	Design	Volume (cc)	Pressure (cm. H_2O)
M3000	Metal box	Volume	300–3,000	+10 to +65
MV Multivent	Metal box	Pressure (positive or negative)	n.a.	−70 to +80
Minilung M15	Suitcase	Volume	200–1,500	+5 to +65
Minilung M25 Assist (also available without the assist feature)	Suitcase	Volume	600–2,500	+5 to +65
Bantam GS	Suitcase	Pressure (positive)	n.a.	+15 to +45
Compact CS	Metal box	Pressure (positive)	n.a.	+15 to +45
Compact C	Metal box	Pressure (positive)	n.a.	+15 to +45

Model	Breaths per minute	Weight (lbs.)	Size (ft.^{3})	Features
M3000	6 to 30	39	0.85	Sigh, four alarms, automatic switchover from AC to battery
MV Multivent	8 to 24	41	1.05	Positive or negative pressure, four alarms, AC only
Minilung M15	8 to 22	24	0.70	Three alarms, automatic switchover from AC to battery
Minilung M25 Assist (also available without the assist feature)	5 to 20	24	0.70	Assist, sigh, three alarms, automatic switchover from AC to battery
Bantam GS	6 to 24	19	0.75	Sigh, six alarms, automatic switchover from AC to battery
Compact CS	8 to 24	25	0.72	Sigh, six alarms, automatic switchover from AC to battery
Compact C	6 to 24	19	0.50	Sigh, four alarms, automatic switchover from AC to battery

Note: n.a. = not applicable.
* Five other models considered obsolete by TRP could be supplied if necessary.
Source: Company sales specification sheets.

someone change the dialed breath rate. The sigh feature gave patients a sigh, either automatically or on demand. Depending on the model, up to six alarms were available to indicate a patient's call, unacceptable low pressure, unacceptable high pressure, low battery voltage/power failure, failure to cycle, and the need to replace motor brushes. All models but the MV Multivent also offered automatic switchover from alternating current to either an internal or an external battery (or both) in the event of a power failure. Batteries provided for 18 to 40 hours of operation, depending on usage.

Higgins felt that TRP's respirators were superior to those of Life Products. Most TRP models allowed pressure monitoring in the airway itself rather than in the machine, providing more accurate measurement. TRP's suitcase style models often were strongly preferred by patients, especially the polio patients who had known no others. TRP's volume models offered easier volume adjustments and all TRP models offered more alarms. On the other hand, he knew

EXHIBIT 4 The M3000 Minilung

M3000 MINILUNG
PORTABLE VOLUME VENTILATOR

What it can mean to the User. . . .

• The M3000 is a planned performance product designed to meet breathing needs. It is a significant step in the ongoing effort of a company which pioneered the advancement of portable respiratory equipment

• This portable volume ventilator sets high standards for flexibility of operation and versatility in use. The M3000 has gained its successful reputation as a result of satisfactory usage in hospitals, for transport, in rehabilitation efforts and in home care. This model grew out of expressed needs of users for characteristics which offer performance PLUS. It is engineered to enable the user to have something more than just mechanical breathing.

• Now breathing patterns can be comfortably varied with the use of a SIGH, which can be obtained either automatically or manually.

• Besides being sturdy and reliable, the M3000 can be adjusted readily.

• Remote pressure sensing in the proximal airway provides for more accurate set up of the ventilator pressure alarms.

• This model has the option of a patient-operated call switch.

• AC-DC operation of the M3000 is accomplished with ease because automatic switch-over is provided on AC power failure, first to external battery, then to internal battery.

THOMPSON takes pride in planning ahead.

See reverse for specifications

Innovators in Respiratory Equipment for Over 25 Years
Thompson Respiration Products, Inc.   1680 Range Street   Boulder Colorado 80301   303/443-3350

SPECIFICATIONS:

300 to 3000 ml adjustable volume

10 to 65 cm. water pressure

6 to 30 breaths per minute

Automatic or Manual Sigh

Alarms:
Patient operated call alarm
Low Pressure alarm and light
High Pressure alarm and light
Low Voltage light with delayed alarm
Automatic switchover provided on AC power failure, first to external battery, then to internal battery
Alarm delay switch

Pilot lamps color-coded and labeled

Remote pressure connector

Self-contained battery for 2 hour operation — recharges automatically

Power sources:
120 volt, 60 hz; 12 volt external battery; and internal battery

Size: 12⅝ W x 11¼ D x 10¼ inches H

Weight: 39 pounds (Shipping weight 48 pounds)

M3000 MINILUNG
Portable Volume Ventilator

that TRP had recently experienced some product reliability problems of an irritating—not life threatening—nature. Further, he knew that Life Products had beaten TRP to the market with the assist feature (the idea for which had come from a Puritan-Bennett machine).

TRP's line of accessories was more extensive than that of Life Products. TRP offered the following for separate sale: alarms, call switches, battery cables, chest shells, mouthpieces, plastic tubing, pneumobelts and bladders (equipment for still another breathing method that utilized intermittent pressure on a patient's diaphragm), and other items. Lifecare Services offered many similar items.

Distribution

Shortly after joining TRP, Higgins had decided to switch from selling and renting products directly to patients to selling and renting products to dealers. While it meant lower margins, less control, and more infrequent communication with patients, the change had several advantages. It allowed TRP to shift inventory from the factory to the dealer, generating cash more quickly. It provided for local representation in market areas, allowing patients greater feelings of security and TRP more aggressive sales efforts. It shifted burdensome paperwork (required by insurance companies and state and federal agencies to effect payment) from TRP to the dealer. It also reduced other TRP administrative activities in accounting, customer relations, and sales.

TRP derived about half of its 1981 revenue of $3 million directly from patients and about half from the dealer network. By April 1982, the firm had 22 dealers (see Exhibit 5 with 3 accounting for over 60 percent of TRP dealer revenues. Two of the three serviced TRP products as did two of the smaller dealers; the rest preferred to let the factory take care of repairs. TRP conducted occasional training sessions for dealer repair personnel but distances were great and turnover in the position high, making such sessions costly. Most dealers requested air shipment of respirators, in quantities of 1 or 2 units.

EXHIBIT 5 TRP dealer locations

Bakersfield, Calif.	Salt Lake City, Utah
Baltimore, Md.	San Diego, Calif.
Birmingham, Ala.	San Francisco, Calif.
Chicago, Ill.	Seattle, Wash.
Cleveland, Ohio	Springfield, Ohio
Fort Wayne, Ind.	Tampa, Fla.
Greenville, N.C.	Tucson, Ariz.
Indianapolis, Ind.	Washington, D.C.
Newark, N.J.	
Oklahoma City, Okla.	Montreal, Canada
Pittsburgh, Pa.	Toronto, Canada

Source: Company records.

Price

TRP maintained a comprehensive price list for its entire product line. (Exhibit 6 reproduces part of the current list.) Each respirator model carried both a suggested retail selling price and a suggested retail rental rate. (TRP also applied these rates when it dealt directly with patients.) The list also presented two net purchase prices for each model along with an alternative rental rate that TRP charged to dealers. About 40 percent of the 300 respirator units TRP shipped to dealers in 1981 went out on a rental basis. The comparable figure for the 165 units sent directly to consumers was 90 percent. Net purchase prices allowed an approximate 7 percent discount for orders of three or more units of each model. Higgins had initiated this policy early last year with the aim of encouraging dealers to order in larger quantities. To date one dealer had taken advantage of this discount.

EXHIBIT 6 Current TRP respirator price list

| | Suggested retail | | Dealer | Dealer price | |
Model	Rent/month	Price	Rent/month	1–2	3 or more
M3000	$380	$6,000	$290	$4,500	$4,185
MV Multivent	270	4,300	210	3,225	3,000
Minilung M15	250	3,950	190	2,960	2,750
Minilung M25	250	3,950	190	2,960	2,750
Bantam GS	230	3,600	175	2,700	2,510
Compact CS	230	3,600	175	2,700	2,510
Compact C	200	3,150	155	2,360	2,195

Source: Company sales specification sheets.

Current policy called for TRP to earn a gross margin of approximately 35 percent on the dealer price for 1–2 units. All prices included shipping charges by United Parcel Service (UPS); purchasers requesting more expensive transportation service paid the difference between actual costs incurred and the UPS charge. Terms were net 30 days with a 1.5 percent service charge added to past due accounts. Prices were last changed in late 1981.

Consumers

Two types of patients used respirators, depending on whether the need followed from disease or from injury. Diseases such as polio, sleep apnea, chronic obstructive pulmonary disease, and muscular dystrophy annually left about 1,900 victims unable to breathe without a respirator. Injury to the spinal cord above the fifth vertebra caused a similar result for about 300 people per year. Except for polio, incidences of the diseases and injury were growing at about 3 percent per year. Most patients kept one respirator at bedside and another mounted on a wheelchair. However, Higgins did know of one individual who kept eight

Bantam B models (provided by a local polio foundation, now defunct) in his closet. Except for polio patients, life expectancies were about five years. Higgins estimated the total number of patients using a home respirator in 1981 at

Polio	3,000
Other diseases	6,500
Spinal cord injury	1,000

Almost all patients were under a physician's care as well as that of a more immediate nurse or attendant (frequently a relative). About 95 percent paid for their equipment through insurance benefits or foundation monies. About 90 percent rented their equipment. Almost all patients and their nurses or attendants had received instruction in equipment operation from respiration therapists employed by medical centers or by dealers of durable medical equipment.

The majority of patients were poor. Virtually none were gainfully employed and all had seen their savings and other assets diminished to varying degrees by treatment costs. Some had experienced a divorce. Slightly more patients were male than female. About 75 percent lived in their homes with the rest split between hospitals, nursing homes, and other institutions.

Apart from patients, Higgins thought that hospitals might be considered a logical new market for TRP to enter. Many of the larger and some of the smaller general hospitals might be convinced to purchase one portable respirator (like the M3000) for emergency and other use with injury patients. Such a machine would be much cheaper to purchase than a large Puritan-Bennett and would allow easier patient trips to testing areas, X-ray, surgery, and the like. Even easier to convince should be the fourteen regional spinal cord injury centers located across the country (Exhibit 7). Other medical centers that specialized in treatment of pulmonary diseases should also be prime targets. Somewhat less

EXHIBIT 7 Regional spinal cord injury centers

Birmingham, Ala.	Houston, Tex.
Boston, Mass.	Miami, Fla.
Chicago, Ill.	New York, N.Y.
Columbia, Mo.	Philadelphia, Pa.
Downey, Calif.	Phoenix, Ariz.
Englewood, Colo.	San Jose, Calif.
Fishersville, Va.	Seattle, Wash.

promising but more numerous would be public and private schools that trained physicians and respiration therapists. Higgins estimated the numbers of these institutions at:

General hospitals (100 beds or more)	3,800
General hospitals (fewer than 100 beds)	3,200
Spinal cord injury centers	14
Pulmonary disease treatment centers	100
Medical schools	180
Respiration therapy schools	250

Dealers

Dealers supplying homecare medical products (as distinct from dealers supplying hospitals and medical centers) showed a great deal of diversity. Some were little more than small areas in local drugstores that rented canes, walkers, and wheelchairs in addition to selling supplies like surgical stockings and colostomy bags. Others carried nearly everything needed for home nursing care—renting everything from canes to hospital beds and selling supplies from bed pads to bottled oxygen. Still others specialized in products and supplies for only certain types of patients.

In this latter category, Higgins had identified dealers of oxygen and oxygen-related equipment as the best fit among existing dealers. These dealers serviced victims of emphysema, bronchitis, asthma, and other respiratory ailments, a growing market that Higgins estimated was about 10 times greater than that for respirators. A typical dealer had begun perhaps 10 years ago selling bottled oxygen (obtained from a welding supply wholesaler) and renting rather crude metering equipment to patients at home under the care of a registered nurse. The same dealer today now rented and serviced oxygen concentrators (a recently developed device that extracts oxygen from the air), liquid oxygen equipment and liquid oxygen, and much more sophisticated oxygen equipment and oxygen to patients cared for by themselves or by relatives.

Most dealers maintained a fleet of radio dispatched trucks to deliver products to their customers. Better dealers promised 24 hour service and kept delivery personnel and a respiration therapist on call 24 hours a day. Dealers usually employed several respiration therapists who would set up equipment, instruct patients and attendants on equipment operation, and provide routine and emergency service. Dealers often expected the therapists to function as a sales force. The therapists would call on physicians and other respiration therapists at hospitals and medical centers, on discharge planners at hospitals, and on organizations such as muscular dystrophy associations, spinal cord injury associations, and visiting nurse associations.

Dealers usually bought their inventories of durable equipment and supplies directly from manufacturers. They usually received a 20 to 25 percent discount off suggested list prices to consumers and hospitals. Only in rare instances might dealers instead lease equipment from a manufacturer. Dealers aimed for a payback of one year or less, meaning that most products began to contribute to profit and overhead after 12 months of rental. Most products lasted physically for upwards of 10 years but technologically for only 5 to 6: every dealer's warehouse contained idle but perfectly suitable equipment that had been superseded by models demanded by patients, their physicians, or their attendants.

Most dealers were independently owned and operated, with annual sales ranging between $5 million and $10 million. However, a number had recently been acquired by one of several parent organizations that were regional or national in scope. Such chains usually consisted of from 10 to 30 retail operations located in separated market areas. However, the largest, Abbey Medical, had begun operations in 1924 and now consisted of over 70 local dealers. Higgins estimated 1981 sales for the chain (which was itself acquired by American Hospital Supply Corporation in April 1981) at over $60 million. In general, chains maintained a low corporate visibility and provided their dealers with working capital, employee benefit programs, operating advice, and some centralized purchasing. Higgins thought that chain organizations might grow more rapidly over the next 10 years.

The Issues

Higgins looked at his watch. It was 5:30 and really time to leave. "Still," he thought, "I should jot down what I see to be the immediate issues before I go—that way I won't be tempted to think about them over the weekend." He took a pen and wrote the following:

1. Should TRP continue to rent respirators to dealers?
2. Should TRP protect each dealer's territory (and how big should a territory be)?
3. Should TRP require dealers to stock no competing equipment?
4. How many dealers should TRP eventually have? Where?
5. What sales information should be assembled in order to attract high quality dealers?
6. What should be done about the "best efforts" clause?

As he reread the list, Higgins considered that there probably were still other short-term-oriented questions he might have missed. Monday would be soon enough to consider them all.

Until then, he was free to think about broader, more strategic issues. Some reflections on the nature of the target market, a statement of marketing objectives, and TRP's possible entry into the hospital market would occupy the weekend. Decisions on these topics would form a substantial part of TRP's strategic marketing plan, a document Higgins hoped to have for the beginning of the next fiscal year in July. "At least I can rule out one option," Higgins thought as he put on his coat. That was an idea to use independent sales representatives to sell TRP products on commission: a recently completed two-month search for such an organization had come up empty. "Like my stomach," he thought, as he went out the door.

Case 18

Laramie Oil Company: Retail Gasoline Division*

In April 1980 George Thomas, vice president in charge of domestic automotive gasoline distribution for the Laramie Oil Company, was considering what action he should take with regard to the company's 12,400 franchised and lessee-operated service stations. A number of developments that indicated discontent among franchisees and lessees had recently occurred. Although he was unsure as to what extent these developments indicated real widespread discontent, Mr. Thomas was wondering what might be causing it, and what action he should take at the present time, and in the long run.

Company Background

The Laramie Oil Company was a fully integrated petroleum company with operations in 21 countries. In 1979 domestic sales were $8.79 billion, and net income was $823.4 million. The Laramie product line included automotive gasoline, aviation fuels, distillates, lubricants, and assorted agricultural and industrial chemicals. Sales of automotive gasoline and related products accounted for 52 percent of revenues earned and 64 percent of net profit.

Both the international and domestic American Head Offices were situated in New York City. As distribution vice president, George Thomas had responsibility for the overall maintenance of a strong network of retail outlets. This responsibility involved the setting of policies concerning lease terms, the selection of dealers, the training of dealers, the motivation of dealers, the dismissal of dealers, and any other factors involving the maintenance of dealer morale and overall effectiveness. Mr. Thomas only had responsibility for the company's Laramie brand stations. Laramie Oil also operated about 50 discount outlets and expected to open more in the near future. These outlets operated under a different brand name.

George Thomas described his objective as distribution vice president as follows:

---

* This case was coauthored by C. Merle Crawford, Professor of Marketing, University of Michigan.

We've done a great deal of research to determine why gasoline purchasers use one brand of gasoline or another. In almost every instance, the consumer's perception of the gasoline retail outlet was a very significant determinant in brand selection. It appears that we're halfway to first base if we can keep our outlets modern and clean, plus provide the service that the consumer desires. By service, I mean more than just good, fast, competent pump island work. Service includes having outlets open when consumers need them, and making sure that outlets handle our national promotions. There is nothing more irritating to a customer who expects to receive a glass or coupon than to find that the station that he happens to be in isn't participating in the national promotion. That is one of the best ways to lose customers for good.

Our whole retail distribution policy is directed toward providing a consistent type of physical outlet and service from one end of the country to the other. That's how gasoline is sold.

Implementation of Distribution Policies

George Thomas's control over the implementation of his department's policies was quite indirect. A general manager in each of five geographical divisions had responsibility for all marketing activities in his division, including retail distribution. Each division had a distribution manager whose responsibilities included the day-to-day implementation of corporate policies in regard to service station operations. The division distribution manager reported directly to the division general manager. The corporate and divisional distribution managers did, however, maintain informal contact with each other. Each divisional distribution manager had a number of district sales managers reporting directly to him. Direct contact with service station operators was maintained by company sales representatives, each of whom reported to a district sales manager. The sales representative was the final link in the chain of implementation between George Thomas's office and the service station operator. (See Exhibit 1 for a partial organization chart.)

Type of Service Stations

Laramie Oil Company distributed its automotive products through three types of service stations:

1. *Company operated.* These stations were owned or leased by Laramie Oil who hired the service station personnel to operate them on a straight salary basis. Laramie controlled the retail price and all other aspects of all products sold through these stations. About 100 of Laramie's 12,400 stations were operated in this manner.

2. *Franchised dealers.* The station site and all physical facilities of franchised dealer operations were owned by the dealers themselves. Laramie did, however, provide financing, so that an individual dealer could commence operation by putting up as little as $2,000. The company, or local financial institutions, held mortgages on the land and physical facilities. About 500 outlets were in this category.

EXHIBIT 1 Partial organization chart

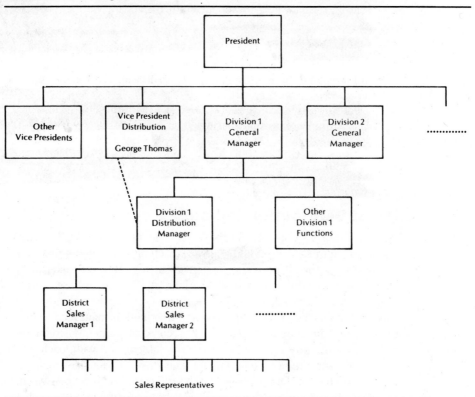

- - - - - Indicates an informal communications link.

3. *Lessee operated.* Lessee operators were dealers who leased their service station from Laramie Oil. The stations, in these cases, continued to be owned by Laramie Oil. The lessee purchased petroleum products from Laramie but was free to set his own operating policies as related to such things as hours, prices, and brands of accessories carried. The lessee's cost price of gasoline was based on a "tank wagon price" which included all taxes and delivery charges to the lessee's station. Typical lessee operators were charged per gallon, as shown in the accompanying table.

Transport price (except tax)	$0.660
Plus: State and federal taxes	0.450
Transport price (including tax)	1.110
Plus: Jobber margin	0.085
Tank wagon price	1.195
Plus: Rent paid to Laramie	0.055
Lessee's margin	0.070
Retail price	$1.320

The cost price of gasoline to franchised dealers closely approximated the lessee cost arrangement, except that rent charges were not included. For most franchisees, interest charges on their mortgages tended to make up this cost difference.

A Closer Look at Two Laramie Lessee Dealers

1. Jerry Williamson's Laramie service station, Dearborn, Michigan. Jerry Williamson's service station was located at one of the main intersections in the Detroit suburb of Dearborn. His customers were drawn mainly from local residents and commuters who drove through Dearborn on their way to and from their work in Detroit. Williamson was a class A automobile mechanic who had worked for a Ford dealership for eight years before becoming a Laramie dealer in 1964. He had put up $9,500 of his own money to obtain the right to be the Laramie lessee for his Dearborn location. Most of the $9,500 had been used to finance product inventories and tools, while some had been used to physically upgrade the station.

Williamson did a large automobile repair business. Over the years he had built up an excellent reputation among the residents of Dearborn for providing competent and reliable repair service. As a result of this business and his good location for attracting gasoline customers, he did an annual sales volume of slightly over $494,000. His profit statement for 1979 is presented in Exhibit 2.

EXHIBIT 2 Percentage profit statements for Jerry Williamson's and Fred Shaw's service stations for 1979

	Jerry Williamson	Fred Shaw
Sales	100.00%	100.00%
Cost of goods sold	75.36	75.24
Gross profit	24.64	24.76
Expenses:		
Labor for outside work	0.46	0.29
Supplies	0.75	0.79
Wages (excluding owner)	8.38	8.69
Repairs and maintenance	0.34	0.24
Advertising	0.79	0.93
Delivery	0.41	0.42
Bad debts	0.02	0.02
Administrative	0.38	0.35
Miscellaneous	0.96	0.72
Rent	2.60	2.00
Insurance	0.47	0.46
Utilities	0.96	1.00
Taxes	0.74	0.66
Interest	0.10	0.11
Depreciation	0.60	0.65
Total expenses	17.96	17.33
Net profit	6.68%	7.43%
Inventory turnover × 1 year	17.26	12.88

Williamson took great pride in the fact that he had been able to build a very successful business operation. He thought of himself as being a part of the community as he took part in community work through his memberships in the Lion's Club, and the Chamber of Commerce. In the latter organization he had risen to the position of vice president, and was looking forward to being president at some time.

When he was asked if there were any negative aspects to being a Laramie dealer, Williamson replied as follows:

> Well . . . not really; it's tough to complain a lot when you're making $33,000 a year. The only thing I really have to complain about is that Laramie pressures me to buy most of my repair parts and accessories from their own supply company or from company-approved jobbers. I think I could get slightly better margins from other jobbers, as the company takes a percentage rake-off from the approved jobbers. However, it's really a small complaint when you consider all the pluses that Laramie gives. Overall, I'm extremely pleased.

2. Fred Shaw's Laramie service station, Detroit, Michigan. Fred Shaw's service station was located in an industrial section of Detroit, with most of his customers being people who worked in the plants in the surrounding area. Prior to becoming the lessee of his current station, Shaw had worked as an employee in a suburban Laramie station. He had always wanted to be in business for himself, and whenever he heard that a station was available, he would approach the sales representative involved to see if he could obtain the station. Most of the stations had required too much capital, but finally he was able to obtain his current station by putting up $8,500 for the required inventories.

Although managing his station required long hours for Shaw, he preferred it to a very great extent over working for another dealer. It was in a very real sense to him the fulfillment of his dream of being his own boss.

Due to the nature of the surrounding environment, Shaw's station was quiet most of the day except when the shifts changed and then it was extremely busy. This constant changing from feast to famine made proper staffing extremely difficult, and required long hours to cover all shift changes.

Shaw's station was not as productive in either gasoline sales or repair service as was Jerry Williamson's. As a result, his 1979 sales volume was just under $95,000. Exhibit 2 presents his 1979 profit statement.

Hank Homes was the Laramie sales representative in Shaw's district, and on one of his weekly visits recently he asked Fred to take part in a special Bicentennial china giveaway promotion. Part of the conversation between the two men went as follows:

Hank: This looks to me to be one of the best promotions the company has ever put together. They're going to put about $2.5 million in advertising behind it. You should draw a pile of customers.

Fred: Come on, Hank. The type of customer who buys from my outlet isn't interested in bone china. It may be fine for other outlets, but I don't want in on this one.

Besides, since the gasoline shortage of '73 and '74, I can't believe anyone wants to start these rotten giveaways again.

Hank: I disagree, Fred. I'm sure you'd do well with it. Why don't you let me sign you up. I think you'd be pleased with the results. We pretested this in Denver and it went well. Think about it for a few minutes while we discuss a few other things. It looks to me as if your station could use a new coat of paint this spring. If we let it go any longer, it will chase customers away.

Fred: I don't think I can afford to put out for the paint right now, Hank. You know what a problem I'm having making ends meet here.

Hank: Well, maybe I can help you out on that score. If I work on them at the regional office, they might let me absorb part or even all of the expense for you. . . . Think about the china promotion, Fred, and I'll drop back tomorrow.

Franchisee and Lessee Discontent

The following dealer comments were taken from meetings of several Laramie retail dealer associations in various parts of the United States. Laramie retail dealer associations were groups of Laramie dealers who had gotten together on their own for such purposes as: the discussion of mutual problems, the collective purchasing of products from independent suppliers, and the undertaking of various social activities. Not all Laramie dealers belonged to associations and the strength and activity level of the associations varied greatly.

Lessee 1: The company claims that we can set our own prices, but that damn sales rep comes into my place and tells me I can't sell at more than a four-cent markup. I can hardly scrape from one week to the next at that rate. . . . I know for sure he'll drop my lease if I don't set these prices. Our dealer association has had economists do studies that showed that on the average it takes a gross profit margin of nine cents a gallon to operate profitably. Margins today run from about three cents to eight cents with the average at about five and a half cents. That's just not enough.

Lessee 2: What really bugs me is those stupid premium offers I have to put up with. They advertise them like mad on TV, so I have to carry them or the customers start screaming. . . . I don't get any more business with them—all my competitors are running some premium too—all they do is add to my costs. It's really frustrating. I thought the oil crisis had finished these things. I guess I was wrong.

Lessee 3: I couldn't be more satisfied. I make a really good living. If some of you guys stopped complaining and started working, you could do the same.

Lessee 4: You know I'd really like to close my place down at night . . . the only reason I'm open nights is 'cause the sales rep said he wouldn't renew my lease if I didn't keep his hours—imagine that, I've worked for Laramie for 15 years as a dealer and they'd drop me just like that. I can't afford to lose my station but I'm losing money by staying open.

Lessee 5: What's really got me worried is that they are going to turn my station into a company-owned and -operated outlet. Where would I be then?

Lessee 6: The company is more interested in their gallonage than our profits, and those one-sided leases let them dictate what we'll charge and what products we'll sell. They also use the lease to ride herd on our prices.

Lessee 7: I had hoped that the Supreme Court rulings prohibiting forcing their TBA (tires, batteries, and accessories) brands on us would have helped; however, all it's done is to make their methods more subtle.

Franchisee 1: I thought when I put up my bucks I was going to be in business for myself—fat chance—that sales rep is in my place all the time suggesting what hours to work, how to work, what price to set. . . . If I object, he starts talking about revoking my franchise. I know the Laramie name draws customer but some of his suggestions are unreasonable.

Franchisee 2: This business of them running their own discount stations in competition with me has really got me bugged, too.

Comments of Sales Representatives (SR)

The following comments were taken from individual interviews with selected sales representatives:

SR 1: Sure, I set hours and prices and procedures; if I didn't, some of those dolts would be out of business tomorrow.

SR 2: To get the volume out of my territory that the district manager demands, I have to pressure the dealers. Talking about the lease is always effective. However, I've never actually threatened any of my dealers with the loss of the lease.

SR 3: If you're honest and friendly with your dealers and show them what they will gain from following what you suggest, then you don't have to threaten them to get cooperation.

SR 4: You can bet your life I'm out pushing our TBA line to dealers. That right hasn't been taken away from us. However, that doesn't mean we're going to club them over the head if they don't.

Comments by George Thomas

(Made before a congressional committee.)

It isn't our policy to require dealers to maintain company directed hours or prices. The whole idea is that the dealer has the right to establish his own hours and prices.

I'd fire any sales representative found pressuring dealers on matters like prices or hours or contests.

It seems to me that what we have here is a situation completely analogous to the normal arrangement between the landlord and tenant. We have up to $200,000 invested in large stations, and if the dealers are mismanaging them we have a right and a duty to protect our investment.

Developments in 1980

A number of developments that concerned George Thomas took place in 1980.

1. A group of dealers in Chicago filed a suit against Laramie, alleging that Laramie violated the Sherman Act by using short-term leases to intimidate the dealers into following suggested retail prices. No decision had been handed down yet by the court.

2. A Laramie Marketing Research Staff report indicated that the turnover rate among Laramie dealers had increased significantly in the last few years. This problem of dealer turnover was common throughout the oil industry. Estimates indicated that approximately one third of all service stations in the United States change management every year. The Laramie turnover rate was below the national average, but was still very high. This high turnover was considered to be a very serious problem by George Thomas. Also disturbing was the fact that a significant number of long-service Laramie dealers had left to join cut-rate chains who guaranteed station managers at least $1,500 income per month.

3. The Automotive Retail Trade Association had requested the Federal Trade Commission (FTC) to charge the seven major oil companies (including Laramie) with misrepresentation, breach of contract, and promotion of price wars. The writ alleged misrepresentation of "exclusive" franchise agreements and breach of contract because the oil companies have opened "off-brand" stations near franchise service stations. The association charged that the off-brand stations sell at prices lower than the wholesale prices charged to the franchise dealers. The association wants an injunction to stop oil companies from creating subsidiary stations in direct competition with franchised dealers.

   The writ also criticized the oil companies for nondisclosure of fees or profits received by oil companies from firms which supply automobile products to the service stations. The association wanted to know this information since service station lessees are requested to buy the accessories only from designated dealers.

   Finally the writ criticized promotional gimmicks and giveaways as a financial burden to operators and alleged that oil companies "demanded" cooperation and participation under threat of nonrenewal of leases.

4. The Central States Automotive Retailers Association presented a brief to the governors of six states asking for legislation to prohibit gimmicks and giveaways connected with gasoline selling. The association alleged that an end to giveaways could reduce the selling price of gasoline by one or two cents a gallon. The brief also asked that oil companies be required to sell gasoline at one price to all customers. At present the wholesale price varies from customer to customer, with the highest being charged to leased gas stations.

5. Laramie had recently closed many marginal stations as a result of gasoline shortages in 1979. A group of dealers dispossessed in this process had brought suit against Laramie charging violations of their franchise agreement and conspiracy to restrain trade.

   Mr. Thomas reflected on these developments and wondered what alternative courses of action were available to him, and what action he should take both in the short run and in the long run. He also wondered what factors had caused the current problems.

Case 19

U.S. Pioneer Electronics Corporation*

In fall 1977 Bernie Mitchell, president of U.S. Pioneer Electronics, placed an ad featuring a portrait of William Shakespeare in several trade magazines. It was an open letter from Shakespeare and Mr. Mitchell to several "dissident" dealers franchised to sell Japanese-made Pioneer products in the United States.[1] The ad, shown in Exhibit 1, alleged that "a few dealers" had resorted to "disparagement of Pioneer products and 'bait and switch' advertising" and threatened dealer investigations to protect Pioneer's reputation.

Mr. Mitchell hoped these "unjustifiable practices" were the sporadic misconduct of only "an unwise few" and could be dealt with individually. But if they represented an overall erosion of dealer support for Pioneer products, he was determined (a) to take immediate steps to prevent further erosion and (b) to establish a new long-run distribution strategy to ensure U.S. Pioneer's continued leadership in the hi-fi industry.

Industry Background

The U.S. hi-fi industry was started in the 1960s by a few engineers who, according to industry legend, left their positions (mostly in the aerospace industry) to pursue their hobby of building amplifiers and speakers in their garages and basements. By the late 1960s, larger component manufacturers were beginning to broaden their product lines.[2] For instance, Scott, previously identified solely

---

* This case was prepared by Assistant Professor Hirotaka Takeuchi with the assistance of William Falkson (MBA 1978) as the basis for class discussion rather than to illustrate either effective or ineffective handling of an administrative situation. Copyright © 1978 by the President and Fellows of Harvard College.

[1] The words "retailers" and "dealers" are used interchangeably in this case.

[2] Components were combinations of different audio equipment, which reproduced sound highly faithful (i.e., high-fidelity or hi-fi sound) to the original record or tape. Consumers created component systems of their choice by combining (a) an inlet source, such as a turntable, tape deck, or FM tuner; (b) a control center, such as an amplifier or receiver, which was an amplifier and FM tuner combined into one unit; and (c) an outlet, such as speakers. In audio terminology, receivers and amplifiers were called "electronics."

EXHIBIT 1

AN IMPORTANT MESSAGE FROM WILLIAM SHAKESPEARE AND PIONEER.

"Who steals my purse steals trash . . .
But he that filches from me
    my good name
Robs me of that which not
    enriches him
And makes me poor indeed."

The Immortal Bard said it over three hundred years ago. It's still true today.

It has come to our attention at Pioneer that a few dealers of high fidelity products, acting in what they believe to be their best interest, have taken up the practice of disparagement of Pioneer products and "bait and switch" advertising, often using Pioneer's hard earned reputation in the industry as the "bait."

This tactic hurts Pioneer, hurts the consumer and ultimately hurts all dealers since it will damage the credibility of our high fidelity business in the eyes of consumers. To protect our legitimate dealers, Pioneer will conduct frequent investigations of this practice, and we will take appropriate steps to protect and defend our reputation on behalf of the great majority of our dealers against the unjustifiable practices of an unwise few.

Respectfully,

William Shakespeare, *Stratford upon Avon*
Bernie Mitchell, *U.S. Pioneer Electronics*

with electronics, was building its reputation in the speaker business. Sherwood, also an electronics manufacturer, introduced an automatic turntable in 1969. KLH, which had started out making speakers, turned to stereo compacts about the same time.[3]

Japanese hi-fi manufacturers such as Pioneer, Kenwood, Sansui, and Teac also entered the U.S. market in the late 1960s. At the same time most original founders of the hi-fi companies, who had operated in a "club-like" business atmosphere, were leaving the industry.

The 1970s saw a new attitude among hi-fi manufacturers. As Mr. Mitchell told one trade magazine reporter,

> Six years ago . . . we only wanted to sell our product to a certain select group of people who had to qualify somehow intellectually and technologically. We didn't want to sell . . . to kids or to ordinary people, only to superpeople. It was a real elitist attitude, and terribly dangerous. We've changed it from an elitist business that didn't really want to grow to an industry that has some pride in itself and its products and says, "These products are so good we won't be happy until we tell everybody." (*Crawdaddy*, July 1976.)

Company Background

Pioneer Electronics Corporation was founded in Tokyo in 1938. It started with capital of $235 and had expanded to $843 million in worldwide sales by 1977. Overseas sales surpassed domestic sales in 1974 and, in 1977, accounted for 65 percent of the total. Net income (pretax) in 1977 was nearly $61 million.

U.S. Pioneer was established in March 1966 under Ken Kai, vice president, then 26 years old. He had joined the parent company in Tokyo after graduating from college and was sent to New York a year later as Pioneer's U.S. liaison. In 1966, U.S. Pioneer had less than $200,000 in sales and fewer than 30 dealers.

Bernie Mitchell joined the company in 1970. He was an economist by training and a music buff, as well as a member of the boards of directors of the New Jersey Symphony and the Metropolitan Opera. He had worked previously with Westinghouse, Toshiba, and Concord Electronics.

To help U.S. Pioneer grow, Mr. Mitchell and Mr. Kai took on the task of developing the market—making more people aware of and knowledgeable about hi-fi products. U.S. Pioneer sponsored hi-fi shows on college campuses and became the first hi-fi company to advertise in such magazines as *Playboy, National Lampoon,* and the *New Yorker.* U.S. Pioneer ads featured music, sports, and other celebrities.

The company also strengthened its distribution network. U.S. Pioneer was supplied by its parent in Japan. Commission sales representatives sold to its

---

[3] Compacts were preassembled audio systems that usually consisted of two units—one containing a turntable, receiver, and/or tape player and the other a pair of speakers. A compact system usually cost less and was smaller than a component system. It reproduced stereo sound (i.e., sound reproduced through two separate channels) but not necessarily high-fidelity sound.

retail dealers. In 1972, U.S. Pioneer had six independent sales representative offices, which sold only Pioneer products (with the exception of accessories, complementary items, and very high-priced lines of electronics that did not directly compete with Pioneer). Each office had its own sales force and served a given region. Each had from four to seven salespeople paid an average annual salary of $20,000. They assisted retailers with merchandising and display, store operations, and sales training. By 1975 U.S. Pioneer had added 10 independent sales representatives offices and 4 company-owned offices—in New York, Washington, D.C., Florida, and Missouri. These "captive" offices were paid the same commission as the independents—but were not allowed to carry product lines of direct or indirect competitors.[4]

By 1977, the number of retail outlets carrying Pioneer products had grown to almost 3,600 from approximately 500 in 1970. Retailers had to sign franchise agreements with U.S. Pioneer. Mr. Mitchell thought they did not hesitate to sign because the company's strong national and local cooperative advertising created considerable consumer pull. Five percent of U.S. Pioneer sales was allocated to local ads featuring its products. In addition, the firm offered dealers attractive gross margins and credit terms.

Fair Trade[5] versus Free Market

FTC Action

Just as market expansion and distribution building were starting to generate higher net sales ($80 million in 1974), the Federal Trade Commission (FTC) issued a complaint against U.S. Pioneer and three other competitors. It alleged that Sansui, Sherwood, Teac, and U.S. Pioneer granted dealerships to retailers only if they agreed to maintain suggested retail prices, directed their sales representatives to report on retailers who failed to maintain such prices, and delayed shipments to retailers who cut prices. These practices violated Section 5 of the Federal Trade Commission Act, which prohibited "unfair methods of competition . . . and unfair or deceptive acts or practices in commerce." Their effect, the FTC charged, was to inflate consumer prices.

---

[4] Before 1974, U.S. Pioneer sales representative offices received a 10 percent commission. That year the rate was reduced to 5 percent, comparable with that of other manufacturers.

[5] Fair-trade (or resale price maintenance) laws permitted a manufacturer or distributor of trademarked products to determine their resale price. Although on the surface such laws seemed to support a manufacturer's desire to influence retail prices, they had initially been advocated by small, independent retailers seeking protection from direct price competition by large chains. The first such state law was passed in 1931, and by 1941 all but three states had such laws. In 13 states a "nonsigner clause" bound all retailers selling a fair-traded product to the contract if one retailer in the state signed an agreement. The Miller-Tydings Act, passed in 1937, applied resale price maintenance to interstate commerce.

Fair-trade practice and enforcement began to decline steadily in the early 1950s. By 1975 fair trade was being used only for certain brands of hi-fi equipment, television sets, jewelry, bicycles, clothing, cosmetics, and kitchenware. Major efforts to repeal state laws started in 1974. In December 1975, the Consumer Goods Pricing Act terminated interstate fair-trade regulations.

Consent Decree

In August 1975, the four companies signed consent decrees with the FTC. They did not admit guilt, but did promise not to engage in the alleged practices. Specifically, they were prohibited from fair trading their products for five years in the 21 states where the practice was still permitted and from using suggested list prices for two years in any part of the country. They also could not ask consumers the price of purchased products on warranty registration forms. Finally, the companies were required to distribute copies of the consent order to all their dealers and to give any dealer whose franchise had been terminated an opportunity to regain it.

U.S. Pioneer's Response

Asked why U.S. Pioneer decided not to contest the FTC decree, Mitchell replied:

> I don't mind being a crusader. In fact, I kind of enjoy it. But I like to crusade for something that makes some long-term sense.
>
> The FTC is asking us not to violate the law. It has never been our intention to violate the law. They are asking that we no longer fair trade our products. We had already unilaterally made the decision that fair trade wasn't viable anymore anyhow. . . . The third thing they are asking us is that we not conspire to fix prices, either among dealers or among ourselves, and we had no intention of doing that.
>
> We did try to fix retail prices at the dealer level as long as fair trade lasted; that was the purpose of fair trade statutes. When we fair traded, we did it pretty darn well. But when we decided to go off fair trade, we decided we were going to be the best there was at free market practices. (*Electronics Retailing,* October 1975.)

To implement this new goal, Pioneer replaced the price sheet in effect during fair trade (see Exhibit 2) with a list that replaced the words "fair trade resale price" with "approximate nationally advertised value" and added optional retail prices under gross margins of 15 percent, 20 percent, 25 percent, 30 percent, 35 percent, 40 percent, and 45 percent (see Exhibit 3).

According to *Home Furnishings Daily* (August 27, 1975), "Most of the dealers and manufacturers contacted scorned [Pioneer's] list because they felt it was, in the words of one manufacturer, 'an open invitation to cut the hell out of prices.'" Mr. Mitchell said in the same article that the initial response was fear and that dealers did not understand the significance of the change from fair-trade to free-market prices.

> Too often, under the fair-trade environment, dealers felt, "If we have a very fine mix of products, and people come in and we tell them wonderful stories about each of those products, they will tell us which products they want. They'll sort of self-sell in an enlightened environment."

EXHIBIT 2 Price list of selected products, April 22, 1975

Stereo Receivers	Description	Fair Trade Resale	1-3 pcs.	4-more	Case	Shipping Weight
SX-1010	AM/FM Stereo Receiver	$699.95	$466.60	$420.00	1	60 lbs.
SX-939	AM/FM Stereo Receiver	599.95	400.00	372.00	1	51 lbs.
SX-838	AM/FM Stereo Receiver	499.95	333.40	310.00	1	44 lbs.
SX-737	AM/FM Stereo Receiver	399.95	266.60	248.00	1	35 lbs.
SX-636	AM/FM Stereo Receiver	349.95	233.30	217.00	1	29 lbs.
SX-535	AM/FM Stereo Receiver	299.95	200.00	186.00	1	27 lbs.
SX-434	AM/FM Stereo Receiver	239.95	160.00	148.80	1	22 lbs.

U.A. Series	Description	Fair Trade Resale	1-3 pcs.	4-more	Case	Shipping Weight
Spec 1	Stereo Pre-Amplifier.	$499.95	$333.40	$300.00	1	30 lbs.
Spec 2	Stereo Power Amplifier.	899.95	600.00	540.00	1	60 lbs.
SA-9900	Integrated Stereo Amp.	749.85	500.00	450.00	1	50 lbs.
SA-9500	Integrated Stereo Amp.	499.95	333.40	300.00	1	44 lbs.
SA-8500	Integrated Stereo Amp.	399.95	266.60	240.00	1	32 lbs.
SA-7500	Integrated Stereo Amp.	299.95	200.00	180.00	1	30 lbs.
SA-5200	Integrated Stereo Amp.	138.95	93.30	84.00	1	23 lbs.
TX-9500	AM/FM Stereo Tuner	399.95	266.60	240.00	1	24 lbs.
TX-7500	AM/FM Stereo Tuner	249.95	166.70	150.00	1	21 lbs.
TX-6200	AM/FM Stereo Tuner	139.95	93.30	84.00	1	18 lbs.
RG-1	RG Dynamic Expander	179.95	120.00	108.00	1	15 lbs.
SR-202W	Stereo Reverb. Amp.	139.95	93.30	84.00	1	12 lbs.
SF-850	Electronic Crossover	199.95	133.30	120.00	1	16 lbs.
SD-1100	Quad/Stereo Display	599.95	400.00	360.00	1	34 lbs.
WC-UA1	Walnut Cabinet*	34.95**	23.30	21.00	1	11¼ lbs.

* Walnut Cabinet for SA-8500, SA-7500, TX-9500, TX-7500 only. ** Suggested Resale

Turntables	Description	Fair Trade Resale	1-3 pcs.	4-more	Case	Shipping Weight
PL-71	2-Speed, DC Brushless Servo Motor, Anti-skating Direct-Drive	$299.95	$200.00	$180.00	1	33 lbs.
PL-55X	2-Speed, DC Brushless Servo Motor, Anti-skating, Direct-drive Automatic Turntable	249.95	166.60	150.00	1	31 lbs.
PL-A45D	2-Speed, Automatic Turntable 2-motor, Belt-drive, Anti-skating	169.95	113.30	105.40	1	26 lbs.
PL-15D/II	2-Speed, Automatic Turntable with Hysteresis Synchronous Motor, Belt-drive, Anti-skating	129.95	87.10	83.20	1	20 lbs.
PL-12D & PL-12D/II	2-Speed, Hysteresis Synchronous Motor, Belt-drive, Anti-skating	99.95	70.00	66.00	1	19 lbs.

EXHIBIT 3 Price list of selected products, July 1, 1975

STEREO RECEIVERS	Description	DEALER COST 1-3 pcs.	4-more	Case	Shp. Wt.	15% Margin	20% Margin	25% Margin	30% Margin	35% Margin	40% Margin	45% Margin	Approx. Nationally Adv. Value	Your Price	Model Number
SX-1010	AM/FM Stereo Rec.	$466.60	$420.00	1	60 lbs.	$494.00	$525.00	$560.00	$600.00	$646.00	$700.00	$764.00	$700.00	_____	SX-1010
SX-939	AM/FM Stereo Rec.	400.00	372.00	1	51 lbs.	438.00	465.00	496.00	531.00	572.00	620.00	676.00	600.00	_____	SX-939
SX-838	AM/FM Stereo Rec.	333.40	310.00	1	44 lbs.	365.00	388.00	413.00	443.00	477.00	517.00	564.00	500.00	_____	SX-838
SX-737	AM/FM Stereo Rec.	266.60	248.06	1	35 lbs.	292.00	310.00	331.00	354.00	382.00	413.00	451.00	400.00	_____	SX-737
SX-636	AM/FM Stereo Rec.	233.30	217.00	1	29 lbs.	255.00	271.00	289.00	310.00	334.00	362.00	395.00	350.00	_____	SX-636
SX-535	AM/FM Stereo Rec.	200.00	186.00	1	27 lbs.	219.00	233.00	248.00	266.00	286.00	310.00	338.00	300.00	_____	SX-535
SX-434	AM/FM Stereo Rec.	160.00	148.80	1	22 lbs.	175.00	185.00	198.00	213.00	229.00	248.00	271.00	250.00	_____	SX-434

U.A. SERIES	Description	DEALER COST 1-3 pcs.	4-more	Case	Shp. Wt.	15% Margin	20% Margin	25% Margin	30% Margin	35% Margin	40% Margin	45% Margin	Approx. Nationally Adv. Value	Your Price	Model Number
Spec 1	Stereo Pre-Amplifier	$333.40	$300.00	1	30 lbs.	$353.00	$375.00	$400.00	$429.00	$462.00	$500.00	$545.00	$500.00	_____	Spec 1
Spec 2	Stereo Power Amp.	600.00	540.00	1	60 lbs.	635.00	675.00	720.00	771.00	831.00	900.00	982.00	900.00	_____	Spec 2
SA-9900	Integ. Stereo Amp.	500.00	450.00	1	50 lbs.	529.00	563.00	600.00	643.00	692.00	750.00	818.00	750.00	_____	SA-9900
SA-9500	Integ. Stereo Amp.	333.40	300.00	1	44 lbs.	353.00	375.00	400.00	429.00	462.00	500.00	545.00	500.00	_____	SA-9500
SA-8500	Integ. Stereo Amp.	266.60	240.00	1	32 lbs.	282.00	300.00	320.00	343.00	369.00	400.00	436.00	400.00	_____	SA-8500
SA-7500	Integ. Stereo Amp.	200.00	180.00	1	30 lbs.	212.00	225.00	240.00	257.00	277.00	300.00	327.00	300.00	_____	SA-7500
SA-5200	Integ. Stereo Amp.	93.30	84.00	1	23 lbs.	99.00	105.00	112.00	120.00	129.00	140.00	153.00	140.00	_____	SA-5200
TX-9500	AM/FM Stereo Tuner	266.60	240.00	1	24 lbs.	282.00	300.00	320.00	343.00	369.00	400.00	436.00	400.00	_____	TX-9500
TX-7500	AM/FM Stereo Tuner	166.70	150.00	1	21 lbs.	176.00	189.00	200.00	214.00	231.00	250.00	273.00	250.00	_____	TX-7500
TX-6200	AM/FM Stereo Tuner	93.30	84.00	1	18 lbs.	99.00	105.00	112.00	120.00	129.00	140.00	153.00	140.00	_____	TX-6200
RG-1	RG Dyn. Expander	120.00	108.00	1	15 lbs.	127.00	135.00	144.00	154.00	166.00	180.00	196.00	175.00	_____	RG-1
SR-202W	Stereo Reverb. Amp.	93.30	84.00	1	12 lbs.	99.00	105.00	112.00	120.00	129.00	140.00	153.00	150.00	_____	SR-202W
SF-850	Electronic Crossover	133.30	120.00	1	16 lbs.	141.00	150.00	160.00	171.00	185.00	200.00	218.00	200.00	_____	SF-850
SD-1100	Quad/Stereo Display	400.00	360.00	1	31 lbs.	424.00	450.00	480.00	514.00	554.00	600.00	655.00	600.00	_____	SD-1100
WC-UA1	Walnut Cabinet†	23.30	21.00	1	11 lbs.	25.00	26.00	28.00	30.00	32.00	35.00	38.00	35.00	_____	WC-UA1
													†Walnut cabinet for SA-8500, SA-7500, TX-9500 & TX-7500 only		
WC-UA2	Walnut Cabinet‡	26.70	24.00	1	11 lbs.	28.00	30.00	32.00	34.00	37.00	40.00	44.00	40.00	_____	WC-UA2
													‡Walnut cabinet for SA-9900 & SA-9500 only		

TURN-TABLES	Description	DEALER COST 1-3 pcs.	4-more	Case	Shp. Wt.	15% Margin	20% Margin	25% Margin	30% Margin	35% Margin	40% Margin	45% Margin	Approx. Nationally Adv. Value	Your Price	Model Number
PL-71	2-Sp., DC Brushless Servo Motor, Anti-skating, Direct drive	$200.00	$180.00	1	33 lbs.	$212.00	$225.00	$240.00	$257.00	$277.00	$300.00	$327.00	$300.00	_____	PL-71
PL-55X	2-Sp., DC Brushless Servo Motor, Anti-skating, Direct drive, Auto. Turntable	166.60	150.00	1	31 lbs.	176.00	188.00	200.00	214.00	231.00	250.00	273.00	250.00	_____	PL-55X
PL-A45D	2-Sp., Auto. Turntable 2-motor, Belt drive, Anti-skating	113.30	105.40	1	26 lbs.	124.00	132.00	141.00	151.00	162.00	176.00	192.00	175.00	_____	PL-A45D
PL-15D/ıı	2-Sp., Auto. Turntable w/Hysteresis Synch Motor, Belt drive, Anti-skating	87.10	83.20	1	20 lbs.	98.00	104.00	111.00	119.00	128.00	139.00	151.00	125.00	_____	PL-15D/ıı
PL-12D & PL-12D/ıı	2-Sp., Hysteresis Synch. Motor, Belt drive, Anti-skating	70.00	66.00	1	19 lbs.	78.00	83.00	88.00	94.00	102.00	110.00	120.00	100.00	_____	PL-12D PL-12D/ıı

I don't really think that's a very good way to run a business. Dealers have to identify what needs the consumer has, acquaint him very quickly with options, suggest an option they think he ought to take and bear down very hard to lead him to take that option. That's called selling.

Effects on Sales and Prices

The immediate impact of the consent decree, according to *Home Furnishings Daily,* was a "price war which lowered dealer profit margins to 5 or 6 percent in many parts of the country." The newspaper also said that "many retailers began to criticize manufacturers for 'abandoning' them and called for them to control the fluctuating markets." Some softening of the market, according to an FTC spokesperson, was expected as a "backlash." But "prices won't stay as low as they are now and higher margins will eventually return. [In the meantime] I expect to see greater sales at discount prices and the good dealers will survive."

In 1976 retail dollar sales jumped 12.6 percent and unit sales increased 9.4 percent over the previous year (see Exhibit 4). In 1975, on the other hand, the increases had been 1.6 percent and 2.2 percent, respectively. According to Mr. Kai, the much smaller percentage increase between 1974 and 1975 probably resulted from the recession and consumer decisions to delay purchases until fair-trade laws were repealed. In New York and New Jersey repeal had been rumored as early as August 1975.

EXHIBIT 4 Unit and dollar sales of hi-fi components, 1974–1977

	1974	1975	1976	1977
Unit sales (000s)				
Total components	7,799	7,971	8,719	9,539
Receivers	960	970	1,050	1,185
Amps, pre-amps, tuners	231	263	275	320
Turntables (except OEM)	1,767	1,709	1,866	2,015
Speakers	2,500	2,550	2,800	3,125
Tape decks (cassette and open reel)	341	399	428	494
Headphones	2,000	2,080	2,300	2,400
Dollar sales ($ millions)				
Total components	$1,056	$1,073	$1,208	$1,390
Receivers	336	306	341	392
Amps, pre-amps, tuners	69	76	81	97
Turntables (except OEM)	168	179	222	252
Speakers	300	319	350	416
Tape-decks (cassette and open reel)	113	120	133	147
Headphones	70	73	81	86

Source: *Merchandising,* March 1978, p. 51.

In the meantime, U.S. Pioneer net sales increased from $80 million in 1974 to $87 million in 1975. In addition, its market share increased between 1974 and 1975 in all hi-fi product categories except turntables and speakers (see Exhibit 5). All Pioneer's market share percentages in 1976 were equal to or higher than those of 1974.

EXHIBIT 5 U.S. Pioneer market share data*

Product category	1971	1972	1973	1974	1975	1976
Receivers	7%	15%	23%	22%	25%	25%
Tuners	3	5	25	18	23	18
Amplifiers	3	5	8	9	12	10
Turntables	3	3	3	11	10	11
Speakers	2	1	4	5	3	7
Headphones	10	5	4	7	9	9
Cassette decks	—	—	4	11	26	20
Open reel tape decks	—	—	—	5	9	9

* Pioneer's overall market share in the hi-fi component market was 18 percent to 20 percent in 1977.
Source: Company data.

Market Growth and Changes

The hi-fi market was growing, and there was evidence that buyer profiles for component parts were changing. As shown in Exhibit 6, there were fewer women, more young adults (ages 18 to 24), more Pacific area residents, more college graduates, and more households with incomes of $25,000 and over purchasing stereo component parts in 1975 than in the previous year.

Realizing a shift in buyer demographics, U.S. Pioneer undertook extensive research to determine (a) the market potential of hi-fi products compared with low-fi products, such as compacts or consoles[6] and (b) the purchasing behavior of hi-fi component buyers.

An independent research firm found that sales of components were growing faster than sales of compacts and consoles. But in sheer volume, compacts outsold components and consoles by a wide margin. In 1975, 3.5 million units of compacts were sold in the United States, compared with 1.5 million component systems and 400,000 consoles. To Mr. Mitchell, this meant that 3.9 million U.S. buyers were taken off the hi-fi market. Once they had purchased compacts and consoles, these customers were not expected to consider replacing them with hi-fi components for several years.

"Also, every time a compact or console is sold, you lose the potential of

---

[6] Consoles were preassembled, all-in-one audio systems that were larger and cost more than most component systems. Their sound reproduction was generally considered poorer than that of components.

EXHIBIT 6 Demographic profile of buyers of stereo component parts*

	1974		1975	
	United States (139,778,000)	Stereo components buyers (3,400,000)	United States (141,622,000)	Stereo components buyers (2,788,000)
Sex				
Men	47.3%	73.4%	49.6%	76.4%
Women	52.7	26.6	50.4	23.6
Age				
18–24	18.1%	42.5%	18.5%	47.6%
25–34	20.6	31.8	21.2	26.9
35–49	24.6	18.0	24.2	15.0
50–64	22.4	6.8	21.7	9.9
65 or over	14.2	1.0	14.4	0.5
Residence				
New England	3.9%	4.4%	5.9%	6.6%
Mid-Atlantic	22.2	18.6	20.6	18.8
East Central	13.1	16.9	14.2	15.1
West Central	16.5	19.8	15.2	16.6
Southeast	18.0	14.0	19.1	14.9
Southwest	10.6	10.4	10.1	7.1
Pacific	15.6	15.9	14.8	20.8
Education				
Graduated college	11.9%	16.3%	12.5%	25.6%
Attended college	14.0	30.8	14.7	27.5
Graduated high shool	37.7	39.5	38.0	36.2
Did not graduate high school	36.4	13.4	34.8	10.7
Household income				
$25,000 or more	8.8%	11.5%	11.3%	20.9%
$20,000–$24,999	7.5	9.3	8.4	9.1
$15,000–$19,999	17.1	21.4	18.6	22.7
$10,000–$14,999	24.1	21.5	23.2	21.1
$ 8,000–$ 9,999	9.2	9.8	8.7	8.5
$ 5,000–$ 7,999	14.4	10.8	13.3	11.3
Less than $5,000	18.8	15.7	16.5	6.4
Family life cycle				
Single	16.2%	38.8%	17.3%	41.9%
Married	69.5	50.4	67.9	52.2
Widowed/divorced/separated	14.3	10.8	14.9	6.0
(Parents)	(43.7)	(36.0)	(42.4)	(37.6)

* Buyers of stereo component parts within the past year.
Source: 1975 and 1976 issues of *Target Group Index,* published by Axiom Market Research Bureau, Inc. Sample sizes were approximately 25,000 for 1974 and 30,000 for 1975.

an additional speaker, add-on tape deck, upgraded receiver, tuner, turntable, and more," said Mr. Mitchell. The research revealed that this add-on market was larger than expected. In 1975, add-on sales accounted for 55 percent of total dollars spent on hi-fi components. New system sales made up the remaining 45 percent.

Buying influences

Consumer research showed that buyers of different audio systems were influenced by different factors, in order of importance:

Component buyers	*Console buyers*	*Compact buyers*
1. Lifelike sound reproduction.	1. Esthetics.	1. Lower price.
2. Superior electronics.	2. Adequate electronics.	2. Small size.
3. Add-on capability.	3. No involved hookup.	3. No involved hookup.
4. Status symbol.	4. A lot for the money.	4. Ease of operation.

The research also found that component buyers:

> Depended heavily on advice of family and friends.
>
> Thought they knew just enough about hi-fi components to get by (only 8 percent thought they knew ''a lot'').
>
> Shopped around, especially for the initial purchase.
>
> Paid either $350–$400 or $650–$750 for initial purchase of system.
>
> Replaced or upgraded components approximately one to two years after their initial purchase.

New Marketing Strategy

On the basis of this research, Mr. Mitchell established the goal of ''doubling the number of people owning and buying any brand of hi-fi components next year.'' He said,

> We'd rather see a consumer buy a Marantz, Sansui . . . yes, and even a Technics than a fancy fruitwood console, or plastic compact, both of which deliver less than true high fidelity.

To implement this goal, he asked dealers to persuade prospective compact or console buyers to consider lower priced hi-fi components. He argued that this could be best accomplished by prominently displaying low-end components and explaining their advantages over compacts and consoles. To support this dealer effort, Pioneer introduced lower priced components. It also allocated $6 million national advertising for 1976. Of this, $2 million was earmarked for persuading consumers that only hi-fi components produced true high-fidelity sound. Head copy for one of the ads read, ''BAD SOUND IS AN UNNECESSARY EVIL.'' The ad referred by name to some of Pioneer's competitors—Marantz, Kenwood, and Sansui—as dedicated companies trying to reproduce high-quality sound.

Mr. Mitchell also asked dealers to use direct mail to tap the replacement and add-on markets. Ads were mailed to customers who had purchased audio systems one and two years before.

Results

Mr. Mitchell and Mr. Kai were very satisfied with their new strategy as Pioneer's sales increased from $87 million in 1975 to $135 million in 1976. Although their goal of doubling the number of hi-fi owners and buyers was not achieved, they felt that more people were buying components than compacts and consoles. The number of compact systems sold in the United States increased from 3.4 million in 1975 to 3.6 million in 1976, whereas component *unit* (not system) sales increased from 8.7 million in 1975 to 9.5 million in 1976 (see Exhibit 7).

EXHIBIT 7 Unit sales of compacts and components, 1974–1977 (000s)

Compact systems	1973	1974	1975	1976
Cassette tape recorder bimode	32	36	38	44
Cassette tape recorder trimode	103	190	197	233
8-track tape player bimode	652	528	525	527
8-track tape player trimode	1,234	798	843	910
8-track tape recorder bimode	549	590	555	569
8-track tape recorder trimode	480	1,024	1,100	1,183
Changer bimode	377	325	324	337
Total	3,427	3,491	3,582	3,803
Components parts (total)	7,799	7,971	8,719	9,539

Source: *Merchandising,* March 1978, p. 51.

They were also impressed by the findings of a Gallup Organization consumer survey for U.S. Pioneer.[7] The survey, conducted in the first half of 1977, measured consumer brand preference for different hi-fi component categories (receiver, FM tuner, amplifier, turntable, speaker, and tape deck). As shown in Exhibit 8, prospective component purchasers preferred Pioneer over all other brands in every category except tape decks.

EXHIBIT 8 Brand preference data for hi-fi components

Brand of receiver	All prospective purchasers (percent)	Brand of FM tuner	All prospective purchasers (percent)
Pioneer	26	Pioneer	28
Marantz	15	Marantz	18
Sony	13	Sansui	14
Sansui	12	Fisher	6
Kenwood	7	Kenwood	6
Fisher	2	Dynaco	3
Harman-Kardon	2	Technics	1
Technics	1	Sherwin	0
Sherwood	1	Rotel	0
Other	2	Other	1

---

[7] Gallup Organization was an independent research firm that specialized in survey research and had gained its reputation through political polls.

EXHIBIT 8 *(concluded)*

	All prospective purchasers (percent)		All prospective purchasers (percent)
Brand of receiver		Brand of FM tuner	
Don't plan to buy	5	Don't plan to buy	5
Don't know	14	Don't know	18
Total	100	Total	100
Brand of amplifier		Brand of turntable	
Pioneer	29	Pioneer	24
Marantz	17	Garrard	19
Sansui	9	Dual	12
Kenwood	8	BSR	8
Harman-Kardon	5	Technics	6
Superscope	3	Sansui	5
Crown	1	Bang & Olufsen	2
Dynaco	1	B.I.C.	1
Technics	1	JVC	1
Other	2	Other	3
Don't plan to buy	6	Don't plan to buy	4
Don't know	18	Don't know	15
Total	100	Total	100
Brand of speaker*		Brand of tape deck	
Pioneer	32	Teac	21
Jensen	11	Pioneer	17
JBL	11	Sony/Superscope	15
AR	5	Sansui	9
Infinity	5	Fisher	6
KLH	4	Akai	5
B.I.C.—Venturi	3	Bekorder	1
Technics	3	Harman-Kardon	1
Dynaco	1	Technics	0
Other	3	Other	2
Don't plan to buy	4	Don't plan to buy	9
Don't know	18	Don't know	14
Total	100	Total	100

Note: National probability sample of 196.

* Among the different component parts, speakers usually offered the highest gross margin to dealers. One industry source estimated the margin spread between speakers and other components (branded products) to be 10 percent to 20 percent. This spread differed by brand and by type of retail outlets.

Source: Gallup Organization, July 12, 1977.

Retailer Dissidence

Just as Pioneer's "franchise" with consumers was strengthening, Mr. Mitchell came across a number of reports suggesting that relationships with its franchised dealers were starting to deteriorate. In particular, he was concerned about sales representatives' reports about (*a*) disparaging Pioneer products by misrepresenting product specification sheets or manipulating sound demonstrations, and (*b*) using an illegal and unethical tactic known as "bait and switch."[8]

---

[8] "Bait and switch" refers to advertising a product at bargain price to draw customers into the store and sell them something similar to, but more expensive than, the advertised item. Pioneer products were good *bait* because of their strong consumer pull—created through national advertising and favorable word-of-mouth communication. In one Pioneer survey, 98 percent of Pioneer component owners interviewed said they were satisfied and would buy the brand again.

Pioneer Field Investigation

Disparagement of Pioneer products was spotted in continuous field work by employees (mostly part time) who visited Pioneer's franchised stores posing as interested shoppers for Pioneer products, interacted with store personnel, and prepared "shopping reports" for the company. (See Exhibit 9.)

EXHIBIT 9 Shopping report

1. *Shopper's name:* John Smith
2. *Store visited:* ABC Sounds
3. *Salesperson and/or store attitude toward Pioneer:* Store's attitude generally negative. Salesperson was not really negative but went along with negative comment by another salesperson.
4. *Products they tried to get you to buy and discouraged:* Pushed Sankyo STD-1900 (a tape deck on sale for $218) and discouraged Pioneer CT-F7272 (a tape deck on sale for $208).
5. *Unfavorable statements toward Pioneer:* The salesperson made no derogatory remarks about Pioneer to me but became involved in a conversation with another store salesperson and prospective customer in which the other salesperson stated that he could produce copies of letters dealers had written to Pioneer complaining about service.
6. *Favorable statements toward competition:* Sankyo unit had much better frequency response and much cleaner sound. Sankyo was the second largest manufacturer of tape decks and manufactured components for Teac.
7. *How were Pioneer products displayed in comparison to competition?* I did not see any of the Pioneer equipment advertised in the paper displayed in the normal manner. Specifically, CT-F7272 was missing from where all other Pioneer decks were displayed. It was in another room with a Sankyo unit sitting on top of it.
8. *Other comments:* When the salesperson set up to play the tapes back I noted that the Sankyo playback control was set at maximum volume and that he adjusted the Pioneer control to about 6. He began playing the tapes back, switching from one deck to the other and commented on the very audible difference of sound created by the higher frequency response of the Sankyo deck. I made no comment but asked to see the spec sheets on the two units. He came back with the spec sheet on the Sankyo but not the Pioneer.

   During the time I spent in the store I overheard no less than six customers ask specifically for one of the Pioneer products advertised in the paper. In each case the customer was told that the particular item had been sold out but that they had lesser or better products in the Pioneer line or comparable products in other lines. I also heard another customer ask if ABC Sounds could order Pioneer's HMP-100s. The salesperson replied, "No, we can't." The customer dropped the idea at that point.

Source: Company data.

In one report, a U.S. Pioneer employee visited a midwestern hi-fi specialty store and asked for a Pioneer tape deck, but was persuaded by the salesperson to buy a competing brand (see Exhibit 9). The report noted that (a) the store salesperson made a comment on how "he could produce copies of letters that dealers had written to Pioneer complaining about service"; (b) Pioneer's tape deck (CT-F7272) was missing from its display area; (c) the store salesperson, when asked for a CT-F7272 specification sheet, handed him that of a competing brand but did not have one for Pioneer; and (d) the store salesperson set the playback sound control at maximum volume for the competing brand but at less than maximum for Pioneer.

To counter these objectionable practices, Pioneer placed the Shakespeare ad (Exhibit 1) in major trade publications to appeal to dealers. The company also asked the presidents of all its sales representative offices to identify the "most blatant, most persistent" disparagement and bait-and-switch offenders in their territories.

Audio Warehouse Suit

U.S. Pioneer filed a suit against Audio Warehouse, a five-store chain with 1977 sales of $10 million, and its advertising agency, both of Akron, Ohio in July 1977. It charged them with using bait-and-switch tactics, advertising without sufficient inventory, and disparaging Pioneer products to customers. A temporary restraining order barred Audio Warehouse from engaging in these practices.

Ed Radford, the 34-year-old president of Audio Warehouse, told *Retail Home Furnishings* (September 26, 1977),

> Yeah, we're being sued (by U.S. Pioneer), but we're not taking this lying down— we're going to fight it. Pioneer surprised me because they got a temporary restraining order, and within one day, they had it in every newspaper in my state. As far as I'm concerned, Pioneer's trying to make me look bad. The public doesn't understand that a temporary restraining order doesn't mean anything. Anybody who puts up a bond can get one.

To prove his point, Mr. Radford (who was called "Fast Eddie" because of his hurried speech and quick rise to fortune) placed a full-page advertisement in two Ohio newspapers (see Exhibit 10).[9] The ad contained Audio Warehouse's version of the suit filed by U.S. Pioneer and offered sharply reduced prices on a number of Pioneer products.

Mr. Radford contended that "many dealers around the country were having difficulty maintaining margins on Pioneer equipment" and charged that Pioneer didn't "seem to care whether we make a profit or not" *(Retail Home Furnishings)*.

---

[9] According to the *Sunday Tribune* (February 12, 1978), Ed Radford, who was orphaned at age five, was planning a "fast" retirement at age 49. He had started his business in 1973 with his life savings of $10,000. In 1978 "Fast Eddie" was a millionaire who still came to work in jeans and an "exploding blond Afro."

EXHIBIT 10 Audio Warehouse advertisement

EXHIBIT 11

Dealer Franchise Agreement

AGREEMENT made _____ this _____ day of _____ 19___ , by and between
U. S. PIONEER ELECTRONICS CORP. a Delaware Corporation, having its principal place of business in Moonachie, New Jersey (hereinafter called "PIONEER"), and

hereinafter called "Dealer"

Signer's name: _____

Corporate name: _____

dba _____

Address _____

City _____ State _____ Zip _____

Telephone No. (____) _____

WITNESSETH:

WHEREAS Pioneer is the Distributor of certain quality products which are sold under the Pioneer brand name and trade marks (hereinafter referred to as "Products"); and

WHEREAS, Dealer desires to engage in the sale of Products at retail.

NOW, THEREFORE, Pioneer and Dealer mutually agree as follows:

1. Pioneer hereby appoints Dealer one of its Franchised Dealers in the continental limits of the United States only, and Dealer hereby accepts such appointment and agrees conscientiously and diligently to promote the sales of the above mentioned products.

2. Dealer shall purchase from Pioneer such Products for resale but all sales or agreements by Dealer for the resale of Pioneer Products shall be made by Dealer as principal and not as agent of Pioneer.

3. Prices to Dealer for such Products shall be set forth in the Pioneer Dealer Cost Schedules issued from time to time by Pioneer. Pioneer shall have the right to reduce or increase prices to Dealer at any time without accountability to Dealer in connection with Dealer's stock of unsold products on hand at the time of such change. When a new price schedule is issued by Pioneer it shall automatically supersede all such schedules on and after its effective date.

4. Dealer has represented to Pioneer, as an inducement to Pioneer for entering this agreement, that Dealer is at the time of entering into this agreement solvent and in a good and substantial financial position. Dealer shall from time to time when requested by Pioneer furnish such financial reports and other financial data as may be necessary to enable Pioneer to determine Dealer's financial condition.

5. Pioneer shall have the right to cancel any orders placed by Dealer or to refuse or to delay the shipment thereof if Dealer shall fail to meet payment schedules or other credit or financial requirements established by Pioneer and the cancellation of such orders or the withholding of shipments by Pioneer shall not be construed as a termination or breach of this agreement by Pioneer.

6. Pioneer will use its best efforts to make deliveries with reasonable promptness in accordance with orders accepted from Dealer, but it shall not be liable for any damages, consequential or otherwise, for its failure to fill orders or for delays in delivery or for any error in the filling of orders.

7. No territory is assigned exclusively to Dealer by Pioneer. Pioneer reserves the absolute right, for any reason whatever, to increase or decrease the number of Franchised Dealers in Dealer's locality or elsewhere, at any time without notice to Dealer.

8. Pioneer shall have the right at any time to discontinue the manufacture or sale of any or all of its Products and parts without incurring any liability to Dealer.

9. Pioneer is at liberty to change its service policies, its financial requirements and the design of its Products and parts thereof at any time without notice, and the Dealer shall have no claim on Pioneer for damage by reason of such change or changes.

10. Dealer agrees to forward promptly to Pioneer information concerning all charges, complaints or claims involving Products, by customers or accounts, that may come to its attention.

11. Dealer shall at no time engage in any unfair trade practices and shall make no false or misleading representations with regard to Pioneer or its Products. Dealer shall make no warranties or representations to customers or to the trade with respect to Products except such as may be approved in writing by Pioneer. Dealer shall hold Pioneer harmless from all damages caused by Dealer's violation of this paragraph. Any written representations respecting Pioneer products must first be submitted to Pioneer for its written approval.

12. Dealer will use its best efforts to resell Products purchased from Pioneer.

Although Mr. Mitchell was confident that the suit would be settled in Pioneer's favor (especially because the attorney general of Ohio became a coplaintiff), he was concerned about the impact of Audio Warehouse's publicity on Pioneer's dealer outlets. At the same time he wondered whether to initiate legal action against other offenders and/or terminate their franchises.[10] (See Exhibit 11 for sample agreement.)

---

[10] Most of these dealer franchise agreements had been signed during the "fair-trade" days and did not fully reflect the changes resulting from the FTC consent order.

EXHIBIT 11 *(concluded)*

13. Dealer shall have no rights in the names or marks owned, used, promoted by Pioneer or in the names or marks of Products, except to make reference thereto in selling, advertising and promoting the sale of Products, which right shall be completely terminated upon the termination of this agreement.

14. Nothing herein contained shall be deemed to establish a relationship of principal and agent between Pioneer and Dealer, Dealer being an independent contractor, and neither Dealer nor any of its agents or employees shall be deemed to be an agent of Pioneer for any purpose, whatsoever and shall have no right or authority to assume or create any obligation of any kind, express or implied, on behalf of Pioneer except as specifically provided herein, nor any right or authority to accept service of legal process of any kind on behalf of Pioneer nor authority to bind Pioneer in any respect whatsoever.

15. All negotiations, correspondence and memoranda which have passed between Pioneer and Dealer in relation to this agreement are merged herein and this agreement constitutes the entire agreement between Pioneer and Dealer. No representations not contained herein are authorized by Pioneer and this agreement may not be altered, modified, amended, changed, rescinded or discharged, in whole or in part, except by a written memorandum executed by Pioneer and Dealer in the same manner as is provided for the execution of this agreement, except that the agreement may be terminated by either party as herein provided.

16. This agreement shall become effective only upon its execution by Pioneer in its executive offices at Moonachie, New Jersey, and no changes, additions or erasure of any printed portion of this agreement shall be valid and binding unless such change, addition or erasure is initialled by both Pioneer and Dealer.

17. This agreement supersedes and terminates any and all prior agreements or contracts, written or oral, if any, entered into between Pioneer and Dealer as of the effective date of this agreement with reference to all matters covered by this agreement.

18. Dealer is appointed a Franchised Pioneer Dealer by reason of Pioneer's confidence in Dealer, which appointment is personal in nature, and consequently this agreement shall not be assignable by Dealer, nor shall any of the rights granted hereunder be assignable or transferable in any manner whatsoever without the consent in writing of Pioneer.

19. This agreement shall be governed and construed in accordance with the laws of the State of Delaware. In the event of the provisions of this agreement, or the application of any such provisions to either Pioneer or Dealer with respect to its obligations hereunder, shall be held by a court of competent jurisdiction to be contrary to any State or Federal Law, the remaining portions of this agreement shall remain in full force and effect.

20. Either Dealer or Pioneer may terminate this agreement at any time by giving five days' written notice to the other and such termination may be made either with or without cause. Neither Dealer nor Pioneer shall be liable to the other for any damages of any kind or character whatsoever on account of such termination. Pioneer, at its option, shall have the right to repurchase from Dealer any or all Products in Dealer's inventory within a reasonable period from said notice of termination, at the net prices at which such Products were originally invoiced to Dealer less any allowances which Pioneer may have given Dealer on account of such Products. If such option to repurchase is exercised by Pioneer, Dealer agrees to deliver the inventory of Products so purchased to Pioneer, Moonachie, New Jersey, immediately after receipt of the exercise of such option.

21. Any notice which is required to be given hereunder shall be given in writing and shall either be delivered in person or sent by registered letter via United States mail to the respective addresses of the parties appearing above. If mailed, the date of the mailing shall be deemed to be the date such notice has been given.

22. Dealer shall not return merchandise without Pioneer's prior written authorization; and Pioneer shall assume no responsibility for returns made without prior written authorization.

IN WITNESS WHEREOF, the parties hereto have caused these presents to be executed the day and year first above written.

DEALER:

BY: _____   U.S. PIONEER ELECTRONICS CORP.

Title: _____   BY: _____

Dealer Communication Program

Sales representatives suggested that U.S. Pioneer organize an extensive communication program to convince dealers that the company was concerned about their well-being and to demonstrate how effective selling of Pioneer products could improve their profits. The sales reps were increasingly confronted with complaints from dealers such as

> Most of my customers ask for Pioneer. But I can't make money with Pioneer.

How can we compete with discounters or mail-order guys who are selling Pioneer for as low as 10 percent above cost?

We'd be better off selling products of smaller manufacturers like Advent and Bose, which still sell at list prices.

I'm making 50 percent to 60 percent margin on house brands; why should I push Pioneer?

Such comments concerned Mr. Mitchell, because he thought dealer support was crucial. When a recent consumer survey asked, "What factors had the greatest influence in your most recent purchase of hi-fi products?" respondents replied,

	Percent of respondents*
Recommendations of friends	29%
Dealers/salespeople	27
Advertising by manufacturers	15
Recommendations of family members	12
Advertising by dealers	8
Store display	7
All others	14
No answer	(n = 1,290)

* Percentages total over 100 because of multiple answers.

In a sales representatives' meeting, Bob Gundick, president of the company sales office in Florida, displayed a presentation package he had used successfully. A set of flip charts was shown to dealers during regular visits and handouts (similar in content) were left after the presentations. As shown in Exhibit 12, the package suggested ways the dealers could (*a*) cope with their competitors, (*b*) determine their product mixes, (*c*) creatively sell Pioneer products in combination with other brands, and (*d*) improve their businesses in general. Mr. Gundick offered his package for nationwide use.

Other suggestions during the meeting included

1. Direct mail brochures to all dealers.
2. More salespeople to increase the frequency of dealer visits.
3. Cash rebates or other incentive programs (such as a contest for dealers).
4. Organizing a "national dealers conference" at a resort.

Although the format of the sales communication program was yet to be determined, Mr. Mitchell felt it justified a budget of $3 million. He was uncertain, however, whether the budget should be incremental or whether some funds should be transferred from consumer advertising.

EXHIBIT 12 Sunshine Audio sales presentation program

MOST OF MY CUSTOMERS ASK FOR PIONEER!!!

I CAN'T MAKE MONEY WITH PIONEER!!!

HOW OFTEN HAVE WE HEARD, OR HAVE YOU MADE, THESE VERY STATEMENTS. IF YOU ARE INTERESTED IN INCREASING YOUR OVERALL BUSINESS AND YOU WANT TO INCREASE YOUR OVERALL PROFIT DOLLARS—READ ON.

You and your competitor

Your business is really not that different from that of the store down the street. You both sell hi-fi, you both are after the same consumer, you both have to make a profit, you both want your business to grow, and you both are competing against each other. Why?

View your competitor as an ally and see what happens to your perspective of the business. You are both fighting to get consumers' disposable income dollars from the TV dealer, the motorcycle dealer, the travel agent, the car dealer, and any number of places they can spend that extra $300–$700. You and other hi-fi retailers should run ads to make the hi-fi market in your town grow—not to "get the other guy" with a low-ball price. Think about it—how many people in your market know that a RZ105 receiver at $136 is a good buy (cost in fact)? Much less, how many know what a receiver is?

You and your sales

Think about this for a minute. Most of your business should be in systems—about 70 percent. Single-piece sales account for the 30 percent balance. Fifteen percent are high margin pieces or accessory sales, and 15 percent are low margin promotional pieces. Now, think about that margin. If you only sell 40 percent margin products and you are not a "discount" house, how come your balance sheet only shows your gross margin between 28 percent and 32 percent? Interesting.

You and Pioneer

Now for the sales pitch. When you put a Pioneer piece in a system you will sell more systems (better brand name recognition) at your usual system margin. Pioneer has plenty of products that sell at full margin all the time—SG-9500, RG-1, turntables with cartridges, component ensembles, RT-2022, and so on. Of course, we have promotional pieces too, CTF 2121, Project 60, 100a, and others. But how low a margin is a CTF 2121 at a cost of $124—with an advertised price of $139—when you sell the deck and its case for $179. This makes the margin 26 percent; sell tape and your margin is higher. I can't make money on Pioneer. Don't believe it! How about the SX1250 at $595—only a $50 profit. With the $50 rebate recently offered your real profit is $100. Sell an extra three SX1250s each week and we add over 15,000 profit dollars to your bottom line in a year. Even without the $50 rebate, the contribution to profit is $7,500 in one year.

EXHIBIT 12 *(concluded)*

Instead of using your energy not to sell, to down sell, or to sell off Pioneer, what would happen if you put that effort into creatively selling it?

You and your business

Some suggestions:

Put together systems with brand name products that can't be duplicated by any dealer in your market.

Sell the accessories with the promotional pieces or make them part of a system to increase profitability.

Sell brand name goods that customers want.

Think in terms of profit dollars, not always gross profit margin.

You and the industry

Pioneer will spend close to $7 million in advertising. Take advantage of this tremendous support. Without advertising and without brand names your business would dry up. Most hi-fi dealers have some exclusive lines. But limited distribution can mean limited market and limited growth. Pioneer in a system will help sell more JVC receivers; Bose, JBL, or Advent speakers; Technics turntables; or whatever your exclusive is, and your business will grow. Pioneer has a product and a model that will fit almost any system you can design. The quality has never been questioned. Sandy Ruby from Tech HiFi in a recent *Home Furnishings Daily* was quoted as saying, "We're actually not doing as much business in limited distribution lines as we were a few years ago. We've tried to look more toward what the market wants. We see surveys of what people are buying or what they say they plan to buy around the country . . . and then we get that equipment. You can't just look at your sales figures. Sure, you may be selling a lot of private brand equipment, but what about the people who didn't buy from you?" What brand do they want? You've got to have a handle on the customers who walked. Pretty interesting stuff. How many of your customers walked? How many did your salespeople's paranoia scare away?

We can help.

Long-Run Strategy Options

Citing the broad changes occurring in the industry, several sales reps argued that the existing situation provided a timely opportunity to reconsider U.S. Pioneers' long-run distribution strategy.

Distribution Shift

One possibility was to shift retail distribution away from specialty stores to department stores and catalog showrooms. In 1977, 75 percent to U.S. Pioneer's dollar sales were accounted for by hi-fi specialty stores, 5 percent by department stores, 7 percent by catalog showrooms, and 13 percent by appliance/TV/hardware/furniture stores.[11] Department stores and catalog showrooms did not generally offer the extensive customer services provided by specialty stores, including professional sales assistance, demonstration, extended store warranty,[12] on-the-premises repair, home delivery and installation, and loaner component programs. They usually had, however, extensive credit facilities, strong consumer "pull" advertising, and lower prices. Industry sources predicted a substantial increase in the market shares of department stores and catalog showrooms.

Multiple Branding

Some sales reps suggested that one way to take advantage of the trend toward more mass-oriented retail outlets and, at the same time, "keep specialty stores reasonably happy" would be multiple branding. U.S. Pioneer would offer several product lines of varying quality and price points under separate brand names. Different product lines would be carried by different types of retail outlets. The "department store" line would presumably be of lower quality and price than a "regular" line. Supporters pointed out that multiple branding had been used in other industries[13] and that it would enable U.S. Pioneer to adapt most effectively to future changes in retail distribution.[14] Others were more concerned that such a strategy would tarnish Pioneer's reputation for selling only top-of-the-line products.

Company-Owned Stores

Another strategic option was to move toward operating its own retail stores. Some retailers in the low-fi market (such as Radio Shack and Sears) had been selling their own house brands for some time. More recently, house brands were starting to make inroads in the hi-fi market. For example, house brand sales by Pacific Stereo (a chain of 80 West Coast stores) were estimated to be 25 percent (unit basis). In other hi-fi specialty stores, house brands were believed to account for 5 percent to 10 percent of unit sales.

---

[11] In terms of the number of existing U.S. Pioneer retail outlets, 69 percent were hi-fi specialty stores, 2 percent department stores, 3 percent catalog showrooms, and 26 percent other stores.

[12] Many specialty stores extended the two-year Pioneer guarantee on parts and labor on its electronics to three years.

[13] For example, it was used in the watch industry. The Bulova Watch Company had three brand names—Bulova, Accutron, and Caravelle. The Bulova line was intended for jewelry and department stores, Accutron for the best stores carrying the Bulova line, and Caravelle predominantly for quality drugstores and specialty gift shops. In fact, Bulova had experienced considerable difficulty maintaining discrete channels for these lines.

[14] Should discount stores become a major force in hi-fi components sales, a new line with a new brand name could be added. Pioneer Electronics of America, a separate, wholly owned subsidiary of Pioneer Electronics Corporation of Japan, currently sold compacts and car stereos to discount stores under the "Centrex" brand name.

Some sales reps felt that house brands would seriously threaten U.S. Pioneer. Because the primary promoters of house brands were large specialty store chains, Pioneer risked being "squeezed out" of them. One way to counter this prospective threat would be to start Pioneer retail stores by acquiring existing one- or two-unit family-owned stores or converting nonaudio stores into "Pioneer shops."

The estimated U.S. Pioneer initial fixed investment for starting up, say, a 5,000-square-foot hi-fi store was to be about $50,000. Given the operating data for a comparable existing specialty store, shown in Exhibit 13, the initial invest-

EXHIBIT 13
HI-FI SPECIALTY STORE*
Income Statement

	1976
Income	$680,069
Cost of sales	509,182
Expenses:	
Advertising	34,803
Sales commissions (4 salespeople)	36,048
Payroll home office (administration)	12,875
Payroll home office (clerical)	767
Payroll taxes	1,770
Rent	18,780
Depreciation	1,831
Insurance	2,937
Taxes—other	237
Freight out	2,017
Store security	1,168
Outside labor	3,374
Travel and entertainment	1,336
Bad debts	3,313
Repairs and maintenance	579
Repairs to merchandise	57
Credit plan service charges	872
Telephone	5,318
Heat, light, and power	1,242
Bad checks	4,108
Recruiting expenses	889
Store supplies and expenses	3,055
Selling and promotion	115
Cleaning and rubbish removal	45
Cash over and short	442
Office supplies and expenses	1,058
Group insurance	257
Interest expense	857
Legal and accounting	3,648
Auto and truck expense	2,070
Rental commissions	130
Computer service expenses	44
Bank service charges	147
Officers' life insurance	193
Miscellaneous	916
Total expenses	146,120
Operating income before federal taxes	$ 24,767

* One of a four-unit chain on the East Coast.

EXHIBIT 14
U.S. PIONEER ELECTRONICS CORPORATION
(A wholly owned subsidiary of Pioneer Electronics Corporation)
Statement of Income and Retained Earnings
($000)

	1976*		1975*	
Net sales	$134,836		$87,105	
Other operating revenue	258		235	
Total revenue		135,094		87,340
Cost of goods sold (CGS) (primarily purchases from the parent company)	91,707		60,470	
Selling, general and administrative expenses (SG&A)	30,608		23,409	
Total CGS and SG&A		122,315		83,879
Income before income taxes		12,779		3,461
Provision for income taxes		6,530		1,716
Net income		6,249		1,745
Retained earnings at beginning of year		4,985		3,240
Retained earnings at end of year		¹11,234		$ 4,985

* Fiscal year ended September 30.
Source: Company data.

ment appeared to be recoverable in a short time. (U.S. Pioneer's income statement is provided in Exhibit 14.)

Conclusion

A few months after the sales rep meeting, Mr. Mitchell met with Mr. Kai to decide what action, if any, to take in the short run and the long run to ensure U.S. Pioneer's growth and profitability.

Part 6

Promotion Decisions

A. Advertising Decisions

Advertising is the most visible and controversial activity carried on in marketing. The first seven cases in this section focus their attention on this function.

Advertising is defined as all paid, nonpersonal forms of communication that are identified with a specific sponsor. It, therefore, includes expenditures on radio, television, newspaper, magazines, and outdoor billboards, plus the yellow pages. The largest absolute dollar spenders on advertising tend to be big consumer products companies, like Procter and Gamble, General Foods, and General Motors. The industries that spend the highest percentage of their sales on advertising are the drug and cosmetic companies, followed closely by packaged food products and soaps.

The marketing decision maker has a number of decisions to make with respect to advertising for a product. These include:

1. Setting advertising objectives.
2. Determining the advertising budget.
3. Deciding on what creative presentation should be used.
4. Selecting what media vehicles to use.
5. Selecting what scheduling pattern should be used.
6. Deciding how the advertising should be evaluated.

In the cases that follow in this section, the reader will work to make decisions in most of these areas. The next section of this note is a short reminder of some of the concepts related to each of these decision points.

Advertising Objectives

Advertising objectives should be stated in qualified terms with a specific time period designed for a specific market target. The objective may be in terms of profits, sales, or communications measures such as awareness, interest, and preference. The objective: "increase brand awareness" is obviously not as good a statement as "increase brand awareness to 85 percent of all women 18–40, in the next six months."

Advertising Budgets

Advertising budgets are difficult to set. That is why companies have fallen into using rule of thumb methods such as (1) the "all we can afford" method; (2) the percentage of sales method; and (3) the matching competitors method. We would prefer decision makers to proceed by defining the task they hope to accomplish and then have them calculate the cost of doing this. This is called the task approach. To do this method the advertiser must understand the functional relationship between his or her task and advertising expenditures.

Creative Development

Creative activity is usually done by an advertising agency. The final product is usually the result of much copy testing on dimensions such as attention getting and persuasiveness.

Media Decision

Media decisions are of two types. The first is the selection of broad classes of media to be considered for future analysis. This is done by matching the media characteristics with the needs of the advertiser. For example, television allows for good visual demonstration. This may be a desired characteristic for the campaign at hand.

The second stage involves the selection of specific media vehicles, for example, the NFL football game versus "All in the Family" versus a page in *Fortune*. The procedures for doing this are complex. Simply stated, vehicles are compared on the basis of their cost per thousand (CPM) target audience persons reached. The vehicle with the lowest CPM is selected. Audience sizes are then adjusted to allow for duplication between vehicles and new CPMs are calculated. Then the lowest CPM vehicle at that point is selected. This process continues until the budget is used up. A number of computer algorithms have been developed to handle the many calculations made in this process.

Scheduling Patterns

The advertisers must decide whether to (1) spend their budget continuously throughout the period; (2) concentrate it at a short interval; or (3) spend it intermittently throughout the period. There are no good rules of thumb to answer this question. The advertisers must experiment to find out which pattern makes the most sense for their products.

Evaluating Advertising

If the advertiser has specified quantitative objectives, one is then in a position to measure to see if the objectives were met. The procedure used should be specifically designed to fit the type of objective stated.

B. Sales Management Decisions

The last three cases in this section of the book deal with the management of the personal selling function. Personal selling is defined as all paid, personal forms of communication that are identified with a specific organization.

Organizations in the United States spend over one and one half times as much money on personal selling as they do on advertising. Effective management of personal selling activity is thus very important.

The marketing decision maker has a number of decisions to make with respect to personal selling for a product. These include:

1. Defining the selling job to be performed.
2. Establishing the desired characteristics of the salespersons who will do this job.
3. Determining the size of the sales force.
4. Recruiting and selecting salespersons.
5. Training salespersons.
6. Organizing the sales force.
7. Designing sales territories.
8. Assigning salespersons to territories.
9. Motivating salespersons.
10. Compensating salespersons.
11. Evaluating salespersons.

In the three sales management cases that are in this section, the reader will work to make decisions in most of these areas. Again, the next section of this note is a short reminder of some of the concepts related to each of these decisions.

Definition of the Selling Job

The beginning point of all sales management decisions is the definition of the selling job to be performed. For example, is the job basically just order taking or are there complex engineering presentations involved? In defining a particular selling job, one must keep in mind the role of personal selling in the overall marketing strategy and understand well the needs of the buyer or buyers involved. The competitive and physical environments of the job are also important considerations.

Desired Characteristics for Salespersons

Out of the definition of the selling job, the manager is able to establish a set of criteria for determining the type of person who should perform the selling job. One should list the personal background and individual skills and qualifications that are necessary to effectively perform the defined job. For example, in selling complex electrical equipment, the criteria might include the holding of a degree in electrical engineering, with strong oral communications skills to make presentations to customers.

Sales Force Size

Determining the necessary size of a sales force involves determining the effort level capabilities of an average salesperson and dividing that into a measure of the total selling job to be done. In doing so, judgments must be made on how many total accounts to serve, how often to call on them, and how many accounts an average salesperson can effectively handle.

Recruiting and Selecting Salespersons

The selection of the right salespersons basically involves generating a pool of prospects and evaluating those prospects using the criteria established for the selling job. Information is collected on prospects using application forms, personal interviews, and psychological tests.

Training

The basic objective of training is to bring a salesperson up to the required level of competence in those areas of the defined selling job that were deficient upon hiring. These might include product knowledge, oral presentation skills, field procedures, and so on. Decisions must be made as to who should do the training and where it should be done. Do we let current salespersons do the training in the field or have special people to do it at the office, or some combination?

Organizing the Sales Force

The sales force may be organized on a geographical, product, market, or some combination of these factors basis. If a salesperson can effectively handle all the company's products in a given geographic area then the geographical structure probably makes the most sense. Otherwise, the product or market basis seem appropriate. The selection between these two approaches depends on whether product or market knowledge is the most important.

Designing Sales Territories

No matter how a sales force is organized, each salesperson is assigned a product or market or geographic territory. The determination of the size of a territory involves the trade-off between equalizing the sales potential in each territory and equalizing the required salesperson effort in each territory. It is usually impossible to have all one's territories with equal potential and equal effort. Both potential and required effort change with time, requiring territories to be changed. The reaction of current salespersons must be considered in doing this.

Assigning Salespersons to Territories

Just who is assigned to a particular territory is a tough issue. The criteria necessary for success may vary by territory for a given company. Chicago is different from Provo, Utah. Individuals may be selected for a particular territory, requiring that the selection criteria reflect these differences.

Motivating Salespersons

Many techniques are used to motivate salespersons. These include sales meetings, nonfinancial incentives, special recognition, and just the interpersonal style of the sales manager. However, these activities are not likely to be effective unless the selection, training, organization, territory designing, and assignment procedures are effective.

Compensation

Compensation is a key motivator that deserves special attention. The compensation plan (salary and/or commission, and/or bonuses for sales over quota) must fit the defined selling task, and the behavior one is trying to stimulate. For example, it would seem to make little sense to pay one's salespersons all on commission if the selling requires a great deal of new customer work with long purchase decision lead times.

Evaluating Salespersons

Evaluation provides important feedback to the salespersons as to how they are performing against the standards that management holds to be important. These standards may include sales levels, sales versus quota, call frequencies, new accounts opened, work habits, and so on. Some subjective judgments are a necessity for some of these standards. The proper handling of this type of feedback is a strong motivator.

Case 20

South-West Pharmaceutical Company*

In August of 1974, Frank Van Huesen, vice president of the New Orleans-based advertising agency, Advertising Associates, was sitting in his skyscraper office contemplating a meeting scheduled for the next week. At that time, he was to meet with Mr. Lewis Spring, president of South-West Pharmaceutical Company (S.W.P. Company), to discuss agency recommendations for Gentle Care advertising in 1975. Although advertising expenditures for Gentle Care, a skin conditioner for pregnant women, were relatively small, the client was an important account for Advertising Associates, with about $700,000 in billings. Even though the number of pregnant women had been declining, Gentle Care had been experiencing a sudden, unexpected surge in sales. Therefore, planning its future strategy posed a definite challenge to Van Huesen's marketing and advertising expertise. Before the meeting, he had to come up with sound answers to such questions as: "How much to spend for advertising?"; "What media mix to employ?"; and "What to say in messages for Gentle Care?"

Company Background

The S.W.P. Company of New Orleans, La., is the oldest manufacturer of proprietary medicine products in the United States. It all began in Iberville, La., in 1826 when Captain N. L. Denard obtained the "formula" for a tonic from the Choctaw Indians. Formulation took place on south Louisiana plantations for many years until 1860 when Charles Thomas Spring, a pharmacist, bought the formula for $25 and started making and selling bottles of the tonic for $5. The company was moved to New Orleans in 1874 because of the city's better transportation facilities, and growth continued in a sporadic way. In 1955, the Stanfield Company was absorbed and with it another unique product, Gentle Care, joined the S.W.P. product line.

---

* This case was coauthored by John S. Wright, Professor of Marketing, Georgia State University.

The company now manufactures and sells three principal products: Spring's Tonic, Ease Eye Drops, and Gentle Care. Exhibit 1 shows a partial product list, which includes package sizes, prices charged to retailers per dozen items, suggested "list" prices to be charged customers by retailers, as well as case sizes and weights. Wholesalers selling the products receive an 18 percent discount for performing their functions. Sales volume for the company was at an annual rate of less than $5 million in July 1974, and had been growing about 10 percent per year.

EXHIBIT 1 Product and price list for S.W.P. Company

Wholesale discounts: 18 percent on net billing	Quantity: 150-pound minimum prepaid shipment. Any assortment of S.W.P. Company products in original case lots can be combined to meet these shipping requirements.	Resale to retailers. At list less applicable wholesaler's cash discount when earned. Terms: 2 percent if paid within 30 days from date of invoice. Net and due after discount period.

Product	Unit size	List dozen	List	Packed case	Case weight
Gentle Care liquid	3 oz.	$14.80	$1.85	3 doz.	9½ lbs.
Gentle Care cream	2 oz.	14.80	1.85	1 doz.	3 lbs.

The firm's products have traditionally been sold in retail drug stores which received the merchandise through drug and specialty wholesalers. The company employs one salesman who calls upon present and prospective customers, primarily in the Southwest. Mr. Spring is active in several trade associations and spends much time traveling to cement trade relations. Management is keenly aware that customer buying patterns are changing and, therefore, efforts are being made to have company products stocked in discount stores, supermarkets, and chain drugstores. Consequently, many "direct" sales are made to large retailers and to rack jobbers. Of its 3,000 active accounts, 500 are large retail chains, and the remaining 2,500 are to a variety of middlemen including wholesale grocers, rack jobbers, and specialty jobbers.

The Product and Its Market

Gentle Care is also very old as products go, having been first sold in 1869. The product, which is a skin conditioner especially formulated for use during pregnancy to relieve tight, dry skin, was originally provided in liquid form. When massaged on the skin, it has a very soothing and relaxing effect on the muscles. Gentle Care's basic ingredients include winter-pressed cottonseed oil, soft-liquid soap, camphor, and menthol.

In 1967, a line extension of the product was devised in the form of Gentle Care cream, whose ingredients include cottonseed oil, laury, myrestyl, cetyl, stearyl in absorption base, glycerin, sorbitol, perfume, and color. Currently the cream form comprises a small but growing percentage of Gentle Care sales.

Mr. Van Huesen describes the industry as "body lotions and creams for use during pregnancy." Exhibit 2 shows the few other companies in the industry, along with the pricing they employ. It should be noted that the other brands are very small in comparison to Gentle Care, are sold primarily through maternity shops, and have only regional or local distribution. None advertises, nor do the brands pose a competitive threat to Gentle Care, which is believed to have better distribution for its sales volume than any other drug product in the United States. By its very nature, the product is a "slow-mover" at the store level, and smaller outlets order the product in half-dozen lots. No deals have been made available to the middlemen in the past; however, an experiment was planned for the fall of 1974 when retailers would be offered a "one free in five" package deal.

EXHIBIT 2 Industry and pricing structure—body lotions and creams for use during pregnancy

Company	Product	Size	Retail price	Wholesale price per dozen
S.W.P. Company, New Orleans, La.	Gentle Care (liquid)	3 oz.	$1.85	$12.80
	Gentle Care (cream)	2 oz.	1.85	12.80
Leading Lady Foundations, Inc., Cleveland, Ohio	Anne Alt Body Lotion	8 oz.	1.50	n.a.
Mothers Beautiful, Miami Beach, Fla.	Mothers Beautiful Body Lotion	8 oz.	1.25	n.a.
Shannon Manufacturing Co., North Hollywood, Calif.	Mary Jane Maternity Lotion	8 oz.	1.50	n.a.
Maternity Modes, Niles, Ill.	Maternity Modes Protein Body Creme	4 oz.	1.50	n.a.

n.a. = not available.

Isolating the target market for Gentle Care may appear to be an obvious exercise—it consists of all pregnant women. Within that category of womankind, however, Mr. Van Huesen thought the prime target for such lotions and creams should be the first-time mother-to-be. If she decides to use such a product at that time, it is quite likely she will again use it during succeeding pregnancies. What role is played by "influencers" (the expectant mother's mother, older mothers in the neighborhood, aunts, nurses, maternity shop personnel, and so forth) in the purchase and use decision is not known.

Birthrates in the United States have been declining precipitously, and the United States is approaching a state of Zero Population Growth, a point where deaths and births are in balance. Reference to Exhibit 3 shows, nevertheless, that one woman in seven in the 20–24 age range does have a baby in a given year. The declining number of women in the target market is further documented in an article which appeared in the July 13, 1974, issue of *Business Week*, which states:

> the total number of babies born in the U.S. last year [1973] dropped to 3.1 million, the lowest level since World War II. That compares with 4.2 million to 4.3 million births per year from 1956 through 1962, the peak of the postwar baby boom and 3.7 million as recently as 1970.[1]

EXHIBIT 3 Birthrate by age of mother and color, United States, 1961–1971

Age (years)	Nonwhite			White		
	1961	1971	Percent change 1961–71	1961	1971	Percent change 1961–71
15–19	15.3%*	12.9%	−16%	7.9%	5.4%	−32%
20–24	29.3	18.5	−37	24.8	14.5	−42
25–29	22.2	13.6	−39	19.4	13.5	−30
30–34	13.6	8.0	−41	11.0	6.6	−45
35–39	7.5	4.0	−47	5.3	2.7	−49
40–44	2.2	1.2	−45	1.5	0.6	−60

* Table is read as follows: In 1961, of all nonwhite women between 15 and 19 years of age, 15.3 percent gave birth.

Little is known about the consumer decision to use these lotions and creams during pregnancy. How do women learn about such products? Are influencers important to the decision, or does advertising inform the expectant mother of the product's availability? In the absence of specific research into this area of consumer behavior, it was assumed by both Mr. Spring and Mr. Van Huesen that advertising plays a significant, if not *the* critical, role. The product recently had been experiencing large increases in sales, with 1974 sales expected to be about 50 percent greater than the 1972 level, in spite of a decline in the market potential for the product category. Exhibit 4 gives the sales of Gentle Care from 1967 to 1974, as well as the advertising to sales ratio for that period. The large sales increases were being achieved by both the liquid and cream forms of Gentle Care.

---

[1] "The Baby Food Market," *Business Week*, July 13, 1974, p. 45.

EXHIBIT 4 Gentle Care—advertising-to-sales ratios, 1967–1974

	Sales	Advertising	A/S Ratio
1967	$ 94,789	$70,256	0.74
1968	97,832	41,046	0.42
1969	102,551	34,695	0.34
1970	125,157	34,525	0.28
1971	126,909	20,451	0.16
1972	132,143	34,088	0.26
1973	157,959	32,853	0.21
1974	200,000	37,500	0.19
	(projected)		

Marketing Strategy

The marketing strategies employed by S.W.P. Company are reflections of the maketing philosophy of its president, Lewis Spring. Before joining the firm in 1957, Spring worked in promotional jobs in the petroleum and entertainment industries and he views promotion as an important part of his job. Technical people are hired to handle the manufacturing and physical distribution sides of the business, while Spring concentrates on the marketing-sales-advertising operations.

This circumstance simplifies Van Huesen's job. There are no layers of bureaucratic approval of S.W.P. Company. Once Van Huesen and Spring agreed on a strategy to be followed, it was implemented. The process involved a combination of Spring's ideas on how proprietary drugs should be promoted and Van Huesen's understanding of how advertising can be used to achieve the company's goals.

For a long time, Spring has maintained great faith in the importance of package design to the sales success of the kind of products manufactured by his company. The company once changed advertising agencies over this issue; Spring thought the Gentle Care package needed changing, while agency personnel felt that such a change would destroy the product's "image with the consumer."

Another of Spring's marketing guidelines is that the smaller company "must find the one single most important use for the product" and build the promotional program around that point. Closely related is another philosophical belief, namely that the firm "should do what the competition is not doing," whether it is in the area of media selection, creative strategy, or other promotional concerns.

The Advertising Budget

The company management does not have any "cut-and-dried" formula for arriving at the advertising budget. Advertising's importance to the sales of company products is recognized by Lewis Spring; nevertheless, as Exhibit 4 reveals, the advertising-to-sales ratio has been declining over the past decade without a consequent decline in sales. The relatively large budget for 1967 was due to the simultaneous introduction of the cream and a change in package design, which was accompanied by an increased budget to help secure greater distribution. The drastic cutback in advertising expenditures for 1971 was due to an unsuccessful diversification into the cosmetic business which necessitated a recoupment of financial resources. The relative cutbacks in 1973 and 1974 were in response to tight money conditions at the time and to a management decision to "make 1974 a year of profit." Spring believes, however, that such cutbacks can be only a temporary phenomenon; in respect to advertising he holds that "you must be everlastingly at it."

Media Strategy

As has been characteristic of the proprietary drug industry for generations, Gentle Care was traditionally advertised by means of small space ads placed in newspapers. Twenty years ago it was realized that for a product whose market is as highly segmented as that for Gentle Care, this media strategy resulted in a great deal of "wasted circulation" of the advertising message; thereafter, advertising for the product was concentrated solely in magazines.

As shown in Exhibit 5, there exists an appreciable number of magazines which can be characterized as "baby oriented." Of course, within the category, those read during the prenatal stage are desired by the producers of pregnancy body skin conditioners. Once the child is born, the product is no longer needed, although it is possible that the woman will continue to use the product for other skin care purposes.

For many years, Gentle Care was featured in smaller-sized ads (one-sixth page to one-half page) in 8 or 10 magazines, one or two insertions per year. In

EXHIBIT 5 Baby-oriented magazines

	Frequency of publication	Circulation	CPM (B/W)	Page rate (B/W) one insertion
American Baby	Monthly	1,108,700	8.92	$ 9,890
Baby Care	Quarterly	575,785	7.49	4,310
Baby Talk	Monthly	1,021,693	8.28	8,460
Congratulations	Annually	2,624,120*	n.a.†	20,670
Expecting	Quarterly	855,013	9.11	7,790
Good Housekeeping	Monthly	5,703,732	3.94	22,765
Modern Romances	Monthly	752,339	3.48	2,645
Mothers' Manual	Bimonthly	913,085	8.77	8,010
Parents' Magazine and Better Family Living	Monthly	2,017,029	6.52	13,565
Redbook's Young Mother	Annually	1,519,888	4.77	19,345

* Distributed to specific places; CPM not determinable.

† n.a. = not available.

Source: SRDS *Consumer Magazines and Farm Publications*, April 26, 1974.

other words, the emphasis was placed on the *reach* strategy—trying to get the message before as many different prospects as possible for a given expenditure of advertising dollars. This strategy was replaced with one aiming at greater *frequency;* fewer publications were used with more insertions in each magazine over the year. The rationale behind this change was based upon the fact that there is no seasonality in the products use; women become pregnant throughout the 12 months.

The 1974 advertising schedule for Gentle Care is shown in Exhibit 6. One key change made in 1973 was switching out of *Redbook* where the product had been advertised every other month adjacent to the magazine's "expectant mother's" column. To ensure that position, larger space had to be purchased, so for the same amount of money, the entire McFadden Group of eight magazines was available, although for small-sized ads. The agency's media department felt that the McFadden Group would be a better match with the target market for Gentle Care than would *Redbook. Parents' Magazine* was included in the media schedule primarily to allow the company to use the seal of approval in Gentle Care advertising, even though its impact on sales was undetermined.

EXHIBIT 6 Gentle Care—1974 advertising plan

Magazine	Size ad	Cost per ad	Number ads	Total cost
Expecting	½ page (2¼ × 6¹⁵⁄₁₆ inches) (71 lines)	$3,310	2	$ 6,620
American Baby	½ col. (2⅜ × 5 inches) (71 lines)	1,820	3	5,460
Mothers' Manual	⅓ page (4⁹⁄₁₆ × 5 inches) (1 col.)	1,800	2	3,600
Parents' Magazine	½ col. (2¼ × 5 inches) (71 lines)	2,665	2	5,330
McFadden's Group *True Story Photoplay TV-Radio Mirror True Confessions Motion Picture True Romance True Experience True Love* Redbook Reserve for special regional availabilities	⅙ page (2¼ × 5¹⁄₁₆ inches) (¼ col.)	3,041	4	12,164 2,000 $35,174
Estimated production				2,326 $37,500

Creative Strategy

Before Advertising Associates took over the account in 1969, Gentle Care was advertised through ads which featured the product jar. A typical ad, as created by the former agency, is shown in Exhibit 7. This ad shows an attractive woman's head with her hand apparently rubbing her shoulder. The headline is very general in content; it is not until the reader sees the subheading does she learn that Gentle Care is for use during pregnancy. Seals of approval from two well-known certification agencies were also featured, which meant that advertisements had to be placed in *Good Housekeeping* and *Parents' Magazine*. Exhibit 8 shows the first advertisement in company history which prominently displays that the product is for use during pregnancy.

The new campaign inaugurated by Advertising Associates in 1970, an example of which is shown in Exhibit 9, was more direct; the reader could read-

EXHIBIT 7 Pre-Advertising Associates ad for Gentle Care

EXHIBIT 8 First Gentle Care ad prominently featuring use during pregnancy

PREGNANT?

MAKE YOURSELF COMFORTABLE.

Treat your skin to a soothing beauty massage with Gentle Care. The rich lubricating liquid helps tight, dry skin stay soft and supple. It brings you ease and comfort while you wait. Look for Gentle Care at your Drug Counter It's the Body Skin Conditioner that's especially recommended during pregnancy.

Gentle Care

EXHIBIT 9 First ad in the Advertising
Associates campaign
of 1970

Make Yourself Comfortable.

Treat your skin to a soothing beauty
massage with GENTLE CARE. It's the
body skin conditioner that's especially
recommended during pregnancy. The rich,
lubricating liquid helps tight, dry
skin stay soft and supple. It
brings you ease and comfort
while you wait. Look for
GENTLE CARE
at your drug
counter.

Gentle
Care

EXHIBIT 10 Example of 1974 advertising for Gentle Care

Don't let your tummy get out of shape while you're pregnant.

Give your tight, dry skin a soothing massage with Gentle Care. Its special formula will help relieve the taut feeling and minimize itching. And it will help your skin stay soft and supple. So make yourself comfortable. Look for Gentle Care in cream or liquid form at your drug counter.

ily determine who used the product and for what purpose. One seal of approval, that of *Good Housekeeping* magazine, was dropped in the belief that the magazine's audience was much older than the target market for Gentle Care. The decision was discussed at length because the role of older women in the purchase and use of the product was not known.

Changing standards and values in our society are reflected in the 1974 campaign as shown in Exhibit 10. Here a nude model is seen actually applying the product as it would be done by the purchaser. Furthermore, the headline is direct and to the point. The *Parents' Magazine* seal is again featured, and the product package is illustrated in a subordinate position.

The 1975 Advertising Plan

In mulling over the advertising history of his client, Van Huesen jotted down several questions which he felt needed answering before he could design the 1975 advertising plan for Gentle Care:

1. What level of advertising should be recommended for 1975?
2. What changes, if any, should be made in media strategy? Are specialized magazines the best media choice for Gentle Care? If so, are "baby-oriented" publications the best choice?
3. Is the frequency rather than the reach strategy to be continued for Gentle Care advertising in 1975?
4. Should the *Parents' Magazine* seal be retained?
5. What changes, if any, should Mr. Van Huesen recommend in the creative strategy for the product?

Once these questions were answered, Mr. Van Huesen felt he was ready to meet with Mr. Spring to present his recommendations for 1975 Gentle Care advertising. Van Huesen knew from past experience that he could anticipate some probing questions from Mr. Spring concerning how the effectiveness of the advertising for Gentle Care could be measured.

Case 21

The Phoenix Suns (B)*

As opening day of the 1981–82 National Basketball Association season approached, Phoenix Suns' General Manager Jerry Colangelo found himself in an enviable, but frustrating, position. Colangelo was at the helm of one of the most successful and progressive franchises in the entire NBA. The Phoenix Suns had just completed their most successful campaign ever in terms of club wins (57 wins, .695 percent), fan attendance (92.9 percent of arena capacity), and the final standings (Pacific Division Champions).

The team was exceeded only by the World Champion Boston Celtics (62 wins, .756 percent), the Philadelphia 76'ers (62 wins, .756 percent), and the Milwaukee Bucks (60 wins, .732 percent) in total number of wins and won-lost percentage. In overall percent of arena capacity filled, the Portland Trail Blazers (100 percent), Milwaukee Bucks (98.9 percent), and Boston Celtics (94.8 percent), were the only NBA clubs to attain higher marks (see Table 1). In addition to these successes, Colangelo himself had been named NBA Executive of the Year by *The Sporting News*—the second time that he had been the recipient of this honor.

Yet, with all of this good fortune, Colangelo remained somewhat dissatisfied. The primary source of this dissatisfaction was the fact that his team had once again been disappointed in the NBA playoffs. A gritty Kansas City Kings club had defeated his Suns, four games to three, in the 1980–81 Western Conference semifinals. For Colangelo and the Suns the defeat represented the fifth time in the last six years that the Suns had made the playoffs but had failed to bring home the championship.

The upcoming season also posed a number of difficult off-the-court decisions that Colangelo did not look forward to making. The team's advertising agency had recently presented their recommendations for the 1981–82 Suns' advertising/promotional campaign and Colangelo found himself in disagreement with many of the agency's proposals. The agency had called for a substantial increase in the Suns' media budget and for a much expanded promotional

---

* This case was prepared by Professor Vincent J. Blasko, Arizona State University. The original version of the Phoenix Suns case was written by Charles H. Patti and appeared in *Advertising Management: Cases and Concepts*, by Charles H. Patti and John H. Murphy, (Columbus, Ohio: Grid, 1978).

TABLE 1 1980–1981 NBA attendance figures and percent of arena capacity filled

		Total attendance	Average attendance	Arena capacity	Percent capacity
1.	Portland Trail Blazers	519,306	12,666	12,666	100.0
2.	Milwaukee Bucks	448,366	10,936	11,052	98.9
3.	Boston Celtics	595,454	14,523	15,320	94.8
4.	Phoenix Suns	482,693	11,773	12,660	92.9
5.	Golden State Warriors	413,480	10,084	13,239	76.2
6.	Los Angeles Lakers	537,865	13,119	17,505	74.9
7.	San Antonio Spurs	440,553	10,745	15,964	68.4
8.	New York Knicks	544,641	13,284	19,591	67.8
9.	Philadelphia 76'ers	469,355	11,448	18,276	62.6
10.	Utah Jazz	307,825	7,508	12,143	61.8
11.	Houston Rockets	385,354	9,399	15,676	59.9
12.	Denver Nuggets	423,307	10,325	17,271	59.8
13.	Seattle Supersonics	675,097	16,466	27,894	59.0
14.	Indiana Pacers	408,839	9,996	16,924	59.0
15.	Atlanta Hawks	595,454	8,846	15,700	56.3
16.	Chicago Bulls	389,718	9,505	17,374	54.7
17.	Kansas City Kings	336,585	8,209	16,638	49.3
18.	Washington Bullets	375,360	9,155	19,035	48.1
19.	Dallas Mavericks	319,347	7,789	17,134	45.4
20.	San Diego Clippers	257,597	6,283	13,841	45.4
21.	New Jersey Nets	302,059	7,367	21,100	34.9
22.	Cleveland Cavaliers	224,489	5,475	19,548	28.0
23.	Detroit Pistons	228,348	5,569	22,366	23.9

effort. In view of the Suns' many accomplishments the previous year, Colangelo had serious doubts concerning the need for such an extensive program.

In evaluating the agency's performance over the last few seasons, Colangelo had also decided that the team's advertising had lacked a basic continuity and focus. This represented an additional area of concern for the Suns' management since the agency recommended the same overall strategies for the upcoming campaign.

Marketing Considerations

The Product

Jerry Colangelo and the Suns' top management have always strived to improve their product offering from year to year. Since the beginning of the franchise's history in 1968 (when the team struggled through their worst season ever—16 wins), Colangelo has worked tirelessly to improve all areas of the business. Fortunately, he has seen those efforts pay major dividends. That first season, a grand total of 753 season tickets were sold and attendance ran at a rather embarrassing 4,340 fans per home game. The team's second year saw season ticket sales jump to 1,752 and average home game attendance nearly doubled (7,617). From that point to the present, with the exception of the 1974–75 season, the Suns have steadily increased both their individual game ticket sales and their season ticket figures (see Table 2).

TABLE 2 Phoenix Suns' home attendance: 1968-1969 through 1980-1981

Year	Season ticket sales	Dates	Attendance	Average
1968-1969	735	37	160,565	4,340
1969-1970	1,752	37	280,868	7,617
1970-1971	3,204	41	332,945	8,120
1971-1972	3,510	41	342,922	8,364
1972-1973	4,396	41	342,117	8,444
1973-1974	4,503	41	284,424	6,934
1974-1975	2,900	41	253,103	6,173
1975-1976	3,500	41	295,293	7,202
1976-1977	5,030	41	411,294	10,032
1977-1978	5,500	41	470,009	11,463
1978-1979	6,800	41	465,010	11,342
1979-1980	8,010	41	480,659	11,723
1980-1981	8,026	41	482,693	11,773

The chief reason for the team's success at the gate is, of course, the overall success that the Suns have realized on the court over the past 13 seasons. Like most teams, the Suns have experienced their highs and lows—with most of the lows occurring between the dismal first year and the 1974–75 season. In that period, the Suns' record (including playoff contests) was 255 wins and 326 losses (.434 percent). The Suns had five coaches in those seven years and managed to make it to the playoffs one time—in the 1969–70 season.

The next six seasons (1975–76 through 1980–81) however, provided a totally different scenario. In that period, under Coach John MacLeod, the team notched an outstanding record. The Suns gained a playoff berth five times in those six years and earned a trip to the NBA World Championship Series in the 1975–76 season. In addition, the Suns' won–lost percentage, including playoff competition, rose to .575—a record exceeded by only Philadelphia, Los Angeles, and Boston for that same time period.

What is perhaps most impressive is the fact that this record was achieved without the presence of a true superstar on the team. While the Suns have had some very solid players, they have never built their attack around a specific individual. As a result, the Suns have gained the reputation for exciting team, rather than individual, performance.

In preparing for the coming 1981–82 season, the Suns' management made a number of transactions that they believe will add even more strength to the team's already impressive roster. Larry Nance and Craig Dykema, the Suns' number one and three draft picks in the 1981 college draft, were signed and second-year guard Dudley Bradley was acquired in a deal with the Indiana Pacers. Returning to the Suns are a number of standout performers including All-NBA defensive performer Dennis Johnson, all-star forward Walter Davis, and last year's impressive rookie, Kyle Macy. The Suns' aggressive, breakaway style and well-balanced attack, combined with these individual player personalities, make the Suns a very marketable product.

The Market

Fan Loyalty

In the formative years of the team's existence, General Manager Colangelo felt that the Phoenix market contained a number of negative characteristics with regard to the establishment of a successful NBA franchise. The most disturbing of these was the fact that the Phoenix area has been growing so rapidly that it was difficult to build true fan allegiance to the Suns. Many of the new Phoenix area residents (from the East and Midwest) still felt a strong loyalty to teams such as the Milwaukee Bucks, New York Knickerbockers, or Boston Celtics. In fact, a study conducted for the Suns in 1975 supported Colangelo's beliefs. Over one third of the study's respondents selected a team other than the Suns as their favorite NBA club.[1]

The problem of building a loyal following, however, seems to have been rectified as witnessed by the recent success of the team, near capacity attendance figures, and a later study which reported only 9 percent of the respondents selecting a team other than the Suns as "their favorite."[2] The study sampled 525 attendees at the first three home games of the 1978–79 season and was conducted by marketing research students at Arizona State University. The study was designed to answer the following two questions:

1. What demographic characteristics do the Phoenix Suns' fans possess?
2. What effect do various promotional activities have upon the fans' decision to attend the games?

See Tables 3 through 7 for the results of the study.

TABLE 3 Occupation characteristics of population attending Suns' first three home games in 1978

Occupation	Total number of responses	Percent of total
Laborer	28	5.3
Clerical	31	6.0
Professional	168	32.0
Technical	34	6.4
Service worker	26	5.0
Farm worker	4	.8
Sales	64	12.2
Student	54	10.3
Self-employed	48	9.1
Unemployed	21	4.0
Retired	19	3.6
Other	28	5.3
Totals	525	100.0

[1] McGuire Research Co., Dallas, Texas, December 1975.
[2] *Phoenix Suns Marketing Research Study,* College of Business Administration, Department of Marketing, Arizona State University, Tempe, Arizona, October 1978.

TABLE 4 Education characteristics of population attending Suns' first three home games in 1978

Education	Total number of responses	Percent of total
Finished grade school	16	3.0
1–3 years high school	37	7.0
Graduated high school	105	20.0
1–3 years college	189	36.0
Graduated college	178	34.0
Totals	525	100.0

TABLE 5 Income characteristics of population attending Suns' first three home games in 1978

Income	Total number of responses	Percent of total
No response	26	5.0
Under $8,000	52	10.0
$8,000–$14,999	100	19.0
$15,000–$24,999	137	26.0
$25,000–$39,999	121	23.0
$40,000 and more	89	17.0
Totals	525	100.0

TABLE 6 Age distribution of population attending Suns' first three home games in 1978

Age	Total number of responses	Percent of all sampled		
		Males	Females	Total
Under 18	39	4.8	2.6	7.4
18–24	78	9.8	5.2	15.0
25–35	141	17.5	9.3	26.8
35–49	179	22.0	12.0	34.0
50–64	64	8.1	4.1	12.2
65 and over	24	3.1	1.5	4.6
Total	525	65.3	34.7	100.0

TABLE 7 Effectiveness of promotions on fans' decision to attend Suns' games (data collected at Suns' first three home games in 1978)

	Reduced price tickets (percent)	Giveaways, T-shirts, etc. (percent)	Opposing team (percent)
Always influenced	36.0	16.0	53.0
Occasionally influenced	9.0	12.0	4.0
Never influenced	55.0	72.0	43.0
Total	100.0	100.0	100.0

Lack of Blue-Collar Market

Another major hurdle that the Suns have managed to negotiate successfully is the fact that a large portion of the Suns' spectators are employed in a professional capacity. This means the makeup of the Suns' target audience is quite a bit different from most NBA franchises. Typically, the blue-collar worker represents the largest portion of the professional sports team market; however, 32 percent of the Suns' audience are employed in a professional category. In addition, 70 percent of the Suns' home game attendees have attended college for one to three years or are college graduates.

Colangelo has been successful in turning this "disadvantage" into a marketing opportunity by employing an approach emphasizing season ticket institutional buys. Under this program, a large company purchases a block of season tickets and then uses the seats for various marketing and promotional activities (public and customer relations, employee incentives, customer contests, etc.). The Suns were the first NBA club to adopt this strategy—an approach now considered standard in the marketing of professional sports teams.

Stadium Expansion

Suns' management expects both season and individual ticket sales to be boosted even further with the expansion of the Phoenix Coliseum that was completed at the start of the 1981–1982 NBA season. A $1.2 million loan, approved by the Arizona State Legislature, allowed for the addition of 2,100 seats to the existing arena. The new capacity brings the total seating to approximately 15,000, a figure that closely parallels that of other NBA arenas.

Colangelo believes that the addition will increase season ticket sales by 1,000 and that overall attendance will be increased by 2,000 per game. It is estimated that an increase of 2,000 fans per game will mean over a half million dollars to the Suns in gate receipts.

Effects of a Championship

Colangelo feels that the best way for the Suns to increase attendance revenues would be to win the NBA World Championship. The experience of the Portland Trail Blazers, NBA Champions of 1977, would seem to confirm Colangelo's beliefs. The Portland club has consistently sold out their home dates since winning the championship and shows no signs of any attendance loss four years later (see Table 1). Colangelo also cites the 1976–77 season (the year following the Suns' defeat by Boston in the championship series) as proof of what that title could mean. Average attendance per game during the 1976–77 season jumped 39 percent (from 7,202 in 1975–76 to 10,032) and season ticket sales increased 25 percent (from 3,500 in 1975–76 to 5,030).

In addition to improving performance at the gate, Colangelo feels the championship would increase the profitability of the team's television market also. The Suns sell television rights to KPNX, a Phoenix TV station, and have also entered into a contract with the American Cable Company. American

Cable will televise a total of 37 Suns' games (20 home, 17 away) beginning with the 1981–82 season. The NBA championship would undoubtedly increase the price of these rights substantially. The Suns' radio market is controlled by the team, who purchase the air time from KTAR, a Phoenix radio station. The Suns then sell the advertising time to produce profit from the broadcast. An NBA championship title would, of course, raise the price of that advertising time.

The Competition

The Suns find themselves in an excellent marketing position because there is only one other major league team in the Phoenix metropolitan area. The other professional sports franchise competing with the Suns is the Phoenix Inferno, a member of the Major Indoor Soccer League. The Inferno, who also play in the Phoenix Coliseum, began their second full season in 1981 and compete in 22 contests at home. Two other professional sports franchises, the Phoenix Racquets (World Team Tennis) and the Phoenix Roadrunners (World Hockey League), had been located in the market but both teams experienced only limited success, for various reasons, and were forced to discontinue play.

The Suns must also compete with a major collegiate sports power, Arizona State University, an institution located in nearby Tempe and well known for its top-flight baseball, football, and basketball teams. ASU is a member of the competitive PAC-10 Conference. In addition, ASU's stadium is the home of the Fiesta Bowl football game, which takes place every December.

In the spring four major league baseball teams (Oakland A's, Milwaukee Brewers, San Francisco Giants, and Chicago Cubs) make the Phoenix area their annual training ground. Also, the Phoenix Giants (the AAA minor league baseball team of the San Francisco Giants) play a 70-game home schedule that extends from April through August. See Exhibit 1 for a summary of team sports located in the Phoenix metropolitan area.

In addition to the organized team sports in the Phoenix area, Suns management realizes that the many outdoor recreational activities that the

EXHIBIT 1 Team sports in Phoenix

Team	Season	Home games	Average attendance	Ticket price*
Phoenix Suns	October–April	41	11,723	$4.50
Phoenix Giants	April–August	70	5,255	2.50
Phoenix Inferno	November–April	22	7,191	4.00
ASU football	September–December	6	63,683	7.25
ASU baseball	January–May	35	2,160	2.50
ASU basketball	November–March	14	8,703	5.00
Major league baseball (spring training)	February–April	40	2,500	3.00

* Denotes general admission ticket price.

Phoenix area is well-known for must also be considered direct competition for the sports enthusiast's dollar. Because the weather in the area is comfortable throughout most of the year, the many activities (golf, hiking, boating, tennis, etc.) available to Phoenix residents comprise a negative factor with regard to professional sports attendance.

Past Marketing Efforts

Promotional Strategy

Basically, the Suns' management conducts two promotional campaigns. The first is geared toward the building of season ticket sales and the second attempts to increase individual game ticket purchases. Season ticket sales are promoted primarily through personal sales calls made by a Suns' representative on large Phoenix area businesses. The primary purpose of these visits is to discuss with company executives the advantages connected with the purchase of a large block of Suns' season tickets. The Suns' representative outlines a variety of promotional ideas and programs that these organizations can implement through the use of season tickets. Many large Phoenix firms (such as Armour Dial, Carnation, and First National Bank) take advantage of this program and have used the season seats to accomplish a variety of their own marketing and promotional objectives (increased traffic, better customer relations, and others). The Suns have also used newspapers and direct mail in the promotion of season tickets. These media, however, play a much less important role in the marketing of these seats since the majority (78 percent) of season purchases are made by area businesses.

Although the 1978 survey profiles the Suns' primary target audience quite well, Suns management believes that the market for individual home games is, in actuality, much broader than this. The Suns feel that any sports enthusiast who lives in the area and has the means available ($4.50) for a general admission ticket is an excellent prospect for a single game ticket sale. The Suns have used a number of promotions to help encourage attendance at individual games, including giveaway nights (team posters, T-shirts) and numerous discount ticket nights in cooperation with local businesses (Basha's Night, Circle K Night and the like).

Other secondary markets that the Suns management feels are important in individual game sales are out-of-town businesses that will be holding conventions in the Phoenix area and the many area clubs and organizations that might be interested in a Suns outing. These prospects (convention directors and club officers) receive a mailer that offers selected home games at specific group rates. Since the target market for individual game tickets is a good deal broader than that for season tickets, the Suns rely more heavily on a wider range of media (television, newspaper, radio, and outdoor) to deliver their advertising message.

Creative Strategy and Execution

In attempting to increase attendance, for both season ticket sales and individual game ticket sales, the Suns have adopted a number of creative concepts which have served as a basis for their advertising executions. These concepts and executions have been built around a number of consumer sales points and consumer benefits. The majority of the Suns' advertising messages are delivered through radio and newspaper, with television, magazine, and outdoor also used but to a much lesser degree (see Table 8). A description of the creative themes and executions are outlined below.

TABLE 8 Phoenix Suns' media expenditures: 1977–1981

Medium	1977–78*	1978–79†	1979–80‡	1980–81§
Newspaper	$52,100	$49,614	$40,984	$44,382
Radio	21,523	19,786	21,260	20,380
Magazine	855	988	71	185
Television	750	2,380	1,970	2,560
Outdoor	1,756	—	1,037	1,065
Totals	$76,984	$72,768	$65,322	$68,572

* Does not include $42,625 of media purchased by trading tickets for space and/or time.

† Does not include $40,757 of media purchased by trading tickets for space and/or time.

‡ Does not include $41,145 of media purchased by trading tickets for space and/or time.

§ Does not include $44,320 of media purchased by trading tickets for space and/or time.

1. Stars on other teams. Frequently, Suns' ads have featured prominent players on other teams, such as Julius ''Dr. J'' Erving of the Philadelphia 76'ers (see Exhibit 2) and Ervin ''Magic'' Johnson of the Los Angeles Lakers (see Exhibit 3). Used to promote individual games, this theme has highlighted the playing ability of NBA superstars as well as the personality of their respective teams.

2. Suns player/company discount promotions. The Suns have also used ads featuring their own team members (such as Walter Davis and Alvin Scott) in conjunction with company promotional nights to boost individual game attendance (see Exhibits 4 and 5). The strategy behind these ads is to capitalize on the performance/personality of the Suns players and to promote the company ticket discount. In addition, the Suns have promoted company discount nights quite frequently on radio.

3. Season ticket promotions. Ads intended to increase season ticket sales have generally centered around a specific Suns player (see Exhibit 6) or on the Suns' team personality (see Exhibit 7). Because the majority of season ticket sales are made to businesses (through personal sales and direct mail), these themes have been used rather infrequently in Suns advertising.

EXHIBIT 2

EXHIBIT 3

SUNS VS. LAKERS
SATURDAY / 7:35

Magic Johnson

PHOENIX
SUNS

TICKETS:
Suns Office—2910 N. Central
Coliseum Box Office
Diamonds Box Office*

50¢ service charge per ticket at Diamonds

EXHIBIT 4

SUNDAY/7:05

SUNS
VS. WARRIORS

Walter Davis

ARMOUR DIAL NIGHT

Bring a wrapper from Dial soap to the Suns office and get a $3 discount on $8 tickets, a $2 discount on $6 or $7 tickets. Offer good only at the Suns ticket office and is subject to ticket availability.

PHOENIX SUNS

2303 N. Central

EXHIBIT 5

THURSDAY / 7:35
SUNS
VS. HAWKS

Only Coliseum appearance by Atlanta this season

Alvin Scott

BASKIN·ROBBINS
31 FLAVORS NIGHT
Ticket discount coupons available at
Baskin-Robbins 31 Flavors Ice Cream stores

$8 tickets — $3 discount per ticket with coupon
$6 & $7 tickets — $2 discount per ticket with coupon

Redeem coupons at any Suns ticket outlet,* including the
Coliseum right up till gametime. Subject to ticket availability. Children 12 years & under get $8, $7, or $6 adult
tickets FOR HALF PRICE.

PHOENIX
SUNS

TICKETS:
Suns office – 2303 N. Central
Coliseum
Diamonds Box Office*

*35¢ service charge per ticket at Diamonds

EXHIBIT 6

In Indiana, his high school talents earned Kyle Macy the title of "Mr. Basketball." At the University of Kentucky, he was a three-time All American. As a pro with the Suns...the beat goes on.

And the best way to see it, is with your own season tickets. For your family. For your business.

Tomorrow, call or visit the Suns office to get complete information on the many season ticket packages available. It's the best entertainment around.

2303 N. Central
258-7111

EXHIBIT 7

Intensity!

You see it in every Phoenix Suns fast break, in every steal, in every John MacLeod time-out. And it's contagious!

Catch it yourself, 41 nights a year, with season tickets. There isn't a better entertainment act in town.

PHOENIX

2303 N. Central   258-7111

SUNS

4. Giveaway promotions. The Suns agency has also included the team's many giveaway nights in advertising designed to build single game attendance. These ads have featured such promotions as Team Poster Night (see Exhibit 8) and Suns T-Shirt Night (see Exhibit 9). These giveaways are usually advertised as part of an overall promotion being sponsored by a local company (other giveaway promotions include Coors Cup Night and Pepsi-Cola Tote Bag Night).

5. Family-oriented promotions. Top management has always felt it important to reinforce the belief that Phoenix Suns basketball is family entertainment, packaged in a highly appealing team, and augmented by numerous family-oriented promotion nights. This theme has been advertised through a variety of executions and in a variety of media (see Exhibit 10).

EXHIBIT 8

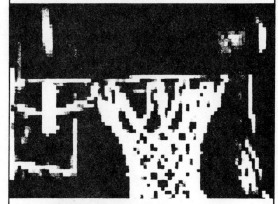

HOME OPENER!
PHOENIX   SAN ANTONIO
SUNS VS. SPURS
TUESDAY, NOV. 3 / 7:35 p.m.

CIRCLE K NIGHT
Save on tickets to the Suns' home opener with special discount coupons available at Circle K stores throughout the Valley. Or use the coupon below.

FREE SUNS CALENDAR POSTERS
to everyone attending the game, compliments of Circle K!

TICKETS:
Coliseum Box Office, Diamonds Box Office*
Suns Ticket Office—2303 N. Central
    (2910 N. Central effective Nov. 2)

SUNS TICKET DISCOUNT COUPON

SUNS VS. SPURS / Nov. 3

This coupon good for a $2.00 discount on $7.00 adult tickets or a $2.50 discount on $9.50 adult tickets purchased for the above game. Discount ticket prices for children 12 years & under are one half the regular adult ticket price. To receive discount, coupon must be redeemed at the time of ticket purchase. Redeem the coupon at the Suns office, Diamonds Box Office* or at the Coliseum Box Office right up until game time. Offer is subject to ticket availability.

*50¢ service charge per ticket at Diamonds   Code B   1

EXHIBIT 9

Mike Bratz

CIRCLE K NIGHT
**Ticket discount coupons available
at all Valley Circle K locations**

$8 tickets — $3 discount per ticket with coupon
$6 & $7 tickets — $2 discount per ticket with coupon

Redeem coupons at any Suns ticket outlet,* including the
Coliseum right up till gametime. Subject to ticket availability. Children 12 years & under get $8, $7, or $6 adult
tickets FOR HALF PRICE.

FREE SUNS T-SHIRTS
to the first 3,000 16 years & under at the game, compliments
of Circle K.

PHOENIX SUNS

TICKETS:
Suns office — 2303 N. Central
Coliseum
Diamonds Box Office*

*35¢ service charge per ticket at Diamonds

EXHIBIT 10

Alvan Adams

SMITTY'S FAMILY PLAN

Pick up Family Plan ticket discount coupons at any Valley Smitty's location. Redeem at a Suns ticket outlet and save $3 on $8 tickets; $2 on $6 & $7 tickets. Subject to ticket availability.

PHOENIX SUNS

TICKETS:
Suns office—2303 N. Central
Coliseum
Diamonds Box Office*

*35¢ service charge
 per ticket at Diamonds

Current Situation

As the Suns face the 1981–82 season, very few obstacles would seem to stand in the way of successful ticket sales and further improvement in attendance figures. However, there are two negative factors that must be considered when one begins to construct an objective-oriented advertising plan. These problem areas, as outlined by the Suns' advertising agency, are as follows:

1. *Lack of "choice" season tickets.* Because of excellent team performance in the past few seasons and a low season ticket attrition rate, many of the best season seats are no longer available for purchase.
2. *Economic factors.* Double-digit inflation, possible fuel shortages, and other demands on personal income are likely to cut into discretionary funds and impact leisure-time activities.

The Suns' agency has also pointed out that the team has a number of items in its favor. These are:

1. *Increase in attendance.* The previous year saw the team enjoy their best season in terms of overall attendance and season ticket sales.
2. *Team performance.* The Suns are also coming off their best year in terms of on-court performance, with the team recording a mark of 57 wins against only 25 defeats.
3. *Team charisma.* The Suns are a team characterized by youth, personality, and a breakaway style of play. These attributes combine to make the team a very marketable product.
4. *Realignment of NBA schedules.* The weighting of schedules toward more frequent play within conferences and divisions will serve to create two areas of opportunity:
   a. The more frequent exposure to teams within the division will heighten rivalries and place more significance on intradivision contests.
   b. One time visits by top teams outside the conference (Boston, Milwaukee, Washington, and Chicago) will give tickets to these games a premium status.
5. *Promotional nights.* The various premium and discount offers conducted with local businesses provide an incentive for the occasional ticket buyer to become exposed to Suns basketball more frequently. This may heighten a fan's interest in the Suns and may also make the individual a prospect for future season tickets. (See Exhibit 11 for the agency's proposed promotion game schedule).
6. *Healthier local economic outlook.* Despite the many negative influences nationwide, the Phoenix economy is likely to suffer less than other parts of the country. Local economic indications are quite strong, with personal income and employment figures at all-time highs.
7. *Additional 2,000 coliseum seats.* The expansion of the Veteran's Memorial Coliseum provides an excellent market opportunity for the Suns in both season and individual game ticket sales.

EXHIBIT 11 Suns' promotion games: 1981–1982 Phoenix Suns

Date	Opposing team	Promotion
November 3	San Antonio	Circle K Night
		Poster Calendar Night
November 5	Dallas	Armour Dial Night
November 25	Houston	Bashas' Night
November 27	Chicago	Pepsi-Cola Night
December 1	San Diego	Armour Food Night
December 5	Utah	Phoenix Gazette Night
December 10	Portland	Sun Giant Night
		Coors Cup Night
December 12	Washington	Circle K Night
		Carnation YMCA Night
December 19	Kansas City	Pepsi-Cola Team Poster Night
December 23	Golden State	J. C. Penney Poster Night
December 30	Portland	Rossie Ford Night
January 2	Seattle	Greyhound Night
		Gorilla T-Shirt Night
January 14	New York	Carnation Night
January 16	San Diego	Circle K T-Shirt Night
January 19	San Antonio	Bashas' Night
January 22	New Jersey	Pepsi-Cola Tote Bag Night
January 23	Detroit	Carnation Girl Scout Night
February 3	Golden State	Checker Auto Night
February 10	Boston	Coors Cup Night
February 12	Atlanta	Earl's Sporting Goods Night
		Wristband Night
		Carnation Boy Scout Night
February 26	Denver	Circle K T-Shirt Night
March 3	Utah	Armour Food Night
March 5	Kansas City	Pepsi-Cola Night
March 7	Houston	Armour Dial Night
March 21	Seattle	Pioneer Take-Out Night
March 24	Dallas	Circle K Night
March 26	Milwaukee	Nike Poster Night
April 4	Kansas City	Bashas' Night
April 8	Portland	Circle K Night

8. *Influx of new residents.* As the Phoenix metropolitan area continues to grow, new markets for both season tickets and individual game ticket sales will be further expanded.

After evaluating the advertising and promotion plans prepared by the Suns' advertising agency for the 1981–82 season, General Manager Jerry Colangelo finds himself hesitant in approving the agency's recommendations. For the past three years the Suns have been spending between $65,000 and $73,000 for advertising media (see Table 8). The cost of giveaways, salaries, production, and media time and space purchased in exchange for tickets is not included in these figures. To further increase both season ticket sales and individual game ticket sales, the Suns' advertising agency is recommending (based on the aforementioned positive factors) a substantial increase both in the media budget (see Table 9) and in individual game promotions. (See Exhibit 11).

TABLE 9 Proposed Phoenix
Suns' media budget:
1981–1982

Medium	Proposed budget*
Newspaper	$55,000
Radio	31,000
Magazine	6,000
Television	6,000
Outdoor	2,000
Total	$100,000

* Does not include approximately
$45,000 of media space and/or time
that will be purchased by trading tickets.

The agency is recommending a $100,000 media budget and is also re-
questing an expanded promotional effort consisting of 29 promotion games.
(This is an increase of 38 percent over the previous year, in which 21 promotion
nights were held.) The agency feels that the Suns are a very salable commodity
and that the current situation warrants increased expenditures to take full
advantage of an excellent market opportunity. Mr. Colangelo, on the other
hand, is not convinced that the agency's media and promotion recommendations are particularly sound. It is his feeling that the team is now in a position to
rely more on its excellent record and proven personnel to increase attendance.

Mr. Colangelo has always believed that a team's success at the gate is
directly related to its performance on the court. He backs up this contention by
citing the 1970–71 and 1971–72 seasons, when team attendance was growing
rapidly without large advertising expenditures (about $30,000) and with about
half the number of promotions that are currently being recommended. During
these two seasons the team had excellent records and therefore generated
expanded interest and support. He also brings out the fact that after the Suns'
exciting 1975–76 season, ticket sales soared and the team was spending only
$50,000 on advertising media. It is Mr. Colangelo's contention that, after the
Suns' best season ever, the fans will not have to be coaxed into coming to see
the team play.

In addition, Mr. Colangelo has his doubts concerning the viability of the
giveaway and discount ticket promotions. His feeling is that teams with excellent records should not have to rely so heavily on giveaways and discounts to
attract fans. A successful team, in Colangelo's opinion, is the best promotion
that management can possibly have. For these reasons, and the fact that the
Suns are currently the only proven major league sports franchise in the area,
Mr. Colangelo would like to see the media budget set at $50,000 and the
number of promotions reduced by half of what the agency suggests.

Finally, the Suns' management feels that a clear statement of advertising
objectives is needed to provide the team's overall communications effort with a

basic focus and direction. Without these goals, Colangelo feels that a unified program is impossible.

Questions for Discussion

1. What is your opinion of the advertising and promotion programs used by the Phoenix Suns?
2. What is the opportunity for advertising to contribute to the stimulation of demand for both season ticket and individual game ticket sales?

Case 22

Law Offices of Gary Greenwald*

Gary Greenwald leaned back in his chair, daydreaming about what it was going to be like to become a daddy. His law practice had been growing since he started it at the end of 1980, and he was pleased that 1982 gross income looked like it would be about 50 percent higher than he earned during his first year. He recognized, however, that he would have to convert some of his excess capacity to increased business if he was to be able to buy a house and adequately support his family. He decided to review the actions he had taken to increase the business over the past 18 months and do some thinking about marketing activities for 1983. He also thought he should review the Bar Association Canon of Ethics regarding marketing practices.

Background

From 1908 until 1977, the legal profession in the United States operated under a canon of ethics that formally banned any method of advertising or client solicitation. The ban, enforced by the American Bar Association (ABA), had historic precedent. Since the days of ancient Greece and Rome, solicitation by attorneys and judges had been both a written and unwritten taboo.

The prohibition of legal service advertising was initiated in the United States in 1908 for several reasons. First, it was felt that the advertising of certain legal services would cause an increase in the events that prompted the need for such service. For example, members of the legal profession thought that advertising of legal services for divorce proceedings would cause an increase in the number of divorces. Second, the American Bar Association felt that the demographic profile of the United States (at that time primarily a rural popula-

---

* This case was coauthored by Bruce Bassett, Graduate Research Assistant, Georgia State University. Copyright © 1984 by Kenneth L. Bernhardt.

tion) did not have a legitimate need for advertising. Most lawyers were general practitioners in small communities, and legal services were rendered with a one-to-one relationship between people who were known to each other and the community.

By the mid-1970s, the demographics of the country had changed dramatically from what they were in 1908. An equally important change had occurred in the legal process of society and in the legal needs of the population. Gone were the days of general practitioners and one-to-one relationships between lawyers and clients/friends. Instead, there was a complex society in which legal regulations were rampant and legal specialization was a necessity. One thing that had not changed, however, was the advertising/solicitation prohibition in the ABA Canon of Ethics.

Changes in the Legal Environment

In 1973 and 1974, the ABA conducted a survey to analyze the public's level of knowledge about lawyers, the law, and the legal process. The survey showed that the public had difficulty recognizing when they needed legal services, finding a lawyer to provide such services, and determining what a lawyer would cost. This survey led the ABA to reexamine its restrictions against advertising.

In December 1975, the ABA Committee on Ethics and Professional Responsibility proposed a change in the Canon of Ethics which would allow advertising not containing a false, fraudulent, misleading, deceptive, or unfair statement or claim. However, at the 1976 midyear meeting of the ABA House of Delegates, the advertising proposal was rejected in favor of a limited code amendment. Under the revised amendment, lawyers were allowed to communicate certain information about themselves and their practice (such as name, address, nature of practice, and consultation fees) in legal directories, bar association directories, and the Yellow Pages of telephone books. Concerned that the ABA had not gone far enough, in June 1976, the U.S. Department of Justice initiated an antitrust suit against the ABA, alleging a conspiracy to prohibit advertising.

Responding to changes in the environment, there emerged in the late 1960s and early 1970s clinics of various sorts to meet the needs of society. These clinics ranged from psychological counseling centers to abortion clinics to health services clinics to legal clinics. Each type of clinic had as its avowed purpose the rendering of specific high-quality services to a large number of people at a low cost to the individual. The clinic concept had initially been part of the social and human rights movements and had been financed in large part with government funds. It slowly evolved from a publicly funded orientation into a private enterprise orientation—this was especially true for legal clinics. Private legal clinics sprang up to handle such routine matters as uncontested divorces, adoptions, simple personal bankruptcies, simple wills, and name changes.

The Bates Case

From 1974 through 1976, John Bates and Van O'Steen ran a legal clinic in Phoenix, Arizona. Their clinic handled routine legal matters and was able to keep costs low by utilizing standardized office procedures and forms. They also used automated typing equipment and relied heavily on paralegals.[1] Their idea was to charge low prices for their legal services but to make money by doing a high volume of work.

The issue of advertising was a hot topic in most local ABA circles, and Bates and O'Steen decided to use advertising to secure a steady flow of new business, which they felt was critical to the success of their clinic. They placed an ad in the February 26, 1976, *Arizona Republic Newspaper,* offering "legal services at very reasonable fees." The ad listed their fees for the various legal services they provided (see Exhibit 1). The ad violated the Arizona Bar Association Disciplinary Rule 2-101(B), which prohibited lawyers from publicizing themselves through print, radio, and television advertisements or any other means of commercial publicity.

Bates and O'Steen were summoned before the local ABA disciplinary committee which recommended that they be suspended for six months. The Board of Governors of the Arizona Bar Association, upon reviewing the proceedings, recommended a one-week suspension. The two lawyers took the case to the Arizona Supreme Court which held that the state board had acted within its rights. Bates and O'Steen then sought review of the decision by the United States Supreme Court.

In 1977, the U.S. Supreme Court agreed to review the case. In the opinion of the Court, there were several issues that dealt with the U.S. Justice Department's antitrust suit against the ABA and several issues that concerned advertising. It was the opinion of the Court that the public's need for information about availability and costs of legal services outweighed the concerns expressed by the Arizona bar that advertising would have a negative impact on professionalism, on the quality of service provided, and on the administration of justice.

Although allowing lawyers to advertise, there were certain restrictions on legal services advertising that the Court did not strike. The Court allowed continued restrictions on ads that were false, deceptive, or misleading and ruled that the time, place, and manner of lawyer advertising could be subjected to reasonable restrictions. In addition, the Court felt that in order to assume that a consumer would not be misled a disclaimer might be needed. In concluding, the Court avoided a stand on radio and television advertising, stating that "the special problems of advertising in the electronic broadcast media would warrant special consideration." In-person solicitation was not an issue in the Bates case and was reserved for future consideration by the Supreme Court.

---

[1] Paralegals are individuals who have had some specialized legal training but have not graduated from law school and are not certified by the ABA to practice law. They typically are paid much less than a new attorney just out of law school.

EXHIBIT 1
Ad at issue in *Bates* v. *State Bar of Arizona*

Changes after Bates

In August 1977, the ABA responded to the Bates decision by creating the ABA Commission on Advertising. The commission developed two alternative proposals for the regulation of legal advertising, allowing each state bar the option of adopting or not adopting each proposal. The states also had some latitude in changing the recommended codes to reflect their own perceived needs.

Proposal A was described as regulatory. It specifically authorized certain prescribed forms of lawyer advertising, listing the type of information that could be provided in attorney ads. The proposal permitted advertising in print, on radio, and (following a 1978 amendment) on television.

A less restrictive proposal, Proposal B was also developed. Proposal B, which could be termed ''directive,'' allowed publication of all information not ''false, fraudulent, misleading, or deceptive.'' It provided guidelines for the determination of improper advertisements, which were subject to ''after-the-fact'' discipline by state authorities. Neither proposal allowed one-to-one solicitation.

A majority of states, including Georgia, adopted Proposal A, and developed ''laundry lists'' specifying the terms that could be used in ads. Some state codes included long lists of information about what was permissible within lawyer advertising; others created equally long lists of prohibited information. An attorney from Alabama ran into trouble with his state's regulations, for example, because he included the words *free parking* in his advertising, a term not on the state's list of approved terms.

But in a 1982 case, In re RMJ, the Supreme Court loosened restrictions by state bar associations on legal advertising, stating that they could be no broader than reasonably necessary to prevent deception. The case involved a young attorney who had opened for business in St. Louis, Missouri, in 1978, using advertising containing terms such as *personal injury* instead of the required *tort law*, and *real estate* instead of *property law*.

The attorney also used a mailing that went to potential new customers, not just friends and relatives as required by the Missouri law. After being reprimanded by the Missouri Supreme Court, the attorney appealed to the U.S. Supreme Court, which threw out Missouri's rule limiting lawyer mailings to ''lawyers, clients, former clients, personal friends, and relatives.'' The Supreme Court indicated the state had not justified its interferences with truthful commercial speech and also rejected Missouri's insistence that lawyers limit ad claims to specific state-approved phrases.

In February 1983, the ABA House of Delegates approved a proposal to allow ''written communication not involving personal contact'' but also adopted a proposal that forbids a lawyer to ''solicit professional employment from a prospective client by mail, in person, or otherwise, when a significant motive for the lawyer's doing so is the lawyer's pecuniary gain.'' Direct mail advertising thus would be permitted when distributed to ''persons not known to need legal services, but who are so situated that they might in general find such services useful.'' This was interpreted by legal advertising scholars to indicate that a lawyer could not send direct mail pieces to 50 known survivors in an airplane crash, but he or she could send the mailing to heavy users of airline travel. By mid-1983, direct mail advertising was specifically allowed in only 11 states, with Georgia being one of the ones that had not changed its regulations in response to the Supreme Court decision and subsequent ABA code revision. Greenwald felt sure that the Georgia restrictions against direct mail would be loosened soon. In any case, he believed the restrictions would not hold up if challenged in the courts.

There were substantial variances in legal advertising regulations from state to state. The ABA had no authority to establish advertising policies at the state level, even though they had considerable influence on the state bar association's decisions regarding advertising policies. The state of Georgia followed the ABA Proposal A closely, requiring that the ads be dignified and allowing the listing of routine services offered. In-person solicitation, direct mail, billboards, handbills, and advertising of contingency fees were all prohibited. TV, radio, Yellow Pages, and newspapers were all specifically permitted.

Most attorneys were still opposed to advertising by lawyers. A recent survey of ABA members funded by the *American Bar Association Journal* revealed that only 3 percent of lawyers had advertised in 1978, only 7 percent had in 1979, and in 1981 only 10 percent had. The bulk of the advertising that had been done had been in the Yellow Pages or in newspapers. Many lawyers, especially established ones, felt that advertising lowers the professionalism of lawyers. The likelihood of advertising decreased as an attorney's income increased, with lawyers earning less than $25,000 five times as likely to advertise as those making over $50,000.

Background on Gary Greenwald

Gary Greenwald moved to Atlanta in late 1979 after graduating from Potomac School of Law in Washington, D.C. During his first year in Atlanta, he served as a Public Defender practicing in the State Court of Fulton County, Georgia. During the first year as a public defender, he handled more than 200 court-appointed cases, with about 80 percent being criminal cases. After two years in business for himself, his practice had changed considerably. He had attained the state bar designation for practice in tax law, had several small-business clients, and had only about 20 percent of his business in criminal cases. His storefront office was on Peachtree Road, the main route from downtown to the affluent residential area called Buckhead.

Within a mile of his office on one side of Peachtree Road were several affluent residential areas made up of single-family homes worth well in excess of $100,000. On the other side of Peachtree Street were many apartments and condominiums housing young urban professionals. All along Peachtree Road were many retailers and office buildings containing small businesses of all types. Although his office was very visible from the street, with ''Law Offices of Gary Greenwald'' and his telephone number painted in large letters on the window, virtually no clients had come to him as a result of that visibility. Most of the cases that he did have, typically 15–20 at any one time, were referred to him by other attorneys. They sent him certain cases that were types their firms didn't handle such as criminal and personal injury cases.

In addition to the good location, another advantage of his offices was the low overhead. The rent was $290 per month. Telephone expenses were $200 per month. He spent $200 per month on law books and updates and had spent $5,000 initially for the books in his law library. Other expenses, including a part-time secretary, amounted to about $5,000 per year. The office was not plush, but it was functional. Greenwald believed that it was important for an attorney to meet the expectations people had of a successful lawyer, and therefore he did not see his long-term future in this office. Until he built up the practice, however, the large amount of space and very low rent were extremely attractive.

Greenwald enjoyed the flexibility and freedom associated with running his own law office. Currently, however, his case load was only taking about 25 percent of his time. Greenwald was anxious to increase the business and reduce his idle time and had tried many different things to accomplish this goal.

Recent Marketing Activities

About nine months earlier, Greenwald had put up a poster advertising his services on bulletin boards in about 60–70 locations in the area including supermarkets and apartment building laundryrooms. Each of the posters contained a number of his business cards which could be taken for later reference (see Exhibit 2). Greenwald had paid $100 for 400 of these posters. The effort generated six clients and about $2,000 in legal fees.

Several months earlier Greenwald had distributed 10,000 copies of the 8½" × 3½" advertisement shown in Exhibit 3, using a "Dow Pack" mailing for the distribution. The Dow Pack contained 10 other advertisements and cost him $400. Four people had come in for a free initial consultation, but as yet no new clients had been developed from the mailing.

Greenwald had also undertaken some advertising in the Georgia Tech and Georgia State University student newspapers and in *Creative Loafing*, a weekly tabloid newspaper containing entertainment listings which was distributed for free. The ads had not been successful in generating new business. For example, 8–10 weeks of classified advertising in *Creative Loafing*, which cost $100, had only generated one new client—a $650 divorce case.

He had also used a two-line classified ad for 10 weeks at a cost of $75 in a neighborhood weekly newspaper. The ad offered to write one letter on his stationery for a client for $12.50. The series of ads generated demand for five letters and four new clients.

EXHIBIT 2 Poster advertisement

LEGAL SERVICES

THE LAW OFFICES
OF
GARY GREENWALD

1831 Peachtree Road
Atlanta, Georgia 30309
(404) 352-1567

LEGAL SERVICES PROVIDED

CIVIL

AUTO ACCIDENTS
BUSINESS INCORPORATION
CHILD CUSTODY
COLLECTION OF ACCOUNTS
CONTRACTS
DIVORCE
EMPLOYMENT DISCRIMINATION
LANDLORD-TENANT
PARTNERSHIP AGREEMENT
PERSONAL INJURY
REAL ESTATE
TAX/IRS PROBLEMS
WILLS
ESTATE PLANNING
WORKMENS COMPENSATION

CRIMINAL

MOTOR VEHICLE OFFENSES
MISDEMEANOR OFFENSES
FELONY OFFENSES
PROBATION VIOLATION
APPELLATE WORK

OFFICE HOURS:

Mon - Fri 9:00 - 9:00
Sat - 10:00 - 5:00

Take One
For Later Reference

GARY GREENWALD
ATTORNEY AT LAW

1831 PEACHTREE ROAD, N.E.
ATLANTA, GEORGIA 30309
(404) 352-1567

EXHIBIT 3 Direct mail ad

LEGAL SERVICES

THE LAW OFFICES OF GARY GREENWALD

A COMPREHENSIVE COORDINATED LEGAL PRACTICE FOR FAMILIES & BUSINESSES
TRIAL PRACTICE IN STATE & FEDERAL COURTS

LEGAL SERVICES PROVIDED

Personal
- Auto Accidents
- Family Law
- Personal Injury
- Estate Planning / Wills
- Taxation / IRS Problems
- Workmen's Compensation

Business
- Contracts
- Collection of Accounts
- Partnership Agreements
- Incorporations
- Taxation / IRS Problems

Criminal
- Traffic Offenses
- Misdemeanor Offenses
- Felony Offenses
- Probation Violations
- Appeals

Present This Ad For Your FREE Initial Consultation

1831 Peachtree Rd. • Atlanta • Mon. - Fri. 9 - 9, Sat. 10 - 5 • By Appointment Only • 352-1567

Current Marketing Considerations

In thinking about his 1983 marketing plan, a lot of things were going through Greenwald's mind. He wondered what rates he should charge, if and how to target his market, and what promotion strategy he should use to communicate to his potential market.

Originally he had offered new clients an initial consultation for free. Recently he had been charging $15 for an initial consultation for individuals and $25 for businesses. His hourly rate varied considerably, depending upon the client and the task. For example, for tax work he charged some clients $40 per hour. He charged others $75 per hour and billed two clients at $120. He was on the list of attorneys taking cases from the juvenile court, and he received only $25 per hour for this work. Greenwald did take a few cases for a fixed fee, typically $500–$600. He only did this when he could accurately forecast the amount of time it would take for the case. Also, he did a number of cases for free when a client could not afford his services, telling the client to pay him when he or she could scrape up the money.

The biggest fee he ever received was $32,000 for a criminal case which lasted 14 months. His next biggest fee was $6,000. He had 10 personal injury cases pending, including a rape, a broken tooth incident, and several car accidents. He anticipated eventually receiving about $20,000 in total from these cases which were all being handled on a contingency basis.[2]

Greenwald had grossed $40,000 his first full year and expected in the second year to gross $60,000. He knew there was considerable room for growth here, particularly if the number of clients could be increased. That led him to

[2] With a typical contingency case, an attorney received no fees if the client lost the case, but received one third of the damages awarded if the client won the case.

thinking about the types of legal services he liked to perform. He had no interest in handling real estate or bankruptcy cases. He felt that the biggest money was to be made in personal injury cases. He liked doing tax work. Greenwald commented that criminal work was fantastic because the work was easy, most cases were plea bargained, and clients always paid in cash. Overall, Greenwald most liked the diversity of work that was possible in his profession.

Advertising

Greenwald reviewed the information he had gathered on various advertising alternatives. He had gathered information on direct mail, newspapers, business publications, radio, television, and the Yellow Pages. Some of this information is presented in Exhibit 4.

There were approximately 10,000 households within a couple of miles of his office. Greenwald could send out a postcard format advertisement, using third-class mail, to 5,000 households for $610, including the cost of the mailing list. He could send out a mailing to 10,000 households for $1,150. It was also possible to include a postcard advertisement in a Valpack. This was a mailing containing the ads from a number of different advertisers who shared the cost of the mailing, resulting in a cost less than half of a solo mailing. Valpack mailings were sent quarterly.

An ad in the Yellow Pages would cost about $4,000 for a small (2″ × 2″) ad. A large ad would cost approximately $10,000 per year. About 40–50 of the 9,000 lawyers in Atlanta had large ads in the Yellow Pages.

It would cost Greenwald about $1,500 to have a television ad produced before he even ran the ad one time. Ads on the major networks would cost

EXHIBIT 4 Media costs per advertisement

1. *Atlanta Journal* and *Constitution* (major daily newspapers)

	Sunday	Morning and evening combination
Ad 4¼″ × 3⁷⁄₁₆″	$734.00	$660.96
Ad 2¹⁄₁₆″ × 2″	142.80	128.52
Services classified ad	5.55/line	4.52/line

TV Week supplement:	1 time	2 times	6 times
⅕ page	$735.00	$684.00	$625.00
¹⁄₂₀ page	212.00	197.00	180.00

2. *Atlanta Business Chronicle* (weekly tabloid business newspaper)

	1 time	4 times	13 times
1 inch	$ 49.00	$ 47.00	$ 44.00
⅛ page	290.00	275.00	260.00
Classified 1 inch	24.00	21.00	18.00

3. *Business Atlanta* (monthly business magazine)

	1 time	3 times	12 times
¹⁄₁₆ page	$275.00	$260.00	$225.00

EXHIBIT 4 *(concluded)*

4. Radio

	Morning drive time	Evening drive time
WGST (all news station):		
30 seconds	$ 96.00/spot	$ 68.00/spot
60 seconds	120.00	85.00
WPCH (easy listening):		
30 seconds	88.00	92.00
60 seconds	110.00	115.00
WSB–FM (middle of the road):		
30 seconds	323.00	191.00
60 seconds	380.00	225.00

5. TV (exclusive of production costs)

	Prime time	Late news
WAGA (CBS station):		
30 seconds	$2,200–$7,000/spot	$1,100/spot
WTBS (Channel 17 superstation):		
30 seconds	650–850/spot	450/spot
WANX (Channel 46 independent station):		
30 seconds	150–550/spot	n.a.

n.a. = not available.

thousands of dollars for each spot, although he could buy time on low-rated stations after midnight for about $50 per spot. Radio advertising was cheaper. He felt that he would have to run an ad at least twice per day, five days per week, for a month to have any impact. This would cost about $3,000, the minimum he felt was appropriate for a fair test. Greenwald knew that Hyatt Legal Services had been very successful with television advertising in Atlanta. Although the six offices in Atlanta had only been open for nine months, he had heard that each office was bringing in about 200 new clients per month as a result of the ads. Hyatt was spending about $8,000 per month on television. In addition, they had a very large ad in the Yellow Pages. Hyatt did not handle personal injury and certain other kinds of cases. They tended to concentrate on simple legal matters like wills, name changes, and uncontested divorces, and Greenwald felt that the average legal fees per client was under $200.

Consumer Analysis

Greenwald had seen the results of several studies that had been conducted to determine the consumer perspective on legal advertising. The studies typically showed that most users of legal services selected their attorney using recommendations by friends or personal acquaintance. Consumers also used the lawyer's area of specialization, integrity, quality of service, past experience, and reputation as selection criteria. Recommendations by other lawyers, promptness of service, and location of office were other selection criteria used.

Listings in the Yellow Pages, name of law school attended, years in practice, convenience of office hours, and cost of legal services were not among the top 10 selection criteria used by consumers. Overall, personal acquaintance and recommendation by a friend were overwhelmingly the most frequently used means of selecting an attorney.

It is not clear from the studies exactly why other criteria such as cost or advertising are not used more frequently. Unavailability of these sources of information in the past is one possible explanation. It is interesting to note, for example, that cost of legal services is mentioned as being very important to consumers, yet very few consumers use this as a factor in selecting their attorney.

Conclusion

Greenwald wondered whether he should invest some of the money that he had saved up for the down payment on a house in an advertising campaign to increase his business. With the baby coming, he and his wife really wanted to buy a house, so he didn't want to blow it all on advertising that might not work. He wondered how much he should spend and whether the advertising he had been using could be used or whether he should develop new copy. He wondered what media would be most appropriate and what services would be best to promote. He was also concerned about how big his ads should be and how frequently they should run. He also wondered how he could benefit more from the excellent storefront location he had and how he could generate more referrals.

After thinking about the effort that would be required to generate an effective marketing program, Greenwald wondered whether he should pack it in and go to work for a big law firm instead. He decided that he better not postpone thinking about these issues any longer and reached for the phone to call his wife to tell her that he would be late for dinner.

Case 23

Cliff Peck Chevrolet*

Whenever a new Chevrolet automobile dealership was opened, a thorough amount of front-end planning was required. The Cliff Peck dealership established in Austin, Texas, several years ago was no exception. The relatively new dealership was located in the growing northwest section of Austin with over 10 acres of cars and 900 feet of frontage on a major traffic artery.

The two principals who established the dealership, Mr. Harold Pannel and Mr. Jack Izard, were extremely pleased about the prospects for their new dealership. They were confident that widespread consumer acceptance of the Chevrolet product line coupled with the healthy Austin market would produce a winning combination. In fact, the success the dealership had enjoyed during its first few years had supported their confidence, and prospects for even greater success in the future appeared bright.

The Auto Industry

No motor vehicle manufacturer has control of any part of the market. There are striking variations in customer acceptance of each manufacturer's products— variations by product groups, car lines, and geographic area. Although repeat sales are highly prized, the evidence has been overwhelming that customer preference must be earned anew with each sale.

Motor vehicle producers also face competition from the large stock of used vehicles in the United States. The great reservoir of unused mileage and the repairability of motor vehicles give customers the option of continuing to use existing vehicles rather than purchasing new ones. This interaction between new and used vehicles is an integral part of competition in the industry. Since motor vehicles are durable and represent a major family decision, cyclical swings in employment and in consumer confidence created amplified swings in new car demand.

---

* This case was prepared by John H. Murphy, Professor of Advertising, University of Texas. Used with permission.

The Austin Market

According to published estimates, the Austin Standard Metropolitan Statistical Area (SMSA) ranked in the top 100 markets, while the city of Austin was ranked in the top 50 of the U.S. Commerce Department's list ranking cities by population. Automobile dealer sales per capita for the Austin SMSA were estimated to be at or slightly above the national average.

Austin had been breaking growth records over the past few years for population increases, although the tide of immigration had eased from its peak period. The city's economic picture had continued to be bright, and a recent survey by The University of Texas's Bureau of Business Research indicated that Austin led all major Texas cities in economic growth. With an almost recession-proof economy firmly rooted in government, education, tourism, and a growing industrial complex, Austin officials were optimistic about the city's continued growth.

A study conducted by a respected national news magazine listed Austin as among the top 15 "most pleasant places to live." The magazine pointed to its recreational opportunities, combined with one of the lowest cost-of-living indexes in the country, which had proved to be an irresistible lure to both re-tirement people and industries looking for attractive leisure facilities for their employees.

Austin Auto Dealers

The two Austin Chevrolet dealers in competition with Cliff Peck were Capitol and Henna Chevrolet. Henna led in sales, with Capitol at an estimated 85 percent of Henna sales and Peck at 80 percent of Henna sales. Capitol has been in Austin for over 50 years, and they tended to use more TV advertising than Peck or Henna. Capitol called themselves "Your Chevrolet Capitol."

Henna Chevrolet was located in the nearby town of Round Rock for 30 years before they moved to Austin more than a decade ago. Henna tended to advertise heavily in newspapers, and their slogan was "Austin's Favorite Dealer."

Austin dealerships selling other makes of cars included Austin Toyota, Covert Buick, Cen-Tex Datsun, Charles Maund Cadillac-Olds, George Coffey Lincoln-Mercury, McMorris Ford, Leif Johnson Ford, Town Lake Chrysler-Plymouth, Rio Dodge, Bob Miller and Lamar Volkswagen, Continental Cars—Mercedes/Honda, and Bill Munday Pontiac/AMC. In addition to these Austin dealers, dealers in surrounding communities such as Round Rock, San Marcos, and Georgetown provided a fair amount of competitive pressure on the Austin auto market.

Cliff Peck's Past Advertising Efforts

Since the dealership opened, Peck had changed advertising agencies twice. For approximately the first three months of the dealership's operation the firm had

EXHIBIT 1 Representative newspaper advertisement

CLOSE OUT 82...

1982 CITATIONS—CHEVETTES—CAVALIERS

Our Entire Citation, Chevette and
Cavalier Inventory on Sale.
Take your Pick
At $1.00 Over Invoice
More Than 100 Available For
Immediate Delivery.

$1.00
ONE
DOLLAR

OVER INVOICE*

*Original factory invoice. Does not include holdbacks
or possible future rebates. Plus tax, title and license
and financing charges, where applicable.

NOW
OVER 400
NEW CHEVY CARS & TRUCKS PRICED FOR LESS!

CLOSE OUT PRICES CAPRICES

CLOSE OUT PRICES CELEBRITYS

CLOSE OUT PRICES PICK-UPS

CLOSE OUT PRICES MONTE CARLOS

CLOSE OUT PRICES CAMAROS

1982 CORVETTES

FANTASTIC SAVINGS

GOOD CLEAN USED CARS

81 MALIBU WAGON 4800 Miles, Immaculate	$6999	80 THUNDERBIRD Weekend Special	$5777	81 GMC ¼ TON 8 Cyl. — Special	$5444
81 CORVETTE 3800 Miles — A Puff	$15,750	80 PHOENIX HATCHBACK Low Mileage — Clean	$4666	80 FORD COURIER Camper — Sharp	$4999
80 CORVETTE Black — Glass Tops	$13,500	79 FORD LTD WAGON Clean — 43,000 Miles	$4555	77 CHEV. SCOTTSDALE Air — Power — Clean	$3888

CLIFF PECK CHEVY COUNTRY

Northwest on Hwy 183 at 11400 Research Blvd.   345-7890   Across From Balcones Woods
Open Evenings till 8:00 p.m.

used an out-of-state agency but it quickly became apparent that this arrangement was unsatisfactory. Next, an agency based in Austin was hired to facilitate communication and to add a new creative punch to the firm's advertising.

Exhibit 1 presents a representative Austin *American-Statesman* newspaper ad for the dealership. Exhibit 2 presents representative radio spots.

Two major reasons were cited for the decision to drop the second agency in favor of another local agency. These reasons were: (1) Peck owners' feeling that the agency had failed to produce creative flair on behalf of the dealership and (2) their feeling that the agency's casual attitude toward research resulted in a failure to properly initiate and utilize research in planning Peck's advertising efforts.

EXHIBIT 2 Representative radio spots

"Jingle"

Chorus:	Pick a Peck Chevrolet—you can do it today—with a Cliff Peck Chevrolet. Take it from the folks who save. Pick a Cliff Peck Chevrolet. The dealer who will help keep your car new. It's waiting here for you to help you keep your car new. Cliff Peck's waiting here for you. Cliff Peck Chevrolet.

"Crazy Day Sale"

Anncr:	Time is running out at Cliff Peck Chevrolet. Chevy's national sales campaign ends April 5, and we are desperate to meet our goal. So we've gone a little crazy. We want to move cars more than make profits. So this is your chance to save big on a beautiful new Peck Chevrolet car or truck. We're forgetting the sticker price—it's what you can buy it for. Now that's what really counts. Come on out—we've got hundreds in stock. Cliff Peck Chevrolet, on 183 north at eleven four hundred Research.

"Door Slammer Sale"

Anncr:	Cliff Peck Chevrolet is slammin' the door . . .
Sfx:	(DOOR SLAMS)
Anncr:	. . . on inflation with a door slammer sale. Because all new Chevys coming in are factory priced one hundred dollars higher than those now in stock, the cars and trucks we have at the old price will go fast, so hurry in now. New Monte Carlos are priced from _____
Sfx:	(DOOR SLAMS)
Anncr:	Citations from _____
Sfx:	(DOOR SLAMS)
Anncr:	Come to Peck's door slammer sale for your best deal in Austin.
Chorus:	(SINGS JINGLE)

"Image Trucks"

Anncr:	The trucking life in Texas starts at Cliff Peck Chevrolet. Cliff Peck knows what a Texan wants in a pickup, and handles the trucks at the prices to fit that lifestyle. Chevy pickups are built to stay tough, and tough in the right places. Cliff Peck has the Chevy truck to fit your needs, whether it's rugged ranch work, or comfortable in-town cruising. For your best truck deal in Austin, come to Cliff Peck Chevrolet.
Chorus:	(SINGS JINGLE)

Research Project

In order to provide continuous research input for use in advertising planning and evaluation, the dealership and the new agency commissioned a series of on-going research studies. A local advertising and marketing research firm was retained to conduct an initial benchmark study and additional follow-up surveys. After a series of meetings with the client and the agency, the research firm developed a research plan to collect the necessary data. This program is described in the following paragraphs.

The ongoing research project was identified as, "Awareness, Knowledge, and Attitudes toward Automobile Dealers among Adults Residing in Selected Areas of Austin." Phase I had just been completed. This initial study provided a benchmark measure of the awareness, knowledge, and attitudes of target prospects toward Cliff Peck Chevrolet and the competition. Such measures, repeated at regular intervals, were to be used in establishing objectives and as a control device for evaluating the effectiveness of the promotional communications activities of the dealership.

In each phase a random sample of target prospects in selected geographic areas of Austin located reasonably close to the dealership were to be interviewed. In addition to being relatively accessible to the dealership, these areas contained the best prospects for the dealership based on socioeconomic considerations.

Telephone interviews were used to collect the data. Three hundred male and female adult household-heads were contacted by using a random sampling procedure. A structured questionnaire was used to measure respondents' un-aided recall and aided recall of automobile dealerships and of Cliff Peck Chevrolet.

Identification of slogans, attitudes toward automobile dealerships, automobile purchase decisions, and several demographic variables were also included in the questionnaire. Selected portions of the research instrument are presented in the Appendix. Tables 1 to 8 present the findings of Phase I of the continuing research project.

Phase II of the research program was to be conducted 12 months after a new advertising campaign was launched. During the time between Phase I and Phase II the advertising slogan and the theme used by Cliff Peck in its campaign was to be modified. Also, other changes were to be introduced, such as the models being advertised at different times, the total budget being allocated to the campaign, and the emphasis on specific variables, such as location, service, and price, which were to be promoted in Peck's advertising.

Phase II would use the same data collection methodology as Phase I (although a new random sample would be interviewed). The purpose of the Phase II study would be to evaluate whether or not differences had occurred in the way potential buyers perceive local dealers and specifically Cliff Peck. Also, other attitudinal and demographic measures that were made in Phase I and repeated in Phase II and later phases would provide a longitudinal study of the

TABLE 1 Top of mind awareness, all car dealers (Q.1)

	First mention	Any mention*
Capitol	13%	28%
Covert	4	10
Henna	18	29
Johnson	13	22
Coffey	7	15
Maund	10	22
McMorris	5	17
Peck	5	11
Other	25	47
Don't know	0	
	100%	

* Multiple responses (first three mentions recorded)

TABLE 2 Why dealership was selected (Q.2)

1.	Offered "best deal," cheapest, best price	32%
2.	Only dealer in town	15
3.	Had car wanted, model, etc.	15
4.	Convenient location	8
5.	Friends with owner or employee	8
6.	Dealt with dealer before	5
7.	Reputable, honest	4
8.	Service	4
9.	Friend or relative recommended	3
10.	Sales personnel	2
11.	Good trade-in	2
12.	Easy credit	1
13.	Advertising	1
14.	Others	—
15.	Work there	—
16.	No reason	—
		100%

TABLE 3 Most important qualities of car dealers—any mention (Q.3)

Service	77%
Location	5
Reputation	13
Price	33
Sales staff	13
Personal attention	13
Other	32

TABLE 4 Top of mind awareness, Chevy dealers—(Q.4)

	First mention	Any mention*
Capitol	44%	65%
Henna	37	66
Peck	15	33
Other	4	21
	100%	

* Multiple responses (first three mentions recorded)

TABLE 5 Slogan identification (Q.5)

	Correct	Incorrect	Don't know
Capitol	50	9	41
Henna	27	13	60
Peck	0	2	98

TABLE 6 Awareness of Cliff Peck Chevrolet (Q.6)

(A)	Ever heard of Cliff Peck	
	Yes	66%
	No	34
		100%
(B)	Make of cars Cliff Peck handles (among those who had heard of Cliff Peck)	
	Chevrolet	90%
	Other	3
	Don't know	7
		100%
(C)	Cliff Peck location (among those who had heard of Cliff Peck)	
	Correct ID	82%
	Incorrect ID	3
	Don't know	15
		100%

TABLE 7 Cliff Peck compared to other Chevrolet dealers*

(A) Best service department (Q.7)		(B) Best prices (Q.8)	
Capitol	9%	Capitol	9%
Henna	12	Henna	7
Peck	8	Peck	9
All same	1	All same	3
Don't know	70	Don't know	72
	100%		100%

(C) Best selection (Q.9)	
Capitol	8%
Henna	10
Peck	15
All same	4
Don't know	63
	100%

* Three dealers compared were Capitol, Henna, and Peck.

TABLE 8 Sample demographics

(A) Household size (Q.12)		(B) Age (Q.13)	
1	9%	Under 18	0%
2	37	18–24	8
3	18	25–34	27
4	23	35–49	32
5+	13	50–64	18
	100%	65+	12
		Refused	3
			100%

(C) Annual household income (Q.14)		(D) Race (Q.15)	
Under $10,000	9%	White	95%
10,000–14,999	13	Other	5
15,000–24,999	26		100%
25,000	28		
Don't know/refused	24	(E) Sex	
	100%	Male	55%
		Female	45%
			100%

effectiveness of Cliff Peck's campaign and would be useful in monitoring other changes in the market.

Phase II would provide a comparison which it was hoped would indicate both the past success and future directions for changes in advertising by Cliff Peck. In addition, information from the study would help management to determine whether current advertising expenditures were sufficient, given the firm's objectives.

Future Directions for Cliff Peck's Advertising

Set against the background of this research project, the new agency's task was to develop a complete advertising campaign for the upcoming fiscal year. For initial planning purposes the agency was told that they could make any reasonable assumptions about the level of the advertising appropriation for the coming year. It was noted that in past years the firm had invested between $150,000 and $200,000 in their total advertising budget.

In developing campaign recommendations, the agency's first step was to develop a set of specific, appropriate, and realistic advertising objectives. More specifically, the agency was asked to prepare a written statement of advertising objectives for Peck which met Steuart Britt's four criteria of sound advertising objectives: (1) what basic message is to be delivered, (2) to what audience, (3) with what intended effects, and (4) what specific criteria are to be used to measure the success of the campaign.[1]

Mr. Izard and Mr. Pannel both firmly believed that by developing advertising objectives consistent with Britt's philosophy and using a comparison of the Phase I and II research findings, some valid conclusions could be reached regarding the effectiveness of the new advertising campaign. Both of the principals in the dealership had indicated that they were eager to confer with the agency to go over the agency's proposed statement of objectives. Individuals at the agency realized how important this task of formulating objectives was, not only in terms of directing all of the other decisions in the campaign planning process but also in terms of proving to the owners of Cliff Peck that they could handle the account properly.

Questions for discussion
1. What are the limitations and strengths of the Phase I research study? What modifications or additions would be appropriate? Why?
2. What additional data from the Phase I study beyond what is presented in the case would be useful?
3. How can the data presented in Tables 1 to 8 be used to develop a statement of advertising objectives?
4. Which of the four component parts of advertising objectives identified by Britt is most important? Why? Which involves the most uncertainty? Why?

---

[1] See "Are So-Called Successful Advertising Campaigns Really Successful?" *Journal of Advertising Research*, June 1969, pp. 3–9.

Appendix   **Data Collection Instrument**

Capitol City Research Services   **Auto dealers attitudes study**

Telephone no. _____

Questionnaire _____

Census Tract _____

Interviewer _____

Note day and time of contact _____ 2d contact _____

May I speak with the male or female head of the household? (If neither head is available, arrange a call back.)

Hello, my name is _____. I work for Capitol City Research Services, a public opinion survey firm. We are interested in finding out what selected Austin residents think about automobile dealers.

1. **When you think of new car dealers, what are the first three that come to mind?**

	Capitol	Covert	Henna	Johnson	Coffey	Maund	McMorris	Peck	Other	Don't Know
1st mention	1	2	3	4	5	6	7	8	9	0
2d mention	1	2	3	4	5	6	7	8	9	0
3d mention	1	2	3	4	5	6	7	8	9	0

---

2. **Have you ever purchased a new car?**   Yes   1

   No (skip to Q.3)   2

   From which dealership did you buy the car?

   Write name of dealership in blank _____

   Why did you select _____ (name of dealership)? _____

3. **What do you feel are the three most important qualities of a good new car dealer?**

	Service	Location	Reputation	Price	Sales staff	Personal attention	Other	(Specify)
1st mention	1	2	3	4	5	6	7	_____
2d mention	1	2	3	4	5	6	7	_____
3d mention	1	2	3	4	5	6	7	_____

---

4. **When you think of Chevrolet automobile dealers, what are the first three that come to mind?**

	Capitol	Henna	Peck	Other
1st mention	1	2	3	4
2d mention	1	2	3	4
3d mention	1	2	3	4

5. **Now I'd like to know if you recall which specific new car dealer uses the following slogans?**

   First, what about "The Tradin' Place"? Which new car dealer uses "The Tradin' Place" as its slogan?

	Capitol	Henna	Johnson	Coffey	McMorris	Peck	Other	Don't know
McMorris Ford's slogan	1	2	3	4	5	6	7	8
Henna's slogan	1	2	3	4	5	6	7	8
Coffey's slogan	1	2	3	4	5	6	7	8
Capitol's slogan	1	2	3	4	5	6	7	8
Peck's slogan	1	2	3	4	5	6	7	8

6. **Have you ever heard of the Cliff Peck car dealership?**

Yes	1
No (skip to Q.10)	2

   If yes, what make of new cars does Cliff Peck handle?

Chevrolet	1
Other	2
Don't know	3

   Where is the Cliff Peck dealership located?

Correct ID	1
Incorrect ID	2
Don't know	3

7. **Now thinking about the service department of the three Austin Chevrolet dealers, which of the three—Capitol, Henna, or Cliff Peck—do you feel would have the best service department?**

Capitol	1
Henna	2
Cliff Peck	3
All same	4
Don't know	5

8. **Again, thinking about the three Austin Chevrolet dealers, which one of the three do you feel would have the lowest prices on new cars?**

Capitol	1
Henna	2
Cliff Peck	3
All same	4
Don't know	5

9. **Now thinking about the selection of cars on hand at the three Austin Chevrolet dealers, which one of the three do you feel would have the largest selection of cars on hand?**

Capitol	1
Henna	2
Cliff Peck	3
All same	4
Don't know	5

Now, a few questions to help classify this questionnaire.

10. **Do you own or rent your home?**

Own	1
Rent	2

11. **How long have you lived at your present address?**

Less than 1 year	1
1–2 years	2
3–4 years	3
5–9 years	4
10 years or more	5
Don't know, unsure	6

12. **Counting yourself, how many persons now live in your household, including babies?**

Number _____

13. **What is your age?**

Under 18	1
18–24	2
25–34	3
35–49	4
50–64	5
65 and over	6
Refused	7

14. **What was the approximate annual income for all members of your household before taxes last year . . . would it be $15,000 or more or would it be less than that?**

$15,000 or more, Ask:		Less than $15,000, Ask:	
Would it be:		Would it be:	
Under $25,000 or	3	Over $10,000 or	2
Over $25,000	4	Under $10,000	1
Don't know	5		
Refused	6		

15. **Finally, would you please tell me your race?**

White	1
Black	2
Mexican-American	3
Other	4

May I have your name, please, in case my office wants to check my work?

NAME _____

Note sex:

Male	1
Female	2

Thank you very much!

VERIFICATION: BY_____ DATE _____

Case 24

Doncaster*

As he was sitting in his office on the top floor of an Atlanta skyscraper late one fall afternoon, Fritz Van Winkle picked up the phone to receive a call from Rutherfordton, North Carolina. Charles Benedict, president of Doncaster, a women's clothing manufacturing firm, was on the line. A broad smile creased Van Winkle's Robert Redfordish face as he listened, for Benedict had some good news: Doncaster was placing its business with Tucker Wayne, the national advertising agency which Van Winkle served as senior vice president.

In addition to the normal elation over adding a new client to the agency's roster, Van Winkle was especially pleased about adding the Doncaster account. For one thing, the firm was engaged in the textile clothing manufacturing business, and Tucker Wayne wished to expand in that product area. Furthermore, the new client was active in the specialized form of marketing known as "direct selling" which poses special challenges for the advertising agency, particularly on the creative side of the business. Moreover, Doncaster appeared to be a company about to experience accelerated growth; thus, if Tucker Wayne could contribute to that growth, the agency could reasonably anticipate increased business for the firm. It all added up to an intriguing opportunity for the advertising agency.

Van Winkle immediately set up a meeting for the following Monday. Attending would be the new account team consisting of an account representative and persons from the agency's creative and media departments. At that meeting the account group would start to map out the strategy for next year's Doncaster advertising.

The Direct Selling Method of Distribution

When contrasted to the volume of goods reaching consumers through retail outlets, direct selling to consumers is unimportant in the overall structure of American retailing. Nevertheless, for some manufacturers direct selling is the

---

* This case was coauthored by Professor John S. Wright, Georgia State University.

only method of distribution used to reach consumers. This is the case for Doncaster.

Direct selling organizations ordinarily use one of two selling methods: (1) door-to-door or (2) the party plan. Manufacturers using the door-to-door plan include such familiar companies as Avon Products, Inc., Fuller Brush Company, Stanley Home Products, World Book Encyclopedia, Electrolux, and Sarah Coventry. With the door-to-door method the sale is made to the prospect in her home by a representative of the manufacturer, usually operating as an independent contractor. This arrangement frees the manufacturer from the legal responsibilities which come with the employer-employee relationship.

Under the party-plan selling method one customer acts as the hostess of a party to which she invites several friends. The salesperson actually stages the party and makes a sales presentation to the several guests at the party. Tupperware is a well-known user of this approach.

One practical problem for the manufacturer seeking to employ the direct selling avenue to the market is the recruitment and retention of a sales force. For example, Avon Products, Inc., needs more than 300,000 Avon representatives to cover the United States and Canada. With an annual turnover rate exceeding 100 percent among its salespeople, Avon must spend a great deal of effort and money in attracting new groups of women to join its sales force.

Company Background

Doncaster is a manufacturer of fine custom clothing for women with its factory and home office located in Rutherfordton, North Carolina. The company was founded in 1931 by the late S. B. Tanner, Jr., and originally engaged in the manufacture of men's shirts. During the following year Mrs. Tanner designed two shirtwaist-style dresses which were made of men's shirting material. This experiment met with good success and launched the company into the world of fashion.

The company has remained family-owned with the three sons of the founders now active in the management of both Doncaster and a sister firm, Tanner of North Carolina, which manufactures a line of casual dresses for sale in specialty shops and better department stores throughout the country. Doncaster's president, Charles Benedict, came to the company more than two decades ago as sales manager. His original specialization was in the field of direct selling.

The Doncaster organization manufactures two separate lines: Doncaster, which is a collection of made-to-order (custom) pants, suits, coats, skirts and similar items of women's wear; and Young Traditions (YT) which consist of ready-made sportswear items. Doncaster clothes are made to order for the customer from materials which she has selected; a pair of pants sells for about $60, a coat for $275, with the average of all items in the line coming at about

$120. The Young Traditions line is lower priced with a T-shirt selling in the $10–12 range, a coat for $130, with an average price of about $40.

The Doncaster Selling Method

Doncaster clothes for women are sold directly to the consumer by approximately 1,000 Doncaster saleswomen. This sales force is spread throughout the nation with some concentration in sunbelt states. These salespeople work on commissions of 25 percent for Doncaster items and 20 percent for YT items. Special bonuses augment earnings for successful salespeople. As with most direct selling organizations, the sales force operates under the independent contractor form of contractual arrangement. The field force is supervised by 50 district managers who are compensated with "overrides" (commissions) of 8 percent of the sales generated by those saleswomen working under this supervision.

Doncaster employs a unique variation to the door-to-door method of direct selling. Instead of the Doncaster saleswoman calling at the prospect's home to make a sales presentation, the prospect is invited to a "showing" which is held in the home of the saleswoman. Four times a year such showings of the Doncaster line are made. Each Doncaster saleswoman sends a formal invitation to the women on her prospect list. The mailing is followed by a phone call to make a specific appointment when the prospect will come to the home of the Doncaster saleswoman to view the new offerings. Each showing lasts from one-half hour to two hours for each prospect who comes alone. The typical showing period runs from one to two weeks depending on the number of prospects available to the particular salesperson.

On display in the saleswoman's home are more than 100 physical samples of finished items, and there is some opportunity to try on clothing. A swatch book containing the fine materials available for use in Doncaster custom-made clothing is also on hand, as is a book of drawings featuring the current styles available for customer choice during the current season. The prospect chooses the dress, skirt, coat, and/or pants that she desires, as well as the fabric to be used in its construction. The Doncaster saleswoman assists the prospect in making the correct size choice, and the order is sent to Rutherfordton to be returned approximately six weeks later.

If the Young Traditions line is also featured, it is displayed in another room. Upon viewing these YT offerings, the prospect orders desired items which are delivered several weeks later. Shipments come either directly to the customer or to the salesperson who then calls the customer and arranges for delivery and fitting adjustments if needed.

Thus, it can be seen that the sale is a very personal event. The prospect is there because of a specific invitation from the Doncaster saleswoman whom she probably knows from a social contact. Selections are made in a relaxed setting with very little sales pressure exerted. Many sales are made to established customers.

The Doncaster Saleswoman

Doncaster management has a good idea of the type of woman who buys their expensive line of clothing. The target market profile reads:

> Suburban.
>
> Affluent ($40,000 plus income).
>
> Nonworking.
>
> Traditional lifestyle.
>
> Well-dressed, but not a fashion leader.
>
> Average age, 45 years.

To reach this market Doncaster seeks women from the same social class—social equals, as it were. Obviously special appeals need to be made to attract the right kind of women into the Doncaster sales force; money incentive is secondary as the reason for signing up. The following excerpt from the company's Information Manual illustrates the appeals used:

> Bringing Doncaster service to women in your community is fun, a pleasant experience, for lots of reasons. For many women there is simply the thrill of showing beautiful clothes. For others, it is a combination of the thrill and the opportunity opened to make new friends. For all, it is a combination of these and the opportunity to earn excellent additional income. Obviously, there are innumerable reasons for desiring additional incomes, but for most women there is a specific goal. We are sure you have one, too.

The typical Doncaster saleswoman earns $1,500 in commissions annually for four to six weeks of work. A good portion of her earnings are often used for the purchase of a personal wardrobe of Doncaster clothing.

The Recruitment Problem

Although direct selling organizations often encounter turnover rates in their sales forces which exceed 100 percent annually, the Doncaster experience is a modest 30 percent. Nevertheless, those replacements must be made. Furthermore, the company management believes that the only way for company sales to grow significantly is through an expansion in the size of the sales force. Getting increased sales volume from existing salespeople is difficult and expensive to achieve. Thus, recruitment of new Doncaster saleswomen has a very high priority in management thinking.

District managers, because of the potential implicit in sales overrides, are interested in recruiting new salespeople. Present sales force members may recommend the program to friends who live in different territories, and present customers do write in to company headquarters occasionally to ask for appointments to the sales force. Although company officials estimate that only 21 percent of new additions to the sales force result from media advertising at the present time, such advertising is probably the most important avenue—other than word-of-mouth—of recruitment available to Doncaster.

Recruitment Advertising

Doncaster has advertised in quality magazines for many years. For instance, in the past year advertisements were run in *New Yorker, Vogue, "W", Southern*

EXHIBIT 1 An ad representative of Doncaster advertising before the change in agency

"As a professional model, I've worn all kinds of fashions. My personal choice is Doncaster."

"I prefer Doncaster because every garment has the look and feel of quality.

"The designs are exclusive. I'm free to choose the fabric and the color. And my clothes are custom-cut.

"I can tell you first-hand that these special touches aren't available in off-the-rack clothes. Even in comparable fashions in the Doncaster price range—from $80 to $250.

"I also like the way Doncaster presents its collections. I go to a private showing in my Doncaster saleswoman's home.

"I can take my time looking over the dresses, suits and ensembles from Doncaster. And if I need separates and coordinates, I can choose from Young Traditions, Doncaster's quality sportswear line.

"Because I'm a model, I'm very conscious of my appearance. People expect me to look like I just stepped out of a fashion magazine.

"Doncaster lets me look and feel exactly that way."

doncaster

Mike Tanner
Doncaster, Dept. V94
Rutherfordton, N.C. 28139

___ I'd like to be invited to the next Doncaster showing in my area.

___ I'd like information on becoming a Doncaster saleswoman.

Name _____

Address _____

City _____

State _____ Zip _____

Photographed at the Gazebo II

Living, and *Smithsonian.* Media choices are made on the basis of readership demographics which correspond to the target profile described earlier.

Exhibit 1 is a reproduction of a one-column ad which appeared in the past September issue of *Vogue* and is representative of the advertising done during the past two years.

In evaluating the effectiveness of these magazine advertisements, Doncaster management was interested in two things: first of all, the raw number of inquiries resulting from each advertisement, and more important, the actual number of Doncaster saleswomen appointments emanating from each advertisement. Results from advertising during the previous spring follow:

	Inquiries	Appointments
New Yorker	74	6
Vogue	76	4
"W"	59	5
Southern Living	86	2
Totals	295	17

A Switch in Advertising Agency

Benedict and other members of the Doncaster management team recently concluded that the company was not getting the best possible results from its media advertising. The advertising program for the past several years had been developed by a Virginia-based agency which specialized in direct selling messages. Interpersonal relations between the advertiser and agency personnel had deteriorated, and a search for a new advertising agency was launched. Several regional advertising agencies were interviewed, and it was decided that commencing with next year's campaign Doncaster's advertising would be created by Tucker Wayne, a large national advertising agency based in Atlanta, Georgia.

The agency was placed on a fee basis. The budget would remain the same as last year (approximately $40,000). Doncaster management's dissatisfaction with the previous agency probably springs in part from the fact that advertising objectives had not been spelled out completely enough. The former agency's approach, because of its basic orientation, was aimed at the generation of inquiries. The principal objective for the new campaign was set down as "Bringing about a significant increase in the number of new Doncaster saleswomen." Thus, Tucker Wayne was authorized to use all of the new budget for this purpose.

Van Winkle realized that the new ads would have to be created and placed in a very short period of time. He wanted to be able to present the agency's recommendation by the end of the month when a trip to Rutherfordton was scheduled.

Case 25

Rich's Department Store

The Executive Committee meeting had been a lengthy session, lasting through most of the morning, but Mr. Dick Mills, vice president and sales promotion director of Rich's Department Store, had returned to his office knowing that a major advertising decision was still not ready to be made. And Mr. Mills realized that it would be his responsibility to submit a final recommendation on media strategy at the next meeting.

Mr. Mills stared at the two neatly bound research reports that he had placed side-by-side on his desk. The pair of documents represented summaries of the two presentations that had been made to the Rich's Executive Committee that morning. These studies had been based on exactly the same data, drawn from the same in-store survey of Rich's customers. Each report had been prepared by an experienced and professional marketing researcher. Mr. Mills had expected the strong self-interests of the researchers to be reflected in their presentations and interpretations of the survey results, but he was confident that neither man would misrepresent the actual facts.

Mr. Mills had to admit to himself that he had been very surprised at the apparent major contradictions between the two presentations that he had heard earlier that morning. Mr. Mills and the research director of Rich's, who had also attended the morning presentations by the two outside researchers, had discussed the situation briefly after the meeting. The two men had decided to separately review the written reports and, then, to meet later in the afternoon to decide what additional steps to take.

Before rereading the reports, Mr. Mills thought back over the events of the past three months that had eventually led to this situation.

Rich's Department Store was both the largest merchant and the largest single advertiser in Atlanta, Georgia. The store had been founded in 1867 and had grown to an annual sales volume of approximately $200 million through its downtown store and six branch stores located in major suburban shopping centers. The Rich's market share was 40 percent of department store sales in Atlanta and 25 percent of all general merchandise sales.

The Rich's advertising strategy in the past had been to emphasize newspaper advertising for specific sales items and to utilize broadcast media primarily for image purposes. Newspaper was also used for some image-oriented advertising, with occasional direct mailings used to promote specific sales items of merchandise. Rich's is the largest local advertiser in both print and broadcast media.

The two principal daily newspapers in Atlanta are *The Atlanta Journal* (evenings) and the *Atlanta Constitution* (mornings). These are two of the largest circulation newspapers in the South, and both have distinguished journalism traditions, including Pulitzer Prizes. Although both newspapers are owned by the same company, Atlanta Newspapers, Inc., there is little overlap of readership except for the combined Sunday morning edition.

There are 6 TV stations and 40 radio stations in the Atlanta market. However, broadcast media are dominated by WSB-TV and WSB Radio, both of which are owned by Cox Broadcasting Corporation.

Mr. Mills recalled that several months earlier, executives of Cox Broadcasting and of their two local stations had met with key executives of Rich's. One topic discussed at that meeting had been possible use of broadcast media to promote individual sales items. WSB had offered to participate with Rich's in a market test to determine the abilities of different media to sell specific items of merchandise.

As a result of these discussions, Mr. Mills had held a series of meetings with Mr. Jim Landon, research director of WSB-TV and Radio, and Mr. Ferguson Rood, research director of the Atlanta Newspapers, Inc., to design the market test. It was eventually decided to conduct the test during Rich's annual Harvest Sale, which has been the merchandising highlight of the year since 1925. This sale runs for two weeks each fall. The test was to center on 10 specific items of merchandise which would be advertised in both print and broadcast media during the first three days of the sale. During this same period, in-store interviews would be conducted by professional interviewers, with all purchasers of these 10 items in three representative stores (see appendixes for detailed survey design, sample questionnaire, and media plan).

At the conclusion of the survey period, the Research Departments of both Atlanta Newspapers, Inc., and WSB were furnished duplicate computer card decks by Rich's containing survey data. It was this data that served as the basis for the presentations that Jim Landon and Ferguson Rood had made to the Rich's Executive Committee. Excerpts from *The Atlanta Journal* and *Constitution* report are in Appendix A, and excerpts from the WSB report are presented in Appendix B.

These were the two presentations that Mr. Mills would have to reconcile to arrive at a decision about future media strategy for Rich's. Mr. Mills knew that a decision would have to be made quickly, in view of TV production lead times, if any change in media mix were to be considered for the upcoming Christmas sales season.

Appendix A   **An Analysis of a Rich's In-Store Study of Advertising Effectiveness on Specific Purchase Decisions***

Foreword

This report is the result of an innovative research study conducted by Rich's Department Store in partnership with Atlanta Newspapers, Inc. and Cox Broadcasting Corporation.

The study was designed to measure:

1. The relative performance of newspapers, television, and radio as a source of influence on shoppers' decisions to purchase specific items.
2. Shoppers' exposure to specific item advertising messages.

The advertising period covered in this study consisted of three days (beginning Sunday, September 20) prior to Rich's annual Harvest Sale.

A total of 2,176 interviews were made on Monday and Tuesday, September 21 and 22. The interviews were made in three of Rich's seven stores—Downtown, Lenox Square, and Greenbriar, and focused on the 10 departments in each store where the advertised items were sold.

An Atlanta interviewing firm was employed by Rich's to interview shoppers in each department immediately after they made their purchase. To qualify for the survey, shoppers had to purchase the specific advertised item or a directly related item.

Summary and Interpretation

More than 9 out of 10 shoppers covered in this survey had the specific purchase in mind before going to Rich's, or knew it was *on special*.

Three fourths of all shoppers recalled being recently exposed to advertising messages for specific items.

More than half of all shoppers' decisions to purchase specific items were attributed to advertising.

Attributions to newspapers were more than twice those of television and radio combined in influencing specific item purchase decisions (71 percent versus 33 percent).

Dollar for dollar . . . newspapers delivered more than three times the influence on specific item purchase decisions than television and radio combined.

The advertising schedule placed in newspapers . . . was conspicuously more effective and more efficient . . . in influencing specific purchase decisions . . . than the saturation schedule placed on television and radio.

---

* Presented by *The Atlanta Journal* and *Constitution* Research & Marketing Department.

See Exhibits A–1 through A–16.

EXHIBIT A-1 Newspaper advertising schedule*

	Sunday Journal and Constitution (inches)	A.M. Constitution (inches)	P.M. Journal (inches)
Sunday	1,064		
Monday		172	247
Tuesday		0	505
Total	1,064	172	752

* 1,989 column inches, the equivalent of 11.6 pages, made up the newspaper schedule covered in this survey.

EXHIBIT A-2 Broadcast schedule*

	Television			Radio		
	Sunday	Monday	Tuesday	Sunday	Monday	Tuesday
6 A.M.		X			X	X
7		X			X	X
8		X	X		X	X
9		X	X	X	X	X
10		X		X	X	X
11		X			X	X
12		X	X	X	X	X
1 P.M.	X	X	X	X	X	X
2	X	X	X	X	X	X
3	X	X	X	X	X	X
4	X	X	X	X	X	X
5	X	X	X	X	X	X
6	X	X		X	X	
7	X	X		X	X	
8	X	X				
9	X	X				
10	X	X				
11	X	X				
Total spots	42	86	49	53	121	87
Average number per schedule hour	3.8	4.8	6.1	5.3	8.6	7.2

* 438 30-second spots were scheduled to run on five television and five radio stations, for an average of eight spots per hour, between 6 A.M. and 11 P.M., over the three-day period.

EXHIBIT A-3 Comparison of advertising schedule and budget

	Broadcast spots			Newspaper space (inches)
	TV	Radio	Total	
Hard goods				
Mattress	12	19	31	35
Carpeting	12	23	35	150
Draperies	16	26	42	407
Vacuum sweeper	15	22	37	172
Color television*	0	0	0	150
Soft goods				
Handbags	15	27	42	189
Girdles†	15	27	42	0
Shoes	15	27	42	398
Shirts*	56	64	120	86
Pant suits	21	26	47	400
Total 10 departments				
Sunday	42	53	95	1,064
Monday	86	121	207	420
Tuesday	49	87	136	505
Total	177	261	438	1,989
Budget			$27,158	$16,910

* The original broadcast schedule included 20 TV and 24 radio spots for the color television sets to run Tuesday. Since all the sets were sold on Monday, this commercial time was switched to shirts.

† While no Playtex girdle ads were scheduled to run in newspapers, other foundation advertising during the test period supported the influence.

EXHIBIT A-4 Interviews

	Number	Percent
Total	2,175	100%
Women	1,764	81
Men	380	18
Couples	31	1
Under 35	963	44
35–49	817	38
50 and older	394	18
White	1,966	90
Nonwhite	209	10
Hard goods	527	24
Mattress	71	3
Carpeting	45	2
Draperies	123	6
Vacuum sweeper	134	6
Color television	154	7
Soft goods	1,649	75
Handbags	284	13
Girdles	249	11
Shoes	393	18
Shirts	483	22
Pant suits	240	11
Distribution of interviews by store		
Downtown	683	31
Lenox Square	848	39
Greenbriar	645	30

EXHIBIT A-5

"Before coming to Rich's today, did you have in mind buying this specific brand/item, or did you decide after you came into the store?"

63 percent of all shoppers had the specific purchase in mind before going to Rich's.

These shoppers described the following as sources of influence on their buying decision when asked: "What was it that gave you the idea to buy this brand/item?"

Advertising	52%
Needed or wanted it	23
Past experience with it	16
Outside source suggestion	6
Other	7

EXHIBIT A-6

"Was the store having a special on this specific brand/item today, or were they selling at the regular price?"

84 percent of all shoppers said the brand/item was on special.

These shoppers gave the following sources when asked: "Where did you learn about that?"

Advertising	63%
Store display/crowds	27
Outside source	6
Other	4

EXHIBIT A-7 Advertising influence

55 percent of all shoppers attributed their specific purchase decision to advertising. Of these, 71 percent attributed their purchase to newspapers, 33 percent to broadcasts (28 percent to television and 9 percent to radio), and 9 percent to mail circulars.

Newspapers and broadcast accounted for 94 percent of all advertising influence. 61 percent of these influences were attributed to newspapers exclusive of broadcast. 23 percent were attributed to broadcast exclusive of newspapers, and 10 percent were attributed to both.

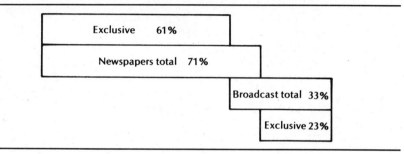

EXHIBIT A-8 Advertising influence

Newspapers and television accounted for 90 percent of all advertising influence. 62 percent of these influences were attributed to newspapers exclusive of television. 19 percent were attributed to television exclusive of newspapers, and 9 percent were attributed to both.

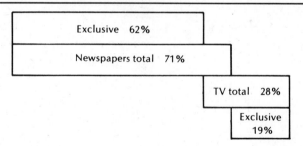

Newspapers and radio accounted for 77 percent of all advertising influence. 68 percent of these influences were attributed to newspapers exclusive of radio. 6 percent were attributed to radio exclusive of newspapers, and 3 percent were attributed to both.

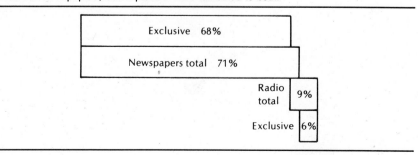

EXHIBIT A-9 Advertising influence—by shopper demographics (among the 55 percent of all shoppers who were influenced by advertising)

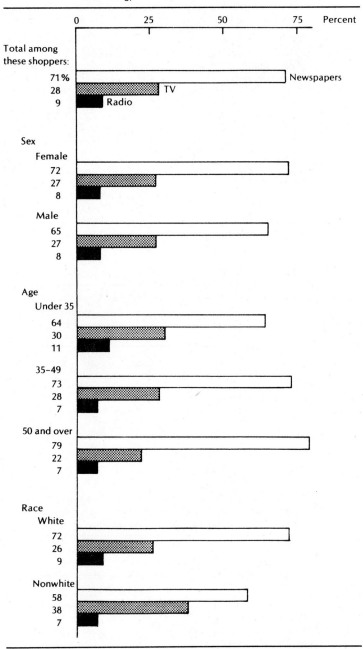

EXHIBIT A-10 Advertising influence—by shopping patterns (among the 55 percent of all shoppers who were influenced by advertising)

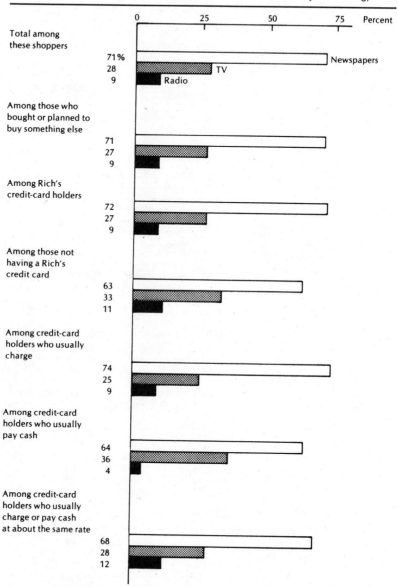

EXHIBIT A-11 Share of budget versus share of influence

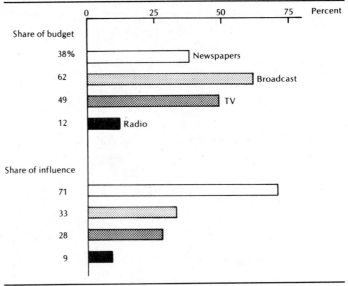

EXHIBIT A-12 Newspapers/broadcast—share of influence
versus share of budget by departments

	Newspapers		Broadcast	
	Share of influence	Share of budget	Share of influence	Share of budget
Total	71%	38%	33%	62%
Hard goods	77	45	30	55
Mattress	43	11	69	89
Carpeting	83	39	23	61
Draperies	83	56	22	44
Vacuum sweeper	70	25	45	75
Color TV	99	100	1	—
Soft goods	68	34	34	66
Handbags	68	41	27	59
Girdles	28	—	74	100
Shoes	87	54	25	46
Shirts	63	12	36	88
Pant suits	82	53	16	47

EXHIBIT A-13 Comparison of advertising schedule/budget/
shopper influence*

	Total 10 departments				
	Broadcast spots		Newspaper space		
	TV	Radio	Journal— Constitution	Constitution	Journal
Schedule					
Sunday	42	53	1,064		
Monday	86	121		172	248
Tuesday	49	87		0	505
	177	261	1,064	172	753

* 438 broadcast spots versus 1,989 inches; budget—$27,158 for broadcast
spots versus $16,910 for newspaper space; and shopper influence—33 per-
cent for broadcast spots versus 71 percent for newspaper space.

EXHIBIT A-14 Advertising exposure

74 percent of all shoppers recalled being exposed to specific advertising messages within the
past day or two. Of these, 79 percent recalled newspapers, 53 percent recalled broadcasts (46
percent television, 18 percent radio), and 24 percent recalled mail circulars.

Newspapers and broadcast accounted for 96 percent of all advertising messages. 43 percent
recalled newspapers exclusive of broadcast. 17 percent recalled broadcast exclusive of newspapers, and 36 percent recalled both.

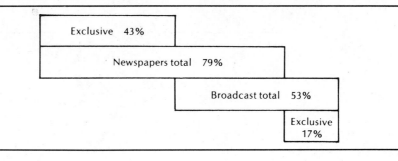

EXHIBIT A-15 Advertising exposure

Newspapers and television accounted for 93 percent of all advertising messages. 47 percent recalled newspapers exclusive of television. 14 percent recalled television exclusive of newspapers, and 32 percent recalled both.

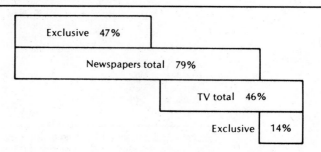

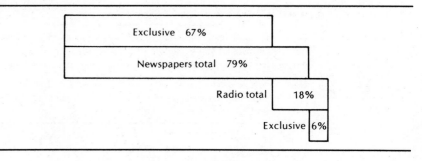

Newspapers and radio accounted for 85 percent of all advertising messages. 67 percent recalled newspapers exclusive of radio. 6 percent recalled radio exclusive of newspapers, and 12 percent recalled both.

Questionnaire   HARVEST SALE IN-STORE CUSTOMER SURVEY

Interviewer Name: _____ (1-2)   STORE: . . . . . . Downtown . . . . . Lenox . . . . . Greenbriar   (3)
                                                              1   2   3

DATE: M   T   W   TIME OF INTERVIEW: _____ DEPARTMENT: _____   (6)
        1   2   3 (4)   (5)

Hello. We're conducting a short survey among RICH'S customers: _____

1. What did you happen to buy in this department today? _____
                                          (PROBE, BRAND, STYLE)   (7-8)

2. Before coming to RICH'S today, did you have in mind buying this specific brand/item, or did you decide after you came into the store?

        HAD IN MIND . . . . (☐) 1   DECIDED IN STORE . . . . . (☐) 2   SKIP TO Q. #3   (9)

        What was it that gave you the
        idea to buy this brand/item? _____

        _____

        (IF APPROPRIATE, ASK: Where did you learn about that?) _____

        _____ (10-11)

3. Was the store having a special on this specific brand/item today, or were they selling at the regular price?

        SPECIAL . . . . . . (☐) 1   REGULAR PRICE . . . . (☐) 2   SKIP TO Q. #4   (12)

        Where did you learn about that? _____

        _____ (13-14)

4. Do you recall seeing or hearing any advertising within the past day or two on radio or television or in the newspapers or in a mail circular that may have reminded you or helped you decide to buy this _____ today?

        YES . . . . (☐) 1   NO . . . . (☐) 2   SKIP TO Q. #5   (15)

        a. Where did you see or hear it? _____   (16)

	4a. UNAIDED RECALL	5. AIDED RECALL	
		YES	NO, DK
RADIO	1	1	2	(17)
NEWSPAPERS	2	1	2	(18)
TELEVISION	3	1·	2	(19)
MAIL CIRCULAR	4	1	2	(20)
OTHER, DON'T KNOW	5			

ASK FOR EACH MEDIUM NOT CHECKED IN Q. #4a.

5. Did you happen to see or hear any of the following within the past day or two:
   A radio commercial for this specific _____? A newspaper ad for this
   specific _____? A television commercial for this specific _____?
   A mail circular for this specific _____? _____

6. Have you bought anything else at RICH'S today, or do you plan to buy anything else at RICH'S today?

        YES . . . . (☐) 1   NO . . . . (☐) 2

7. Do you (or your wife/husband) have a RICH'S credit card?   (21)

        YES . . . . (☐) 1   NO . . . . (☐) 2   (22)

        a. Do you usually charge or pay cash for most of your purchases at RICH'S?

        CHARGE . . . . (☐) 1   CASH . . . . (☐) 2   SAME . . . . . (☐) 3   (23)

8. What is the name of the county where you live? _____ OUT-OF-STATE . . (☐) (24-25-26)

ESTIMATE AGE: UNDER 35 YEARS . . (☐) 1   SEX: FEMALE . . . (☐) 1   RACE: WHITE . . . . (☐) 1   (27)
               35 - 49 . . . . (☐) 2   MALE . . . . . (☐) 2   NON WHITE . (☐) 2   (28)
               50+ . . . . (☐) 3   (29)

Appendix B Analysis of Rich's In-Store Survey*

Introduction

First, we would like to state that WSB television and radio were pleased to have the opportunity to participate in this research effort with Rich's. We have one basic characteristic in common with Rich's—both WSB-TV and WSB Radio, like Rich's, are dominant in the Atlanta market. Like Rich's, we are an Atlanta institution and have enjoyed dominance since our origination.

In this presentation, we will not attempt to interpret the results of your research from a marketing standpoint. You have your own market research department, and we are sure that they have done a capable job of analyzing and interpreting the results of the study from that aspect. Instead, we will concentrate on interpreting the results from a media standpoint, which is our particular area of experience.

The following pages contain our detailed analysis of this research for Rich's management.

Pre-Harvest Sale Advertising Weight

Rich's Pre-Harvest Sale was heavily promoted with a "mix" of three media: radio, TV, and newspaper.

On the broadcast side, Rich's ran 261 radio spots on five stations and 177 TV spots on five stations promoting 10 different items during a three-day period. It can be estimated that the total radio campaign reached about 90 percent of the Atlanta adult metro population, with the average listener exposed to seven commercial announcements (all products combined). The total television campaign also reached an estimated 90 percent of the Atlanta adult population, with the average viewer exposed to 10 commercial announcements.

The newspaper campaign consisted of 13 ads for the specific items and 11 ads for related[1] items, or a total of 24 ads representing 1,987 inches of space in the *Journal* and *Constitution*. Rich's also ran 6,140 inches of other newspaper advertising during the three-day period. We have no way of estimating the reach and frequency of the newspaper ads.

Pre-Harvest Sale a Success

Rich's total advertising effort helped make the store's pre-Harvest Sale a tremendous success.

Monday, September 21, and Tuesday, September 22, were two of Rich's biggest days of the year according to traffic and sales volume. As far as we

---

* Presented by WSB-TV, WSB Radio, and Cox Broadcasting Research.
[1] Same item but different price than in the radio and TV commercial.

know, the departments participating in the test were all up considerably in sales volume compared to a year ago.

Unfortunately, sales results for the *specific items* tested were not available. However, it is our understanding that the departmentwide sales results reflected the success of the individual items in those departments that were tested.

The advertising effort for the pre-Harvest Sale represented one of the few times that Rich's has used a media-mix for *item selling*. Radio and TV have been used extensively by Rich's for institutional advertising and to announce sale events, but item selling has been limited in the past primarily to newspaper and direct mail. *The media-mix for item selling worked from a sales results standpoint.*

Summary of Media Recall Findings

After analyzing the results of the survey, we found the following to be the most significant findings:

1. Because of the confusion and particularly the conditioning factor regarding newspaper, the three media cannot be completely compared in recall.
2. Recall for both radio and TV was significantly higher on Tuesday versus Monday, indicating that the broadcast media were building in impact on customers. Sales results were also generally better on Tuesday versus Monday.
3. Both radio and TV did *best* in recall (compared to newspaper) for items having the *least* amount of newspaper advertising. Radio and TV did *poorest* for items having the *greatest* amount of newspaper advertising.
4. In general, items where radio and TV did *best* in recall (compared to newspaper) had better sales results than items where radio and TV did poorest.
5. All three media performed better among high-priced items and for items where customers decided to buy before coming into the store.
6. Radio and TV balanced newspaper quite well by reaching younger adults than the print medium.

See Exhibits B–1 through B–3.

EXHIBIT B-1 Summary of newspaper recall

Item	Budget	Day/ads	Got idea	Learned of special	Direct recall
Draperies	$4,412	Sun.-2, Tues.-2	48%	68%	81%
Pant suits	3,359	Sun.-2, Mon.-1, Tues.-3	50	56	63
Shoes	2,834	Sun.-1, Mon.-2, Tues.-1	48	55	72
Handbags	1,670	Sun.-1, Tues.-1	30	30	60
Carpeting	1,503	Sun.-1	61	63	80
Color TV	1,503	Sun.-1	62	68	66

EXHIBIT B-1 *(concluded)*

Item	Budget	Day/ads	Got idea	Learned of special	Direct recall
Dress shirts	$859	Sun.–1	40%	40%	54%
Vacuum cleaner	780	Mon.–4	36	62	64
Mattresses	260	Tues.–1	30	37	54
Career shirts	—	—	19	27	45
Girdles	—	—	12	15	16
Averages, all items*			42	51	64

* Excludes girdles (no ads), but includes career shirts because of ads for dress shirts, a related item.

EXHIBIT B-2 Summary of television recall

Item	Budget	Adult audience (000)	Got idea	Learned of special	Direct recall
Career shirts	$2,998	1,373.4	15%	16%	27%
Draperies	2,714	776.5	11	15	37
Pant suits	2,494	885.4	8	9	39
Playtex girdles	2,364	752.1	25	34	32
Dress shirts	2,028	824.8	16	16	29
Handbags	1,922	649.2	10	10	34
Shoes	1,909	724.7	11	14	41
Vacuum cleaner	1,867	627.4	19	36	42
Carpeting	1,790	624.5	8	12	29
Mattresses	1,627	691.9	40	48	49
Color TV	—	—	0	0	5
Averages, all items*			16	21	36

* Excludes color TV (no commercials).

EXHIBIT B-3 Summary of radio recall

Item	Budget	Adult audience (000)	Got idea	Learned of special	Direct recall
Career shirts	$903	489.1	2%	6%	17%
Draperies	560	654.3	1	2	8
Shoes	544	566.8	5	6	14
Pant suits	539	633.9	1	2	12
Carpeting	513	590.9	8	7	24
Dress shirts	498	496.4	4	5	12
Girdles	482	553.0	6	9	11
Mattresses	477	527.6	11	23	29
Handbags	476	475.1	2	3	20
Vacuum cleaner	453	482.1	7	8	10
Color TV	—	374.2	—	1	2
Averages, all items*			5	7	16

* Excludes color TV (no commercials).

Three Types of Media Recall in the Study

The questionnaire used in Rich's in-store survey obtained information about customers' recall of advertising media in three areas:

1. Idea to Buy

For customers purchasing the item being tested, those that indicated having in mind buying that specific merchandise before coming to the store were asked *what gave them the idea to buy the item.* In this question, answers involving media came from top-of-mind recall (not aided). Nonmedia answers to this question, such as "needed" item, "wanted" item or "had past experience" with item were accepted.

2. Learned of Special

Those customers who were aware of the store having a special on the specific item purchased were asked *where they learned about it.* In this question, answers involving media also came from top-of-mind recall and nonmedia responses such as "saw on display" or "friend told me" were accepted.

3. Direct Recall

Customers were also asked if they recalled seeing or hearing any advertising that may have reminded them or helped them decide to buy the specific item. If they answered in the affirmative, they were then asked *where they saw or heard it.* If radio, newspaper, TV or mail circular were not mentioned by the respondent, they were also asked if they happened to hear a radio commercial, see a newspaper ad, and so on (aided recall). For purposes of analyzing the results, the unaided and aided answers to direct recall have been combined in this question.

Effect of Confusion and "Conditioning"

First, we would like to emphasize three points that should be taken into consideration when evaluating each advertising medium's performance based on the recall results of the study:

1. Because of the heavy amount of Rich's advertising activity in all media during the three-day period of interviewing, there was a certain amount of confusion that occurred among the customer-respondents regarding where they saw or heard advertising. This fact will be documented in the pages to follow.

2. Because Rich's traditionally has done the vast majority of its *item* advertising in newspaper, customers are "conditioned" to this particular medium; i.e., more inclined to think of Rich's merchandise being advertised in a newspaper.

3. During the three-day period of the study, *other department stores* were also running *newspaper* ads for items similar to Rich's items being tested. Some newspaper ad recall in this study could have been due to confusion with other stores' ads.

These points can all be substantiated by the following results.

Only Slight Confusion for Radio Commercials

There were *no* radio commercials for color TV sets, since the spots were canceled before they were scheduled to run on Tuesday afternoon.

0%	Claimed they got the idea to buy a color TV set from radio commercials.
1%	Thought they learned of color TV sets being on sale from radio commercials.
2%	Said they recalled hearing radio commercials for color TV sets.

Only Slight Confusion for TV Commercials

There were *no* TV commercials for color TV sets, since the spots were canceled before they were scheduled to run on Tuesday afternoon.

0%	Claimed that they got the idea to buy a color TV set from TV commercials.
0%	Thought they learned of color TV sets on sale from TV commercials.
5%	Said they recalled seeing TV commercials for color TV sets.

Some Confusion and "Conditioning" for Mail Circular

In the mail circular that Rich's distributed to its customers the week prior to the survey, there were *no* ads for any specific items, yet among the total sample of customer-respondents purchasing any of the 11 items tested:

3%	Claimed they got the idea to buy the specific item from a mail circular.
5%	Thought they learned of the specific item being on sale from a mail circular.
18%	Said they recalled seeing a mail circular for the specific item.

Greater Confusion and "Conditioning" for Newspaper Ads

There were *no* Rich's newspaper ads for Playtex girdles, yet:

12%	Claimed they got the idea to buy girdles from newspaper ads.
15%	Thought they learned of girdles being on sale from newspaper ads.
16%	Said they recalled seeing newspaper ads for girdles.

There were *no* Rich's newspaper ads for mattresses on either Sunday or Monday of the survey, yet among customers interviewed on Monday:

27%	Claimed they got the idea to buy a mattress from newspaper ads.
30%	Thought they learned of the mattress being on sale from newspaper ads.
49%	Said they recalled seeing newspaper ads for mattresses.

Caution in Comparing Media by Recall!

As you can see, the extent of erroneous recall of newspaper advertising ranged from a low of 12 percent to a high of 49 percent. For this important reason, it is impossible to derive any accurate yardstick for measuring the separate value of each medium, dollar for dollar. In addition, these results cannot be converted to any type of advertising-to-sales ratio.

Radio May Have Been Higher with More WSB Spots

Due to the problem created by trying to find enough availabilities on WSB only in morning and evening drive time (because of the agency's buying criteria) to handle commercials for 11 different items in three days, Atlanta's dominant radio station was not able to contribute as much weight as it should have to most of the media schedules. As a result, a higher proportion of spots ran on WQXI (primarily teens), WAOK (primarily ethnic) and WRNG (primarily 50 + listeners), and WPLO (lower socioeconomic level). A brief analysis of the number of radio commercials that ran for each item, showing the light proportion of WSB spots, is shown in the accompanying table.

	Total spots	WSB spots	WSB morning drive spots*
Career shirts	48	10	0
Carpeting	23	6	3
Color TV	—	—	—
Draperies	26	7	2
Dress shirts	15	6	2
Girdles	27	5	1
Handbags	27	5	1
Mattresses	19	6	2
Pant suits	26	8	2
Shoes	27	6	2
Vacuum cleaner	22	5	2
Total	260	64	17

* Monday or Tuesday.

Television versus Newspaper

While TV budgets were fairly even, newspaper budgets ranged from $260 for mattresses up to $4,412 for draperies. TV versus newspaper performance in all types of recall showed a good relationship to the amount of money spent in newspaper. The smaller the newspaper budget versus TV, the better TV performed versus newspaper in recall, and vice versa:

1. TV did *best* in all types of recall *compared to newspaper* for mattresses, career shirts, and vacuum cleaners. These items had the *smallest amount* of advertising space in the newspaper compared to the others.
2. TV did *poorest* in all types of recall *compared to newspaper* for draperies, pant suits, shoes, and carpeting. These items had the *greater amount* of advertising space in the newspaper.

Radio versus Newspaper

Again, radio budgets were fairly even compared to the wide range in newspaper budgets. Radio versus newspaper performance in all types of recall also showed a fairly strong relationship to the amount of money spent in newspaper. The smaller the newspaper budget versus radio, the better radio performed versus newspaper in recall, and vice versa:

1. Radio did *best* in all types of recall *compared to newspaper* for mattresses, vacuum cleaners, and career shirts. These items generally had the least newspaper space.
2. Radio did *poorest* in all types of recall *compared to newspaper* for draperies, pant suits, and handbags. These items generally had the greatest newspaper space.

Less Newspaper Space—No Harm to Sales Volume

We have just indicated that, as newspaper space was reduced, both radio and TV did better in recall.

How about Rich's Sales Volume?

There appeared to be little, if any, correlation between the amount of newspaper space and sales volume as measured by department sales increases. If anything, the reverse occurred:

	Monday	*Tuesday*
TV and radio did best (least newspaper space):		
Girdles	+7%	+92%
Career shirts	+151	+349
Mattresses	+43	+76
Vacuum cleaners	+98	+222
TV and radio did poorest (most newspaper space):		
Draperies	−0	+9
Pant suits	+17	+46
Shoes	−19	+14
Carpeting	−9	+526

Idea to Buy versus Direct Recall

One probable indication of the "conditioning" of Rich's customers to newspaper advertising comes from comparing initial "idea to buy" recall, where media responses came purely from top of mind, to the direct recall that came later in the interview, concentrating on each medium. All three media gained in regard to the proportion of customers recalling (from idea to buy to direct recall), but newspaper, having been recalled more from top of mind, gained the least, while TV and especially radio, in the background during top of mind "idea to buy," came to the surface more in the direct recall.

	Average recall, all items*		
	Idea to buy	Direct recall	Percent increase
Newspaper	42%	64%	+52%
TV	16	36	+125
Radio	5	16	+220

* Girdles were eliminated for newspaper and color TV sets were eliminated for radio and TV because of no advertising.

First Day versus Second Day Recall

Analysis of the direct recall results by day of interview produced an interesting fact. The impact of newspaper was initial, while both radio and TV performed significantly better on the second day. This is probably due to the nature of the broadcast media, which gain impact and effectiveness with *increased frequency* (as listeners and viewers are exposed to more commercials). In addition, sales results for all items were generally better on Tuesday than on Monday, compared to a year ago. This also indicates that, if spots had been spread more evenly over Sunday, Monday, and Tuesday (rather than concentrated on Sunday and Monday in most cases), and if interviewing had been extended through Wednesday, both radio and TV would have performed better in recall, at no increase in budget for either medium.

	Average recall, all items*		
	Monday	Tuesday	Tuesday percent difference
Newspaper	66%	62%	−6%
TV	33	38	+15
Radio	13	18	+38

* Mattresses were eliminated for newspaper as an invalid comparison, since there were no ads on Sunday or Monday. However, even though there were no radio or TV commercials for career shirts on Sunday or Monday, and no newspaper ads at all, this item was included in this comparison because there was advertising for dress shirts, a related item. Also girdles were eliminated for newspaper and color TV for radio and TV because of no advertising.

High-Priced versus Low-Priced Items

In order to analyze media performance by item *price range,* the items were divided into either a high-price (carpeting, color TV, draperies, mattresses, and vacuum cleaners) or a low-price (career shirts, dress shirts, girdles, handbags, pant suits, and shoes) group. All three media performed better among high-priced items compared to low-priced merchandise, especially radio and TV. However, the differences were greater regarding "idea to buy" recall and "learned of special" recall than with the direct recall. Customers who had made up their minds to buy a large ticket item were apparently more persuaded by advertising than those coming to Rich's for lower priced merchandise. However, whether in the market for high- or low-priced items, both type customers were exposed to advertising, as indicated in the direct recall.

	High-priced items	Low-priced items	High-priced percent difference
Idea to buy:			
Newspaper	47%	37%	+27%
TV	20	14	+43
Radio	7	3	+133
Learned of special:			
Newspaper	60	42	+43
TV	28	16	+75
Radio	10	5	+100
Direct recall:			
Newspaper	69	59	+17
TV	39	34	+15
Radio	18	14	+29

"Had in Mind" versus "Decided in Store"

In order to analyze media performance by the extent to which customers had in mind to buy the item before coming to the store, the items were divided into two groups: "had in mind" and "decided in store," based on results to the question covering this aspect of purchasing. The four items where roughly half of the customers indicated deciding in the store (pant suits, dress shirts, career shirts, and handbags) were placed in the "decided in store" group. The other seven items, where significantly less customers indicated deciding in store, were placed in the "had in mind" group. All three media performed significantly better among items in the "had in mind" group, that is, for items where a greater proportion of customers made their decision in advance. The differences were greater regarding "idea to buy" and "learned of special" recall than with the direct recall.

	"Had in mind" items	"Decided in store" items	"Had in mind" percent difference
Idea to buy:			
Newspaper	48%	35%	+37%
TV	19	12	+58
Radio	6	2	+200
Learned of special:			
Newspaper	59	38	+55
TV	26	13	+100
Radio	9	4	+125
Direct recall:			
Newspaper	70	56	+25
TV	38	32	+19
Radio	16	15	+7

Broadcast Media Recall Reflected Younger Adults

By analyzing media recall by age of customer, it was determined that radio and TV balanced newspaper quite well by reaching younger adults. In all three types of recall, the under 35 age group was proportionately higher for broadcast, especially radio, than for newspaper. These figures are based on all items combined.

Age	Radio	TV	Newspaper
Got idea:			
Under 35	56%	44%	36%
35–49	31	38	44
50 and over	13	18	20
Learned of special:			
Under 35	50	43	36
35–49	34	41	41
50 and over	16	16	23
Direct recall:			
Under 35	49	44	41
35–49	33	38	41
50 and over	18	18	18

Note: Read Table. Of those customers indicating that they "got the idea" to buy an item from radio commercials, 56 percent were in the under 35 age group.

Rich's Dominant Position in Atlanta

In concluding this presentation, we would like to announce the results of separate research that we have just completed that indicates the extent to which

Rich's dominates the department store market in Atlanta, a domination that we feel is due to:

Outstanding management.

Quality of merchandise.

Attention to customer service and satisfaction.

Efficient use of advertising and promotion, *especially the use of a media-mix.*

Presentation Summary

1. With use of media-mix for item selling, the pre-Harvest Sale was a success. All departments participating in the test were up in sales volume.
2. Because of confusion and conditioning factors, recall results are not completely comparable between media.
3. In general, as the amount of newspaper space was reduced, the proportion of recall for both TV and radio was increased, and sales results were generally more favorable.
4. Sales volume was up significantly on Tuesday versus Monday in all departments, indicating a relationship with broadcast media recall, also up significantly on Tuesday as frequency increased.
5. All media had higher recall for higher priced items and items where customer generally decided in advance.
6. Separate research confirms Rich's dominance of the Atlanta market, especially versus Davison's. Rich's uses radio and TV effectively, Davison's uses very little broadcast media.

Exercise in Print Advertising Assessment

One of the most important and most difficult marketing decisions is the choice of creative executions in advertising. The purpose of this exercise is to help you develop skills in determining what is a good and a bad creative execution.

In preparation for your class session using this exercise, we would like you to spend time looking at *print* advertising (newspaper and magazine advertising). We would like you to select what you think is the "best ad" you have seen and the "worst ad" you have seen. To aid you in this task you might ask yourself the following questions:

1. What is the sponsor's apparent target segment(s)?
2. What are the objectives of the ad?
3. Is the basic appeal, theme, and copy approach appropriate for these purposes?

To the bottom of each ad you selected attach a small piece of paper containing the following information:

1. Sponsor of the ad.
2. Publication in which the ad appeared.
3. Publication date.
4. Your reason(s) for selecting that ad as the best or worst.
5. Your name.

Staple or tape this information to the bottom of the ad but don't obscure any of the ad. Turn in your ads to your professor as required. In the class session you will get a chance to compare your choice of ads with those of your classmates.

Case 27

Allied Food Distributors

In April 1977, Ms. Elizabeth Ramsey, the district sales manager for the upper Midwest district of Allied Food Distributors, was preparing to hire a new salesperson for the southwest Indiana sales territory. The current salesperson in this territory was leaving the company at the end of June. Ms. Ramsey had narrowed the list of potential candidates to three. She wondered which of these applicants she should select.

Company Background

Allied Food Distributors was one of the largest food wholesalers in the United States. The company carried hundreds of different packaged food items (fruits, vegetables, cake mixes, cookies, powdered soft drinks, and so on) for sales to supermarkets and grocery stores. Allied carried items in two different circumstances. First, some small food companies had Allied carry their entire line in all areas of the United States. Allied was in essence their sales force. Second, some large food companies had Allied carry their lines in less populated parts of the country. These areas were not large enough to sustain a salesperson for each food company.

Allied operated in all 50 states. The country was divided into 20 sales districts. Ms. Ramsey's sales district included Michigan, Indiana, and Illinois. Each district was divided into a number of sales territories. A salesperson was assigned to each territory.

The Southwest Indiana Territory

The sales territory for which Ms. Ramsey was seeking a salesperson was located in the southwest corner of Indiana. Exhibit 1 presents a map of the territory. It was bordered on the south by the Ohio River and the state of Kentucky, on the west by the Wabash River and the state of Illinois, and on the east by the Hoosier National Forest. The northern boundary ran a few miles north of Highways 50 and 150 that ran from Vincennes in the west through

EXHIBIT 1 A map of the southwest Indiana territory

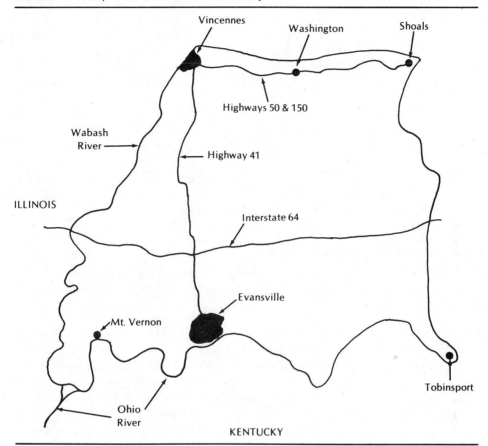

Washington to Shoals in the east. Evansville was the largest city in the area with a population of about 140,000. The salesperson for the territory was expected to live in Evansville, but would spend about three nights a week on the road. The only other reasonably large population concentration was in Vincennes with a population of about 20,000. Vincennes was located about 55 miles straight north of Evansville on Highway 41. Interstate Highway 64 ran the 80 miles east-west through the territory about 15 miles north of Evansville. Evansville was 165 miles southwest of Indianapolis, 170 miles east of St. Louis, Missouri, and 115 miles southwest of Louisville, Kentucky. The territory was very rural in character with agriculture being the dominant industry. The terrain was quite hilly, with poor soil. As a result, the farms in the area tended to be economically weak. There were many small towns and villages located throughout this basically rural environment.

The Selling Task

Allied maintained 75 active retail accounts in the southwest Indiana territory. About 10 of these accounts were medium- to large-sized independent supermarkets located in Evansville and Vincennes. The rest of the accounts were small, independent general food stores located throughout the territory.

The salesperson was expected to call on these accounts about every three weeks. The salesperson's duties included: checking displays and inventory levels for items already carried, obtaining orders on these items, informing retailers about new items, attempting to gain sales orders on these items, setting up special displays, and generally servicing the retailers' needs. Often, the salesperson would check the level of inventory on an item, make out an order, and present it to the retailer to be signed. The salesperson generally knew the store owner on a first name basis. The ordered goods were sent directly to the retailer from a warehouse located in Indianapolis.

The Selection Process

The responsibility for recruiting salespersons for the territories within a district was given to the district sales manager. The process consisted of the following steps:

1. An advertisement for the job was placed in newspapers in the state in question.
2. Those responding to the ad were sent job application forms.
3. The returned application forms were examined and certain applicants were asked to come to the district sales office for a full day of interviews.
4. The selection was then made by the district sales manager, or all applicants were rejected and the process started again.

Training

Allied did all its salesperson training on-the-job. The salesperson on the territory that a new person would be assigned to, was given the task of training. Basically, this involved having the new person travel the territory to meet the retailers and to be shown how to obtain and send in orders. The district sales manager usually assisted in this process by traveling with the new salesperson for a few days.

Compensation

The current salesperson on the southwest Indiana sales territory was earning a straight salary of about $16,000 per year plus fringe benefits. Ms. Ramsey indicated that she was willing to pay between $10,000 and $17,000 for a new person depending on the qualifications presented.

The Choices

On the basis of application forms and personal interviews, Ms. Ramsey had narrowed the field of applicants down to three. A summary of the information on their application forms along with the comments she had written to herself are contained in Exhibits 2, 3, and 4. She wondered which person she should select for the position.

EXHIBIT 2 Information on Mr. Michael Gehringer

Personal information

Born July 15, 1935; married; three children ages 14, 16, and 19; height 5 feet, 10 inches; weight 205; excellent health; born and raised in Indianapolis.

Education

High school graduate; played football; no extracurricular activities of note.

Employment record

1. Currently employed by Allied Food Distributors in the warehouse in Indianapolis; two years with Allied; job responsibilities include processing orders from the field and expediting rush orders; current salary $650 per month.
2. In 1974–75 employed by Hoosier Van Lines in Indianapolis as a sales agent; terminating salary was $550 per month; left due to limits placed on salary and lack of challenge in the job.
3. In 1972–74 employed by Main Street Clothiers of Indianapolis as a retail salesperson in the men's department; terminating salary $500 per month; left due to boring nature of this type of selling.
4. Between 1955 and 1972 held six other clerical and sales type jobs, all in Indianapolis.

Applicant's statement

I feel that my true employment interest lies in selling in a situation where I can be my own boss. This job seems just right.

Ms. Ramsey's comments

Seems very interested in job as a career.
Well recommended by his current boss.
Reasonably intelligent.
Good appearance.
Moderately aggressive.

EXHIBIT 3 Information on Mr. Carley Tobias

Personal information

Born February 12, 1947; married; two children ages 1 and 4; height 6 feet, 2 inches; weight 170; excellent health; born in San Francisco; raised in Cleveland, Ohio.

Education

High school and Community College graduate in business administration; student council president at Community College; plus belonged to a number of other clubs.

Employment record

1. Currently employed by The Drug Trading Company in Cincinnati as a salesperson; job responsibility involves selling to retail drug stores; seven years with Drug Trading; current salary $1,100 per month.
2. In 1969–70 U.S. Army private; did one tour of duty in Vietnam.

Applicant's statement

I am seeking a new position because of the limited earning potential at Drug Trading, plus my family's desire to live in a less populated city.

Other information

He is very active in civic and church organizations in Cincinnati; he is currently president of the Sales and Marketing Executives of Cincinnati.

Ms. Ramsey's comments

Very personable.

Reasonably intelligent.

Good appearance.

He seems to like Cincinnati a lot.

Good experience.

EXHIBIT 4 Information on Mr. Arthur Woodhead

Personal information

Born May 26, 1955; single; height 6 feet; weight 180; excellent health; born and raised in Chicago.

Education

Will graduate in May 1977 from the University of Illinois, Chicago Circle with a B.B.A. Active in intramural athletics and student government.

Employment record

Summer jobs only; did house painting and gardening work for his own company. Earned $700 per month in summer of 1976.

Applicant's statement

I really like to run my own affairs, and selling seems like a good position to reach this objective.

Ms. Ramsey's comments

Well dressed and groomed.
Very intelligent.
Management potential, not career salesperson.
Not very aggressive.

Case 28

Outdoor Sporting Products, Inc.*

The annual sales volume of Outdoor Sporting Products, Inc., for the past six years had ranged between $3.2 million and $3.4 million. Although profits continued to be satisfactory, Mr. Hudson McDonald, president and chief operating officer, was concerned because sales had not increased appreciably from year to year. Consequently, he asked a consultant in New York City and the officers of the company to submit proposals for improving the salesmen's compensation plan, which he believed was the basic weakness in the firm's marketing operations.

Outdoor's factory and warehouse were located in Albany, New York, where the company manufactured and distributed sporting equipment, clothing, and accessories. Mr. Hudson McDonald, who managed the company, organized it in 1956 when he envisioned a growing market for sporting goods resulting from the predicted increase in leisure time and the rising levels of income in the United States.

Products of the company, numbering approximately 700 items, were grouped into three lines: (1) fishing supplies, (2) hunting supplies, and (3) accessories. The fishing supplies line, which accounted for approximately 40 percent of the company's annual sales, included nearly every item a fisherman would need such as fishing jackets, vests, caps, rods and reels of all types, lines, flies, lures, landing nets, and creels. Thirty percent of annual sales were in the hunting supplies line which consisted of hunting clothing of all types including insulated and thermal underwear, safety garments, shell holders, whistles, calls, and gun cases. The accessories line, which made up the balance of the company's annual sales volume, included items such as compasses, cooking kits, lanterns, hunting and fishing knives, hand warmers, and novelty gifts.

While the sales of the hunting and fishing lines were very seasonal, they tended to complement one another. The January–April period accounted for the bulk of the company's annual volume in fishing items, and most sales of hunt-

---

* Adapted from a case written by Zarrel V. Lambert, Auburn University, and Fred W. Kniffin, University of Connecticut, Stamford. Used with permission.

ing supplies were made during the months of May through August. Typically, the company's sales of all products reached their lows for the year during the month of December.

Outdoor's sales volume was $3.34 million in the current year with self-manufactured products accounting for 35 percent of this total. Fifty percent of the company's volume consisted of imported products which came principally from Japan. Items manufactured by other domestic producers and distributed by Outdoor accounted for the remaining 15 percent of total sales.

Mr. McDonald reported that wholesale prices to retailers were established by adding a markup of 50 to 100 percent to Outdoor's cost for the item. This rule was followed on self-manufactured products as well as for items purchased from other manufacturers. The resulting average markup across all products was 70 percent on cost.

Outdoor's market area consisted of the New England states, New York, Pennsylvania, Ohio, Michigan, Wisconsin, Indiana, Illinois, Kentucky, Tennessee, West Virginia, Virginia, Maryland, Delaware, and New Jersey. The area over which Outdoor could effectively compete was limited to some extent by shipping costs, since all orders were shipped from the factory and warehouse in Albany.

Outdoor's salesmen sold to approximately 6,000 retail stores in small- and medium-sized cities in its market area. Analysis of sales records showed that the firm's customer coverage was very poor in the large metropolitan areas. Typically, each account was a one- or two-store operation. Mr. McDonald stated that he knew for a fact that Outdoor's share of the market was very low, perhaps 2 to 3 percent; and for all practical purposes, he felt the company's sales potential was unlimited.

Mr. McDonald believed that with few exceptions, Outdoor's customers had little or no brand preference and in the vast majority of cases they bought hunting and fishing supplies from several suppliers.

It was McDonald's opinion that the pattern of retail distribution for hunting and fishing products had been changing during the past 10 years as a result of the growth of discount stores. He thought that the proportion of retail sales for hunting and fishing supplies made by small- and medium-sized sporting goods outlets had been declining compared to the percent sold by discounters and chain stores. An analysis of company records revealed Outdoor had not developed business among the discounters with the exception of a few small discount stores. Some of Outdoor's executives felt that the lack of business with discounters might have been due in part to the company's pricing policy and in part to the pressures which current customers had exerted on company salesmen to keep them from calling on the discounters.

Outdoor's Sales Force

The company's sales force played the major role in its marketing efforts since Outdoor did not use magazine, newspaper, or radio advertising to reach either the retail trade or consumers. One advertising piece that supplemented the work of the salesmen was Outdoor's merchandise catalog. It contained a complete listing of all the company's products and was mailed to all retailers who were either current accounts or prospective accounts. Typically, store buyers used the catalog for purposes of reordering.

Most accounts were contacted by a salesman two or three times a year. The salesmen planned their activities so that each store would be called upon at the beginning of the fishing season and again prior to the hunting season. Certain key accounts of some salesmen were contacted more often than two or three times a year.

Management believed that product knowledge was the major ingredient of a successful sales call. Consequently, Mr. McDonald had developed a "selling formula" which each salesman was required to learn before he took over a territory. The "formula" contained five parts: (1) the name and catalog number of each item sold by the company; (2) the sizes and colors in which each item was available; (3) the wholesale price of each item; (4) the suggested retail price of each item; and (5) the primary selling features of each item. After a new salesman had mastered the product knowledge specified by this "formula" he began working in his assigned territory and was usually accompanied by Mr. McDonald for several weeks.

Managing the sales force consumed approximately one third of Mr. McDonald's efforts. The remaining two thirds of his time was spent purchasing products for resale and in general administrative duties as the company's chief operating officer.

Mr. McDonald held semiannual sales meetings, had weekly telephone conversations with each salesman and had mimeographed bulletins containing information on products, prices, and special promotional deals mailed to all salesmen each week. Daily call reports and attendance at the semiannual sales meetings were required of all salesmen. One meeting was held the first week in January to introduce the spring line of fishing supplies. The hunting line was presented at the second meeting which was scheduled in May. Each of these sales meetings spanned four to five days so the salesmen were able to study the new products being introduced and any changes in sales and company policies. The production manager and comptroller attended these sales meetings to answer questions and to discuss problems which the salesmen might have concerning deliveries and credit.

On a predetermined schedule each salesman telephoned Mr. McDonald every Monday morning to learn of changes in prices, special promotional offers, and delivery schedules of unshipped orders. At this time the salesman's activities for the week were discussed, and sometimes the salesman was asked by Mr. McDonald to collect past due accounts in his territory. In addition, the salesmen submitted daily call reports which listed the name of each account contacted and the results of the call. Generally, the salesmen planned their own itineraries in terms of the accounts and prospects that were to be contacted and the amount of time to be spent on each call.

Outdoor's sales force during the current year totaled 11 full-time employees. Their ages ranged from 23 to 67 years and their tenure with the company from 1 to 10 years. Salesmen, territories, and sales volumes for the previous year and the current year are shown in Exhibit 1.

EXHIBIT 1 Salesmen: Age, years of service, territory, and sales

Salesmen	Age	Years of service	Territory	Sales Previous year	Current year
Allen	45	2	Illinois and Indiana	$ 165,132	$ 164,608
Campbell	62	10	Pennsylvania	596,096	690,120
Duvall	23	1	New England	—	207,328
Edwards	39	1	Michigan	—	209,708
Gatewood	63	5	West Virginia	179,264	179,276
Hammond	54	2	Virginia	207,468	207,364
Logan	37	1	Kentucky and Tennessee	—	283,860
Mason	57	2	Delaware and Maryland	322,516	412,544
O'Bryan	59	4	Ohio	271,964	286,196
Samuels	42	3	New York and New Jersey	368,512	412,236
Wates	67	5	Wisconsin	185,356	171,100
Salesmen terminated in previous year				914,408	—
House account				128,692	122,240
Total				$3,339,408	$3,347,408

Compensation of Salesmen

The salesmen were paid straight commissions on their dollar sales volume for the calendar year. The commission rate was 5 percent on the first $150,000, 6 percent on the next $50,000 in volume, and 7 percent on all sales over $200,000 for the year. Each week a salesman could draw all or a portion of his accumulated commissions. McDonald encouraged the salesmen to draw commissions as they accumulated since he felt the men were motivated to work harder when they had a very small or zero balance in their commission accounts. These accounts were closed at the end of the year so each salesman began the new year with nothing in his account.

The salesmen provided their own automobiles and paid their traveling expenses, of which all or a portion were reimbursed by per diem. Under the per diem plan, each salesman received $60 per day for Monday through Thursday and $28 for Friday, or a total of $268 for the normal workweek. No per diem was paid for Saturday, but a salesman received an additional $60 if he spent Saturday and Sunday nights in the territory.

In addition to the commission and per diem, a salesman could earn cash awards under two sales incentive plans that were installed two years ago. Under one which was called the Annual Sales Increase Awards Plan, a total of $10,400 was paid to the five salesmen having the largest percentage increase in dollar sales volume over the previous year. To be eligible for these awards, a salesman had to show a sales increase over the previous year. These awards were made at the January sales meeting, and the winners were determined by dividing the dollar amount of each salesman's increase by his volume for the previous year with the percentage increases ranked in descending order. The salesmen's earnings under this plan for the current year are shown in Exhibit 2.

Under the second incentive plan, each salesman could win a Weekly Sales Increase Award for each week in which his dollar volume in the current year exceeded his sales for the corresponding week in the previous year. Beginning with an award of $4 for the first week, the amount of the award increased by $4 for each week in which the salesman surpassed his sales for the comparable week in the previous year. If a salesman produced higher sales during each of the 50 weeks in the current year, he received $4 for the 1st week, $8 for the 2d week, and $200 for the 50th week, or a total of $4,100 for the year. The salesman had to be employed by the company during the previous year to be eligible for these awards. A check for the total amount of the awards accrued during the year was presented to the salesmen at the sales meeting held in January. Earnings of the salesmen under this plan for the current year are shown in Exhibit 2.

The company frequently used ''spiffs'' to promote the sales of special items. The salesman was paid a spiff, which usually was $4, for each order he obtained for the designated items in the promotion.

For the past three years in recruiting salesmen, Mr. McDonald had guaranteed the more qualified applicants a weekly income while they learned the business and developed their respective territories. During the current year five salesmen, Allen, Duvall, Edwards, Hammond, and Logan, had a guarantee

EXHIBIT 2 Salesmen's earnings and incentive awards in the current year

Salesmen	Sales Previous year	Sales Current year	Annual sales increase awards Increase in sales (percent)	Annual sales increase awards Award	Weekly sales increase awards (total accrued)	Earnings*
Allen	$165,132	$164,608	(0.3%)	—	$1,012	$20,000†
Campbell	596,096	690,120	15.8	$3,000 (2d)	2,244	44,808
Duvall	—	207,328	—	—	—	20,000†
Edwards	—	209,708	—	—	—	20,000†
Gatewood	179,264	179,276	(0.1)	400 (5th)	1,104	9,256
Hammond	207,468	207,364	—	—	420	20,000
Logan	—	283,860	—	—	—	20,000
Mason	322,516	412,544	27.9	4,000 (1st)	3,444	25,378
O'Bryan	271,964	286,196	5.2	1,000 (4th)	1,512	16,534
Samuels	368,512	412,236	11.9	2,000 (3d)	1,300	25,356
Wates	185,356	171,100	(7.7)	—	612	8,766

* Exclusive of incentive awards and per diem.
† Guarantee of $400 per week or $200,000 per year.

of $400 a week which they drew against their commissions. If the year's cumulative commissions for any of these salesmen were less than their cumulative weekly drawing accounts, they received no commissions. The commission and drawing accounts were closed on December 31 so each salesman began the new year with a zero balance in each account.

The company did not have a stated or written policy specifying the maximum length of time a salesman could receive a guarantee if his commissions continued to be less than his draw. Mr. McDonald held the opinion that the five salesmen who currently had guarantees would quit if these guarantees were withdrawn before their commissions reached $20,000 per year.

Mr. McDonald stated that he was convinced the annual earnings of Outdoor's salesmen had fallen behind earnings for comparable selling positions, particularly in the past six years. As a result, he felt that the company's ability to attract and hold high-caliber professional salesmen was being adversely affected. He strongly expressed the opinion that each salesman should be earning $40,000 annually.

Compensation Plan Proposals

In December of the current year, Mr. McDonald met with his comptroller and production manager, who were the only other executives of the company and solicited their ideas concerning changes in the company's compensation plan for salesmen.

The comptroller pointed out that the salesmen having guarantees were not producing the sales that had been expected from their territories. He was concerned that the annual commissions earned by four of the five salesmen on guarantees were approximately half or less than their drawing accounts.

Furthermore, according to the comptroller, several of the salesmen who did not have guarantees were producing a relatively low volume of sales year after year. For example, annual sales remained at relatively low levels for Gatewood, O'Bryan, and Wates, who had been working four to five years in their respective territories.

The comptroller proposed that guarantees be reduced to $200 per week plus commissions at the regular rate on all sales. The $200 would not be drawn against commissions as was the case under the existing plan but would be in addition to any commissions earned. In the comptroller's opinion, this plan would motivate the salesmen to increase sales rapidly since their incomes would rise directly with their sales. The comptroller presented Exhibit 3 which showed the incomes of the five salesmen having guarantees in the current year as compared with the incomes they would have received under his plan.

From a sample check of recent shipments, the production manager had concluded that the salesmen tended to overwork accounts located within a 50-mile radius of their homes. Sales coverage was extremely light in a 60- to 100-mile radius of the salesmen's homes with somewhat better coverage beyond 100

EXHIBIT 3 Comparison of earnings in current year under existing guarantee plan with earnings under the comptroller's plan*

		Existing plan			Comptroller's plan		
Salesmen	Sales	Com- missions	Guar- antee	Earnings	Com- missions	Guar- antee	Earnings
Allen	$164,608	$ 8,376	$20,000	$20,000	$ 8,376	$10,000	$18,376
Duvall	207,328	11,012	20,000	20,000	11,012	10,000	21,012
Edwards	209,708	11,180	20,000	20,000	11,180	10,000	21,180
Hammond	207,364	11,016	20,000	20,000	11,016	10,000	21,016
Logan	283,860	16,370	20,000	20,000	16,370	10,000	26,376

* Exclusive of incentive awards and per diem.

miles. He argued that this pattern of sales coverage seemed to result from a desire by the salesmen to spend most evenings during the week at home with their families.

He proposed that the per diem be increased from $60 to $72 per day for Monday through Thursday, $28 for Friday, and $72 for Sunday if the salesman spent Sunday evening away from his home. He reasoned that the per diem of $72 for Sunday would act as a strong incentive for the salesmen to drive to the perimeters of their territories on Sunday evenings rather than use Monday morning for traveling. Further, he believed that the increase in per diem would encourage the salesmen to spend more evenings away from their homes which would result in a more uniform coverage of the sales territories and an overall increase in sales volume.

The consultant from New York City recommended that the guarantees and per diem be retained on the present basis and proposed that Outdoor adopt what he called a "Ten Percent Self-Improvement Plan." Under the consultant's plan each salesman would be paid, in addition to the regular commission, a monthly bonus commission of 10 percent on all dollar volume over his sales in the comparable month of the previous year. For example, if a salesman sold $40,000 worth of merchandise in January of the current year and $36,000 in January of the previous year, he would receive a $400 bonus check in February. For salesmen on guarantees, bonuses would be in addition to earnings. The consultant reasoned that the bonus commission would motivate the salesmen, both those with and without guarantees, to increase their sales.

He further recommended the discontinuation of the two sales incentive plans currently in effect. He felt the savings from these plans would nearly cover the costs of his proposal.

Following a discussion of these proposals with the management group, Mr. McDonald was undecided on which proposal to adopt, if any. Further, he wondered if any change in the compensation of salesmen would alleviate all of the present problems.

Case 29

Pure Drug Company*

Mr. David Thomas had been transferred to the Syracuse, New York, Division of Pure Drug Company in the first week of May 1970. At this time he was appointed sales manager of the Syracuse wholesale drug division. Formerly he had been an assistant to the vice president in charge of sales at the company's headquarters in New York.

At the month-end sales meeting on the first Friday of June 1970, Mr. Harvey Brooks, a salesman in one of the division's rural territories, informed Mr. Thomas that he wished to retire at the end of July when he reached his 65th birthday. Mr. Thomas was surprised by Mr. Brooks's announcement because he had been informed by the division manager, Mr. Robert Jackson, that Mr. Brooks had requested and received a deferment of retirement until he reached his 66th birthday in July 1971. The only explanation offered by Mr. Brooks was that he had "changed his mind."

The retirement of Mr. Brooks posed a problem for Mr. Thomas, in that he had to decide what to do with Mr. Brooks's territory.

Background of the Syracuse Division

When Mr. Thomas became the divisional sales manager, he was 29 years old. He had joined Pure Drug (as the firm was known in trade circles) as a sales trainee after his graduation from Stanford University in 1964. During the next two years he worked as a salesman. In the fall of 1966, the sales manager of the company made Mr. Thomas one of his assistants. In this capacity Mr. Thomas helped the sales manager to arrange special sales promotions of the lines of different manufacturers.

Mr. Thomas' predecessor, Mr. Harry L. Schultz, had served as divisional sales manager for 15 years before his death in April. "H. L.," as Mr. Schultz

* This case was written by T. Levitt, Professor of Business Administration, Harvard University, R. Sorenson, President, Babson Institute, and U. Wiechman, Professor of Business Administration, Harvard University. Copyright 1972, the President and Fellows of Harvard College. Reproduced by permission.

had been known, worked as a salesman for the drug wholesale house that had been merged with Pure Drug to become its Syracuse Division. Although Mr. Thomas had made Mr. Schultz's acquaintance in the course of business, he did not know Mr. Schultz well. The salesmen often expressed their admiration and affection for Mr. Schultz to the new sales manager. Several salesmen, in fact, made a point of telling Mr. Thomas that "Old H. L." knew every druggist in 12 counties by his first name. Mr. Schultz had died of a heart attack while trout fishing with the president of the Syracuse Pharmacists' Association. The Syracuse Division manager said that most of the druggists in town attended Mr. Schultz's funeral.

The Syracuse Division of Pure Drug was one of 74 wholesale drug houses in the United States owned by the firm. Each division acted as a functionally autonomous unit having its own warehouse, sales department, buying department, and accounting department. The divisional manager was responsible for the performance of the unit he managed. There were, however, line functions performed by the regional and national offices that pertained directly to the individual departments. A district sales manager, for instance, was associated with a regional office in Albany for the purpose of implementing marketing policies established by the central office in New York.

As a service wholesaler, the Syracuse Division sold to the retail drug trade a broad line of approximately 18,000 items. The line might be described most conveniently as consisting of everything sold through drugstores except fresh food, tobacco products, newspapers, and magazines. In the trading area of Syracuse, Pure Drug competed with two other wholesalers; one of these carried substantially the same line of products; the other, a limited line of drug products.

The history of the Syracuse Division had been a profitable family-owned wholesale drug house before its merger with Pure Drug in 1950. The division had operated profitably since that date, although it had not shown a profit on sales equal to the average for the other wholesale drug divisions of Pure Drug. Since 1961, the annual net sales of the division had risen each year. Because the competitors did not announce their sales figures, it was impossible to ascertain, however, whether this increase in sales represented a change in the competitive situation or merely a general trend of business volume in the Syracuse trading area. Mr. Schultz had been of the opinion that the increase had been at the expense of competitors. The district drug sales manager, however, maintained that, since the trend of increase was less than that of other divisions in the northern New York region, the Syracuse Division may have actually lost ground competitively. A new measuring technique of calculating the potential wholesale purchasing power of retail drugstores, which had been adopted shortly before Mr. Thomas' transfer, indicated that the share of the wholesale drug market controlled by the Syracuse Division was below the median and below the mean for Pure Drug divisions.

Only a few of the present employees working in 1970 for the Syracuse Division had also been employed by the predecessor company. Mr. Schultz was the one remaining man of the executive echelon whose employment in the Syracuse Division antedated the merger. Most of the executives and salesmen currently active in the organization had been employed as executives or salesmen in the organization during the 1950s and 1960s. Two salesmen, however, Mr. Brooks and Mr. Clifford Nelson, had sold for the predecessor company before the merger.

Of the men who were employed as executives or salesmen before the 1960s, only Mr. Robert Jackson, the division manager, had a college degree which he had earned at a local YMCA night school. All the more recently employed young men were university or pharmacy college graduates. None of the younger men had been promoted when vacancies had occurred for the job of operations manager (who was in charge of the warehouse) and merchandise manager (who supervised buying) in the Syracuse Division; however, two of the younger men had been promoted to similar positions in other divisions when vacancies had occurred.

The Syracuse Division Sales Force

From the time when Mr. Thomas took over Mr. Schultz's duties he had devoted four days a week to the task of traveling through each sales territory with the salesman who covered it. He had, however, made no changes in the practices or procedures of the sales force. The first occasion on which Mr. Thomas was required to make a decision of other than routine nature was when Mr. Brooks asked to be retired.

When Mr. Thomas took charge of the Syracuse Division sales force, it consisted of nine salesmen and four trainees. Four of the salesmen, Frederick Taylor, Edward Harrington, George Howard, and Larry Donnelly, had joined the company under the sales training program for college graduates initiated early in the 1960s. The other five salesmen had been with the company many years. Harvey Brooks and Clifford Nelson were senior to the others in terms of service. William Murray joined the company as a warehouse employee in 1946 when he was 19. He became a salesman in 1951. Walter Miller was employed as a salesman in 1951 when the wholesale drug firm that he had previously sold for went out of business. Mr. Miller, who was 48 years old, had been a wholesale drug salesman since he was 20. Albert Simpson came to Pure Drug after working as a missionary salesman for a manufacturer. Mr. Simpson, who was 26 when he joined the company in 1954, had served as an officer in the Army Medical Corps during the Korean War. He was discharged as a captain in hospital administration in 1958.

The four trainees were men who had graduated from colleges the preceding June. When Mr. Thomas arrived in Syracuse, these men were in the last phase of their 12-month training program. The trainees were spending much of their time traveling with the salesmen. Mr. Thomas, who now had the full responsibility for training these men, believed that Mr. Schultz had hired four trainees to cover anticipated turnover of salesmen, to cover anticipated turnover among the trainees themselves, and to implement the New York office's policy of getting more intensive coverage of each market area. The trainees, he understood, expected to receive territory assignments either in the Syracuse Division or elsewhere on the completion of their training period.

Mr. Thomas had not seen very much of the salesmen. His acquaintance with them had been formed at the sales meetings and while traveling with them through their territories.

Mr. Thomas was of the opinion that Walter Miller was a very easygoing, even-tempered person. He seemed to be very popular with the other salesmen and with his customers. Miller was very proud of his two sons, the younger one of whom was in high school while the other was the father of a son named after Mr. Miller. Mr. Thomas thought that the salesman liked him because Miller had commented to him several times that the suggestions offered by Mr. Thomas had been very helpful to him.

Harvey Brooks had not, in Mr. Thomas' opinion, been particularly friendly. Mr. Thomas had observed that Brooks was well-liked because of his good humor and friendly manner with everyone; however, Mr. Thomas had noticed that on a number of occasions Brooks had intimated that his age and experience should cause the sales manager to defer to his judgment. Mr. Brooks and his wife lived in the town of Oswego.

On June 4, 1970, Mr. Thomas had traveled with Mr. Brooks, and they had visited five of Mr. Brooks's accounts. On a routine form for sales managers' reports on fieldwork with salesmen, which was filed with the district sales manager and New York sales manager, Mr. Thomas made the following comments about Mr. Brooks:

> *Points requiring attention.* Not using merchandising equipment; not following weekly sales plan. Pharmaceutical business going to competitors because of lack of interest. Too much time spent on idle chatter. Only shows druggist what "he thinks they will buy." Tends to sell easy items instead of profitable ones.
>
> *Steps taken for correction.* Explained shortcomings and demonstrated how larger, more profitable orders could be obtained by following sales plan—did just that by getting the biggest order ever written for Carthage account.
>
> *Remarks.* Old-time "personality." Should do terrific volume if trained on new merchandising techniques.

On a similar form made out by Harry L. Schultz on the basis of working with Mr. Brooks on March 3, 1970, the following comments were made:

> *Points requiring attention.* Not getting pharmaceutical business. Not following promotion plans.
>
> *Steps taken for correction.* Told him about these things.
>
> *Remarks.* Brooks made this territory—can sell anything he sets his mind to—a real drummer—very popular with his customers.

George Howard, 29 years old, was the oldest of the group of salesmen who had passed through the formal sales training program. Mr. Thomas considered him earnest and conscientious. He had increased his sales each year. Although Mr. Thomas did not consider Howard to be the "salesman type," he noted that Howard had been quite successful in the use of the merchandising techniques which Mr. Thomas was seeking to implement.

William Murray handled a number of the big accounts in downtown Syracuse. Mr. Thomas believed that Murray was an excellent salesman who considered himself "very smooth." Mr. Thomas had been surprised at the affront Murray had taken when the sales manager had offered a few suggestions about the improvement of his selling technique. Mr. and Mrs. Murray were good friends of the Jacksons. The Murrays were social friends of the merchandise and operations managers and their wives. Mr. Thomas suspected that Murray had expected to be Mr. Schultz's successor.

Clifford Nelson seemed to Mr. Thomas to be an earnest and conscientious salesman. He had been amiable, though not cordial, toward Mr. Thomas. Mr. Thomas' report on calls on 10 accounts on June 5, 1970, with Mr. Nelson contained the following statements:

> *Points requiring attention.* Rushing calls. Gets want book and tries to sell case lots on wanted items. Carries all merchandising equipment but doesn't use it.
>
> *Steps taken for correction.* Suggested change in routing; longer, better planned calls; conducted presentation demonstration.
>
> *Remarks.* Hardworking, conscientious, good salesman, but needs to be brought up to date on merchandising methods.

Mr. Schultz's comments on observations of Mr. Nelson on March 4, 1970, reported on the same form, were as follows:

> *Points requiring attention.* Uses the want book on the basis of most sales. Not pushing promotions.
>
> *Steps taken for correction.* Discussed shortcomings.
>
> *Remarks.* Nelson really knows how to sell—visits every customer each week. Hard worker—very loyal—even pushes goods with very low commission.

On the day Mr. Thomas had traveled with Nelson, the salesman suggested that Mr. Thomas have dinner at the Nelson's home. Mr. Thomas accepted the invitation, but at the end of the day Nelson took him to a restaurant in Watertown, explaining that he did not want to inconvenience his wife because his two daughters were home from college on vacation.

Albert Simpson had caused Mr. Thomas considerable concern. Simpson complained about sales management procedures, commission rates, the "lousy service of the warehouse people," and other such matters at sales meetings. Mr. Thomas believed that most of the complaints were founded in fact, but that the matters were usually trivial in that the other salesmen did not complain of these matters. Mr. Thomas mentioned his difficulties with Simpson to Mr. Jackson. Mr. Jackson's comment was that Simpson had been very friendly with Mr. Schultz. Simpson seemed to be quite popular with his customers.

Frederick Taylor was, in Mr. Thomas's opinion, the most ambitious, aggressive, and argumentative salesman in the Syracuse Division. He had been employed by the company since his graduation from the University of Rochester in 1966, first as a trainee and then as a salesman. Taylor had substantially increased the sales volume of the territory assigned to him. He had persuaded Mr. Schultz to assign him six inactive hospital accounts in July of 1968. In six months, Taylor made sales to these accounts in excess of $50,000. The other salesmen considerd him ''cocky'' and a ''big spender.'' Mr. Thomas thought his attitude was one of independence. If Taylor agreed with a sales plan, he worked hard to achieve its objectives, but if he did not agree, he did not cooperate at all. Mr. Thomas thought that he had been very successful in working with Taylor.

Larry Donnelly impressed Mr. Thomas as being unsure of himself. Donnelly seemed to be confused and overworked. Mr. Thomas attributed this difficulty to Donnelly's trying to serve too many accounts in too large an area. Donnelly was very solicitous about Mr. Thomas's suggestions on improvement of his work. Donnelly was 24 years old. Mr. Thomas believed that he would improve in time with proper help. Donnelly had raised his sales to the point where he was on commission instead of salary in March of 1970.

Edward Harrington was the only salesman who worked on a salary. His sales volume was not sufficient to sustain an income of $600 a month which was the company minimum for salesmen with more than one year's experience. Harrington was very apologetic about being on a salary. Mr. Thomas believed that Harrington's determination to ''make good'' would be realized because of the latter's conscientiousness. The salesman was 25. When he had been assigned the territory two years before, it had consisted largely of uncontacted accounts. The volume of sales had tripled in the meantime. Mr. Thomas felt that Harrington appreciated all the help he was given and that in time Harrington would be an excellent salesman.

Sales commission rates were as follows:

	Percent
Brooks and Nelson	2.375%
Miller and Donnelly	2.25
Murray and Simpson	2.125
Howard and Taylor	2

Mr. Thomas said that expense accounts amounted to about 0.75 percent of sales for both city and country salesmen. The differences in percentage rates of commissions were explained by Mr. Thomas in terms of the differential commissions set by the company. Higher commission rates were given on items the company wished to ''push,'' such as pharmaceuticals and calendar promotion items.

The trainees were something of an unknown quantity to Mr. Thomas. He had training conferences with them in which he had thought they had performed rather poorly. He believed that Mr. Schultz had neglected the training of the new men. All four of them seemed to be good prospects. They were eager to be assigned territories, as they informed Mr. Thomas as often as possible.

The turnover of the Syracuse Division sales force has been very low among the senior salesmen. Six of the sales training program men had left the division since 1965. Two had been promoted to department heads in other divisions. Four had left to work for manufacturers. Because manufacturers valued salesmen with wholesaling experience and competing wholesalers did not have training programs for young men, there were many opportunities for a salesman who desired to leave.

Sales Management

Since Mr. Thomas had replaced Mr. Schultz, he had devoted considerable thought to the problem of improving the sales performance of the Syracuse Division. He had accepted a transfer to the new job at the urging of Mr. Richard Topping, the vice president in charge of sales. Mr. Thomas was one of a dozen young men whom Mr. Topping had brought into the New York office to work as assistants to the top sales executives. None of the young assistants had remained in the New York office for more than three years, for Mr. Topping made a policy of offering the young men field assignments so that they could ''show their stuff.'' Mr. Thomas believed that the sales performance of the Syracuse Division could be bettered by an improved plan of sales management. He knew that the share of the Syracuse market for wholesale purchases of retail drugstores[1] held by Pure Drug was only 20.05 percent as against a 48 percent share for some of the other divisions.

Mr. Topping, for whom Mr. Thomas worked immediately before his transfer, had focused his staff's attention upon the qualitative aspects of sales policy. Mr. Thomas had assisted Mr. Topping in implementing merchandising plans intended to utilize the salesmen's selling efforts in such a way as to minimize the handling cost of sales and maximize the gross margin.

The company encouraged the salesmen to use a threefold plan for increasing profitability:

1. Sales of larger average value per line of the order were encouraged because the cost of processing and filling each line of an order was practically constant.

---

[1] The potential wholesale sales for retail drugstores were calculated by the New York office market analysis section. This market estimate, called the PWPP (potential wholesale purchasing power) was calculated for each county by adjusting retail drugstore sales to an estimate of the purchases of goods from wholesalers.

2. Sales of larger total value were encouraged because the delivery cost for orders having a total weight between 20 and 100 pounds were practically constant.

3. Because some manufacturers offered margins considerably larger than others, sales of products carrying higher margins were encouraged. Salesmen's commissions varied with the margins available to Pure Drug on the products they sold.

The executives of the company also sought to increase the effectiveness of Pure Drug promotions by setting up a sales calendar. The sales calendar coordinated the activities of all Pure Drug divisions so that during a given calendar period every account would be solicited for the sale of particular items yielding satisfactory profits. The type of activity represented by the sales calendar required that the salesmen in each division follow a pattern in selling to every individual account. The sales manager was responsible for coordinating the activities of his salesmen.

The matter of selling patterns was largely the responsibility of the division sales manager. Mr. Thomas believed that his predecessor had never really accepted the changes that had taken place in the merchandising policy of the New York office.

Mr. Thomas had inherited from his predecessor a system of sales department records which had been carefully maintained. The national offices required each division to keep uniform sales and market analysis records. During the period of Mr. Thomas's work in the New York office, he had developed a familiarity with the uses of these records.

The basis of the sales and market analysis record was the division trading area. The limits of the trading area were determined by the economics of selling costs, and the factors on which the costs were based were transportation costs of delivery and salesmen's traveling expenses. Mr. Thomas knew from his own experience that delineation of trading areas was influenced by tradition, geographic conditions, the number of salesmen, the number of calls a salesman could make, the estimated market potential, competition, and agreements with adjacent Pure Drug divisions. The Syracuse Division was bordered by the trading areas of Pure Drug divisions located in Rochester and Albany on the east, south, and west; to the north was the Canadian border. A map of this division is included here in Exhibit 1.

Exhibit 2 gives information on sales and sales potential by county. Exhibits 3 and 4 show selected data on salesmen's territory assignments and performance. During the time since his arrival, Mr. Thomas had formed the opinion that the present salesmen's territories had been established without careful regard for the number of stores in the area, the sales potential, or the amount of traveling involved. Although Mr. Thomas had not yet studied any one territory carefully, he suspected all his salesmen of skimming the cream from many of their accounts because they did not have adequate time to do a thorough selling job in each store.

EXHIBIT 1 Syracuse Division trading area

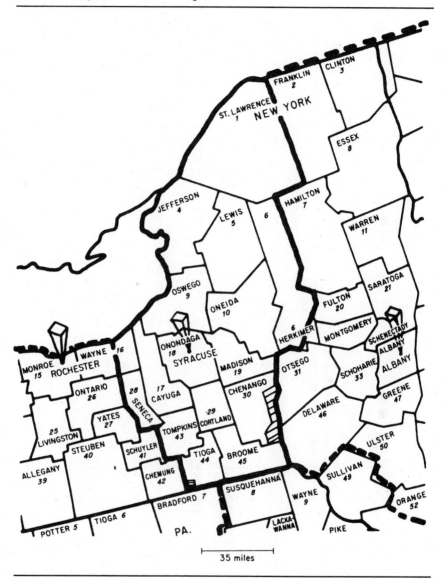

35 miles

EXHIBIT 2 Selected data on sales and sales potentials, by counties

County	Code	Popu-lation (000s)	Per-cent	Retailers				Potential wholesale purchasing power* ($000)	Per-cent area PWPP	Sales† ($000)	Sales per-cent PWPP	Hospitals			Miscella-neous sales ($000)
				Sold	Inactive accounts	Accounts not sold	Total					Sold	Not sold	Sales ($000)	
St. Lawrence	1	117.2	6.3%	23	1	2	26	$1,090	4.4%	$408	26.9%	2	4	$ 8	$ 6
Jefferson	4	90.2	4.9	34	—	—	34	1,306	5.3	367	28.2	2	2	4	3
Lewis	5	24.8	1.3	8	—	—	8	261	1.0	86	32.2	—	1	—	—
Herkimer	6	69.3	3.7	10	6	1	17	624	2.5	98	15.7	1	2	—	10
Oswego	9	97.8	5.3	25	1	—	26	1,340	5.5	373	27.1	—	2	—	7
Oneida	10	285.4	15.5	46	14	12	72	3,480	14.2	375	10.5	—	13	—	—
Wayne	16	76.6	4.1	4	—	1	5	247	1.0	55	22.3	—	—	—	—
Cayuga	17	75.6	4.1	12	4	—	16	561	2.3	101	18.0	2	—	4	27
Onondaga	18	474.8	25.8	98	9	13	120	7,647	31.2	2,166	28.7	6	9	108	192
Madison	19	59.7	3.2	12	2	3	17	1,250	5.1	261	20.9	—	2	—	—
Seneca	28	34.4	1.9	6	1	3	10	558	2.3	84	15.0	2	1	6	24
Cortland	29	45.4	2.5	6	2	1	9	510	2.1	161	31.5	—	2	—	—
Chenango	30	48.2	2.6	4	2	6	12	568	2.3	63	11.1	—	3	—	—
Tompkins	43	75.7	4.1	9	1	4	14	815	3.3	132	16.2	—	5	—	—
Tioga	44	46.2	2.5	4	—	7	11	322	1.3	80	24.8	—	—	—	—
Broome	45	225.3	12.2	22	2	13	37	3,970	16.2	253	6.4	—	8	—	18
		1,846.6	100.0%	323	45	66	434	$24,549	100.0%	$5,063	20.5%	15	54	$130	$287

* Includes miscellaneous but not hospital or house sales.
† Excludes miscellaneous sales, sales to hospitals, and house sales.

EXHIBIT 3 Selected data on salesmen's territory assignments by county

Salesman	County	Sales, 1969*	Active† accounts	Esti-mated‡ potential (000s)	Assigned† accounts
Miller	Chenango	$ 61,902	4	$ 567	15
	Tompkins	132,900	9	815	19
	Tioga	79,678	4	322	11
	Broome	270,300	22	3,971	45
	Total	544,780	39	5,675	90
Brooks	Jefferson	146,034	16	906	18
	Lewis	86,394	8	261	9
	Oswego	369,860	25	1,070	28
	Total	602,288	49	2,237	55
Howard	Onondaga	229,017	14	910	14
	Madison	260,850	12	1,250	19
	Cortland	161,000	6	510	11
	Total	650,867	32	2,670	44
Murray	Onondaga	756,153	33	2,225	44
	Total	756,153	33	2,225	44
Nelson	St. Lawrence	408,176	25	1,090	32
	Jefferson	222,519	20	400	20
	Oswego	2,780	1	270	1
	Total	633,475	46	1,760	53
Simpson	Onondaga	733,926	29	3,008	48
	Total	733,926	29	3,008	48
Taylor	Onondaga	638,073	29	1,504	29
	Total	638,073	28	1,504	29
Donnelly	Herkimer	97,060	10	624	19
	Oneida	375,000	46	3,480	85
	Total	472,060	56	4,104	104
Harrington	Wayne	54,400	4	247	5
	Cayuga	127,000	14	561	18
	Seneca	108,780	8	558	13
	Total	290,180	26	1,366	36
Hospitals	Taylor-Syracuse	108,000			
	All others	22,000			
House accounts		$ 529,012			
Total division sales		$5,980,764			

* The figures by salesmen include sales to chain and independent drugstores, and to miscellaneous accounts, but do not include sales to hospitals or house accounts indicated at the foot of the table.

† Includes hospitals and other recognized drug outlets in the territory.

‡ No potential is calculated for hospitals or miscellaneous sales. However, where a county is divided among several salesmen, the potential sales figure for each salesman is obtained by allocating the county potential in proportion to the total number of potential drugstore and miscellaneous accounts in that county assigned to that salesman.

EXHIBIT 4 Summary data on salesmen's performance

	1969 sales ($000)	Per-cent	1969 Potential* ($000)	Per-cent	Sales percent of potential	1969 active accounts†		1969 assigned accounts†		Active accounts percent of assigned	1969 sales per account	Potential per assigned account‡
						No.	Percent	No.	Percent			
I:												
Miller	$ 545	10.2%	5,675	23.2%	9.6%	39	11.5%	90	17.9%	43.4%	$14,000	$63,100
Brooks	$ 602	11.3%	2,237	9.1	27.0	49	14.5	55	10.9%	89.0	14,000	40,600
Murray	756	14.2	2,225	9.1	34.0	33	9.8	44	8.8	75.0	22,900	50,500
Nelson	634§	11.9	1,760	7.2	36.0	46	13.6	53	10.5	85.0	13,800	33,200
Simpson	734	13.8	3,008	12.2	24.5	29	8.6	48	9.5	60.5	25,350	62,700
Subtotal	$3,271	61.4%	14,905	60.8%	22.0	196	58.0%	290	57.6%	67.2	16,700	51,400
II:												
Howard	651	12.2	2,670	10.9	24.4	32	9.5	44	8.7	72.7	20,360	60,600
Taylor	638§	12.0	1,504	6.1	42.4	28	8.3	29	5.8	96.5	26,700	51,800
Donnelly	472	8.9	4,104	16.7	11.5	56	16.5	104	20.7	53.8	8,420	39,500
Harrington	290§	5.5	1,366	5.5	21.3	26	7.7	36	7.2	72.3	11,150	38,000
Subtotal	$2,051	38.6%	9,644	39.2%	21.3	142	42.0%	213	42.4%	66.7	14,470	45,300
Total	$5,322§	100.0%	24,549	100.0%	21.7	338	100.0%	503	100.0%	67.0	15,730	48,800

Hospital sales by:
Taylor 108
Nelson 12
Harrington 10
House sales: 529
Grand total $5,981

* No potential is calculated for hospital or miscellaneous sales. However, where a county is divided among several salesmen, the potential sales figure for each salesman is obtained by allocating the county potential in proportion to the total *number* of potential drugstore and miscellaneous accounts in that county assigned to that salesman.

† Includes hospitals and other recognized drug outlets in the territory.

‡ Understated since hospitals and miscellaneous accounts are included in the assigned accounts listed but not in the potential.

§ Excluding hospital sales.

2/Exhibit 6. Mr. Brooks' accounts that Mr. Nelson wants total $417,985 (87.7 percent of Mr. Brooks's sales in Jefferson County, 80 percent in Oswego County, or 69.4 percent of the territory total). Added to Nelson's 1969 sales, would increase his volume 65 percent to $1,063,207. Brooks' old territory would be left with $184,303 in sales.

3/Using commission rates as given, earnings are: Miller, $12,270; Brooks, $14,290; Murray, $16,080; Nelson, $15,400; Simpson, $15,600; Howard, $13,020; Taylor, $12,760; Donnelly, $10,620; Harrington, $7,200.

Mr. Thomas had been able to observe the performance records of other divisonal sales managers while he worked in New York. He knew that some sales managers had achieved substantial improvements on the past performances of their divisions.

Sales Territories of Brooks and Nelson

The territory that Mr. Brooks covered included accounts scattered through small towns in four counties of the rural area northeast of Syracuse (see Exhibit 5).

EXHIBIT 5 Counties sold by Messrs. Brooks and Nelson

Mr. Brooks had originally developed the accounts in the four-county area for the predecessor company. At the time he undertook this task the competing service wholesaler already had established a mail-order business with the rural druggists in this area. Mr. Brooks had taken to the road in 1940 to build up the sales in all four counties. He had been hired specifically for this job because he was a native of the area and an experienced "drummer."

Five years later Mr. Clifford Nelson, a friend of Mr. Brooks, became a division salesman, and, at the suggestion of Mr. Brooks, covered other accounts in the same four-county area. Mr. Nelson had been a salesman for a proprietary medicine firm before he joined the wholesale drug house. He was seven years younger than Mr. Brooks. Since that time Mr. Brooks had serviced a number of accounts in the four-county area. The list of accounts that each of these men handled appears in Exhibit 6 and 7. Mr. Thomas noticed that the incomes which Messrs. Brooks and Nelson had received from commissions were very stable over the years.

EXHIBIT 6 Accounts sold by Harvey Brooks, by counties, with 1969 purchases

Jefferson County:		
Adams Center	D	$ 3,570
(Alexandria Bay	D	18,300)
(Alexandria Bay	D	15,790)
Bellville	D	2,100
(Carthage	D	61,000)
Chaumont	D	604
(Clayton	D	10,630)
(Clayton	D	16,400)
Deferiet	D	369
Dexter	D	11,670
Ellisburg	D	236
LaFargeville	D	522
Plessis	D	880
Redwood	M	108
Rodman	D	3,210
Sackets Harbor	D	645
County total		$146,034
Lewis County:		
Beaver Falls	D	$ 3,810
Croghan	D	24,597
Harrisville	D	18,516
Lowville	D	23,688
Lowville	D	4,314
Lyons Falls	D	6,024
Port Leydon	D	2,325
Turin	M	3,120
County total		$86,394
Oswego County:		
Calosse	D	$ 1,709
Central Square	D	1,857
Constantia	M	72
Cleveland	M	390

EXHIBIT 6 (*concluded*)

Oswego County (*continued*)		
(Fulton	D	$ 15,120)
(Fulton	D	24,510)
(Fulton	D	27,800)
(Fulton	D	38,400)
Hannibal	D	3,890
Hastings	M	3,840
Lacona	M	462
Mexico	D	15,900
Oswego	D	12,075
(Oswego	D	20,760)
(Oswego	D	24,100)
(Oswego	D	41,000)
(Oswego	D	43,900)
(Oswego	D	22,430)
Oswego	H	15
Parish	M	5,160
Phoenix	D	9,730
(Pulaski	D	8,750)
(Pulaski	D	29,080)
Sandy Creek	D	14,130
West Monroe	D	4,780
County total		$369,860
Territory total		$602,288

Code: D = independent drugstore; C = chain drugstore; M = miscellaneous account; H = Hospital.

Note: Accounts in parentheses are those wanted by Mr. Nelson.

EXHIBIT 7 Accounts sold by Clifford Nelson, by counties, with 1969 purchases

St. Lawrence County:		
Canton	D	$ 39,240
Edwards	D	2,016
Edwards	M	5,655
Gouverneur	D	678
Gouverneur	D	28,149
Gouverneur	D	49,559
Heuvelton	D	324
Messena	D	33,777
Messena	D	10,191
Messena	C	7,344
Messena	C	6,675
Messena	H	114
Madrid	D	4,296
Morristown	D	8,193
Norfolk	D	8,985
Norwood	D	9,417
Ogdensburg	D	24,270
Ogdensburg	D	67,665
Ogdensburg	D	21,609

EXHIBIT 7 (concluded)

St. Lawrence		
County: (continued)		
Ogdensburg	D	$ 10,140
Ogdensburg	M	447
Ogdensburg	H	7,959
Potsdam	D	46,332
Potsdam	C	22,113
Potsdam Falls	D	1,101
County total		$416,249
Jefferson County:		
Adams	C	$ 1,885
Carthage	C	2,130
Evans Mills	D	2,210
Philadelphia	D	3,780
Watertown	D	30,200
Watertown	D	4,740
Watertown	D	8,800
Watertown	D	30,680
Watertown	D	18,440
Watertown	D	26,300
Watertown	D	38,200
Watertown	D	23,000
Watertown	D	9,700
Watertown	D	854
Watertown	D	11,320
Watertown	C	3,630
Watertown	C	5,970
Watertown	M	680
Watertown	H	126
Watertown	H	3,600
County total		$226,245
Oswego County:		
Pulaski	C	2,730
Territorial total		$645,224

Code: D = independent drugstore; C = chain drugstore; M = miscellaneous account; H = hospital.

A Visit from Mr. Nelson

On the Wednesday morning following the June sales meeting, Mr. Thomas saw Mr. Nelson come in the front door of the Syracuse Division offices. Although the salesman passed within 30 feet of Mr. Thomas' desk, he did not appear to notice the sales manager. Mr. Nelson walked through the office area to the partitioned space where Mr. Jackson's private office was located. Twenty minutes later Mr. Nelson emerged from the division manager's office and made his way to Mr. Thomas' desk.

"Hi there, young fellah!" he shouted as he approached.

"Howdy, Cliff. Sit down and chat awhile," Mr. Thomas replied. "What got you out of bed so early?" he asked, knowing that the salesman must have risen at 6 o'clock to make the drive to Syracuse from his home in Watertown.

Mr. Nelson squeezed his bulky frame into the armchair next to the desk. "It's a shame Harvey is retiring," he said. "I never thought he could stand to give it up. I never knew anyone who enjoyed selling as much as Harvey—'cept, maybe me." Mr. Nelson continued praising Mr. Brooks and telling anecdotes which illustrated his point until Mr. Thomas began to wonder whether Mr. Nelson thought that the sales manager was biased in some way against the retiring salesman. Mr. Thomas recalled that he had made some critical remarks about Mr. Brooks to Mr. Jackson, but he could not recall any discussion of Mr. Brooks' shortcomings with the man himself or any of the other salesmen. Mr. Nelson ended his remarks by saying "Old 'H. L.,' God rest his soul, always said that Harvey was the best damn wholesale drug salesman we'd ever known."

There was a brief silence as Mr. Thomas did not realize that Mr. Nelson was finished. Finally Mr. Thomas said, "You know, Cliff, I think we ought to have a testimonial dinner for Harvey at the July sales meeting."

Mr. Nelson made no comment on Mr. Thomas' suggestion; instead, he went on to say, "None of these green trainees will ever be able to take Harvey's place. Those druggists up there are old-timers. They would resent being high pressured by some kid blown up to twice his size with college degrees. No sir! You've got to sell 'em right in those country stores."

Mr. Thomas did not believe that Mr. Nelson's opinion about the adaptability of the younger, college educated salesmen was justified by the evidence available. He recalled that several of these men in country territories had done better on their May sales quotas than either Mr. Brooks or Mr. Nelson. He was proud of his self-restraint when he commented, "Selling in a country territory is certainly different."

"That's right, Dave, I wanted to make sure you understood these things before I told you." Mr. Nelson was nervously massaging his double chin between his thumb and forefinger.

Mr. Thomas looked at him with a quizzical expression. "Told me what."

"I have just been talking to Mr. Jackson. Well, I was talking to him about an understanding between Harvey and me. We always agreed that if anything should happen to the other, or he should retire, or something—well, we agreed that the one who remained should get to take over his choice of the other's accounts. We told 'H. L.' about this and he said, 'Boys, what's OK by you is OK by me. You two developed that territory and you deserve to be rewarded for it.' Well, yes sir, that's the way it was."

Without pausing, Mr. Nelson went on, "I just told Mr. Jackson about it. He said that he remembered talking about the whole thing with 'H. L.' 'Yes,' he said, 'Tell Thomas about it,' he said, 'Tell Thomas about it.' Harvey and I went over his accounts on Sunday. I went over his list of accounts with him and checked the ones that I want. Here is the list with the accounts all checked off.[2] I already know nearly all the proprietors. You'll see that—"

---

[2] Mr. Nelson's selected accounts are the accounts in parentheses in Exhibit 6.

"Wait a minute, Cliff! Wait a minute!" Mr. Thomas interrupted. "You've lost me completely. In the first place, if there is any assignment of accounts to be made I'll do it. It will be done on a basis that is fair to the salesmen concerned and profitable to the company. You know that."

"Dave, I'm only asking for what is fair." Mr. Nelson's face was flushed. Mr. Thomas noticed that the man he had always believed to be deliberately confident and self-possessed was now so agitated that it was difficult for him to speak. "I don't want my territory chopped up and handed to some green kid!"

Mr. Thomas noticed that everybody in the office was now watching Mr. Nelson. "Calm down, Cliff," he whispered to the salesman, indicating with a nod of his head that others were watching.

"Don't talk to me that way, you young squirt!" replied Mr. Nelson. "I don't care. A man with 25 years' service deserves some consideration."

"You're absolutely right, Cliff. You're absolutely right." As Mr. Thomas repeated his words, Mr. Nelson settled back in his chair. The typewriters started clattering again.

"Now, first of all, Cliff," queried Mr. Thomas, as he tried to return the conversation to a friendly basis, "where did you get the idea that your territory was going to be chopped up?"

"You said so yourself. You said it at the very first sales meeting when you made that speech about how you were going to boost sales in Syracuse." Mr. Nelson emphasized his words by pounding on the side of the desk with his Masonic ring.

Mr. Thomas reflected for a moment. He recalled giving a talk at his first sales meeting at the end of May called, "How we can do a better job for Pure Drug." The speech was a restatement of the merchandising policy of the New York office. He had mentioned that getting more profitable business would require that a larger percentage of the purchases of each account would have to come to Pure Drug; that receiving a larger share of the business from each store would require more selling time in each store; and that greater concentration on each account would require reorganization of the sales territories. He realized that his future plans did entail reorganization of the territories; he had not anticipated, however, any such reaction as Mr. Nelson's.

Finally, Mr. Thomas said, "I do plan to make some territorial changes—not right away—at least not until I have looked things over pretty darn carefully. Of course, you understand that our first duty is to make greater profits for the company. Some of our territories would be a great deal more profitable if they were organized and handled in a different manner."

"What are you going to do about Harvey's territory?" asked Mr. Nelson.

"Well, I just haven't had a chance to study the situation yet," he replied. "If I could make the territory more profitable by reorganizing it, I guess that is what they would expect me to do." Since Mr. Thomas had not yet looked over the information about the territory, he was anxious not to commit himself to any course of action relating to it.

"What about the promises the company made to me about letting me choose the accounts I want?" the salesman asked.

"You don't mean the company's promise; you mean Mr. Schultz's promise," Mr. Thomas corrected him.

"Well, if Mr. Schultz wasn't 'the company,' I don't see how you figure that you are!" Mr. Nelson's face resumed its flush.

"OK, Cliff. How about giving me a chance to look over the situation. You know that I want to do the right thing. Let me go over your list of the accounts you want. In a few days I can talk intelligently about the matter." Mr. Thomas felt that there was no point in carrying on the discussion.

"All right, Dave," said Mr. Nelson, rising. The two men walked toward the front entrance of the office. As they reached the top of the steps leading to the front door, Mr. Nelson turned to the sales manager and offered his hand. "Look, Dave. I'm sorry I got so mad. You just can't imagine what this means to me. I know you'll see it my way when you know the whole story." Mr. Nelson's voice sounded strained.

Mr. Thomas watched the older man leave. He felt embarrassed at the realization that Mr. Nelson's parting words had been overheard by several manufacturers' representatives standing nearby.

A Conversation with the Division Manager

Mr. Thomas decided to talk at once to Mr. Jackson about his conversation with Mr. Nelson. He walked over to Mr. Jackson's office. He hesitated in the doorway; Mr. Jackson looked up and then indicated with a gesture that Mr. Thomas was to take a seat.

The sales manager sat down. He waited for Mr. Jackson to speak. Mr. Jackson was occupied for the moment with the problem of unwrapping a cigar. Mr. Thomas opened the conversation by saying, "Clifford Nelson just stopped by to speak to me."

"Yeah?" said Mr. Jackson, removing bitten flakes of tobacco from the end of his tongue.

"He said something about getting some of Harvey Brooks's accounts when Harvey retired," Mr. Thomas said in a deliberately questioning manner.

"Yeah."

The sales manager continued, "Well, this idea of his was based on a promise that he said 'H. L.' had made."

"Yeah. He told me that, too."

"Did Schultz make such a promise?" Mr. Thomas inquired.

"Hell, I don't know. It sounds like him." He tilted back in his swivel chair.

"What shall I do about it?"

"Don't ask me; you're the sales manager." Mr. Jackson paused, holding his cigar away from his lips as if he were about to speak. Just as Mr. Thomas was about to say something, Mr. Jackson lurched forward to flick the ashes from his cigar into his ashtray. "Look here, Dave. I don't want any morale problems around here. You're the first of the 'wonder boys' to be put in charge of a department in this division. I don't want you to do anything to mess up the morale. We never had any morale problems when Schultz was alive. We don't want anything like that in this division.''

Mr. Thomas was momentarily bewildered. He knew by the way that Mr. Jackson used the phrase ''wonder boys'' that he was referring to the college men who had been brought into the organization by Mr. Topping, the vice president in charge of sales.

Mr. Jackson went on, ''Why the devil did you tell the men that you were going to reassign the sales territories without even telling me?''

''But you were there when I said it.''

''Said what?''

''Well, at my first sales meeting, that one of the ways we were going to get more business was to reorganize the sales territory,'' Mr. Thomas replied.

''I certainly don't remember anything like that. Dave, you gave a good inspirational talk; but I sure can't remember anything about reassigning territories.''

''Actually, I just mentioned the reorganization of territories in passing,'' the sales manager smiled.

''I'll be damned. That sort of thing is always happening. Here everybody is frothing at the mouth about something that they think we are going to do and we haven't the slightest idea why they think we're going to do it. You know, the real reason Harvey Brooks asked to be retired instead of staying on as he planned was probably this fear of having his territory reorganized. Both he and Nelson know that their pension on retirement is based on their earnings in the last five years of active employment. Now that I think of it, three or four of the other salesmen have stopped in during the last couple of weeks to tell me what a fine job they were doing. They probably had this territory reassignment bogey on their minds.''

Mr. Jackson's cigar was no longer burning. He began groping under the papers on his desk for a match.

Mr. Thomas took advantage of this pause in the conversation. ''Mr. Jackson, I think there are some real advantages to be won by an adjustment of the sales territories. I think—''

''You still think that after today?'' the division manager asked in a sarcastic tone.

''Why, yes! The profit we make on sales to an individual account is related closely to delivery expense. The larger the total proportion of the account's business we get, the more profit we make because the delivery expense remains more or less constant.''

''Look, Dave. You college men always have everything all figured out with slide rules, but sometimes that doesn't count. Morale is the important thing. The salesmen won't stand for having their territories changed. I know that you have four trainees that you'd like to put out on territories. You put them out on parts of the territories belonging to some of the more experienced men— bam! God knows how many of our good salesmen would be left. Now, I've never had any trouble with sales force morale since I've been manager of this division. Old Schultz, bless his soul, never let me down. He wasn't any damn Ph.D., but, by golly, he could handle men. Don't get off on the wrong foot with the boys, Dave. With the labor situation in the warehouse being what it is, I've just got too much on my mind. I don't want you to be creating more problems than I can handle. How 'bout it, boy!''

Mr. Jackson ground out his half-smoked cigar, looking steadily at Mr. Thomas.

Mr. Thomas was upset because the division manager had imputed to him a lack of concern for morale problems. He had always thought of himself as being very considerate of the thoughts and feelings of others. He realized that at the moment his foremost desire was to get away from Mr. Jackson.

Mr. Thomas rose from his chair saying, ''Mr. Jackson, you can count on me. I know you are right about this morale business.''

''Atta boy,'' said the division manager. ''It does us a lot of good to talk like this once in a while. Now, you see if you can make peace with the salesmen. I want you to handle everything yourself.''

''Well, thanks a lot,'' said the sales manager, as he backed out of the office door.

As he walked through the office after talking with Mr. Jackson, he saw two manufacturers' representatives with whom he had appointments already seated near the receptionist's desk. His schedule of appointments that day did not permit him to do more than gather the material pertaining to the Nelson and Brooks territories.

Mr. Thomas Goes Home

Mr. Thomas left the office shortly after five o'clock to drive to his home in a suburb of Syracuse. It was a particularly hot and humid day. Pre-Fourth-of-July traffic lengthened the drive by nearly 20 minutes. When he finally turned into his own driveway, he felt as though his skin were caked with grime and perspiration. He got out of the car and walked around the house to the terrace in the rear. Betsy, his wife, was sewing in a deck chair under the awning.

''Hello, Dave. You're late,'' she said, looking up with a smile.

''I know it. Even the traffic was bad today.'' He dropped his coat on a glass-topped table and sprawled out full length on the glider. ''Honestly, I'm so exhausted and dirty that I am disgusted with myself.''

''Bad day?''

''Awful. You just can't imagine how discouraging it is trying to get this job organized. You would think that it would be obvious to everybody that what ails the Syracuse Division is the organization of the sales force,'' said Mr. Thomas, arranging a pillow under his head.

''I didn't realize that you thought anything was wrong with the Syracuse Division.''

''Well, what I mean is that we get only 20 percent of the potential wholesale business. If I could organize the sales force my way—well, God knows, maybe we could get 40 percent of the business. That is what the New York office watches for. The sales manager who increases his division's share of the market gets the promotions when they come along. I know Mr. Topping transferred me to this division because he knew these possibilities existed.''

"I don't understand. Is Mr. Topping still your boss, or is Mr. Jackson?'' asked his wife.

"Betsy, it's terribly discouraging. Mr. Jackson is my boss, but I'll never get anywhere with Pure Drug unless Mr. Topping and the other people in New York promote me.''

"Don't you like Mr. Jackson?''

"I had a run-in with him today.''

"You didn't!'' she said crossly as she laid her sewing aside.

Mr. Thomas had not anticipated this reaction. He gazed up at the awning as if he did not notice his wife's intent expression. "We didn't argue particularly. He just—well, he doesn't know too much about sales management. He put his foot down on my plans to reorganize the territories.''

"I can't understand why you would go and get yourself into a fight with your boss when you haven't been here even two months. We should never have bought this house!''

"Honestly, honey, I didn't have any fight. Everything is OK. He just—well, do you want me to be a divisional sales manager all my life?''

She smiled and said nothing.

He continued, "I'm sorry you married such a grouch, but I just get plain mad when somebody calls me a wonder boy.''

"You're tired,'' she said sympathetically. "Why don't you go up and take a shower while I feed the children. We can have a drink and then eat our dinner whenever we feel like it. It's only meat loaf, anyway.''

"That sounds wonderful,'' he said, raising himself from his prone position.

An Unexpected Caller

Mr. Thomas had just stepped out of the shower when he heard his wife calling to him. "Dave, Fred Taylor is here to see you.''

"Tell him I'll be down in just a minute. Give him a drink, Betsy.''

As he dressed, Mr. Thomas wondered why the salesman had chosen the dinner hour to call. During the month since he had moved into his new home, no salesman had ever dropped in uninvited.

When Mr. Thomas came downstairs, he found Mr. Taylor on the living room couch with a gin and tonic in his hand.

"Hello, Fred,'' said Mr. Thomas crossing the room with his right hand extended. "You look as if you had a hot day. Why don't you take off your coat? If we go out to the terrace, you may get a chance to cool off.''

"Thanks, Dave,'' the visitor said as he moved out to the terrace. "I'm sorry to come barging in this way, but I thought it was important.''

"Well, what's on your mind?" said Mr. Thomas as he sat down.

Mr. Taylor started to speak but hesitated as Mrs. Thomas came out of the door with two glasses in her hand. She handed one glass to Mr. Thomas, then excused herself saying, "I think I better see if the children are all right."

After she had disappeared into the house, Mr. Taylor said, "I heard about what happened at the office today, so I thought I'd come over to tell you that we stand 100 percent behind you."

Mr. Thomas was perplexed by Mr. Taylor's words. He realized that the incident to which the salesman referred was probably his meeting with Mr. Nelson. Mr. Thomas said, "I'm not sure what you mean, Fred."

"I heard that you and Nelson had it out this morning about changing the sales territories," Mr. Taylor replied.

Mr. Thomas smiled. Two thoughts entered his mind. He was amused at the proportions that the brief conversation of that morning had assumed in the minds of so many people; but, at the same time, he was curious as to how Mr. Taylor, who had presumably been in the field selling, had heard about the incident so soon. Without hesitation he asked, "Where did you hear about this, Fred?"

"Bill Murray told me! He was down at the warehouse with Walter Miller when I stopped off to pick up a special narcotics order for a customer. They are all excited about this territory business. Murray said Nelson came out to his house at lunch time and told him about it. Everybody figured that you were going to change the territories when you started traveling around with each of the boys, especially after what you said at your first sales meeting."

"Well, the reason I went on the road with each of the men, Fred," said Mr. Thomas, "was so that I could learn more about their selling problems and, at the same time, meet the customers."

Mr. Taylor smiled, "Sure, but when you started filling out a rating sheet on each account, I couldn't help thinking you had some reason for it."

Mr. Thomas realized that the salesman had spoken with irony in his voice, but he thought it was better to let the matter pass as if he had not noticed it. Since he was planning to use the information that he gathered for reorganization of the sales territories, he decided that he would be frank with Mr. Taylor in order to find out what the young salesman's reaction might be on the question of territorial changes. He said, "Fred, I've thought a lot about making some changes in the territories—"

Mr. Taylor interrupted him. "That's terrific. I'm sure glad to hear that. I don't like to speak ill of the dead, but old Schultz really gave the trainees the short end of the stick when he put us on territories. He either gave a man a territory of uncontacted accounts so he beat his head against a stone wall until he finally quit, and that is just what happened to two guys who trained with me, or else he gave him a territory where somebody had to be replaced and where some of the best accounts had been handed over to one of the older salesmen. Well, I know for a fact that when I took over my territory from Mike Green, Bill Murray and Albert Simpson got 12 of Green's best accounts. And, damn it,

I got more sales out of what was left than Green ever did, but Murray and Simpson's total sales didn't go up at all. It took me a while, but, by golly, I had the laugh at every sales meeting when our monthly sales figures were announced.''

''Is that right?'' said Mr. Thomas.

''Damn right! And I wasn't the only one. That's why those old duffers are so down on the four of us that have come with the division since the mid-1960s. We've beaten them at their own game.''

''Do you think that Harrington and Howard and Donnelly felt the same way?'' asked Mr. Thomas.

''Think, hell! I know it! That's all we ever talk about. If you reorganize those territories and give us back the accounts that Schultz took away, you'll see some real sales records. Take, for example, the Medical Arts Pharmacy out by Mercy Hospital. Bill Murray got that one away from my territory and he calls there only once a week. If I could get that one back, I'd get in there three times a week and get five times as much business.''

Mr. Thomas had to raise his hands in a gesture of protest. ''Don't you have enough accounts already, Fred, to keep you busy?''

''Dave, I spend 50 hours a week on the road and I love it; but I know damn well that if I put some of the time I spend in 'two-by-four' stores into some of those big juicy accounts like Medical Arts Pharmacy, I'd do even more business.''

Mr. Thomas commented, ''I'm not particularly anxious to argue the point now, but if you start putting your time into Medical Arts Pharmacy, what's going to happen to your sales to the 'two-by-four' stores?''

The salesman replied, ''Those druggists all know me. They'd go right on buying.''

Mr. Thomas did not agree with Mr. Taylor, and he thought that the salesman realized this.

After a moment of silence Mr. Taylor rose from his chair saying, ''I'd better scoot home. My wife will be waiting for me with a rolling pin for being late so I'd better get out before your wife gets at me with a skillet.'' Mr. Taylor laughed heartily at his own joke.

The two men walked around the house to Mr. Taylor's car. As the salesman climbed into the car, he said, ''Dave, don't forget what I said. Harrington, Howard, Donnelly, and I stand 100 percent behind you. You won't ever hear us talk about going over to a competitor!''

''Who's talking about that?'' asked Mr. Thomas.

''Well,'' said Mr. Taylor as he started the motor and shifted into gear, ''I don't want to tell tales out of school.''

''Sure,'' Mr. Thomas said quickly. ''I'm sorry I asked. So long, Fred. I'll see you soon.''

Mr. Thomas watched the salesman back out of the driveway and drive away.

Part 7

Pricing Decisions

The cases in the pricing section of this book involve several different kinds of decisions. A firm's pricing strategy is extremely important because of the quickness with which a change can be implemented, because of the importance of price to consumers in their purchase decisions, and because of the direct impact of prices on profits.

The first important consideration in establishing a price for a product is the firm's pricing objectives. A firm striving for growth may utilize a totally different strategy from one who is seeking to discourage others from cutting prices or to desensitize consumers to price. Firms with objectives oriented around maximizing long-run profits may utilize different strategies than firms who are seeking to maximize short-run profits. Thus, the first step in establishing a price should be to clearly identify what the objectives are.

Two alternative strategies often utilized are skimming and penetration. A skimming strategy is one in which a high initial price is set, and the product is sold to all those consumers willing to pay this price. The price is then lowered somewhat, and the product is sold to those consumers willing to pay that price. This process continues for some time, "skimming the cream" off the top of the market with each price change. For example, when electronic calculators were first introduced, they were priced at more than $300. A number of scientific and engineering related organizations were willing to purchase the product at this price. The price was then lowered to the neighborhood of $150 to $200, and a number of other organizations were willing to purchase the product. Later, the price was reduced to the $50 to $100 range and very many more buyers entered the market. Eventually, the price was lowered still further and many more consumers entered the market.

A skimming strategy is appropriate when there are no close substitutes for the product and the demand is inelastic with respect to price. It is a very

439

conservative policy allowing the marketer to recover as much of the costs as possible quickly in the event that demand is not that great. It also allows the marketer to accumulate money for aggressive penetration later when competition enters the market. A skimming strategy is an effective way to segment the market, as in the calculator example and in the case of the book market where a skimming strategy is used for hardcover books, and the paperback edition is later introduced using a penetration strategy.

A penetration strategy utilizes a low initial price in the hopes of penetrating a large proportion of the market in a short period of time. This strategy would be used when one or more of the following conditions existed:

a.   High short-run price elasticity [for example, the low price of the Model-T Ford allowed many people to purchase a car for the first time].
b.   Large economies of scale in production.
c.   The probability of quick public acceptance.
d.   The probability of quick competitive imitation.

The specific pricing decisions that have to be made include the price level to set, price variation including discount structure and geographic price differences, margins to be given to various intermediaries in the channels of distribution, and the determination of when to change the price structure.

A number of different pricing methods are utilized by organizations. Some use the cost-plus method, whereby a certain percentage is added to the firm's costs to establish their pricing. This method is often used by industrial marketers and by wholesalers and retailers. Other organizations use break-even analysis, marginal cost analysis, and/or marginal revenue analysis to determine their pricing structure. Still other organizations are price followers and use a strategy of meeting the prices of competitors.

The ideal way to determine the price that should be charged involves analyzing a number of variables before actually setting the price. Included would be:

1.   *Consumer buying patterns.* What price would consumers expect to pay for this type of product? What are the important price points or price lines that different segments of the market desire?
2.   *Product differentiation.* In what ways is the company's product different from the others on the market? What advantages does the product offer the consumer?
3.   *What is the competitive structure* of the industry, and what stage of the product life cycle is the product in?
4.   *How price sensitive* is total industry demand, and how price sensitive is demand for the individual firm's product? What is the size of the total market and what is the likelihood of economies of scale?
5.   *What is the economic climate forecast,* and how sensitive is the demand of the product to changes in the economic climate?

6. *Legal and social considerations.* New interpretations of the Robinson-Patman Act (prohibiting price discrimination) and various state laws governing pricing must be taken into consideration.

7. *Cost structure of the firm.* The relationship between fixed costs and variable costs is extremely important in pricing decisions, as is the cost structure of the firm compared to competitors' pricing structure. Pricing strategy for a hotel, with a very low variable cost ratio, will of neccessity be quite different than pricing strategy for a clothing manufacturer which has a very high variable cost ratio.

8. *The overall marketing strategy for the product.* It is important to recognize that the pricing strategy must be consistent with all the other elements of the firm's marketing strategy.

Case 30

Twins Peaks National Bank*

On February 2, 1976, Mr. James Clark, vice president in charge of marketing, Twin Peaks National Bank, received a telephone call from the president of the bank, Mr. Frank Horman, regarding the bank's All-in-One Account. Mr. Horman mentioned that he had been looking at the different services that the bank offered. Mr. Horman indicated that he was contemplating changes in pricing policies for the bank's services that would increase the bank's profitability without jeopardizing its market share. Mr. Horman felt that since Twin Peaks National Bank had the lowest price of all competitors for the All-in-One type account he would like a review of the All-in-One account to determine if a change in pricing or service should be made.

After the telephone conversation with Mr. Horman, Mr. Clark met with the product manager, Mr. Joe Will, who was in charge of the All-in-One Account and the marketing research manager, Mr. Steve Hale, to explain Mr. Horman's concern regarding the pricing policy for the All-in-One Account. Mr. Will had worked with the account since its inception in July 1973. Mr. Hale had started with the bank in 1974 and had formulated some data on the All-in-One Account.

Mr. Will felt that Mr. Hale should conduct further research on the customer demographics in order to evaluate the service since its inception to determine if the All-in-One Account had met the objectives that were initially set up for the program. The three managers decided to meet again at a later date to make a recommendation on any change that could be made to the account to increase the bank's profitability without affecting Twin Peaks' market share.

Background

The Twin Peaks National Bank was the lead bank in the Twin Peaks Holding Corporation which had 12 other banks located in the state of Ohio. The Holding Company was the eighth largest in the state with total assets of $1.4 billion.

* This case was written by Subhash C. Jain, Associate Professor of Marketing, University of Connecticut and Iqbal Mathur, Associate Professor of Marketing, University of Pittsburgh. Used with permission.

less commercial now to aggressive market

Twin Peaks National Bank was the second largest in Frank County which had a population of 900,000. Twin Peaks had been primarily a wholesale bank serving commercial customers and correspondent banks throughout the state. However in 1960, management recognized the opportunity in the retail market and the bank opened its first branch and then proceeded to its present level of 33 branches located in prime market areas in the county. In keeping with the changing needs of the retail customer, Twin Peaks was the first bank in the community to introduce a package account. This was called the All-in-One Account, consisting of seven banking services with a single charge per month.

The package included the following:

1. Write all the checks you want for a $2 monthly fee.
2. Free personalized checks.
3. A Passbook Savings Account with $1 deposited by the bank.
4. Ten percent rebate of the finance charge on qualifying installment loans.
5. Free traveler's checks.
6. A 24-hour bank at the automated banking machines.
7. Overdraft protection with checking reserve. Lets you write a check for more money than you have in your checking account, up to your credit line.

The exclusiveness of the All-in-One Account lasted for six months until other banks in town introduced their package accounts. Exhibit 1 shows the services and charges of the various banks in the community.

EXHIBIT 1 Package comparison

	Twin Peaks	Bank 1	Bank 2	Bank 3	Bank 4
Price	$2.00	$2.50	$2.75	$2.25	Free* $100 min
Checks included	Yes	Yes	Yes	Yes	No
Charge card	Yes	Yes	Yes	Yes	No
24-hour banking	Yes	Yes	Yes	Yes	No
Identification card	Yes	Yes	Yes	Yes	No
Savings	$1.00	$2.50	0	$1.00	No
Installment loan rebate	10%	0.50% add†	Average month‡	0.50% add†	No§
Safe deposit box included	No	Yes	No	No	No
Overdraft demand deposit	Yes	Yes	Yes	Yes	No
Official checks	No	Yes	No	No	No
Travelers checks	Yes	Yes	No	Yes	No
Check cashing	Yes	Yes	Yes	Yes	No
Money orders	No	Yes	No	Yes	Yes
Budget	No	Yes	No	No	No

* $100 minimum deposit required.

† The regular add-on interest rate is reduced by 0.50 percent (from 6 percent add-on to 5.50 percent, for example).

‡ The rebate is equal to the average interest paid per month during the time period of the loan.

§ Regular rates are comparable to rates of the other banks after deducting their rebates.

Source: Company records.

EXHIBIT 2 Number growth of All-in-One—related accounts

	Year-end number of accounts					Number change				Percent change			
	1971	1972	1973	1974	1975	71–72	72–73	73–74	74–75	71–72	72–73	73–74	74–75
Scenario 1— with All-in-One													
All-in-One	0	0	6,180	18,931	30,500	n.a.*	6,180	12,751	11,569	n.a.	0%	206.3%	61.1%
Regular DDA†	54,082	57,321	63,344	72,118	82,427	3,239	6,023	8,774	10,309	6.0%	10.5	13.9	14.3
Regular savings	80,475	90,311	102,557	116,566	133,244	9,836	12,246	14,009	16,678	12.2	13.6	13.7	14.3
MasterCard	46,264	47,150	58,063	63,158	70,000	886	10,913	5,095	6,842	1.9	23.1	8.8	10.8
Checking reserve	6,900	7,884	14,028	27,417	40,000	984	6,144	13,389	12,583	14.3	77.9	95.4	45.9
Scenario 2—without All-in-One (control)													
Regular DDA	54,082	57,321	62,193	67,479	73,215	3,239	4,872	5,286	5,736	6.0	8.5	8.5	8.5
Regular savings	80,475	90,311	99,509	107,966	117,114	9,836	9,198	8,457	9,148	12.2	10.2	8.5	8.5
MasterCard	46,264	47,150	52,864	57,357	62,233	886	5,714	4,493	4,876	1.9	12.1	8.5	8.5
Checking reserve	6,900	7,884	9,067	10,427	11,991	984	1,183	1,360	1,564	14.3	15.0	15.0	15.0

Note: Regular DDA control projected based on review of 1969–70, 1970–71, and 1971–72 percent changes of 7.2, 8.5, and 6, respectively. Then arbitrarily selected highest of the three (8.5 percent). Regular savings control projected by assuming that it would run 160 percent of regular DDA numbers outstanding. MasterCard control projected by assuming that it would run 85 percent of regular DDA numbers outstanding. Checking reserve control projected by arbitrarily selecting an annual percent change of 15 percent which is slightly higher than the 14.3 percent rate experienced one year prior to All-in-One.

* n.a. = not applicable.

† DDA = Demand deposit account (checking).

Source: Company records.

All-in-One Account Growth

When the All-in-One Account was introduced in July 1973, it was projected that by the end of the third year there would be 10,000 All-in-One Accounts. This projection was based on a review of the previous three years and the highest percentage rate change was used. Regular savings account growth was projected at 160 percent of the regular demand deposit accounts outstanding at year-end. Checking reserve accounts were projected at 15 percent annual growth which compared to a growth of 14.3 percent in the prior year.

The success of the All-in-One Account is shown in Exhibit 2, which illustrates the actual growth of the All-in-One Account and related accounts as compared with the growth without the All-in-One Account and related accounts using the above assumptions.

All-in-One Account Impact on Market Share

Using weekly Federal Reserve Bank data and averaging weeks into months, Twin Peaks' market share was compared with the other two major banks within Frank County. The figures were available for regular savings, MasterCard, and checking reserve. Exhibits 3, 4, and 5 indicate that the bank's market share increased each year since the inception of the All-in-One Account. Exhibit 6 was developed by utilizing a survey taken by the bank's Research Department to show the impact of the All-in-One Account on the total demand deposit accounts as well as the new demand deposit accounts market.

EXHIBIT 3 Market shares: Regular savings

	Share of market				Share of market increase			
	1972	1973	1974	1975	1972	1973	1974	1975
Twin Peaks	28.9	29.2	29.5	30.3	33.1	33.6	34.0	34.3
Other	71.1	70.8	70.5	69.7	66.9	66.4	66.0	65.7

Source: Federal Reserve Bank data.

EXHIBIT 4 Market shares: Frank County MasterCard cards

	Share of market				Share of market increase			
	1972	1973	1974	1975	1972	1973	1974	1975
Twin Peaks	20.92	21.99	22.68	23.68	23.7	25.8	24.1	44.6
Other	79.08	78.01	77.32	76.32	76.3	74.2	75.9	55.4

Source: Federal Reserve Bank data.

EXHIBIT 5 Market shares: Overdraft checking

	Share of market			Share of market increase	
	1972	*1973*	*1974*	*1973*	*1974*
Twin Peaks	29.3	27.7	34.3	11.8	67.8
Bank 1	31.6	34.0	32.7	57.4	25.9
Bank 2	39.0	38.0	33.0	30.8	6.3

Source: Federal Reserve Bank data.

EXHIBIT 6 Market shares: Demand deposit acounts

	New account market		General market	
	3/73	*3/75*	*11/73*	*2/75*
Twin Peaks	27.9	38.8	29.1	35.4
Bank 1	34.9	37.6	29.1	31.7
Bank 2	37.2	23.5	41.8	32.9

Source: Company records.

Retention of Accounts

A major objective of the All-in-One Account was the cross-selling of bank services. The assumption was that the more services a bank customer had, the harder it would be for him to leave the bank. Net growth was determined as follows: Acquisition − Attrition = Net growth. The bank's performance in reducing the number of closed accounts increased its net growth.

Exhibit 7 shows the attrition rate for demand deposit and savings accounts since 1972. Their retention performance had allowed Twin Peaks to have a positive increase (14.3 percent versus 13.9 percent) in overall acquisition rate in 1975 even though the percentage of open rate decreased from 1974.

EXHIBIT 7 Attrition rate for selected product lines, 1971–1975

	Regular demand deposit accounts				Regular savings accounts			
	Opened	*Closed*	*Accounts outstanding*	*Attrition rate**	*Opened*	*Closed*	*Accounts outstanding*	*Attrition rate**
1971			54,082				80,475	
1972	14,654	11,415	57,321	21.1	28,314	18,478	90,311	23.0
1973	18,347	12,324	63,344	21.5	31,977	19,731	102,557	21.8
1974	20,771	11,997	72,118	18.9	35,964	21,955	116,566	21.4
1975	22,298	11,989	82,427	16.6	37,910	21,232	133,244	18.2

* Calculated as a percentage of previous year's outstanding.

Source: Company records.

Customer Survey

A survey of 3,997 All-in-One Accounts was made in order to determine the customer demographics and evaluate the service and its components. This was accomplished through the mailing of a questionnaire and the investigating of the account activity through the Central Information File for these customers. A total of 2,278 replied for a 57 percent return which represented 11.3 percent of the total All-in-One Accounts.

The All-in-One Account service had attracted the young, highly educated white-collar worker with above average income. Specifically the predominant characteristics were:

41 percent are 25–34 years of age.

19 percent are 35–44 years of age.

49 percent have a college degree.

67 percent are white-collar workers.

47 percent have income of $15,000 or more.

59 percent were Twin Peak conversions.

The mail-out survey indicated that 59 percent of the All-in-One Account customers were conversions from existing Twin Peaks checking account holders.

An additional 18 percent of the customers switched from other Frank County banks. This was followed by 13 percent new moves, 6 percent change in marital status, 4 percent other, and 3 percent additional account and first account. Analysis was done on the 18 percent of the customers who switched banks. Of these respondents, 25 percent switched for convenient location, 24 percent due to dissatisfaction at another bank, 24 percent based on the $2 price, and 21 percent due to the All-in-One package.

The participants in the survey were asked to give their opinions on the four most important features of the All-in-One Account. The most important feature turned out to be the price followed by checking reserve. The results of this open-end question are shown in Exhibit 8.

EXHIBIT 8 All-in-One—most important features

Attribute	Percent mentioned
Price	62%
Checking reserve	59
Free checks	46
24-hour banking	32
Unlimited checking	31
10% loan rebate	22
Traveler's checks	20
No minimum balance DDA	10
MasterCard	8
Convenience	2
Savings account dollars deposited	2
Easy to understand	1
No answer/no opinion	13

Source: Company records.

Account Profitability

The All-in-One Account study included the measurement of account activity through the CIF (Central Information File). Based on this measurement, the average All-in-One Account customer was then analyzed for profit/loss. This income and expense analysis (Exhibit 9) shows that the average All-in-One Account customer contributed $19.09 before tax, profits and indirect overhead. If this analysis were applied to the 30,500 All-in-One Account customers the operating profit contributed from these accounts would be $582,245.00, which is $0.238 per share.

EXHIBIT 9 Income and expense analysis (account customer average for All-in-One)

Income:		
All-in-One fee	$ 24.00	
Installment loan	131.47	
MasterCard	24.34	
Checking reserve	12.45	
		$192.26
Expense:		
Travelers checks	$ 0.27	
DDA*		
Operation cost	38.27	
Personal checks	4.29	
Savings:		
Operation cost	4.59	
Interest	34.59	
Installment:		
Operation cost	37.48	
Rebate	12.85	
MasterCard—operation cost	10.88	
Checking reserve—operation cost	1.56	
Cost of borrowed funds	13.78	
Bad debt:		
Installment (1%)	9.37	
MasterCard (2%)	3.58	
Checking reserve (2%)	1.66	
		$173.17
Net contribution before tax to profit and indirect overhead		19.09 ✗ 30,500 =

* DDA = Demand deposit account.
Source: Company records.

$ 582,245

A review of this information showed that the All-in-One Account had tremendous impact on the growth of the bank's market share. It had accomplished all of the objectives set up in July 1973 when the service was first introduced. It had increased the cross-selling of the bank's services. It had proved to be a checking account that was unique versus other competitors'. It reduced the attrition rate of Twin Peaks' customers and it was a marketable service which reflected an aggressive retail-oriented corporate image that Twin Peaks desired to project.

Mr. Will and Mr. Hale agreed that the fee charged for the All-in-One Account was inelastic and since the service was still in its growth stage that a small change in price and/or service would not affect the demand for the All-in-One Account. They also felt that if a substantial change in price were made, a service should also be added to somewhat offset the price change. They recommended to Mr. Clark that he present the following proposals to Mr. Horman:

1. The All-in-One Account fee may be increased to $3 per month and a safe deposit box included.
2. The All-in-One Account fee may be increased to $2.50 per month with no additional service.
3. The All-in-One Account fee may be increased to $2.50 per month and the installment loan rebate reduced to 5 percent.
4. The All-in-One Account charge may be left at $2 with the installment loan rebate reduced to 5 percent.

Case 31

United Techtronics

In June 1977, United Techtronics faced a major pricing decision with respect to its new video screen television system. "We're really excited here at United Techtronics," exclaimed Mr. Roy Cowing, the founder and president of United Techtronics. "We've made a most significant technological breakthrough in large screen, video television systems." He went on to explain that the marketing plan for 1978 for this product was now his major area of concern, and that what price to charge was the marketing question that was giving him the most difficulty.

Company History

United Techtronics (UT) was founded in Boston in 1959 by Mr. Cowing. Prior to that time Mr. Cowing had been an associate professor of electrical engineering at M.I.T. Mr. Cowing founded UT to manufacture and market products making use of some of the electronic inventions he had developed while at M.I.T. Sales were made mostly to the space program and the military. Sales grew from $100,000 in 1960 to $27 million in 1976. Profits in 1976 were $3.2 million.

The Video Screen Project

For a number of years beginning in the late 1960s, Mr. Cowing had been trying to reduce the company's dependency on government sales. One of the diversification projects that he had committed research and development monies to was the so-called video screen project. The objective of this project was to develop a system whereby a television picture could be displayed on a screen as big as 8 to 10 feet diagonally. In late 1976, one of UT's engineers made the necessary breakthrough. The rest of 1976 and the first few months of 1977 were spent producing working prototypes. Up until June 1977, UT had invested $600,000 in the project.

Video Screen Television

Extra-large screen television systems were not new. There were a number of companies who sold such systems both to the consumer and commercial (taverns, restaurants, and so on) markets. Most current systems made use of a special magnifying lens that projected a regular small television picture onto a special screen. The result of this process is that the final picture lacked much of the brightness of the original small screen. As a result, the picture had to be viewed in a darkened room. There were some other video systems that did not use the magnifying process. These systems used special tubes, but also suffered from a lack of brightness.

UT had developed a system that was bright enough to be viewed in regular daylight on a screen up to 10 feet diagonal. Mr. Cowing was unwilling to discuss how this was accomplished. He would only say that the process was protected by patent, and that he thought it would take at least two to three years for any competitor to duplicate the results of the system.

A number of large and small companies were active in this area. Admiral, General Electric, RCA, Zenith, and Sony were all thought to be working on developing large-screen systems directed at the consumer market. Sony was rumored to be ready to introduce a 60-inch diagonal screen system that would retail for about $2,500. A number of small companies were already producing systems. Advent Corporation, a small New England company, claimed to have sold 4,000, 84-inch diagonal units in two years at a $4,000 price. Muntz Manufacturing claimed one-year sales of 5,000, 50-inch diagonal units at prices from $1,500 to $2,500. Mr. Cowing was adamant that none of these systems gave as bright a picture as UT's. He estimated that about 10,000 large-screen systems were sold in 1976.

Cost Structure

Mr. Cowing expected about 50 percent of the suggested retail selling price to go for wholesaler and retailer margins. He expected that UT's direct manufacturing costs would vary depending on the volume produced. Exhibit 1 presents these estimates. He expected direct labor costs to fall at higher production volumes due to the increased automation of the process and improved worker skills.

EXHIBIT 1 Estimated production costs of UT's video screen system

	Volume		
	0–5,000	5,000–10,000	10,001–20,000
Raw materials	$ 480	$460	$410
Direct labor	540	320	115
Total direct costs	$1,020	$780	$525

Material costs were expected to fall due to less waste due to automation. The equipment costs necessary to automate the product process were $70,000 to produce in the 0–5,000 unit range, an additional $50,000 to produce in the 5,001–10,000 unit range, and an additional $40,000 to produce in the 10,001–20,000 unit range. The useful life of this equipment was put at five years. Mr. Cowing was sure that production costs were substantially below those of current competitors including Sony. Such was the magnitude of UT's technological breakthrough. Mr. Cowing was unwilling to produce over 20,000 units a year in the first few years due to the limited cash resources of the company to support inventories, and so on.

Market Studies

Mr. Cowing wanted to establish a position in the consumer market for his product. He felt that the long-run potential was greater there than in the commercial market. With this end in mind he hired a small economic research consulting firm to undertake a consumer study to determine the likely reaction to alternative retail prices for the system. These consultants undertook extensive interviews with potential television purchasers, and examined the sales and pricing histories of competitive products. They concluded that: "UT's video screen system would be highly price elastic across a range of prices from $500 to $5,000, both in a primary and secondary demand sense." They went on to estimate the price elasticity of demand in this range to be between 4.0 and 6.5.

The Pricing Decision

Mr. Cowing was considering a number of alternative suggested retail prices. "I can see arguments for pricing anywhere from above Advent's to substantially below Muntz's lowest price," he said.

Case 32

Consolidated-Bathurst Pulp and Paper Limited*

On the morning of September 28, 1973, Mr. John Andrew, president of Consolidated-Bathurst Pulp and Paper Limited, was evaluating the current price charged for newsprint to U.S. customers. A number of recent developments in the newsprint market had provoked this evaluation. Newsprint was in much shorter supply than in previous years due to a large increase in demand in the last two years. This increase had not been matched by increased industry capacity to produce. Also, a number of competitors' newsprint mills were shut down by strikes. Mr. Andrew was considering a change from Consolidated-Bathurst's current price of U.S. $175 per ton. He was aware that he would have to carefully consider both the customers' reactions and the competitions' reactions to any changes that he might make.

Company Background

Consolidated-Bathurst Pulp and Paper Limited was a wholly owned subsidiary of Consolidated-Bathurst Limited, a fully integrated, multiproduct paper company. Mr. Andrew was a senior vice president of the parent company, besides holding the operating responsibility for the newsprint division.

In 1972, Consolidated-Bathurst Limited had sales of $348 million and had assets of $430 million. The company's sales and earnings performance record for the period 1966–72 is shown in Exhibit 1. In 1970 and 1971, the company operated at a loss. Throughout this period the newsprint operation, the firm's major product line, had remained profitable, but with insufficient return on investment to warrant the investment of additional capital to purchase a new newsprint machine. These machines cost about $120,000 per daily ton, if built at an existing mill site with wood handling facilities available. At a new site, the costs of developing this wood handling capacity would raise the cost to about $150,000 per daily ton. Thus, a machine that could produce 500 tons per day would cost about $75 million. Consolidated-Bathurst had made some capital

---

* Copyright 1974, the University of Western Ontario. Reproduced with permission.

EXHIBIT 1 Sales and earnings results ($000)

	1972	1971	1970	1969	1968	1967	1966
Net sales	$348,055	$343,362	$353,944	$348,087	$295,472	$242,198	$234,485
Earnings (before extraordinary items)	6,496	442	589	10,554	13,126	17,788	21,108
Per common share*	0.55	(0.45)	(0.42)	1.23	1.69	2.48	3.05
Net earnings (loss) per share after extraordinary items*	0.56	(8.70)	(2.30)	1.40	1.36	2.40	3.00

* Per common share earnings are stated after deducting application of preferred dividend requirements.

investments in the last few years and as a result anticipated that their capacity would increase by 70,000 tons per year at the end of 1973. This increase in capacity would come from an extension of their Belgo Division Mill in Shawinigan, Quebec. An old newsprint machine had been purchased and modified at a cost of $11 million to give this increase in capacity.

Governments, particularly provincial, had frequently distorted the industry's normal growth pattern. By means of grants and tax incentives, they had promoted expansion when it was not needed, sometimes in a locale which was not and never could be economic. Many of these ventures had proven to be disastrous. (Developments in Newfoundland and Manitoba were outstanding examples of this.)

Mr. Andrew was concerned that increased prices would be an incentive for competitors to develop new mills. The risks were that expansion by competitors would decrease Consolidated-Bathurst's share of the market and also that rapid expansion by many companies could result in significant overcapacity such as had existed some few years before.

In 1972, Consolidated-Bathurst recorded a newsprint sales volume of 912,000 tons, of which about two thirds was sold in U.S. markets. About 10 percent was sold overseas and the rest in Canada. Other Consolidated-Bathurst products included pulp, container board, kraft paper, boxboard, lumber, and packaging products. Overall, the company's total business was 56 percent basic mill products, 41 percent packaging, and 3 percent lumber.

The Newsprint Industry

Consolidated-Bathurst ranked fifth in newsprint capacity in Canada with 9.2 percent of the total capacity. Exhibit 2 shows the capacity and shares of the other Canada-based competitors in the industry. Operating capacity rates for the past nine years as shown in Exhibit 3, were a major element in pricing decisions by members of the industry. There were also a number of significant U.S. producers of newsprint. Exhibit 4 shows their estimated capacities. The U.S. companies were very important in the pricing process for newsprint. Consolidated-Bathurst sales personnel felt that American publishers attached a higher

EXHIBIT 2 Canadian newsprint producers (>200,000 tons) in order of size, by capacity and residual total (<200,000 tons) lumped

	Producer	Capacity (tons)	Share of industry (percent)
1.	MacMillan-Bloedel Ltd.	1,364,100	13.4%
2.	Canadian International Paper	1,154,100	11.3
3.	The Price Company Ltd.	1,058,400	10.4
4.	Abitibi Paper Co. Ltd.	1,044,200	10.2
5.	Consolidated-Bathurst Ltd.	936,600	9.2
6.	Ontario Paper Co. Ltd.	765,000	7.5
7.	Bowaters Canadian Corp. Ltd.	546,200	5.4
8.	Domtar Newsprint Ltd.	540,300	5.3
9.	Great Lakes Paper Co. Ltd.	432,200	4.2
10.	Anglo-Canadian Pulp & Paper	336,800	3.3
11.	Spruce Falls Power & Paper Co.	332,100	3.3
12.	Ontario-Minnesota Pulp & Paper Co.	322,200	3.2
13.	Donohue Co. Ltd.	257,000	2.5
14.	Crown Zellerbach Can. Ltd.	254,100	2.5
15.	B. C. Forest Products Ltd.	242,700	2.4
	Balance of producers (<200,000 ton producers)	607,600	5.9
		10,193,600	100.0

EXHIBIT 3 Canadian newsprint industry: Capacity, operating ratio, production, reserve capacity (1965 through 8 months 1973)

Year	Official capacity*	Indicated operating ratio	Production	Indicated reserve capacity
1965	8,420,800	91.7	7,719,700	701,100
1966	8,878,100	94.8	8,418,800	459,300
1967	9,293,900	86.6	8,051,500	1,242,400
1968	9,655,400	83.2	8,031,300	1,624,100
1969	9,611,500	91.1	8,758,400	853,100
1970	9,718,900	88.6	8,607,500	1,111,400
1971	10,050,400	82.6	8,297,000	1,753,400
1972	10,117,900	85.6	8,660,800	1,457,100
8 months—1973	6,795,100	90.5	6,130,100	665,000
12 months—1973	10,193,600†			

* Capacity figures shown are official, theoretically possible amounts. An approximate 95 percent is considered practically possible. Note also that these figures represent nondutiable (U.S. tariff) grades only and do not incorporate Groundwood Printing and Specialty Grades (dutiable) of which some 500,000 tons per annum are produced. Detailed capacities of the latter are not published and, indeed, some part of the above capacities can be shifted to produce dutiable grades as demand dictates and profit incentives exist.

† Estimated.

EXHIBIT 4 Major U.S.
newsprint
producers

Producer	Capacity (tons)
Southland Paper	470,000
Kimberly-Clark	420,000
Publishers Paper	360,000
Great Northern	360,000
Boise Cascade	135,000
Boise Price	150,000
Others	<100,000

degree of legitimacy to price increases originating with U.S.-based producers. At the present time, only Great Northern, Crown Zellerbach, and Publishers Paper of the U.S. producers were placing their major sales emphasis in the prime market areas of the Canadian producers.

Most pulp and paper companies were experiencing increasing production costs. As shown in Exhibit 5, manufacturing costs as a percentage of sales were higher in 1972 than most of the previous seven years. Consolidated-Bathurst's

EXHIBIT 5 Ratio of
manufacturing
costs to gross
sales: Index
1965 = 100

Year	Industry
1972	108
1971	107
1970	103
1969	106
1968	108
1967	106
1966	102
1965	100

manufacturing costs as a percentage of sales had risen sharply in the previous three years and in 1973 were above the industry average. An increase in the cost of labour in 1974 was expected to increase production costs even more. Although Consolidated-Bathurst did not have any workers on strike, the demands of wage parity with other firms that were on strike would certainly be a major factor in future negotiating sessions. The current industry labour position is shown in Exhibit 6. The seriousness of the situation was reported in the *Globe and Mail* on Friday, September 28, 1973:

EXHIBIT 6 Eastern Canadian newsprint mills—strikes situation as of September 28, 1973

Company	Date strike began	Status
MacMillan Rothesay Ltd. (MacMillan-Bloedel Mill at Rothesay, Quebec)	September 9	Still out
E. B. Eddy	August 29	Ratified Sept. 14
Canadian Cellulose	August 1	Settled Aug. 5
C.I.P.—Gatineau, LaTuque, Trois Rivieres	July 27	Still out
C.I.P.—Hawkesbury	August 3	Still out
New Brunswick International Paper	August 8	Still out
Ontario and Minnesota Pulp and Paper—Fort Frances	July 3	Still out
—Kenora	July 9	Still out
Price Company—Alma and Kenogami	August 10	Still out

Despite recent settlements in Ontario, strikes in the Quebec pulp and paper industry continue to present a bleak contrast to an otherwise rosy prospect for that key Quebec industry.

No end is in sight to strikes involving about 5,000 workers that began several weeks ago at five mills, three of them in Quebec, owned by Canadian International Paper Co. of Montreal, nor to strikes by about 1,800 employees that began in August at two Quebec mills of Price Co. Limited of Quebec City.

Meanwhile, the UPIU (United Paperworkers International Union) has resumed contract negotiations with the Eastern Canada Newsprint Group, which is bargaining on behalf of five mills owned by four Quebec companies and one in Nova Scotia. Negotiations involving several other Quebec mills remain in abeyance in their preliminary stages.

These strikes come at a time when sales have generally been "Terrific" for pulp and paper producers, says Paul E. Lachance, President of the Council of Pulp and Paper Producers of Quebec.

He considers the strikes particularly unfortunate because the industry could have been selling so much. He estimates that between CIP and Price, about $1 million a day of sales are being lost.

Dr. Lachance expects strong markets to continue in 1974.

The Market for Newsprint

About 50 percent of newsprint in the United States was consumed by major metropolitan papers and the rest by much smaller dailies and weeklies. Papers like the *New York Times* and the *Detroit News,* for example, would consume about 400,000 tons and 100,000 tons of newsprint every year, respectively. Consolidated-Bathurst sold mostly to larger papers or groups of papers. Their yearly contracts with the larger papers or groups of papers ranged from 20,000 tons to over 100,000 tons with an average of about 50,000 tons. Consolidated-Bathurst had a total of about 170 accounts with 10 percent of these accounting for almost 70 percent of sales and 25 percent accounting for over 90 percent of sales. In the United States some of the larger contracts were held with the *Baltimore Sun,* The Newhouse Group (including *Long Island Daily* and *Cleveland Plain Dealer*), the Knight Newspapers (including *Miami Herald, Beacon Journal,* Akron, Ohio, *Detroit Free Press*), the *Detroit News, Philadelphia Bulletin, Boston Globe, The Wall Street Journal* and the *New York Daily News.* Major Canadian customers included *La Presse Trans-Canada Newspapers,* the *Montreal Star* and the *Toronto Star.* For large accounts, newsprint contracts were negotiated by Mr. Andrew and his immediate subordinates. The publisher and financial vice president usually represented the newspaper in these negotiations. Most other newsprint producers had about the same amount of account concentration as Consolidated-Bathurst.

In determining which newsprint producer received a particular volume of newsprint contract, publishers considered the printability and runability (amount of breakage in the press), delivery time, sales terms, and customer technical service to correct any problems. Personal relationship among negotiators was also considered to be very important. Almost all publishers had two or three sources of supply. Also, they quite often purchased some cut-price newsprint from smaller suppliers in Scandinavia or the United States.

About 85 percent of Canadian newsprint was produced in eastern Canada with the remaining 15 percent being produced in British Columbia. The major western producers were MacMillan-Bloedel Limited, Crown Zellerbach, and B. C. Forest Products. These producers sold mainly in the western United States and the Orient. MacMillan-Bloedel also had about 25 percent of its total capacity at Rothesay in eastern Canada and so competed directly with the eastern producers. The eastern producers sold mainly in the Northeast and Midwest United States, the United Kingdom, South America, and Canada.

Personnel at Consolidated-Bathurst estimated that in 1974, U.S. production would be 3.4 million tons out of a capacity of 3.6 million tons, and that Canadian production would be 9. 8 million tons out of a capacity of 10.6 million tons. U.S. exports were expected to be about 100,000 tons while Canadian overseas exports were expected to be about 1.7 million tons. Scandinavian imports into the United States were expected to be about 300,000 tons. Total U.S. demand for 1974 was estimated at 10.5 million tons, while Canadian demand was expected to be 900,000 tons. Another 200,000 tons were expected to be sold for inventory.

Mr. Andrew knew that a few competitors had started marketing a 30-pound grade of newsprint. An important factor was that the thinner sheet produced a 6 percent saving in wood consumption. This saving was important as the pulp and paper industry was quickly approaching the limit of low-cost, accessible wood resources. The impact of this thinner paper on publishers was not yet known.

Consolidated-Bathurst also made higher quality newsprint grades which sold at a 3 percent to 10 percent premium over the standard price.

History of Price Changes

Because of the competitiveness in the newsprint market, any price changes were made after much deliberation and with full anticipation of possible competitive moves. An outline of pricing activity in the U.S. newsprint market in recent years is shown in Exhibit 7. This exhibit only lists those firms that were in the first group of firms to act on any price change. After a sorting-out period following a price change, most firms sold at the established market price within a particular geographic market. Usually a change was made effective from a future date which allowed both competitors and purchasers time to analyze and react to the change. The North-South distinction in the exhibit refers to the fact that major publishers in the southeastern states had bargained one firm against another to get a lower market price than existed in the northeastern states. This difference existed despite the increased distance and transportation costs.

Most sales contracts were for 5 to 10 years but provisions for price increases were outlined in clauses tying them to "general although not necessarily universal" industry prices. In relation to these contracts, members of the sales staff generally felt that the customer was not bound if the conditions under which the contract was signed should change.

Newsprint represented about 30 percent of the total costs to newspaper publishers, and consequently, newsprint price increases had to be passed on by the publisher, usually to advertisers, if he was to maintain his profitability. Timing of a price increase therefore was critical—if it came just after the publisher had revised his advertising rates (which were usually fixed for a certain period) then he would have no means of recouping the extra cost. Rate cards for major publishers were set at many different times throughout the year.

Newspaper publishers had in the past reacted in several ways to the announcement of a price increase for newsprint. The first reaction was sometimes emotional. Heated telephone calls, letters pleading for reconsideration or speeches castigating the Canadian newsprint "cartel" were not uncommon.

Publishers could also take direct action by threatening to cancel their contracts. Some contracts actually had been cancelled using the price increase as an excuse, but the real reason might have been something else. More often, customers used the threat of cancellation to extract discounts from suppliers. This pressure was particularly effective when either of the following conditions existed:

a.   The market was soft; that is, the industry was in a general state of oversupply. In this case, the customer would likely be able to find supply elsewhere, often at a reduced price.

b.   The customer had more than one supplier. If one supplier was willing to grant a discount, the customer could use this as leverage to obtain concessions from the others. A prime example of this type of situation existed in the southern United States where a publisher-controlled newsprint company had influenced the establishment of a market price $2 less than the

EXHIBIT 7 Outline of U.S. newsprint price changes (1965–1973) in U.S. dollars per ton

Date	Company (in order of announcement)	Announced increase or decrease	Effective price	Effective date	Notes
March 1, 1966 (est.)	Domtar	$10	$145	April 1, 1966	
	Bowater Sales Corp.	10	145	April 1, 1966	
	Consolidated Paper (Consolidated-Bathurst's 1966 name)	10	145	April 1, 1966	
March 23, 1966	Domtar announces rollback	(5)	140	May 16, 1966	
	Bowater Sales Corp.	(5)	140	May 16, 1966	
	Great Lakes Paper	(5)	140	May 16, 1966	
April 20, 1966	All firms change effective date	(5)	140	June 1, 1966	
September 26, 1966	Crown Zellerbach Corp.	4	138	June 1, 1967	⎫ West Coast
October 25, 1966	MacMillan Bloedel	(3)	137	June 1, 1967	⎬ United States only
November 1, 1966	Crown Zellerbach	3	140	June 1, 1967	⎭
March 15, 1967	Consolidated Paper	3	143	July 1, 1967	
March 17, 1967	International Paper Sales Co.	3	143	July 1, 1967	
September 27, 1968	International Paper Sales Co.	5	148	January 1, 1969	North
		4	147	January 1, 1969	South*
	All others follow immediately after				
September 24, 1969	Bowater Sales Co.	4–5	152	January 1, 1970	Wipes out all price differential— universal price
	(Consolidated-Bathurst is 4th company to announce price increase)				
November 20, 1969	$1 price differential to South reinstated	(1)	152	January 1, 1970	North
			151	January 1, 1970	South

Date	Company	Increase	Price	Effective Date	Market
September 8, 1970	Anglo-Canadian	10	162	January 1, 1971	
	Consolidated-Bathurst	10	162	January 1, 1971	
	International Paper	10	162	January 1, 1971	
September 22, 1970	Boise-Cascade	8	162	January 1, 1971	
	Boise-Cascade	8	160	January 1, 1971	South only
November 3, 1970	Abitibi	8	160	January 1, 1971	All markets
November 4, 1970	Southland Paper	7	159	January 1, 1971	South
November 15, 1970	All majors	8	160	November 15, 1970	
December 6, 1970	All majors	8	160	April 1, 1971	Canada only
August 12, 1971	MacMillan-Bloedel	8	168	November 1, 1971	
	Price Company	8	168	November 1, 1971	
	(Consolidated-Bathurst is 5th company to announce price increase)				
August 15, 1971	Nixon imposes wage-price freeze. Price increase dropped.				
December 10, 1971 (Est.)	International Paper Sales Co. (3.4%, or $5.25 price increase approved by U.S. Price Commission)	8	168	December 1971	North
	Consolidated-Bathurst	5.25	164.25	December 1971	South
		8	168	December 1971	North
December 1, 1972	Great Northern Paper Co.	5	170	February 1, 1973	
	Southland Paper Co.	5	170	February 1, 1973	
	(Consolidated-Bathurst is 4th company to announce price increase (December 19)).				
April 12, 1973	Bowater Sales Co.	5	175	July 1, 1973	
	Kruger Pulp and Paper	5	175	July 1, 1973	
	Consolidated-Bathurst	5	175	July 1, 1973	

* South includes Texas, Oklahoma, Louisianna, Arkansas, Missouri, and Kansas.

rest of the eastern United States. Because of this, Canadian mills charged a lower price to southern customers than to those in the North.

In August 1971, President Nixon imposed universal wage and price controls in the United States for 90 days. As of September 1973, the newsprint industry was operating under voluntary restraint on prices. Price increases were allowed, but were subject to review by the Cost-of-Living Council. If this council considered a price increase to be unreasonable, it could order the price rolled back.

The Future

Mr. Andrew was anxious to avoid any losses in the future especially in view of Consolidated-Bathurst's performance in previous years. In evaluating all the factors, Mr. Andrew knew that he would have to decide what the new price should be and when the change was to be made if he decided to make any price change at all. He also wondered if now was the time to make the investment in a new newsprint machine, and if so, what size of machine. He expected that production costs for newsprint on a new machine would be about 10 percent less than the current average total cost. Mr. Andrew knew that he was operating in a basically conservative commodity business. He was anxious to make good decisions both for his company and for his industry.

Case 33

Big Sky of Montana, Inc.*

Introduction

Karen Tracy could feel the pressure on her as she sat at her desk late that April afternoon. Two weeks from today she would be called on to present her recommendations concerning next year's winter season pricing policies for the Big Sky of Montana, Inc.—room rates for the resort's accommodation facilities as well as decisions in the skiing and food service areas. The presentation would be made to a top management team from the parent company, Boyne U.S.A., which operated out of Michigan.

"As sales and public relations manager, Karen, your accuracy in decision making is extremely important," her boss had said in his usual tone. "Because we spend most of our time in Michigan, we'll need a well-based and involved opinion."

It'll be the shortest two weeks of my life, she thought.

Background: Big Sky and Boyne U.S.A.

Big Sky of Montana, Inc., was a medium-sized destination resort[1] located in southwestern Montana, 45 miles south of Bozeman, and 43 miles north of the west entrance to Yellowstone National Park. Big Sky was conceived in the early 1970s and had begun operation in November 1974.

The 11,000-acre, 2,000-bed resort was separated into 2 main areas: Meadow and Mountain Villages. The Meadow Village (elevation 6,300 feet) was located 2 miles east of the resort's main entrance on U.S. 191 and 7 miles from the ski area. The Meadow Village had an 800-bed capacity in the form of 4

---

* This case was prepared by Anne Senausky and Professor James E. Nelson for educational purposes only. It is designed for classroom purposes and not for purposes of research nor to illustrate either effective or ineffective handling of administrative problems. Some data are disguised. Copyright © 1978 by the Endowment and Research Foundation at Montana State University. Used with permission.

[1] Destination resorts were characterized by on-the-hill lodging and eating facilities, a national market, and national advertising.

condominium complexes (ranging from studios to 3-bedroom units) and a 40-room hostel for economy lodging. Additional facilities included an 18-hole golf course, 6 tennis courts, a restaurant, post office, a convention center with meeting space for up to 200 people, and a small lodge serving as a pro shop for the golf course in the summer and cross-country skiing in the winter.

The Mountain Village (elevation 7,500 feet) was the center of winter activity, located at the base of the ski area. In this complex was the 204-room Huntley Lodge offering hotel accommodations, 3 condominium complexes (unit size ranged from studio to 3-bedroom), and an 88-room hostel for a total of 1,200 beds. The Mountain Mall was also located here, next to the Huntley Lodge and within a five-minute walk of 2 of the 3 condominium complexes in the Mountain Village. It housed ticket sales, an equipment rental shop, a skier's cafeteria, two large meeting rooms for a maximum of 700 persons (regularly used as sack lunch areas for skiers), two offices, a ski school desk, and ski patrol room, all of which were operated by Boyne. Also in this building were a delicatessen, drug store/gift shop, sporting goods store/rental shop, restaurant, outdoor clothing store, jewelry shop, a T-shirt shop, two bars, and a child day-care center. Each of these independent operations held leases, due to expire in two to three years.

The closest airport to Big Sky was located just outside Bozeman. It was served by Northwest Orient and Frontier Airlines with connections to other major airlines out of Denver and Salt Lake City. Greyhound and Amtrak also operated bus and train service into Bozeman. Yellowstone Park Lines provided Big Sky with three buses daily to and from the airport and Bozeman bus station (cost was $4.40 one way, $8.40 round trip), as well as an hourly shuttle around the two Big Sky villages. Avis, Hertz, National, and Budget offered rent-a-car service in Bozeman with a drop-off service available at Big Sky.

In July 1976 Boyne U.S.A., a privately owned, Michigan-based operation, purchased the Huntley Lodge, Mountain Mall, ski lifts and terrain, golf course, and tennis courts for approximately $8 million. The company subsequently invested an additional $3 million into Big Sky. Boyne also owned and operated four Michigan resort ski areas.

Big Sky's top management consisted of a lodge manager (in charge of operations within the Huntley Lodge), a sales and public relations manager (Karen), a food and beverage manager, and an area manager (overseeing operations external to the lodge, including the mall and all recreational facilities). These four positions were occupied by persons trained with the parent company; a fifth manager, the comptroller, had worked for pre-Boyne ownership.

Business figures were reported to the company's home office on a daily basis and major decisions concerning Big Sky operations were discussed and approved by "Michigan." Boyne's top management visited Big Sky an average of five times annually, and all major decisions such as pricing and advertising were approved by the parent for all operations.

The Skiing

Big Sky's winter season usually began in late November and continued until the middle of April, with a yearly snowfall of approximately 450 inches. The area had 18 slopes between elevations of 7,500 and 9,900 feet. Terrain breakdown was as follows: 25 percent novice, 55 percent intermediate, and 20 percent advanced. (Although opinions varied, industry guidelines recommended a terrain breakdown of 20 percent, 60 percent, and 20 percent for novice, intermediate, and advanced skiers, respectively.) The longest run was approximately three miles in length; temperatures (highs) ranged from 15 to 30 degrees Farenheit throughout the season.

Lift facilities at Big Sky included two double chairlifts, a triple chair, and a four-passenger gondola. Lift capacity estimated at 4,000 skiers per day. This figure was considered adequate by the area manager, at least until the 1980–81 season.

Karen felt that the facilities, snow conditions, and grooming compared favorably with that of other destination resorts of the Rockies. "In fact, our only real drawback right now," she thought, "is our position in the national market. We need more skiers who are sold on Big Sky. And that is in the making."

The Consumers

Karen knew from previous dealings that Big Sky, like most destination areas, attracted three distinct skier segments: local day skiers (living within driving distance and not utilizing lodging in the area); individual destination skiers (living out of state and using accommodations in the Big Sky area); and groups of destination skiers (clubs, professional organizations, and the like).

The first category was comprised typically of Montana residents, with a relatively small number from Wyoming and Idaho. (Distances from selected population centers to Big Sky are presented in Exhibit 1.) A 1973 study of four Montana ski areas performed by the advertising unit of the Montana department of highways characterized Montana skiers as:

EXHIBIT 1

A. Population centers in proximity to Big Sky (distance and population)

City	Distance from Big Sky (miles)	Population (U.S. 1970 Census)
Bozeman, Montana	45	18,670
Butte, Montana	126	23,368
Helena, Montana	144	22,730
Billings, Montana	174	61,581
Great Falls, Montana	225	60,091
Missoula, Montana	243	29,497
Pocatello, Idaho	186	40,036
Idaho Falls, Idaho	148	35,776

EXHIBIT 1 (concluded)

B. Approximate distance of selected major U.S. population centers to Big Sky in air miles)

City	Distance to Big Sky*
Chicago	1,275
Minneapolis	975
Fargo	750
Salt Lake City	375
Dallas	1,500
Houston	1,725
Los Angeles	975
San Francisco	925
New York	2,025
Atlanta	1,950
New Orleans	1,750
Denver	750

* Per passenger air fare could be approximated at 20 cents per mile (round trip, coach rates).

1. In their early 20s and males (60 percent).
2. Living within 75 miles of a ski area.
3. From a household with two skiers in it.
4. Averaging $13,000 in household income.
5. An intermediate to advanced ability skier.
6. Skiing five hours per ski day, 20 days per season locally.
7. Skiing four days away from local areas.
8. Taking no lessons in the past five years.

Karen was also aware that a significant number of day skiers, particularly on the weekends, were college students.

Destination, or nonresident skiers, were labeled in the same study as typically:

1. At least in their mid-20s and males (55 percent).
2. Living in a household of three or more skiers.
3. Averaging near $19,000 in household income.
4. More an intermediate skier.
5. Spending about six hours per day skiing.
6. Skiing 11–14 days per season with 3–8 days away from home.
7. Taking ski school lessons.

Through data taken from reservation records, Karen learned that individual destination skiers accounted for half of last year's usage based on skier days.[2] Geographic segments were approximately as follows:

---

[2] A skier day is defined as one skier using the facility for one day of operation.

Upper Midwest (Minnesota, Michigan, North Dakota)	30 percent
Florida	20 percent
California	17 percent
Washington, Oregon, Montana	15 percent
Texas, Oklahoma	8 percent
Other	10 percent

Reservation records indicated that the average length of stay for individual destination skiers was about six or seven days.

It was the individual destination skier who was most likely to buy a lodging/lift package; 30 percent made commitments for these advertised packages when making reservations for 1977–78. Even though there was no discount involved in this manner of buying lift tickets, Karen knew that they were fairly popular because it saved the purchaser a trip to the ticket window every morning. Approximately half of the individual business came through travel agents, who received a 10 percent commission.

The third skier segment, the destination group, accounted for a substantial 20 percent of Big Sky's skier day usage. The larger portion of the group business came through medical and other professional organizations holding meetings at the resort, as this was a way to "combine business with pleasure." These groups were typically comprised of couples and individuals between the ages of 30 and 50. Ski clubs made up the remainder with a number coming from the southern states of Florida, Texas, and Georgia. During the 1977–78 season, Big Sky drew 30 ski clubs with membership averaging 55 skiers. The average length of stay for all group destination skiers was about four or five days.

A portion of these group bookings were made through travel agents, but the majority dealt directly with Karen. The coordinator of the professional meetings or the president of the ski club typically contacted the Big Sky sales office to make initial reservation dates, negotiate prices, and work out the details of their stay.

The Competition

In Karen's mind Big Sky faced two types of competition, that for local day skiers and that for out-of-state (i.e., destination) skiers.

Bridger Bowl was virtually the only area competing for local day skiers. Bridger was a "nonfrills," nonprofit, and smaller ski area located some 16 miles northeast of Bozeman. It received the majority of local skiers including students at Montana State University, which was located in Bozeman. The area was labeled as having terrain more difficult than that of Big Sky and was thus more appealing to the local expert skiers. However, it also had much longer lift lines than Big Sky and had recently lost some of its weekend business to them.

Karen had found through experience that most Bridger skiers usually "tried" Big Sky once or twice a season. Season passes for the two areas were mutually honored at the half-day rate for an all-day ticket, and Big Sky occasionally ran newspaper ads offering discounts on lifts to obtain more Bozeman business.

For out-of-state skiers, Big Sky considered its competition to be mainly the destination resorts of Colorado, Utah, and Wyoming. (Selected data on competing resorts is presented in Exhibit 2.) Because Big Sky was smaller and newer than the majority of these areas, Karen reasoned, it was necessary to follow an aggressive strategy aimed at increasing its national market share.

Exhibit 2 Competitors' 1977–1978 package plan rates,* number of lifts, and lift rates

	Lodge double (2)†	Two-bedroom condo (4)	Three-bedroom condo (6)	Number of lifts	Daily lift rates
Aspen, Colo.	$242	$242	$220	19	$13
Steamboat, Colo.	230	230	198	15	12
Jackson, Wyo.	230	242	210	5	14
Vail, Colo.	230	242	220	15	14
Snowbird, Utah	208	none	none	6	11
Bridger Bowl, Mont.	(no lodging available at Bridger Bowl)			3	8

* Package plan rates are per person and include seven nights lodging, 6 lift tickets (high season rates).

† Number in parentheses denotes occupancy of unit on which price is based.

Present Policies

Lift Rates

It was common knowledge that there existed some local resentment concerning Big Sky's lift rate policy. Although comparable to rates at Vail or Aspen, an all-day lift ticket was $4 higher than the ticket offered at nearby Bridger Bowl. In an attempt to alleviate this situation, management at Big Sky instituted a $9 "chair pass" for the 1977–78 season, entitling the holder to unlimited use of the three chairs, plus two rides per day on the gondola, to be taken between specified time periods. Because the gondola served primarily intermediate terrain, it was reasoned that the chair pass would appeal to the local, more expert skier. A triple chair serving the bowl area was located at the top of the gondola, and two rides on the gondola would allow those skiers to take ample advantage of the advanced terrain up there. Otherwise, all advanced terrain was served by another chair.

However, if Big Sky was to establish itself as a successful, nationally prominent destination area, Karen felt the attitudes and opinions of all skiers must be carefully weighed. Throughout the season she had made a special effort to grasp the general feeling toward rates. A $12 ticket, she discovered, was thought to be very reasonable by destination skiers, primarily because Big Sky was predominantly an intermediate area and the average destination skier was of intermediate ability; also because Big Sky was noted for its relative lack of lift lines, giving the skier more actual skiing time for the money. "Perhaps we should keep the price the same," she thought, "we do need more business. Other destination areas are likely to raise their prices and we should look good in comparison."

Also discussed was the possible abolition of the $9 chair pass. The question in Karen's mind was if its elimination would severely hurt local business or would it sell an all-lift $12 ticket to the skier who had previously bought only a chair pass. The issue was compounded by an unknown number of destination skiers who opted for the cheaper chair pass too.

Season-pass pricing was also an issue. Prices for the 1977–78 all-lift season pass had remained the same as last year, but a season chair pass had been introduced which was the counterpart of the daily chair lift pass. Karen did not like the number of season chair passes purchased in relation to the number of all-lift passes and considered recommending its abolition as well as an increase in the price of the all-lift pass. "I'm going to have to think this one out carefully," she thought, "because skiing accounted for about 40 percent of our total revenue this past season. I'll have to be able to justify my decision not only to Michigan but also to the Forest Service."

Price changes were not solely at the discretion of Big Sky management. As is the case with most larger western ski areas, the U.S. government owned part of the land on which Big Sky operated. Control of this land was the responsibility of the U.S. Forest Service which annually approved all lift pricing policies. For the 1976–77 ski season, Forest Service action kept most lift rate increases to the national inflation rate. For the 1977–78 season, larger price increases were allowed for ski areas which had competing areas near by; Big Sky was considered to be such an area. No one knew what the Forest Service position would be for the upcoming 1978–79 season.

To help her in her decision, an assistant had prepared a summary of lift rates and usage for the past two seasons (Exhibit 3).

EXHIBIT 3

A. 1977–78 lift rates and usage summary (136 days operation)

Ticket	Consumer cost	Skier days*	Number season passes sold
Adult all day all lift	$ 12	53,400	
Adult all day chair	9	20,200	
Adult half day	8	9,400	
Child all day all lift	8	8,500	
Child all day chair	5	3,700	
Child half day	6	1,200	
Hotel passes†	12/day	23,400	
Complimentary	0	1,100	
Adult all lift season pass	220	4,300	140
Adult chair season pass	135	4,200	165
Child all lift season pass	130	590	30
Child chair season pass	75	340	15
Employee all lift season pass	100	3,000	91
Employee chair season pass	35	1,100	37

EXHIBIT 3 (concluded)

B. 1976–77 lift rates and usage summary (122 days operation)

Ticket	Consumer cost	Skier days	Number season passes sold
Adult all day	$ 10	52,500	
Adult half day	6.50	9,000	
Child all day	6	10,400	
Child half day	4	1,400	
Hotel passes†	10/day	30,500	
Complimentary	0	480	
Adult season pass	220	4,200	84
Child season pass	130	300	15
Employee season pass	100	2,300	70

* A skier day is defined as one skier using the facility for one day of operation.

† Hotel passes refers to those included in the lodging/lift packages.

Room Rates

This area of pricing was particularly important because lodging accounted for about one third of the past season's total revenue. It was also difficult because of the variety of accommodations (Exhibit 4) and the difficulty in accurately forecasting next season's demand. For example, the season of 1976–77 had been unique in that a good portion of the Rockies was without snow for the initial months of the winter including Christmas. Big Sky was fortunate in receiving as much snow as it had, and consequently many groups and individuals who were originally headed for Vail or Aspen booked in with Big Sky.

Pricing for the 1977–78 season had been made on the premise that there would be a good amount of repeat business. This came true in part but not as much as had been hoped. Occupancy experience had also been summarized for the past two seasons to help Karen make her final decision (Exhibit 5).

EXHIBIT 4

A. Nightly room rates,* 1977–1978

	Low season range	High season range	Maximum occupancy
Huntley Lodge			
Standard	$ 42–62	$ 50–70	4
Loft	52–92	60–100	6
Stillwater Condo			
Studio	40–60	45–65	4
One-bedroom	55–75	60–80	4
Bedroom w/loft	80–100	90–100	6
Deer Lodge Condo			
One-bedroom	74–84	80–90	4
Two-bedroom	93–103	100–110	6
Three-bedroom	112–122	120–130	8
Hill Condo			
Studio	30–40	35–45	4
Studio w/lot	50–70	55–75	6

EXHIBIT 4 (concluded)

B. Nightly room rates, 1976–1977

	Low season range	High season range	Maximum occupancy
Huntley Lodge			
Standard	$ 32–47	$ 35–50	4
Loft	47–67	50–70	6
Stillwater Condo			
Studio	39–54	37–52	4
One-bedroom	52–62	50–60	4
Bedroom w/loft	60–80	65–85	6
Deer Lodge Condo			
One-bedroom	51–66	55–70	4
Two-bedroom	74–94	80–100	6
Three-bedroom	93–123	100–130	8
Hill Condo			
Studio	28–43	30–45	4
Studio w/loft	42–62	45–65	6

* Rates determined by number of persons in room or condominium unit and do not include lift tickets. Maximums for each rate range apply at maximum occupancy.

EXHIBIT 5

A. 1977–1978 Lodge-condominium occupancy (in room-nights*)

	December (26 days operation)	January	February	March	April (8 days operation)
Huntley Lodge	1,830	2,250	3,650	4,650	438
Condominiums†	775	930	1,350	100	90

B. 1976–1977 Lodge-condominium occupancy (in room-nights)

	December (16 days operation)	January	February	March	April (16 days operation)
Huntley Lodge	1,700	3,080	4,525	4,300	1,525
Condominiums‡	600	1,000	1,600	1,650	480

C. Lodge-condominium occupancy (in person-nights§)

December 1977 (1976)	January 1978 (1977)	February 1978 (1977)	March 1978 (1977)	April 1978 (1977)
7,850 (6,775)	9,200 (13,000)	13,150 (17,225)	17,900 (17,500)	1,450 (4,725)

* A room-night is defined as one room (or condominium) rented for one night. Lodging experience is based on 124 days of operation for 1977–78 while Exhibit Three shows the skiing facilities operating 136 days. Both numbers are correct.
† Big Sky had 92 condominiums available during the 1977–78 season.
‡ Big Sky had 85 condominiums available during the 1976–77 season.
§ A person-night refers to one person using the facility for one night.

As was customary in the hospitality industry, January was a slow period and it was necessary to price accordingly. Low season pricing was extremely important because many groups took advantage of these rates. On top of that, groups were often offered discounts in the neighborhood of 10 percent. Considering this, Karen could not price too high, with the risk of losing individual destination skiers, nor too low, such that an unacceptable profit would be made from group business in this period.

Food Service

Under some discussion was the feasibility of converting all destination skiers to the American Plan, under which policy each guest in the Huntley Lodge would be placed on a package to include three meals daily in a Big Sky-controlled facility. There was a feeling both for and against this idea. The parent company had been successfully utilizing this plan for years at its destination areas in northern Michigan. Extending the policy to Big Sky should find similar success.

Karen was not so sure. For one thing, the Michigan resorts were primarily self-contained and alternative eateries were few. For another, the whole idea of extending standardized policies from Michigan to Montana was suspect. As an example, Karen painfully recalled a day in January when Big Sky "tried on" another successful Michigan policy of accepting only cash or check payments for lift tickets. Reactions of credit card carrying skiers could be described as ranging from annoyed to irate.

If an American Plan were proposed for next year, it would likely include both the Huntley Lodge Dining Room and Lookout Cafeteria. Less clear, however, were prices to be charged. There certainly would have to be consideration for both adults and children and for the two independently operated eating places in the Mountain Mall (see Exhibit 6 for an identification of eating places in the Big Sky area). Beyond these considerations, there was little else other than an expectation of a profit to guide Karen in her analysis.

The Telephone Call

"Profits in the food area might be hard to come by," Karen thought. "Last year it appears we lost money on everything we sold." (See Exhibit 7.) Just then the telephone rang. It was Rick Thompson, her counterpart at Boyne Mountain Lodge in Michigan. "How are your pricing recommendations coming?" he asked. "I'm about done with mine and thought we should compare notes."

"Good idea, Rick—only I'm just getting started out here. Do you have any hot ideas?"

"Only one," he responded. "I just got off the phone with a guy in Denver. He told me all of the major Colorado areas are upping their lift prices one or two dollars next year."

EXHIBIT 6 Eating places in the Big Sky area

Establishment	Type of service	Meals served	Current prices	Seating	Location
Lodge Dining Room*	A la carte	Breakfast	$2–5	250	Huntley Lodge
		Lunch	2–5		
		Dinner	7–15		
Steak House*	Steak/lobster	Dinner only	6–12	150	Huntley Lodge
Fondue Stube*	Fondue	Dinner only	6–10	25	Huntley Lodge
Ore House†	A la carte	Lunch	.80–4.00	150	Mountain Mall
		Dinner	5–12		
Ernie's Deli†	Deli/restaurant	Breakfast	1–3	25	Mountain Mall
		Lunch	2–5		
Lookout Cafeteria*	Cafeteria	Breakfast	1.50–3.00	175	Mountain Mall
		Lunch	2–4		
		Dinner	3–6		
Yellow Mule†	A la carte	Breakfast	2–4	75	Meadow Village
		Lunch	2–5		
		Dinner	4–8		
Buck's T–4†	Road house restaurant/bar	Dinner only	2–9	60	Gallatin Canyon (2 miles south of Big Sky entrance)
Karst Ranch†	Road house restaurant/bar	Breakfast	2–4	50	Gallatin Canyon (7 miles north of Big Sky entrance)
		Lunch	2–5		
		Dinner	3–8		
Corral†	Road house restaurant/bar	Breakfast	2–4	30	Gallatin Canyon (5 miles south of Big Sky entrance)
		Lunch	2–4		
		Dinner	3–5		

* Owned and operated by Big Sky of Montana, Inc.
† Independently operated.

EXHIBIT 7 Ski season income data (percent)

	Skiing	Lodging	Food and beverage
Revenue	100.0	100.0	100.0
Cost of sales:			
Merchandise	0.0	0.0	30.0
Labor	15.0	15.9	19.7
Maintenance	3.1	5.2	2.4
Supplies	1.5	4.8	5.9
Miscellaneous	2.3	0.6	0.6
Operating expenses	66.2	66.4	66.7
Net profit (loss) before taxes	11.9	7.0	(25.2)

"Is that right, Rick? Are you sure?"

"Well, you know nobody knows for sure what's going to happen but I think it's pretty good information. He heard it from his sister-in-law who works in Vail. I think he said she read it in the local paper or something."

"That doesn't seem like very solid information," said Karen. "Let me know if you hear anything more, will you?"

"Certainly. You know, we really should compare our recommendations before we stick our necks out too far on this pricing thing. Can you call me later in the week?" he asked.

"Sure, I'll talk to you the day after tomorrow; I should be about done by then. Anything else?"

"Nope—gotta run. Talk to you then. Bye," and he was gone.

"At least I've got some information," Karen thought, "and a new deadline!"

Part 8

Marketing and Public Policy

The current environment of the marketing manager is one undergoing rapid change and transition. Probably the most noteworthy of these developments, whether for better or for worse, is the increasing pervasiveness of "public" influences on marketing institutions and decision making. In this context, public influences are generally defined to include different levels of government (acting through legislation, regulation, or moral suasion), organized public groups (the consumerism movement, for example), individual advocates of change, and the force of changing public attitudes and opinion.

The cases in this section seek to develop an improved understanding of some of these trends and developments, and to provide practice for students in rendering decisions in the contemporary environment. The specific objectives of the cases are as follows:

1. To improve capacity for marketing decision making in situations where public influences are involved.
2. To explore the nature and extent of public influences on marketing institutions and decision making.
3. To develop conceptual foundations leading to an improved understanding of contemporary developments in marketing.

Approaches to decision making in the area of marketing and public policy are not well established. One possible approach makes three assumptions. They are as follows:

1. Marketing and public policy decisions are made in a bargaining arena containing many interest groups.

This note draws heavily on the work of Professor Michael Pearce of the University of Western Ontario.

2. Either explicit or implicit bargaining takes place among the interest groups in this arena whenever a marketing decision involves public influences.
3. Better decisions will be made if the objectives, motivations and behaviors of each interest group are understood.

   With the assumptions in mind, we now shall present an approach to decision making in this area:

1. List and/or diagram the interest groups involved in a particular decision context. Note the interrelationships among them.
2. Identify the behavior of each group.
3. Attempt to explain this behavior by examining the objectives, motivations, and values of the people comprising the groups.
4. Identify what each group stands to lose or gain in the bargaining.
5. Identify what each group might be most willing to give up. What would they most want in return?
6. Based upon this analysis, predict the likely strategies of each group.
7. Make a decision based upon the anticipated reaction of each group to the alternatives you are considering. Be sure to have a contingency in case their reactions are not as you anticipated.

Case 34

F&F Sales Company

Tom Frolik leaned back in his chair and reflected upon the events that had taken place earlier that day. His first day back to work after a long weekend over New Year's had really been hectic. Apparently while he had been on his skiing vacation, an article had appeared in the morning newspaper indicating that the Georgia State Troopers were upset about the effectiveness of radar detectors such as the Fuzzbusters that he marketed, and had encouraged several legislators to introduce a bill for the upcoming General Assembly outlawing these devices in Georgia. The phone had been ringing all day with many people calling to order a Fuzzbuster before their sale became illegal. Recognizing the potential consequences of this act for his company, he decided to develop a complete plan of action in the next few days.

Background on Radar Detector

The first radar detectors were marketed in the early 1960s. Typically, the units were not very high quality and sold for a price between $19.95 and $29.95. These units clipped onto the visor and would emit a beep when police radar was detected, allowing the driver to slow down before being caught in a radar trap. Although these units were relatively unsophisticated, several companies were somewhat successful in marketing them through mail-order advertising. With speed limits of 70 or 75 mph on most highways, however, most people did not have a need for these units.

Things changed dramatically beginning in 1973 with the fuel crisis and oil embargo. Speed limits were reduced nationally to 55 mph and were often enforced. The first response to this development was a dramatic increase in the sale of Citizens Band (CB) radios, which had been in existence for a number of years, but had experienced a very low level of sales. Many truckers purchased these units, and soon thereafter salesmen and other individuals who had to drive a great deal began purchasing CB units. By 1975, the general public started buying CB radios in great numbers.

EXHIBIT 1

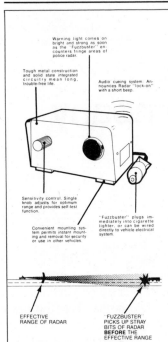

Warning light comes on bright and strong as soon as the "Fuzzbuster" encounters fringe areas of police radar.

Tough metal construction and solid state integrated circuitry mean long, trouble-free life.

Audio cueing system: Announces Radar "lock-on" with a short beep.

Sensitivity control. Single knob adjusts for optimum range and provides self-test function.

Convenient mounting system permits instant mounting and removal for security or use in other vehicles.

"Fuzzbuster" plugs immediately into cigarette lighter, or can be wired directly to vehicle electrical system.

EFFECTIVE RANGE OF RADAR

"FUZZBUSTER" PICKS UP STRAY BITS OF RADAR **BEFORE** THE EFFECTIVE RANGE

Complete protection for
$ **109.**⁹⁵

FUZZBUSTER
IS MADE EXCLUSIVELY BY
ELECTROLERT, inc.
Troy, Ohio 45373

DISTRIBUTED BY:

FUZZBUSTER
TURNS A RADAR
BEAM TO LIGHT

RADAR

WHEN YOU SEE IT...
REACT!

WHEN YOU DON'T...
RELAX~

FUZZBUSTER
Parametric Radar Receiver

Put a **Fuzzbuster** on your Dash and you can drive relaxed again. No watching for Radar lurking in the bushes, or trying to make sense out of the C.B. Radio chatter. And you don't have to put up with squeals or growls that warn you too late, or when there isn't any Radar around. Now you can enjoy the drive, anytime, anyplace . . . tension free.

The **Fuzzbuster** has been proven by tens of thousands of truckers over billions of miles, nationwide...so effective it has become a highway legend!

The **Fuzzbuster** was designed by a Speed Radar Manufacturer, and is a thoroughly engineered military type parametric radar receiver. Its performance is absolutely unparalleled. All solid-state integrated circuit construction insures extreme sensitivity and reliability.

The **Fuzzbuster** is equipped with a revolutionary audio cueing system which alerts you with a short beep each time the receiver locks on to a Radar signal. At the same time: the **Fuzzbuster** gives you positive visual indication of stationary or moving Radar ("New Vascar") two to ten times farther than the range of the Radar. You'll have ample time to slow down. With a little practice, the visual indicator can even tell you where and what kind of speed trap you are encountering.

The **Fuzzbuster** mounts quickly on the Dashboard and plugs directly into your cigar lighter, or you can wire it directly. It automatically adapts to positive or negative ground systems. The black matte finish prevents glare, and blends with any interior.

It works!

- **Sensitive** to **1/100th** of a **millionth** of **one watt** microwave energy.
- **Many times** more **sensitive** and **selective** than nearest pretender.
- **Works two** to **ten times** farther than Radar **without** the frequent **false alarms** of other detectors.
- **Draws** less than **¼ watt...indefinite life.**
- **12 volt positive** or **negative** ground.
- **No antenna — no involved installation.**
- **Receives** all **X-Band Radars** in **all** states.
- Especially **effective** on new **Moving Radar,** used by 40 states.
- **Works day** or **night...city** or **highway.**
- **Half** the cost of a good **C.B. Radio.**

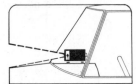

Give the **Fuzzbuster** a good view of the road ahead, and it will spot those electronic ambushes long before the Radar can spot you!

There were several problems with the CB radios as a means of avoiding speeding tickets. First, as more and more amateurs started using their radios, the channels became very cluttered. Often it was hard to hear what people were saying, as many people tried to use the same channel. Second, the CB radio became less and less reliable as the police (Smokey the Bear) put CB radios in their cars also. Thus, they could receive the same messages that truckers and other drivers were sending to each other. Third, the CB radio became much less reliable at night with the users' inability to see the police speed trap in the dark.

In addition to the problems with the effectiveness of CB radios, the state of the art on radar increased substantially about this time. With the old police radar units, about all they could do was set up a radar trap. New mobile radar units were developed that allowed the policemen to get a radar reading on a speeding car while the police car was moving. Another dramatic development was the ability of police radar to determine the speed of a car even though the police car was going in the opposite direction. Thus, a police officer could detect a speeding car going in the other direction, make a U-turn and arrest the speeder, something that was unheard of previously.

It was in this environment of reduced speed limits, increased enforcement, reduced effectiveness of CB radios, and increased effectiveness of police radar that the Fuzzbuster was introduced by the Electrolert Company in 1975. The Fuzzbuster, a military-type, parametric radar receiver, is sensitive to one/one hundredth of one-millionth of one watt, approximately the strength of radar at three miles if not blocked or otherwise attenuated. The Fuzzbuster receives in the 10.5 GHz Amateur (ham microwave) Band.

Drawing less than one quarter of a watt power, the Fuzzbuster can be left on indefinitely. It is installed on the dash of the car and has a self-contained antenna. The unit plugs into the cigarette lighter. When radar is picked up by the receiver, a warning light goes on and at the same time, a high-pitched tone is generated. The tone cuts off after two to three seconds, but the lamp remains bright until the radar signal ceases. The Fuzzbuster provides this identification of radar up to three miles distant. A pamphlet describing the Fuzzbuster is reproduced in Exhibit 1.

Background on Tom Frolik and F&F Sales Company

Tom Frolik first became aware of Fuzzbusters in January 1976, when he was working as a consultant to a large truck stop on Interstate 75 in Georgia. At that time Fuzzbusters had a suggested retail price of $99.95 and were sold to the retailer for $75. The truck stop ordered one dozen and sold them. They then ordered another dozen, and these also sold quite rapidly. Mr. Frolik then contacted the Electrolert Company and worked out an arrangement to become a distributor. The truck stop had a warehouse distribution subsidiary which bought replacement parts for trucks, and this subsidiary became an Electrolert distributor. About this time some product improvements were made, the most important being the introduction of a flashing light in addition to the beep when radar was detected, and the retail price was increased to $109.95. The whole-sale price was $79.

The price to the distributor was $59 per unit, but they had to order in gross (a gross is 144 units). The manufacturer provided sample advertising mats and allowed $3 per unit for co-op advertising allowances. In March 1976, the truck stop ordered its first gross and at the same time, reduced the retail price to $84.95. Mr. Frolik recalled that they sold like hotcakes at this price, but because of complaints from those who had paid $109.95, and a feeling that a higher price would not hurt sales, they decided to raise the price to $89.95.

The truck stop distributor subsidiary made no attempt to sell Fuzzbusters through any other outlets, but did sell them through a second truck stop which they had recently purchased.

By October they had sold five gross (720 units) and were told that they had a big backup on the co-op advertising allowance. At the same time, the owner of the truck stop began to have some guilt feelings about marketing the product and decided he did not want to advertise it using his company name.

In late October, Tom Frolik announced that he was leaving the truck stop company to move to Atlanta to establish his own consulting firm and start several entrepreneurial enterprises. The owner of the truck stop suggested that Frolik market in the Atlanta area some of the products that the truck stop's distributor subsidiary handled. Frolik suggested that he be given the use of the advertising allowance credit for the Fuzzbuster, that he put in the time on the project, and that the truck stop owner and he split the profits on an equal basis. His proposal was accepted by the truck stop owner, and thus F&F Sales Company was created.

In November when Frolik came to Atlanta, the advertising allowance was up to $2,200. The Electrolert Company would pay 50 percent of all advertising expenditures for the Fuzzbuster up to this amount, but they would pay 100 percent of the expenses for newspaper advertising. Because of this provision, Frolik decided to take out some ads in *The Atlanta Journal* and *Constitution*. Exhibit 2 contains the ad that was approved by Electrolert. Mr. Frolik decided to run the ad four times—Sunday, December 12, the evening of December 16, the morning of December 17, and Sunday, December 19. These four ads, at an average of approximately $550 each, would utilize the full co-op advertising allowance available.

After the December 12 ad ran, with minimal response, Mr. Frolik changed the ad by inserting the telephone number of his office where people could call for further information or to place an order which would be charged to a bank credit card (using the truck stop's bank credit card mechanism). The four ads resulted in the immediate sale of 60 Fuzzbusters, with approximately half the people calling in for information before sending in their order. Mr. Frolik indicated that most of these buyers were salesmen, rather than truckers.

Three other outlets in Atlanta were advertising Fuzzbusters at this time. Two of these were retailers which took out small ads at a price of $99.95 and $109.95, with both stores requiring the consumer to come to the retail outlet to purchase the Fuzzbuster. The third source was a firm in Alabama that offered a

EXHIBIT 2

toll-free number together with a coupon in the ad for ordering. This firm, which accepted credit cards, charged $89.95 plus tax and handling ($3.50 for the tax and handling, the same as F&F Sales charged).

Although there were several other companies which marketed similar kinds of products, Mr. Frolik felt that the Fuzzbuster was the best radar detector available on the market. In the Atlanta area, these competitors had virtually no distribution.

Current Situation

As a result of the four ads in the middle of December, Mr. Frolik had been quite optimistic about sales of the Fuzzbuster. He had a number of ideas which he was planning to implement to increase sales, including taking out some classified advertising in the CB radio section of the classified ads. He also knew that Radio Shack stores did not stock Fuzzbusters or competitors, so he planned to write to the 43 Radio Shack store managers in his area and ask them to send any customers who requested this product to him.

Thus, all was very rosy for F&F Sales Company and Mr. Frolik when he left on Friday, December 24 for a 10-day skiing vacation. By the time he returned to the office on January 3, things were quite different. Exhibit 3 contains the article which ran in the morning *Atlanta Constitution* on Friday, December 31 describing the plan by the Georgia State Troopers to outlaw Fuzzbusters. Exhibit 4 contains the proposed legislation that would be intro-

EXHIBIT 3 Fuzzbuster newspaper article

Fuzz Busters Really Work—
Troopers Want Radar Detectors Outlawed

By Keeler McCartney

Georgia state troopers are up in arms over the latest gadgets some motorists are using to detect highway radar speed timers, and they want the upcoming General Assembly to do something about it.

Bill Wilson, information officer of the state Department of Public Safety, said the gadgets in question detect the presence of radar machines and warn drivers before the troopers have a chance to detect speeders.

"It just isn't fair," Wilson said.

He said the warning devices, usually mounted on the dashboards of autos and trucks, can be purchased for $99.95 under the suggestive trade names of "Fuzz Busters," "Bear Finders" and "Trooper Snoopers."

As they approach radar stations, drivers equipped with the devices are alerted by a variety of noises ranging from the wail of an upended talking doll to the buzz of an angry bee and the beep of a telephone answering service.

The safety department has prepared a bill to submit to the next General Assembly which would make it a misdemeanor to possess, manufacture or sell the devices in Georgia.

EXHIBIT 3 *(concluded)*

Troopers have checked the devices and found that they do, indeed, give the driver ample warning to slow down to the legal 55-mile limit before he enters a radar field, Wilson declared.

State Patrol Capt. R. C. Womack, who conducted a series of the tests in the Thomson and Savannah areas, concluded his findings this way:

"These devices are very demoralizing to the trooper who works the road day after day attempting to enforce the national speed limit. It is also a pathetic situation when a $100 device can counteract a $2,000 piece of equipment being used by law enforcement officers."

The troopers may be down because of the radar warning detectors, but they definitely are not out. They've worked up a trick or two of their own to beat the gadgets.

One of their favorites is to keep the radar speed timer turned off until the driver is well within range and then flick it on.

"The warning device will sound, all right," Wilson grinned. "But it's too late. The driver has already been caught."

And troopers have figured out the Citizens' Band (CB) lingo that goes with the use of radar detectors.

A favorite among truck drivers is, "My bird dogs are barking."

While awaiting legislative action, the troopers are collecting advertisements of the warning gadgets.

"Put a——on your dash and you can drive relaxed again," one ad suggests.

"No watching for radar lurking in the bushes or trying to make sense out of the CB radio chatter," says another. "And you don't have to put up with squeaky bleeps that warn you too late. Now you can enjoy the drive."

Wilson said legislation which the safety department is seeking is similar to laws already passed in the states of Virginia and Connecticut and the cities of Denver, Colo., and Washington, D.C.

Reprinted with permission from *The Atlanta Constitution*, December 31, 1976, p. 1.

EXHIBIT 4 Proposed legislation

H.B. No. 545
By: Representatives Milford of the 13th, Coleman of the 118th, Smith of the 42nd, McDonald of the 12th and Childs of the 51st

A BILL TO BE ENTITLED

AN ACT

To prohibit the use of devices on motor vehicles used to detect the presence of radar upon highways; to prohibit the operation of motor vehicles so

EXHIBIT 4 *(concluded)*

equipped; to prohibit the sale of such devices; to provide for penalties; to provide an effective date; to repeal conflicting laws; and for other purpses.

BE IT ENACTED BY THE GENERAL ASSEMBLY OF GEORGIA:

Section 1.   Prohibiting use of devices on motor vehicles to detect presence of radar upon highways or operation of motor vehicles so equipped or sale of such devices. It shall be unlawful for any person to operate a motor vehicle upon the highways of this State when such vehicle is equipped with any device or mechanism to detect the emission of radio microwaves in the electromagnetic spectrum, which microwaves are employed by police to measure the speed of motor vehicles upon the highways of this State for law enforcement purposes; it shall be unlawful to use any such device or mechanism upon any such motor vehicle upon the highways; it shall be unlawful to sell any such device or mechanism in this State. Provided, however, that the provisions of this section shall not apply to any receiver of radio waves of any frequency lawfully licensed by any State or federal agency.

Section 2.   Any person, firm, or corporation violating the provision of this Act shall be guilty of a misdemeanor and, upon conviction thereof, shall be punished as for a misdemeanor, and any such prohibited device or mechanism shall be forfeited to the court trying the case.

Section 3.   The presence of any such prohibited device or mechanism in or upon a motor vehicle upon the highways of this State shall constitute prima facie evidence of the violation of this section. The State need not prove that the device in question was in an operative condition or being operated.

Section 4.   This section shall not apply to motor vehicles owned by the State or any political subdivision thereof and which are used by the police of any such government nor to law enforcement officers in their official duties, nor to the sale of any such device or mechanism to law enforcement agencies for use in their official duties.

Section 5.   This Act shall become effective upon its approval by the Governor or upon its becoming a law without his approval.

Section 6.   All laws and parts of laws in conflict with this Act are hereby repealed.

duced in the Georgia legislature. Mr. Frolik had read that the Virginia legislature had banned the devices several years earlier, but that the public outcry against such action had been so strong that legislation lifting the ban on radar detectors was under consideration in that state, and had a high likelihood of passing.

Mr. Frolik realized that his vacation was over and that he would have to develop a plan of action for the next few weeks. His first thought was that none of the cases he had studied during his M.B.A. program at a well-known eastern business school had dealt with this type of problem.

Case 35

AUTOCAP*

On November 7, 1977, William Carey, vice chairman of the Georgia Automotive Consumer Action Panel (AUTOCAP), was reviewing files on the five cases to be discussed at AUTOCAP's regular monthly meeting the following day. Carey was one of three consumer representatives on the panel; the other four members of the seven-person panel, including the chairman, were automobile dealers. Each member came to the meetings prepared to discuss each of the cases and to suggest resolutions to the disputes involved.

The five cases to be discussed represented consumer complaints that had not already been successfully resolved by the staff of AUTOCAP. Each month several times this number of cases were successfully resolved by the staff without review by the full panel. In fact, it had been found that about 80 percent of the consumer complaints received by AUTOCAP could be resolved simply by establishing direct communication between the customer and the dealership's owner or general manager (rather than the sales or service departments). More often than not, the dealer was simply unfamiliar with the problem, and customer dissatisfaction could be traced to improper handling by dealership personnel, poor customer-dealership communication, or manufacturer defects.

In addition to reviewing the case files, Carey was reflecting upon the role of AUTOCAP in general, its effectiveness since its inception six months earlier, and consumer awareness of AUTOCAP, issues which he planned to bring up for discussion at the meeting.

History of AUTOCAP

In the past few years there has been rapid expansion in the number of consumer complaints. A variety of alternative complaint resolution mechanisms have been established, including state and local government agencies, trade association organizations such as the Better Business Bureaus and consumer action

---

* This case was coauthored by Sherri McIntyre. Copyright © 1980 by Kenneth L. Bernhardt. Names of consumers and auto dealers in the case have been changed.

panels, private, nonprofit consumer organizations, corporate complaint handling departments, and the President's Office of Consumer Affairs in Washington. At the same time, the number of consumer-oriented bills introduced in Congress and major pieces of consumer legislation enacted by Congress have skyrocketed.

AUTOCAP is an example of the attempt made in several industies (including the automobile, major appliance, and furniture industries) to handle their own consumer complaints by establishing consumer action panels and to reduce thereby the need for government intervention in industry affairs. The first AUTOCAP was introduced as a pilot program in 1973, developed by the National Automobile Dealers Association and the Automotive Trade Association of the Nation's Capital, with the endorsement of the White House Office of Consumer Affairs. The basic objectives of AUTOCAP are:

1. To establish channels at the state and local levels for automotive customers to voice their complaints and obtain action.
2. To take automotive complaints out of the offices of congressmen and federal and state consumer agencies.
3. To demonstrate to government and consumers that automobile dealers can and will resolve customer problems.
4. To promote an improved dealer image, more satisfied customers, and less government interference in the affairs of the retail automobile business.

AUTOCAP strives to make the automotive retailing industry more responsive to the needs and desires of the consuming public and to alleviate the breakdown in communication between business and the public largely responsible for the frustration consumers can experience in today's marketplace.

The Georgia AUTOCAP, established in June 1977, was one of 35 AUTOCAPs throughout the country (22 state organizations and 13 city organizations) in operation by November 1977. Establishment of the Georgia AUTOCAP by the Georgia Automobile Dealers Association in cooperation with the governor's office was met with some opposition. The controversy involved whether an industry can handle its own complaints or if state, local, and federal agencies are better able to resolve these consumer complaints, an issue that has caused a great deal of disagreement.

The major opponent of the Georgia AUTOCAP was the administrator of the governor's Office of Consumer Affairs, who was quoted as claiming that: (1) the panel was an "industry ploy" to dilute the effectiveness of his own agency; (2) if the panel met only once a month and had only one full-time staff member, it could not be effective; (3) the panel would be weighted toward the industry since four of its seven members would come from the automobile dealership business; and (4) information from consumer affairs offices around the country indicated that AUTOCAP did not work. The major proponent of the panel, the governor's chief assistant, argued that business was capable of resolving its own problems and should be encouraged to do so.

Operating Procedures of Georgia AUTOCAP

The Georgia AUTOCAP was established as a free-of-charge community service of the Georgia Automobile Dealers Association for handling complaints concerning its members. An 800 WATS line number was established for calling AUTOCAP toll-free from anywhere in the state of Georgia. Consumers were made aware of AUTOCAP's services mainly by means of brochures available at the dealerships and periodic announcements pertaining to the program released to the public by the Georgia Automobile Dealers Association through news releases sent to the various media.

The AUTOCAP panel was appointed by the president of the Georgia Automobile Dealers Association with the advice and approval of the board of directors. The chairman of the panel was selected from the board of directors and was appointed by the board. The terms of the chairman and each consumer panelist expired on the 31st day of December each year. The dealer members' terms were not specified, but it was expected that their terms would be less than a year to enable more dealers to have experience as a panel member.

The by-laws of the Georgia AUTOCAP stipulate that each of the three consumer panelists "shall be directly affiliated with an organization actively involved in the field of consumerism and shall not be employed in the automobile industry." The vice chairman of the panel was always to be a consumer panelist. Dealer panelists are selected from the approximately 600 members of the Georgia Automobile Dealers Association (GADA).

The chairman of AUTOCAP was assisted in his duties by the executive vice president of GADA and the full-time AUTOCAP staff person, who was responsible for administration of the activities of AUTOCAP and the preparation and dissemination of all communications relating to those activities.

Upon receiving a telephone call from a consumer voicing a complaint, AUTOCAP sent a form to the consumer to register the complaint. When AUTOCAP received the written complaint, it was immediately acknowledged and forwarded to the dealer concerned for a response. Dealers were given a maximum of 15 days to respond to official notification of a complaint from AUTOCAP before the complaint was automatically forwarded to the panel for consideration at its regular monthly meeting.

The staff person officially closed all cases which appeared to be resolved to the satisfaction of both parties, as indicated on a return postcard sent in by the consumer. When the consumer and the dealer could not agree on a satisfactory solution, the problem was referred to the AUTOCAP panel for informal arbitration and mediation. The staff person prepared a complete file on each case for the panel to examine before their regular monthly meeting. Personal interviews and meetings with complainants were not usually conducted by the chairman or any panel member. However, in special cases the complaint was assigned to one member of the panel who investigated the circumstances by meeting with both parties together and reported the case back to the full panel.

At any meeting a total of four panelists constituted a quorum; of this number, two had to be consumer panelists and two had to be dealer panelists. The panel attempted to arrive at recommendations by consensus, which had been possible in virtually all of the cases handled by the full panel since its inception. In the event that a consensus could not be obtained, an "official" AUTOCAP recommendation was determined by a majority vote of those present.

AUTOCAP did not attempt to determine the legal rights of the parties to any dispute and could choose not to attempt to mediate any dispute which had been litigated, was currently in litigation, or in which litigation appeared inevitable. In all instances, AUTOCAP strove to be objective. Under no circumstances was the status or economic condition of any party to a dispute considered relevant in reaching a solution.

The essence of AUTOCAP was the resolution of disputes to the mutual satisfaction of the customer and the dealer. In achieving this goal, all panelists were expressly charged with protecting the confidentiality of all information originating from AUTOCAP. Any panelist could be dismissed at any time for whatever reason if regular panelists determined that such a member was a detriment to the viability of AUTOCAP.

During the first four months of operation, AUTOCAP had closed 91 cases. As shown in Exhibit 1, 58 of these resulted in customer satisfaction, as indicated on the return postcards sent in by the consumers. In only 4 cases did AUTOCAP rule that the complaint was not valid and the desired remedy should be denied. The number of requests for assistance forms had been increasing recently and was expected to continue to increase as "the word got around."

EXHIBIT 1 AUTOCAP status report, October 25, 1977

Customer request for assistance forms mailed on request		229
Customer request for assistance forms not returned		92
Cases closed to customer satisfaction:		
Manufacturer's warranty repairs	21	
Dealer repairs	23	
New car sales	9	
Used car sales	5	
Cases closed—customer satisfaction unknown:		
Vehicle stolen from service lot (insurance claim)	1	
Customer no longer owns vehicle	3	
Customer retained an attorney	4	
Unable to contact consumer	3	
Panel concluded that complaint was not valid	4	
Complaint for record only—no action requested	5	
Dealer not a member of AUTOCAP	2	
Referred complaint to other organizations	11	
	91	91
Pending cases		46
		229

Cases to Be Discussed at the November Meeting

The first case William Carey had to review in preparation for the next day's meeting involved the complaint of one Gene Mitchell concerning the gas mileage he was getting with his new 1976 Mercury Monarch. Mitchell's complaint form and the subsequent correspondence are reproduced in Exhibit 2. In essence, Mitchell claimed that his 6-cylinder Monarch only averaged 12 to 12.5 miles per gallon and that he could not afford a car that got such low gas mileage. In order to solve his problem, he suggested that the dealership replace his 6-cylinder engine with an 8-cylinder engine and stated that he would be willing to pay the difference in the cost of the two engines. A service engineer from the parts and service division of the Ford Motor Company examined and adjusted Mitchell's Monarch but was unable to decrease the gas consumption of the car. In reply to Mitchell's suggestion, John Harris, the dealer's service manager who had been handling the problem stated that such an exchange of engines would not only be economically unfeasible but would possibly be illegal. Harris concluded and wrote AUTOCAP that there was nothing that could be done to increase the gas mileage of this particular automobile or any so equipped.

EXHIBIT 2

CUSTOMER REQUEST FOR ASSISTANCE

AUTOCAP File #00118

Date___8/29/77___

Dealership:__Kimbro Lincoln-Mercury_____

Address:__70 Pine Boulevard, Atlanta, Georgia_____

Customer's name:__Gene Mitchell_____

Address:__2019 Village Circle, #4, Atlanta, Georgia___ Phone:__821-4167___

Make and model car:__Mercury Monarch_____ Year:__1976___

In warranty? Yes ___X___ Factory _____ (check one)
No _____ Used _____

Bought from:__Kimbro Lincoln-Mercury_____ When:__June 1976___

With whom at the dealership have you discussed the problem:
Service manager John Harris and salesman Bob Wilson

Nature of problem:__Averaging 12 mpg to 12.5 mpg. Have been informed by the above gentlemen that the 6-cylinder Mercury Monarchs are overloaded and nothing can be done. I also spoke to a Mr. Jack Kinard, owner of a Lincoln-Mercury dealership known as Kinard's Lincoln-Mercury in Birmingham, Alabama, and he informed me that he will not handle the 6-cylinder Mercury Monarch because of the low miles per gallon. He further stated that in one case he changed carburetors several times and the best mileage he was able to get was 15 mpg on a trip.

NOTE: ATTACH COPIES OF ANY DOCUMENTS YOU FEEL PERTINENT.

EXHIBIT 2 *(continued)*

KIMBRO LINCOLN-MERCURY INC.

70 Pine Boulevard   Phone 226-4000

ATLANTA, GEORGIA 30321

September 1, 1977

Mr. Herman Watkins
Executive Vice President
AUTOCAP
1380 West Paces Ferry Road, N.W.
Atlanta, Georgia 30327

Dear Mr. Watkins:

I am writing in reference to your letter dated the 29th day of August and AUTOCAP File #00118. I am quite familiar with Mr. Gene Mitchell's problem. Initially, let me say that Mr. Mitchell has been extremely patient and cooperative throughout this experience. I hope he feels that we have reciprocated that cooperation.

My experience with this particular model automobile, equipped with a 250 C.I.D. engine, consistently falls short of any mileage estimates. After several attempts on our part to decrease Mr. Mitchell's gas consumption problem, we contacted the representatives of Ford Motor Company's parts and service division. They, in turn, sent Mr. Jack Adams, a service engineer, to examine and adjust as necessary Mr. Mitchell's automobile. After Mr. Adams had worked on the car, there again was no change in the gas consumption.

I contend that there is nothing that can be done to increase the gas mileage of this particular vehicle, or any so equipped. However, I am always open to any suggestions you may be able to offer in this matter.

Sincerely,

John Harris
Service Manager

cc: Mr. Bruce Kimbro
      Mr. Gene Mitchell

EXHIBIT 2 *(continued)*

2019 Village Circle, #4
Atlanta, Georgia 30309
September 12, 1977

Ms. Jean Spears
AUTOCAP
1380 West Paces Ferry Road, N.W.
Atlanta, Georgia 30327

Dear Ms. Spears:

I received a letter from Kimbro Lincoln-Mercury addressed to your Mr. Herman Watkins which indicated that nothing could be done to improve the mileage on my 1976 Mercury Monarch automobile. As I have stated in previous correspondence to the Ford Motor Company, I am perfectly willing to pay the difference in cost between my 6-cylinder and an 8-cylinder model, since I cannot afford a car which gives only 12 miles per gallon.

My car was checked at the Kimbro Mercury dealership by a service engineer for the Lincoln-Mercury parts and service division in order that they might check on the problem of mileage. He also said that nothing could be done to better the gas mileage on this model car.

I would greatly appreciate any assistance you may be able to afford me in this matter.

Very truly yours,

Gene Mitchell

EXHIBIT 2 *(concluded)*

KIMBRO LINCOLN-MERCURY INC.
70 Pine Boulevard   Phone 226–4000
ATLANTA, GEORGIA 30321

October 11, 1977

Ms. Jean Spears
AUTOCAP
1380 West Paces Ferry Road, N.W.
Atlanta, Georgia 30327

Dear Ms. Spears:

I am writing in response to your letter of October 2, 1977. You had enclosed a copy of a letter you received from Mr. Gene Mitchell concerning his 1976 Mercury Monarch.

In the letter Mr. Mitchell mentioned that he would be agreeable to replace his 6-cylinder engine with an 8-cylinder engine and he would pay the difference. Initially, let me say that we are eager to resolve Mr. Mitchell's problems. However, the proposal that you have suggested is not only economically unfeasible but possibly illegal.

The changeover would cost as much as $900 for the new engine alone. Then, in order to meet EPA specifications, new catalytic converters, exhaust pipes, and possibly a new differential would need to be installed.

I hope that I have shed some light on this particular problem and hope that we can work together in order to resolve Mr. Mitchell's problem.

Sincerely,

John Harris
Service Manager

The second case to be discussed at the monthly meeting of AUTOCAP involved the complaint of Dr. Charles Marvin (see Exhibit 3). Marvin had purchased a used 1976 Chevrolet Camaro with 3,914 miles on it for the use of his sons in college. The car was not covered by a warranty. Less than a month after purchase, Marvin's sons were on a weekend trip in the car when they looked out the window and saw the left rear wheel wobbling. Upon inspection, it was discovered that the car had a bent axle, apparently the result of a serious accident. The necessary repairs cost Marvin approximately $350. Although Marvin realized he had purchased the car out of warranty, he felt that the dealership had an obligation to insure that this and other cars were at least safe, and he felt that the dealer should be willing to pay for one half of the damages out of good faith. The dealer replied that although he regretted Marvin's problems he felt no obligation to repair any vehicle sold without a warranty.

EXHIBIT 3

CUSTOMER REQUEST FOR ASSISTANCE

AUTOCAP File #00131
Date: 9/5/77

Dealership: Fussell Volkswagen
Address: 4980 King Drive, Atlanta, Georgia 30216
Customer's name: Dr. Charles Marvin
Address: 747 Shannon Circle, Decatur, Georgia   Phone: 471-9140
Make and model car: Chevrolet Camaro   Year: 1976
In warranty? Yes_____   Factory_____
            No _____   Used   X   (check one)
Bought from: Ben Johnson, salesman at Fussell VW When: July 30, 1977
With whom at the dealership have you discussed the problem:
Ben Johnson and the sales manager (Mike O'Henry)

Nature of problem: The car was bought for my sons to use while attending school at the University of Virginia, Charlottesville, Virginia. The car had very low mileage (3,914 miles) when I bought it. I stated that this was unusual and said, "It hasn't been in a wreck, has it?" Ben Johnson said, "Not that I know of." I drove the car and it performed very well. My sons came home from summer school on the 6th of August and then drove the car back to Charlottesville on the 8th of August. They called me that night to say that they had arrived safely, and they said the car had performed fine; they got 20.2 mpg, etc. They did mention that when they stopped for gas and checked the tires, the left rear wheel lug nuts were loose; they could turn them with their fingers. They tightened them and had no further problem. I just assumed they were not tight to start with. On the 19th of August, I received a call from my sons who were en route to Alexandria, Virginia, for the weekend. They said while driving along the highway, they heard a clicking noise and looked out the window of the car, and the left rear wheel was wobbling. They checked the wheel, and the nuts were so loose they were about to drop off. They again tightened the lug nuts and proceeded 25 miles more to Alexandria, where they took the car to a garage and it was determined that the car had a bent axle. The garage stated that the bent axle had been caused by the car being in a fairly serious accident and proceeded to show my sons the tell-tale signs of repaired body work, etc. In addition, he stated that it would have been evident to anyone who had looked or examined the underside of the car, i.e., bottom was all scraped, gas tank bent, etc. I called Fussell VW on August 19th and informed them of the above. While they were sympathetic, they stressed that they had sold the car to me with no warranty and there was nothing they could do about it. I called them again on August 29th and advised that I was submitting this complaint to the Georgia Automobile Dealers Association. I have presently told my sons to have the car fixed, and the bill is going to be about $350. I feel an automobile dealer has the obligation to insure that a car he sells is at least safe. As the mechanic stated, all they had to do is look under the car, and it would have been immediately apparent that the car had been in a wreck. I feel Fussell should be willing to pay at least half of the costs I have incurred out of good faith. Hope you can help me out.

EXHIBIT 3 *(concluded)*

FUSSELL VOLKSWAGEN, INC.
4980 King Drive   622-9000
ATLANTA, GEORGIA 30216

September 14, 1977

Mr. Herman Watkins
Executive Vice President
AUTOCAP
1380 West Paces Ferry Road, N.W.
Atlanta, Georgia 30327

Dear Mr. Watkins:

This letter is a reply to yours dated September 9, 1977, concerning AUTO-CAP File #00131.

Fussell Volkswagen, Inc., sold the subject vehicle with no warranty, expressed or implied. Dr. Marvin had ample opportunity to check out and drive subject vehicle prior to purchase. We do not offer a warranty of any type on any vehicles except Volkswagens.

We sympathize with Dr. Marvin and regret he has experienced a problem but we do not feel that we have any obligation to repair a vehicle that was sold without a warranty.

Sincerely,
FUSSELL VOLKSWAGEN, Inc.

R. L. Fussell, President

The third case awaiting review by the panel also involved a warranty problem although in this case a limited warranty on the vehicle had been issued and had expired (see Exhibit 4). Jack Cole, president of Cole and Patterson Battery Company, had purchased a used Ford van with 30,073 miles on it for his company. The van was covered by a 30-day or 1,000-mile warranty. Ten days after the warranty expired, the van broke down and required a complete transmission overhaul. Cole contacted both the dealer and Ford Motor Company concerning possible compensation for the repairs. He contended that no Ford van should require a major transmission overhaul 957 miles after purchase. The dealer and the manufacturer were unwilling to pay for any of the repairs, stating that the full extent of their obligation was set forth in the Dealer Limited Warranty accepted by Cole at the time of purchase.

EXHIBIT 4

CUSTOMER REQUEST FOR ASSISTANCE

AUTOCAP File #00180

Date 10/4/77

Dealership: Bow-Mar Ford, Inc.

Address: 4000 Buchanan Highway, Atlanta, Georgia

Customer's name: Cole and Patterson Battery Company (Jack Cole)

Address: 614 Woodside Way, N.E., Conyers, Georgia   Phone: 696-1840

Make and model car: Ford E-100 Van   Year: 1976

In warranty? Yes   X   Factory _____
              No _____ Used   X   (check one)

Bought from: Bow-Mar Ford   When: 5/14/77

With whom at the dealership have you discussed the problem:
Salesman Roger Searcy

Nature of problem: See my letter of October 4, 1977, attached.

NOTE: ATTACH COPIES OF ANY DOCUMENTS YOU FEEL PERTINENT.

EXHIBIT 4 *(continued)*

COLE AND PATTERSON BATTERY COMPANY
614 Woodside Way, N.E.   Conyers, Georgia 30610
Telephone 696-1840

October 4, 1977

AUTOCAP
1380 West Paces Ferry Road, N.W.
Atlanta, Georgia 30327

Dear Sirs:

On May 14, 1977, my firm purchased a used 1976 Ford E-100 van from Bow-Mar Ford in Atlanta. At the time of the purchase there were 30,073 miles on the vehicle. On June 27, 1977, the vehicle was operating in the south Atlanta area and had total transmission failure. I personally called Roger Searcy, our salesman at Bow-Mar, to ask what could or should be done with the van. He advised me, after conferring with others at Bow-Mar, that they could do nothing since the vehicle was legally out of warranty. We then had the vehicle towed to the nearest Ford dealership, Mid-South Ford Truck Sales, Inc., who told us the transmission needed overhauling. I again called Searcy at Bow-Mar to see if they would like to send someone to look at the transmission prior to repairs, and when they declined, repair work was commenced.

On July 5, 1977, I mailed copies of all pertinent documents to Ronald Pickens at Ford's parts and service division and talked with him on the phone concerning possible compensation for the repairs. He told me that the matter would be researched and we should hear something in two or three weeks. A month later Mr. Pickens was again contacted, and he stated that in error he had forwarded the matter to the wrong person or division. Around September 2, 1977, I again contacted Mr. Pickens and was informed that the matter was still in progress. On October 3, 1977, Mr. Pickens was contacted and said that Mr. Bob Bates was now handling the matter. On October 4, 1977, I called and talked with Mr. Bates, who flatly stated that there was no possibility of aid and there never had been. I was left with the feeling after our brief conversation that he had neither researched nor heard of our case. On this same date I called Mr. Pickens again to tell him what had occurred and to ask him what else could be done. He stated that nothing else could be done.

What we are seeking is at least partial compensation for the repairs to the van. I realize that legally the van was 10 days out of warranty, but morally I feel that any Ford van should not require a transmission overhaul 957 miles after it rolls off a Ford dealer's used lot. Thank you in advance for your help in this matter.

Sincerely,

Jack Cole, President

EXHIBIT 4 *(continued)*

BOW-MAR FORD, INC.
4000 Buchanan Highway
ATLANTA, GEORGIA 30609
(404) 942–1900

October 28, 1977

AUTOCAP
Georgia Automobile Dealers Association
1380 West Paces Ferry Road, N.W.
Atlanta, Georgia 30327

Gentlemen:

Enclosed is a copy of the "Dealer Limited Warranty" which Mr. Jack Cole of Cole and Patterson Battery Company signed and accepted at the time of purchase of his vehicle.

Since our position is fully stated on the enclosed document, it would seem that no further reply would be required.

Very truly yours,
BOW-MAR FORD, INC.

Enclosure   Robert H. Bower, President

EXHIBIT 4 *(continued)*

DEALER LIMITED WARRANTY

ODOMETER MILEAGE ON DATE OF VEHICLE SALE __30,073__ VEHICLE SALE DATE __5/14/77__ DEALER: (WARRANTOR) __Bow-Mar Ford, Inc.__ ADDRESS: __4000 Buchanan Highway, Atlanta__ PURCHASER: __Cole and Patterson Battery Company__ ADDRESS: 614 Woodside Way, N.E. Conyers DEALER SELLS TO PURCHASER THE VEHICLE BELOW IDENTIFIED SUBJECT TO THE FOLLOWING TERMS AND CONDITIONS:

VEHICLE INFORMATION

MAKE __Ford__   SERIAL NUMBER __F02AMD48011__

YEAR __1976__   MODEL __E-100 Van__

1. Persons Capable of Enforcing the Limited Warranty. Dealer extends this warranty to any person who may reasonably be expected to use, or be affected by the goods, and who is injured by breach of the warranty.

2. Parts Covered by the Limited Warranty. The following parts are covered by this warranty, but only if their defect or malfunction is caused by a mechanical breakdown or failure (defined as inability of any covered part to perform its designed function) and only to the extent provided for in section 3.

A. Engine, including: Cylinder block Head Internal parts Water pump Intake manifold	B. Transmission, including: Case Internal parts Torque converter	C. Rear axle, including: Differential Internal parts

D. Propeller shaft, including: E. Other parts covered: __N.A.__
Universal joints

3. Percentage of Repair Costs Covered. This warranty covers __50%__ of the total costs (parts and labor) for repairs under sections 2A, 2B, 2C, and 2D; and covers __N.A.__ % of the total costs (parts and labor) for repairs under section 2E.

4. Exclusions from the Warranty: All parts and systems that are not included in section 2 above are excluded from coverage under this warranty. Any malfunction resulting from failure to perform periodic maintenance in accordance with manufacturer's recommendations is excluded from this warranty. Any damage resulting to the vehicle that is not caused from a defect or malfunction is also excluded from this warranty.

5. Dealer's Obligations. During the period of this limited warranty (see section 6 below), Dealer will repair the parts as provided in section 2 above, and the only cost to Purchase for these repairs will be the balance of the percentage amounts stated in section 3 above of the total repair costs (parts and labor), plus applicable sales taxes.

6. Period of the Warranty.

A. The warranty coverage commences on the delivery date of the vehicle and extends to __30__ days after the delivery date, or for __1,000__ miles beyond the odometer reading, whichever occurs sooner.

7. Obligations of the Purchaser.

A. Purchaser shall give notice to Dealer of any breach of contract or breach of express or implied warranty applicable to the goods within __twenty__

EXHIBIT 4 *(concluded)*

(20)   days after the notice of breach to allow the seller the opportunity to cure the said breach or the Purchaser shall be barred from any remedy for the breach.

   B.   Purchaser must authorize the Dealer to make the repairs, and Purchaser must, upon redelivery of the repaired vehicle to Purchaser, pay the balance of the percentage amounts stated in section 3 above of the total repair costs (parts and labor), plus applicable sales taxes.

   C.   If Purchaser is dissatisfied because he feels that Dealer has failed to conform to this warranty, he should contact:

   Philip Sanderson   Phone Number   404/942–1900

at Dealer's above address.

IMPORTANT

   8.   *Limitations on Implied Warranties and Exclusions as to Consequential Damages and Incidental Damages.* ALL IMPLIED WARRANTIES, INCLUDING THE IMPLIED WARRANTIES OF MERCHANTABILITY AND FITNESS FOR A PARTICULAR PURPOSE, ARE HEREBY LIMITED TO THE SAME DURATION OF TIME AS THE EXPRESS WRITTEN WARRANTY ABOVE STATED. PURCHASER SHALL NOT BE ENTITLED TO RECOVER FROM THE SELLING DEALER ANY CONSEQUENTIAL DAMAGES, DAMAGES TO PROPERTY, DAMAGES FOR LOSS OF USE, LOSS OF TIME, LOSS OF PROFITS, OR INCOME, OR ANY OTHER INCIDENTAL DAMAGES, EXCEPT IN JURISDICTIONS WHERE THE PROVISIONS OF ANY LAW PROHIBIT OR MAKE UNCONSCIONABLE THESE LIMITATIONS, AND THEN THAT PORTION OF THESE LIMITATIONS WHICH IS PROHIBITED OR DECLARED TO BE UNCONSCIONABLE SHALL BE OF NO EFFECT. SOME STATES DO NOT ALLOW LIMITATIONS ON HOW LONG AN IMPLIED WARRANTY LASTS, SO THE ABOVE LIMITATION MAY NOT APPLY TO YOU. SOME STATES DO NOT ALLOW THE EXCLUSION OR LIMITATION OF INCIDENTAL OR CONSEQUENTIAL DAMAGES, SO THE ABOVE LIMITATION OR EXCLUSION MAY NOT APPLY TO YOU.

   9.   Purchaser's Legal Rights. This warranty gives you specific legal rights, and you may also have other rights which vary from state to state.

   10.   Limited Warranty. This is limited warranty. It is not a service contract.

   There is no other express warranty on this vehicle, and there is no agreement between Purchaser and Dealer relating to repairs of the vehicle except as set forth in this warranty.

   Purchaser acknowledges that he has read, understands and accepts all of the provisions of the warranty statement covering the used vehicle above identified.

5/14/77	/s/ Jack Cole
Date	Purchaser's Signature
/s/ Roger Searcy	/s/ Robert H. Bower
Witness	Dealer's Signature
	(not valid unless signed by Dealer or his authorized representative)

The fourth case involved service performed on Mrs. Lynn Luxemburger's 1973 Lincoln-Continental. Pertinent correspondence is reproduced in Exhibit 5. Mrs. Luxemburger left her car for servicing at the dealership, along with a list of items needing repair, and asked that she be provided an estimate. After the car was checked, it was determined that repairs costing in the neighborhood of $1,000 were needed. The dealer claims that Mrs. Luxemburger authorized the service department to proceed with the most needed repairs, not to exceed $500–$520. Mrs. Luxemburger denies this, claiming that she never authorized the $500 and was expecting the repairs to be around $300–$350. Furthermore, she says that she only authorized the repairs on her list, plus one additional repair authorized over the phone, and not the "most needed repairs" at the discretion of the service department. She also claims that much of the work she was charged for was not done. Mrs. Luxemburger's car broke down before she got home the day she picked it up from the dealership. She contends this was

EXHIBIT 5

CUSTOMER REQUEST FOR ASSISTANCE

AUTOCAP File #00072

Date   7/1/77

Dealership: Haverty Lincoln-Mercury Sales Inc.
Address: 2450 Peachtree Road, N.E., Atlanta, Georgia 30302
Customer's name: Mrs. Lynn Luxemburger
Address: 443 Janice Drive, Stone Mountain, GA 30348   Phone: 996–0619
Make and model car: 1973 Lincoln Continental Towncar   Year: 1973

| | Yes ____ | Factory ____ | (check one) |
| In warranty: | No   X | Used ____ | |

Bought from: Venture Lincoln-Mercury Co., Spartanburg, S.C. When: 1973
With whom at the dealership have you discussed the problem: Neil Simpson, service advisor, and Mr. Green, sales manager, at Haverty Lincoln-Mercury
Nature of problem: I left my car at Haverty Lincoln-Mercury for service on May 30, 1977, along with a written list of things to be done, which I gave to the service advisor, Mr. Simpson. Although I had an appointment for the work to be done and was promised one day service, I had to wait a week before my car was ready. My car broke down on my way home from the service department. Furthermore, I was charged for things that were not done and that I did not authorize instead of the work I requested. My car is in worse condition now than when I brought it in. I recommend that someone from AUTOCAP examine my car to demonstrate that my charges are true, that the entire service bill be canceled, and that Haverty Lincoln-Mercury pay me for the hardship and inconveniences caused me by their negligence and inferior workmanship. I do not intend to carry my car back to Haverty for anything.

NOTE: ATTACH COPIES OF ANY DOCUMENTS YOU FEEL PERTINENT.

due to the negligence and inferior workmanship of the service department; the service department believes that the breakdown was probably caused by the need for further alternator repairs that could not be made under the $500 limitation. AUTOCAP's file included several letters containing accounts of a number of subsequent contacts between the dealership and Mrs. Luxemburger that had been unsuccessful in clearing up the differences of opinion and fact discrepancies reported above. In settlement of her claim, Mrs. Luxemburger felt that the dealership should cancel the service bill and also should pay her for the inconveniences and hardship it had caused her.

EXHIBIT 5 *(continued)*

HAVERTY LINCOLN-MERCURY SALES, INC.
Telephone 821–6111   2450 Peachtree Road, N.E.
Atlanta, Georgia 30302

August 2, 1977

Georgia Automobile Dealers Association
1380 West Paces Ferry Road, N.W.
Atlanta, Georgia 30327

Attention: AUTOCAP

Gentlemen:

We have received your letters dated July 8 and 22, 1977 regarding a consumer complaint filed by Mrs. Lynn Luxemburger (AUTOCAP File #00072). The delay in responding to your letters has been occasioned by the fact that we have not been able to get Mrs. Luxemburger to bring her car in or to let us have it towed in. We enclose a report filed by our service manager concerning our contacts with Mrs. Luxemburger.

We feel that we have acted diligently and in good faith in our efforts to resolve this complaint. We stand ready to answer any questions Mrs. Luxemburger may have at any time; our offer to have the car brought into our dealership to be checked by the several consumer affairs representatives she has contacted, along with our mechanic, is still open.

If Mrs. Luxemburger is not willing to meet us halfway or even part way in the interest of resolving this problem, we are prepared to defend whatever legal action she may take.

Sincerely,

G. M. Marvin
Executive Vice President and
General Manager

cc: Office of Consumer Affairs
      (Attention: Mr. Sumner)

EXHIBIT 5 (continued)

Mr. Ralph Bumgarner
WXTM—Atlanta

TO WHOM IT MAY CONCERN:

On May 30, 1977, Mrs. Lynn Luxemburger brought her 1973 Lincoln to Haverty for service. When she brought the car in, Mrs. Luxemburger requested that we check the car over and provide her with an estimate. She provided a list of items she felt needed to be done, as listed below:

Rear end bumpy
Using lots of oil
Power steering does not seem to work
Repair right rear arm rest
Brakes squeak
Check exterior lights, both front and rear
Check windshield washer fluid
Check starter

After checking the car, it was discovered that the following items needed to be done:

Shock absorbers
Upper inner shaft bushings
Power steering pump and steering gear
Brake job
Alternator
Fuel pump
Hoses
Alignment

Mrs. Luxemburger was called and advised of these repair needs and that these repairs alone would involve a repair bill of approximately $991. She authorized us to proceed with the most needed repairs with the stipulation we not exceed $500–$520.

Accordingly, we proceeded and performed the following repairs:

Replaced upper inner shaft bushings
Adjusted steering gear preload
Completed brake job
Replaced bearing on alternator (*)
Replaced fuel pump
Replaced all hoses and flushed system
Aligned wheels

(*) A notation was made on the repair order by the mechanic that the alternator still needed a stator and rotor; however, this was not done due to limitations placed on the repair bill to be incurred.

EXHIBIT 5 *(continued)*

The total repair bill for the work performed was $527.57, which Mrs. Luxemburger paid when she picked up her car on July 5, 1977. On the same day she called and stated that her car had stopped running—which was probably the result of the faulty alternator, although we cannot be sure because Mrs. Luxemburger has not permitted us to bring the car back in to our shop. Mrs. Luxemburger was told to have the car towed back to Haverty, and that if we had done something wrong we would pay the towing bill and would make the repair at no charge, but that if the cause was due to the *additional* work needed to be done, she would be responsible for the repair charges. I then gave her the number of our towing service. Later in the day Mrs. Luxemburger called and said she had taken the car to a service station and that *none* of the things she had paid for had been done. I told her I would like to verify this for myself and again asked her to have the car towed to Haverty, reminding her that an additional $500 in repairs was still necessary to put the car in good condition. She had been forewarned by the service writer and the mechanic that she could possibly have problems. She said that she was going to contact some consumer groups and file a legal action and that she would never bring her car back to Haverty Lincoln-Mercury. I replied that we would be perfectly willing to have her car checked at our dealership with whatever consumer representatives she desired present. Since that time, we have tried unsuccessfully on numerous occasions to meet with Mrs. Luxemburger and to resolve this complaint.

Neil Simpson
Service Manager

EXHIBIT 5 *(concluded)*

443 Janice Drive
Stone Mountain, Georgia 30348
August 8, 1977

AUTOCAP
Georgia Automobile Dealers Association
1380 West Paces Ferry Road, N.W., Suite 230
Atlanta, Georgia 30327

RE: AUTOCAP File #00072

Gentlemen:

Thank you for your letter of August 4 and the information therein.

The accounts given by Mr. Simpson and Mr. Marvin are inadequate and filled with half-truths and nontruths. My complaint is a simple one. I feel that I have been charged for parts and services allegedly done on my car which I did not authorize. The work which I authorized was submitted to the service department by me in written form at the time I left my car for service, with the exception of the alternator, which I authorized by telephone. In addition, I have been charged for work which was not done. The starter is an example. I was specifically told that the starter had been repaired when I picked the car up. The car stalled on me before I could get home from Haverty Lincoln-Mercury on July 5 with the same starter problem.

When I left my car, I was told specifically that a rough estimate of the repairs on my list would be approximately $300–$350. A couple of days later I called and was told my car was not ready; even at that time I was not told that the car would be over $500. My first knowledge of this amount was when I went to pick the car up on Tuesday, July 5.

I do not see how my car could possibly have needed $1,000 of work since it is a one-owner car, and I have always had it serviced in accordance with the manual and by a Lincoln-Mercury dealership.

Mr. Marvin did invite me to his office to discuss the matter. As I told him then, transportation is a problem for me. I have been without the use of my car now for over a month.

I am willing to have the car inspected by any impartial inspector, but I will not take it back to Haverty Lincoln-Mercury. I do hope you will put my case on the agenda for your next meeting and appreciate the interest you have put forth in trying to work out a solution to this frustrating problem.

Respectfully,

Lynn Luxemburger (Mrs.)

The last case is somewhat different from the rest in that it involved a complaint alleging deceptive and misleading advertising (see Exhibit 6). Ben Harrell, the complainant, had seen a newspaper advertisement advertising a new 1978 F–100 pickup truck for only $3,395. Harrell had been comparing prices on the F–100 pickup, and $3,395 was considerably lower than anything he had seen elsewhere. For this reason Harrell went to Stokes Ford the following day planning to purchase the truck. As he examined the sticker price on the truck at the dealership, Harrell noticed a list price of $3,895, rather than the $3,395 he had seen in the ad. When he asked a salesman about this, it was pointed out that the $3,395 did not include the $500 down payment and that the cash price listed in the ad was $3,895 rather than $3,395. Harrell did not purchase the truck. However, he filed a complaint with AUTOCAP claiming

EXHIBIT 6

CUSTOMER REQUEST FOR ASSISTANCE

AUTOCAP File #00194

Dealership: Stokes Ford, Inc.

Address: 7280 Russell Road, Atlanta, Georgia

Customer's name: Ben F. Harrell

Address: 929 Rosedale Avenue, Atlanta Georgia 30308   Phone: 862-0126

Make and model car: Ford F–100 Pickup   Year: 1978

In warranty?   Yes _____   Factory _____   (check one)
No _____   Used _____

Bought from: Not Applicable   When: _____

With whom at the dealership have you discussed the problem:
Charlie Stikeleather, salesman

Nature of problem: I went to Stokes Ford on Monday, October 9, 1977, planning to purchase a 1978 F–100 pickup I had seen advertised in the Sunday paper (10/8) for $3,395; a copy of the advertisement is attached. I had been shopping around, and this price was quite a bit lower than any I had seen. At the dealership I was examining the items included on the sticker on the truck when I noticed a list price of $3,895, rather than the $3,395 I had seen advertised. When I asked a salesman about this, I was informed that the $3,395 price did not include the $500 down payment and that I had misread the ad. It was pointed out to me by Mr. Stikeleather that the cash price of the truck included in the ad was $3,895. This price was included in the *fine print.* In my opinion, this ad clearly says, "You pay only $3,395." I do not as a habit read the fine print in advertisements, nor do I believe that this is where important facts should be revealed. I feel this type of advertising is misleading and ought to be stopped. I would not do business with a company that uses such deceptive practices. I believe AUTOCAP's review of this matter is warranted.

NOTE: ATTACH COPIES OF ANY DOCUMENTS YOU FEEL PERTINENT.

EXHIBIT 6 *(continued)*

STOKES FORD, INC.
7280 Russell Road, Atlanta, Georgia 30601
404/759–9050

October 23, 1977

Mr. Herman Watkins
Executive Director
AUTOCAP
1380 West Paces Ferry Road, N.W.
Atlanta, Georgia 30327

Dear Mr. Watkins:

This is in response to your letter of October 19, 1977, concerning the complaint of Mr. Ben Harrell. Mr. Harrell questions our advertising practices, in particular the advertisement we included in the *Atlanta Journal* on Sunday, October 8, 1977, a copy of which is already in your file.

We disagree that this advertisement is in any way deceptive. The terms advertised of "$500 down" are in very large print at the top of the ad, and the cash price clearly reads $3,895. Mr. Harrell obviously misread the ad; we have had no other problems or misunderstandings concerning it.

Please don't hesitate to call me at 759-9050 if you have any further questions in this regard.

Sincerely,

Kenneth Stokes

that such advertising was misleading and should not be permitted. Stokes Ford replied to AUTOCAP that its advertisement was not deceptive, that all of the information was included in the advertisement, and that Harrell had simply misinterpreted it.

EXHIBIT 6 *(concluded)*

Case 36

Nestlé and the Infant Food Controversy (A)*

In October 1978, Dr. Fürer, managing director of Nestlé S.A., headquartered in Vevey, Switzerland was pondering the continuing problems his company faced. Public interest groups, media, health organizations, and other groups had been pressuring Nestlé to change its marketing practices for infant formula products, particularly in developing countries. Those groups had used a variety of pressure tactics, including consumer boycott in the United States over the past eight years. Critics of Nestlé charged that the company's promotional practices not only were abusive but also harmful, resulting in malnutrition and death in some circumstances. They demanded Nestlé put a stop to all promotion of its infant formula products both to consumers and health personnel.

Nestlé management had always prided itself on its high quality standards, its efforts to serve the best interests of Nestlé customers, and its contribution to the health and prosperity of people in developing countries. Nestlé management was convinced their infant formula products were useful and wanted; they had not taken the first signs of adverse publicity in the early 1970s very seriously. By 1978, massive adverse publicity appeared to be endangering the reputation of the company, particularly in Europe and North America. Despite support from some health officials and organizations throughout the world, Nestlé Management in Vevey and White Plains, New York (U.S.A. headquarters) were seriously concerned. Dr. Fürer had been consulting with Mr. Guerrant, President of Nestlé U.S.A. in an effort to formulate a strategy. Of immediate concern to Nestlé Management was the scheduled meeting of the National Council of Churches (USA) in November 1978. On the agenda was a resolution to support the critics of Nestlé who were leading the consumer boycott against

* This case was written by Aylin Kunt, research assistant under the supervision of Professors Christopher Gale and George Taucher in 1979. The earlier work of Professor James Kuhn of Columbia University is gratefully acknowledged. This version is a substantial revision of the earlier case and was prepared by Professor Michael R. Pearce. Copyright © 1981 by l'Institut pour l'Etude des Methodes de Direction de l'Enterprise (IMEDE), Lausanne, Switzerland and The School of Business Administration, University of Western Ontario, London, Ontario, Canada. It is intended for classroom discussion and is not intended as an illustration of good or bad management practices.

Nestlé products in the United States. The National Council of Churches was an important, prestigious organization which caused Nestlé management to fear that NCC support of the boycott might further endanger Nestlé.

Also of concern was the meeting of the World Health Organization (WHO) scheduled in the fall of 1979 to bring together the infant food manufacturers, public interest groups, and the world health community in an attempt to formulate a code of marketing conduct for the industry. Nestlé management, instrumental in establishing this conference, hoped that a clear set of standards would emerge, thus moderating or eliminating the attacks of the public pressure groups.

Dr. Fürer was anxious to clear up what he thought were misunderstandings about the industry. As he reviewed the history of the formula problem, he wondered in general what a company could do when subjected to pressure tactics by activist groups, and in particular, what Nestlé management should do next.

Nestlé Alimentana S.A.

The Swiss-based Nestlé Alimentana S.A. was one of the largest food products companies in the world. Nestlé had 80,000 shareholders in Switzerland. Nestlé's importance to Switzerland was comparable to the combined importance of General Motors and Exxon to the United States. In 1977, Nestlé's worldwide sales approximated 20 billion Swiss francs. Of this total, 7.3 percent were infant and dietetic products; more specifically, 2.5 percent of sales were accounted for by infant formula sales in developing countries.

Traditionally a transnational seller of food products, Nestlé's basic goal had always been to be a fully integrated food processor in every country in which it operated. It aimed at maintaining an important market presence in almost every nation of the world. In each country, Nestlé typically established local plants, supported private farms and dairy herds and sold a wide range of products to cover all age groups. By the end of 1977, Nestlé had 87 factories in the developing countries and provided 35,610 direct jobs. Nestlé management was proud of this business approach and published a 228-page book in 1975 entitled *Nestlé in Developing Countries*. The cover of this book carried the following statement:

> While Nestlé is not a philanthropic society, facts and figures clearly prove that the nature of its activities in developing countries is self-evident as a factor that contributes to economic development. The company's constant need for local raw materials, processing, and staff, and the particular contribution it brings to local industry, support the fact that Nestlé's presence in the Third World is based on common interests in which the progress of one is always to the benefit of the other.

Although it neither produced nor marketed infant formula in the United States, the Nestlé Company, Inc. (White Plains) sold a variety of products such as Nescafé, Nestea, Crunch, Quik, Taster's Choice, and Libby and McNeil & Libby products throughout the United States.

With over 95 percent of Nestlé's sales outside of Switzerland, the company had developed an operating policy characterized by strong central financial control along with substantial freedom in marketing strategy by local managers. Each country manager was held responsible for profitability. Through periodic planning meetings, Nestlé management in Vevey ("the Centre") reviewed the broad strategy proposals of local companies. One area of responsibility clearly reserved by Vevey was the maintenance of the overall company image, although no formal public relations department existed. Marketing plans were reviewed in part by Vevey to see if they preserved the company's reputation for quality and service throughout the world.

Nestlé and the Infant Formula Industry

The international infant formula industry was composed of two types of firms, pharmaceutically oriented ones and food processing ones. The major companies competing in the developing countries were as follows:

Company	Brands
A. Pharmaceutical	
(U.S.) Wyeth Lab (American Home Products)	SMA, S26, Nursoy
(U.S.) Ross Lab (Abbott Laboratories)	Similac, Isomil
(U.S.) Mead Johnson (Bristol-Myers)	Enfamil, Olac, Prosobee
B. Food processing	
(U.S.) Borden	New Biolac
(Swit.) Nestlé	Nestogen, Eledon, Pelargon Nan, Lactogen
(U.K.) Unigate	

In addition to these six firms, there were about another dozen formula producers chartered in 1978 throughout the world.

The basic distinction between pharmaceutically oriented formula producers and food processing oriented producers lay in their entry point into the formula business. In the early 1900s, medical research laboratories of major pharmaceutical firms developed "humanized formulas," leading their parents into marketing such products. Essentially, a humanized formula was a modification of normal cow's milk to approximate more closely human milk. Generally speaking, the food processing companies had begun offering infant food as an extension of their full milk powdered products and canned milk.

As early as the 1800s, Nestlé had been engaged in research in the field of child nutrition. In 1867, Henri Nestlé, the founder of the company and the great-grandfather of infant formula, introduced the first specifically designed, commercially marketed infant weaning formula. An infant weaning formula is basically a cereal and milk mixture designed to introduce solids to a child of five–six months of age.

As of the 1860s, both Nestlé and Borden had been producing sweetened and evaporated milk. Nestlé very quickly recognized the need for better artificial infant food and steadily developed a full line of formula products in the early 1900s (for example, Lactogen in 1921, Eledon in 1927, Nestogen in 1930). Although it was a food processing company, Nestlé's product development and marketing were supervised by physicians.

In the United States in the early 1900s, the infant formula products developed by the medical laboratories were being used primarily in hospitals. Over time, the industry developed the distinction of formula products for "well babies" versus for "sick babies." In the latter category would be included special nutritional and dietary problems, such as allergies to milk requiring babies to have totally artificial formulas made from soybeans. Approximately 2 percent of industry volume was formula designed for "sick babies."

In the late 19th century and early years of the 20th century, Nestlé had developed a commanding position in the sweetened and evaporated milk market in the developing countries (also referred to as "the Third World"). Demand for these products was initially established among European colonials and gradually spread throughout the world and into the rising middle classes in many nations. Nestlé's early marketing efforts focused on switching infant feeding from the previously common use of sweetened and condensed milk to a more appropriate product, humanized infant formula.

By promoting a full product line through doctors (medical detailing), Nestlé achieved an overwhelmingly dominant market position in the European colonies, countries which later became independent "Third World" countries. Meanwhile, most of the competition developed quickly in the industrialized countries, so much so that Nestlé stayed out of the U.S. formula market entirely. Only late in the 1950s did significant intense competition, mainly from American multinationals, develop in Nestlé's markets in developing countries. These markets with their high birth rates and rising affluence became increasingly attractive to all formula producers. After the entry of American competitors, Nestlé's share of markets began to erode.

As of 1978, Nestlé accounted for about one third to one half of infant formula sales in the developing countries while American companies held about one fifth. The size of the total world market for infant formula was not exactly known because data on shipments of infant formula were not separated from other milk products, especially powders. Some sources guesstimated world sales to be close to $1.5 billion (U.S.), half of that to developing countries.

Traditional Methods of Promotion

Several methods had been used over the years to promote infant products in developing countries. Five major methods predominated:

1. Media advertising—all media types were employed including posters in clinics and hospitals, outdoor billboards, newspapers, magazines, radio, television, and loudspeakers on vans. Native languages and English were used.

2. Samples—free sample distribution either direct to new mothers or via doctors was relatively limited until competition increased in the 1960s. Mothers were given either formula or feeding bottles or both, often in a "new mother's kit." Doctors in clinics and hospitals received large packages of product for use while mother and baby were present. The formula producers believed this practice helped educate new mothers on the use of formula products, and hopefully, initiated brand preference. In some instances, doctors actually resold samples to provide an extra source of income for themselves or their institutions.

3. Booklets—most formula marketers provided new mothers with booklets on baby care which were given free to them when they left the hospitals and clinics with their newborn infants. These booklets, such as Nestlé's *A Life Begins,* offered a variety of advice and advertised the formula products and other infant foods, both Nestlé and home made.

4. Milk nurses—milk nurses (also known as mothercraft nurses) were formula producer employees who talked with new mothers in the hospitals and clinics or at home. Originally, they were all fully-trained nurses, instructed in product knowledge, then sent out to educate new mothers on the correct use of the new formula products. This instruction included the importance of proper personal hygiene, boiling the water, and mixing formula and water in correct quantities. These became a major part of many firms' efforts; for example, at one time Nestlé had about 200 mothercraft employees worldwide. The majority of milk nurses were paid a straight salary plus a travel allowance, but over time, some were hired on a sales-related bonus basis. Some companies, other than Nestlé, began to relax standards in the 1960s and hired nonnursing personnel who dressed in nurses' uniforms and acted more in a selling capacity and less in an educational capacity.

5. Milk banks—milk bank was the term used to describe a special distribution outlet affiliated with and administered by those hospitals and clinics which served very low income people. Formula products were provided to low income families at much reduced prices for mothers who could not afford the commercial product. The producers sold products to those outlets at lower prices to enable this service to occur.

PAG 23

Nestlé management believed the controversy surrounding the sale of infant formula in developing countries began in the early 1970s. Many international organizations were concerned about the problem of malnourishment of infants in the developing countries of South Asia, Africa, and Latin America. In Bogota (1970) and Paris (1972), representatives of the Food and Agricultural

Organization (FAO), the World Health Organization (WHO), UNICEF, the International Pediatric Association, and the infant formula industry including Nestlé all met to discuss nutrition problems and guidelines. The result was a request that the United Nations Protein-Calorie Advisory Group (PAG), an organization formed in 1955, set guidelines for nutrition for infants. On July 18, 1972, the PAG issued Statement 23 on the "Promotion of special foods for vulnerable groups." This statement emphasized the importance of breast-feeding, the danger of over-promotion, the need to take local conditions into account, the problem of misuse of formula products, and the desirability of reducing promotion but increasing education.

Statement 23 included the following statements:

> Breast milk is an optimal food for infants and, if available in sufficient quantities it is adequate as the sole source of food during the first four to six months of age.
>
> Poor health and adverse social circumstances may decrease the output of milk by the mother . . . in such circumstances supplementation of breast milk with nutritionally adequate foods must start earlier than four to six months if growth failure is to be avoided.
>
> It is clearly important to avoid any action which would accelerate the trend away from breast-feeding.
>
> It is essential to make available to the mother, the foods, formulas, and instructions which will meet the need for good nutrition of those infants who are breast-fed.

Nestlé management regarded PAG 23 as an "advisory statement," so management's stance was to see what happened. None of the developing countries took any action on the statement. Nestlé officials consulted with ministers of health in many developing countries to ask what role their governments wished Nestlé to play in bringing nutrition education to local mothers. No major changes were requested.

At the same time, Nestlé Vevey ordered an audit of marketing practices employed by its companies in the developing nations. Based on reports from the field, Nestlé Management in Vevey concluded that only a few changes in marketing were required which they ordered be done. In Nigeria, the Nigerian Society of Health and Nutrition asked Nestlé to change its ads for formula to stress breast-feeding. Nestlé complied with this request, and its ads in all developing countries prominently carried the phrase "when breast milk fails, use . . ."

The British Contribution

In its August 1973 issue, the *New Internationalist,* an English journal devoted to problems in developing countries, published an article entitled "The Baby Food Tragedy." This was an interview with two doctors: Dr. R. G. Hendrikse, Director of the Tropical Child Health Course, Liverpool University, and medical researcher in Rhodesia, Nigeria, and South Africa and Dr. David Morley, Reader in Tropical Child Health, University of London. Both doctors expressed concern with the widespread use of formula among impoverished, less literate families. They claimed that in such cases, low family incomes prevented mothers from buying the necessary amount of formula for their children. Instead, they used smaller quantities of formula powder, diluting it with more water than recommended. Further, the water used was frequently contaminated. The infant thus received less than adequate nutrition, indeed often was exposed to contaminated formula. The malnourished child became increasingly susceptible to infections, leading to diarrheal diseases. Diarrhea meant the child could assimilate even less of the nutrients given to him because neither his stomach nor intestines were working properly. This vicious cycle could lead to death. The two doctors believed that local conditions made the use of commercial infant formula not only unnecessary, but likely difficult and dangerous. Breastfeeding was safer, healthier, and certainly less expensive.

The article, in the opinion of many, was relatively restrained and balanced. However, it was accompanied by dramatic photographs of malnourished black babies and of a baby's grave with a tin of milk powder placed on it. The article had a strong emotional impact on readers and reached many people who were not regular readers of the journal. It was widely reprinted and quoted by other groups. The journal sent copies of the article to more than 3,000 hospitals in the developing nations.

The two doctors interviewed for the article had mentioned Nestlé and its promotional practices. Accordingly, the editors of the *New Internationalist* contacted Nestlé S.A. for its position. The company response was published in the October issue of the *New Internationalist* along with an editorial entitled "Milk and Murder."

Nestlé S.A. responded in part as follows:

> We have carefully studied both the editorial and the interviews with Dr. Hendrickse and Dr. Morley published in the August edition of the *New Internationalist*. Although fleeting references are made to factors other than manufacturers' activities which are said to be responsible for the misuse of infant foods in developing countries, their readers would certainly not be in a position to judge from the report the immense socioeconomic complexities of the situation. . . .
>
> It would be impossible to demonstrate in the space of a letter the enormous efforts made by the Nestlé organization to ensure the correct usage of their infant food products, and the way in which the PAG guidelines have been applied by the Nestlé subsidiaries. However, if the editor of the *New Internationalist* (or the author of the article in question) wishes to establish the complete facts as far as we are concerned, then we should be happy to receive him in Vevey on a mutually agreeable date in the near future. We should certainly welcome the opportunity to reply to some of the sweeping allegations made against Nestlé either by implication or by specific references.

The editor of the *New Internationalist* refused the invitation to visit Nestlé's Vevey headquarters. Further they maintained that PAG 23 guidelines were not being observed and did not have any provisions for enforcement.

In March 1974, War on Want published a pamphlet entitled *The Baby Killer*. War on Want was a private British group established to give aid to Third World nations. In particular, they were devoted "to make world poverty an urgent social and political issue." War on Want issued a set of recommendations to industry, governments, the medical profession, and others to deal with the baby formula problem as they saw it. See Exhibit 1.

EXHIBIT 1 War on Want's recommendations

Industry
1. The serious problems caused by early weaning onto breast milk substitutes demand a serious response. Companies should follow the Swedish example and refrain from all consumer promotion of breast milk substitutes in high risk communities.
2. The companies should cooperate constructively with the international organisations working on the problems of infant and child nutrition in the developing countries.
3. Companies should abandon promotions to the medical profession which may perform the miseducational function of suggesting that particular brands of milk can overcome the problems of misuse.

Governments of developing countries
1. Governments should take note of the recommendations of the Protein Advisory Group for national nutrition strategies.
2. Where social and economic conditions are such that proprietary infant foods can make little useful contribution, serious consideration should be given to the curtailment of their importation, distribution, and/or promotion.
3. Governments should ensure that supplies are made available first to those in need—babies whose mothers cannot breast feed, twins, orphans, etc.—rather than to an economic elite, a danger noted by the PAG.

British Government
1. The British Government should exercise a constructive influence in the current debate.
2. The Government should insist that British companies such as Unigate and Glaxo set a high standard of behaviour and it should be prepared to enforce a similar standard on multinationals like Wyeth who export to developing country markets from Britain.
3. The British representative on the Codex Alimentarius Commission should urge the commission to consider all aspects of the promotion of infant foods. If necessary, structural alterations should be proposed to set up a subcommittee to consider broader aspects of promotion to enable the commission to fulfill its stated aims of protecting the consumer interests.

Medical profession
There is a need in the medical profession for a greater awareness of the problems caused by artificial feeding of infants and of the role of the medical profession in encouraging the trend away from breast-feeding.

EXHIBIT 1 *(concluded)*

Other channels

Practicing health workers in the Third World have achieved startling, if limited, response by writing to local medical journals and the press about any promotional malpractices they see and sending copies of their complaints to the companies involved. This could be done by volunteers and others not in the medical profession but in contact with the problem in the field.

In Britain, student unions at a number of universities and polytechnics decided to ban the use of all Nestlés products where they had control of catering following the initial exposé by the *New Internationalist* magazine. Without any clear objective, or coordination, this kind of action is unlikely to have much effect.

However, if the companies involved continue to be intransigent in the face of the dangerous situation developing in the Third World, a more broadly based campaign involving many national organisations may be the result. At the very least, trade unions, women's organisations, consumer groups, and other interested parties need to be made aware of the present dangers.

There is also a clear need to examine on a community scale, how infant feeding practices are determined in Britain today. There is a long history of commercial persuasion, and artificial feeding is now well entrenched.

As has been shown, there are still risks inherent in bottle feeding even in Britain. The available evidence suggests that both mother and child may do better physically and emotionally by breast-feeding. An examination of our own irrational social practices can help the Third World to throw a light on theirs.

The Baby Killer was written by Mike Muller as an attempt to publicize the infant formula issue. Mr. Muller expanded on the *New Internationalist* articles, and in the view of many observers, gave reasonable treatment to the complexity of the circumstances surrounding the use of formula products in the developing countries. On the whole, it was an attack against bottle-feeding rather than an attack against any particular company.

Part of *The Baby Killer* was based on interviews the author had with three Nestlé employees: Dr. H. R. Müller, G. A. Fookes, and J. Momoud, all of Nestlé S.A. Infant and Dietetics Division. These Nestlé officials argued that Nestlé was acting as responsibly as it could. Further, they said, that abuses, if they existed, could not be controlled by single companies. Only a drastic change in the competitive system could check abuses effectively. Mr. Muller apparently was not impressed by this argument, nor did he mention Nestlé management's stated willingness to establish enforceable international guidelines for marketing conduct. In *The Baby Killer,* Mr. Muller revealed he was convinced that Nestlé was exploiting the high birth rates in developing countries by encouraging mothers to replace, not supplement, breast-feeding by formula products. Mr. Muller offered as support for his stance a quotation from Nestlé's 1973 Annual Report:

. . . the continual decline in birth rates, particularly in countries with a high standard of living, retarded growth of the market. . . . In the developing countries our own products continue to sell well thanks to the growth of population and improved living standards.

Dr. Fürer's reaction to *The Baby Killer* was that Mr. Muller had given too much weight to the negative aspects of the situation. Mr. Muller failed to mention, for example, that infant mortality rates had shown very dramatic declines in the developing countries. Some part of these declines were the result of improved nutrition, Dr. Fürer believed, and improved nutrition was partly the result of the use of formula products. Despite his strong belief that Nestlé's product was highly beneficial rather than harmful, Dr. Fürer ordered a second audit of Nestlé's advertising and promotional methods in developing countries. Again, changes were made. These changes included revision of advertising copy to emphasize further the superiority of breast-feeding, elimination of radio advertising in the developing world, and cessation of the use of white uniforms on the mothercraft nurses.

At the same time, on May 23, 1974, WHO adopted a resolution that misleading promotion had contributed to the decline in breast-feeding in the developing countries and urged individual countries to take legal action to curb such abuses.

The Third World Action Group

In June 1974, the infant formula issue moved into Switzerland. A small, poorly financed group called the Third World Action Group located in Bern, the capital of Switzerland, published in German a booklet entitled *Nestlé Kills Babies (Nestlé Totet Kinder).* This was a partial translation of the War on Want publication *The Baby Killer.* Some of the qualifying facts found in Mr. Muller's booklet were omitted in *Nestlé Kills Babies,* while the focus was changed from a general attack on bottle-feeding to a direct attack on Nestlé and its promotional practices.

Nestlé top management was extremely upset by this publication. Dr. Fürer immediately ordered a follow-up audit of Nestlé's marketing practices to ensure stated corporate ethical standards were being observed. Nestlé management also believed that the infant formula issue was being used as a vehicle by leftist, Marxist groups intent on attacking the free-market system, multinational companies in general, and Nestlé in particular. Internal Nestlé memoranda of the time reveal the material available to management that supported their belief that the issue went beyond infant formula promotion. For example:

Having a closer look at the allies of the AG3W in their actions, we realize that they happen to have the same aim. There are common actions with the leninist progressive organizations (POCH), who are also considered to be pro-Soviet, with the Swiss communist party (PdA) and the communist youth organization (KJV), as well as with the revolutionary marxist alliance (RML). Since the

AG3W has tried to coordinate the support of (only pro-communist) liberation movements with representatives of the communist block, it is not surprising that they also participate at the youth festival in Eastern Berlin.[1]

Believing the issue to be clearly legal, Nestlé management brought suit in July 1974 against 13 members of the Third World Action Group and against two newspapers who carried articles about *Nestlé Kills Babies*. Nestlé charged criminal libel, claiming that the company had been defamed because "the whole report charges Nestlé S.A. with using incorrect sales promotion in the third world and with pulling mothers away from breast-feeding their babies and turning them to its products." More specifically, Nestlé management claimed the following were defamatory:

The title "Nestlé Kills Babies."

The charge that the practices of Nestlé and other companies are unethical and immoral (written in the introduction and in the report itself).

The accusation of being responsible for the death or the permanent physical and mental damage of babies by its sales promotion policy (in the introduction).

The accusation that in less developed countries, the sales representatives for baby foods are dressed like nurses to give the sales promotion a scientific appearance.

The trial in Bern provided the Third World Action Group with a great deal of publicity, giving them a forum to present their views. Swiss television in particular devoted much time to coverage of the trial and the issues involved. The trial ended in the fall, 1976. Nestlé management won a judgment on the first of the libel charges (because of lack of specific evidence for the Third World Action Group), and the activists were fined 300 Swiss Francs each. Nestlé management dropped the remaining charges. In his judgment, the presiding judge added an opinion that became well-publicized:

the need ensues for the Nestlé company to fundamentally rethink its advertising practices in developing countries as concerns bottle-feeding, for its advertising practice up to now can transform a life-saving product into one that is dangerous and life-destroying. If Nestlé S.A. in the future wants to be spared the accusations of immoral and unethical conduct, it will have to change its advertising practices.

The Controversy Spreads

While the trial was in process, various interest groups from all over the world became interested and involved in the infant formula controversy. In London, England Mr. Mike Muller founded the Baby Foods Action Group. Late in 1974, the World Food Conference adopted a resolution recommending that developing-nation governments actively support breast-feeding. The PAG had been

---

[1] Third World Action Group (AG3W) *Der Zürichbieter*, August 15, 1973.

organizing a number of international regional seminars to discuss all aspects of the controversy. For example, in November 1974, during the PAG regional seminar in Singapore, the PAG recommended that the infant formula industry increase its efforts to implement Statement 23 and cooperate to regulate their promotion and advertising practices through a code of ethics.

The world health organizations kept up the pressure. In March 1975, the PAG again met:

> to discuss together the problem of deteriorating infant feeding practices in developing countries and to make recommendations for remedying the situation. The early discontinuance of breast-feeding by mothers in low-income groups in urban areas, leading to malnutrition, illness, and death among infants has been a serious concern to all.

In May, 1975 WHO at its 14th plenary meeting again called for a critical review of promotion of infant formula products.

In response, representatives of the major formula producers met in Zürich, Switzerland in May 1975 to discuss the possibility and desirability of establishing an international code of ethics for the industry. Nine of the manufacturers, with the notable exceptions of Borden, Bristol-Myers, and Abbott, created an organization called the International Council of Infant Food Industries (ICIFI) and a code of marketing conduct. This code went into effect November 1, 1975. Some firms also adopted individual codes, including Nestlé, with standards higher than the ICIFI code.

The ICIFI code required that ICIFI members assume responsibility to encourage breast-feeding, that milk nurses be paid on a strict salary basis and wear company uniforms, and that product labels indicate breast milk as the best infant food. At this time, Nestlé began to phase out use of mass media for infant formula in developing countries, but continued to distribute educational materials and product information in the hospitals and clinics. Nestlé management believed such advertising and promotion was of educational value: to ensure proper use of formula and to decrease usage of sweetened and condensed milk for infant feeding.

ICIFI submitted its code of ethics to the PAG who submitted it to a number of third parties. On the basis of their opinions, the PAG refused to endorse the code saying it did not go far enough, that substantial amendments were required. ICIFI rejected these suggestions because of difficult antitrust considerations, so the PAG withheld its approval of the code.

An important exception to ICIFI membership was Abbott Laboratories. While Abbott representatives had attended the meeting that led to the establishment of ICIFI, they decided not to join. Abbott, having recently had difficulties with the U.S. Food and Drug Administration regarding the marketing of cyclamates and artificial sweeteners, felt ICIFI was not an adequate response to the public pressure:

> the most important area is to reduce the impact of advertising on the low-income, poorly educated populations where the risk is the greatest. The ICIFI code does not address this very important issue.

> Our company decided not to join ICIFI because the organization is not prepared to go far enough in answering this legitimate criticism of our industry. We feel that for Abbott/Ross to identify with this organization and its code would limit our ability to speak on the important issues.

Abbott acted largely independently of the other producers. Later in 1977, Abbott management announced its intention to commit about $100,000 to a breast-feeding campaign in developing nations and about $175,000 to a task force on breast-feeding, infant formula, and Third World countries.

Developments in the United States

Although Nestlé U.S. neither manufactured nor marketed formula, management found itself increasingly embroiled in the controversy during the mid-1970s. The first major group to bring this matter to the public was the Interfaith Center on Corporate Responsibility (ICCR). The ICCR, a union of 14 protestant denominations and approximately 150 Catholic orders and dioceses, was a group concerned about the social responsibility behaviour of corporations. The ICCR advised its members on this topic to guide decisions for the members' combined investment portfolio of several billion dollars. Formerly known as the Center of Corporate Responsibility, the ICCR was established under the tax-exempt umbrella of the American National Council of Churches when the U.S. Internal Revenue Service revoked the CCR tax exemption.

The ICCR urged its members to investigate the marketing practices of the leading American formula producers, American Home Products, Abbott Laboratories, and Bristol-Myers. Stockholder groups demanded from these companies, as they were entitled to do by American law, detailed information regarding market shares, promotion and advertising practices, and general company policies concerning the infant formula business.

Nestlé management believed that the ICCR was interested in ideology more than in baby formula. As support, they pointed to a statement made in a January edition of ICCR's *The Corporate Examiner:*

> the motivations, ethos, and operations of transnational corporations are inimical to the establishment of a new economic order. Both justice and stability are undermined in the fulfillment of their global vision.

Perhaps the major vehicle used by ICCR to get attention was a half-hour film entitled *Bottle Babies*. Well-known German filmmaker Peter Krieg began this film shortly after the Bern trial began. Nestlé Vevey management believed that the film was partially sponsored by the World Council of Churches to provide a public defence for the Third World Action Group position. Most of the filming was done in Kenya, Africa in 1975 in a "documentary" style, although Nestlé management pointed out that the film was scripted and in their opinion, highly emotional and misleading. A letter (Exhibit 2) that Nestlé management later received written by Professor Bwibo of the University of Nairobi supported management's views about the *Bottle Babies* film.

EXHIBIT 2

14th April, 1978

Miss June Noranka
644 Summit Avenue
St. Paul
Minnesota 55105

Dear Miss Noranka:

Following your visit to Kenya and my office I write to inform you, your group, your colleagues, and any other person interested that the film Peter Krieg filmed in this department and the associated teaching areas, did not represent the right aspects of what we participated in during the filming.

The film which was intended to be a scientific and educational film turned out to be an emotional, biased, and exaggerated film—and failed to be a teaching film. It arouses emotions in people who have little chance to check these facts. No wonder it has heated the emotions of the Activists groups in America and I understand now spreading to Europe. I wish I was in an opportunity to be with your groups and we view the film together and I comment.

As a pediatrician, I would like to put on record that I have not seen the Commercial baby food companies pressure anybody to use their brands of milk. As for Nestlé, we have discussed with their Managing Directors, starting much earlier than the time of the film in 1971, as to the best way of approaching baby feeding and discussed extensively advertisement especially the material to be included. The directors have followed our advice and we are happy with their working conditions.

We are interested in the well being of our children and we are Medical Scientists. So anything of scientific value we will promote but we will avoid imagined exaggerated and distorted views.

I am taking the liberty to copy this letter to Mr. Jones, managing director of Food Specialty in Nairobi who produce and make Nestlé's products here, for his information.

Yours sincerely,

NIMROD O. BWIBO
Professor & Chairman

ICCR distributed copies of the *Bottle Babies* film to church groups throughout the United States. Typically, the film was shown to a gathering of church members followed by an impassioned plea to write letters of protest and a request for funds to further the campaign. Since the film singled out Nestlé for attack in its last 10 minutes, Nestlé became symbolic of all that was wrong in the infant formula controversy in the minds of these religious groups. Nestlé management, however, was seldom asked for, or given an opportunity to present, its position on the issues.

While Nestlé felt the growing pressure of *Bottle Babies,* the major American formula producers faced a variety of ICCR-shareholder initiatives. ICCR requested detailed information from American Home Products, Abbott Laboratories, and Bristol-Myers. Each company responded differently.

American Home Products.   After refusing to release all the information ICCR requested, AHP faced a resolution to be included in its proxy statement. ICCR dropped the resolution the day before printing, when AHP management agreed:

To provide the requested information.

To send a report to its shareholders saying that many authorities believe misuse of infant formula in developing countries could be dangerous, that the company promotes breast-feeding while making available formula for mothers who cannot or do not choose to breast-feed, that the company would promote to medical professionals only and that AHP was a member of ICIFI which was developing a voluntary code of promotional practices.

Abbott Laboratories.   After a year and a half of meetings with ICCR, Abbott released most of the information ICCR wanted. Still, to obtain the rest of the data, ICCR shareholders filed a shareholder resolution. This proposal received less than the three percent of the vote required by the Securities and Exchange Commission (SEC) in order to resubmit the proposal at a later time. Thus, it was not resubmitted.

Bristol-Myers.   Bristol-Myers would not cooperate with ICCR so one church shareholder with 500 shares, Sisters of the Precious Blood, filed a shareholder resolution in 1975 asking that the information be released. After receiving 5.4 percent of the vote and having aroused the concern of the Ford Foundation and the Rockefeller Foundation, it appeared the resolution would be launched again the next year. In August 1975, Bristol-Myers management published a report "The Infant Formula Marketing Practices of Bristol-Myers Co. in Countries outside the United States." The 1976 proxy included the Sisters' resolution and a statement entitled "Management's Position." The Sisters maintained the statement was false and misleading and filed suit against management; statements appearing in a proxy statement are required by law to be accurate.

In May 1977, a U.S. district court judge dismissed the case, saying the Sisters had failed to show irreparable harm to themselves as the law requires.

The judge would not comment on the accuracy of the company's proxy report. The nuns appealed with the support of the SEC. In early 1978, the management of Bristol-Myers agreed to send a report outlining the dispute to all shareholders and to restrictions on company marketing practices including a ban on all consumer-directed promotion in clinics, hospitals, and other public places and a stop to using milk nurses in Jamaica.

In 1977, Abbott management agreed to revise their code of marketing conduct and to eliminate the use of nurses' uniforms by company salespeople despite the fact some were registered nurses.

ICCR and its supporters also persuaded Representative Michael Harrington, Democrat–Massachusetts to cosponsor a federal resolution requiring an investigation of U.S. infant formula producers.

The campaign against the formula producers took on a new dimension in mid-1977. A group called the Third World Institute, led by Doug Johnson at the University of Minnesota, formed the Infant Formula Action Coalition "INFACT" in June 1977. INFACT members were encouraged by ICCR and the Sisters, but felt that significant progress would not be made until Nestlé was pressured to change. INFACT realized that legal and shareholder action against a foreign-based company would be futile, so on July 4, 1977 INFACT announced a consumer boycott against those infant formula companies whose marketing practices INFACT found abusive. Despite the boycott's original target of several companies, Nestlé was the main focal point especially after the other major companies made concessions to ICCR. INFACT began the boycott in front of Nestlé's Minneapolis offices with a demonstration of about 100 people. INFACT urged consumers to boycott over 40 Nestlé products.

Nestlé management in White Plains was not sure what response to take. Nestlé U.S. was not at all involved with infant formula, but was genuinely concerned about the publicity INFACT was getting. Nestlé S.A. management on the other hand originally did not think the boycott campaign would amount to anything, that it was a project of some college kids in the United States based on misinformation about events in other parts of the world.

In September and October 1977, Nestlé senior managers from Vevey and White Plains met with members of INFACT, ICCR, the Ford Foundation, and other interested groups. Nestlé management had hoped to resolve what they thought was a problem of poor communication by explaining the facts. Nestlé management argued the company could not meet competition if it stopped all promotion, which would mean less sales and less jobs in the developing nations. Further, management claimed: "We have an instructional and educational responsibility as marketers of these products and, if we failed in that responsibility, we could be justly criticized." INFACT members stated they found the talks useful in clarifying positions, but concluded Nestlé was unwilling to abandon all promotion of its formula products.

In November 1977, INFACT decided not only to continue the boycott, but also to increase it to a national scale. INFACT held a conference in Minneapolis on November 2–4, for more than 45 organizers from 24 cities. These organizers represented women's groups, college hunger-action coalitions, health professionals, church agencies, and social justice groups. A clearinghouse was established to coordinate boycott efforts and information collection. The group also agreed to assist ICCR in its shareholder pressure campaign and to press for congressional action. Later, INFACT petitioned all U.S. government officials, state and federal, for support of the boycott. On November 21, the Interfaiths Hunger Coalition, a group affiliated with INFACT, demonstrated in front of Nestlé's Los Angeles sales office with about 150 people chanting "Nestlé kills babies." This demonstration received prominent media coverage as did other boycott activities. The combination of INFACT's boycott, ICCR's shareholder efforts, the exhibition of *Bottle Babies*, and the strong support of other U.S. activists (including Ralph Nader, Cesar Chavez, Gloria Steinem, and Dr. Benjamin Spock), resulted in an increasingly high profile for the infant formula controversy, even though Nestlé management believed there had been as yet no adverse effect on sales.

In early 1978, an unofficial WHO working group published the following statement:

> The advertising of food for nursing infants or older babies and young children is of particular importance and should be prohibited on radio and television. Advertising for mother's milk substitutes should never be aimed directly at the public or families, and advertising for ready-made infant food preparations should show clearly that they are not meant for less than three-month old infants. Publicity for public consumption, which should in any case never be distributed without previous recommendation by the competent medical authority, should indicate that breast milk should always constitute the sole or chief constituent of food for those under three months. Finally, the distribution of free samples and other sales promotion practices for baby foods should be generally prohibited.

Nestlé management met again with INFACT representatives in February 1978. No progress was made in reconciling the two sides. Nestlé management could not accept statements from INFACT such as:

> The corporations provide the product and motivate the people to buy it, and set into motion a process that may cause the death of the baby. The corporations are responsible for that death. When the outcome is death, the charge against the corporation is murder.

Nonetheless, management learned what INFACT wanted:

> Stop all direct consumer promotion and publicity for infant formula.
>
> Stop employing "milk nurses" as sales staff.
>
> Stop distributing free samples to clinics, hospitals, and maternity hospitals.
>
> Stop promoting infant formula among the medical profession and public health profession.

To further publicize their campaign, INFACT representatives and their allies persuaded Senator Edward Kennedy, Democrat–Massachusetts, to hold Senate hearings on the infant formula issue in May 1978. CBS decided to make a TV report of the entire affair. To prepare for the hearings, INFACT organized a number of demonstrations across the United States. At one meeting on April 15, 1978, Doug Johnson said:

> The goal of the Nestlé's Boycott Campaign and of the entire infant formula coalition is to get the multinationals to stop promotion of infant formula. We're not asking them to stop marketing; we're not asking them to pull out of—out of the countries; we're simply asking them to stop the promotion, and in that I think we're—we're in agreement with a number of prestigious organizations. The World Health Organization recently asked the corporations to stop consumer advertising and to stop the use of free samples, and the International Pediatric Association did that several years ago. So, I think we're asking a very reasonable thing: to stop promoting something which is inappropriate and dangerous.

CBS filmed these demonstrations, but did not air them until after the Kennedy hearings.

The Kennedy Hearings and CBS Report

Senator Kennedy was chairman of the Subcommittee on Health and Scientific Research on Infant Nutrition. Both critics and members of the infant formula industry appeared before the Kennedy Committee in May 1978. Nestlé S.A. management decided not to send headquarters management or management from Nestlé U.S. Instead, they asked R. Oswaldo Ballarin, president and chairman of Nestlé, Brazil to represent Nestlé at the hearings. Dr. Ballarin began with a statement prepared by Nestlé U.S., but Senator Kennedy soon interrupted him as the following excerpt from the testimony indicates:

Dr. Ballarin: United States Nestlé's Company has advised me that their research indicates this is actually an indirect attack on the free world's economic system: a worldwide church organization with its stated purpose of undermining the free enterprise system is at the forefront of this activity.

Senator Kennedy: Now you can't seriously expect . . . [Noise in background: gravel banging] We'll be in order . . . we'll be in order now please. We'll be in order. Uh, you don't seriously expect us to accept that on face value, after we've heard as . . . as you must've, Doctor . . . if I could just finish my question . . . the . . . the testimony of probably 9 different witnesses. It seemed to me that they were expressing a very deep compassion and concern about the well-being of infants, the most vulnerable in this . . . face of the world. Would you agree with me that your product should not be used where there is impure water? Yes or no?

Dr. Ballarin: Uh, we give all the instructions . . .

Senator Kennedy: Just . . . just answers. What would you . . . what is your position?

Dr. Ballarin: Of course not. But we cannot cope with that.

Senator Kennedy: Well, as I understand what you say, is where there's impure water, it should not be used.

Dr. Ballarin: Yes.

Senator Kennedy: Where the people are so poor that they're not gonna realistically be able to continue to purchase it, and which is gonna . . . that they're going to dilute it to a point, which is going to endanger the health, that it should not be used.

Dr. Ballarin: Yes, I believe . . .

Senator Kennedy: Alright, now . . . then my final question is . . . is what do you . . . or what do you feel is your corporate responsibility to find out the extent of the use of your product in those circumstances in the developing part of the world? Do you feel that you have any responsibility?

Dr. Ballarin: We can't have that responsibility, sir. May I make a reference to . . .

Senator Kennedy: You can't have that responsibility?

Dr. Ballarin: No.

Dr. Ballarin's testimony continued (for example of excerpts, see Exhibit 3), but Nestlé management believed little attention was paid to it. Mr. Guerrant, president of Nestlé U.S. was very angry and wrote a letter to Senator Kennedy

EXHIBIT 3 Further excerpts from Dr. Ballarin's testimony

Nestlé recognized that even the best products will not give the desired results if used incorrectly. We, therefore, placed great weight on educational efforts aimed at explaining the correct use of our product. Our work in this field has received the public recognition and approval of the official Pediatric Associations in many countries. Such educational efforts never attempt to infer that our product is superior to breast milk. Indeed, we have devoted much attention to the promotion of breast-feeding, and educational material has always insisted that breast-feeding is best for the baby.

Nevertheless, many factors militate against exclusive breast-feeding in the rapidly growing cities of Brazil as well as other developing countries, and our products are seen today as filling a valid need, just as they did when they were first introduced over 50 years ago. In recognition of this, all such products are subject to strict price control, while in many countries which do not have a local dairy industry, they are classified as essential goods and imported free of duty. In many cases, official agencies establish what they consider to be a fair margin for the manufacturers.

It must be stressed that many problems remain to be solved. Our production is far from reaching the total needs of the population. Hence, many mothers in the poorer population groups continue to supplement breast-feeding with foods of doubtful quality. Owing to the lack of adequate medical services, especially in the rural areas, misuse of any supplement can occur and we are very conscious of the need to improve our efforts. These efforts depend on continued cooperation between the infant food industry and health professionals. We have to be more and more conscious of our responsibility to encourage breast-feeding while researching new foods and safer methods for feeding babies who cannot be exclusively breast-fed. The dilemma facing industry and the health service alike, is how to teach these methods without discouraging breast-feeding.

on May 26, 1978 protesting against the way he had treated Dr. Ballarin (Exhibit 4).

CBS aired its program on July 5, 1978. Again, Nestlé management was upset. In their view CBS had selected portions of the testimonies to make Nestlé management look inept and confused. Mr. Guerrant wrote a letter of protest to CBS president Richard Salant (Exhibit 5).

EXHIBIT 4 Excerpts from Mr. Guerrant's letter to Senator Kennedy

---

I am angry but more important deeply concerned about the example of our governmental processes exhibited this week by the Human Resources Subcommittee on Health and Scientific Research.

It was the general consensus of several people in the audience that your position toward the manufacturers was "you are guilty until you prove your innocence." Objectivity would have been more becoming, Senator.

Secondly, it seemed equally probable that prior to the hearing the prepared statements were reviewed and you were quite prepared to rebuff Dr. Ballarin on his statement "undermining the free enterprise system." Unaccustomed to television and this type of inquisition, Dr. Ballarin, who appeared voluntarily, was flustered and embarrassed.

Probably, for this gathering, the statement was too strong (though nothing to compare with their theme "Nestlé kills babies") and should have been more subtle. But the point is well made, and your apparent denial of this possibility concerns me.

As you may know, this whole issue gained its greatest momentum a few years ago in Europe fostered by clearly identified radical leftist groups. Their stated purpose is opposition to capitalism and the free enterprise system. I submit that they are not really concerned with infants in the third world but are intelligent enough to know that babies, especially sick and dying, create maximum emotional response. Further, they are clever enough to know that the people most easy to "use" for their campaign, to front for them, are in churches and universities. These are good people, ready to rise against oppression and wrong-doing without, regrettably, truthful facts for objective research. I know, as my father is a retired Presbyterian minister, and I have a very warm feeling toward members of the church, Protestant and Catholic.

People with far left philosophies are not confined to Europe and are certainly represented in many accepted organizations here and abroad. (Please take the time to read the enclosed report of the 1977 Geneva Consultation of the World Council of Churches.) Associated with the World Council is the National Council of Churches, and one of their units is the Interfaith Centre for Corporate Responsibility. One of their major spokespersons appears to be Leah Margulies, who was present in your hearing.

Now, just briefly to the very complex infant food issue. As the U.S. Nestlé Company does not manufacture or sell any infant food products, we are unhappy with the attempted boycott of our products—at least 95 percent of these manufactured in the United States. The jobs and security of about 12,000 good U.S. employees are being threatened.

From our associates in Switzerland, and Nestlé companies in the Third World, we

EXHIBIT 4 *(concluded)*

have gathered hundreds of factual documents. Neither Nestlé nor the U.S. companies in this business claim perfection. Companies are comprised of human beings. However, virtually every charge against Nestlé has proved to be erroneous. Distorted "facts" and just pure propaganda have been answered by people with undeniable integrity and technical credentials. Quite some time ago, because of the accusations, Nestlé world headquarters in Switzerland studied every facet of their total infant food business, made immediate changes where warranted and established new and very clear policies and procedures regarding the conduct of this business.

I might add that Nestlé infant foods have undoubtedly saved hundreds of thousands of lives. There is not even one instance where proof exists that Nestlé infant food was responsible for a single death. The products are as essential in the Third World as in the industrialized world. Though the accusers use some statements by apparently qualified people, there is an overwhelming amount of data and number of statements from qualified medical, technical, and government representatives in the Third World confirming Nestlé's position.

At your hearing this week were the same identical charges made against Nestlé and the others years ago. These people will not recognize the changes made in marketing practices nor the irrefutable facts of the real infant health problems in the Third World. They continue to push the U.S. Nestlé boycott and continue to distribute the fraudulent film "Bottle Babies." (Please read Dr. Bwibo's letter enclosed.) Sincere, well-meaning church people continue to be used, as they have not had all the real facts available for analysis.

The above situation made me believe that the organizers must have some motivation for this campaign other than what appears on the surface. If it could possibly be what I think, then our representatives in government should proceed with caution, thorough study, and great objectivity, as your ultimate position can be of critical consequence. I am not a crusader, but I do feel the free enterprise system is best.

Following the Kennedy hearings, representatives of Nestlé S.A., Abbott, Bristol-Myers and American Home Products met privately with Senator Kennedy to explore a suggestion for a further hearing. Meanwhile, the president of ICIFI wrote Kennedy, pointing out that this was an international and not a U.S. domestic issue—and should therefore be discussed at a forum sponsored by WHO. Kennedy accepted ICIFI's suggestion and requested the Director General of WHO to sponsor a conference at which the question of an international code could be discussed.

A consensus emerged that a uniform code for the industry was required and that Kennedy and ICIFI would suggest that WHO sponsor a conference with that aim in mind. The conference would be comprised of WHO officials, ICIFI members and other companies, health and government officials from the developing countries, and all appropriate concerned public groups. WHO accepted the idea and announced the conference date in the fall of 1979. Shortly

EXHIBIT 5 Excerpts from Mr. Guerrant's letter to CBS President Salant

In the first minute of the program the infant formula industry has been tried and convicted of causing infant malnutrition. The remainder of the program is devoted to reinforcing Mr. Myer's conclusion. Tools of persuasion include the emotionality of a needle sticking in a child's head and the uneasy answers of cross-examined industry witnesses who are asked not for the facts but to admit and apologize for their "guilt."

But CBS Reports chose to concentrate on the "rhetoric of concern" and the claims which permeate the rhetoric. Industry's response to the rhetoric is not glamorous but hits into the root causes of infant malnutrition—the poverty, disease, and ignorance existing in the areas of developing and developed countries. Those conditions are not easy for anthropologists, economists, scientists, or medical people to trace or explain. And certainly the reasons for them are not as identifiable as a major corporation. But in 30 minutes Mr. Myers and Ms. Roche identified four companies as a major reason for infant malnutrition.

One way Nestlé has attempted to meet the responsibility is by making capital investments in and transferring technology to the developing countries. Nestlé began this effort in 1921 in Brazil and now has almost 40,000 local employees working in 81 manufacturing facilities in 25 developing countries. Not only does Nestlé have a beneficial impact on those directly employed, the company also encourages and assists the development of other local supporting industries, such as the dairy industry and packaging plants.

Another way Nestlé meets its responsibility is to work with local governments and health authorities in educating consumers. Clinics, pamphlets, posters, books, and product labels emphasize the superiority of breast-feeding, demonstrate proper sanitation and diet for breast-feeding, and show in words and pictures how to correctly use formula products.

Neither of these positive approaches was covered in CBS Reports nor was there mention of the fact that infant mortality has declined worldwide over the past 30 years, nor that lack of sufficient breast milk is a major cause of infant malnutrition, nor that tropical diseases cause millions of deaths per year in developing countries. Any one of these facts would have provided some balance to the Myers-Roche report.

---

after Nestlé management met with Kennedy, the National Council of Churches, comprised of about 30 major religious groups in the United States, announced that the question of supporting INFACT and ICCR would be discussed and decided at the NCC national conference in November 1978.

The Situation in October 1978

Dr. Fürer knew all senior Nestlé management felt personally attacked by critics of the industry. Not only was this the first major public pressure campaign ever encountered by Nestlé, but also Nestlé management felt its critics were using unfair tactics. For example, again and again they saw in boycott letters and articles a grotesque picture of a wizened child with a formula bottle nearby.

Eventually this picture was traced to Dr. Derrick Jeliffe, an outspoken critic of the industry. He admitted to *Newsweek* he had taken the picture in a Caribbean hospital in 1964. Even though it seemed the media and many respected companies were against Nestlé, Dr. Fürer stated publicly:

> No one has the right to accuse us of killing babies. No one has the right to assert that we are guilty of pursuing unethical or immoral sales practices.

Nonetheless, under U.S. law a company is regarded as a public person which meant that the First Amendment applied; that is, Nestlé could not get legal relief against charges made by the critics unless the company could prove those charges were both wrong and malicious.

Further, Dr. Fürer was struck by the fact that all the demands for change were coming from developed countries. In fact, Nestlé had received many letters of support from people in the developing countries (Exhibit 6). Mr. Ernest Saunders, Nestlé vice president for infant nutrition products summarized his view as follows:

> Government and medical personnel tell us that if we stopped selling infant foods we would be killing a lot of babies.

EXHIBIT 6 Examples of support for Nestlé

1. I have been associated with the medical representatives of Nestlé in Kenya for the last five years. We have discussed on various occasions the problems of artificial feeding, in particular the use of proprietary milk preparations. We have all been agreed that breast-feeding should always come first. As far as I am aware, your representatives have not used any unethical methods when promoting Nestlé products in this country.

   M. L. Oduori, Senior Consultant
   Pediatrician
   Ministry of Health
   Kenyatta National Hospital, Nairobi
   Kenya, Dec. 23, 1974

2. You are not "killing babies," on the contrary your efforts joined with ours contribute to the improvement of the Health Status of our infant population.
   We consider your marketing policies as ethical and as not being opposite to our recommendations. We note with pleasure that you employ a fully qualified nurse and that during discussions with mothers she always encourages breast-feeding, recommending your products when only natural feeding is insufficient or fails.

   Dr. Jerry Lukowski
   Chief Gynecologist, Menelik Hospital
   Ethiopia, Dec. 3, 1974

3. Over several decades I have had direct and indirect dealings with your organisation in South Africa in relation to many aspects of nutrition among the

EXHIBIT 6 *(continued)*

nonwhite population who fall under our care, as well as the supply of nutriments to the hospital and peripheral clinics.

I am fairly well aware of the extent of your Company's contributions to medical science and research and that this generosity goes hand in hand with the highest ethical standards of advertising, distribution of products, and the nutrition educational services which you provide.

At no time in the past have my colleagues or I entertained any idea or suspicion that Nestlé have behaved in any way that could be regarded as unethical in their promotions, their products or their educational programmes. On all occasions when discussion of problems or amendments to arrangements have been asked for, full cooperation has been given to this department.

Your field workers have given and are giving correct priorities in regard to breast feeding, and, where necessary, the bottle feeding of infants.

The staff employed to do this work have shown a strong sense of responsibility and duty towards the public whom they serve, no doubt due to the educational instruction they have themselves received in order to fit them for their work.

> S. Wayburne, Chief Pediatrician
> Baragwanath Hospital
> Associate Professor of Pediatrics,
> Acting Head of Department of
> Pediatrics, University of
> Witwaterbrand/South Africa
> Dec. 18, 1974

4. I have read about the accusation that "Nestlé Kills Babies" and I strongly refute it, I think it is quite unjustifiable.

   On my experience I have never seen any mother being advised to use artificial milk when it was not necessary. Every mother is advised to give breast foods to her baby. It is only when there is failure of this, then artificial foods are advised.

   I, being a working mother have brought up my five children on Nestlé Products and I do not see anything wrong with them. I knew I would have found it difficult to carry on with my profession if I had nothing to rely on like your products.

   Your marketing policies are quite in order as I knew them and they are quite ethical. As they stress on breast milk foods first and if this is unobtainable then one can use Nestlé's Products.

> Mrs. M. Lema, Nursing Officer
> Ocean Hospital
> Dar-es-Salaam/TANZANIA
> Dec. 16, 1974

5. On behalf of the Sisters of Nazareth Hospital, I thank you heartily for your generous contribution in giving us the Nestlé products in a way that we can assist and feed many undernourished children freely cured and treated in our hospital.

EXHIBIT 6 *(concluded)*

Trusting in your continuous assistance allow me to express again my sincerest thanks, and may God bless you.

Nazareth Hospital
Nairobi, Kenya
September 9, 1978

6.   I am very grateful for this help for our babies in need in the maternity ward.

Another mission has asked me about this milk gift parcels, if there would be any chance for them. It is Butula Mission and they have a health centre with beds and maternity and maternal child health clinics. There is a lot of malnutrition also in that area, so that mothers often do not produce enough milk for their babies. It would be wonderful if you could help them also.

Nangina Hospital
Medical Mission Sisters
Funyula, Kenya
June 15, 1976

7.   As a doctor who has practiced for 18 years in a developing country, I was angered by the collection of half-truths, judiciously mixed with falsehoods put out by the Infant Formula Action Coalition as reported in the *Newsweek* article on breast-feeding. Whether we like it or not, many mothers cannot or will not resort to breast-feeding. I do not believe that advertising has played any significant part in their decision. It is an inescapable necessity that specific, nutritionally balanced formulas are available. Otherwise, we would witness wholesale feeding with products that are unsuitable.

I carry no brief for companies like Nestlé, but have always found it to be a company with the highest regard to ethical standards. Infant formulas have saved many thousands of lives. What alternative are their critics proposing?

D. C. Williams, M.D.
Kuala Lumpur
Malaysia

8.   Surely, Nestlé is not to blame. There have been similar problems here but through the efforts of the Save the Children Fund and government assistance, feeding bottles can only be purchased through chemists or hospitals by prescription. In this way, the decision of whether to breast-feed or not is decided by qualified personnel.

I would think that Americans would have better things to do than walk around disrupting commerce with placards.

Gail L. Hubbard
Goroka, Papua New Guinea

Dr. Fürer also believed that the scientific facts underlying the breast versus bottle controversy were not being given adequate attention (for example, see Exhibit 7) nor were the changes Nestlé and the other companies had made. Nestlé's policies regarding infant formula products were apparently not well known. Exhibit 8 includes excerpts from the latest edition, dated September 1, 1977.

EXHIBIT 7 Examples of supplementary information on breast-feeding versus bottle-feeding

1. Findings of the Human Lactation Center (HLC).

The HLC is a scientific research institute, a nonprofit organization dedicated to worldwide education and research on lactation. The HLC entered the breast/bottle controversy between the infant formula industry and the anti-multinational groups in an attempt to clarify certain issues. Eleven anthropologists, all women, studied infant feeding practices in 11 different cultures, ranging from a relatively urbanized Sardinian village to a very impoverished Egyptian agricultural village. Their findings:

> Poverty is correlated with infant morbidity (disease). Child health is associated with affluence.
>
> Infant mortality had decreased in the three decades prior to 1973 when food prices began to escalate.
>
> Breast milk is the best infant food but breast-feeding exclusively for most *undernourished* women in the less developed countries is inadequate beyond the baby's third month. Lack of sufficient food after this time is a major cause of morbidity and mortality whether or not the infant is breast-fed.
>
> Mixed feeding is an almost universal pattern in traditional cultures; that is, breast-feeding and supplementary feeding from early on and often into the second year.
>
> The preferred additional food for the very young child is milk. Most milk is fresh milk, unprocessed.
>
> *Most* women still breast-feed though many do not. The popular assumption that breast-feeding is being reduced has not been verified.
>
> Third World women with the least amount of resources, time or access to health care and weaning foods, have no choice but to breast-feed.
>
> More than half the infants they bear do not survive due to lack of food for themselves and their children.
>
> Women who are separated from close kin, especially the urban poor, lack mothering from a supportive figure. They find themselves unable to lactate adequately or lose their milk entirely. Without suitable substitutes, their infants die.
>
> Middle class women in the less-developed countries, market women, the elite and professional women are moving towards bottle feeding with infant formula in much the same way women turned from breast to bottle feeding in the western countries.

EXHIBIT 7 *(continued)*

The current literature on breast-feeding in the developing countries is meager. Information on mortality, the incidence of breast-feeding, the content of infant food, and the amount of breast milk, tend to be impressionistic reports by well-meaning western or western trained persons often unaware of the complexities of feeding practices and insensitive to the real-life situation of the mothers. Judgments for action based on these inconclusive data could be dangerous.

Mothers have a sensitive and remarkable grasp of how best to keep their infants alive. Neither literacy nor what has been called "ignorance" determine which infants live and which die except as they are related directly to social class.

In seeking solutions to the problems of infant well-being in the developing world, we must listen to the mothers and involve them in the decisions which will affect their lives.

2. *The Feeding of the Very Young: An Approach to Determination of Policies,* report of the International Advisory Group on Infant and Child Feeding to the Nutrition Foundation, October 1978:

"Two basic requirements of successful feeding are: (1) adequate milk during the first four to six months of life, and (2) adequate complementary foods during the transition to adult diets. It is imperative that all societies recognize these requirements as a major component of nutrition policy. The extent to which mothers are able to meet both of these requirements will vary under different cultural and sociological circumstances. In all societies there will be some proportion of mothers who will not be able to meet them without assistance, and policy must be developed to protect those children who are at risk of malnutrition resulting from inadequacy in either one or both of these basic requirements."

Source: Nestlé memoranda.

EXHIBIT 7 *(concluded)*

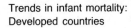

Trends in infant mortality:
Developed countries

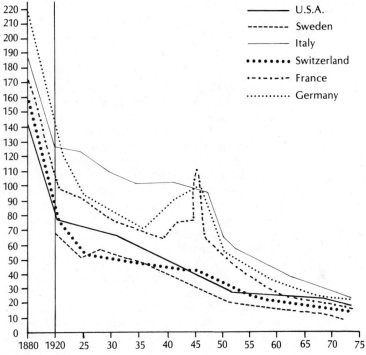

Trends in infant mortality:
Developing countries

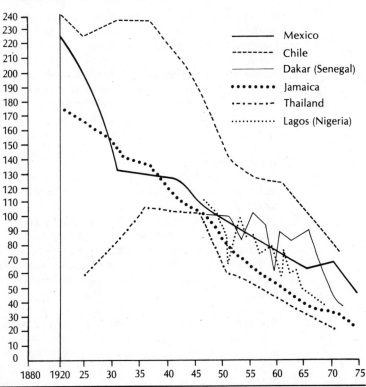

Source: Demographic Yearbook, United Nations.

EXHIBIT 8 Excerpts from Nestlé directives on infant and dietetic products policy

Infant milks

It is recognized that breast milk is the best food for a baby. Our baby milks are therefore not intended to compete with breast milk, but to supplement breast feeding when the mother's own milk can no longer cover the baby's needs or to replace it when mothers cannot, or elect not to breast feed.

Three to four months after birth, the quantities of breast milk produced by the average mother become insufficient to satisfy the growing needs of the baby. The baby needs a supplement of water and food. From this moment on, in the poor communities of developing countries this baby is in danger because water is sometimes polluted and local foods, like plantain or manioc, are nutritionally inadequate. They are starchy foods with little food value and a young baby cannot digest them. Thus the highest infant mortality occurs precisely in areas where babies receive only mother's milk plus a supplement of unboiled local water and/or starchy decoctions.

This is not a Nestlé theory. This is a fact known by every Third World doctor and recently scientifically demonstrated by British researchers working in Africa.

The alternative to traditional local supplement is a properly formulated breast milk substitute, preferably a humanized formula. It is true that there is a risk of misuse, but these risks exist with a local supplement too, although the baby has a better chance of survival when the starting point is of high quality.

It is precisely to reduce the risks of misuse and thereby increase the chances of survival that we had developed over the years a comprehensive programme of information and education: contact with doctors, educative advertising, booklets, nurses; all this had the purpose of making the alternative to local supplements known and ensuring a proper and safe use of our products when needed. Nestlé policies are designed to avoid the unnecessary replacement of breast milk.

The real issue is not breast milk versus formula, as so often pictured, but breast milk plus formula plus education versus traditional foods like manioc.

Products must be in line with internationally recognized nutritional criteria and offer definite consumer benefits.

Distribution policy

It is a rule that PID products are never sold to mothers directly by us; distribution aims at making products available to prescribers and users under optimum safety and price conditions.

Within the limits set by the law and by the distribution structure, we practice mixed distribution (pharmacies and general food stores) and use the normal market channels. On the other hand, dietetic specialities and products designed for delicate or sick babies, which are basically sold on medical prescription, are sold only through pharmacies, unless special local conditions warrant mixed distribution.

Communication policy—direct contact with mothers

Medical representatives must not enter into direct contact with mothers, unless they are authorized to do so in writing by a medical or health authority and provided that they are properly qualified. Films may be shown with the agreement of the medical or public health authorities concerned.

EXHIBIT 8 *(concluded)*

Visits to mothers in their homes are not allowed unless the responsible medical authority has made a written request for a visit to take place.

Personnel policy

The main task of the medical promotion personnel consists in contacting the medical and paramedical professions and hospitals. They are not concerned with direct sales to mothers and cannot sell dietetic products other than, exceptionally and exclusively, to the trade or institutions.

Specialized training must be given to such staff, to enable them to render a genuine service to the medical and paramedical professions and give them scientific and unbiased information on product characteristics and utilization.

No sales-related bonus will be paid to any staff engaged in medical promotion or having direct contact with mothers. If a bonus is to be paid, it must depend on elements other than sales, such as personal qualities and qualifications.

Many members of management believed the attack against Nestlé was ideologically based. They gathered information about and quotations from many of the activist groups to support their position (for example, see Exhibit 9). Whatever their foundation, the critics seemed to Dr. Fürer to be gaining publicity and momentum. INFACT claimed at least 500 separate action committees in the United States, support in about 75 communities in Canada, as well as support in about 10 other countries. "The movement is snowballing," reported Gwen Willens of INFACT. "We're getting over 300 letters of support every day."

As Dr. Fürer consulted with senior management in Nestlé, he wondered what further steps Nestlé might take to deal with the controversy surrounding the marketing of infant formula products in the developing countries.

EXHIBIT 9 Examples of comments concerning the ideology of the activist group

Sue Tafler and Betsy Walker, "Why Boycott Nestlé?" in *Science for the People,* January/February 1978.

> Unfortunately, the power in many developing countries is not held by the people themselves, and local ruling elites often want to encourage corporate investment. . . . What the boycott will not do is overthrow capitalism. . . . The boycott can unite well-meaning groups that see themselves as apolitical with more openly political groups. . . . We can have the effect of politicizing others working in the coalition. If Nestlé does make some concessions to the demands of the boycott, the sense of victory can give encouragement to the organizers of the boycott to continue on to larger struggles.

T. Balasusiya, Centre for Society and Religion, Colombo, Sri Lanka, participant at the World Council of Churches meeting, January 1977.

EXHIBIT 9 *(concluded)*

The capitalist system is the main cause of the increasing gap and within that system multinationals are a main form. Ideology of wealth is the practical religion of capitalist society. Churches are legitimizers of the system, so their first job is self-purification. There can be no neutrality between money and God.

Our function is not to judge persons, but we have to judge systems. . . . What alternative solutions do countries propose that have rejected the capitalist system, e.g., USSR, China, Cuba, Tanzania? Capitalism is inherently contradictory to the Gospel.

M. Ritchie, at a conference, "Clergy and Laity Concerned," August 1978.

It's not just on babies, it's not just multinational corporations, it's class conflict and class struggle. Broadening the constituency both of people interested in the infant formula issue . . . how the infant formula campaign and the people there link up completely in terms of support and action with other types of campaigns. . .

I think ultimately what we're trying to do is take an issue-specific focus campaign and move it in conjunction with other issue-specific campaigns into a larger very class-wide very class-conscious campaign and reasserting our power in this country, our power in this world.

Douglas Johnson of INFACT, at an address in Washington, September 1978.

Our hope is that we can use this [boycott] campaign as the forerunner of legislation for control of multinational corporations.

Source: Nestlé internal memoranda.

Case 37

Litton Industries, Inc.*

Introduction

Fridays were always the worst day of the week for Marc Stillwell. As an administrative law judge for the Federal Trade Commission, he frequently considered his workload burdensome, but Fridays always seemed the worst. While many civil servants spent the afternoon clearing off their desks preparing to start off fresh the following Monday, Stillwell was cramming his briefcase with case files and court briefs that would require his attention over the weekend. He felt he'd be lucky if he could spare the time to watch a little football on Sunday, judging by the bulge in his briefcase.

The Litton Industries case decision had to be made soon, and as the presiding administrative law judge, he would have to prepare a detailed decision including his reasoning for the conclusions reached. The FTC staff attorneys and the Litton attorneys had both filed their final statements containing their arguments and findings of fact, and he would have to sort out from these conflicting documents what was actually correct.

Although it was not surrounded by the heavy publicity that characterized some of the more dramatic cases he had worked on in the past, the Litton case was important because it contained some important issues concerning the use of surveys in advertising, and the increasing use of comparisons between competitors in advertising with actual names of competitors being used. He knew it was commission policy to encourage advertising that uses factual data such as that obtained from surveys and that the agency also wanted to encourage comparison advertising. At the same time he had to decide if in this case these goals conflicted with another FTC policy—that no advertising should be unfair or deceptive.

In addition to deciding if Litton had engaged in unfair or deceptive advertising and if they had adequate substantiation for the claims made, he also

---

* This case was coauthored by Larry M. Robinson, Assistant Professor of Marketing, Georgia State University.

had to determine an appropriate remedy if the company was found guilty. A proposed order had been recommended by the FTC staff attorneys, and he would have to decide if it was reasonable or whether some other order would be better.

The Company

Litton Industries, Inc., was founded in November 1953 as a small electronics firm in San Carlos, California. Revenues that year were less than $3 million. By the end of fiscal 1978, Litton was the 99th largest U.S. corporation with revenues exceeding $3.65 billion.[1] But Litton's management still held to a strategy laid out in the company's first annual report:

> The company's management [has] planned first to establish a base of profitable operations in advanced electronic development and manufacturing. Utilizing this base, the plan contemplates building a major electronics company by developing new and advanced products and programs and by acquiring others having potential in complementing fields. . . . This plan is designed to establish strong proprietary product values and a "broad base" on which to grow—a profitable balance between commercial and military customers and an integrated but diversified line of electronic products.[2]

By 1980, Litton had grown to become a widely diversified, international industrial conglomerate with 175 manufacturing and research facilities in the United States and around the world employing over 90,400 people. The corporation produced such products as business computer systems, business furniture, calculators, copiers, Royal typewriters, Sweda cash registers and POS/retail information systems, machine and hand tools, material-handling systems, specialty metal products, electronic components, biomedical equipment, paper and printed products, medical professional publications including the *Physicians Desk Reference,* textbook publications, airborne navigation systems, electronic signal surveillance equipment, and so on. Litton's Ingalls Shipbuilding subsidiary built U.S. Navy destroyers and nuclear submarines. Exhibit 1 contains Litton's sales by product line.

As can be seen, Litton Industries produced primarily commercial, industrial, and defense-related products. However, the company's electronic and electrical products division successfully produced and marketed at least one major consumer good—microwave ovens.

Microwave Ovens

Microwave cooking was first developed shortly after World War II as an offshoot of advancements in radar technology. Although microwave ovens were introduced as early as 1954 principally for institutional and commercial use,

---

[1] "The Forbes 500s," *Forbes,* May 14, 1979, p. 234.

[2] Litton Industries, Inc., *Annual Report, Fiscal 1978,* p. 4.

EXHIBIT 1 Litton's sales breakdown ($000)

Sales and service revenues by product line—continuing operations (unaudited)

	Year ended July 31				
	1978	*1977*	*1976*	*1975*	*1974*
Business systems and equipment					
Business machines and retail information systems	$ 448,109	$ 373,489	$ 389,970	$ 431,941	$ 450,805
Typewriters and office copiers	321,970	302,078	284,903	284,385	302,344
Office products, furniture, and fixtures	177,510	157,899	147,408	143,396	151,638
Intrasegment eliminations	(855)	(1,134)	(1,394)	(9,821)	(2,881)
	946,734	832,332	820,887	849,901	901,906
Industrial systems and services					
Machine tools	282,475	252,238	223,678	242,909	219,453
Resource exploration	235,494	161,206	159,632	177,436	135,705
Material handling	95,559	79,705	81,513	91,423	96,677
	613,528	493,149	464,823	511,768	451,835
Electronic and electrical products					
Microwave cooking products	179,640	160,104	129,400	69,431	50,585
Medical and electronic products	160,964	187,762	220,776	217,163	192,527
Electronic and electrical components	398,241	336,742	305,389	313,395	306,880
Intrasegment eliminations	(6,759)	(8,492)	(7,527)	(4,800)	(3,346)
	732,086	676,116	648,038	595,189	546,646
Paper, printing, and publishing					
Specialty paper, printing, and forms	215,561	194,108	199,630	190,517	165,126
Educational and professional publishing	74,924	64,676	57,888	61,593	64,488
	290,485	258,784	257,518	252,110	229,614
Advanced electronic systems					
Navigation and control systems	315,045	276,719	286,278	248,034	212,935
Communications and electronic data systems	222,427	203,809	187,236	205,154	185,761
Intrasegment eliminations	(7,520)	(5,502)	(4,797)	(4,725)	(5,241)
	529,952	475,026	468,717	448,463	393,455
Marine engineering and production	616,069	792,213	794,142	906,851	642,618
	3,728,854	3,527,620	3,454,125	3,564,282	3,166,074
Intersegment eliminations	(89,935)	(96,852)	(120,429)	(153,433)	(164,191)
Miscellaneous	14,290	12,156	20,856	1,340	898
Sales and service revenues— continuing operations	$3,653,209	$3,442,924	$3,354,552	$3,412,189	$3,002,781

The above table sets forth the sales and service revenues of continuing operations by classes of similar products or services within the business segments.

Source: Litton Industries, Inc., 1978 Annual Report.

consumer models were not mass marketed until early 1970. Improvements in production technology corresponded in time with tremendous demand for convenience goods and fast-food services. In 1970 the industry sold about 40,000 microwave ovens. The Association of Home Appliance Manufacturers estimated that by the end of 1978 market penetration for microwave ovens in American households would reach 10 percent. Over 2.8 million ovens were sold in 1979, representing sales of over $1.25 billion.

The working principle of microwave cooking is actually quite simple. Microwaves are electromagnetic or radio waves in the gigahertz (in excess of one billion hertz or cycles per second) frequency range with wave lengths between one and one hundred centimeters. The Federal Communication Commission, which regulates all forms of electromagnetic transmissions, has set aside a frequency range equal to 2.45 gigahertz for the use of microwave ovens.

The device inside of these ovens that emits the microwave energy is known as a "magnetron microwave generator." Microwaves, if applied with sufficient energy, will cause the water molecules within food substances to become agitated and start to vibrate. This vibrating action generally begins, unlike conventional cooking, deep within the middle of whatever is being cooked. The vibrating molecules create friction which heats the food, generally in one fourth the time it would take conventionally.

All microwave ovens work on this simple principle, although most manufacturers have added features to facilitate the process further or that overcome some of the inherent problems in microwave cooking. Generally, foods cooked in a microwave oven are more nutritional and have a better, more natural flavor than conventionally prepared foods due to less water and natural vitamin content loss. Of course, the most desired feature remains the faster cooking speed.

Microwave cooking is not suitable for all types of food, a factor that ensures conventional ovens will not become obsolete in the near future. Meats and bread products are notable "problem" foods: Meat because it cooks from the inside out in a microwave oven and tends not to brown on the outside; and bread products because the water content quickly evaporates causing it to harden or not to rise properly. Manufacturers are trying to overcome these problems. Older model ovens generally were powered at a fixed energy level. Newer models, with a variable temperature feature, can emit microwaves intermittently or at different power settings up to the FCC maximum of 625 watts, which assists in more uniform cooking.

In the 1970s advancements in another type of technology took place that vastly affected the nature of microwave cooking. The development of silicon chips and microcircuitry was quickly adopted by the appliance industry to simplify and automate many procedures. Many of today's microwave ovens incorporate such "minicomputers" to facilitate cooking processes. For example, Litton's newest microwave oven, the model 560 Meal-In-One Oven, uses a microprocessor with four levels of memory. This oven "knows" how to cook, reheat, or defrost 47 types of frequently prepared foods with just a touch of a button on a keyboard-like control panel.

Litton's history in electronic technology allowed the company to be one of the first manufacturers of consumer microwave ovens. By 1979 the company was the largest manufacturer with a 25-percent market share. Amana, a division of the Raytheon Corporation and also an early pioneer in the microwave cooking field, was the second largest producer with 20 percent of the market, followed by Sharp, General Electric, and Tappan with 15, 10 and 10 percent shares respectively. Litton's microwave sales contributed almost $180 million in revenues to the company in 1978.

Primary Demand

Until 1978 microwave oven sales for the industry had been increasing at an annual rate exceeding 45 percent, and it has been estimated that by 1985 almost 50 percent of American households would be using the product. Microwave ovens were capable of handling over 80 percent of a household's normal cooking.

Demand for microwaves began to fall off sharply in mid-1978, surprising analysts who expected sales to begin to decline only after market penetration of America's 80 million households exceeded the 20-percent level. In the first six months of 1978, unit sales were only 14 percent ahead of the same period in the previous year. Comparatively, the growth rate for the first six months of 1977 was 43 percent. This represented a shakeout period in the industry with two manufacturers, Farberware and Admiral, dropping out of the American microwave market.

Industry experts generally concurred on several reasons for the unexpected slump. By 1978 there were 35 different manufacturers with microwave models on the U.S. market. The proliferation of brands, each with its own array of special features, was believed to have injected a great deal of confusion into consumer purchasing decisions. The complicated controls on many of the models also was believed to have scared off potential buyers.

Because it was a new and fairly expensive product, the proper marketing strategy called for knowledgeable salespeople to explain and demonstrate the microwave oven's many uses. Industry analysts pointed out that by 1978 most dealers were not putting enough effort into actual cooking demonstrations and other "push type" marketing strategies. This became especially true as mass merchandise retail chains began selling the product. Such stores had neither the time nor the trained salespeople to devote to the kind of personal selling required for such a product.

Another speculation as to the cause for the sudden slump in sales was related to market segmentation. As the manufacturers struggled to differentiate their products from those of their competitors, they began to upgrade their products by adding such items as probes that could automatically cook meat to the correct temperature, rotating carousels to ensure uniform cooking, browning units, defrosting cycles, variable temperature controls, memory storage, delayed timing controls, and so forth. Most manufacturers continued to market the basic, no frills oven models, but emphasis was placed on the deluxe-type models with all the added features. There was a good reason for this, since the fastest growing market segment, representing 32 percent of dollar volume sold, was for the expensive model ovens with retail prices of $450 and up. Litton's Model 560, for example, retailed for $629 and had been very popular.

To date, therefore, there had been very little incentive for manufacturers and retailers to lower prices to encourage demand. Members of the market segment for the more expensive models tended to have higher incomes and better educations, and were more likely to be familiar with the microwave principle, and to have seen it in actual use by friends or relatives. Such consumers were less likely to misunderstand the safety-related factors that had caused much apprehension in the early introductory stages.

Industry experts had begun to wonder whether sales to this particular market segment had reached the saturation level. Many felt that it was time that microwave manufacturers began to concentrate on selling to the larger, more price-conscious market segment which had remained mostly untapped. Research studies over a period of several years showed that there was a large segment of the market (86 percent) who consistently had stated that they had no plans to purchase a microwave oven. Trade analysts felt that many of these people could be encouraged to buy if prices were lower.

Although it remained slightly ahead of the industry with a 20-percent growth rate in 1978, Litton felt the effects of the general sales slump. The company reacted aggressively. The 1978 advertising budget already had been increased by 13.5 percent to over $21.5 million. To counter declining demand, the 1979 ad budget was increased to about $50 million. The company decided to stress product education as the key to market growth, and a large portion of the budget was earmarked for sales training, dealer promotions, and in-store demonstrations. Over 2,000 home economists were hired across the country to demonstrate the product in appliance and department stores, shopping malls, and grocery chains.

The Federal Trade Commission complaint

On January 31, 1979, the Federal Trade Commission formally issued a complaint against Litton stating that some of their earlier advertisements constituted "unfair and deceptive acts or practices in or affecting commerce and unfair methods of competition in or affecting commerce in violations of Section 5 of the Federal Trade Commission Act."[3] The complaint concerned a series of 1976 and 1977 ads in such publications as *Newsweek* and *The Wall Street*

---

[3] Federal Trade Commission Complaint, Docket No. 9123, January 31, 1979, p. 5.

Journal that featured the results of an ''independent'' survey. The FTC charged the ads claimed that:

1. The majority of independent microwave oven service technicians would recommend Litton to their customers.
2. The majority of independent microwave oven service technicians are of the opinion that Litton microwave ovens are superior in quality to all other brands.
3. The majority of independent microwave oven service technicians are of the opinion that Litton microwave ovens require the fewest repairs of all microwave brands.
4. The majority of independent microwave oven service technicians have Litton microwave ovens in their homes.[4]

The FTC stated that such claims were deceptive and unfair and that there was ''no reasonable basis of support for the representations in those advertisements, at the time those representations were made.''[5]

The FTC formally alleged that the survey in no way could be described as ''independent.'' They claimed that Litton hired Custom Research, Inc., to conduct the survey but that Litton designed the survey instrument and analyzed the results themselves and that Custom Research had only engaged in telephoning the respondents who were selected from a list of names supplied by Litton.

The FTC also claimed that the list of respondents were drawn exclusively from a list of Litton-authorized microwave service agencies. The surveys also failed to show that the respondents knew enough about competing brands of microwave ovens to make a comparison to Litton's ovens. The commission also stated that the base number of respondents was too small to have any statistical significance.

In summary, ''the sample surveyed was not representative of the population of independent microwave oven service technicians and the survey was biased.''[6] (Refer to Exhibit 2 for a copy of the Federal Trade Commission complaint. Exhibit 3 shows a sample copy of the Litton advertisements in question.)

The filing of the FTC complaint was accompanied with the usual notice stating the time and place of an administrative hearing at which time Litton had to show cause why it should not be subject to a cease and desist order. Litton did not choose to enter into a consent agreement, whereby the company would not have admitted any of the charges and would have negotiated an order outlining an agreed upon remedy.

At the time the complaint was originally issued, a Litton spokesman made the following public response to the charges:

---

[4] Ibid., p. 2.

[5] Ibid., p. 4.

[6] Ibid.

EXHIBIT 2 Litton complaint and proposed order

UNITED STATES OF AMERICA
BEFORE FEDERAL TRADE COMMISSION

In the Matter of
LITTON INDUSTRIES, INC.,
a corporation.

DOCKET NO. 9123

COMPLAINT

Pursuant to the provisions of the Federal Trade Commission Act, and by virtue of the authority vested in it by said Act, the Federal Trade Commission, having reason to believe that Litton Industries, Inc., a corporation (hereafter "Respondent" or "Litton"), has violated the provisions of said Act, and it appearing to the Commission that a proceeding by it in respect thereof would be in the public interest, hereby issues its complaint stating its charges in that respect as follows:

PARAGRAPH ONE: Litton Industries, Inc., is a corporation, organized, existing, and doing business under and by virtue of the laws of the State of Delaware, with its executive office and principal place of business located at 360 North Crescent Drive, Beverly Hills, California 90210. Litton's Microwave Cooking Products Division is located at 1405 Xenium Lane North, Minneapolis, Minnesota 55441.

PARAGRAPH TWO: Litton is now, and for some time in the past has been, engaged in the manufacture, distribution, advertising, and sale of various products including microwave ovens.

PARAGRAPH THREE: Respondent Litton causes the said products, when sold, to be transported from its place of business in various states of the United States to purchasers located in various other states of the United States and in the District of Columbia. Respondent Litton maintains, and at all times mentioned herein has maintained, a course of trade in said products in and affecting commerce. The volume of business in such commerce has been and is substantial.

PARAGRAPH FOUR: In the course and conduct of said business, Litton has disseminated and caused the dissemination of advertisements for microwave ovens manufactured by Litton, by various means in or affecting commerce, including magazines and newspapers distributed by the mail and across state lines, for the purpose of inducing and which were likely to induce, directly or indirectly, the purchase of said microwave ovens.

PARAGRAPH FIVE: Typical and illustrative of the advertisements so disseminated or caused to be disseminated by Litton are the advertisements attached as Exhibits A, B, C and D, designated as the "initial consumer microwave independent technician survey advertisement," the "revised consumer microwave independent technician survey advertisement," the "initial commercial microwave independent technician survey advertisement," and the "revised commercial microwave independent technician survey advertisement," respectively.

EXHIBIT 2 *(continued)*

PARAGRAPH SIX: In Exhibit A, the "initial consumer microwave independent technician survey advertisement," printed in *The Wall Street Journal,* October 25 and December 13, 1976, and elsewhere, and in Exhibit B,* the "revised consumer microwave independent technician survey advertisement," printed in *HFD Retailing Home Furnishings,* August 22, 1977, and in other advertisements substantially similar thereto, Litton has represented, directly or by implication, that:

1. The majority of independent microwave oven service technicians would recommend Litton to a friend.
2. The majority of independent microwave oven service technicians are of the opinion that Litton microwave ovens are the easiest to repair of all microwave oven brands.
3. The majority of independent microwave oven service technicians are of the opinion that Litton microwave ovens are superior in quality to all other microwave oven brands.
4. The majority of independent microwave oven service technicians are of the opinion that Litton microwave ovens require the fewest repairs of all microwave oven brands.
5. The majority of independent microwave oven service technicians have Litton microwave ovens in their homes.
6. Representations 1–5 were proved by a survey independently conducted by Custom Research, Inc., in June 1976.

PARAGRAPH SEVEN: In Exhibit C,* the "initial commercial microwave independent technician survey advertisement," printed in *Hospitality (Restaurant),* November 1976, and elsewhere, and in Exhibit D,* the "revised commercial microwave independent technician survey advertisement," printed in *Restaurant Business,* September 1977, and elsewhere, and in other advertisements substantially similar thereto, Litton has represented, directly or by implication, that:

1. The majority of independent microwave oven service technicians would recommend Litton to their customers.
2. The majority of independent microwave oven service technicians are of the opinion that Litton commercial microwave ovens are superior in quality to all other microwave oven brands.
3. The majority of independent microwave oven service technicians are of the opinion that Litton commercial microwave ovens are the easiest to repair on location of all microwave oven brands.
4. The majority of independent microwave oven service technicians are of the opinion that Litton commercial microwave ovens require the fewest repairs of all microwave oven brands.
5. The majority of independent microwave oven service technicians are of the opinion that Litton commercial microwave ovens are the least costly to maintain in operation over time of all microwave oven brands.

* Not included here.

EXHIBIT 2 *(continued)*

6. Representations 1–5 were proved by an April 1976 survey independently conducted by Custom Research, Inc.

In addition, in Exhibit C,* Litton has represented, directly or by implication, that Litton is the best commercial microwave oven to buy and that this representation was proved by the above referenced survey.

PARAGRAPH EIGHT: In Exhibits A and B,* and in other advertisements substantially similar thereto, Litton has represented, directly or by implication, that:

1. Litton microwave ovens are superior in quality to all other microwave oven brands.
2. Litton microwave ovens are the easiest to repair of all microwave oven brands.
3. Litton microwave ovens require the fewest repairs of all microwave oven brands.

PARAGRAPH NINE: In Exhibits C* and D,* and in other advertisements substantially similar thereto, Litton has represented, directly or by implication, that:

1. Litton commercial microwave ovens are superior in quality to all other microwave oven brands.
2. Litton commercial microwave ovens are the easiest to repair on location of all microwave oven brands.
3. Litton commercial microwave ovens require the fewest repairs of all microwave oven brands.
4. Litton commercial microwave ovens are the least costly to maintain in operation over time of all microwave oven brands.

PARAGRAPH TEN: In truth and in fact, the April and June 1976 technician surveys conducted for Litton by Custom Research, Inc., do not prove the representations listed in PARAGRAPHS SIX and SEVEN, for reasons including but not limited in the following:

a. The survey respondents were drawn exclusively from the list of Litton authorized microwave oven service agents. As such, the sample surveyed was not representative of the population of independent microwave oven service technicians and the surveys were biased.
b. The surveys failed to establish that the survey respondents possessed sufficient expertise with either (1) microwave ovens or (2) competitive brands of microwave ovens to qualify as respondents for a microwave oven comparative brand survey.
c. In some paired comparisons, the results lacked statistical significance because the base number was too small.

* Not included here.

EXHIBIT 2 *(continued)*

d. The surveys conducted for Litton by Custom Research, Inc., were not in fact independent surveys. The surveys were designed and analyzed by Litton employees. The role of Custom Research was limited to placing the telephone calls, from a list of names supplied by Litton, and conducting the interviews, from a questionnaire supplied by Litton.

For the above reasons, representation 6 in PARAGRAPHS SIX and SEVEN is false. Therefore, representation 6, contained in Exhibits A, B,* C,* and D,* was, and is, deceptive and unfair.

PARAGRAPH ELEVEN: In Exhibits A, B,* C,* and D,* and other advertisements substantially similar thereto, Litton has represented, directly or by implication, that it had a reasonable basis of support for the representations contained in those advertisements at the time those representations were made. In truth and in fact, for the reasons enumerated in PARAGRAPH TEN, Litton had no reasonable basis of support for the representations listed in PARAGRAPHS SIX, SEVEN, EIGHT, and NINE at the time those representations were made. Therefore, the representations listed in PARAGRAPHS SIX, SEVEN, EIGHT, and NINE were, and are, deceptive and unfair.

PARAGRAPH TWELVE: In the course and conduct of the aforesaid business, and at all times mentioned herein, Litton has been and is now in substantial competition in commerce with corporations, firms, and individuals engaged in the sale and distribution of microwave ovens of the same general kind and nature as those sold by Litton.

PARAGRAPH THIRTEEN: The use by Litton of the aforesaid unfair and deceptive statements, representations and practices has had, and now has, the capacity and tendency to mislead members of the consuming public into the purchase of substantial quantities of microwave ovens manufactured by Litton.

PARAGRAPH FOURTEEN: The aforesaid acts and practices of Litton, as herein alleged, were, and are, all to the prejudice and inquiry of the public and of respondent's competitors and constituted, and now constitute, unfair and deceptive acts or practices in or affecting commerce and unfair methods of competition in or affecting commerce in violation of Section 5 of the Federal Trade Commission Act.

WHEREFORE, THE PREMISES CONSIDERED, the Federal Trade Commission on this 31st day of January 1979 issues its complaint against said respondent.

NOTICE

Notice is hereby given to the respondent hereinbefore named that the 19th day of March 1979 at 10:00 o'clock A.M. is hereby fixed as the time and Federal Trade Commission Offices, Gelman Building, 2120 "L" Street, Northwest, Washington, D.C. 20580, as the place when and where a hearing will be had before an administrative law judge of the Federal Trade Commission, on

* Not included here.

EXHIBIT 2 *(continued)*

the charges set forth in this complaint, at which time and place you will have the right under said Act to appear and show cause why an order should not be entered requiring you to cease and desist from the violations of law charged in this complaint.

You are notified that the opportunity is afforded you to file with the Commission an answer to this complaint on or before the thirtieth (30) day after service of it upon you. An answer in which the allegations of the complaint are contested shall contain a concise statement of the facts constituting each ground of defense, and specific admission, denial, or explanation of each fact alleged in the complaint or, if you are without knowledge thereof, a statement to that effect. Allegations of the complaint not thus answered shall be deemed to have been admitted.

If you elect not to contest the allegations of fact set forth in the complaint, the answer shall consist of a statement that you admit all of the material allegations to be true. Such an answer shall constitute a waiver of hearings as to the facts alleged in the complaint, and together with the complaint will provide a record basis on which the administrative law judge shall file an initial decision containing appropriate findings and conclusions and an appropriate order disposing of the proceeding. In such answer you may, however, reserve the right to submit proposed findings and conclusions and the right to appeal the initial decision to the Commission under Section 3.52 of the Commission's Rules of Practice for Adjudicative Proceedings.

Failure to answer within the time above provided shall be deemed to constitute a waiver of your right to appear and contest the allegations of the complaint and shall authorize the administrative law judge, without further notice to you, to find the facts to be as alleged in the complaint and to enter an initial decision containing such findings, appropriate conclusions and order.

The following is the form of order which the Commission has reason to believe should issue if the facts are found to be as alleged in the complaint. If, however, the Commission should conclude from the record facts developed in any adjudicative proceedings in this matter that the proposed order provisions as to Litton Industries, Inc., a corporation, might be inadequate to protect fully the consuming public, the Commission may order such other relief as it finds necessary or appropriate.

ORDER

IT IS ORDERED, that respondent Litton Industries, Inc., a corporation, (hereinafter "Litton") and its successors, assigns, officers, agents, representatives, and employees, directly or through any corporation, subsidiary, division or other device, in connection with the advertising, offering for sale, sale, or distribution of any commercial microwave oven, any consumer microwave oven, or any other consumer product, in or affecting commerce, as "commerce" is defined in the Federal Trade Commission Act, do cease and desist from:

EXHIBIT 2 *(continued)*

1. Representing, directly or by implication, that any commercial microwave oven or consumer microwave oven or any other consumer product:
   a. Is able to perform in any respect, or has any characteristic, feature, attribute, or benefit; or
   b. Is superior in any respect to any or all competing products; or
   c. Is recommended, used, chosen, or otherwise preferred in any respect more often than any or all competing products,
   unless and only to the extent that respondent possesses and relies upon a reasonable basis for such representation at the time of its initial and each subsequent dissemination. Such reasonable basis shall consist of competent and reliable scientific surveys or tests, and/or other competent and reliable evidence.

2. Advertising the results of a survey unless the respondents in such survey are a representative sample of the population referred to in the advertisement, directly or by implication.

3. Representing, directly or by implication, by reference to a survey or test, that experts recommend, use, or otherwise prefer any commercial microwave oven, any consumer microwave oven, or any other consumer product unless:
   a. Such individuals or experts in fact possess the expertise to evaluate such product(s) with respect to such representation;
   b. Such experts actually exercised their expertise by comparatively evaluating or testing the product(s) and based their stated preferences, findings, or opinions on such exercise of their expertise;
   c. Such representation, to the extent it expresses or implies that such product(s) is superior to competing products, is supported by an actual comparison by such experts, and a conclusion therefrom that such product(s) is superior in fact to the competing products with respect to the feature(s) compared.
      For purposes of this order, an "expert" is an individual, group, or institution held out as possessing, as a result of experience, study or training, knowledge of a particular subject, which knowledge is superior to that generally acquired by ordinary individuals.

4. Making representations, directly or by implication, by reference to a survey and/or test, or to any portions or results thereof, concerning the performance or any characteristic, feature, attribute, benefit, recommendation, usage, choice of, or preference for any commercial microwave oven, any consumer microwave oven, or any other consumer product unless:
   a. Such survey and/or test is designed, executed, and analyzed in a competent and reliable manner so as to prove the claims represented;
   b. In regard to any claims of superiority based thereon, such survey and/or test establishes that such product is superior to each compared product in respect to which the specific representation is made to a

EXHIBIT 2 *(continued)*

degree that will be discernible to or of benefit to the persons to whom the representation is directed; and

c.   Such survey and/or test is represented as fully as necessary to assure that all results which are material to the consumer with respect to the specific representations made are disclosed.

For purposes of this order, a survey or test conducted in a "competent and reliable manner" is one in which one or more persons, qualified by professional training and/or education and/or experience, formulate and conduct the survey or test and evaluate its results in an objective manner, using procedures which are generally accepted in the profession, to attain valid and reliable results. The survey or test may be conducted or approved by *(i)* a reputable and reliable organization which conducts such surveys or tests as one of its principal functions, *(ii)* an agency or department of the government of the United States, or *(iii)* persons employed or retained by Litton Industries, Inc. Provided, however, such organization, agency, or persons must be qualified (as defined above in this paragraph) and conduct and evaluate the survey or test in an objective manner.

5.   Misrepresenting in any manner, directly or by implication, the purpose, content, validity, reliability, results, or conclusions of any survey and/or test.

6.   Failing to maintain accurate records, which may be inspected by Commission staff members upon reasonable notice,

a.   Which contain documentation in support or contradiction of any claim included in advertising or sales promotional material disseminated or caused to be disseminated by respondent insofar as the text is prepared, authorized, or approved by any person who is an officer or employee of respondent, or of any division, subdivision or subsidiary of respondent, or by any advertising agency engaged for such purpose by respondent, or by any of its divisions or subsidiaries;

b.   Which provided or contradicted the basis upon which respondent relied at the time of the initial and each subsequent dissemination of the claim; and

c.   Which shall be maintained by respondent for a period of three years from the date such advertising or sales promotional material was last disseminated by respondent or any division or subsidiary of respondent.

IT IS FURTHER ORDERED, that the respondent shall, within sixty (60) days after service upon it of this order, file with the Commission a report in writing, setting forth in detail the manner and form in which it has complied with this order.

IT IS FURTHER ORDERED, that the respondent shall forthwith distribute a copy of this order to each of its operating divisions.

IT IS FURTHER ORDERED, that respondent notify the Commission at least thirty (30) days prior to any proposed change in the corporate respondent such as dissolution, assignment or sale resulting in the emergence of a suc-

EXHIBIT 2 *(concluded)*

cessor corporation, the creation or dissolution of subsidiaries, or any other change in the corporation which may affect compliance obligations arising out of this order.

By the Commission

S E A L

ISSUED: January 31, 1979

Carol Thomas
Secretary

EXHIBIT 3

Quality is No. 1 at Litton!

76% of the independent microwave oven service technicians surveyed* recommend Litton.

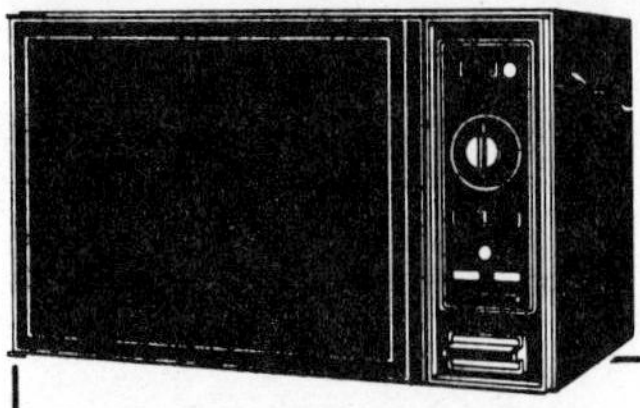

Litton Model 419 microwave oven.

Litton leads all brands.

PREFERENCE FOR SPECIFIC BRANDS AMONG TECHNICIANS SERVICING THOSE BRANDS

Brand To Brand	Litton vs. G.E.	Litton vs. Amana	Litton vs. Magic Chef	AVERAGE PREFERENCE FOR LITTON VS. ALL COMPETITION – (weighted average)
Which Microwave Oven Brand would you recommend to a friend?	59% vs. 23%	66% vs. 18%	81% vs. 1%	76% vs. 8%
Which Microwave Oven Brand is easiest to repair?	68% vs. 5%	65% vs. 8%	71% vs. 0%	72% vs. 4%
Which Microwave Oven Brand is the best quality?	48% vs. 16%	50% vs. 26%	69% vs. 1%	63% vs. 9%
Which Microwave Oven Brand requires fewest repairs?	38% vs. 22%	42% vs. 24%	59% vs. 3%	53% vs. 12%
Which Microwave Oven Brand do you have in your home?	48% vs. 19%	59% vs. 18%	70% vs. 5%	67% vs. 10%

Among independent technicians servicing Litton and competitive microwave ovens, an average of 76% of those surveyed said they would recommend Litton to a friend. And an average of 63% identified Litton brand ovens as having the best quality.

You'll find it in our full line of advanced countertop microwave ovens, double-oven and combination microwave ranges.

Respondents represent independent microwave oven service agencies, who service at least two brands of microwave ovens, (one of them Litton) and do not represent a factory owned service agency. Percentages add to less than 100% due to other responses (other brands and no preference).

*Survey conducted by Custom Research, Inc. Complete survey results available on request.

And in such Litton features as Vari-Cook® oven control, Vari-Temp® automatic temperature control and new Memorymatic™ microwave program cooking. Innovative ways to microwave more foods better.

Need any more reasons to buy Litton? Ask your Litton dealer for a microwave cooking demonstration. For his name and number, call us right now, toll free **800-328-7777.**

LITTON
Microwave Cooking
1405 Xenium Lane No. Minneapolis, Minnesota 55440

Litton... changing the way America Cooks.

We employed an independent research firm to survey our authorized independent microwave service agencies numbering over 500 throughout the U.S. Litton surveyed only those servicemen who repaired at least two brands of ovens and tabulated their response only as to the brands they serviced. Litton feels the claims made in the ads, that up to 80 percent of the servicemen would recommend purchase of Litton microwave ovens, were accurately represented, and that the FTC's concerns are unfounded.[7]

The Federal Trade Commission

The Federal Trade Commission is an independent law enforcement agency charged by the Congress with protecting the public—consumers and business-men alike—against anticompetitive behavior and unfair and deceptive business practices.

The commission has authority to stop business practices that restrict competition or that deceive or otherwise injure consumers, as long as these practices fall within the legal scope of the commission's statutes, affect inter-state commerce, and involve a significant public interest. Such practices may be terminated by cease and desist orders issued after an administrative hearing or by injunctions issued by the federal courts upon application by the commission.

In addition, the FTC defines practices that violate the law so that business-men may know their legal obligations and consumers may recognize those business practices against which legal recourse is available. The commission does this through Trade Regulation Rules and Industry Guides issued peri-odically as "dos and don'ts" to business and industry and through business advice—called Advisory Opinions—given to individuals and corporations re-questing it.

When law violations are isolated rather than industrywide, the FTC exercises its corrective responsibility also by issuing complaints and entering orders to halt false advertising or fraudulent selling or to prevent a businessper-son or corporation from using unfair tactics against competition. The commis-sion itself has no authority to imprison or fine. However, if one of its final cease and desist orders or trade regulation rules is violated, it can seek civil penalties in federal court of up to $10,000 a day for each violation. It can also seek redress for those who have been harmed by unfair or deceptive acts or practices. Redress may include cancellation or reformation of contracts, refunds of money, return of property, and payment of damage.

The commission defines its role, in its literature, as:

> protecting the free enterprise system from being stifled or fetted by monopoly or anticompetitive practices and protecting consumers from unfair or deceptive practices.[8]

---

[7] "Litton Industries, Inc.'s Microwave Oven Ads Deceptive, FTC Says," *The Wall Street Journal,* February 2, 1979, p. 4.

[8] This section is based on *Your FTC: What It Is and What It Does* (Washington, D.C.: The Federal Trade Commission).

The remedies available to the FTC are described in Exhibit 4.

EXHIBIT 4 FTC remedies

I. Assurance of voluntary compliance (nonadjudicative)

 If the commission believes the public interest will be fully safeguarded, it may dispose of a matter under investigation by accepting a promise that the questioned practice will be discontinued. A number of factors are considered by the commission in the rare cases in which it accepts such a promise, including (1) the nature and gravity of the practice in question, and (2) the prior record and good faith of the party.

II. Consent order

 Instead of litigating a complaint, a respondent may execute an appropriate agreement containing an order for consideration by the commission. If the agreement is accepted by the commission, the order is placed on the public record for sixty (60) days during which time comments or views concerning the order may be filed by any interested persons. Upon receipt of such comments or views, the commission may withdraw its acceptance and set the matter down for a formal proceeding, issue the complaint and order in accordance with the agreement, or take such action as it may consider appropriate. Respondents in consent orders do not admit violations of the law, but such orders have the same force and effect as adjudicative orders.

III. Adjudicative order

 An adjudicative order is based on evidence of record obtaining during an adjudicative proceeding that starts when a complaint is issued. The proceeding is conducted before an administrative law judge who serves as the initial trier of facts. After the hearings the judge within 90 days issues his initial decision, which is subject to review by the commission on the motion of either party or on the commission's own motion. Appeals from a final commission decision and order may be made to any proper court of appeals and ultimately to the Supreme Court.

IV. Preliminary injunctions

 The Federal Trade Commission has statutory authority to seek preliminary injunctive relief in federal district court against anyone who is violating or about to violate any provision of law enforced by the FTC.

Source: *Your FTC: What It Is and What It Does* (Washington, D.C.: Federal Trade Commission), p. 26.

Deceptive Practices

Deceptive or fraudulent trade practices affecting consumers have centered around the misuse of advertising. The trend in the agency has been to identify and counter the more subtle forms of false advertising. Businesses, in arguing against the FTC's jurisdiction, have relied heavily on the First Amendment's protection, specifically freedom of speech. In 1976 the U.S. Supreme Court held in *Virginia State Board* v. *Virginia Citizens Consumer Council* that:

> Although an advertiser's interest is purely economic, that hardly disqualifies him from protection under the First Amendment. . . . It is a matter of public interest

that [private economic] decisions, in the aggregate, be intelligent and well informed. To this end, the free flow of commercial information is indispensable.[9]

The Court was reaffirming the First Amendment rights of business enterprises through the right of the public to know facts relevant to decision making in the marketplace.

The Supreme Court, however, held in *Bates* v. *State of Arizona* in 1977 that this First Amendment protection of advertising was entirely dependent upon its truthfulness. ''The public and private benefits from commercial speech derive from confidence in its accuracy and reliability.''[10] In other cases the courts have gone on to say that truthfulness in advertising includes completeness of information, as well as the absence of misleading or incorrect information.

The key legal requirement of advertising is that the advertiser have a ''reasonable basis'' to substantiate the claims made before an ad has been run. Not having a reasonable basis beforehand has been found by the courts to be a violation of Section 5 of the FTC Act as an unfair marketing practice, even if the ad is not deceptive.

It has long been argued that the FTC's simple enforcement power to issue cease and desist orders in regard to false advertising was largely ineffectual since it occurred after the fact and offered no remedial sanctions. Unscrupulous advertisers could get by with a simple admonition to ''go and sin no more.'' Recently, however, the FTC has been increasing the use of such remedial actions as corrective advertising, the most severe of possible penalties facing legitimate marketers.

In 1975, for example, the FTC ordered the Warner-Lambert Company to include a corrective message in their $10 million of advertising. The message would have to say that Listerine was not effective against colds and sore throats, a statement which contradicted the company's earlier advertising. The commission argued that if, under Section 5(b) of the FTC Act, it had:

> the authority to impose the severe and drastic remedy of divestiture in antitrust cases in order to restore competition to a market, surely it had the authority to order corrective advertising to restore truth to the marketplace.[11]

On April 3, 1978, the Supreme Court upheld the FTC order by denying a request to review a lower court's decision.

The FTC, as a rule, has required corrective advertising only when it found that such ads are necessary to present to the public ''the honest and complete information'' about an advertised product to dispel ''the lingering effects of years of false advertising.''[12] Without such measures, advertisers would:

---

[9] William Sklar, ''Ads Are Finally Getting Bleeped at the FTC,'' *Business and Society Review*, September 1978, p. 41.

[10] Ibid., p. 42.

[11] ''Corrective Ad Order not Antifree Speech: FTC,'' *Advertising Age*, September 13, 1976, p. 2.

[12] Ibid.

remain free to misrepresent their products to the public, knowing full well that even if the FTC chooses to prosecute they will be required only to cease an advertising campaign which by that point will, in all likelihood, have served its purpose.[13]

Summary of FTC's Arguments against Litton

In a national advertising campaign which stretched over a year and a half in at least 26 states, Litton Microwave Cooking Products promoted the results of a survey of microwave oven service technicians. (See the sample ad in Exhibit 3.) The advertisements represented the majority of service technicians as recommending Litton microwave ovens on the basis of quality, fewest repairs, and ease of repairs. These advertisements are held by the Federal Trade Commission to be unfair and deceptive in that the survey as conducted does not substantiate the advertisements' claims.

The survey is represented as an independent survey conducted by Custom Research, Inc. In fact, Litton designed the survey, developed the questionnaire, provided the sampling frame, and analyzed the results. Custom Research personnel made the actual phone interviews.

Errors exist in the survey design which biased the results of the study, thus precluding the results being projected to the population of service technicians as represented in the ads. Litton was aware of these biases prior to the implementation of the ad campaign but ran the advertisements anyway. A memorandum sent to executives by Litton's manager of marketing analysis noted that the surveys were likely to be biased and recommended that the source of the sample be kept confidential. The sample used for survey was limited to those service technicians on a list of 500 Litton authorized service agencies. No attempt was made to draw a sample from technicians authorized to service other brands of microwave ovens.

Only one technician from each agency and that technician selected by the person answering the phone was interviewed. Even with this limited, easily accessible sample, response rates were between 42 and 47 percent. Little was done to improve the response rate, and what was done is uncertain since no written interviewer instructions were provided.

With the majority of respondents authorized only by Litton, their familiarity with Litton products would tend to bias their responses. In addition, no screening was conducted to determine if the respondent had recently or ever serviced Litton or the brand compared, thereby failing to establish a level of expertise necessary for answering the questionnaire.

With the survey biased to the point that it cannot be held to substantiate the advertisements' claims, the FTC has proposed an order for Litton Industries, the parent corporation, and all divisions to cease and desist advertisements and representations based on faulty survey techniques or testing. This "strong

---

[13] Ibid.

order'' which refers to all of Litton's consumer products and representations is necessary to ''protect the public interest and to deter respondents from future unfair and deceptive acts.''

Details of the specific FTC arguments are included in Exhibit 5.

EXHIBIT 5 FTC case against Litton

The findings as developed by the FTC are summarized by the following outline:

A. The FTC has *jurisdiction* over the alleged misleading advertisements since substantiation provided by Litton does not constitute a reasonable basis for the advertisement claims.
B. The advertisements are misleading in representing the results of the survey as *projectable to the total population.* Problems exist relative to:
   1. Survey design and statistical significance of the results.
   2. Deficiencies in sampling.
   3. Low response rate.
   4. Representing survey as "independent" survey.
   5. Respondents' possession of "necessary expertise."
   6. Respondents' familiarity with Litton as basis for answers.
   7. Definition of "independent technician."
C. The FTC has the right to issue a "strong order."
   The national advertisement distributed by Litton has represented, directly or by implication, that the majority of independent microwave service technicians:
   Would recommend Litton to a friend.
   Are of the opinion that Litton microwaves are the easiest to repair.
   Are of the opinion that Litton microwaves are superior in quality to other brands.
   Are of the opinion that Litton microwave ovens require the fewest repairs.
   Have Litton microwaves in their homes.

A. Jurisdiction
   Litton is "engaged in the manufacture, distribution, advertising, and sale of various products including microwave ovens."
   Litton causes their products "to be transported from their place of business . . . to purchasers located in various other states."
   Litton has been and is now "in substantial competition in commerce with corporations, firms, and individuals engaged in the sale" of microwave ovens similar to those sold by Litton.
   National advertisements based on the service technician surveys were disseminated in 4 magazines, 28 newspapers, and 6 trade publications.
   One hundred fourteen ads ran during a year and a half period.
   Litton Industries is a proper respondent to this proceeding since it owns and controls Litton Systems of which Litton Microwave Cooking Products is a division.

B. Survey results as advertised are misleading
   The advertisements represent the results of the surveys as projectable to the entire population of independent microwave oven service technicians.
   The disclaimer attempts (the use of "technicians surveyed" or "of those surveyed") in no way limit the representations of the ads as projectable to all technicians.

EXHIBIT 5 *(continued)*

"The ad does not state that those service technicians actually interviewed . . . are in any way different from or might hold differing views than the general population of service technicians."

The many defects in the surveys preclude their results from being capable of supporting "*any* conclusions about the attitudes of . . . microwave oven service technicians."

The surveys do not substantiate the advertised claims.

1. Deficiencies in survey design limit the use of the survey.

There were no written interviewer instructions.

The screening questions on Litton's survey were ambiguous in whether the questions applied to "your company" or "you yourself."

Litton failed to test whether the survey results were statistically significant.

2. Deficiencies in *sampling* procedure preclude projecting results to the population.

The surveys "do not provide accurate and reliable results because the surveys suffer from basic deficiencies in sample design."

All sampling was from lists of Litton approved service agencies. (Litton had in its possession but did not use lists of Magic Chef and Sharp technicians. Lists were also available for other technicians. Technicians not on Litton's authorized list had no chance of being interviewed.)

Litton asserted that samples obtained from their lists of authorized technicians were representative of all independent service technicians.

Litton vastly underestimated the universe of independent microwave oven service agencies. Litton's national field service manager estimated their list of 500 Litton authorized technicians represented 85–90 percent of all microwave service technicians and that there were not more than 100 independent agencies servicing microwave ovens that were not on the Litton list. But, in addition to the list of 500 used as a sampling frame, Litton had a list of 1,700 servicing dealers who repaired Litton microwave ovens under warranty. Other dealers' service networks included numerous additional service agencies: Sharp, 1,480; General Electric, 5,000; Amana, 2,500; Magic Chef, 1,323. These numbers do not include service networks for additional suppliers such as Tappan, Panasonic, Frymaster and Hobart.

From the results of a survey by an independent research company for the FTC, it is estimated that Litton excluded from its consumer survey between 414 and 715 (low and high projections) agencies which serviced Litton plus at least one other brand. At most, 421 service agencies were included in Litton's study. Therefore, Litton excluded at least as many service agencies which service Litton and another brand as it included.

Less than half the technicians surveyed were authorized to service the brand they compared to Litton. They were therefore comparing a brand for which they were authorized with one for which they were not authorized, a source of substantial bias.

Litton's survey methodology of interviewing only one technician per agency and that technician selected by the person answering the phone further limited the possibility of a technician in the population being interviewed and led to biases:

EXHIBIT 5 *(concluded)*

---

    a. Small firms may have been overrepresented.

    b. Technicians who work in the field would have been excluded (Litton's policy was to do warranty work in the home).

    3. The *response rates* in the Litton surveys were low (47 percent for the consumer survey, 42 percent for the commercial survey) leading to nonresponse biases.

    4. "The Litton consumer and commercial surveys were not independent surveys," as the ads suggested. Custom Research merely placed telephone calls to agencies on a list provided by Litton and asked questions from a questionnaire designed by Litton.

    5. "Litton failed to establish that the respondents to the . . . surveys possessed the necessary expertise or relied upon that expertise to compare various brands of microwave ovens."

    6. The Litton survey respondents, as Litton-authorized technicians, were likely to have expressed preferences for Litton microwave ovens because they were most familiar with that brand.

    7. The term "independent microwave oven service technicians" in the ad headlines conveys the meaning of technicians working for independent agencies not owned by a manufacturer. The footnote stating only technicians who served Litton microwaves were interviewed does not qualify the representation of the headline. In fact, a Litton executive was unable to read the fine print of the footnote when asked to do so in court.

C. "The proposed order is required to protect the public from further deceptive and unfair practices." The respondents' conduct justifies a broad order to protect the public, since:

    1. Litton disseminated a large-scale deceptive advertising campaign.

    2. The survey claims are a prominent and material component of the advertisements.

    3. Litton knowingly disseminated results of a biased study.

    4. Litton is a leader in the advertising and marketing of microwave ovens.

    5. Litton sells a number of consumer products to the public.

Summary of Litton's Defense

The original complaint in this action challenged certain advertisements run by Litton Industries as being in violation of Section 5 of the Federal Trade Commission Act. The complaint was preceded by a two-year investigation of a limited number of magazine and newspaper ads run in October through December of 1976 and August and September of 1977.

    Complaint counsel has not met the burden of proving that the advertisements were "deceptive" within the meaning of Section 5. Complaint counsel and their witnesses did nothing more than identify "potential" deviations from *ideal* survey procedures which "might" have influenced the survey results. The procedures used were perfectly reasonable, were in accord with generally accepted survey practice, and yielded reliable results.

Even if one were to assume that a technical violation of Section 5 has occurred, the unintentional, minor nature of any such violation, and the public policy implications of the proposed order dictate that no order should be issued. The proposed order covers all products of Litton Industries. As such, it is punitive in nature, sweeping far beyond the violations, if any.

In essence, the complaint charges that the ads contained three categories of representations: (1) alleged representations concerning the actual superiority of Litton microwave ovens over competitor brands, (2) alleged representations concerning the opinions of the "majority" of independent microwave oven service technicians relative to the superiority of Litton microwave ovens over competitive brands, and (3) alleged representations that the Litton surveys "proved" the first two representations. Only the third category is alleged to be false and misleading. Complaint counsel did not seek to prove that Litton was *not* superior to competitive brands on the attributes listed or even that independent service technicians were *not* of that opinion. The main issue was not the specific allegations in the ads but, rather, the sufficiency of the surveys upon which the ads were based.

The key issues, then, are (1) were the ads interpreted by the readers of those ads in the manner alleged in the complaint and (2) if so, did the survey provide a "reasonable basis" for any representations which were made. On both issues, complaint counsel bears the burden of proof. A careful examination of the record reveals that complaint counsel misconceived the nature of their burden of proof and fell far short of meeting it. What the record does reveal is that Litton Industries attempted in good faith to conduct reliable surveys aimed at guiding its future marketing and engineering decisions. The surveys were designed and conducted in a manner which would lead to results upon which a "reasonably prudent businessman" could rely.

The surveys were designed and conducted as part of the business planning function at Litton. Specifically, the surveys were in response to advertising and point-of-sale literature by Amana which directly and implicitly raised questions concerning the quality of Litton microwave ovens. These Amana ads emphasized the fact that Amana had received an exemption from a warning label requirement and caused certain Litton dealers to question the quality of Litton microwave ovens. As a result of the Amana ads, Litton dealers began encountering problems on the sales floors. Their concerns were communicated to Litton management.

The problems caused by Amana's attacks on the quality of Litton microwave ovens persisted. As a result, product quality became a frequent subject of discussion. The Litton marketing division president and Litton microwave consumer products president became very concerned that perhaps the quality of Litton microwave ovens was in fact deteriorating and that they were not being adequately informed. Thus, in the early spring of 1976, Litton decided to investigate the quality of Litton microwave ovens through market research studies.

It was only after Litton conducted its studies for internal management purposes and analyzed the results that the idea of incorporating the results into advertising germinated. That possibility was not even seriously considered until September 1976. In fact, the ads were not included in the advertising budget for 1976–77. As a result, special approval had to be obtained from the president of Litton microwave consumer products in order to prepare the ads.

The advertising copy which ultimately emerged from the surveys fairly presented the results, at a level of detail so complete that it threatened their effectiveness as an advertising tool. The decision to present the data fully was made so that the ads would withstand any subsequent scrutiny.

This case was chosen by Federal Trade Commission staff as a "test" case for establishing industrywide standards for the advertising of survey results and for the procedures which must be followed in such surveys. Indeed, the commission press release announcing the issuance of the complaint identified it as a test case which would set standards for advertising surveys and tests. Thus, the key issue is whether Litton had a "reasonable basis" upon which to make the claims included in the ads.

The arguments made by Litton as their defense are summarized in Exhibit 6.

EXHIBIT 6 Summary of Litton's defense

A. Litton acted in good faith in designing and conducting the surveys.

Litton confined the surveys to independent microwave oven service agencies servicing multiple brands, including Litton.

Litton followed the definition of independent microwave service agency commonly used in the industry: one which services but does not sell microwave ovens (this definition excluded over 1,700 Litton dealers who serviced Litton microwave ovens).

Independent service technicians eliminated a potential source of bias since they have no special tie to one manufacturer and are experienced in servicing many makes of microwave ovens.

Litton used a list of independent service agencies identified by a nationally known expert as the most reliable source. This list was nearly exhaustive and thus was representative of the universe of independent service agencies.

Interviewers were specifically instructed to ask for an experienced service technician. The respondent had to have worked for the agency for at least one year. The agency had to have serviced microwave ovens for at least one year. Only technicians who serviced at least two brands, including Litton, were interviewed.

To ensure unbiased representation of all brands serviced by the technicians surveyed, those comparisons were made between Litton and other brands only if the respondents serviced both brands.

A reputable outside organization, Custom Research, Inc., conducted the surveys.

Litton's identity as the research sponsor was never disclosed to the respondents. Also, the interviewers were not aware of the survey purpose.

In each ad, the headline prominently states that results pertain only to those "independent microwave service technicians surveyed."

EXHIBIT 6 *(continued)*

The ads carefully delineate the groups surveyed and that the survey was conducted by Custom Research, Inc.

The ads were targeted to a special audience of businessmen and microwave oven purchasers who were characterized by complaint counsel witnesses as upscale, sophisticated, and knowledgeable.

The total cost of all the survey ads was $215,384.29, only 2.1 percent of the Litton microwave advertising budget for the 1976–1977 year.

When the FTC challenged the initial ads, Litton modified the ads in response to the criticisms.

B. The specialized audience interpreted the representations in a distinctly limited manner.

Complaint counsel, under Section 5 of the FTC Act must prove that the ads were interpreted by the audience in a way which suggests "the capacity or tendency to mislead." Yet complaint counsel developed no empirical data nor called any expert to testify on the issue.

Expert testimony concluded that the small portion of the audience which attached any significance to the ads would merely perceive that a study had been done, that it involved people with major biasing ties to a manufacturer who were qualified to service microwave ovens, and that their opinions were obtained on various characteristics of microwave ovens.

The most which the ads could have possibly done was to convince a small number of readers who were otherwise uncertain that Litton was one of the brands worthy of further consideration.

The ads did not state, as alleged in the complaint, that a "majority" of *all* independent service technicians preferred Litton.

The combination of *low* public trust in surveys, the *lower* public trust in surveys conducted by private companies, the inherent cautiousness of readers of ads generally, and the even greater caution exercised by "upscale" readers lead to the conclusion the interpretations alleged in the complaint did not occur.

C. The surveys were conducted in accordance with generally accepted practices in the survey research community.

To prove that the Litton surveys did not provide a "reasonable basis" for representations made in the ads, complaint counsel had to establish that (1) generally accepted standards for survey and market research exist within the industry, (2) the procedures followed by Litton represent substantial, unreasonable deviations from those standards, and (3) such deviations resulted in demonstrable biases favoring Litton and thus in advertising which was "deceptive" within the reasoning of Section 5 of the FTC Act. Complaint counsel met *none* of the three requirements.

Expert witnesses were unable to define generally accepted survey research standards.

The Litton survey was, in the opinion of expert witnesses, "indicative of typical industry practice."

EXHIBIT 6 *(concluded)*

D. The surveys were conducted in an accurate and unbiased manner.

The universe was carefully defined to eliminate any significant risk or bias.

The Litton surveys were an attempted census of the ascertainable agencies in the universe.

The procedures to respond to the survey were reasonable and produced reliable results.

The use of Litton's authorized service agency lists was proper and introduced no bias into the survey results.

The questionnaires used adequately qualified respondents and produced accurate results.

Response rates were within normal and accepted ranges and did not create any biases.

Tests of statistical significance were neither necessary nor proper.

Litton's role in the surveys was consistent with normal survey procedures and with the advertised claims.

Interviewer instruction and supervision was entirely adequate.

Part 9

Marketing Programs and Strategy

This section contains seven cases which are comprehensive in nature, requiring the student to make a number of decisions in several different marketing decision areas. Thus, a great deal of integration is necessary. A decision in one of the marketing areas may have a significant impact on the other decisions which must be made to complete the marketing program.

In developing a complete marketing program for a product, one must start with the firm's overall goals and objectives. Then all the environmental factors such as demand, competition, marketing laws, distribution alternatives, and cost structure must be analyzed. At this point, a number of opportunities as well as potential problems will have been identified, and specific marketing objectives can be established.

The marketer must make a clear definition of the target market(s) to be served. This can be determined only after a thorough evaluation of all the alternative segments of the market, their needs, wants, attitudes and behavior, the strengths and weaknesses of the firm's products and those of competitors, and the potential profitability of various alternatives.

The next step in developing the marketing program is to search for the optimal marketing mix; that is, what is the best combination of product strategy, pricing strategy, promotion strategy, and distribution strategy? Typically, there will be a number of possible alternatives for each of these, so the marketer must determine the interrelationships among them and choose the optimal combination based upon a complete situation analysis.

The last step in the development of a marketing program is to create a plan for implementing the program. Without adequate implementation, even the best designed plans will fail.

Case 38

A&W Drive-Ins (Fundy) Limited*

"It is all psychological—when he picks up that burger it feels pretty good. The merchandising appeal of that larger hamburger and the weight in comparison to McDonald's is significant—it is noticed by the customer. A&W isn't strong enough in the market that we can afford to tinker with the portioning, which is definitely one of our strong points." These thoughts passed through Mr. Ed Drayson's mind in 1973 as he sat preparing a set of recommendations for the company's board of directors. The company was facing rapidly rising food and operating costs in its A&W outlets in the Atlantic Provinces of Canada. These rising costs were threatening to drastically cut the contribution these outlets made to company overhead and profit.

The cost pressures were particularly severe in A&W's hamburger line, where meat costs were expected to be 40 percent higher in the summer of 1973 than they had been in the fall of 1972. The company's problems were compounded by the increasing competition posed by McDonald's and other fast-food operators, who were aggressively expanding in the A&W (Fundy) market area.

The Company

Mr. Drayson was the president of A&W Drive-Ins (Fundy) Limited, and was directly responsible for the firm's A&W operations. Mr. Drayson's office was located in Moncton, New Brunswick, although the company's head office staff, whose main function was to provide accounting services for the company, was located in Toronto. All the managers of A&W outlets in the Atlantic Provinces reported directly to Mr. Drayson. The company was also involved in a number of non-A&W activities. Mr. Harry Brathwaite, the chairman of the board, spent much of his time supervising these activities.

A&W Drive-Ins (Fundy) was a franchisee of A&W Food Services of Canada Limited which held the A&W franchise for Canada. A&W (Fundy)

---

* This case was written by Adrian B. Ryans, Associate Professor of Marketing, Stanford University. Used with permission of the author and the University of Western Ontario.

operated eight A&W outlets in the Atlantic Provinces, and five outlets in Ontario. There were also a number of other A&W operators in the Atlantic Provinces, but none had franchises in the cities served by A&W (Fundy). The locations of the eight outlets in New Brunswick, Nova Scotia, and Prince Edward Island are shown in Exhibit 1. Monthly sales by outlet for 1971, 1972, and the first three months of 1973 are shown in Exhibit 2. All outlets in the Atlantic Provinces, except Oromocto, were drive-in restaurants. The Oromocto restaurant provided inside seating in a shopping centre.

For each unit A&W (Fundy) had opened, it had entered into a license agreement with A&W Food Sevices of Canada. Basically each franchise agreement granted the franchisee a license to operate a drive-in restaurant and to use the A&W trademarks in advertising and on menus, packaging, and signs in the preparation and sale of A&W beverages, products, and approved menu items. The license agreement remained in effect for a 20-year term, provided the franchisee met the terms of the agreement—the major ones being:

The franchisee was to pay an initial fee of $2,500 and an annual service fee of approximately 1 percent of gross sales.

EXHIBIT 1 Location of A&W (Fundy) units

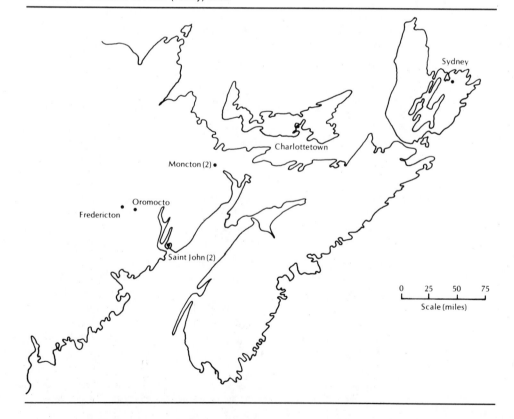

EXHIBIT 2 Monthly sales by unit (1971–1973)

	Jan.	Feb.	March	April	May	June	July	Aug.	Sept.	Oct.	Nov.	Dec.	Total
1971 Sales													
Charlottetown	$ 17,503	$ 18,740	$ 21,594	$ 27,139	$ 29,235	$ 28,806	$ 43,320	$ 43,435	$ 31,357	$ 31,965	$ 29,879	$ 23,387	$ 346,360
Fredericton	20,405	18,706	24,182	32,027	36,675	29,639	38,810	38,230	35,954	37,354	37,144	25,553	374,679
Sydney	22,196	21,594	26,534	31,785	34,851	34,709	36,242	35,535	29,139	29,923	29,244	24,853	356,605
Saint John No. 1	20,157	19,928	24,548	28,563	31,432	30,338	34,766	34,562	31,062	34,545	34,390	24,836	349,127
Saint John No. 2	—	—	—	—	—	—	—	—	—	—	—	26,295	26,295
Moncton No. 1	11,787	12,268	13,782	18,096	21,074	20,433	24,587	24,895	21,757	22,366	20,635	17,074	228,754
Moncton No. 2	9,380	9,956	11,573	15,006	17,959	18,267	24,518	24,164	19,634	20,095	18,926	14,818	204,296
Oromocto	16,408	14,006	15,886	16,182	16,710	18,042	25,307	23,465	17,665	21,212	16,818	16,833	218,534
	$117,836	$115,198	$138,099	$168,798	$187,936	$180,234	$227,550	$224,286	$186,568	$197,460	$187,036	$173,649	$2,104,650
1972 Sales													
Charlottetown	$ 20,702	$ 21,728	$ 25,690	$ 34,638	$ 34,776	$ 40,496	$ 61,649	$ 58,361	$ 38,499	$ 36,301	$ 33,877	$ 33,707	$ 440,424
Fredericton	19,091	18,890	23,569	35,592	36,048	38,181	43,070	40,555	38,478	33,413	28,789	24,639	380,315
Sydney	21,176	17,739	25,025	30,202	35,998	39,186	43,082	43,353	33,848	30,096	31,167	31,329	382,201
Saint John No. 1	21,067	19,975	24,655	33,339	36,497	35,001	40,783	37,660	31,339	31,543	28,687	25,957	366,503
Saint John No. 2	22,523	19,712	24,090	32,407	35,245	34,725	36,994	36,164	30,128	28,956	27,123	25,384	353,451
Moncton No. 1	14,942	13,559	16,764	24,350	26,673	28,319	32,738	31,598	27,013	24,540	21,266	19,620	281,382
Moncton No. 2	12,572	11,246	14,197	20,314	22,611	25,765	31,822	31,520	24,857	21,693	18,864	16,976	252,437
Oromocto	13,875	13,399	15,950	16,255	16,953	20,531	24,951	22,573	17,253	17,224	16,903	16,424	212,291
	$145,948	$136,248	$169,940	$227,097	$244,801	$262,204	$315,089	$301,784	$241,415	$223,766	$206,676	$194,036	$2,669,004
1973 Sales													
Charlottetown	$ 30,390	$ 28,243	$ 42,264										
Fredericton	21,754	23,534	34,311										
Sydney	26,636	20,719	30,095										
Saint John No. 1	24,860	23,245	28,031										
Saint John No. 2	23,473	22,369	29,970										
Moncton No. 1	17,737	16,878	23,578										
Moncton No. 2	15,898	14,257	22,830										
Oromocto	14,825	14,528	19,482										
	$175,573	$163,773	$230,561										

EXHIBIT 3 April 1973 menu

BURGERS

PAPA BURGER .64
2 Patties Meat

MAMA BURGER 44
Single Patty

BABY BURGER 24
(Cheese on above 5¢, Bacon 5¢)

TEEN BURGER 59
SINGLE PATTY · LETTUCE · TOMATO
BACON · MAYONNAISE · CHEESE ·
TOASTED SESAME SEED BUN

**ALL SERVED WITH YOUR CHOICE OF
MUSTARD, KETCHUP, PICKLES
and ONIONS**

BEVERAGES

A & W ROOT BEER 20   .15
Baby Root Beer free to children under 6

A & W ORANGE 20   .15

ICE CREAM FLOAT . . . . .10 extra

MILK SHAKES 35

MILK 30   .20

COFFEE 15

TEA 15

HOT CHOCOLATE 15

	Gal.	½ Gal.	Qt.
Root Beer	.95	.60	.35
Orange	1.00	.80	.50
	Plus Deposit		

SIDE ORDERS

COLE SLAW, side order 15

HOT DOG 34

WHISTLE DOG 49
With bacon, cheese & relish

FRENCH FRIES, side order 19   .29

ONION RINGS 35

FISH & CHIPS 65

FRIED CLAMS (When available) 75

FRIED CLAMS & CHIPS 95

**CONEY SAUCE, on Hot Dogs
Burgers and Fries** 15

STRAWBERRY SHORTCAKE 39

APPLE TURNOVER 20

SUNDAE 25
Chocolate or Strawberry

ICE CREAM 15

CHICKEN

CHUBBY DINNER 1.19
3 Pcs. Chicken, French Fries

CHUBBY JUNIOR 89
2 Pcs. Chicken, French Fries

CHUBBY "6" 1.79
6 Pcs. Chicken

CHUBBY "12" 2.99
12 Pcs. Chicken

CHUBBY "18" 4.49
18 Pcs. Chicken

FAMILY PAK FRENCH FRIES 95

COLE SLAW
½ pint 30   1 pint 50

**ALL ORDERS CAN BE PREPARED
FOR TAKE OUT**

A & W DRIVE-INS (FUNDY) LIMITED

(See List of Maritime Locations on Back)

The restaurant was to be constructed, at the franchisee's expense, in accordance with plans and specifications provided by A&W Food Services of Canada.

The equipment for the restaurant had to be purchased from the franchisor.

The operator of the restaurant was required to attend an A&W restaurant management training course.

The franchisee was required to purchase all uniforms, packaging materials and special A&W concentrates, syrups, bases, and spices from the franchisor.

The recent agreements required the franchisee to contribute 1.50 percent of his gross sales to a national advertising and promotional fund. Some of the agreements required contributions to a regional advertising fund. Most agreements also specified a minimum percentage of gross sales that must be spent on local promotion and advertising.

Unlike a number of other fast-food franchisors, A&W Food Services of Canada did allow the franchisee some latitude in the selection of his menu. He was required to serve certain products, such as the "Burger Family," but he was also allowed to select items from a list of optional products, and he could, if authorized by A&W Food Services of Canada, offer specialty items. "Fried clams" was one such item on the menu of the A&W (Fundy) outlets. The menu in use in the A&W (Fundy) outlets in April 1973 is shown in Exhibit 3.

Commenting on the terms of the franchise agreement, Mr. Drayson noted that the costs of supplies, while marked up by the franchisor, were not greatly different from the prices A&W (Fundy) would have to pay in the market, given its smaller purchasing power. With regards to the requirements for local advertising and promotion Mr. Drayson noted that it was not constraining, since A&W (Fundy) typically allocated a much higher percentage of sales to local advertising and promotion. In summarizing, Mr. Drayson pointed out that the value of a franchise and the reasonableness of the terms depend ultimately on the attention to, and the skill of the national firm in, building the A&W image, creating effective national advertising and promotion, and providing operating and menu suggestions. He indicated that he felt that the national advertising and promotion programme of A&W Food Services of Canada could be improved.

The Competition

Most of the A&W outlets operated in a highly competitive environment, with competition ranging from local takeouts to such national chains as McDonald's, Harvey's, and Kentucky Fried Chicken. Some of the local chains such as Deluxe French Fries in Moncton were well established with good local reputations.

The toughest competitive environment existed in Moncton, where there were two A&W's, two McDonald's, one Harvey's, two Kentucky Fried Chicken stores and three Deluxe French Fries outlets. A&W (Fundy) had opened its first drive-in in the Atlantic Provinces in Moncton in July 1965. Harvey's had been the first national competitor to follow A&W into Moncton, which it did in 1968. The second A&W drive-in was opened in 1969 and was located about two miles from the first one. The opening of the second outlet had a significant impact on the sales of the first one. McDonald's entered Moncton with two outlets in 1970. The McDonald's were both located within one-quarter mile of the two A&W outlets. In fact every major competitor in Moncton had a store located within about one-half mile of A&W's Moncton No. 1 drive-in. Until McDonald's entered Moncton, the sales in the two A&W drive-ins had been expanding steadily. After the opening, A&W's sales in Moncton dropped and then gradually began to rise again. The impact of the opening was such that A&W's sales in the year following the opening were about equal to those in the previous year.

In April 1973, there were approximately 300 A&W outlets in Canada. By comparison there were less than 100 McDonald's units, although McDonald's had announced that by the end of 1973 they planned to have 140 units in operation. Mr. Drayson knew that the McDonald's operation was in many ways different from his own A&W operation. He felt that some of these differences were reflected in two McDonald's pro forma income statements shown in Exhibit 4. These income statements were from 1972 material provided by McDonald's to prospective franchisees, and were said to represent typical pro forma statements for McDonald's units in Canada.

In April 1973, McDonald's had one outlet in Fredericton which had opened in June 1971 and one in Saint John that had only been open about two weeks. The McDonald's unit in Saint John was located within a quarter mile of

EXHIBIT 4 McDonald's typical Canadian pro forma statement

		Percent		Percent
Net sales	$400,000	100.0%	$600,000	100.0%
Food	134,000	33.5	201,000	33.5
Paper	20,000	5.0	30,000	5.0
Total cost	154,000	38.5%	231,000	38.5%
Gross profit	246,000	61.5	369,000	61.5
Controllable expenses:				
Crew labor	69,200	17.3	94,200	15.7
Management labor	19,200	4.8	19,200	3.2
Payroll deductions	5,500	1.4	6,500	1.1
Travel expenses	750	0.2	750	0.1
Advertising	16,000	4.0	24,000	4.0
Promotion	4,000	1.0	6,000	1.0
Outside services	2,800	0.7	2,900	0.5
Linen	2,000	0.5	2,200	0.4
Operating supplies	3,500	0.9	4,000	0.7
Maintenance and repairs	4,000	1.0	4,500	0.7
Utilities	8,000	2.0	8,500	1.4
Office and telephone expenses	900	0.2	1,000	0.2
Miscellaneous	750	0.2	850	0.1
Total controllables	136,600	34.2%	174,600	29.1%

EXHIBIT 4 *(concluded)*

		Percent		*Percent*
Noncontrollable expenses:				
Rent*	$ 34,000	8.5	$ 51,000	8.5
Service fee	12,000	3.0	18,000	3.0
Legal and accounting	700	0.2	700	0.1
Insurance	1,600	0.4	1,600	0.3
Taxes and licenses	4,800	1.2	4,800	0.8
Equipment lease	720	0.2	720	0.1
Depreciation and amortization†	9,625	2.4	9,625	1.6
Total noncontrollables	63,445	15.9%	86,445	14.4%
Total operating expenses	200,045	50.0	261,045	43.5
Net operating income	45,955	11.5	107,955	18.0
Cash flow	$ 55,580	13.9%	$117,580	19.6%

Note: All the above figures are estimates and can change due to many factors.

* Note that McDonald's owns the land and building.

† Based over 10 years on assets, 20 years on fees.

A&W's Saint John No. 1 drive-in. In the two weeks since the McDonald's unit had opened, sales in the Saint John No. 1 outlet had been about 20 percent lower than in the corresponding period in 1972. Mr. Drayson had heard rumours that a second McDonald's was soon to be built in Saint John. Mr. Drayson had also just learned that McDonald's had purchased a site in Sydney directly across the street from the A&W drive-in. This store was expected to open in October 1973. McDonald's was also reported to be looking for a site in Charlottetown. Again, it seemed quite likely that the McDonald's would be close to the A&W.

McDonald's April 1973 prices and those for the most nearly comparable A&W products were as shown in the accompanying table:

McDonald's		*A&W*	
Hamburger	0.25	Baby Burger	0.24
(1 ¹⁄₁₀ lb. patty)*		(1 ¹⁄₁₀ lb. patty)	
Cheeseburger	0.30	Baby Burger with cheese	0.29
(1 ¹⁄₁₀ lb. patty)		(1 ¹⁄₁₀ lb. patty)	
¼ lb. Burger	0.60	Papa Burger	0.64
(1 ¼ lb. patty)		(2 ½ lb. patties)	
¼ lb. Cheeseburger	0.70	Papa Burger with cheese	0.69
(1 ¼ lb. patty)		(2 ½ lb. patties)	
Big Mac	0.65	Teenburger	0.59
(2 ¹⁄₁₀ lb. patties)		(1 ½ lb. patty)	
Fries	0.23 & 0.39	Fries	0.19 & 0.29
Milk shakes	0.30	Milk shakes	0.35
Drinks	0.15 & 0.20	Drinks	0.15 & 0.20

* All weights are uncooked weight.

The competitive situation in each of the six cities is summarized in Exhibit 5.

EXHIBIT 5 Major A&W competitors (in operation and expected—March 31, 1973)

Moncton, N.B.
McDonald's—two units (1970)
Harvey's (1968)
Kentucky Fried Chicken—two units
Deluxe French Fries—three units
Independents

Saint John, N.B.
McDonald's (March 1973, second unit expected)
Deluxe French Fries—two units
Kentucky Fried Chicken—two units
Independents

Fredericton, N.B.
McDonald's (June 1971)
Kentucky Fried Chicken—two units
Dixie Lee Fried Chicken
Independents

Sydney
Kentucky Fried Chicken
Independents
McDonald's (expected October 1973)

Charlottetown
Kentucky Fried Chicken
Independents
McDonald's (expected)

Oromocto
None

Mr. Drayson had received in 1971 a report conducted for A&W's national advertising agency by a firm of consultants. A total of 1,200 people had been interviewed by telephone, with equal sample sizes in Moncton, Montreal, Toronto, Edmonton, Kamloops, and Vancouver. Quota sampling had been used in each city to ensure that 50 married adult males, 50 married adult females, 50 males 16–20 years old and 50 females 16–20 years old would be interviewed. The research had been undertaken to determine the awareness, trial, and usage of various drive-in eating places. Some results from this study are reported in Exhibit 6.

A&W (Fundy) and other A&W operators in the Maritimes spent over $150,000 in media advertising in the Maritimes, using materials produced and made available by A&W's national advertising agency. The advertising fea-

EXHIBIT 6 Excerpts from consultant's report

A. Reasons for preferring favourite
   eating place

	A&W	Deluxe	Mc Donald's	Harvey's	All other burgers	All chicken	All pizza	All other	Total
Number of respondents	451	46	118	78	209	111	38	87	1,138
Food:									
Quantity of	6%	11%	3%	4%	3%	5%	3%	3%	5%
Variety of	5	4	1	5	5	—	8	2	4
Type of	15	—	8	8	4	10	21	7	10
Quality/taste of	54	28	20	42	42	34	26	56	44
Other specific	2	—	—	1	1	5	3	1	2
Other nonspecific	—	—	10	—	10	1	—	3	3
Service:									
Speed of	6	13	19	9	10	13	13	14	10
Efficiency	16	7	8	4	4	10	5	6	10
Other specific	1	—	2	—	3	2	—	2	2
Other nonspecific	*	—	3	—	4	2	—	—	1
Premises:									
Clean	4	2	3	3	7	5	—	6	4
Decor/atmosphere	2	—	1	3	8	2	8	5	3
Facilities/seating/ fixtures, etc.	13	—	2	3	9	2	16	5	8
Parking/parking lot	1	—	2	1	*	3	—	1	1
Other specific	1	—	1	—	*	1	3	1	1
Other nonspecific	—	—	—	—	*	2	—	1	*
Location:									
Convenience of/no. of/ location	28	33	36	31	35	41	24	44	33
Other specific	1	—	—	—	—	—	—	—	*
Other nonspecific	*	—	—	—	—	—	—	—	*
Price/value, etc./all mentions	6	30	52	10	15	13	5	15	15
Other:									
Opportunity	*	—	2	—	—	2	—	—	1
Desire	*	—	—	—	—	—	—	—	*
Availability of transportation	1	—	—	—	*	1	8	2	1
Usual spot/place	6	2	3	1	1	—	—	1	3
Where friends go	15	7	10	14	8	1	11	8	11
Staff of eating place	6	—	3	—	4	—	5	8	4
Other comments	5	—	5	4	3	5	—	8	4
Nothing	*	—	—	—	—	—	—	—	*
Don't know	1	—	1	3	—	—	—	—	1
No answer	3	2	2	5	2	2	3	5	3

Note: Column percentages may add up to more than 100 percent due to multiple responses by some respondents.
* Less than 0.5 percent.

EXHIBIT 6 *(continued)*

B. Things disliked about A&W by those who do not visit A&W most frequently (by municipality)

	Monc-ton	Mon-treal	To-ronto	Edmon-ton	Kam-loops	Van-couver
Number of respondents	121	117	142	69	72	166
Food:						
Quantity of	4%	2%	1%	—	8%	4%
Variety of	3	3	2	—	3	5
Type of	2	5	—	10%	1	3
Quality/taste of	15	8	15	22	18	16
Other specific	—	2	1	—	—	5
Other nonspecific	—	—	—	—	—	3
Service:						
Speed of	3	—	10	14	17	13
Efficiency	7	—	2	7	3	5
Other specific	1	1	1	3	—	4
Other nonspecific	—	—	—	—	—	1
Premises:						
Clean	—	—	1	1	—	2
Decor/atmosphere	1	2	1	3	4	4
Facilities/seating/ fixtures, etc.	5	3	12	6	6	10
Parking/parking lot	2	1	—	3	1	1
Other specific	—	—	3	1	—	—
Other nonspecific	—	—	—	—	—	—
Location:						
Convenience of/no. of/ location	4	20	8	10	1	2
Other specific	—	—	—	—	—	—
Other nonspecific	—	—	—	—	—	—
Price/value, etc./all mentions	31	4	12	7	29	20
Other:						
Opportunity	—	—	—	—	—	—
Desire	—	3	—	—	—	—
Availability of transportation	4	2	2	6	1	—
Usual spot/place	—	2	1	—	—	1
Where friends go	—	—	—	—	4	—
Staff of eating place	—	3	2	1	1	5
Other comments	1	3	3	16	1	2
Nothing	25	24	25	22	13	14
Don't know	2	10	19	1	—	11
No answer	7	15	5	6	12	3

Note: Percentages may add to more 100 percent as some respondents gave more than one answer.

EXHIBIT 6 *(concluded)*

C. Things liked about A&W by those who do not visit A&W most frequently (by municipality)

	Monc-ton	Mon-treal	To-ronto	Edmon-ton	Kam-loops	Van-couver
Number of respondents	121	117	142	69	72	166
Food:						
Quantity of	2%	—	—	6%	1%	1%
Variety of	2	4%	5%	4	6	2
Type of	—	8	13	9	4	25
Quality/taste of	45	18	19	49	54	23
Other specific	1	3	4	4	1	11
Other nonspecific	—	—	—	—	—	—
Service:						
Speed of	19	4	4	10	15	6
Efficiency	7	11	8	25	11	4
Other specific	1	3	1	—	—	5
Other nonspecific	1	—	—	—	—	2
Premises:						
Clean	6	—	3	3	3	2
Decor/atmosphere	—	—	1	1	3	—
Facilities/seating/ fixtures	17	23	8	4	6	3
Parking/parking lot	—	4	1	3	3	1
Other specific	—	—	—	1	1	—
Other nonspecific	—	—	—	—	—	—
Location:						
Convenience of/no. of/ location	4	—	4	4	8	4
Other specific	—	—	—	—	—	—
Other nonspecific	—	—	—	—	—	—
Price/value, etc./all mentions	2	1	2	7	8	1
Other:						
Opportunity	—	—	—	—	1	—
Desire	—	—	—	—	—	—
Availability of trans-portation	2	—	—	—	—	—
Usual spot/place	—	—	—	—	—	—
Where friends go	1	—	—	3	—	—
Staff of eating place	10	1	2	10	13	4
Other comments	1	4	3	4	—	4
Nothing	10	3	18	10	4	12
Don't know	5	9	21	9	—	9
No answer	9	32	11	1	8	5

Note: Percentages may add to more than 100 percent as some respondents gave more than one answer.

tured two fictional characters, Albert and Walter, who were used to promote the high quality of A&W's products and particular items on the A&W menu. The overall theme was "Two great ideas are better than one"—which referred to the root beer and burger combinations. Little was known about McDonald's spending plans except that they provided heavy advertising support when they opened new units. McDonald's advertising and promotion was generally regarded by those in the fast-food trade as being of the highest quality, with its varied emphasis on children's promotions and the overall theme of "You deserve a break today."

Each A&W (Fundy) outlet completed a daily report of operations. Hour-by-hour sales and customer count were two of the items included in these reports. Summaries of two of these forms for different outlets and different days are included in Exhibit 7.

EXHIBIT 7 Summary of selected data from daily operations reports

Ending hour	Unit A (Sunday)		Unit B (Friday)	
	Hourly sales	Hourly customer count	Hourly sales	Hourly customer count
Noon	$ 23.92	13	$ 10.19	6
1 P.M.	92.02	34	84.94	41
2 P.M.	71.63	27	26.65	15
3 P.M.	64.15	33	16.75	12
4 P.M.	100.10	41	19.33	20
5 P.M.	137.72	51	20.53	13
6 P.M.	220.57	70	91.38	34
7 P.M.	221.68	77	86.80	33
8 P.M.	127.67	47	55.78	25
9 P.M.	125.71	50	34.96	17
10 P.M.	174.70	70	52.46	34
11 P.M.	155.03	60	76.85	40
Midnight	139.13	57	92.98	50
1 A.M.	83.56	32	104.36	57
2 A.M.	56.68	28	105.08	53
Totals	$1,794.27	690	$879.04	450

"We feel that we have done the best job of any A&W operator in competing with McDonald's," Mr. Drayson had remarked. "We reduced our prices substantially in 1971 and we were successful in building volume." He noted that other A&W operators had retained their historical pricing policies which resulted in April 1973 with many units charging 75 cents for a Teenburger, versus the 59 cents charged by A&W (Fundy).

A&W (Fundy) had extensively publicized its price reductions in 1971. The publicity had included a small card which had been distributed to customers. A sample is included as Exhibit 8 on page 581. In Mr. Drayson's opinion,

EXHIBIT 8 1971 price reduction announcement

A & W's New Look of "Total Value" for 1971!

At first glance our new menu may not seem much different. But take a second look, because there's a story to tell. Many of our prices are down. Why have we done this? Well, some people think when costs go up the only thing to do is raise prices. Sometimes that's true, but at A & W we think the best way to overcome our own rising costs is to do more business, and we think the best way to do more business is to increase the value to our customer. We refuse to compromise on quality, the size of our portions, or our service. So, as you look over the menu on the reverse side you will note we have lowered some of our prices—at first glance they may not appear large, but when your bill is totalled you will be pleasantly surprised. So that's the story, the same high standards of quality and service but greater value to you.

A & W DRIVE-INS (FUNDY) LIMITED

The BURGER FAMILY

PAPA BURGER	.64
2 Patties Meat	
MAMA BURGER	.44
Single Patty	
BABY BURGER	.24
(Cheese on above 5¢, Bacon 5¢)	
TEEN BURGER	.59

(Single Patty with Cheese, Bacon, Lettuce, Tomato, Mayonnaise, Toasted Sesame Seed Bun)

All served with your choice of Mustard, Ketchup, Pickles and Onions

CHUBBY CHICKEN

CHUBBY DINNER	1.35
3 Pcs. Chicken, French Fries, Cole Slaw	
CHUBBY JUNIOR	.90
2 Pcs. Chicken, French Fries	
CHUBBY NINE	2.75
9 Pcs. Chicken	
CHUBBY FIFTEEN	3.75
15 Pcs. Chicken	
CHUBBY TWENTY-ONE	4.95
21 Pcs. Chicken	
FAMILY PAK FRENCH FRIES	1.00
Cole Slaw, 4 oz. 15¢, ½ pint 30¢, 1 pint 50¢	

OTHER A & W FEATURES

Hot Dog	.34
Whistle Dog, Bacon, Cheese & Relish	.49
French Fries	.25
Onion Rings	.35
Fish and Chips	.65
Fish on a Bun	.15
Fried Clams (When Available)	.75
Fried Clams and Chips	1.00

BEVERAGES — DESSERTS

A & W ROOT BEER	.25 - .15
A & W ORANGE	.25 - .15
Baby root beer free to children under 6	
ICE CREAM FLOAT	.35 - .25
MILKSHAKES	.35
MILK	.30 - .20
COFFEE	.15
TEA	.15
HOT CHOCOLATE	.15
APPLE TURNOVER	.25
(With cheese or ice cream 10¢ extra)	
SUNDAE	
Chocolate or Strawberry	.20
ICE CREAM	.10

A&W (Fundy) had not been entirely successful in dispelling the high-price image.

Prices had stayed relatively constant from 1971 to late in 1972. In September 1972, the company had conducted an extensive cost of sales study for each item on its menu for each outlet to estimate the theoretical food and packaging cost as a percentage of sales. Portions of this report for the Saint John's drive-ins are shown in Exhibit 9.

In late 1972 prices, especially meat prices, began to rise across Canada, and a number of A&W franchisees in Canada began to lobby for a move to smaller hamburger patties. A&W had always had a standard of six hamburger patties to the pound (uncooked weight) in Canada. By January 1973, however,

EXHIBIT 9 Cost of sales (Saint John), September 1972

Teen Burger—59¢	
Meat	10.33
Bun	3.25
Seasoning	0.10
Onion	1.46
Mustard	0.15
Ketchup	0.33
Pickles (2)	0.66
Bacon	1.76
Cheese	2.00
Mayonnaise	0.86
Lettuce	0.60
Tomato	0.90
Bag	1.71
	24.11¢–40.8%
Chubby Dinner—$1.19	
3 pcs. chicken	42.90
3 oz. fries	5.22
Ketchup	0.66
Portion cup	0.20
Plastic fork	0.35
Salt	0.01
Grease-proof paper	0.41
Box	4.47
	54.22¢–45.6%
Jumbo root beer—mug	3.72¢–18.6%
Jumbo root beer—take out	6.21¢–31.0%
Baby Burger—24¢	
Meat	6.20
Bun	2.83
Seasoning	0.02
Mustard	0.08
Ketchup	0.17
Pickle	0.33
Onion	0.73
Bag	1.24
	11.60¢–48.3%

several of the largest A&W operators in Canada, including A&W (Fundy), had moved to seven patties to the pound.

The Situation in April 1973

By March 1973, the cost situation had deteriorated further. In a March 21 memo to senior executives in the company and members of the board of directors, Mr. Drayson noted: "Our meat prices from suppliers have increased from approximately 61 cents per pound last September to the current 70 cents in New Brunswick and 81½ cents in Charlottetown. Sydney is the only unit with any kind of a break at the present time and is paying 61 cents per pound, but I am sure this will not last long. All indications are that beef will cost us 85 cents per pound in all units before the summer is over. Therefore, I feel any changes we make should be based on the assumption we will be paying 85 cents per pound shortly and this will probably not decrease very much by the end of the year. If we are to meet our profit objectives I feel we must move our cost of sales percentages back to last September's level. To do this, there appear to be at least three options: (1) raise prices, (2) decrease the patty size by moving to eight patties per pound, or (3) decrease the patty size as well as increasing prices."

Later in the memo Mr. Drayson added: "I think we must also bear in mind the fact that we have had to absorb increases not only in food costs, but also in all other operating costs." Mr. Drayson was particularly conscious of the rise in labor costs. He had pointed out: "If you look back to 1965, when we first opened up, wages in our stores on an annual basis amounted to 17 to 18 percent of gross sales, exclusive of the manager's salary. Today we are looking at wage percentages anywhere from 20 to 24 percent, with the average being 22 to 23 percent." He remarked that the increases were mainly due to increases in the minimum wage. The 1973 and the planned 1974 minimum wages in the Atlantic Provinces are noted in Exhibit 10. A&W (Fundy) paid on the average about 30 cents per hour higher than the minimum wage.

Mr. Drayson also attached to the memo a photocopy of a sales mix study done on one of the Moncton A&W drive-ins on a Saturday earlier in March. A

EXHIBIT 10 Past and planned minimum hourly wage rate in New Brunswick, Nova Scotia, and Prince Edward Island

	New Bruns-wick	Nova Scotia	Prince Edward Island
April 1, 1972	$1.40	$1.35 ($1.20)*	$1.25 ($0.95)
April 1, 1973	1.50	1.55	1.25 ($1.10)
July 1, 1973	1.50	1.65	1.65 ($1.40)
January 1, 1974 (planned)	1.75	1.65	1.65

* Hourly rate in parentheses is for females, where this differs from the male hourly rate.

copy of the study is contained in Exhibit 11. Mr. Drayson felt that the sale mix was quite representative of the sales mix in the company as a whole.

EXHIBIT 11 Analysis of sales Moncton No. 1, March 1973 (Saturday)

Item	Selling price	Units	Sales
Pa	$0.64	107	$ 68.48
Pa Ch*	0.69	17	11.73
Grandpa	0.94	4	3.76
Pa Ch Bac†	0.79	6	4.74
Ma	0.44	77	33.88
Ma Ch	0.49	20	9.80
Ma Ch Bac	0.59	2	1.18
Teen	0.59	312	184.08
Pa Teen	0.89	5	4.45
Grandpa Teen	1.19	1	1.19
Baby	0.25	135	33.75
Baby Ch	0.30	9	2.70
Hot Dog	0.39	17	6.63
Whistle Dog	0.49	34	16.66
French fries	0.19 & 0.29	115	30.16
Onion rings	0.39	118	46.02
Fish & Chips	0.69	40	27.60
Fried clams	0.85	14	11.90
Fried clams & F.F.	1.05	17	17.85
Burger Platters‡	Various	139	116.91
Chicken	Various	—	82.38
Drinks	Various	—	176.83
Other	Various	—	18.25
			$910.93

* Ch—with cheese.
† Bac—with bacon.
‡ Consists of a burger, fries, and coleslaw.

Mr. Drayson had already discussed the options at some length with Mr. Brathwaite, and he knew that Mr. Brathwaite had some strong opinions about what should be done. Mr. Brathwaite believed A&W (Fundy) should try to position itself very close to McDonald's, by reducing the portions, if this was necessary to keep prices roughly comparable. Mr. Brathwaite felt that the customer didn't notice small differences in hamburger sizes. He pointed out, for example, that no customer appeared to have noticed A&W's switch from six to the pound to seven to the pound. Mr. Brathwaite felt that A&W could move quite easily to eight to the pound without the customer knowing, since it was a common practice in the fast-food trade to scale down the bun size by a proportional amount. Mr. Drayson disagreed with this. He felt that eight patties to the pound would be sufficiently different from six patties to the pound that many customers would notice.

As he once again reviewed the options, Mr. Drayson turned to the 1973 profit plan for one of the Saint John's units (Exhibit 12) which had been prepared in November 1972, based on the food cost data prepared in September 1972. He knew that it was a reasonably representative outlet and he realized that if the company were to meet its profit objectives for 1973, he would have to obtain approximately the same contribution from this outlet irrespective of the rising costs. He realized the board of directors would expect him to have a concrete set of recommendations.

EXHIBIT 12 1973 profit plan—Saint John No. 1

Net sales	$330,000
Food (including paper)	123,100
Gross profit	206,900
Controllable expenses:	
Wages and fringe benefits	83,900
Management salaries	16,600
Advertising and promotion	
National (1.5%)	5,000
Local	19,800
Uniforms	1,200
Utilities	4,400
Miscellaneous unit expenses*	17,100
Total controllables	148,000
Noncontrollable expenses:	
Lease of land and building	18,800
Franchise fee (1.5%)	5,000
Accounting services	3,000
Insurance and taxes	1,400
Equipment depreciation	5,400
Administration†	8,900
Total noncontrollables	42,500
Total operating expenses	$190,500
Unit contribution	$ 16,400

* Includes cleaning supplies, maintenance, snow removal, refuse collection, telephone, and so on.

† Allocated by head office.

Case 39

Dutch Food Industries Company (A)*

In early September, Jan de Vries, product manager for Dutch Food Industries' new salad dressing product, was wondering what strategy to follow with respect to this new product. His assistant had prepared information concerning alternative promotional methods to use to introduce the new product, and he was concerned with exactly which of these he should recommend for the product's introduction. He also wondered what price the new product should retail for and when the company should introduce the new product. Mr. de Vries had to decide these issues in the next couple of days, as his report containing his recommendations on the introduction of the new salad dressing was due on the desk of the director of marketing the following Monday.

Company Background

The Netherlands Oil Factory of Delft, The Netherlands, was founded in 1884. This firm, which supplied edible oils to the growing margarine industry, merged in 1900 with a French milling company. The new firm then operated under the name Dutch Food Industries Company (DFI).

From this origin, the brand name DFI became increasingly strong and was eventually given to all of the company's branded products. More recently, the name was registered for use internationally.

In the course of the 1920s, DFI became an important factor in the margarine market. The company was a troublesome competitor for the Margarine Union, the company formed by the merger in 1927 of the two margarine giants, Van den Bergh and Jurgens. In 1928, an agreement was reached by which DFI joined the Margarine Union.

In 1930, the interests of the Margarine Union were merged with those of International Industries Corporation—a large, diversified, and international

---

* The authors were assisted in writing this case by Jos Viehoff, graduate student, Netherlands School of Economics.

organization. It was in this way that DFI became a part of the International Industries complex of companies.

International Industries Corporation (IIC) is a worldwide organization with major interests in the production of margarine, other edible fats and oils, soups, ice cream, frozen foods, meats, cheeses, soaps, and detergents.

The total sales of IIC were more than $1 billion.[1] Profits before taxes were $56 million.

Within IIC, DFI proceeded with its original activities after its margarine factory was closed, namely developing its exports of oils and fats, its trade in bakery products, as well as a number of branded food products. The following list indicates the range of consumer products which the company marketed: table oil, household fats, mayonnaise, salad dressing (several varieties), tomato ketchup, peanut butter, and peanuts.

DFI's total annual sales were between $14 million–$28 million. Profits before taxes were between $1.4 million–$2.8 million.

Background on the Dressing Market

A large and growing percentage of Holland's population eats lettuce, usually with salad dressing, with their meals. Estimates indicated that 82 percent of the people ate lettuce with salad dressing regularly. The salad dressing market has extreme seasonal demand as shown in Exhibit 1. This seasonal pattern coincides with the periods of greatest production of lettuce in Holland. Thus, 50 percent of the total year's volume for the salad dressing market occurs in the four months beginning in April. During this period, lettuce is plentiful and sells for approximately $0.46 per head.

The total salad dressing market was growing at approximately 7 percent per year. DFI's share of the market had declined from 20.7 percent to 16.6 percent over the last five years. The total market for salad dressings at manufacturer's level was currently estimated at between $7 million and $8.4 million. The company was looking for ways to halt the decline in market share and, in fact, increase DFI's share of the growing market.

Historically, the salad dressing market was composed of two segments. The first was a 25 percent oil-based salad dressing, which comprised 90 percent of the total market. The other 10 percent of the market consisted of 50 percent oil-based salad dressing, a slightly creamier product. Previously, DFI, in an effort to increase its market share, had introduced a new product which was 50 percent oil based. Up to that time, DFI sold only 25 percent oil-based salad dressing. The product, called Delfine, was not successful in obtaining the desired volume and profit. While DFI still marketed Delfine, almost all of DFI's volume came from its 25 percent oil-based product, Slasaus.

A research study was conducted to help the DFI marketing executives determine why Delfine was not successful. Several reasons emerged:

[1] All financial data in this case are presented in U.S. dollars.

EXHIBIT 1 Seasonal analysis of salad dressing market (percentage of annual total market sales—bimonthly periods)

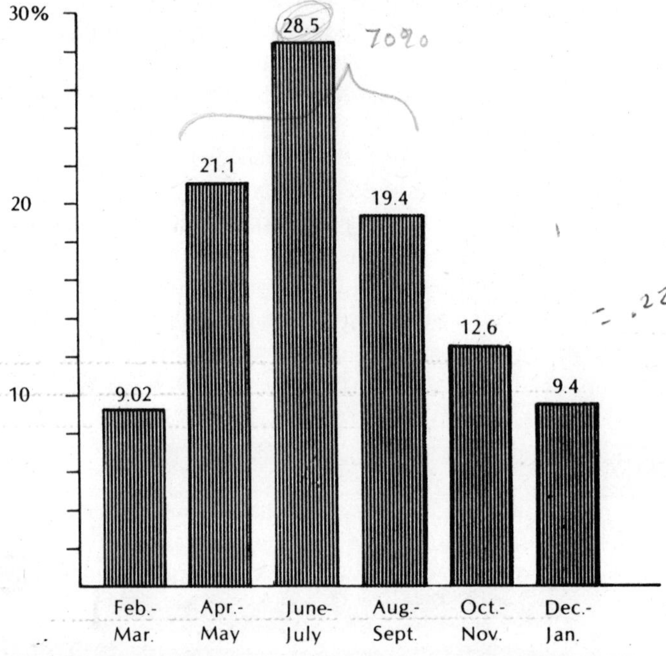

1. The potential of the 50 percent oil-based market was much smaller than originally anticipated, and only a small percentage of the total population was even interested in this product.
2. The consumers could detect only a small difference between the 25 percent oil-based and the 50 percent oil-based varieties when blind-tested. The difference was not noticeable enough for the consumers to prefer the 50 percent oil-based product.
3. The 50 percent oil-based salad dressing was more expensive, and the consumer was not willing to pay the difference for an apparently almost imperceptible difference.

Because the Delfine sales were well below expectations, DFI removed the heavy promotion support which it had been giving the product. The executives decided to wait for a significant breakthrough of a product with unique advantages. The Delfine experience indicated to them that it would take a totally new type of product for DFI to increase its market share significantly.

Background and Development of Slamix

Every two years, the company conducted a housewives' habits study in which a panel of 700 consumers was asked about their household and their food preparation habits. In August two years before, the company received the most recent study, called PMC-11. The housewives were asked how they prepared their lettuce and what ingredients they used. The results showed that an extremely large percentage of the housewives added not only salad dressing to lettuce, but also added other ingredients such as salt, pepper, eggs, onion, gherkins, and so on. Thus DFI executives got the idea that putting some of these ingredients in the salad dressing would result in a real convenience for the housewife, and DFI would have the significant new product for which they had been searching. The laboratory, in August of the same year, began developing a "dressed" salad dressing which included some of the ingredients which many housewives were accustomed to adding.

Early in the next year, a committee called the Slamix Committee,[2] was formed to make sure that every part of the company was involved in the development of this new product. The committee, which was headed up by the product manager, had representatives from various parts of the company, including development, production, and marketing. The committee studied production problems, laboratory findings, and in general, was charged with the responsibility of seeing that the development progressed as scheduled. The committee did not have decision-making powers but either invited decision makers to important meetings or wrote reports to the people who were in a position to make the required decisions.

After several product tests concerned with taste and keeping properties were conducted at the factory, the company, one year after laboratory work began, undertook its first consumer test of the new "dressed" salad dressing. A panel of housewives was shown a bottle of the new product which was a salad dressing containing pieces of gherkins, onions, and paprika. Several conclusions emerged from this study:

1. The "dressed" salad dressing was seen by the housewives as more than a salad dressing with ingredients. It was seen as a completely new product.
2. There were two sides to this newness:
   a. By looking at the product, they thought that it had a new taste.
   b. The convenience aspect was strongly stressed by the housewives.
3. The housewives thought that the new product would be good for decorating the lettuce. With its new color (light red with colorful ingredients), they thought that they could decorate the lettuce much better than with present salad dressings which were creme-colored and very similar to mayonnaise.
4. When asked about the ingredients, one half of the housewives were favorable toward paprika, and half were against it. This apparently was a troublesome ingredient. However, because of the convenience aspect, gherkins and onions were favored by the housewives.

Later, a second consumer study was conducted by the Institute of Household Research in Rotterdam. A sample of 140 housewives who actually used

---

[2] Literally translated, Slasaus means "lettuce sauce," and Slamix is literally "lettuce mix."

salad dressing on lettuce was given a bottle of the new product to take home. Then, they were visited in their homes. Much useful information emerged from this study. After looking at the product, but before trying it, the housewives said that it looked like a fun product, it made them happy, and they thought that it would taste good. When asked what they thought the product contained, they said tomatoes, red paprika, celery, gherkins, and green paprika.

However, the company was disappointed with the housewives' overall evaluation of the product. Only 20 percent of the housewives said that they thought the product was very good, 11 percent did not like the product, and 69 percent of the housewives said that there were some favorable and some unfavorable aspects of the product. The main reason for the 80 percent unfavorable reaction was the consistency of the new salad dressing. It was too thin. The housewives could pour it too easily and it rapidly went to the bottom of the bowl. Because it fell to the bottom, the housewives said that it was much harder to decorate their salad. It was also uneconomical because they felt that they would put too much on if the product was that thin. There were also problems with taste. Many of the housewives thought it was too sour or too sharp. The paprika was the main reason for the dissatisfaction.

In spite of the above problems, there were several aspects of the study which encouraged the company to proceed with the development of this new product. When asked how they would change the ingredients in the "dressed" salad dressing, only 47 percent of the housewives suggested changes. Most recommended that more onions be added. The housewives were asked for their preference between DFI's Slasaus and the new "dressed" salad dressing. As shown in Exhibit 2, the housewives preferred the new product, except for its consistency. Sixty percent of the housewives said that they would buy the product if it were possible to buy it in the store. Since this was a very high positive response, the company was very encouraged.

EXHIBIT 2 Preference test: Slasaus versus "dressed" salad dressing

Prefer	Taste	Appearance	Decoration aspects	Consistency	Convenience
"Dressed" salad dressing	59%	73%	46%	18%	50%
Slasaus	38	20	44	65	20
No preference/no difference	3	7	10	17	30
	100%	100%	100%	100%	100%

The marketing, production, and development groups, coordinated by the Slamix Committee, began work on incorporating the required changes made evident by this consumer study. DFI's development group experimented with changes in the consistency, taste, and ingredients. The production group experimented with a new production process. DFI had intended to introduce the new "dressed" salad dressing in a few months. However, the top corporate executives decided that, before the new product could be introduced, an extensive test of its keeping properties (vulnerability to deterioration) would have to be conducted.

The keeping-properties test showed that after several months the light red-colored product changed to a pink color. The difference in color was only slight, but DFI executives thought that the consumer reaction to this change should be tested. They decided that at the same time they would conduct a consumer test to find a name for this new product. A sample of 180 housewives from the Institute of Household Research was used to get at these questions. Only 2 out of the 180 housewives saw that there was a difference in color between the two bottles of the new product. When they were told that there was a slight difference and were shown the two bottles together, most of the housewives could not see the color change, and those that could were not unhappy about it.

The housewives were then asked what the name for this product should be. The phrase "mixed salad dressing" kept coming up. The housewives were then asked what they thought of two names which the company had screened, "Slamix" (lettuce mix) and "Spikkeltjessaus" (sauce with little spots). Eighty-one percent thought that Slamix was a very good name. Only 26 percent thought that Spikkeltjessaus was a good name. The name Slamix was chosen for the new product. Interestingly, that was the name that the company had used internally for the new product when it was first being developed.

A short time later, DFI had solved the color-change problem. The company now thought that it had a product ready to be marketed, so a final consumer test was undertaken to test the effect of all of the changes that had been made during the previous year.

Two versions of Slamix, a white one and a pink one, were tested at the Institute for Household Research. One hundred eighty housewives were asked what they thought of the product and whether they would buy it or not. The negative reactions to the product were minimal. Almost no negative comments were voiced. The problems of consistency, color, taste, and ingredients had apparently been solved. When asked if they would buy the product, 76 percent of those shown the pink product, and 70 percent of those shown the white product responded in a positive manner. After tasting the two versions of Slamix, the housewives revealed a strong preference for the pink Slamix. The DCI executives felt that the product was now ready to be marketed.

DFI executives next reviewed the financial projections prepared by Mr. de Vries, the product manager. Almost no capital investment would be required as the Slamix would be produced by using present production facilities. Only a few machines, at a total cost of $11,000, would be required.

At an early stage in the development of the product, Slamix sales had been forecasted at 3.7 percent of the total market at the end of the first year. Encouraged by the results of the consumer tests, DFI executives revised their estimate of sales. The new forecast was for approximately 6.7 percent of the market. (See Exhibit 3.)

The directors of the company thought that they finally had the product for

EXHIBIT 3 Forecast sales of
Slamix

Year	Share of market (percent)
Original estimates	
Year 1	3.7%
Year 2	3.9
Year 3	4.4
Revised estimates	
Year 1	6.7
Year 2	11.7

11.7

which they had been waiting. The consumer tests were complete, and the product had found very high favor with the consumers. There was significant technological development involved in the product, and DFI executives thought that it would take considerable time for the competition to duplicate the product. The product manager's projected sales seemed reasonable. Mr. de Vries was asked to prepare a comprehensive report concerning the introductory marketing strategy to be used to introduce the new product.

Pricing Strategy

The first problem that the product manager had to resolve concerned the suggested retail price that the company should charge for Slamix. To help Mr. de Vries make his recommendation, the assistant product manager had made a list of the following considerations:

1. The company's total cost for a 0.30-liter-size bottle of Slamix was $0.20. This was 20 percent higher than DFI's regular salad dressing, Slasaus.
2. The gross margin for Slasaus was 22 percent. Because of the unique qualities of Slamix, large development costs, and possible substitution with Slasaus, a higher gross margin for Slamix might be considered.
3. DFI gave the wholesalers a 12.5 percent margin and retailers a 14.3 percent margin for Slasaus. Possibly these should be increased for Slamix to encourage greater acceptance and promotion by the trade channels of distribution.
4. The two leading salad dressings, Salata by Duyvis and Slasaus, both had a retail price of $0.28 for the 0.30-liter bottle. The retail price for the 0.60-liter bottle was $0.48. Private label salad dressings were $0.22 for a 0.30-liter bottle. The average price for all salad dressings was approximately $0.26.
5. DFI had conducted some research on the optimal price of Slamix. After using a sample of the product, 140 housewives were asked what price they would be willing to pay for Slamix. Their responses, by percent, were:

	Percent
$0.31 or less	45%
Between $0.31 and $0.40	41
$0.40 or more	14
Total	100%

The average price mentioned was $0.34.

The assistant product manager also prepared the table shown in Exhibit 4. The first column shows the retail price, and gives data that allows one to calculate trade margins and gross margin for Slasaus. The remaining six columns show alternative retail prices for Slamix, resulting from different trade margins and gross margins. Mr. de Vries wondered which of these prices he should recommend to the board of directors.

EXHIBIT 4 Alternative prices for Slamix*

PENETRATION

	Slasaus	1	2	3	4	5	6
Retail price	$0.28	$0.32	$0.34	$0.34	0.36	$0.37	$0.38
Price to retailer	0.24	0.28	0.28	0.29	0.295	0.31	0.316
Price to wholesaler	0.21	0.25	0.25	0.26	0.26	0.28	0.28
Cost	0.165	0.20	0.20	0.20	0.20	0.20	0.20

Selected figures in this table have been disguised.

gross margin

Promotion Alternatives

The board of directors told the product manager that he had $203,000 for his promotion budget. Of this, $7,000 was to be allocated as Slamix's share of the general corporate advertising which aided all DFI products. The $203,000 was determined by using a percentage of the "expected gross profit of the first year" for Slamix.[3] DFI's policy was to break even in the third year of the new product, attaining a total payback within five years. The company was generally willing to spend the gross profit for the first year as part of the total investment.

The company had already given considerable thought to the sales message and the brand image desired for Slamix. The information below was sent to the advertising agency to help in planning the promotional program of the company:

> *Sales message.* It is now possible, in a completely new way, to make delicious salad. Sla + Slamix = Sla Klaar. (Lettuce + Slamix = Lettuce Ready)

---

[3] It was possible that the percentage could be greater than 100 percent. This would mean that the company was willing to spend more than the first year's gross profit for initial promotion.

Supporting message. Slamix is a salad dressing with pieces of onion, gherkins, and paprika.

Desired brand image. With Slamix you can make, very easily and very quickly, a delicious salad that also looks nice. Slamix is a complete, good, handy product. DFI is a modern firm with up-to-date ideas.

Thus, the company wanted to get across three principal points. They are (1) that Slamix is a completely new product, (2) that it is convenient, and (3) that it is a salad dressing with ingredients making it a complete salad dressing.

The product manager was undecided as to how to divide the $196,000 among the following alternatives:

1. Television.   *52 000*
2. Radio.
3. Newspaper advertising.
4. Magazines.
5. Sampling.
6. Coupons.   *1398*
7. Price-off promotion.
8. Key chain premiums.
9. Trade allowances.
10. SAMPLE PROMOTION

Television

The product manager thought that television would be advantageous because of the ability to show the product in actual use—a housewife pouring Slamix onto the lettuce. The cost of using the television medium is shown in Exhibit 5. The company did not have a choice among the seven blocks of time, but had to take whatever was available. For planning, however, they figured an average cost of a 30-second ad would be $1,800. Mr. de Vries felt that at least 25 advertisements were necessary before the TV advertising would have maximum impact.

EXHIBIT 5 Data on Dutch television media

$ 45,000
7 000
$ 52,000

Station	Block number	Time	Cost of 30-second ad
Nederland 1	1	Before early news	$2,300
Nederland 1	2	After early news	2,300
Nederland 1	3	Before late news	2,950
Nederland 1	4	After late news	2,950
Nederland 2	5	After early news	500
Nederland 2	6	Before late news	840
Nederland 2	7	After late news	840
Average cost per 30-second TV ad			$1,800
Production cost for a TV ad			7,000

TV coverage per 1,000 households = 850 or 85 percent. Only about one half of the homes can receive Nederland 2.

Radio

The chief attraction of radio was its extremely low price. Each 30-second radio ad cost $126 on Radio Veronica, a popular station during the daytime. Production costs for a radio ad were approximately $840. Only 60 percent of the households could receive Radio Veronica, mainly in the western part of the country. Mr. de Vries felt that if radio were used, a minimum of 100 spots should be purchased.

Newspapers

Mr. de Vries thought the main advantages of newspapers would be the announcement effect and its influence with the local trade. Nationally, the cost of each half-page insertion would be $14,000.

Magazines

Magazines would be a desirable addition to the promotional program for several reasons. Due to the ability to use color, the company could show the product as it actually looked on the shelf. By using several women's magazines, the company could reach a select audience of people reading the magazine at its leisure. Data on selected Dutch magazines are shown in Exhibit 6. Mr. de Vries thought that if they were to use a magazine campaign, at least 10 insertions would be necessary before the advertising would be very effective. Of the possibilities in Exhibit 6, the agency thought that the combination of *Eva*,

EXHIBIT 6 Data on selected Dutch magazines

Magazines	Type	Circulation	Frequency	Price for full-page ad Black and white	Price for full-page ad Color	Cost per 1,000 circulation*
Eva	Women's	375,000	Weekly	$ 770	$1,408	$3.75
Margriet	Women's	825,000	Weekly	2,100	3,440	4.15
Libelle	Women's	570,000	Weekly	1,416	2,340	4.10
Prinses	Women's	213,000	Weekly	660	1,175	5.55
Panorama	General	403,000	Weekly	1,300	2,150	5.40
Nieuwe Revu	General	261,000	Weekly	920	1,540	5.90
Spiegel	General	175,000	Weekly	710	1,325	7.55
Het Beste	Digest	325,000	Monthly	965	1,615	4.90
Studio	TV guide	575,000	Weekly	1,525	2,420	4.20
NCRV-gids	TV guide	482,000	Weekly	1,420	2,290	4.75
Vara-gids	TV guide	504,000	Weekly	1,500	2,370	4.70
AVRO-Televizier	TV guide	950,000	Weekly	2,600	3,870	4.05
Combination of Eva, Margriet, and AVRO-Televizier				4,900	7,785	3.65

* Cost of one-page color ad, divided by circulation in thousands. With *Eva* as an example, cost per 1,000 circulation = $1,408/375 = $3.75.

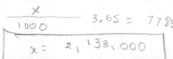

Margriet, and *AVRO-Televizier* would be most effective for DFI, since the combination would reach a large number of people at a relatively low cost.

Sampling

Although he realized that it was very expensive, Mr. de Vries considered the use of direct-mail sampling. A small 12 cm. by 18 cm. (approximately 5 × 7 inches) folder could be mailed to Holland's 3.7 million households for $20,000. The cost, however, would increase substantially if a small bottle of the product were to be included in the direct mailing. This cost would be 20 cents for handling, plus 75 cents for the actual sample. Thus, it would cost $980,000 to sample the whole country.

Coupon

Mr. de Vries was considering whether or not to include a coupon good for $0.04 off the purchase of Slamix with one of the other DFI products—mayonnaise, for example. He estimated that 900,000 coupons would be distributed. At a redemption rate of 5 percent, the cost would, thus, be approximately $1,700.

Price-Off Promotion

DFI made use of a reduced retail price for most of its new product introductions. Thus, the product manager thought it quite normal to consider the use of reducing the retail price by U.S. $0.07 per bottle and identifying this price reduction on the label of the product. It was felt that this reduced price would encourage the housewives to try Slamix. It was also quite normal to follow up this sales promotion with a similar price reduction approximately five months after the product was introduced. This would encourage those who had still not tried the product to purchase a bottle and would encourage those who had already bought one bottle to continue purchasing the new product. The cost of this price-off promotion is shown in Exhibit 7.

EXHIBIT 7

Introduction:	
720,000 bottles at 25 cents (U.S. $0.07) off each	$50,400
Handling and display materials	2,800
Total	$53,200
Follow-up five months later:	
600,000 bottles at 25 cents (U.S. $0.07) off each	$42,000
Handling and display materials	2,800
Total	$44,800

Key Chain Premium

It was very unusual to use a free premium to introduce a new product, but Mr. de Vries was considering this alternative for several reasons. Many products in Holland at this time were using key chains as a premium. As shown in Exhibit 8, an extremely large percentage of the people in Holland were collecting key chains. The details of the research showed that mothers and daughters were more likely to collect key chains, especially if the children were between 8 and 11 years of age. Mr. de Vries felt that if he used key chains as premiums for the introduction of Slamix he could have a follow-up promotion five months later using either key chains or price-off deals. Selected cost information on the key chain promotion is shown in Exhibit 9.

EXHIBIT 8 Percentage of households collecting key chains

	June	July	September
Households with children	45	n.a.	n.a.
Households without children	5	n.a.	n.a.
Total (weighted average)	34	37	41

n.a. = not available.

EXHIBIT 9

Introduction:	
720,000 bottles = about 220 metric tons	
750,000 key chains at $0.056	$42,000
Handling costs and display materials	16,800
Total	$58,800
Follow-up five months later:	
600,000 bottles = about 180 tons	
625,000 key chains at $0.056	$35,000
Handling costs and display materials	14,000
Total	$49,000

14,000
16,000
floor displays. 137,800

Trade Allowances

The product manager also considered the use of trade allowances to encourage the retailers to accept and promote the new product. The company traditionally offered $0.28 per case of 12 bottles. Thus, if it was decided that trade allowances were desirable, the cost would be $16,800 for the initial introduction and an additional $14,000 used during the follow-up promotion five months later. Trade allowances could be used together with either the price-off promotion or the key chain promotion. The product manager felt that trade allowances would not be very effective without one of the two consumer sales promotions.

Distribution

Outside of the question of what trade margins to use and whether or not to use trade allowances during the consumer sales promotions discussed above, Mr. de Vries did not see any problems with distribution. DFI had a sales force of approximately 50 persons who regularly called on 10,000 outlets in Holland. It was felt that the sales force could handle the introduction of the new product with no problem.

The last problem the product manager faced concerned the timing of the introduction of Slamix. The product would be ready for introduction in October. Mr. de Vries wondered whether the seasonal nature of the demand for the product would make it more desirable to hold off the introduction until March of the next year.

NO - APPEAL TO EASE OF PREPARATION IN UPCOMING HOLIDAY SEASON (CHRISTMAS)

Case 40

The Video Game Industry—1983*

History

The exact time of birth of the video game industry is cloudy at best. It is likely that several forward thinkers dabbled at different times with the same idea of combining entertainment and electronics on a television screen. *Video and Arcade Games* magazine gives credit to Willy Higinbotham,[1] a senior scientist at Brookhaven Laboratory. As early as 1958, Higinbotham, while working for the government, used an analog computer to create a simulated tennis match. The screen looked like an upside-down "T" and each player used a knob to control and angle direction of the ball. When asked why he didn't patent the game, Higinbotham replied, "It was fun . . . but it wasn't something the government was interested in. It's a good thing, too. Today all video game designers would have to license their games from the Federal government!"[2]

Much to the subsequent regret of Fairchild Cameras and Semiconductors, the company withdrew funding of one of its chief engineers, Jerry Lawson, who developed the product concept and business plan for the first video game with high quality graphics in 1977. After Fairchild's divestiture of the project, Lawson attempted unsuccessfully to pull together venture capital for his product but had to let it drop.[3]

Several years earlier, in 1969, a young engineering graduate of the University of Utah was continuing his work on a similar idea. Upon graduation, Nolan Bushnell had been unable to secure a position in research for Disney, and had accepted a job with Ampex, a recording tape company, as a research engineer. During his off-work hours he tinkered at home in his workshop, a converted bedroom. Earlier while at the University, Bushnell and friends had

---

* This case was coauthored by Adrienne L. Kelly.

[1] John Anderson, "Who Really Invented the Video Game?" *Creative Computing: Video and Arcade Games,* Spring 1983, p. 8.

[2] Ibid., p. 11.

[3] Lee Hilliard, "Cash in on the Video Game Craze," *Black Enterprise,* December 1982, p. 44.

rigged the school's mainframe computer to simulate space wars on a video screen. Although commercially appealing, the economics (an $8 million setup) were far too unrealistic for a mass market toy. This major obstacle disappeared several years later with the introduction of low-priced (computer-on-a-chip) technology.

Bushnell's first commercial game, "Computer Space"[4] was well received by his engineering comrades. It mirrored many of today's action space games, but was not a winner in the public domain. Less than 2,000 of the electronic arcades were sold. Those that made it to the street were unused. They were just too complex for the average player in 1972. Bushnell started over, this time with the strategy of making games "easy to learn and difficult to master."[5] He obtained $50,000 from savings, relatives, and bank loans. He started his own company, Atari, borrowed from the Japanese game of strategy, meaning "You are about to be engulfed"[6]—and produced an electronic version of Ping-Pong, entitled Pong. The game combined a small computer and a modified black-and-white television screen. Graphics consisted of a cartoonist table tennis court with paddles and a ball that bounced back and forth across the screen. Movement of the paddles was controlled by each player, scoring when his opponent missed the ball. This game was an overnight success in the bars and stores which acquired it. These games sold for $1,200, about 50 percent more than existing electromechanical games, but the lower labor costs associated with video games (they are easily assembled solid state components that last for years) would drop their price below pinballs within a year of purchase. The success of Pong was not restricted to the Atari company. Distributors who channel arcade games from the manufacturer to store and restaurant owners were usually responsible for maintenance. Their savings in labor costs greatly increased their margins. Copy-cat companies also profited from Atari's market success, so much so that of the 100,000 Pongs sold by 1974, only 10 percent were Atari originals, the others were American and Japanese counterfeits.[7]

The $500,000 profit realized by Bushnell was merely "the tip of the iceberg."[8] A new idea and new financing was necessary to expand the viability and longevity of the company. It happened that while Bushnell was in California reaping profits from Pong, another man on the East Coast, Ralph Baer, took a game console prototype to Magnavox, a television manufacturer. Magnavox licensed the console, attached it to one of the black-and-white models, and the unit became the first home video game on the market (Christmas 1972). The product, named Odyssey, was supported with heavy promotion and 200,000 units were sold by year end 1975.

---

[4] Colin Covert, "Video Gamesmanship: The Rise and Fall and Rise of Atari," *TWA Ambassador,* August 1982, p. 30.

[5] Anne Krueger, "Videogame Veteran Larry Kaplan Looks into His Designer's Crystal Ball," *Merchandising,* September 1982, p. 45.

[6] Covert, "Video Gamesmanship," p. 29.

[7] Ibid., p. 32.

[8] "A Red-Hot Market for Video Games," *Business Week,* November 1973, p. 212.

Bushnell picked up on this concept of a home video game as a natural extension of his product. His major obstacle was to obtain the financing to manufacture, promote, and distribute the product which he planned to unveil at an upcoming toy industry conference. Before the conference, he was approached by Sears, Roebuck & Company (mass market retail chain) and offered financing in return for exclusive distribution rights for the chain. Bushnell promised 150,000 units for that year and obtained instant access to national advertising and 900 outlets across the United States. In fiscal 1975, the company's revenues were $39 million; net income was $3.5 million.[9]

The growth and development of the Atari company after that point was unique. Bushnell's own relaxed, fun-loving personality pervaded the organization where engineers wore T-shirts, worked any hours they chose, and brainstormed for new products over beer and marijuana. The culture and strategy of the organization seemed stable and business progressed smoothly for a time. However, 1976 brought in two major changes that would alter the tide of the industry. First, consumer demand had rapidly increased (now all TV owners made up the potential market), so much so that the two-competitor industry (Magnavox and Atari) could not meet the production requirements necessary to fill demand. Second, new competitors with established marketing expertise and financial resources were beginning to enter this infant industry. Again, Atari was in need of financial backing. The company had several alternatives: assuming huge loans, going public, or selling out to an established company. Bushnell chose the latter.

An attractive offer was made by Warner Communications which at the time was experiencing falling or no profits in several of its businesses. The record industry was in a severe downturn, film production profits had fallen to their lowest level in several years and the company's cable joint venture (Warner-Amex) was not projected to make profits until 1985. Atari could be the catalyst to spur new and substantial revenues for the entertainment giant.

Bushnell completed the deal at age 33 with $15 million more in his pockets. The agreement included a noncompetition clause disallowing Bushnell to compete in video games effective through October 1983.[10] He stayed on for a time as board chairman but his lack of interest in management issues proved to be an irritant to Warner management. After several restructurings, a new management team emerged including Raymond Kassar as CEO, Joseph Keenen as chairman, and Bushnell as director. Bushnell was to take a more distant advisory role and would have nothing to do with daily management operations.

By Christmas 1977, Atari had introduced the Video Computer System, a $200 programmable system with color graphics, but they were no longer uncontested in this booming market. In 1976, Bally, RCA and Fairchild Instrument and Camera Corporation (number three manufacturer in the semiconductor industry) entered the market. Christmas sales for all programmable

[9] Covert, "Video Gamesmanship," p. 33.

[10] "Nolan Bushnell's Newest Brainstorms," *Business Week*, February 28, 1983, p. 54.

video units were sluggish in 1977, however, due to system bugs and incompatibility problems, and the overwhelming popularity of hand-held electronic games.

Mattel, Incorporated Toy Products Group held the industry lead in hand-held electronic games, a segment which had grown from $35 million to $86 million over the period 1977 to 1978. From its beginning in 1945, the company followed a product strategy of making toy and toy-related products. By 1973, three major product categories existed: the Toy Products Group, with such famous toys as Barbie Doll, the Leisure Products Group including audio cassette equipment, and the Entertainment Group which for many years owned ''The Greatest Show on Earth''—Ringling Bros. and Barnum & Bailey Circus.[11]

EXHIBIT 1 Toy industry electronic products sales

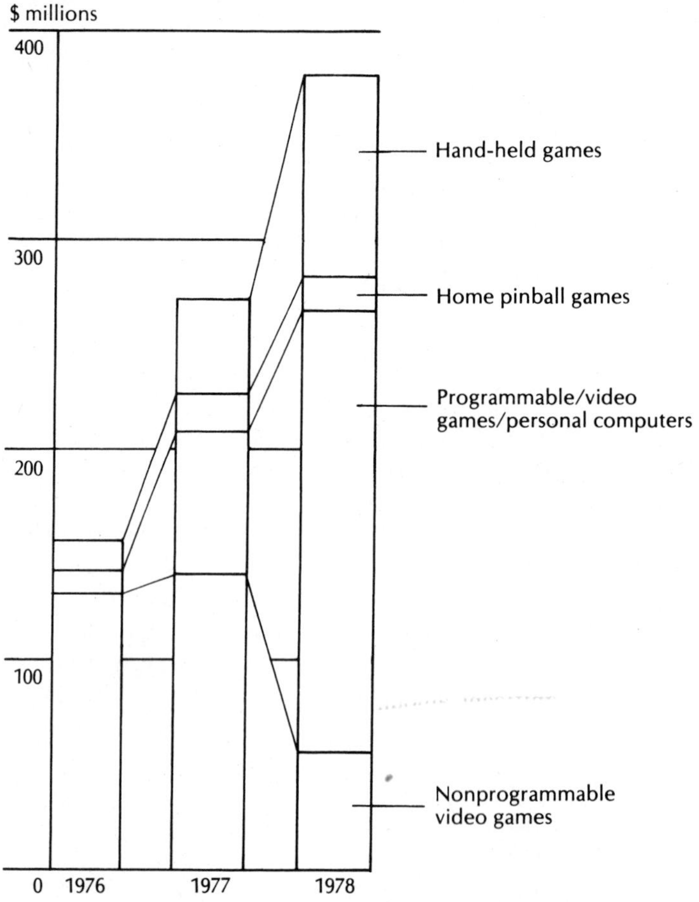

Source: Mattel Toys Division.

---

[11] *1973 Annual Report, Mattel, Incorporated,* Hawthorne, Calif.: Mattel, Inc., p. 9.

With the advent of electronic game entertainment and its unprecedented growth in the late 70s, the company established Mattel Electronics within the Toy Products Group in 1978 to develop products using electronic technology. The division's charter included the manufacturing and marketing of home pinball games, programmable video games, and personal computers. In 1978, the division emphasized their hand-held electronic games which held a 40 percent market share in the industry.[12] Six new games were introduced in fiscal year 1978–79 to bring the total line to 12 products. Game titles included Football II, Soccer, Horoscope Computer, and Brain Baffler. Growth in electronic games during this period was impressive (see Exhibit 1).

In 1979, Mattel entered the video game and home computer markets, together totaling $210 million in sales. By December 1979, Mattel had introduced Intellivision which the company chairman touted as "technologically superior to any comparably priced product currently on the market."[13] The growing significance of the electronic toy segment of Mattel's business is indicated from the accompanying chart which identifies total company net sales and income, and sales and income attributable to the electronic toy business only.[14]

	1978	1979	1980	1981	1982
Sales					
Total	436	493	805	915	1,134
Electronic	n.a.	n.a.	92	119	387
Electronic as					
percent of total			11.4	13.0	25.3
Income (profit after tax)					
Total	28	30	30	8	39
Electronic	n.a.	n.a.	n.a.	8	73

One can readily see the growing percentage of electronic sales (25 percent in 1982) in relation to the rest of Mattel's businesses, several of which have lost significant amounts of money in the last several years. For a comparison of Atari and Mattel home video game operating profits, see Exhibit 2.

Important events over this period included the beefing up of the research and development staff—over 300 inventors, artists, engineers, and designers gave Mattel one of the largest R&D staffs in the toy industry. Because the

---

[12] *1978 Annual Report, Mattel, Incorporated*, Hawthorne, Calif.: Mattel, Inc., p. 34.

[13] *1979 Annual Report, Mattel, Incorporated*, Hawthorne, Calif.: Mattel, Inc., p. 3.

[14] *1982 Annual Report, Mattel, Incorporated*, Hawthorne, Calif.: Mattel, Inc.

EXHIBIT 2 Home video games' share of operation profits

Atari's share at Warner Communications

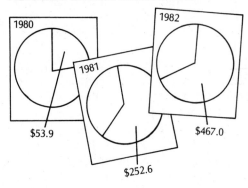

Intellivision's share at Mattel

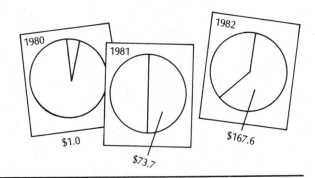

Source: *Fortune,* November 15, 1982.

demand for hand-held games slowed considerably in 1980 due to market saturation, the focus of the talented staff shifted to videogames. In mid-1981, a keyboard attachment was made available in limited quantities to allow the video game console to be used as a home computer. Software development and market testing continued. Twenty-six cartridges were marketed by Mattel in 1982 using both existing sales staff in the Toys, USA division and their own consumer electronic representatives.[15]

It is impossible to discuss the emergence of the video game industry without including Activision, a small Silicon Valley start-up. On October 1, 1979, five seasoned designers at Atari left the company, pooled their talents and began a new organization. Activision was the first independent company to design, manufacture, and market home video game cartridges. The company

[15] Ibid.

did not intend or attempt to make console units but rather produced cartridges that would play on the Atari VCS system. This strategy followed the recognition that the home video game is another "razor blade" industry (profits are made by selling blades, not razors). The heavy development and manufacturing costs of consoles slimmed profit margins considerably, while the extremely low

EXHIBIT 3

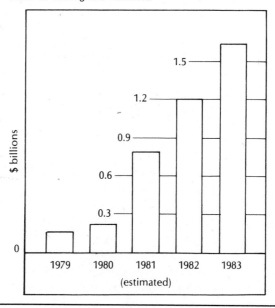

Video game cartridge sales

Units (millions)

| | 1977 | 1978 | 1979 | 1980 | 1981 | 1982 |

1.0   1.7   3.6   9.5   35.9   65.0

(estimated)

Note: Not drawn to scale.

Sales of video game cassettes

$ billions

1.5
1.2
0.9
0.6
0.3
0

1979   1980   1981   1982   1983
(estimated)

Source: R. Simon, Goldman Sachs Research. Activision, Inc.

cost of manufacturing game cartridges (consisting of merely a computer chip encased in plastic) left lots of room for ''other'' expenditures and large profits.

At this time, Atari, Inc. led the cartridge market selling more than 20 million games at approximately $20 or more each. But the forecast growth in this segment of the business called for a sevenfold increase in consumer purchases of game cartridges (see Exhibit 3). The lure of quick profits on modest investments made Activision the first to leap into this market, and with great success. With only $700,000 in venture capital invested, revenues increased from $6,226,000 in fiscal 1981 to $65,987,000 in fiscal 1982, and net income went from $744,000 to $12,918,000 over the same period—a 1636 percent increase. (The fiscal year ends in March.) This success has generated revenues over 60 times the original investment.

Entrants

Atari and Mattel were the front runners of this industry. 1981 sales of console units for the two companies were 3.2 million and 65 thousand respectively (see Exhibit 4). Atari came to the market unopposed initially with modest advertising and built a consumer franchise for its product. Mattel's strategy was to capitalize on its historical strength as a toy manufacturer, its creative product development organization, and its financial clout. Mattel Electronics spent $2 million in major media advertising in the first half of 1980. Intellivision was backed by a $200,000 magazine campaign, $880,000 in network TV and $300,000 in spot TV.[16] The system combined highly sophisticated microprocessor technology with more intricate games to produce the highest level resolution of color graphics available at the time. Activision was the pioneer in software-only development. Their razor blade strategy allowed the tiny firm significant profits within 18 months of the first customer order.

Once the signal of potential profitability was loud and clear, players large and small entered the lucrative market. A partial listing of manufacturers is shown in Appendix B. The makeup of entrants into the industry is varied by size, existing product focus, age of the corporation, and personality of the organization's leader. One type of entrant was existing toy manufacturers. In 1979 consumers spent $5.8 billion on toys and games, $500 million of that in electronic games (excluding video games).[17]

The shift toward electronic games in general opened the eyes of many toy manufacturers as the markets for the future. Manufacturers of traditional games began to market electronic games once the miracle chip became available. While sales of Barbie dolls and monopoly boards remained strong (although level) the battleground centered on electronic introductions. Parker Brothers, subsidiary of General Mills and maker of Risk, Clue, and Monopoly introduced Merlin in 1978, a hand-held electronic game offering six games in one. In

---

[16] ''Toys and Games,'' *Marketing and Media Decisions*, December 1980, p. 141.

[17] Ibid., p. 136.

EXHIBIT 4

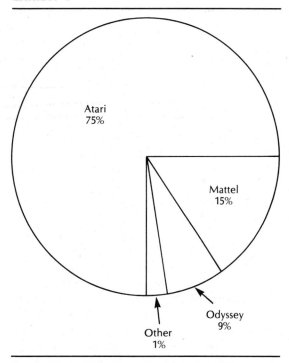

Source: *The Wall Street Journal*, November 27, 1982.

March 1982, Parker entered the video game market with Frogger, compatible with the Atari VCS.

Two other game and toy companies took the acquisition route: Quaker Oats Co., owner of Fisher-Price Toys, acquired U.S. Games Corporation in Santa Clara (Atari-compatible cartridges) and Milton Bradley Company bought General Consumer Electronics Corporation (game machine with its own video monitor) in Santa Monica. In 1980, Coleco (incorporated as Connecticut Leather Company in 1932), now a $100 million toy manufacturer, followed Mattel into the hand-held electronic market managing to secure a 20 percent share. Their Electronic Learning machine, introduced that year, was a computer for children which made learning "fun." By August 1982 Coleco had taken the plunge into the market providing its own console system, ColecoVision, and cartridges also compatible with Atari and Mattel.

A second type of industry entrant were those involved in the film industry. By the end of 1982, six of the seven major film producers were either in the market or seriously considering entry. None, however, with the exception of Warner Communications (owner of Atari) planned to manufacture game consoles. The strategy of these contenders was to manufacture cartridges based on movie titles or characters, as in the case with CBS Inc., Paramount, and

Twentieth Century Fox, or to license movie characters to other game manufacturers (e.g., Walt Disney productions). Although this strategy for entry is less involved and therefore less risky, the firms mentioned have huge financial resources that can be dedicated to the promotion of their game titles. Furthermore, their participation permitted the broadening of the product content concept from mostly generic sports to games having a specific character or personality attached to them.

Many of the licensing agreements of film companies are with existing arcade manufacturers of which Atari and Bally Manufacturing are the largest. The companies are entering joint ventures or are acquiring companies that can improve their home cartridge distribution network. They are acting as middlemen between the product concept (from film company) and the consumer.

Finally, in the spirit of the Activision start-up, a second California-based company, Imagic, has begun marketing video game cartridges. The cartridges are compatible with both Mattel and the Atari VCS. The first customer shipments were in March 1982 and in the first six months after shipment sales equaled $34,950,000 with a net income of $6,108,000.[18] When asked to remark about the growth of the industry, Imagic's founder (and former marketing VP of Activision) said, "Any market with this much opportunity is bound to attract people."[19] With that recognition, it's important to note that this includes the Japanese who have already entered through designing such games as Space Invaders and Pac-Man and licensing them to U.S. manufacturers. It's entirely likely and probable that Japanese participation will span the manufacture of cartridges as well.

With such a sprouting of participants in the industry with widely different backgrounds, one may wonder if there is no end to the craze.

> Don Valentine, who was shrewd enough to invest in Atari nearly a decade ago as president of Capital Investment Services Inc. in Menlo Park [answers this when he says that] Start-up companies in video games are "an area to be avoided. I think it's too late." Frank Caufield, a partner in the San Francisco firm of Kleiner Perkins Caufield & Byers, also says he wouldn't invest in a new video game venture now, although "I think Imagic may have been the last opportunity to get through that closing window," although he added that larger corporations such as CBS still may profit as late entrants because "they can afford to spend more money" than a venture capitalist on a new enterprise.[20]

In considering the diversity of entrants to this market, it is important to look at what barriers may or may not have to be overcome by the players. Access to distribution channels is probably the greatest barrier for a manufacturer of either consoles or game cartridges. The early entry of Atari, and the

---

[18] *IMAGIC Prospectus,* Los Gatos, Calif., December 1982, p. 7.

[19] "The Riches Behind Video Games," *Business Week,* November 9, 1981.

[20] Kathryn Harris, "Video Games: Is It Too Late to Play?" *Los Angeles Times,* November 21, 1982, p. 3.

existing retailer base of Mattel toys gives any entering competitor a tough sell for gaining access to channels.

With the proliferation of game titles in 1982, shelf space became a major consideration for buyers. Product differentiation is normally a key concern when attempting to overcome consumer loyalty to one market leader. In more cases than not, however, manufacturers have tied themselves to the Atari product (i.e., cartridge compatibility). Those who have not, like Mattel and Coleco, have had to aggressively advertise their product advantages (better graphics, computer upgradeable) and be extremely competitive on price. Capital requirements are low for cartridge-only producers but can be significantly high for companies producing consoles. Mattel ran into severe margin reductions in the fourth quarter of 1982 due to high product development and production costs. Consumer switching costs are moderately high right now. It is unlikely that a consumer would switch from a Mattel to an Atari to a Coleco console. However, switching costs are rapidly coming down as software manufacturers make games that run on *both* Atari and Mattel (e.g., Activision's hit game, Pitfall!), together with Coleco's strategy of having hardware that will play any game.

Economies of scale are certainly a consideration in manufacturing costs and Atari's healthy market share gives it a competitive advantage here. The high margins potentially available in the industry reduced any concern about an entry deterring price. Only since the market has become crowded with competitors have prices gone down and costs (advertising/promotion) gone up, squeezing once fat margins and making this barrier increasingly important.

The ability to exit the industry varies by type of player. Film companies have the least amount of business and resources tied up in video games and therefore exit is relatively easy. Toy manufacturers have significant stakes in other areas of their business albeit these segments are growing less rapidly than electronic games so the impetus to stay and become successful in the market is strong. Mattel, on the other hand (as well as Atari), has staked much of its future financial success in this industry (50 percent of '82 profits are attributable to the video game market) and exit for Mattel is highly unlikely. Activision and Imagic are in the video game business only. It's likely that Activision could cash in its chips now and come out considerably healthy (employees holding stock would be wealthy!) but the corporation's belief in the industry's long-term viability and Activision's major role in it means the chance of exiting is nonexistent at this time. Imagic is probably on much shakier ground (living in the shadow of Activision) given its smaller size and lack of financial clout.

Competitive Dynamics

The factors affecting market share and profitability while participating in the industry include both "expected" variables and some that are more unique to this industry. Intense competition has emerged on six major fronts: pricing, promotion, advertising, designer talent, legal issues, and distribution (see Buyer section).

With increased participation in the video game industry and the introduction of home computers by old and new companies alike, the marketplace began to be cluttered by look-alike machines varying in power, complexity, and initially price. Manufacturers getting caught in the fray of consumers' lack of knowledge about such systems and the fear that they (manufacturers) would not reach economies of scale decided to make the decision to purchase easier and cut their prices. This move only made things worse.

By September 1982, Texas Instruments Corporation had cut the price of its home computer to $199, dangerously close to the existing home video components. In October, Mattel announced it would slash the price of Intellivision to $150, following a recently expired $50 rebate on the product which representatives said successfully sparked sales. Atari's newly introduced 5200 VCS had a retail price of $269, but it was rumored that store owners were likely to be selling the product near dealer cost ($160), taking significant losses to beef up volume.

There was great debate in the industry as to whether home computers would swallow up the video game console market giving more function at a competitive price. Commodore Business Machines internalized this belief and de-emphasized its Max game machine, turning increased attention to the VIC-20 instead. The VIC-20 was being discounted to prices between $150 and $179. Another school of thought existed on this subject however. Ray Kassar, president and CEO of Atari stated that "games and computers are both very important, but they are two distinct markets."[21] Atari chose to develop each market separately and went as far as maintaining separate divisions within the company to do so. Mattel's strategy was to develop a game console that would be convertible to a home computer with the addition of a special keyboard, attempting to span across all fronts of the debate. Arnold Greenberg, president of Coleco, believed "there would be a fusion" of the markets.[22]

Video game cassettes were also coming under pricing scrutiny by the end of 1982. Retailers hesitated to cut into the healthy 25–30 percent margins they realized on cassettes but some price reductions were evident as they tried to build traffic for the Christmas season. Bob Faught, Activision vice president of sales, believed that a quality distinction of "good, better, and best" would determine pricing strategy. "The 'better' and 'best' game cartridges will maintain their price," he said, "but the poor product will be discounted."[23]

Caught in the midst of muddying product definition and pricing confusion was the consumer. How were they to figure out who offered what product fea-

---

[21] Speech by Raymond Kassar, president of Atari, at Harvard Business School, Boston, Mass., October 14, 1982.

[22] Aljean Harmetz, "Makers Vie for Millions in Home Video Games," *New York Times*, January 13, 1983.

[23] Marcia Golden, "Price Wars New Game Entry for This Fall?" *Mart*, September 1982, p.15.

tures and which features were most desirable for them? To answer these questions, manufacturers came to the consumers' aid with a surge in promotions and a blitz of national advertising campaigns in 1982. The advertising agency of Keye, Donne, and Pearlstein (San Francisco) projected a year-end advertising expense of $98 million, to be broken down as follows:[24]

Atari	$60 million	(up from $30 million in 1981)
Mattel	$16	
Activision	$8	
Magnavox	$6	
Imagic	$4	

A second source suggested Atari would spend $75 to $85 million in advertising by year end, and an additional $55 million in cooperative advertising. More than half of this total was allotted for the fourth quarter of 1982. Manufacturers advertised in major periodicals including *Life, Newsweek, Playboy,* and *Sports Illustrated* as well as trade magazines like *Electronic Games* and *Video Game Magazine.* The bulk of expenditures, however, came from television commercials in prime time and on sports programs (both network and spot) to reach the adult buying audience. Television is the natural advertising medium for home video games, since the sight-and-sound medium can capture the suspense, excitement, and challenge of these products and transmit them to viewers in the rooms housing their TV sets."[25]

Industry giants did not quit with traditional mediums for communicating their message to consumers, however. By August, Activision, Atari, and Mattel had spread their advertising battleground to include movie theatres. Capitalizing on heavy summer traffic, each company bought cinema commercial packages from Screenvision which has 1,600 theatre affiliates nationwide. Screenvision bases its ad rates on cost-per-thousand admissions with 60-second spots at $21, and two-minute messages like Mattels at $28 cpm.[26] Often these expenditures run into six figures for a single commercial but they provide still another channel for reaching the consumer.

To encourage trade participation in this business, all manufacturers have participated in Consumer Electronic Shows, held several times a year around the country, displaying their latest technology innovations and creative genius. Additionally, heavy trade promotion has been evidenced at the retailer level with Imagic leading in innovative push technologies. "Defend Atlantis (and Win Its Lost Treasure)" is an Imagic promotion which ran for three months in

---

[24] "Videogame and Equipment Ad Budgets," *Advertising Age,* February 22, 1983, p. 77.

[25] "Home Video Game Warfare Erupts on Television," *Broadcasting,* March 1, 1983, p. 64.

[26] James Forkan, "Videogame Ads Hit Hot Movie Houses," *Advertising Age,* August 2, 1982, p. 6.

'82. According to James Goldberger, vice president of marketing, "Retailers (could) win a week in Bermuda by creating the best looking display or by sending (Imagic) a photo of their high score for the Atlantis video game."[27] Atari and McDonald's launched a joint promotion where prizes ranged from Big Macs to Atari 400 and 800 home computer systems. More conventional trade promotions include creative game displays and the Lefty game cartridge allowances for retailers.

A unique base for competition has been that of designer talent. Good designers provide a unique blend of technological prowess with creative genius, making them hot commodities for game manufacturers. The perpetual splitting of all kinds of talent in this industry provides an incestual tone to the business. The designers in this industry are young; most are under 30, and some are on their way to becoming millionaires, as well as public heroes. Veteran designer Larry Kaplan (three years with Atari, three years with Activision) points to the attraction of the industry because "computer people, for leisure, always create games."[28] Perhaps, but none are so well known as those at Activision who are promoted like "rock stars" with their pictures and comments appearing on cassette packaging. Freelance designers receive royalties for their games which can run 25 to 35 percent allowing some game designers to pull in $75,000 to $175,000 on a single game.[29] Competitors must consider acquiring or developing this kind of talent base to improve the quality of graphic and contextual game play.

The last major front of competition to be considered is less directly related to the video game business itself but has acted as a weapon in slowing or stopping the entry of rivals in the industry. A rash of copyright infringements and antitrust suits abounded in the fourth quarter of 1982. Atari, in particular, used its weight as industry leader to claim that Imagic's Demon Attack was not an original game but rather a copy of the arcade game Phoenix that Atari was producing. The market leader also filed a $350 million suit against Coleco charging that the Coleco (Atari-compatible) adapter contained circuitry "substantially identical to the motion object and sound circuitry of the Atari VCS."[30] Coleco responded with a $500 million antitrust suit against Atari. Legal battles are time-consuming and expensive, and the issues are not clearcut. "Software," says Michael Keplinger of the U.S. Copyright Office, "does not fit neatly into any legal category."[31]

Suppliers

General Instrument Corporation and Rockwell International are the primary suppliers to the video game industry. While they also provide the semiconduc-

---

[27] Anne Krueger, "Videogames Go Hollywood," *Merchandising,* September 1982, p. 46.

[28] Krueger, "Videogame Veteran Larry Kaplan," p. 65.

[29] Kathleen Wiegner, "New Stars, New Firmament," *Forbes,* May 24, 1982, p. 50.

[30] Associated Press, "Atari Accuses Coleco of Patent Infringement," *The Record,* p. E3.

[31] Richard Sandza with Aric Press, "The Bandits vs. the Lawyers," *Newsweek,* December 20, 1982.

tor chips for manufacturers of home computers, neither company seemed fazed by the 40 percent expected growth rate from 1981 to 1982. In fact, Howard Cotterman, vice president for microcomputer products at Rockwell, states that video games are "moving from explosive growth into a merely high-growth phase."[32]

The components needed to manufacture a game cassette are relatively few and inexpensive. Assembly consists of a memory chip, printed circuit boards, a plastic case, a cardboard box for packaging, and the label. These materials in 1982 came to an estimated cost of $4 to $5. At an average manufacturer's selling price of $24.50 ($35.00 at retail and 30 percent retailer margin), the manufacturer of a video game cassette makes out quite nicely. Those industry participants who have chosen to compete in the console segment of the business have a much harder time keeping profitable margins due to hardware costs, development, and manufacturing overhead.

Channels of Distribution

The importance of access to distribution channels should be plainly evident. This is not an industry where personal selling is possible so that pull (advertising) and push (through the trade) strategies are critical. Atari accidently (and much to their good fortune) established a contract with Sears in the early days of this industry which locked up a nationwide channel for the young company.

Initially, once the interest in video games took off, the industry was a seller's market. Manufacturers could not meet the demand of end users (and hence the trade). Retailers sought to stock any and all types of game cartridges without regard to quality or manufacturer. Mattel and other toy companies benefited from existing channels developed for their other toy businesses.

As the number of manufacturers in the industry grew, and game cartridges proliferated, retailers were unable to stock the numerous titles available. In 1981 and 1982 these distributors began to use discretion in those products they accepted. Retailers chose game titles on the basis of degree of game difficulty, graphics, type of game (e.g., sports), and by designer and company. Likewise, shelf space was limited for game consoles. Many retailers chose to stock only Atari and Mattel, limiting the channel outlets for Coleco and smaller console manufacturers. Retailer margins varied from 25 to 40 percent, but generally ran close to 33 percent for game cartridges (retail prices range from $22.95 to $37.95). See Exhibit 5. Consoles on the other hand, only gave a 5 percent margin ($150 to $220 for the consumer). By the end of '82, retailers were returning older games and slower-moving games to manufacturers, preferring to keep higher volumes of hit games instead. Even some of these game sales were "overestimated," causing returns.

While retailers have become more discriminating in their purchases of game cartridges, they have also become more aggressive in their selling to end

---

[32] "Video-Game Boom Continues Despite Computer Price War," *The Wall Street Journal*, October 1, 1982, p. 33.

EXHIBIT 5 Market share of video game players

		80%
Atari		
		60%
Mattel		40%
Coleco		20%

| 1981 | 1982 | 1983 projected |
| year end | | |

Source: *Fortune,* March 7, 1983.

users. Many have created or expanded home entertainment displays in the stores. Gimbels (Pittsburgh, Pennsylvania) has gone to the extent of developing the New Arcade, a spacious, neon-lit, video game center where "customers are given unlimited time to examine, play, and learn."[33] As a committed retailer with a large distribution network, Gimbels has little trouble getting games before its competition. For example, the store had 8,000 Pac-Man cartridges three weeks before anyone else in the Pittsburgh area. (Eventually they cancelled 3,000 of these cartridges).

A somewhat different kind of buyer, also gaining power, is the rental retailer. Video specialty stores have begun to shift their emphasis from movies to video game cartridges. Rentals are running at a three-to-one ratio with sales at Entertainment Systems of America in Phoenix. Rental charges are $2 per night.[34] This kind of endeavor creates an additional channel for the manufacturer while giving the consumer another opportunity to try out games before buying them.

Broader Concept

What can take the place of a home video game is open to debate, depending on how you define the product. In the most general sense they are video entertainment. Therefore, a potential substitute is the movie theatre. It is difficult to

---

[33] Richard Mariani, "Gimbels' New Arcade Triples Video-Game Volume," *Merchandising,* Summer 1982, p. 53.

[34] "Video-Game Cartridge Rental Promotes Sales," *Merchandising,* Summer 1982, p. 9.

quantify the switching costs to a consumer, trading off between a $4 to $5 ticket (adult price) for a movie, and playing a video game at home. Some considerations: there is no transportation cost to play the video games, the same game can be played many times over without additional cost, and video games allow (in fact necessitate) audience participation. On the other hand, it is unlikely that consumers would make a complete switch from the theatre to home video games so the financial tradeoff is not exact.

Perhaps more comparable are other forms of home video entertainment. These may include products like videodisc machines or video cassette recorders which allow the taping and/or playing of movies, sports, and other video entertainment. "However," says an Atari executive, "when you compare the $150 cost of a video game machine with videodisc machines or VCR's that run anywhere from $500 to $1,200, the video game looks like a pretty good entertainment option."[35]

Hand-held electronics enjoyed a huge market success before video games got off the ground. Unfortunately, their simplicity and generic nature caused sales to peak quickly and market saturation leveled off sales. Generic nature refers to the fact that these games are inclined toward math games or sports (how many ways can you play football?).

Probably closest to home, although not in the home, are electronic arcade games. The shift from traditional electromechanical pin-ball machines to electronic arcades came about in the mid-1970s with Nolan Bushnell as the catalyst (developing Pong). By 1981, approximately $7 billion dollars was spent at the consumer level (one quarter at a time) on coin-operated videogames. The accompanying chart compares Richard Simon's (Goldman Sachs) estimate for unit shipments and dollars for arcade and home games in 1981.[36]

Estimated worldwide videogame market, 1981 (millions)

| Videogames | Manufacturer level | | Consumer level |
	Units shipped	Amount	Amount
Coin operated	.5	$1,050	$7,000
Home consoles	5.1	615	670
Home cartridges	38.4	560	800
Total	44.0	$2,225	$8,470

Simon's expectation of home video totaling approximately 21 percent of total consumer dollars spent in this market nearly doubled in 1982, to 34 percent. While coin-operated game sales to distributors showed flat growth in

[35] Laura Landro, "New Video-Game Makers Jump Into Fight," *The Wall Street Journal*, November 27, 1982, p. 1.

[36] Richard Simon, "The Videogame Industry," *Investment Research* (New York: Goldman Sachs, February 22, 1982), p. 2.

1982, the home market expanded considerably. There tend to be wide swings in market share of coin-operated manufacturers because a game's financial success is dependent largely on its ability to be a "hit."

Like the movie industry, games that appeal to a large audience can make millions, while other games may never be played. For example, about 100,000 Pac-Man coin-op games were sold in the United States in 1981. If the average unit generated about $200 per week in the coin drop (box office), the coin drop equivalent of theatrical box-office would be about $1 billion. This is about equal to the *combined* box office of *Star Wars, The Empire Strikes Back, Jaws* and *Grease*.[37] For this reason, games that become hits will have a heavy concentration in locations with multiple machines.

Less popular games will be sparsely scattered and may not even appear in locations that have only a few machines. In December 1982, a shakeout among game operators was evident. Distributors were overstocked and buyers were "becoming very secretive and very conservative."[38] Leisure industry analyst Steven Eisenberg at New York's Bear Sterns and Co. predicts that 1983 sales will be no better than 1982's estimated 450,000 units priced at about $2,000 each.[39]

The most critical element in determining the growth of coin-op games is market saturation (technological innovation and game design are also important). Saturation is difficult to put a handle on because the *potential* market and *probable* market can vary widely. Distribution channels include arcades (10 or more games in a location where this is the primary business), malls, movies, bars, restaurants, and fast-food chains. The fast-food chains are least penetrated now, but growth here is uncertain because of fluctuating ROI and maintenance costs (labor and overhead). Theme restaurants may prove to be the most likely area of expansion. Nolan Bushnell's Pizza Time Theatre currently leads this industry in number of locations and dollar sales. Bushnell is naturally a proponent of arcades in his restaurant operations. Whether growth in coin-op games continues to stabilize or shows some promise of slow growth, it is evident that the home video market is booming and will continue on a faster upward trend.

It is across these arenas described above that video game competitors battle for market share and profitability in the industry. The following section takes a look at three specific companies and their strategies for competition.

Competitive Strategies

Coleco Industries, Inc.

At the year's end in 1982, Coleco was the New York Stock Exchange's best performer, growing from $6.87 to $36.75 a share. The strategy that has led to

---

[37] Ibid., p. 6.
[38] "Arcade Video Games Start to Flicker," *Business Week*, December 6, 1982, p. 39.
[39] Ibid.

this success has been a modification of a "me, too" strategy. Coleco does it too, but they do it better. According to president and chief executive officer, Arnold Greenberg, "We've never prided ourselves on being first, but on our ability to build a better mousetrap at a better price."[40] Coleco seems to have done just that, having entered the market in early 1982 and capturing 10 percent of the cartridge business and slightly less than that for consoles in this greater than $2 billion industry (see Exhibit 5). Sales have reached $510 million from $178 million in '81, profits have increased 420 percent to $40 million from the prior year.

The company's product strategy is one of high quality graphics and high quality games, hitting both Atari (poor graphics) and Mattel (lack of hit games) where it counts. Coleco has five product lines in the video game market. Self-contained games (table-top portable sets measuring 8-by-12 inches and selling at $50) accounted for approximately 32 percent of revenues in '82.

Three other product lines are compatible cartridges, one each for Atari, Mattel, and Coleco, which account for 50 percent of video game revenues. The remainder of sales in this area are for ColecoVision, with practically all 550,000 units shipped in the fourth quarter at $169–$189 (manufacturer's price).

By choosing this type of product strategy, Coleco has bombarded the video game market from all sides. It touts compatibility to the hilt. If you own ColecoVision, you can play Atari and Mattel games, but if you own an Atari VCS, well—better luck next time. The ability to obtain compatibility is a benefit, but by no means a free one. ColecoVision adapters to play Atari-compatible games are $60, no deterrence to the 150,000 ColecoVision owners who bought them within 2 months of availability this year. On the cartridge front, Coleco depends on outside consultants to convert licensed arcade games or cartoon properties to home game cartridges. Greenberg does not scoff at the costliness of licensing. "Outrageous cost notwithstanding, software is outrageously—if not sinfully—profitable."[41] The company currently makes about 50 percent profit on cartridges after manufacturing, advertising, royalty, and other expenditures.

The advertising that supports these product lines, ColecoVision's in particular, has become an increasingly significant cost, somewhat offsetting the high profit margins. The $20 million advertising campaign planned for winter 1982–83 is the largest in the history of the 50-year-old company. Coleco aims its ads at three target audiences:

> ColecoVision commercials target the consumers who do not own a video system yet, while cartridge commercials aim at those 15 percent who do own video systems. The commercials for hand-held units appeal to those consumers who can't afford the entire video system.[42]

---

[40] Lisa Miller Mesdag, "How Coleco Plans to Keep Flying High," *Fortune*, March 7, 1983, p. 118.

[41] "Coleco Hits with Home Video Games," *Business Week*, January 27, 1983, p. 32.

[42] "Coleco Kicks Off Ad Campaign," *Advertising Age*, Fall 1982.

Coleco's objectives are clear and aggressive. The company directly advertises against Atari and Mattel and makes no apologies for its intent to beat out the latter opponent for the number 2 spot in the home console segment. Coleco predicts an increased market share from 8 percent to 25 percent by mid-1983. If Mr. Greenberg has his way, and he usually does, this is exactly what will happen. Greenberg's management style has been described as *totalitarian*—he is slow to delegate authority and is involved in every aspect of operations.[43]

The organization has come a long way from losing $22 million in 1978, knocking on bankruptcy's front door. Coleco's history shows a series of ups and downs in its businesses, which were traditionally seasonal. How Greenberg manages the fast-paced and uncertain video game business will determine whether Coleco can in fact be a winner by "selling a better mousetrap."

Activision

Formed by five ex-Atari designers and James Levy (a former executive of Time, Inc., Hershey Foods, and GRT record company), Activision became the first independent company to design, manufacture, and market home video game cartridges. The company was incorporated in October 1979, when only Atari and Odyssey consoles were on the market. Initially it manufactured cartridges compatible with Atari systems only, far superior in quality to Atari-made games. Intellivision-compatibles were introduced in November of 1982. The company also markets games in 38 countries on every continent except Antarctica.

As initiator of the "razor blade" strategy, Activision enjoyed low overhead (only 50 employees in November 81) and high profit margins. Levy estimated aftertax margins of 15 percent and rising.[44]

Both the company's growth in sales and people has been astonishing. There were 131 employees in August 1982 and 230 employees in December of that year. Activision opened a new 92,500-square-foot manufacturing and distribution center which radically increased production capacity in 1982. The company has grown to more than $100 million in sales since its inception, on an initial investment of a mere $700,000 of venture capital. Activision has not borrowed a dime since then.

The theme of independence rings strongly through the corporate strategy of the company. Although soon after incorporation, the founders were hit with a $20 million suit from Atari, charging unfair competition and conspiracy to appropriate trade secrets,[45] they bounced back after settling out of court, agreeing to pay Atari royalties. Since then, Activision has been its own company.

The company emerged as an outgrowth of the designers' dissatisfaction with their then current employer, Atari. Atari management was too directive for

---

[43] Mesdag, "How Coleco Plans," p. 117.
[44] "The Riches behind Video Games," *Business Week*, November 9, 1981, p. 98.
[45] Ibid.

these designers' tastes, so they formed their own company to guard against being told what to create. Activision has encouraged and enforced this concept of designer independence and even at its current staff size of 31 designers, does little more than present market information to them. *They* decide what games to make. Following this concept of independent creativity, designers are promoted with their game titles in a "rock star" fashion. This strategy is probably a carry-over from Levy's work in the music business.

A designer's picture and comments are packaged with the game and players are encouraged to write fan mail to their favorite designers. This promotional gimmick includes fan club membership and prizes (i.e., game emblems, T-shirts) for obtaining high point scores for particular games. Clubs include "Save the Chicken Foundation" (Freeway) and "Flying Aces" (Barnstorming). Just send in a picture of your video screen with your game score on it. As of the fourth quarter in '82, the company answered more than 6,000 letters per week from fans of all ages. This promotion strategy sets Activision apart from its competitors and has been combined with heavy advertising expenditures.

Game titles are promoted individually, with Pitfall!, Freeway, Stampede, and Kaboom! achieving greatest success so far (see Appendix B). Pitfall! was "number one on the charts" (akin to the record industry) for weeks after its introduction. Activision's series of *hit* games have enabled it to maintain its independence as a player in the industry. Up until now, the company has held a firm stance against game licensing and arcade copycats. It may loosen its position in the future, reveals Tom Pomeroy, vice president of planning,[46] because its position ignores a lucrative segment of the market. But creative, high quality games will continue to be a major asset for the firm in competing against the companies with greater resources.

Concerning its future success, Activision has considered offering Coleco-Vision compatible games; it will seek to expand its participation in the European market; and will produce entertainment software for home computers.

Imagic

Emerging on the heels of Activision, William Grubb (formerly of Activision and Atari) set out to start his own software business in Los Gatos, California. Imagic made compatible cartridges for both Mattel and Atari in March 1982 only nine months after its incorporation. The corporate strategy is to supply consumers with high quality entertainment software compatible with various manufacturers' hardware, in order to reduce dependencies on any one console system.

The marketing slogan "Created by Experts for Experts"[47] publicly states

---

[46] Interview with Mr. Tom Pomeroy, vice president of planning, Activision, Mountain View, Calif., March 29, 1983.

[47] *Imagic Prospectus,* p. 11.

the strategy of high product quality. Along with distinctive packaging and initially word-of-mouth advertising, Imagic realized $3.9 million dollars in sales in its first quarter of shipments. Its Demon Attack game, compatible with Atari, was chosen as 1982's ''Game of the Year'' by *Electronic Games* magazine over popular games like Donkey Kong, Pac-Man, and Frogger.

Initially, Imagic depended on 3 in-house designers for the bulk of its game production but it has since increased that number to 19, spreading its innovation risk more broadly. The company has not chosen to license arcade games or motion picture titles, again taking Activision's lead.

The most critical issue facing Imagic in 1982 was its transition from word-of-mouth to formal advertising, ''the most important part of the marketing mix (in this business),''[48] states Grubb. On this note, the company launched a $10 million ad campaign (spanning September '82 to February '83) covering Saturday morning children's television on ABC and NBC, and prime time programs on all three major networks. It advertises its cartridges on an individual basis, with the heaviest share of spending on Star Voyager and Demon Attack. Additionally, Imagic has been aggressive and creative in trade promotions, gaining access to virtually all the major retail chains in the United States, including J. C. Penney, Sears, Montgomery Ward, and Toys-R-Us. None of these customers account for more than 10 percent of total sales.

The major concern for this tiny firm (less than 200 employees to date) is whether it can keep up aggressive advertising and promotion amidst such giants as Atari, Mattel, Coleco and North American Phillips, all with financial resources substantially greater than itself.

Recent Events: Late '82 to Early '83

In late '82, after doubling the profits of its parent corporation, Warner Communications, Inc., Atari announced that sales of its video game cartridges had fallen below projections, contributing to a 50 percent drop in Warner's earnings. Perry Odak, head of the consumer products group was fired, reportedly due to differences in management style between himelf and Ray Kassar. Shortly thereafter, Mattel disclosed that it would lose money in the fourth quarter even though shipments of games and consoles were significantly higher in that period than the preceding year. These events had a domino effect on Wall Street. Warner stock plunged $30.63 over a two-day period, with Mattel's shares falling 37 percent. In fact, most stocks that were related in any way with video games, including General Instrument and Toys-R-Us experienced some drop in share price.

What went wrong? Some competitors blame the mishap on Atari's rush introduction of the E.T. home game. Atari bought the license for E.T. in late August and pushed out a low quality, simplistic game in time for Christmas

---

[48] Philip Dougherty, ''$10 Million Campaign by Imagic,'' *New York Times,* September 28, 1982.

sale.[49] Consumers were disappointed. Scarring the company's reputation further, it was announced that eight company executives including the president, sold sizeable shares of stock prior to release of fourth quarter earnings projections. These management blunders cost the company considerable money and credibility.

Mattel's woes were caused by both internal and external problems. Product development costs for Intellivision II, a streamlined version of its predecessor and Intellivoice—the voice synthesizer module that attaches to the control unit—were substantial, cutting into projected profits. The company has sought to reduce dependence on outside chip suppliers by bidding for Solid State Scientific, Inc., a small publicly held semiconductor maker. All of this up-front investment is costing the company dearly. And it comes at a time when competitors have aggressively introduced new products and cut prices.

Coleco has quickly gained market share giving Mattel a battle for survival, and software makers are busily introducing Intellivision-compatible games. Says Richard Simon of Goldman Sachs, "The time bomb that hit Atari in 1982 will hit Mattel in 1983."[50] Mattel has attempted to increase consumer loyalty for its games through an agreement with Playcable which allows Intellivision owners to play games through cable TV for $10 a month. However, sales have been disappointing so far.

For other competitors, aggressive advertising, pricing and product introduction continues. Coleco has made an agreement to make CBS its principal foreign distributor in return for developing and marketing home video cartridges licensed by CBS from Bally, for ColecoVision.[51] At the same time, Activision has announced the introduction of Pitfall! and Stampede, Intellivision-compatible games to be made available in 10 European countries. Both Activision and Imagic have announced planned software for Atari Home Computers. Levy states, "We plan to be as significant a factor in the development of home computer software as we have been in the development of video games."[52]

The issues facing this industry fall into three broad categories: technology, market segmentation, and consumer acceptance. From a technological standpoint, the issue of compatibility is a real one. Standardization is coming to the fore, but unfortunately for Atari it has not been chosen as a lone standard. Several technologies are present (Atari, Mattel, and Coleco) and will most likely remain. Each of these competitors has invested to the degree where backing out of this industry is probably not an option, due to financial constraints and management commitment.

The development of the home computer market will also impact the video game industry and each of these players has taken steps to mitigate their vulner-

---

[49] Interview with various personnel at Activision, Mountain View, Calif., January 8, 1983.

[50] "Mattel Struggles to Fix Its Product Woes," *Business Week*, May 9, 1983, pp. 76 and 78.

[51] Mesdag, "How Coleco Plans," p. 120.

[52] Activision company literature for News Release, Mountain View, Calif., January 6, 1983.

ability by developing home computer products as well. Coleco will enter this market in June of 1983 with a system comparable to the Atari 400 or Commodore VIC-20. Video game cartridge makers, as well, are taking precautions to prevent exclusion from the home computer market. Finally, technological revolutions may still occur in this industry. Video game designer veteran and president of Video-Soft in California, Jerry Lawson, plans to introduce a "Smart Cart" system allowing players at home to compete with each other using the telephone.[53] Innovations of this type could create further monumental changes in the industry structure and in its participants.

Market segmentation has evolved through manufacturers' efforts to get a piece of the action. New markets have opened up based on the licensing of film or TV characters (i.e., Atari licensing Sesame Street characters for games), geographical markets (especially Europe), educational games, and those for specific age groups (elderly people as well as youngsters). The additional insight gained from segmenting the consumer base will allow for further penetration of individual groups and increased game sales for companies.

Finally, consumer acceptance must always be considered. In 1981, several outcries of parental concern were heard over children spending too much time and too many quarters at the arcades. Some towns placed curfews on evening hours that arcade machines could operate. That sentiment seems to have died down, although parents' ill will rose again when an X-rated game hit the market. In Custer's Revenge, for instance, a mostly naked General Custer, who dodges menacing cacti and flying arrows, attempts to have his way with an Indian maiden whose hands are tied behind her back.[54] Games like Custer, along with Bachelor Party and Beat 'em and Eat 'em may have a limited following but it is important that major manufacturers in this industry do not gain the disfavor of their mass audience, for the consumer will determine who wins and loses in this volatile marketplace. For any serious competitor, the ability to advertise heavily, lock up retailer shelf-space, and compete aggressively on price will be essential to its long-term health and wealth in the video game industry.

---

[53] Hilliard, "Cash in on Craze," p. 44.

[54] Peter Nulty, "Why the Craze Won't Quit," *Fortune*, November 15, 1982, p. 128.

APPENDIX A Video game consoles and home computer systems

Videogames and computers for your home

Company and game machine	Retail price	Graphic quality	Top-selling games	Size of game library
Atari Video Computer System	$129–$149	Good	Pac-Man, Space Invaders	60
Atari 5200 Home Video Entertainment Center	$150	Very good	Galaxian, Star Raiders	10
Mattel Intellivision	$229–$250	Superior	NFL Football, Tron	30
Coleco Colecovision	Under $250	Superior	Donkey Kong, Cosmic Avengers	24
North American Phillips Odyssey	$139–$150	Excellent	Pick Axe Pete, K.C.'s Crazy Chase	48
Company and Home computers				
Commodore VIC-20	Under $200	Excellent	Gorf, Omega Race	19
Atari 400	$339–$349	Superior	Centipede, Frogger	50
Texas Instruments Home Computer	$299	Good	TI Invader, Hunt the Wumpus	79
Apple II Plus	$1,530	Excellent	Choplifter, Swashbuckler	50

APPENDIX B Video game cassettes by manufacturer*

Atari	Mattel	Coleco	Activision	Imagic	Parker
Space Invaders	Astrosmash	Donkey Kong	Pitfall	Demon Attack	Frogger
Breakout	Auto Racing	Lady Bug	Starmaster	Trickshot	Empire Strikes Back
Night Driver	Blackjack	Venture	Megamania		
Hangman	Utopia	Zaxxon	Kaboom		
Pac-Man	Night Stalker	Smurf	Freeway		
Defender		Turbo	Stampede		
Berzerk		Avenger	Seaquest		
Star Raiders		Mouse Trap	Checkers		
		Carnival	Ice Hockey		

* Partial listing only.

Case 41

Norton Company*

Subject to the business cycle swings of the capital goods industry, Norton Company experienced the usual drop in sales during the economic downturn of 1975. What was unusual for Norton was its ability on this occasion to sustain profits compared to the customary plunge in earnings whenever the economy dipped. Robert Cushman, president and chief executive officer of Norton Company, saw this performance as evidence of the growing effectiveness of Norton's strategic planning.

As of 1976, five years' efforts had gone into developing planning activities that specifically could help top management shape strategies for the firm's diversified business operations. Mr. Cushman was pleased with the results of these efforts:

> Our strategic planning has made a tremendous difference in the way the company is now managed. It gives us a much-needed handle to evaluate strategies for each of our many businesses.

One of the difficult strategic planning decisions faced by top management in 1976 concerned a reevaluation of the long-term strategy for the coated abrasives business operations in the United States. This situation is described following a general explanation of the strategic planning process at Norton Company and how it came to be.

The Company

Norton Company, headquartered in Worcester, Massachusetts, was a multinational industrial manufacturer with 85 plant locations in 21 countries. The firm employed almost 19,000 persons.

As the world's largest abrasives manufacturer, Norton produced both abrasive-grain raw materials and finished products. The latter included such items as sandpaper and grinding wheels. The company also produced a wide

* This case was prepared by Professor Francis Aguilar with the assistance of Norton Company to serve as a basis for class discussion rather than to illustrate either effective or ineffective handling of an administrative situation. Copyright © 1979 by the President and Fellows of Harvard College.

range of other industrial products, including industrial ceramics, sealants, catalyst carriers and tower packings for the chemical process industries, engineered plastic components, tubing and related products for medical applications and for food processing, and industrial safety products. In 1975, these other products accounted for about 27 percent of the reported total sales of $548 million.[1] Exhibit 1 contains a five-year summary of financial results.

EXHIBIT 1

NORTON COMPANY

Five-Year Financial Summary

	1971	1972	1973	1974	1975
Net sales ($ millions)	346	374	475	558	548
Net income ($ millions)*	11.4	14.5	25.4	21.6	20.9
Net income, excluding effect of foreign currency exchange rate changes ($ millions)*	10.3	15.0	21.3	25.1	24.8
By line of business (percent):					
Abrasives					
Sales	70%	75%	75%	75%	73%
Net income	85%	87%	89%	76%	70%
Diversified products					
Sales	30%	25%	25%	25%	27%
Net income	15%	13%	11%	24%	30%
By subsidiaries outside the United States (percent):					
Sales (%)	41%	41%	42%	45%	49%
Net income (%)	39%	33%	56%	56%	40%
Working capital ($ millions)	148	151	155	159	200
Total debt ($ millions)	69	65	66	102	112
Shareholders' equity ($ millions)	211	218	232	244	255
Operating and financial ratios:					
Net income as percentage of sales	3.3	3.9	5.3	3.9	3.8
Net income as percentage of equity	5.4	6.7	10.9	8.8	8.2
Current ratio	3.7	3.6	2.9	2.3	3.3
Percent total debt to equity	33	30	29	42	44
Per share statistics†					
Net income*	2.12	2.70	4.70	4.02	3.85
Net income, excluding effect of foreign currency exchange rate changes*	1.92	2.80	3.94	4.68	4.57
Dividends	1.50	1.50	1.50	1.575	1.70
Stock price (NYSE)	27–37	32–39	23–36	19–29	21–29

* Exchange gains and losses resulting from the translation of foreign currency financial statements were included for the first time in the 1975 annual report in determining net income in accordance with a new procedure recommended by the Financial Accounting Standards Board (FASB). The net income results excluding foreign currency effects conform to prior reporting practices at Norton and generally throughout industry.

† The average number of shares of common stock outstanding varied between 5.37 million and 5.67 million during this period.

Source: Annual reports and *Moody's Industrial Manual,* 1975.

---

[1] On September 9, 1976, Norton Company announced an agreement in principle to merge with Christensen, Inc., for stock valued at $100 million. Christensen, with 1975 sales of $118 million and net income of $9.5 million, manufactured diamond-drilling bits and coring bits for the petroleum and mining industries. With Christensen, nonabrasive products would account for about 40 percent of total sales.

Organization

Norton Company was organized into "low growth" and "high growth" product groups. This organizational structure reflected two basic corporate objectives. The first was to remain the worldwide leader in abrasives. The second was to improve profitability through "a limited number of diversified product lines and without conglomeration."[2]

When introducing this structure in 1971, Cushman had remarked:

> As you look at Norton Co. you see two major areas of business: our traditional abrasives products, which are good cash generators but have low growth, and our newer nonabrasive lines, which need cash but have high growth potential. We need a different type of manager to run each area.

Harry Duane, age 45, headed the abrasives group. His job was characterized as that of "running a large, cyclical-prone, slow-growth business with stiff competition in many different markets." Successful performance in this business was said to depend on careful cost control, keeping products up to date, and holding established markets. Duane had had experience in the abrasives business abroad as well as in the United States since joining Norton in 1957.

Donald R. Melville, age 50, headed Norton's diversified products business group. He had joined the company in 1967 as vice president of marketing after having served in various marketing capacities with Continental Can Company, Scott Paper Company, and Dunlop Tire & Rubber. As reported in *Business Week:*

> Melville's management style relies on creating an entrepreneurial atmosphere that will allow people to operate where they are not bogged down by a formal line-management reporting system. "In the case of abrasives," says Melville, "you compensate your people on the basis of whether or not they make that month's budget. In diversified products, you don't care as much about a month's budget—you try to double your sales in 12 months."[3]

The 1976 company organization structure is shown in Exhibit 2.

Concepts for Strategic Planning

In 1967, as executive vice president in charge of company-wide operations, Cushman faced the problem of assessing the role each of some 75 product lines was to play in Norton's future. The conventional corporate long-range planning then in use at Norton was found wanting for this task. Mr. Cushman conse-

---

[2] The *Norton Company Annual Report* for 1975 also highlighted three other corporate objectives: (1) to maintain responsible corporate citizenship, which at times means accepting lower profits; (2) to maintain a superior employee working environment; and (3) to enhance the value of Norton stock.

[3] *Business Week,* August 7, 1971, p. 80. Reprinted by special permission. © 1971 by McGraw-Hill, Inc., New York, N.Y. 10020. All rights reserved.

EXHIBIT 2 Partial organization chart, June 1976

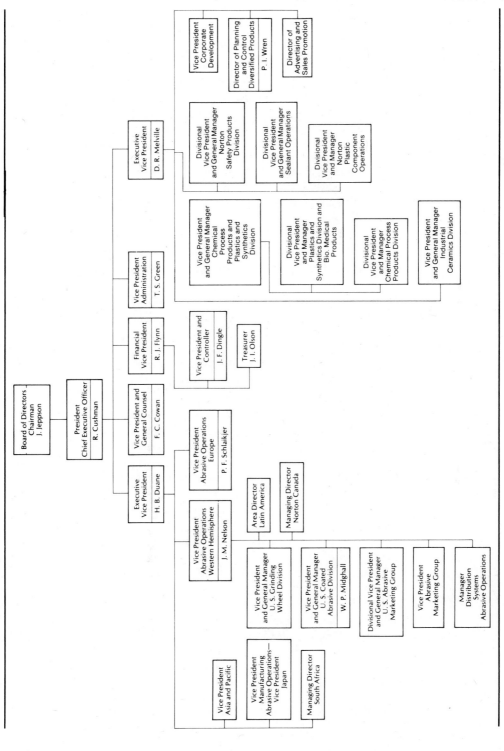

quently began to search for more appropriate ways to plan multibusiness operations. He later remarked:

> During the early 60s, Peter Drucker, widely known spokesman, critic, and analyst to business, began to describe business in terms of certain variables which seemed to determine a company's future. But it was Fred Borch, marketing vice president of the highly diversified General Electric, who in 1960 asked the key question and then assigned two members of his staff, Jack McKitterick and Dr. Sidney Schoeffler, to find the answer. "Why is it," he said, "that through the years some of our businesses fail while others succeed? There must be certain decisions, strategies, or factors which lead to certain results. With hundreds of products ranging from electric pencil sharpeners to diesel engines and nuclear plants, it is difficult to do an effective job of planning. It is, in fact, impossible for management to have a direct, personal feeling and knowledge about so many business environments. We need better guidelines."

In 1967, Dr. Schoeffler was invited to Norton to describe the results of GE's "profitability optimization" study. Based on sophisticated multiple regression analyses covering 10 years' experience for 150 product lines at General Electric, Dr. Schoeffler had been able to identify some 37 factors which accounted for more than 80 percent of the variations in profit results. The findings showed how profitability varied with respect to such factors as market share, market growth rate, and the level of investments required. The findings also showed how profitability varied with respect to policies on such matters as research and development as a percentage of sales, marketing expenditures, product quality, and pricing.[4] Mr. Cushman was struck with the relevance and concreteness of the resulting guidelines.

In his search for better guidelines, Mr. Cushman also became interested in the work of Bruce Henderson, founder and president of the Boston Consulting Group. Based on the premise that costs decreased with experience in a predictable manner, Henderson held that the firm with the greatest volume should have the lowest costs for a given product line. Market share served as a measure of relative volume for planning purposes.

The cash flows associated with growth and mature industries constituted a second element of Henderson's approach. Product lines with leading market shares in mature industries were generators of surplus cash; those in growth industries represented the potential cash generators for future years. For diversified business operations, Henderson urged that attention be given in strategic planning to the creation of a portfolio in which some product lines could generate sufficient cash throw-off to nourish the development and growth of other product lines in growing markets.

---

[4] Examples of profit determinants would include: (1) high marketing expenditures damage profitability when product quality is low; (2) high R&D spending hurts profitability when market share is small but increases ROI in when market share is high; and (3) high marketing expenditures hurt ROI in investment-intensive businesses.

Strategic Planning at Norton

The basic building block for planning continued to be the strategy analysis for individual product lines. This analysis considered a wide range of business factors such as competitive conditions, technology, and future trends, and concluded with a proposed course of action over time. Each strategy was prepared by the manager holding profit responsibility for the product line and was evaluated by group and corporate line management. The customary analysis and review of strategy were extended to include two additional tests based on the somewhat related sets of concepts described above.

One of these additional tests concerned the intrinsic profit potential for a business. Based on experiential data for a wide range of businesses (such as had been generated for General Electric), Norton was able to ascertain a measure of the profit level appropriate for a business as it existed. It was also able to ascertain the extent to which profits and cash flows might be increased under alternative strategies. These financial norms helped management to evaluate how well a business was being run and how much additional potential it had.

A business strategy was also evaluated in the context of total corporate cash flows. The strategy had to conform to the overall availabilities of, or needs for, cash. For this purpose, market share performance served as a major controlling device. In broad terms, businesses were assigned the task of building, holding, or harvesting market share. "Building strategies" were based on active efforts to increase market share by means of new product introductions, added marketing programs, etc. Such strategies customarily called for cash inputs. "Holding strategies" were aimed at maintaining the existing level of market share. Net cash flows might be negative for rapidly growing markets and positive for slowly growing markets. "Harvesting strategies" sought to achieve earnings and cash flows by permitting market share to decline.

In line with this approach, Norton's operations had been divided into some 60 businesses whose characteristics were sufficiently different to warrant the development of individual business strategies. These subdivisions were known as substrategic business units. Combinations of these substrategic business units were grouped into about 30 strategic business units for purposes of top-management review.

Strategy Guidance Committee

In April 1972, Cushman formed a top-management committee to assist in the evaluation of these business strategies. As Cushman later reported to the Norton Board:

> The function of the Strategy Guidance Committee is to review at appropriate levels the strategy of each business unit, to make certain it does fit corporate objectives, and to monitor how effectively its strategy is being carried out. It provides the executive, regional, and division manager an opportunity for an "outside" peer group to examine and advise.

The committee totals 12: the president, the executive vice president, the regional vice presidents, the financial vice president, the controller, the vice president of corporate development, and Graham Wren as secretary. Depending on the circumstances, business units are reviewed on a two-year cycle. Well-documented strategies along standard lines are sent to members for review before meetings.

Each strategic business unit was responsible for preparing a strategy book for review. Copies of this book were distributed to members of the Strategy Guidance Committee at least one week prior to the scheduled review. To focus attention on the critical issues, Cushman had set the following ground rules for the review session:

No formal presentation is required at the meeting because each committee member is expected to have thoroughly studied the strategy book.

Discussion during the meeting will generally center around these questions:

1. Questions of facts, trends, and assumptions as presented in the strategy book.
2. Questions as to the appropriateness of the mission of the business in terms of *Build, Maintain,* or *Harvest.*
3. Questions as to the appropriateness of the strategy in the context of the facts and mission.
4. Questions suggested by PIMS analysis.
5. How does the business unit and its strategy fit and relate to similar businesses within Norton (e.g., coated abrasives Europe versus coated abrasives world-wide)?
6. How does the business unit and its strategy fit within the corporate portfolio and strategy?

Involvement of Line Managers

The involvement of key line managers in the Strategy Guidance Committee and the methodology used in generating the strategy books gave a distinct line orientation to planning at Norton. Management for each business unit had to take a position concerning its mission, strengths and weaknesses, likely competitive developments, trends, and finally its strategy. The analysis and recommendations had to stand the test of critical evaluation by an experienced and involved top management.

Although Cushman was pleased with the planning tools Norton had developed, he felt that the deep involvement of line managers in both the formulation and review of strategies served to prevent a mechanical or otherwise undue reliance on the planning tools themselves. He believed it highly desirable that an operating manager's ''gut feel'' remain an important input to strategic planning.

Other Elements Related to Strategic Planning

In 1976 detailed cash flow models which could be used to support and extend the analysis described above were being completed. Several Norton managers remarked that these models would contribute importantly to the strategic planning efforts.

Also, Norton's incentive system was designed to motivate managers in carrying out their assigned strategic moves—whether to build, maintain, or harvest their business. Cushman reported the use of over 50 different custom-tailored plans for this purpose.

Finally, Cushman's deep-seated involvement in the strategic planning process and the respect he commanded from other senior-level managers at Norton undoubtedly influenced this process in major ways.

Coated Abrasives Domestic[5]

One of the difficult cases for consideration by the Strategy Guidance Committee in 1976 concerned a reevaluation of the strategy to be followed for the U.S. coated abrasives business. Coated Abrasives Domestic (CAD), one of Norton's larger operating divisions, had had a recent history of declining market share and profitability.

In 1974 Norton management had decided to stem further loss of market share by a major restructuring of the CAD division. During the ensuing two years, market share and profitability continued to decline. These unfavorable results raised important questions about the merits of the earlier decision. The case for holding market share (the current strategy) was further challenged by the recommendations resulting from the PIMS regression analysis. The PIMS report had concluded that the CAD business should be moderately harvested (market share permitted to decline) for its cash throw-off.

The remainder of this case presents excerpts from information presented to the Strategy Guidance Committee or otherwise known by its members concerning CAD.

The Abrasives Market

Abrasive finished products were generally classified as bonded or coated. Bonded abrasives were basic tools used in almost every industry where shaping, cutting, or finishing of materials was required. Some of the major uses were in foundries and steel mills for rough grinding of castings and surface conditioning of steels and alloys, in metal fabrication for such products as automobiles and household appliances, in tool and die shops, in the manufacture of bearings, and in the paper and pulp industry. Norton produced more than 250,000 types and sizes of grinding wheels and other bonded abrasive products.

Coated abrasives (popularly referred to as sandpaper) were widely used throughout the metalworking and woodworking industries, in tanneries, and in service industries such as floor surfacing and automobile refinishing. Norton produced more than 38,000 different items in the form of sheets, belts, rolls, discs, and specialties. The most common form of coated abrasives was the

---

[5] Numbers for the remainder of the case are disguised.

endless belt, some major applications of which included the grinding and finishing of automobiles and appliance parts, the precision grinding and polishing of stainless and alloy steel, and the sanding of furniture, plywood, and particle board.

The overlap of customers' requirements for bonded and coated abrasives varied from industry to industry. For example, the woodworking industry used coated abrasives almost exclusively. In contrast, the auto industry purchased large quantities of both bonded abrasives (e.g., for grinding engine parts) and coated abrasives (e.g., for finishing bodies). Industrial distributors, which accounted for a large portion of Norton's abrasive sales, usually carried both bonded and coated abrasive products. Both Norton and Carborundum offered full lines of bonded and coated abrasive products; 3M competed only in coated abrasives.

In management's opinion, the principal factors which contributed to a favorable market position in this industry included quality and reliability of product, completeness of product line, nonpatented technological "know-how," substantial capital investment, length of experience in the business, familiarity and reputation of name, strength of marketing network, technical service, delivery reliability, and price. In 1975 no single customer, including the U.S. government, accounted for as much as 5 percent of Norton's net sales.

CAD in the Corporate Context

As was customary, the meeting of the Strategy Guidance Committee to review the CAD strategy was opened by Mr. Graham Wren, secretary of the committee, with a short presentation showing where the product line in question fitted in the Norton portfolio of businesses. The first chart he presented contained an overview of the market share strategies for 31 strategic business units, as summarized in Figure 1.

Separate charts showed the ranking of all business units with respect to return on net assets (RONA), return on sales (ROS), and asset turnover ratio for

FIGURE 1 Summary of market share strategies for the Norton portfolio of businesses

Market share strategy	Sales ($ millions)	Abrasive operations	Diversified products
Build	96		
Build/maintain	135	In the actual presentation, each strategic business was listed under its appropriate category. For example, CAD and 15 other business units were listed in the abrasives column for the maintain strategy.	
Maintain	257		
Maintain/harvest	60		
Harvest	0		
Total	548	400	148

EXHIBIT 3 Norton portfolio of businesses on growth share matrix (balloon areas proportional to sales)

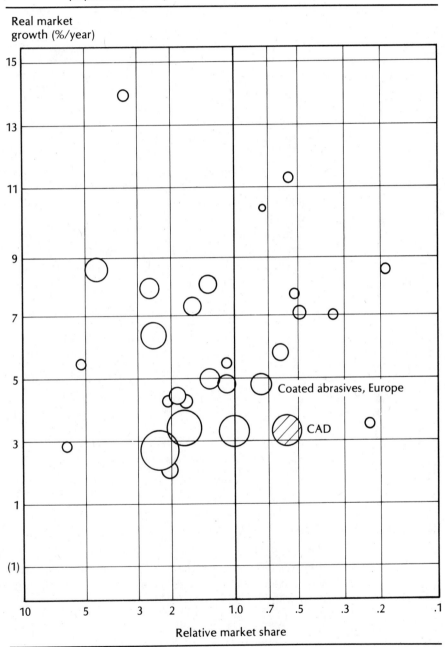

1974 and 1975, and the average for the two years. CAD placed in the ranking as follows:

Coated abrasives domestic

	Rank among 31	Value for 1974–1975 average	Norton Average operations
RONA	27	6.0	10
ROS	26	3.5	6
Asset turnover	23	1.7	1.9

A growth share matrix showed CAD to lie well in the undesirable low-growth/smaller-than-competitor quadrant (see Exhibit 3). A product experiencing both low growth and low market share (relative to the industry leader) would likely be a net user of cash with little promise for future payoff.

Finally, the committee's cash generations versus market share corporate test was applied to the CAD proposed strategy. As shown in Figure 2, the combination of maintaining market share at its present level and generating cash was acceptable.

FIGURE 2 The cash generation/market share strategy test

Cash generation	Market share strategy		
	Build	Maintain	Harvest
Uses cash	A/?	U	U
Provides own cash	A/?	U	U
Disengages cash	A	Ⓐ ↘ CAD	A

A = The combination is an acceptable strategy.
? = The combination is a questionable strategy.
U = The combination is an unacceptable strategy.

CAD Strategy Plan

Paul Midghall, vice president and general manager for Norton's U.S. Coated Abrasives Division, was the principal architect of the strategic plan to maintain market share. His reasoning as laid out in the 1976 strategy book for CAD began with a statement of the division's role and strategy:

Mission: Cash Generation

Norton's long-term objective is to allocate resources to high-growth opportunities while maintaining total world abrasives leadership. CAD's role within that corporate objective is: to be a long-term cash generator; to act as the technical focal point for coated abrasives operations worldwide.

Strategy: Restructure and Maintain

To meet that objective, CAD has in the last two years radically restructured its operations. Its strategy now is to complete the restructuring; to consolidate the organization into a confident, coherent team; and to pursue market segmentation based on the strengths which have emerged from restructuring. To understand how this strategy evolved, one must turn to CAD's history.

The strategy report went on to identify the reasons for the earlier deterioration of market share and profitability. These included:

1. Inadequate reinvestment in the basic coated abrasives business in favor of investments which attempted to build allied businesses.[6]
2. High wage rates and fringe benefits coupled with low productivity and poor work conditions.
3. High overheads.
4. Premium pricing without compensating benefits to the customer.
5. A labor strike in 1966.

Serious attempts to reverse the negative trends for CAD had proved unsuccessful, and in late 1973 management decided a major change had to be made to the business. The current strategy report reviewed the alternative strategies that had been considered earlier:

By late 1973, CAD's condition demanded positive action; share had dropped to 26 percent and RONA to 7.5 percent. A fundamental change had to occur. The principal options were:

1. Sell, liquidate, or harvest. These alternatives were eliminated because: *(a)* a viable coated abrasives business was deemed important to worldwide coated abrasives business; *(b)* a viable coated abrasives business was judged important to U.S. bonded abrasives business.
2. Attempt to regain lost share and with it volume to cover fixed expenses. In a mature industry, with the major competitors financially secure and firmly entrenched, such a strategy was judged too expensive.
3. Greater price realization. We already maintained a high overall price level, and 3M was the price leader in the industry. In later 1974, Norton tried to lead prices up dramatically to restore profitability but the rest of the industry did not follow.

Alternative: Comprehensive Cost Reduction

A new cost structure was the only reasonable choice for a radical change. We had to scale down to a cost level consistent with our volume and our position in the industry.

In 1974 a decision to restructure the CAD business by making major cost reductions was made by Norton's Executive Committee and approved by its

---

[6] According to Mr. Duane, coated abrasives and the other allied businesses had been organized in a single profit center at that time. The focus of attention had been on the total unit's overall performance. With the current approach to strategy analysis, each major product line was examined separately.

board of directors. This move was intended to make CAD more competitive so that it could prevent further erosion of its market share.

Restructuring

The strategy review of 1974 had identified many areas for cost reduction. These touched on almost every segment of operations and included: moving labor-intensive manufacturing operations from New York to Texas; combining the coated abrasives sales force with that for bonded abrasives (e.g., grinding wheels); and reducing fixed assets. The product line was also to be reduced. Earlier about 4,000 product items out of some 20,000 (that is, 20 percent) had accounted for 87 percent of sales.

During the two-year period 1974–75, over $2 million had been invested to implement the restructuring. The changes were eventually expected to result in over $9 million annual direct recurring savings, raising RONA by about 8 percentage points to a total of 14 percent.[7] The number of employees for CAD had declined from 2,000 to 1,300 by 1976.

CAD's Future Environment

The U.S. coated abrasives industry was expected to experience low growth and gradual changes as a rule. The strategy book forecast long-term growth at 2.5 percent per annum. Industrial markets, which constituted 75 percent of Norton's CAD business, were to grow even more slowly. Because of the depressed level of business operations in early 1976, annual growth for industrial markets was forecast to spurt to about 7 percent until 1980.[8]

Product technology was expected to change slowly, but in important ways. The strategy book noted:

> The advent of Norzon grain, new resin bonds, and synthetic backings illustrates the fact that although coated abrasives may be a mature product, it is not a commodity product. Technological evolution is slow but continuous, and a competitor who fails to keep abreast cannot survive.
>
> While product development exhibits highly visible evolution, process development is inconspicuous. No major changes have occurred, or are expected, in manufacturing technology.

---

[7] It was estimated that 3M had a RONA of 17 percent of 20 percent in coated abrasives.

[8] An investment advisory report issued by Loeb Rhoades some months later (August 1976) had this to say about future prospects for the industry as a whole (bonded and coated products):

> We have believed for some time that there were fair prospects for higher profitability in abrasives on a secular and not just a cyclical basis, merely because profitability had been poor for a long enough (seven to nine years) time. In a product that is basic to economic activity and that is capital intensive, and where no unusual reason can be discerned for the poor return on investment, such as foreign competition or technological change, etc., a lengthy period of poor profitability generally will lead to changes by industry factors designed to improve returns. . . . At some point supply and demand come into a better balance, which then supports firmer pricing. And in fact . . . pricing had improved significantly since late 1974 despite declining demand in real terms.

Capacity in all segments of manufacturing will be adequate to fill demand well into the 1980s.

The U.S. coated abrasives market was said to have "healthy, strong, rational competition." With the exception of 3M, the return of most competitors was thought to be below the U.S. industrial average. Figure 3 shows sales and market shares for the principal competitors.

FIGURE 3 U.S. coated abrasives market share estimates

	1975 sales ($ millions)	Total market share	
		1975	1973
3M	$ 99	34%	32%
Norton	76	26	27
Carborundum	40	14	15
Armak	23	8	8
Other U.S. manufacturers	35	12	12
Foreign	21	7	7
Total industry	$294	100%	100%

	Market segment		
	Metal working*	Wood working	General trade†
Market potential, 1975 ($ millions)	$130	$36	$81
Estimated market share, 1975			
3M	30%	27%	65%
Norton	29	26	20
Carborundum	22	10	11

* Includes primary metals, fabricated metals, and transportation equipment (autos, aircraft) industries.

† Includes hardware retail and automobile finishing businesses.

CAD Strategy for 1976

The proposed strategy for CAD contained two principal elements. One element was a continuation of the restructuring and cost cutting that had begun in 1974. CAD management estimated that about 75 percent of this program had been put into effect and that two more years would be required to complete the steps under way.

The second element of the strategy was to focus on those market segments where Norton had competitive advantage. Detailed share/growth balloon charts, such as shown in Exhibit 4, were used to identify specific sectors for attention.

To foster product innovation, the 1976 plan had introduced a recommendation to expand R&D efforts. Twenty-two men had been assigned to CAD product development in 1975.

These strategic moves were predicted to produce favorable results. The CAD report identified the units' future strengths to include: variable costs to be among the lowest in the industry; distribution channel relations to be among the

EXHIBIT 4 CAD growth share matrices (balloon areas proportional to Norton's sales)

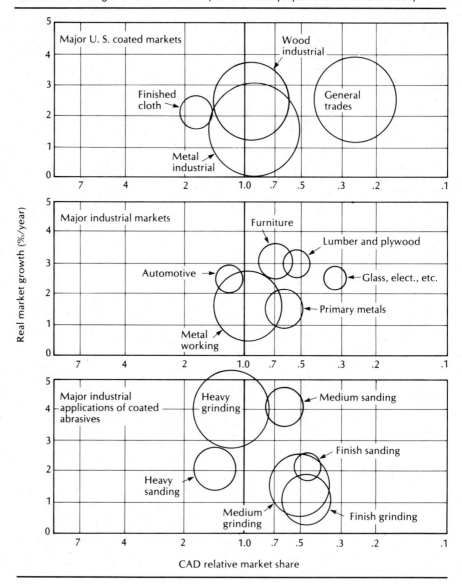

best, especially with the close tie between coated and bonded abrasives; and a technological edge on new products (e.g., Norzon). The ultimate result, the report forecast, would be the generation of more than $7 million cash during 1977–80. Excerpts from the summary of financial results are shown in Figure 4.

FIGURE 4 Summary of financial results (numbers disguised)

	Actual					Expected				
	1971	1972	1973	1974	1975	1976	1977	1978	1979	1980
Market share (percent)	29	28	27	26	25.5	26	27	27.5	27.5	27.5
Net sales (index)	77	90	107	120	100	108	128	150	160	180
Net income (index)	215	220	310	230	100	140	480	760	810	950
Percent return on sales (c/b)	4.4	3.9	4.6	3.0	1.6	2.0	6.0	8.0	8.0	8.0
Percent RONA	8	8	7.5	7	5	4.5	8	13	13	13
Funds generated ($ millions)						(4.7)	0.5	2.5	3.4	1.3

* 7 percent inflation per annum assumed.

The PIMS Report[9]

The PIMS analysis for CAD had resulted in a recommendation at variance with that made by Mr. Midghall. A summary of these findings was included in the strategy book submitted to the Strategy Guidance Committee. The remainder of this section presents excerpts from the PIMS analysis:

> The 1975 PAR report[10] indicates that the Coated-U.S. business is a below-average business in a weak strategic position with a *pretax* PAR-ROI of 12.0 percent. The business' operating performance has been very close to PAR with a 1973–75 average *pretax* actual ROI of 12.2 percent.
>
> The major factors impacting on PAR-ROI and their individual impacts are listed below.[11]

	Major negative factors		Major positive factors
(1.5)	Marketing only expense/sales	1.8	Sales direct to end users
(1.7)	Capacity utilization		
(4.1)	Effective use of investments		

---

[9] As a subscriber to the services of the Strategic Planning Institute, Norton received on a regular basis analysis reports for several of its major businesses. These reports were circulated to divisional and corporate managers concerned with the business in question.

[10] The PAR report specified the return on investment that was normal for a business, given the characteristics of its market, competition, technology, and cost structure.

[11] The figures represent the impact of that factor on PAR-ROI. For example, the higher marketing (excluding sales force) expenses/sales ratio noted in the following paragraph when comparing CAD to all PIMS businesses was said to have an effect of reducing the PAR-ROI by 1.5 percent. In contrast, by selling directly to the end users, PAR-ROI was increased by 1.8 percent compared to all PIMS businesses.

During the three-year period, the *marketing less sales force expenses/sales* ratio averaged 6 percent compared to the 4.1 percent PIMS average. PIMS findings acknowledge that high marketing expenses hurt profitability when relative product quality is low; i.e., it doesn't pay to market heavily a product with equivalent or inferior product quality. The average relative product quality for the business over the three years was estimated as follows: 10 percent superior, 75 percent equivalent, and 15 percent inferior.

For the Coated-U.S. business, the positive impact indicates that selling through distributors instead of direct should lower customer service costs.

Whether the Coated-U.S. business objective is to optimize cash flow or ROI over the long term, the Strategy Sensitivity Report (SSR) suggests a *moderate harvest* strategy. The SSR is based upon how other participating businesses with similar business characteristics have acted to achieve their objectives.

The SSR suggests that the following strategy should be pursued to optimize either cash flow or ROI over the long term.

1. *Prices.* Prices relative to competition should be maintained.
2. *Working capital/sales.* The SSR suggests that this ratio be lowered significantly to about 25 percent through primarily reduced inventory levels.
3. *Vertical integration.* Over the long term, the degree of vertical integration should be reduced.
4. *Fixed capital.* Don't add large segments of capacity, and maintain capacity utilization at the 80 percent level.
5. *R&D marketing expenses.* The SSR recommends that R&D expenditures should be reduced; and consequently, the relative product quality remains inferior. Also, the products should be marketed less energetically during the implementation phase.

The results from this strategy are (1) a gradual loss of market share from 26 percent to 21 percent; (2) an average ROI of 24 percent versus the current PAR-ROI of 12 percent; and (3) a 10-year discounted cash flow value of $2.33 million.

A study was undertaken to compare the PAR-ROI of this business in its steady-state environment (after the recommended strategy has been implemented— 1978–80) with the 1973–75 PAR-ROI. The results indicate that the strategy is successful in moving this business into a much better strategic position. The pretax PAR-ROI increases from 12 percent to 24 percent.

The major factors that had a significant impact on the improved PAR-ROI are *relative pay scale* and *use of investments*. These two factors account for a majority of the 12 percentage point increase in PAR-ROI.

The general message from the SSR for the *restructured* Coated-U.S. business is the same as for the *current* business; i.e., if the objective is to manage the business for cash flow or ROI, a *moderate harvest strategy* is recommended by PIMS.

Management Considerations

Norton's top managers recognized how difficult it was for them to remain objective when deciding the fate of a core part of the company's traditional business. As Mr. John Nelson, vice president abrasive operations western hemisphere, remarked:

> There is no question that this decision has been an emotional one for me and probably for others as well. It would be difficult to turn our backs on CAD. Yet, if the business cannot produce the target return on net assets, I think we are prepared to take the appropriate actions.
>
> I do not think that we are likely to close shop on U.S. coated abrasives. It is too important to other parts of our business to go that far. For example, coated abrasives strengthens our sales of bonded abrasives and is a plus to our distribution system in the United States. It also provides us with a bigger base for R&D on coated abrasives. This benefits our overseas coated abrasives operations. Nonetheless, whether to stay with our earlier decision to maintain market share or to harvest the business was and still is very much at issue.

Both Mr. Duane and Mr. Nelson remarked that the choice of strategy in 1973–74 had been predicated on the belief that the industry could support a profitable number two and that Norton could play that role with its existing market share. The continued loss of market share was a cause of concern to them and to other members of the Strategy Guidance Committee. As noted in the minutes for the CAD review session of June 7, 1976:

> In the shorter term period of late 1973 to the first quarter 1976, CAD market share dropped from 27 percent to 25 percent. Some of this drop was due to intentional de-emphasis of the general trades segment. However, there was also an unintentional loss in the industrial segment. The key question is whether this short-term market share decline in the industrial area can be stopped and reserved.

The PIMS recommendations for an alternative strategy also served to raise questions about the soundness of the present approach. One Norton executive put in context the relative impact of PIMS with the following observation: "We are still learning how to use PIMS. At present, we consider it a useful input, among many, to our thinking. We would not reverse divisional management's position on the basis of PIMS alone."

Mr. Donald Melville, executive vice president, diversified products, made the following comment about the CAD issue:

> You have to consider the dynamics of Norton's situation in 1976. We have done a lot to restructure the company, and the results in 1975—a bad recession year for abrasives—show our progress. But we are not yet in a position where we can harvest a major segment of our abrasives business, because that is the major guts of our company.
>
> By the early 80s our restructuring should be complete and we will not be so dependent on abrasives. If we were faced with the decision in, say, 1982, instead of 1976, we could and probably should be willing to harvest CAD. In the meantime, we might as well repair CAD, because if we succeed, then we won't have to harvest it in the 80s. And if we fail, we will have lost very little.

A relative newcomer to the top management ranks at Norton, Mr. Richard

Flynn, financial vice president, made the following comments about Norton's approach to strategic planning:[12]

> However the Strategy Guidance Committee finally decides on this matter, I think they are at least addressing the right issues, and that itself is something.
>
> The wide use of profit centers in large U.S. corporations has often led to bad analysis when different products were lumped together. Corporate-wide planning did not help the situation. Looking at a single product line family, as we are doing for U.S. coated abrasives, gives management much more meaningful data to work with.
>
> The other thing I like about Norton's strategic planning is that we are doing it repeatedly during the year. This means that we are always called on to think strategy. Looking at different businesses at different times enables us to take on different perspectives to our strategic thinking. This sometimes helps us to gain new insights for other businesses.
>
> All in all, the strategic planning sessions have been very effective in helping top management to think about and to deal with business strategies.

---

[12] Richard J. Flynn joined Norton Company in January 1974, as financial vice president and as a member of the Board of Directors and the Executive Committee. He had been president of the Riley Stoker Corporation, a subsidiary of the Riley Company, manufacturers of steam generating and fuel burning equipment. He previously held executive positions with Ling-Temco Vought and Collins Radio.

Case 42

The Jos. Schlitz Brewing Company*

In 1979 the Jos. Schlitz Brewing Company was facing the fight of its life. So much had happened to the once second largest brewer in the United States in such a short time that a complete overhaul of the company and its marketing activities was required.

Only six years ago in 1973, the future looked great for Schlitz. For the period 1968 to 1973, Schlitz enjoyed the best growth rate of any major brewer with the number of barrels sold growing at an average 13 percent per year. The brewer was bragging of having the most efficient new breweries in the industry. Net earnings for 1973 were an impressive $53.7 million.

The next five years brought near disaster. In 1974, growth slowed to 6.2 percent. The next year, however, volume was down 8.7 percent. Also in 1975, outside legal problems came from two fronts. The Securities and Exchange Commission charged Schlitz with making illegal payments to the people who handle its products.[1] A federal grand jury in Milwaukee charged Schlitz with 747 violations of federal alcohol laws including illegal payments to customers, falsifying and destroying business records, and income tax evasion. Conviction on these could have caused Schlitz to lose its license to sell alcoholic beverages in several states.

The company was in a state of internal turmoil. In the next two and one-half years, Schlitz lost two presidents, a number of vice presidents, and four of its eight top marketing and sales personnel. Most notable among these losses were Robert A. Uihlein and Fred R. Haviland. Uihlein (pronounced E-line) died in 1976. He had been both company president and chairman for most of the period from 1962 until 1975. In this dual role some thought that he had given his managers too much free rein and failed to see some of their most serious mistakes in management. He was also a fourth generation member of the

---

* This case was written by Constance M. Kinnear using published documents and interviews with people knowledgeable about the brewing industry.

[1] The SEC also charged other major U.S. breweries with similar violations.

controlling family in the Schlitz organization.[2] Uihlein's death left the company with no one groomed as his replacement. Haviland was the director of marketing. He had been brought into the firm by Robert Uihlein from Anheuser-Busch in the early 1960s. He was a strong inspirational leader who had instilled confidence and aggressiveness in his sales force. Haviland realized the importance of wholesalers to the brewery industry. He encouraged them to bring their complaints, suggestions, and perceptions of market shifts directly to him freely. The marketing and sales people lost during this time were those held responsible by Schlitz for the illegal activities of which Schlitz was accused.

At the same time those previously bragged-about efficient new breweries were proving themselves to be liabilities rather than assets. At the 1977 annual meeting another member of the Uihlein family, David V. Uihlein, charged the management of brewing beer that "couldn't hold its head." In the name of efficiency, Schlitz had developed a batch brewing method which it claimed assured even fermentation and cut the brewing cycle in half. In the name of cost reduction Schlitz was using less barley malt in its brews, substituting cheaper corn syrup. With its Primo brand beer, which at the time controlled 70 percent of the Hawaiian market, Schlitz used what was called a "revolutionary" process. It stopped brewing the beer entirely in Hawaii, instead performing most of the critical production steps in Los Angeles and shipping a dehydrated mixture back to Hawaii for only the final fermentation, aging, and bottling. The consumer noticed the difference—and did not like it. The first market to respond was the Hawaiian market. By the end of 1975 Primo only enjoyed a 20 percent share of market. The overall Schlitz market was slower to react. The news of the lower quality product that "went flat" was spread by word of mouth, and the customers' selection of Schlitz beer was hit by the most important factor in the beer industry—peer-pressure. By 1977 the results were clear to all. Volume sold was down 2 million barrels from 1976, or 8.4 percent. Capacity utilization, which had been 81.9 percent in 1976, was down to 75 percent. Market share, which had been 16.3 percent in 1976, was down to 13.9 percent. Net earnings were only $19.8 million.

To make matters worse, Schlitz made an ad campaign change in 1977. The long-time successful slogan, "When you're out of Schlitz, you're out of beer" was dropped. In its place, Schlitz used intimidating boozers, boxers, and football player types who seemed to be threatening someone attempting to take away their Schlitz. This campaign only succeeded in alienating consumers already questioning their choice of a Schlitz beer. It became known as the "drink Schlitz or I'll kill you" campaign in the industry.

Relations with wholesalers were deteriorating. Their counsel about conditions and changes in their markets was no longer sought. In fact, it seemed to them that their suggestions were unwelcome and ignored. They claimed that the

---

[2] Some 500 members of the Uihlein family own 75 percent of the Schlitz stock. The family held 11 of 16 board seats in 1978.

resulting management lack of knowledge kept Schlitz out of the fast-growing 7 oz. bottle market for years.

The Beer Industry

But perhaps more important to Schlitz than any of these internal problems was the vastly changing competitive nature of the whole beer industry. In the early 1970s the major beer companies, including Schlitz, began building "super breweries" double the size of previous breweries, enabling them to cut labor costs in half by taking advantage of technological improvements. Huge sums were committed for capital expansion. Available figures show that Schlitz spent $462 million between 1974 and 1979 on expansion.

In 1977 Schlitz began construction on a new 6-million barrel per year facility in Syracuse, New York. Miller spent over $600 million moving its capacity from approximately 7 million barrels in 1972 to 30 million in 1976. Included in this in 1976, Miller broke ground on a new 10-million barrel per year brewery in North Carolina. In total, Miller will spend $850 million by 1980 to bring its capacity up to 40 million barrels per year. Anheuser-Busch was also expanding. In the 1970s new breweries were added in New Hampshire, Virginia, and California, increasing Anheuser-Busch capacity by a total 9.4 million barrels per year. Total 1979 Anheuser-Busch capacity is expected to be 46.4 million barrels. Both Pabst and Coors expanded their production by 10 percent in 1977. In the year 1977 alone, total industry capacity increased by 10 percent or 18 million barrels. In that same year, however, industry sales growth was only 2.5 percent. The extra expansion had to come at the expense of existing brewers.

Traditionally, price competition has been a predominant marketing activity in the beer industry. This was true because most breweries produced only one beer and most marketing departments viewed the market as homogeneous. One beer was considered undifferentiable from another. This presented no problem until the inflation of the 1970s started to put its squeeze on the beer industry. In the six-year period from 1972 to 1978 raw material costs increased approximately 63.3 percent and packaging costs increased almost 75 percent. However, brewers discovered that they could not pass on these rising costs without losing market share. Thus the price of a six-pack of beer had only increased 51 percent in the period from 1967 to 1978 when the overall consumer price index increased 92 percent. The way out of this situation chosen by the large U.S. brewers was to build the larger, more cost-efficient breweries. This made it possible for them to maintain lower prices longer. Before long, the smaller, less efficient regional brewers began to disappear from the scene. The total number of U.S. brewers decreased from 118 in 1965 to only 49 in 1975. In 1978, there were only 45 brewers. Some industry specialists believe this number will dwindle to 15 breweries in the 1980s. At the same time the market share controlled by the top 5 brewers has been steadily increasing. In 1971

Anheuser-Busch, Miller, Schlitz, Pabst, and Coors jointly controlled 53 percent of the market. In 1976, that figure was 69 percent. In the 1980s that figure is expected to be 90 percent.

Another factor changing the environment of the beer industry is demographics. Traditionally, 50 percent of all beer has been purchased by the 18–34 age group. In the 1970s the size of this group reached its peak, a fact that has significant impact on the future growth prospects for the entire industry.

Considering all these factors, continuing expansion must eventually take its toll among the largest brewers.[3] Competition can only get tougher and new ways of maintaining market share have to be found. (See Exhibits 1 and 2.)

EXHIBIT 1 Barrels sold comparisons (millions)

	1976	1979*
Anheuser-Busch	29.1	46.3
Schlitz	24.2	17.9
Miller	18.4	37.8
Pabst	17.0	15.5
Coors	13.7	13.0

* Estimated.

EXHIBIT 2 Market share projections through 1983 (percentages)

	1978	1979	1983
Anheuser-Busch	25.2%	27.1%	32.0%
Miller	19.0	22.1	29.7
Schlitz	11.9	10.5	7.3
Pabst	9.4	9.1	7.0
Coors	7.6	7.6	7.6
Heileman	4.3	6.0	6.3
All others	22.6	17.6	10.1

Source: Industry analysts.

Miller Brewing Company

Undoubtedly the best thing that ever happened to the Miller Brewing Company was its purchase in 1970 by Philip Morris, Inc. This purchase brought Miller a great influx of cash, cash available for needed expansion, modernization, and other capital projects. But what turned out to be more important was the influx of Philip Morris people into Miller's management. Miller's new president was John A. Murphy, who had been with Philip Morris 12 years before taking this

---

[3] For the period 1979 to 1982, industry growth is expected to be 27 million barrels. For the same period Anheuser-Busch plans to increase capacity by 18 million barrels and Miller by 16 million barrels for a combined total increase of 34 million barrels.

post. The new vice president for marketing was Lauren S. Williams, the former brand manager of Virginia Slims cigarette. These men and the others from Philip Morris brought with them the highly tuned marketing expertise that had moved Philip Morris from sixth to second in share of market in the tobacco industry. These people were not raised in the brewing business as was the case with the management of most other breweries. They came in not bound by convention or tradition but ready to experiment and determined to dominate the U.S. brewing industry.

Philip Morris has taken a manufacturing company and turned it into a marketing company. The management started treating beer as any other consumer good. They put money into brewery expansion but also into research and development and marketing research. Their purpose was to develop distinctive brands to meet the needs of specific segments of the beer market.

MARGET SEGMENT.

The first changes made were with Miller High Life. As "The Champagne of Bottled Beers," High Life was only appealing to women and other occasional and low-volume beer drinkers. The beer was given a new image, advertised as being used by blue-collar workers after they have finished their day engaged in "he-man" exploits. The theme line was "Now comes Miller time." Now the beer was being aimed at the big segment of the market, the 30 percent of drinkers who consume 80 percent of the beer.

The most obvious example of Miller's marketing philosophy is the Miller Lite story. Here Miller is credited with creating a market segment. With Lite, Miller took advantage of its acquisition of Meister Brau Lite and the changing attitude among young adults regarding fitness to bring the right beer to the market at the right time. Other "low-calorie" beers had existed before, but all had failed. They had tried to appeal to dieters, but dieters are not beer drinkers. Lite was aimed at the real beer drinkers. It is advertised by convincing beer-drinking personalities. It is easy for a beer drinker to feel confident about his choice of Lite knowing that such "heroes" say it's OK. Miller did not promote the fact that Lite was low calorie so much as that it had great taste and was less filling, both attributes important to the heavy beer user.

As important to the industry as Miller's "discovery" of segmentation was the amount of advertising dollars spent on the introduction of Lite. (See Exhibits 3 and 4 for competitive advertising expenditures.) In 1975 the industry average spent on advertising was $1 per barrel. Miller spent $6.50 per barrel on Lite in that introductory year. This amounted to $10 million between February and October 1975. The level of spending was designed not only to achieve high product awareness and trial but also to discourage competition. Miller wanted to establish its predominance in this segment so well that it could maintain it even when there was competition.

Segmentation had another benefit for Miller that was a real reprieve for the industry. The introduction of a truly differentiated product allowed Miller to differentiate on price. Lite was sold from the start at 10 cents more per six-pack than premium beers even though it is actually slightly cheaper to produce.

Miller's overall results were greatly unexpected by the rest of the industry.

EXHIBIT 3 Advertising expenditures—1973 to 1978

	1978		1977		1976		1975		1974		1973	
	Total	Per BBL	Total	Per BBL	Total	Per BBL	Total	Per BBL	Total	Per BBL	Total	Per BBL
Schlitz	$ 58,213,000	$2.97	$55,080,000	$2.49	$34,131,400	$1.41	$26,530,000	$1.14	$20,910,940	$ .92	$19,722,864	$ .92
Miller	81,312,400	2.60	50,820,000	2.10	29,114,700	1.58	21,252,000	1.65	13,556,133	1.50	10,914,623	1.58
Anheuser-Busch	114,099,000	2.80	79,171,000	2.16	28,535,300	.98	27,354,000	.78	17,839,935	.52	20,522,602	.69
Heileman	12,979,000	1.82	10,151,000	1.63	3,767,300	.72	2,902,200	.62	2,666,400	.62	3,356,043	.76
Coors	33,470,000	2.66	15,523,000	1.21	9,831,000	.72	1,243,000	.10	1,611,931	.13	1,374,929	.13
Pabst	39,823,000	2.59	26,799,000	1.57	9,727,900	.57	9,662,000	.61	8,449,274	.59	7,219,051	.55

Source: *Advertising Age.* Copyright © Crain Publications. Used with permission. Also company sources used.

EXHIBIT 4 Allocation of advertising dollars among media—1978 (percentages)

	Schlitz	Miller	Anheuser-Busch	Coors	Pabst
Magazines	.06%	.51%	4.17%	.29%	—
Newspapers	1.56	.34	1.61	1.68	.33%
Network TV	80.02	81.83	68.33	.68	23.91
Spot TV	10.62	13.36	6.04	54.49	60.95
Network radio	—	—	3.62	—	—
Spot radio	7.57	3.89	13.95	30.65	14.38
Outdoor	.17	.07	2.28	12.21	.43

Source: Industry analysts.

Between 1972 and 1975, Miller increased its beer shipments by 68.7 percent. In 1972, sales were only 5 million barrels and market share only 4 percent. In 1975, sales were 12.5 million barrels, 2 million of which were Lite beer. The company as a whole was at 90 percent capacity, and Miller was allocating its shipments of Lite. In 1976, sales were 18 million barrels and market share was 12 percent. In 1978, sales were over 30 million barrels. Expansion plans are for a capacity of 40 million barrels by 1980, quite close to the capacity of the industry leader, Anheuser-Busch. In 1971, Miller was the seventh largest brewer in the United States. In 1976, Miller was third and by 1978, Miller was second.

The next move for Miller was into the super-premium market, a segment dominated by Anheuser-Busch's Michelob with a 75 percent share of that market. Miller's entry is the domestically brewed Löwenbräu which Miller has priced 25 percent above Michelob (which is already priced 25 cents per six-pack above premium beers). Again, Miller has backed its new entry with exceedingly heavy advertising, approximately $20 million in the first year. Miller is also reportedly ready to test market a lower low-calorie beer than Lite called Players. It has half the calories of regular beer, whereas Lite has two thirds the calories.[4]

In 1978 Miller shipped about 19.7 million barrels of High Life, 8.5 million barrels of Lite, and 1.2 million barrels of Löwenbräu.

Anheuser-Busch, Incorporated

A different approach to the industry changes can be seen in the competitive activities of Anheuser-Busch. The actions taken by its management are in line with the company's position in the industry as number one in share of market and the company's image, held both internally and externally, as a stronghold of tradition and quality of product.

---

[4] Calories in selected brands were: Miller Lite 96, Natural Light 110, and Michelob Light 134. Regular beer has 140 calories.

As of 1978, Anheuser-Busch had been first in the beer industry for 15 consecutive years. Its market share had grown from 7 percent in 1957 to 20 percent in 1972 to 25.7 percent in 1978. The firm's current chairman of the board, president, and chief executive officer is August Busch III, a fourth generation member of the family that controls 25 percent of the company's stock. The generations have instilled a vast knowledge of the business in August Busch III but also a firm dedication to the traditions handed down to him. He is unflinching in his determination to maintain the quality of his products even though this means substantially higher production costs than for other brewers. Indeed, Anheuser-Busch could use corn instead of rice or domestic rather than imported hops or it could cut its production time down from a month to the 20-day industry average, but tradition will not allow it.

Anheuser-Busch points to the facts to justify this position. Budweiser is the best selling beer in the world. Michelob, a super-premium beer, controls 75 percent of its market. 1978 sales were $1.7 billion and earnings were $92.2 million. Both were records for the company. For the period 1970 to 1978 Anheuser-Busch's volume increased from 22.2 million barrels to 41 million barrels, or an average annual increase of 8 percent. In 1978 Anheuser-Busch sold approximately 26.7 million barrels of Budweiser, 7.6 million barrels of Michelob, and 1.2 million barrels of Natural Light. The rest of their sales were of Busch and Michelob Light.

Even though the credit for "discovering" market segmentation in the beer industry has gone to the Miller Brewing Company, the true initiators of this marketing strategy were the people at Anheuser-Busch. In 1975 when Miller brought out its Lite brand, Anheuser-Busch already had three beers on the market. Of these, the premium brew Budweiser and the super-premium Michelob had been in existence for over 100 years. The popular priced brand, Busch Bavarian, was introduced in 1955 as a low-profit item designed to fill production gaps allowing the brewery to produce at capacity.

Anheuser-Busch has been a long-time advocate of the use of marketing research in positioning its products and determining the correct message and media mix in its ad campaigns. They, like most of the industry, were amazed by the quick success of Miller Lite. But Anheuser-Busch waited for marketing research to find it a niche in this new segment before rushing in. In 1977 Natural Light was introduced, not stressing fewer calories as Lite had or taste as Schlitz Light had but appealing to the health conscious consumer, stressing its all natural, nonsynthetic ingredients. Within six months, Natural Light had sales equal to the number two beer in the category, Schlitz Light.

Continuing marketing research helped Anheuser-Busch in the decision to develop its next product as well. Studies showed that the light-beer segment was holding back the growth of Michelob. Michelob and the lights were attracting the same beer drinkers, the young, upscale white-collar drinker. Other studies showed that one half of all beer drinkers had rejected the light-beer segment on the basis of taste. Anheuser-Busch combined these two findings to develop Michelob Light in 1978, a light beer with more calories than the other lights and therefore more real beer taste. It was hoped it would appeal as Michelob did to the young, upscale white-collar market and hopefully gain trial by those who had rejected the category before. It did just that as 80 percent of Michelob Light buyers were coming from competitive brands. After only seven months on the market in 38 states, it had solid hold on fourth position in the light-beer segment which by this point had over 23 entrants in three years.[5]

In both these cases, Anheuser-Busch followed the advertising expenditure levels established by Miller for its introduction of Lite. This was a real change for Anheuser-Busch. In 1977, $11 million was spent on the introduction of Natural Light. The total ad budget for all their brands, which had only been $49 million in 1976, was $115 million in 1978. That is an increase of over 13 percent. But though these advertising entry costs were high for their new products, Anheuser-Busch found that its delay in entry meant that it could spend those dollars more efficiently. Miller and Schlitz had had to bear the costs of establishing and legitimizing the existence of the light-beer segment. For Natural Light and Michelob Light, Anheuser-Busch was able to concentrate solely on the attributes of these brands.

1978 brought another change for Anheuser-Busch. It withdrew from the dwindling popular-priced beer market. Busch Bavarian was reformulated to make it sweeter, repackaged, given a new ad campaign and a new premium beer price. Once again, Anheuser-Busch was successful in getting those higher profit margins that are available with the premium, super-premium, and light-beer markets.

A marketing strategy has become apparent in all this activity. Anheuser-Busch now has two entrants on each of the premium and light beer segments. To continue this trend and to challenge directly Miller's Löwenbräu, plans are underway for Anheuser-Busch to distribute Wurzburger, an imported beer to be priced in the super-premium price range. With this entrant, Anheuser-Busch will have bracketed each major segment with high-profit brands.

This marketing strategy is further aided by the extensive capital expenditure plans of Anheuser-Busch. A total of $1.5 billion has reportedly been committed for expansion for the period 1978 to 1982. Capacity, which in 1978 was expected to be 46.3 million barrels, will be approximately 59 million barrels in 1982. It is hoped by their management that the combination of these two strategies in marketing and expansion will give Anheuser-Busch continuing leadership with a 31 percent share of market in 1982.

G. Heileman Brewing Company

Heileman's is a brewery which has followed a strikingly different growth strategy from that of Miller and Anheuser-Busch. It is estimated that Miller's

---

[5] It is important at this point to realize how fast the light beer segment had grown. In 1975, there were only 5 light beers selling 3 million barrels that year for a 2 percent market share. By the end of 1978 there were more than 23 light beers. These sold a combined 11 million barrels and had a combined 10 percent market share. Rapid growth was expected to continue.

expansion costs approximately \$25 to \$30 for each additional barrel. Anheuser-Busch's expansion is more costly per barrel added due to its longer, more traditional brewing methods. Estimates put its expansion costs in the neighborhood of \$40 to \$45 per additional barrel. These quickly become hefty amounts to have available when a company plans millions and millions of barrels of additional capacity.

Heileman's has exercised a less expensive expansion program through acquisition. Twenty years ago Heileman's was just a small regional brewer selling only two brands of beer in four midwestern states. In 1972 Associated Brewing Company was acquired giving the company larger midwest distribution. In 1977 distribution was gained on the West Coast with the purchase of Rainier Brewing. The latest acquisition was that of the Carling Brewing Company in 1979, giving Heileman its first nationally distributed brands, Black Label beer and Red Cap Ale. In total some 13 breweries have been added to the Heileman fold since 1959. The company now sells over 30 brands[6] of beer, several of them nationally. All this expansion has been done at an amazingly low cost in comparison to the figures quoted for Miller and Anheuser-Busch. Since 1967 it is estimated that Heileman has added capacity at an average cost of \$3.90 per new barrel. On top of this figure Heileman has had to spend another \$52.7 million for the period 1970 to 1979 to modernize these acquired breweries.

The expansion has brought great growth for the company. Volume sold has increased an average of 11 percent per year since 1970. In 1978 sales volume was 7.1 million barrels, yielding \$330 million in sales and earnings of \$18 million. The Carling acquisition in 1979 boosted volume to over the 10 million barrel per year point. The brewer that was ranked ninth in 1975 is expected to be ranked sixth in 1979 with a 4.4 percent share of market.

Heileman's also has a different approach in its ad campaigns. It does not put the emphasis on the type of consumer it is after or on well-known personalities. It puts the emphasis on the product. It also takes the competition head on with taste tests and quality and price comparisons. Since most of its brands, in fact all until the purchase of Carling, are purely regional, Heileman advertising seeks to build a brand mystique by romanticizing this regionalism. Heileman's has made this possible by retaining the original formulations and brand names of its acquisitions, building on their local loyalties.

The proliferation of brands has given Heileman's some unique problems. The brewery has the largest force of wholesalers in the business, some 1,800 strong. This compares to approximately 950 for Schlitz and 959 for Anheuser-Busch. Often Heileman beers do not generate enough sales for exclusive distribution by a wholesaler, a fact which only further complicates the control the company has in this area. Another problem comes from the pressure

---

[6] Brands now sold by Heileman include Old Style, Special Export, Blatz, Rainier, Tuborg, Carling Black Label, and Colt 45. In 1979 it is expected that Heileman will make a deal to become the U.S. distributor for a German import, Beck's Beer, in 21 states.

carrying so many brands puts on capacity and promotional funds. Brands can only be expanded gradually, state by state. The most profitable brands are being slowly introduced into the areas of the new acquisitions. Heileman's has decided to use its limited advertising funds in promoting only its six top labels, its money-making premium and super-premium brands. The rest are only promoted by consumer loyalty and word of mouth. In total, Heileman's ad budget in 1978 was $17 million or an average of $2.39 per barrel sold. In 1979 the budget is expected to increase to $26 million, but that will still be only about $2.40 per barrel. (For 1979 Anheuser-Busch's expenditures for advertising are expected to come to approximately $3.33 per barrel.)

Adolph Coors Company

Yet another strategy is apparent in the activities of the largest regional brewer in the United States, Coors. The company still maintains only its original brewery in Golden, Colorado, although over the years it has continually expanded its capacity. It presently can produce in the neighborhood of 13 million barrels per year. Coors is a more highly integrated brewer than most in that it also produces its own cans, bottles, and other container needs. Until 1978 Coors brewed only one beer.

Coors expansion has been slow, deliberately. In 1977 the beer was distributed in 12 western states and enjoyed, on average, a 40 percent market share in this area. Almost half of its total barrelage was sold in the state of California, and changes were occurring there which caused the company to change its strategy somewhat. In 1976 Anheuser-Busch opened a new California brewery north of San Francisco. The increased availability of Anheuser-Busch products had an immediate effect on Coors. In one year Coors' market share dropped by 4 percent in California. This situation is expected to worsen for in 1978 Miller began building a new brewery in California.

But Coors had a built-in safety valve. The beer was only being sold in 20 percent of the U.S. market. Besides, the product has always possessed a certain mystique, especially in the states on the fringes of its current market. If the company needs to sell more beer due either to increased capacity or loss of market share, all it has to do is expand its territory. This is precisely what Coors has done. In 1977 the states of Iowa and Missouri were added to the elite list of Coors states. In 1978 two more states were added leaving the total area of distribution at 16 states.

The insurgence of Miller and Anheuser-Busch on Coors' territory has had other effects on the brewer as well. For the period 1967 to 1976 Coors enjoyed an average annual sales growth rate of 12.9 percent. This phenomenal growth combined with the product's mystique allowed the brewer to spend considerably less than any other brewer on advertising. For most of that 10 years, Coors spent an average of only 17 cents per barrel sold when the industry average for that period was nearly $2 per barrel. But the increase in competition brought Coors in 1976 to spend eight times the amount of its 1975 ad budget or nearly

$10 million. This figure amounts to 72 cents per barrel sold. In 1978 Coors' advertising figure was $33,470,000 or $2.66 per barrel. This figure was above the industry average which was about $2.25 per barrel that year.

A further effect of increased competition was the 1978 introduction of Coors Light. The brewer had long contended that Coors was already a light beer and it had no intention of segmenting its market. Coors Light has 105 calories, only 25 percent fewer than regular Coors. Rumor also has it that Coors is looking into getting the U.S. distribution rights on a European beer. So segmentation seems to be the strategy of the future for Adolph Coors Company.

Pabst Brewing Company

The Pabst Brewing Company is a brewer currently facing some of the same problems as Schlitz. The brewer's market share has been dropping steadily over the past few years after reaching an all-time high of 11.33 percent in 1976. In 1977 that share dropped to 10.12 percent and in 1978 to 9.38 percent. For the first nine months of 1978 Pabst's profits were down 53 percent from the same period in 1977 to $8.9 million. In 1977 Pabst operated at 87 percent capacity, but in 1978 that figure dropped to 80 percent capacity. The firm sold 15,367,000 barrels out of a total 19,000,000 capacity of barrels. Average advertising expenditure per barrel has drastically changed for Pabst lately as it has for all brewers. For the period 1967 to 1976, Pabst spent only an average of $.61 per barrel on advertising. This figure jumped to an average $2.08 per barrel for the period 1977–1978.

Pabst has beers in all major market segments. Pabst Blue Ribbon is its long-standing premium beer. Eastside brand and Burgermeister brand are sold only in California. Two entries into the light beer segment were made in 1977 with Pabst Extra Light (with one half the calories of Pabst Blue Ribbon) and Pabst Light. A popular priced Red, White and Blue beer and a super-premium Andeker are the company's newest offerings. These new brands have had little impact on the market.

Pabst seems to be following a conservative strategy. The firm has shown little marketing aggressiveness and has embarked on no major expansion activities. Possible acquisition of Pabst by other firms is often mentioned in the press.

Schlitz's Reaction

By 1978 Schlitz had a new management team in place making drastic internal changes in the firm. The new president was Frank Sellinger, previously an executive vice president at Anheuser-Busch with 40 years of experience in the beer industry. Daniel McKeithan, who was once married to an Uihlein, was now chairman, and Allin Proudfoot, a former Coca-Cola Company marketing executive was the new executive vice president for marketing. Under their leadership each Schlitz brand has been reworked. The Schlitz brand has been reformulated, returning to its "classic" formula. Each brand has been turned over to a new advertising agency to receive a new advertising campaign, new packaging, and new promotions. These actions were especially needed for Schlitz, Schlitz Light, and the popular priced Old Milwaukee. Schlitz Malt Liquor dominated its segment, but this segment represented only about 3 percent of the beer market. Old Milwaukee was holding its own in its segment. The problems are that the size of this segment is contracting rapidly and the margin available makes it the least profitable segment. (See Exhibit 5.) Although Schlitz had been the first major brewer to respond to Miller Lite, its Schlitz Light brand had run through five advertising campaigns in three years, never having achieved high enough product awareness to satisfy sales hopes.

EXHIBIT 5 Segment growth in the U.S. beer market (percent of total consumption volume)*

	Popular	Premium	Light	Super-premium	Imports
1972	52.7	42.2	0.0	1.7	0.7
1973	48.2	45.9	0.4	2.2	0.8
1974	44.6	48.0	1.4	2.6	1.0
1975	42.9	48.0	2.1	3.3	1.1
1976	40.2	47.2	4.7	3.8	1.6
1977	33.9	48.7	7.8	5.4	1.6
1978	30.2	49.0	10.1	6.0	2.1
1980 bottle price†	28¢	37¢	40¢	47¢	70¢

* Excludes malt liquor and ale and therefore does not add to 100 percent.
† Estimated average for 12 oz. bottle (approximate).
Source: *Beverage World,* September 1979.

The new management team also reworked several departments within the company. The marketing department which traditionally had a functional setup was transformed to a brand management approach. The sales department was expanded considerably. New emphasis has been placed on the wholesalers. A wholesaler's council was established which meets regularly with top management personnel including the chairman and president. Board of directors meetings are now often held at the different breweries so that wholesalers have a chance to talk directly to the board members. Also, the new management has established a new products department. It has already been productive. Its first new brew is Erlanger, a super-premium now ready for test market. It is reported that this new department is currently working on a light beer to compete with Michelob Light and a menthol-flavored beer expected to be ready for testing in the fall of 1979. The company spent an average of $1.8 million per year in 1977 and 1978 on research and development.

Schlitz has also put emphasis on integrating its production processes. It has built aluminum can production plants and is currently filling 80 percent of its can requirements internally. Commercial sales of aluminum cans increased revenue by $37 million in 1978.

Schlitz's newest strategy seems aimed at trimming its excess capacity. In January 1979 the firm announced its intention to close the 300,000 barrel per year Primo Brewery in Hawaii. It has been rumored that a $100 million deal may be in the works with Anheuser-Busch for the sale of Schlitz's 5.3 million barrel facility in Syracuse, New York. There is also conjecture among industry specialists that Schlitz may follow the Syracuse deal with one regarding its 5.5 million barrel Memphis plant. This would leave the firm with approximately a 20-million barrel capacity. This figure is in line with its current sales prospects.

Or is this capacity trimming only a step toward getting Schlitz down to a saleable size? Each capacity reduction that is rumored is accompanied by acquisition rumors. Firms mentioned as interested in Schlitz include R. J. Reynolds Industries, Liggett Group, Coca-Cola, and Kirin, a Japanese brewer.

Whatever the strategy is meant to do, the latest available figures show that Schlitz has not ironed out its problems (see Exhibits 6, 7 and 8). For the first nine months of 1978, sales were down by two million barrels from the same period in 1977. For the same period, profits were off by $9.4 million to a total of $13.2 million. The new Schlitz team still has work to do. Just what marketing moves can Schlitz management make to reverse its past sales and profit trends?

EXHIBIT 6 Summary of operating results—1976–1978, Jos. Schlitz Brewing Company

	1976	1977	1978
Barrels sold	24,160,000	22,130,000	19,580,000
Capacity utilization	81.9%	75%	62%
Net sales	$999,996,000	$937,424,000	$910,841,000
Net earnings	$ 49,947,000	$ 19,765,000	$ 11,961,000
Market share	16.3%	13.9%	11.9%
Capacity	29,500,000	29,500,000	31,500,000

Source: Company reports.

use to grow at 13%

12,139,600

N.P.M.   .05   .02   .01

EXHIBIT 7

JOS. SCHLITZ BREWING COMPANY
Statements of Consolidated Earnings
($000)

Year ended December 31	1978	1977
Sales, net of discounts and allowances	$ 1,083,272	$ 1,134,079
Less excise taxes	172,431	196,655
Net sales	910,841	937,424
Cost of goods sold	723,199	726,445
Gross profit on sales	187,642	210,979
Marketing, administrative, and general expenses	151,594	150,124
Earnings from operations	36,048	60,855

EXHIBIT 7 *(concluded)*

Year ended December 31	1978	1977
Other income (expense):		
Interest and dividend income	3,311	1,861
Interest expense	(15,359)	(16,724)
Gain (loss) on disposal of assets	(3,045)	(8,325)
Market adjustment of marketable securities	—	—
Miscellaneous, net	(185)	(2,653)
	(15,278)	(25,841)
Earnings before income taxes	20,770	35,014
Provision for income taxes:		
Current—		
Federal	(6,292)	(6,719)
State ....\...............................	1,037	1,019
Deferred	14,064	20,949
	8,809	15,249
Net earnings	$ 11,961	$ 19,765
Average number of common shares outstanding	29,062,982	29,062,982
Net earnings per common share (based on average number of shares outstanding during the period)	$ .41	$ .68
Cash dividends declared per common share	$ .47	.68

EXHIBIT 8

JOS. SCHLITZ BREWING COMPANY AND SUBSIDIARIES
Consolidated Balance Sheets
December 31, 1978, and 1977

Assets	1978	1977
Current assets:		
Cash	$ 8,472,000	$ 8,348,000
Marketable securities, at lower of cost or market	18,173,000	13,756,000
Accounts receivable, less allowances for doubtful accounts of $805,000 and $678,000, respectively	27,161,000	30,441,000
Refundable income taxes	16,516,000	12,770,000
Inventories, at lower of cost or market	58,126,000	58,404,000
Prepaid expenses	7,403,000	10,620,000
Total current assets	135,851,000	134,339,000
Investments and other assets:		
Notes receivable and other noncurrent assets	5,474,000	5,166,000
Investments	16,522,000	16,871,000
Land and equipment held for sale, less reserve	7,492,000	5,766,000
	29,488,000	27,803,000

EXHIBIT 8 *(concluded)*

	1978	1977
Plant and equipment, at cost:		
Land	$ 10,885,000	$ 11,591,000
Buildings	184,498,000	188,021,000
Machinery and equipment	588,383,000	588,199,000
Cooperage and pallets	44,007,000	53,662,000
Equipment not placed in service	8,813,000	8,829,000
Construction in progress	3,107,000	4,977,000
	839,693,000	855,279,000
Less accumulated depreciation and unamortized investment tax credit	313,097,000	290,659,000
	526,596,000	564,620,000
Total assets	$691,935,000	$726,762,000

Liabilities

	1978	1977
Current liabilities:		
Notes payable	$ 5,614,000	$ 768,000
Accounts payable	45,725,000	44,229,000
Dividends payable	2,906,000	4,941,000
Accrued liabilities—		
Salaries and wages	2,490,000	2,014,000
Vacation and welfare	14,659,000	14,756,000
Taxes, other than income taxes, and miscellaneous	19,117,000	12,935,000
Income taxes	2,789,000	3,995,000
	93,300,000	83,638,000
Deposits on containers held by customers	2,297,000	3,007,000
Total current liabilities	95,597,000	86,645,000
Long-term debt	140,362,000	196,506,000
Deferred income taxes	100,970,000	86,906,000
Shareholders' investment		
Common stock, par value $2.50 per share, authorized 30,000,000 shares, issued 29,373,654 shares	73,434,000	73,434,000
Capital in excess of par value	2,921,000	2,921,000
Retained earnings	285,279,000	286,978,000
	361,634,000	363,333,000
Less cost of 310,672 shares of treasury stock	6,628,000	6,628,000
Total shareholders' investment	355,006,000	356,705,000
Total liabilities	$691,935,000	$726,762,000

Case 43

Cool-Ray Sunglasses*

Hugo Powell reached down and picked up the sunglasses from his desk and looked at them one more time, turning them over and over in his hands.

"These are absolutely excellent sunglasses," he said to himself, "yet people seem to be turning away from Cool-Ray and buying Foster Grant's or some other kind. We seem to have the competition beaten on all counts—product quality, distribution, sales force, advertising, and commanding higher prices—yet all the forecasts predict that we will lose market share. If we pick up this Cool-Ray line, we'd have to do something to protect our share of the market."

Hugo Powell was to meet the following week with Steve Wilgar, president of Warner-Lambert Canada Limited. In that meeting on May 5, 1975, Hugo would present his recommendations on what should be done about the possible acquisition of the Cool-Ray line of sunglasses. As he looked out his window at the rush-hour traffic in the street, Hugo recalled the events that had led to this present assignment.

In early 1974 he and the marketing managers of the other divisions of Warner-Lambert had sat down with Mr. Wilgar in the boardroom to discuss the new corporate strategy. They had decided that they wanted to maintain earnings growth at 10 percent per year, and they had developed a three-part strategy to accomplish this. First, they concluded that they could develop their existing brand franchises. This might involve adding advertising support where it was needed, starting new consumer promotions, or improving products. Second, they could develop new brands that met new consumer needs. Third, they could plug gaps in existing product lines by manufacturing products under licence (or by acquiring whole product lines or companies). Acquisitions were quite desirable because they represented a source of cash flow from which funds could be obtained for advertising expenditures on existing products or investment in new product research. Any firm that Warner-Lambert Canada Limited

---

* This case was written by Professor David D. Monieson of Queen's University and by Ronald Jamieson. Used by permission.

659

planned to acquire would have to allow the company to exploit two of what they considered to be their three main resources: selling, marketing, and manufacturing.

Wilgar had handed Hugo a file the company kept on prospective firms for acquisition and asked him to review those firms (and any others he might choose) and to present his recommendations within 12 months. After that meeting Hugo had called a young product manager from consumer products division, Bruce Pope, into his office and asked Bruce to assist him in his search for a firm to acquire.

About three weeks after they had started their search, Hugo had picked up the morning paper and read on the front page that a National Foreign Investment Review Agency (FIRA) was to be established in April of 1974 to oversee acquisitions and mergers involving Canadian companies and foreign-owned operations. The agency was to be empowered to examine any such situation involving a Canadian company with $250,000 in assets and $3 million or more in annual sales. The Foreign Investment Review Act's definition of a takeover was acquisition of 5 percent of the shares of a public company or 20 percent of a private company. Furthermore, FIRA was expected to extend its authority in the future and to start screening expansions into new lines of business by companies that were already foreign controlled. Acquisition of Canadian firms by foreign companies also had to be compatible with provincial development goals. Highest priority was given to the creation of jobs in underdeveloped areas and preservation of existing jobs.

Over the course of the next six weeks Hugo and Bruce had spent considerable time with corporate lawyers, assessing the political sensitivities of several potential acquisitions. After dropping several firms from the list because acquisition would have led almost certainly to a FIRA investigation, Hugo and Bruce had recommended that Warner-Lambert Canada Limited look further into acquiring the Cool-Ray line of sunglasses from American Optical Company. The risk of an investigation by FIRA was minimized because American Optical already was owned by Warner-Lambert's parent company in the United States; thus, it was expected that acquisition of Cool-Ray would be interpreted as the transfer of a business line from one subsidiary to another. Although it was possible that the decision for transfer of management of the Cool-Ray line from American Optical to Warner-Lambert would be done only in Canada, it would have to be cleared by the parent company, involving the presidents of the Pan American management centre and the international division, as well as the president of the Warner-Lambert Company.

The Canadian Market for Sunglasses

Canadian sales of sunglasses in 1972 amounted to 6.5 million units, or $26 million at retail, but dropped to 5.2 million units and $24 million in 1974. Unit sales were expected to grow at only 1.5 percent per year, while dollar sales were forecast to grow at 12 percent each year (see Exhibit 1).

EXHIBIT 1 Canadian sunglass market comparison with the United States

	United States	Canada
Market development		
Reported/estimated sunglass units—1973	87,300,000	6,523,000
1973 population	210,400,000	22,095,000
Market development (sunglasses/ thousand population)	414.9	295.2
Index: Canadian market development versus U.S. market development	100	71
Retail price		
Reported/estimated average retail—1973	$3.53	$4.00
Index: Canadian versus U.S. average	100	113
Cool-Ray average retail price—1973	$5.00*	$536
Index versus total market average	142	134
Index: Canadian versus U.S. average	100	107
Factory price		
Reported/estimated average factory cost—1973	$1.41	$2.14
Index: Canadian versus U.S. average	100	152
Cool-Ray average factory price—1973	N.A.	$2.89†
Index versus total market average	N.A.	135
Factory dollars		
Reported/estimated total factory value—1973	$123,100,100	$13,974,000
1973 population	210,400,000	22,095,000
Market development (factory $/thousand population)	$585.1	$685.4
Index: Canadian market development versus U.S. market development	100	117

N.A. = not applicable.

* Average unit price of polarized sunglasses.

† Before any discounts for early bookings.

Source: Company records.

Cool-Ray was the dominant figure in the market, holding 31 percent of the unit volume but 49 percent of the revenue. Although Foster Grant, Cool-Ray's principal competitor, held a 24 percent market share in the United States, in Canada they held only 4 percent of the market. The rest of the market in Canada was made up of a number of imported products, despite import duties of 12.5 percent plus another 12 percent. Some of the imports were European products, but the majority were manufactured in the Far East.

Sales of sunglasses were typically seasonal, peaking in the summer months. About 45 percent of the sales were made from May to August. However, people in the sunglass trade felt that the seasonality was becoming less pronounced and that sales would be more or less even through the year. "People don't see sunglasses as part of the summer anymore," they said. "Skiers buy them for the winter and automobile drivers buy them for year-round protection from the sun whenever they're driving."

Consumer Behaviour

Hugo had asked Bruce Pope to go out into the field during the summer to see what he could learn about consumers' buying habits through discussion with people in the sunglass trade.

"Well, between 60 and 70 percent of the population wear sunglasses," Bruce stated, "although only about 30 percent buy a new pair in any single year. I spoke with a buyer from one of the big department stores downtown and he said most sunglass purchases were made by women. He mentioned that unisex and neutral styles were also big sellers in his stores. This buyer thought that the major influence on choice was appearance. Price, brand name, and lens quality he thought were of lesser importance. While I was out in the store with him, I noticed that people were trying on six or seven pairs before deciding on one they would buy. According to this chap, that is not unusual."

"Sounds like styling is pretty important."

"Yes. The buyer told me he thought that firms in the sunglass market need to be extremely close to the fashion industry and to be aware of changing fashion trends. Styles can be very faddish—in one year, out the next."

"Did customers just try on different styles of one brand name?"

"That would seem to be very unusual. I approached a few customers and asked them if they came into the store looking for any particular brand. For the most part they said that they were looking for something that appealed to them and bought the style they liked most regardless of brand. When I asked them what they liked about the last pair they owned, they usually talked about colour, style, or protection; while the things they liked least about their last pair usually were such things as quality of construction or materials."

An American study revealed that in 1970 purchasers had mentioned protection and styling with equal frequency as a reason for purchasing. However, in 1972 about 40 percent indicated styling was a major reason for purchasing and only 30 percent mentioned protection. Exhibits 2 and 3 show the data from the American study.

EXHIBIT 2 The sunglass market consumer information*

	1970 (percent)	1972 (percent)
Incidence of sunglass wearing	62%	67%
Incidence of sunglass purchasing	39	41
Unaided brand awareness		
Cool-Ray	61	63
Foster Grant	21	26
Total brand awareness		
Cool-Ray	86	89
Foster Grant	50	57
When sunglasses brand decision made		
While in store	61	56
Before entering store	31	33
Not specified	8	11

EXHIBIT 2 *(concluded)*

	1970 (percent)	1972 (percent)
Major reasons for purchasing		
Protection	38	30
Appearance	36	42
Forced choice: styling versus protection†		
Styling	33	26
Protection	60	70
Average price paid per pair	$4.47	$5.34
Average number of pairs owned	1.6	1.6
Average number of pairs purchased at one time	1.4	1.4

EXHIBIT 3 The sunglass market consumer perceptions of major brands*

	Cool-Ray (percent)	Foster Grants (percent)	Imports (percent)
Brand image			
Best brand overall	48%	12%	10%
Finest lens quality	54	19	18
Fashionable styles	42	31	32
Scratch-resistant lenses	28	10	9
Excellent frame fit	35	18	15
Excellent eye protection	55	17	14
Prestige brand	47	22	18
Expensive	27	12	22
Major reason(s) for purchasing last pair			
Like the style/shape	25	44	57
Eliminate glare/are polaroid; polarized	39	7	10
Fit well/are comfortable	29	7	24
Inexpensive	9	28	27
Lenses are nicely tinted	13	43	21
Why purchase decision made			
Wanted additional/different pair	24	11	28
Broken last pair	25	25	25
Lost or forgotten previous pair	16	17	23
First pair purchased	14	4	9
Major reason(s) for liking last pair purchased			
Fit well/are comfortable	43	42	37
Eliminate glare/are polaroid; polarized	45	11	20
Cut down on glare	44	11	15
Provide protection from sunlight	16	11	20
Like the style/shape	5	20	23

EXHIBIT 3 (concluded)

	Cool-Ray (percent)	Foster Grants (percent)	Imports (percent)
Major reason(s) for disliking last pair purchased			
Are plastic/scratch easily	11	18	8
Not sturdy/fell apart	5	6	9
Consumer perceptions of brand differences			
Eliminate/cut down glare	44	8	2
Are a good (quality) product	11	7	9
Are clearer/offer more visibility	10	1	1
Are better/good for eyes	9	2	—
Provide protection from sun/ protect eyes	8	2	1

* Based on U.S. data.
Source: Company records.

About 35 percent of sunglasses in Canada were sold in drugstores, 40 percent through department stores and mass merchandisers, 8 percent through department stores, and the remaining 17 percent through variety stores, tobacconists, and other small retailers. Over several years buyers in the sunglass trade had noted a decline in the importance of variety stores as outlets for sunglasses and had attributed this to a trend towards higher sunglass prices and the variety of styles available at other outlets.

Distribution and Sales

"When you spoke with people in the sunglass trade, did you find out anything about how the sales force is employed?" Hugo asked.

"Not all of the sunglass manufacturers use a sales force in Canada," said Bruce. "When I spoke with a representative of a larger association of independent wholesalers he said that there were three ways to obtain distribution: sell through a wholesaler and his sales force; employ a sales broker using a central warehouse; or sell direct to retailers with your own sales force. Because sunglasses are sold through so many different kinds of outlets, nearly all sunglass merchants use one or the other of the first two methods I described. This fellow said that Cool-Ray was the only sunglass manufacturer using its own sales force in Canada. Foster Grant and Riviera both used sales brokers. Other suppliers went to Europe to obtain exclusive distributionships in Canada for the high-style, high-price 'prestige' lines.

"The sunglass salesman tries to call on a retail account twice a week during the summer peak period. In the off season, the salesman's call pattern is more random, perhaps once every two months. Call frequency depends a lot on the size of the store. At the wholesale level the sunglass salesman calls three or four times a year on the larger wholesalers and only once a year on the smaller wholesalers.

"The reason for such a low number of calls to wholesalers was that the salesmen, in addition to calling on wholesalers, spent a good portion of their time filling in retail accounts on the latest styles, prices, and so on. They would also drop ship[1] for the wholesaler in order to keep the store's racks full. While the salesman actually made the delivery to the retailer, billing was done through the wholesaler by prior arrangements."

Hugo said, "It sounds like a sunglass salesman's calls are more complicated than our salesmen's calls. At least we don't have to deal with the wholesaler because of our sell-direct policy. How exactly does a sunglass sales call go, Bruce?"

"One of the wholesalers arranged for me to meet some of the Cool-Ray salesmen, and I went with them on a few sales calls. When the salesman entered the store, he went directly to the sunglass display. He'd count the sunglasses on hand and note down the styles and colours that were out of stock. The other sunglass manufacturers put their sunglasses on a Cool-Ray rack wherever they find the space, so the salesman has to look the rack over very carefully to be sure he's counted only the Cool-Rays.

"The salesman then draws up an order based on what he thinks will move most quickly, and then talks with the store buyer. The buyer can either sign the order and wait for delivery from the warehouse or ask the salesman to restock the racks from the stock in his trunk. The buyer tells the salesman if any glasses have been lost or stolen while on the rack and gives him any broken or faulty sunglasses. The sunglass salesman can cover the retailer's losses on the spot and exchange good sunglasses for faulty ones. Often the salesman makes up a credit voucher to compensate the retailer for lost and broken merchandise. If the retailer's requirements are too large for the salesman to handle from his trunk stock, he arranges to drop ship the mechandise on his next visit to the retailer."

The salesman was very important to the manufacturer because his expertise could influence the volume the manufacturer could move through certain outlets. It was usually the salesman who determined the styles displayed on the racks. His knowlege of fashion trends was quite valuable because sunglass styles had a tendency to follow the latest fashions. The larger retail chains wanted to keep their merchandise turning over, and if the salesman did not manage to keep the sunglasses moving, the supplier might be discontinued the following year. If one line of sunglasses was moving faster than another, the retailer might limit the volume the supplier of the slow-moving line could sell through the stores in the chain. The supplier of the fast-moving line might find that the retailer would allow him more space in the store and would allow him to sell a higher volume of sunglasses through the chain.

---

[1] Drop shipment is one means of delivering merchandise to a retailer. The salesman would typically have a supply of merchandise in his car that he could deliver to the retailer to replenish his stocks.

Display and Promotion

Sunglasses were displayed—usually prepriced by the manufacturer—on racks. While the retailer had the option of purchasing a standard display rack for his store(s), very often the retailer bought the rack already filled with sunglasses and the cost of the rack was covered by the cost of the sunglasses. The retailer could also buy on consignment and return unsold sunglasses to the supplier at the end of the season. A counter rack by itself usually cost a manufacturer such as Cool-Ray about $70, while a floor rack cost $150. A floor rack held about 130 pairs of sunglasses.

Couponing, "cents off" deals, and other consumer promotions were not common practice in the sunglass trade. Occasionally promotions were directed at the wholesalers or retailers. A few of the large sunglass manufacturers relied on advertising to complement their coverage by the salesmen and would direct some of this advertising at consumers as well as at the trade.

One wholesale tobacconist said that the most important factors in selecting a supplier of sunglasses were the reputation of the supplier, their advertising policies, and their sales and exchange policy. Retailers wanted reliable suppliers whose merchandise was immediately and readily available so that the racks would be kept stocked. Advertising helped to maintain a high level of consumer brand awareness which would result in a high level of consumer demand. Finally, the retailer wanted a guarantee that the glasses would sell and didn't want to be stuck with unsold or unpopular styles.

Warner-Lambert Company, Inc.

In 1975 Warner-Lambert Company, Inc. (the U.S. parent company), was number 95 on *Fortune's* list of 500 industrials, with sales of $2.17 billion and net income of $165 million. Its earnings had grown at a rate of 10 percent per year since 1965, assisted by several acquisitions during that period. Warner-Lambert was the product of a 1955 merger between the Lambert Company and Warner-Hudnut. The latter company was founded in 1856 as Warner-Chilcott, a manufacturer of prescription drugs, but later expanded to include DuBarry cosmetics and Richard Hudnut toiletries. The Lambert Company marketed toothpastes and toiletries, and it was probably best known for its Listerine mouthwash. The 1956 acquisition of the Emerson Drug Company added Bromo-Seltzer to Warner-Lambert's product line, and the 1962 acquisition of the American Chicle Company added confectionery products such as Chiclets, Dentyne, Rolaids, and Certs. Many other acquisitions were made by Warner-Lambert during this period, but these few illustrate the flavour of the company and outline its major divisions.

One of the largest acquisitions was American Optical Company, which marketed more than two thousand products designed to extend and protect the physical senses of man. Some years prior to the merger, American Optical had sought to expand its lines of optical lenses and frames by diversifying into sunglasses. They had entered into an exclusive agreement with Polaroid Corporation for a process to coat lenses with a polarizing material. The result was the Cool-Ray line of sunglasses.

Warner-Lambert Canada Limited

In 1974 Warner-Lambert Canada Limited had sales of $60 million. The company was organized into four divisions: Warner-Chilcott Pharmaceuticals, Adams Brands Confectioneries, Consumer Products, and DuBarry. Manufacturing took place in three Toronto plants: the Adams plant, the main plant, and the Schick plant. Instead of reporting to Warner-Lambert Canada Limited, the Canadian management of American Optical reported to the head office of American Optical International in Massachusetts. In Canada, American Optical manufactured frames at the Nicolet, Quebec, plant and imported lenses from the United States for assembly at the Belleville plant. During the peak period the Nicolet plant employed about 140 people, of which 70 were part-time employees.

In considering which of the four divisions might adopt the sunglass line, Hugo decided that Cool-Ray would not be compatible with the distribution channels used by Warner-Chilcott Pharmaceuticals. Warner-Chilcott had fairly good penetration in the drug trade but was not really present to a significant extent in food stores or mass merchandisers. Moreover, Warner-Chilcott salesmen spent much of their time detailing physicians rather than selling to retail outlets. As it happened, Warner-Lambert had just divested the DuBarry division. Accordingly, Hugo was considering Adams Brands or Consumer Products as possible sources of management for the Cool-Ray line.

Because of the diversified nature of the Consumer Products and Adams Brands product lines, these divisions had achieved intensive distribution through food chains, department stores, drugstores, and intermediates such as wholesalers and jobbers (see Exhibit 4).

EXHIBIT 4 Distribution channels in Canada, 1974

	Drug	Food	Discount	Department	Wholesalers	Others
Total number of accounts	5,000	31,700	1,000	300	450	
Consumer Products coverage	2,754	3,668	812	220	405	620
Adams Brands coverage	4,775	26,945	N.A.	240	432	
Cool-Ray coverage	3,693	360	624	179	50	260

Warner-Lambert Canada employed 182 salespeople in the Adams and Consumer Products divisions. Exhibit 5 shows the number of salesmen in Consumer Products, Adams Brands, American Optical, and major Canadian competitors. Adams Brands had 46 salesmen who sold gum exclusively (Dentyne, Chiclets, Trident, and the like) and 45 salesmen who sold confectioneries

EXHIBIT 5 Comparison of sales forces, 1974

| | Consumer Product | Adams Brands | | | American Optical Canada (Cool-Ray) | Foster Grant | Polaroid* | Riviera |
		Gum	Candy	Both				
Salesmen	46	46	45	20	8	Use a broker	9	Use a broker
Sales managers	12		15		1		1	
Total	58		126		9		10	

* This represented the camera sales force; film was sold through a broker.

exclusively (such as Certs, Clorets, and Hall's Mentholyptus Cough Drops). Another 20 salesmen handled both gum and confectioneries. Consumer Products had a sales force of 46 men.

The Adams Brands line consisted of a number of confectionery items sold through food, drug, mass merchandisers, and variety stores. The most likely locations for an Adams display were the candy counter or a rack by the checkout counter to enhance last-minute purchases. The retailer usually received a discount of between 30 and 45 percent off the consumer list price as his margin for carrying this line. The risk of pilferage and spoilage contributed to the size of this markup.

The Consumer Products line was quite diverse, and thus this division's products were scattered throughout a store. While some products might be in with home remedies, others such as the Schick line might be in among men's toiletries or displayed on a rack. This meant that a Consumer Products salesman had to visit several areas of a store on one call, whereas a salesman from Adams Brands visited only one or two areas. The discounts on Consumer Products were about the same as on Adams Brands.

Salesmen for Adams Brands made an average of 22 calls per day, whereas salesmen for Consumer Products made roughly 11 calls per day. The difference was attributed to the more complex Consumer Products sales presentation and the need for the Products salesmen to visit several sections of the customer's store. While the Adams salesmen could talk exclusively about gum or candy, the Products salesmen had to be able to talk about mouthwash, toothpaste, razor blades, stomach remedies, and so on. One study on Hugo's desk stated that the addition of sunglasses to the sales call was expected to reduce the call frequency to 16 per day from 22 for Adams salesmen and to 9 per day from 11 for Products salesmen.

Hugo recalled from his past experiences in accompanying salesmen on their sales calls that it seemed to take some special talent for a salesman to service rack merchandise. The salesman had to be able to look over the rack very quickly and identify items low in stock or out of stock. He would then organize the rack so that products were in their proper locations and prepare an order for the items that were out-of-stock. Warner-Lambert was considered to have considerable expertise in rack servicing and rack design and thus made extensive use of this form of product display.

Sales of Adams and Products lines had a slight seasonality, with about one third of sales taking place between September and November. April to July was the ''slow'' period for their sales.

The Cool-Ray Operation

Cool-Ray was the originator of the polarized sunglass as it is known today. They manufactured the lenses using a process that was licensed from Polaroid Corporation. Cool-Ray paid Polaroid a royalty of 4.3 percent of factory sales value and used the Polaroid name prominently in its advertising and on products and labels. The Cool-Ray line was one of many product lines of American Optical, and in Canada the line was sold by eight salesmen and a sales manager. According to people in the sunglass trade, Cool-Ray's major strength was its expertise in rack merchandising and pricing.

Cool-Ray had about 5,100 retail accounts and 130 headquarters accounts,[2] but 70 percent of Cool-Ray sales were to wholesalers. Of the seven or eight calls per day a Cool-Ray salesman might make, two would be to retail outlets. Cool-Ray depended upon the wholesaler's sales force to supplement their coverage of retail accounts and had to accept the fact that the wholesalers sold more than just sunglasses on their sales calls to retailers. Two large wholesalers accounted for 38 percent of Cool-Ray's sales, and the larger of these two had just negotiated a sales agency agreement that was not cancellable until the end of 1976. To improve the coverage of retail accounts by its sales people, Cool-Ray executives had drawn up a plan for a 35-woman part-time sales force to service retail accounts starting in 1976.

Cool-Ray sunglasses were sold through 75 percent of all drugstores and 60 percent of the discount stores in Canada. Cool-Ray was typically strong in drugstores and weak in department stores, while variety stores and mass merchandising sales were close to average. Cool-Ray dealt with only about 10 percent of the food wholesalers and had extremely poor coverage of food stores. Exhibit 6 compares Cool-Ray distribution to the national averages in the United States and Canada.

EXHIBIT 6 Comparison of U.S. versus Canadian sunglass sales distribution, 1974

	U.S Cool-Ray	U.S. market	Cool-Ray Canada	Canadian market
Drug stores	62%	24%	55%	35%
Department stores	1	20	5	8
Mass merchandisers	13	17	15	20
Food stores	2	8	5	20
Variety/other	22	31	20	17
Total	100%	100%	100%	100%

---

[2] Headquarters accounts were usually large national chains that had a center purchasing department and dealt with the Cool-Ray sales manager.

Cool-Ray offered retailers a discount of 40 percent from the suggested list price; Foster Grant, Sahara, and other sunglass marketers offered the retailers a discount of 50 percent. Trade discount to wholesalers averaged between 10 and 15 percent of the prices paid by the retailers. Some marketers, such as Foster Grant, allowed wholesalers a further discount of 5 percent if they placed their orders early (usually before the spring). Cool-Ray offered wholesalers a 10 percent discount and would give a further 10 percent discount for orders booked three to six months early.

Spiffs[3] could be paid to the retailer or to the wholesaler's sales force, depending on how distribution was organized. They were used to compensate the wholesaler or broker salesmen for keeping the racks stocked. Sahara paid a spiff of 3.3 percent of invoiced cost to the retailer or wholesaler; Foster Grant paid 1.75 percent; and Cool-Ray paid about 1.1 percent. Cool-Ray had a fairly generous policy of dating orders[4] anywhere from three to six months. Warner-Lambert did not know what sort of dating policy (if any) was used by other sunglass distributors.

While in theory, discounts of 40 and 10 percent meant that for every dollar of list sales price the retailer got 40 cents and the wholesaler 6 cents, in practice this was not necessarily the case. Chains typically received discounts of more than the usual retailer discount. If merchandise were sold direct to the chain's outlet, the retailer discount applied; if it were shipped to the chain's warehouse, the chain also received some or all of the usual wholesaler's trade discount.

Approximately 60 percent of Cool-Ray's shipments took place during October and November when retailers placed their orders for the following year. The peak period for in-store servicing was from May to August, and business was pretty even over the rest of the year. Exhibit 7 compares the

EXHIBIT 7 Cool-Ray analysis, sales seasonality comparison

	Dollar sales ($000)			Percentage sales		
	Consumer Products	Cool-Ray	Consumer Products plus Cool-Ray	Consumer Products	Cool-Ray	Consumer Products plus Cool-Ray
December 73– February 74	3,020.0	600	3,620.0	19.3%	11.2%	17.2%
March–May	3,708.5	860	4,568.5	23.7	16.1	21.8
June–August	2,560.7	468	4,028.7	22.7	8.8	19.2
September– November	5,367.2	3,420	8,787.2	34.3	63.9	41.8
Total	15,656.4	5,348	21,004.4	100.0%	100.0%	100.0%

Source: Company records.

---

[3] Spiffs, or "push money," were payments made by a manufacturer to a retailer or a salesman to provide an incentive to sell his products rather than a competitor's.

[4] Dating of orders was one means of extending credit to a customer. For example, if a customer receives goods in August and the order is dated November, he doesn't have to pay for the merchandise until November.

seasonality of Cool-Ray and Warner-Lambert sales. About 85 percent of Cool-Ray's sales represented sales to stores of sunglasses on full racks, while the other 15 percent of sales came about as a result of rack replenishment during the May–August period.

To complement the efforts of its sales force, Cool-Ray spent approximately 11 percent of its sales revenue on advertising and promotion. Of the total sales and promotion budget, $250,000 was spent on media advertising, and Cool-Ray was recognized by the sunglass trade as the only major national advertiser of sunglasses in Canada. The Cool-Ray copy platform had traditionally focussed on the glare-reduction (protection) feature of the lens (see Exhibit 8). Styling had been Foster Grant's copy platform for many years.

Cool-Ray typically sold their product at a premium price relative to their competitors. In contrast, the lowest priced sunglasses landed in Canada at as low a price as 50 cents per pair. For Cool-Ray the cost of goods at the factory represented about 50 percent of the factory selling price, while the factory cost of Foster Grant sunglasses was estimated to be 30 percent of the factory selling price. Cool-Ray's cost of goods was higher than Foster Grant's because Cool-Ray attempted to put more ophthalmic features such as top-quality lenses, frames, and materials into their products and manufactured to very close tolerances. In 1973, for example, it was estimated that Cool-Ray's average factory price in Canada was $2.89, which was approximately 35 percent more than the Canadian average and double the U.S. average. It was generally acknowledged in the trade that Cool-Ray's biggest weakness was in its knowledge of styles and fashion. Their sunglasses were believed to be somewhat utilitarian and without great flair to them.

In the highly fragmented sunglass market Cool-Ray considered its main competition to come from Foster Grant. While Foster Grant had a 24 percent share of the U.S. market, they had only 4 percent of the Canadian market. The Foster Grant line was promoted on the basis of styling. For example, Foster Grant caught on to the popularity of aviator-style sunglasses and became the leader in this style, which accounted for 12 percent of Foster Grant's sales and was the most successful of their 60-odd styles. Foster Grant had developed a polarized lens of their own and had begun promoting their line of polarized sunglasses in 1973. They spent about 4 percent of their annual sales on advertising and market promotional cost at a low level by using a sales broker in Canada.

"The latest on Foster Grant is that they plan to establish a direct sales force here in Canada this year or next," Bruce Pope mentioned when Hugo asked him for an update. "I expect that by putting in such effort they will be able to double their share of the market in the first year and add another 60 percent to that in the second year. However, I'm really worried about Polaroid. They're planning on introducing their own line of polarized sunglasses about the same time as Foster Grant puts on its big push. From what I've heard, they expect to grab 5 to 10 percent of the sunglass market in the first year and double that in the second year. Not only that, but they have manufacturing capacity available and a sales force already in Canada. The sales force handles cameras,

EXHIBIT 8 Advertisement for Cool-Ray sunglasses

ADVERTISEMENT FOR COOL-RAY SUNGLASSES

you won't believe your eyes.

You won't believe how great you'll look in Cool-Ray* Sunglasses. Over 125 eye-catching styles and colors! From our new polarized Gradient and Mirrored lenses to our Tortoise Stripe Frames, they're out of sight! They're also specially designed to conform to your face, so they fit just as beautifully as they look. What's more, every pair of Cool-Ray Sunglasses is polarized to give you the glare-protection you simply can't get with ordinary sunglasses. Cool-Ray, with suggested retail prices from $2.50 to $12. They're America's No. 1 sunglasses. And it's easy to see why. COOL-RAY sunglasses. You won't believe your eyes.

and I don't know if they plan to add sunglass salesmen or have the nine salesmen at present handle sunglasses too."

"Since American Optical plans to drop the Polaroid name from the Cool-Ray line about that time, I guess Polaroid is just trying to fill the vacuum by keeping their name present in the sunglass trade," said Hugo. "The competition definitely appears to be more aggressive now. I had some of our salesmen look over the Cool-Ray racks in their territories during the summer. In their spot checks they reported that between 20 and 30 percent of the rack space was empty, and this was in the urban areas. The salesmen said that other times they would go and look at a Cool-Ray rack to find that 25 to 90 percent of the space was filled with competitors' products."

Cool-Ray executives had just completed a series of moves in 1974 intended to strengthen the company's position. They had increased their allowance to the retail trade from 40 percent to 50 percent of retail price and had increased their early booking discount from 10 percent to 15 percent. They had instituted a policy of dating orders for five months after delivery and had added a 5 percent allowance to retailers for cooperative advertising. However, they had increased their wholesale prices by an average of 36 percent during a period in which some customer segments were switching to lower priced products. Finally, they had just decided to expand their product line from 130 to 180 items.

By May of 1975 Cool-Ray executives found that returns, which were as low as 4 percent in 1973, shot up to 18 percent of sales in early 1975. They were also accumulating an inventory worth almost $2 million at retail prices.

In talking with other managers in Warner-Lambert, Hugo learned about the problems in the acquisition of the DuBarry line. Some changes in DuBarry operations had been made so that they would conform to Warner-Lambert practices and standards. As a result of these changes in practices a number of costs were incurred by Warner-Lambert in the year that they acquired DuBarry. Hugo's assessment of the Cool-Ray acquisition was that immediate changes would have to be made in several areas of Cool-Ray's operations.

Based on Bruce Pope's survey of the salesmen and his own judgment, Hugo estimated that 25 percent of Cool-Ray's inventory was unsalable because certain styles were out of fashion. He further estimated that 90 percent of the returned merchandise should be destroyed and not recycled (as had been the Cool-Ray practice) for the same reason. Although Cool-Ray held substantial inventory for delivery to customers the following year, they reported that sale of the merchandise had taken place in the present year. To offset what he thought an excessive price increase, Hugo felt that prices might have to be decreased by 10 to 15 percent. Because most of next year's merchandise had already been delivered to the wholesalers and retailers, credit vouchers would have to be issued to them in order to realize such a price rebate.

Again drawing on the past experiences in Warner-Lambert, Hugo was apprehensive of the consequences of any move from a lengthy distribution channel (one with wholesalers or brokers between manufacturer and retailer) to a "sell-direct" policy. The wholesale trade would not be pleased by such a development.

Hugo was not certain if he had sufficient human resources in Warner-Lambert to accommodate Cool-Ray. There were promotional campaigns planned for 1976 to improve market share for several major brands such as Listerine. Considerable manpower and funds would be dedicated to these efforts. Furthermore, a staff group was studying the implications of the federal government's new Anti-Inflation Board (AIB), which was formed in October 1975. The preliminary guidelines, as published in Canadian financial journals, called for firms to maintain their profit margins at no more than the percentage gross profit margin achieved during the last complete fiscal year before October 14, 1975.

Wage and price increases were limited to a maximum of 12 percent. Firms that achieved "unusual productivity gains" were expected to be allowed to keep the increased profit, although the interpretation of "unusual" was unknown. The AIB regulations did not seem to cover mergers or acquisitions.

If firms could allocate costs to individual products, price changes were expected to match cost changes. Firms that could not allocate costs to individual products were to price their products in such a way as to leave percentage pretax net profit margin no higher than 95 percent of its average percentage pretax net profit margin in the last five completed fiscal years.

Despite these obstacles Hugo felt that Cool-Ray could benefit a great deal from Warner-Lambert control in Canada. By combining the Cool-Ray sales force with the sales force from either Consumer Products division or Adams Brands, Hugo felt that it would be possible to increase replacement sales by 50 percent and to expand distribution through new accounts and improve coverage of existing accounts. For example, he thought it possible to quadruple sales through food stores and to increase sales by 3 percent through other outlets. Such a combined sales force would eliminate the need for discounts to the wholesaler trade and virtually eliminate spiffs. To direct the entire Cool-Ray line, Hugo thought, a product manager would be required to assist the present sales manager. Exhibit 9 shows the structure of the Consumer Products and Adams Brands division.

Finally, Hugo turned to Bruce and said,

> We've really got to pull all this together—and fast! If I'm going to stand up in front of Steve (Mr. Wilgar, the president) and say that we should or should not acquire Cool-Ray, I'd better have some good reasons. Cool-Ray's profits are very large right now, and we could use that money to support our development of new brands. If I say that we should acquire Cool-Ray, Steve is going to want to know which division should handle it and where Cool-Ray is expected to go in the future. He's also going to want to know what we will be able to do to maintain Cool-Ray's profitability if we take it on.

EXHIBIT 9

A. Organization chart for the Consumer Products division, 1975

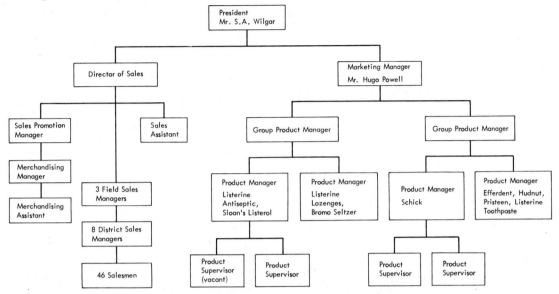

B. Organization chart for Adams Brands divisions, 1975

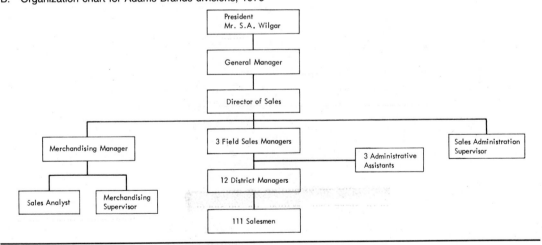

3:00 fish bowl.

Case 44

Canadair Challenger Jet*

TAYLOR— MARKETING.
HALTON — ENGINEERING.
KEARNS — PRES.

Mr. James Taylor and Mr. Harry Halton were taking a last minute look at the marketing strategy developed for Canadair's new Challenger business jet. Mr. Taylor was head of Canadair Inc., the Challenger's marketing arm located in Westport, Connecticut. Mr. Halton, the executive vice president, was the chief engineer, responsible for the design and production of the Challenger at Canadair's Montreal plant. The Challenger was being touted as the world's most advanced business aircraft, incorporating the latest technologies to achieve high speed, longest range, greatest fuel economy, and greatest seating space and comfort. It was early July 1976, and the president of Canadair, Mr. Fred Kearns, wanted senior management's consensus on product design, pricing, advertising, and approach to selling.

The preliminary design of the Challenger was generally complete, but Mr. Halton continued to receive suggestions for additional features from Mr. Taylor and his marketing group, from prospective customers, and from project engineers. Rather than build prototype models by hand, Mr. Halton had decided to begin setting up a full-scale production line. Eventually, three preproduction models of the Challenger would be constructed for testing and demonstration.

pricing

Canadair management was considering a number of pricing options. Some executives advocated a very competitive initial price to hasten customer orders, with subsequent price increases. Another group of top executives believed that the Challenger should bear a premium price to reflect its superiority and to recover $140 million in development costs. The advertising agency's proposed copy for the Challenger's print advertisements was feared to be too controversial and the marketing group wondered whether some "softening" of the copy might be advisable. Selling direct to customers, selling direct to customers with a supplementary dealer network, or selling entirely through a dealer network were three possible approaches to sales. Finally, executives recognized that

Distribution

---

* This case was prepared by Mr. Larry Uniac, research assistant, under the direction of Professor Kenneth G. Hardy. Case material of the Western School of Business Administration is prepared as a basis for classroom discussion. Copyright © 1979, The University of Western Ontario.

676

plans for service facilities required to maintain the Challenger "in the field," which could mean anywhere in the world, were very sketchy.

Canadair executives wanted 50 orders by September 30, 1976, before committing fully to the Challenger program. However, the major marketing decisions had to be finalized before the sales blitz could begin. If sales by September 30 fell in the range of 30 to 40 units, management might grant an extension on the deadline. However, sales of fewer than 30 units probably would result in scrapping the Challenger program.

General Background

Canadair's objective was to sell 410 units, or 40 percent of the market for large business jets over the period from 1978 to 1988. Business jets were changing the way companies conducted business, as executives learned the competitive advantages that a corporate aircraft could provide. What critics had once scorned as a "toy of executive privilege" was increasingly seen as a desirable and advantageous management tool. "Probably more than ever, most businessmen agree with Arco's vice chairman Louis F. Davis, that 'there's nothing like face-to-face communications to keep a business running.' "[1] One observer commented:

> As big as corporate flying has become in recent years, there are strong signs that its role will continue to expand rapidly in years to come. Of the largest 1,000 U.S. companies, only 502 operate their own airplanes versus 416 five years ago. That leaves a sizable virgin market, which sales people from a dozen U.S. and foreign aircraft builders are tripping over each other to develop.[2]

Competitors were skeptical that the Challenger could meet its promised specifications. The unloaded Challenger would weigh only 15,085 pounds compared to 30,719 for the Grumman Gulfstream II (GII), a head-on competitor that was the biggest corporate jet flying, yet still provide a wider cabin. The Challenger would be propelled by less powerful engines than the GII, yet theoretically would fly faster and consume only 50 percent as much fuel. "The Canadians seem to know something the rest of the industry doesn't," commented Ivan E. Speer, group vice president of Aerospace at Garret Corp., the major builder of corporate jet engines.[3] The Challenger was to be powered by Avco-Lycoming engines, a competitor to the Garret Corp.

More simply, it was not known how well the Challenger would fly. Although Canadair had made jets for the military, the company had never built a business jet. Beyond these concerns, production problems could arise with a project of this nature and magnitude, but little could be done to anticipate how and when these problems would occur.

---

[1] "Corporate Flying: Changing the Way Companies Do Business," *Business Week*, February 6, 1978, p. 64.

[2] Ibid., p. 62.

[3] Ibid., p. 64.

Company Background

Originating as the aircraft division of Canadian Vickers Ltd. in the 1920s, Canadair assumed its own identity in 1944 following a reorganization brought about by the Canadian government. In 1947, Canadair was acquired by Electric Boat Company of Groton, Connecticut, forming the basis for an organization that became General Dynamics Corp. in 1952. Canadair reverted to Canadian government ownership in January 1976 under a government plan for restructuring the Canadian aerospace industry. In 1975, *Interavia* magazine described Canadair as follows: "Once a flourishing company, Canadair is the 'sick man' of the national aerospace industry; employment has steadily dropped since 1970, when 8,400 were on the books, and could fall below 1,000 sometime this year unless new work is found rapidly."[4]

However, uneven employment was characteristic of the entire aircraft industry. In terms of deliveries, quality, innovation, and steady profits, Canadair had an enviable record. Located at Cartierville Airport in St. Laurent, Quebec, approximately 10 miles from the center of Montreal, the plant was one of the largest and most versatile aerospace-manufacturing facilities in Canada. Canadair's activities included the design and development of new aircraft, and contracting for major modifications to existing types of aircraft. Subcontracts for the manufactured component parts and subassemblies for military and commercial aircraft in production such as the Boeing 747 accounted for a substantial volume of the company's business (Table 1). Exhibit 1 supplies data on earnings for Canadair from 1973 to 1976. Canadair's President reflected on the activities of the company:

> We at Canadair are not really known as a major influence in the international aerospace industry. For various reasons, we have been a major subcontractor or producer of other people's aircraft over a large span of our existence, and our native designs have not been more than a small portion of our overall effort. You may imagine that the elder statesmen of the aerospace industry smiled indulgently when they heard about this radical new aircraft that Canadair was developing.

TABLE 1 Canadair's estimated sales from 1973 through 1976 by class of business

	1976		1975		1974		1973	
	Dollars (000)	Per-cent	Dollars (000)	Per-cent	Dollars (000)	Per-cent	Dollars (000)	Per-cent
Aircraft	20,410	46	15,520	42	38,808	68	22,006	63
Component subcontracts	7,783	17	6,716	18	2,945	5	2,967	9
Surveillance systems	9,367	21	6,958	19	9,620	17	8,542	25
Other	7,034	16	7,938	21	5,744	10	1,113	3
Total	44,954	100%	37,132	100%	57,117	100%	34,628	100%

---

[4] *Interavia*, February 1975, p. 150.

EXHIBIT 1

CANADAIR LIMITED AND SUBSIDIARIES
Consolidated Statement of Income
($000)

	Year Ended December 31			
	*1976**	*1975*	*1974*	*1973*
Sales	$44,594	$37,132	$57,117	$34,628
Cost of sales	41,325	42,421	53,264	31,702
Income (loss) from operations	3,269	(5,289)	3,853	2,926
Other income (expense):				
Interest income	240	260	248	356
Miscellaneous income	9	30	61	71
Interest expense	(2,056)	(3,203)	(1,755)	(1,001)
	(1,807)	(2,913)	(1,446)	(574)
Income (loss) from operations before provision for income taxes, loss on discontinued operations of a subsidiary, extraordinary items and share of earnings of Asbestos Corporation Limited	1,462	(8,202)	2,407	2,352
Provisions for federal and provincial income taxes	642	6	1,122	1,056
Income (loss) before loss on discontinued operations of a subsidiary, extraordinary items and share of earnings of Asbestos Corporation Limited	820	(8,208)	1,285	1,296
Loss on discontinued operations of a subsidiary	(385)	(165)	(260)	(280)
Income (loss) before extraordinary items and share of earnings of Asbestos Corporation Limited	435	(8,373)	1,025	1,016
Extraordinary items:				
Income tax reduction	638	—	1,100	1,041
Gain on exchange	—	1,957	—	—
Provision for disposal of a subsidiary company's assets	(988)	—	—	—
Total extraordinary items	(350)	1,957	1,100	1,041
Income (loss) before share of earnings of Asbestos Corporation Limited	85	(6,416)	2,125	2,057
Share of earnings of Asbestos Corporation Limited	—	7,368	6,063	520
Net income	$ 85	$ 952	$ 8,188	$ 2,577

Consolidated Statement of Earned Surplus (deficit—$000)

	Year ended December 31			
	*1976**	*1975*	*1974*	*1973*
Balance at beginning of year	$(14,059)	$ 49,683	$41,495	$38,918
Net income	85	952	8,188	2,577
	(13,974)	50,635	49,683	41,495
Dividend paid	—	25,000	—	—
Unrecovered portion of investment in Asbestos Corporation Limited, representing the excess of carrying value over the amount paid by General Dynamics Corporation	—	39,694	—	—
	—	64,694	—	—
Balance at end of year	$(13,974)	$(14,059)	$49,683	$41,495

* Estimated results for 1976.

The Canadian Aerospace Industry[5]

The Canadian aerospace-manufacturing industry had specialized capabilities for the design, research and development, production, marketing, and in-plant repair and overhaul of aircraft aero-engines, aircraft and engine subsystems and components, space-related equipment and air and ground-based avionic systems and components.

Approximately 100 companies were engaged in significant manufacturing work, but 40 companies accounted for 90 percent of the industry's sales in 1975. Three companies (including Canadair) were fully integrated, having the capability to design, develop, manufacture, and market complete aircraft or aero-engines. With aggregate sales of $785 million in 1976, the Canadian aerospace industry shared fifth place in western world sales with Japan, after the United States, France, the United Kingdom, and the Federal Republic of Germany.

It was economically impractical for Canadian industry to manufacture all the diverse aerospace products demanded on the Canadian market. Through selective specialization, the Canadian industry had developed product lines in areas related to Canadian capabilities and export-market penetration. In 1975, 80 percent of the industry's sales were in export markets, an achievement attained under strong competitive conditions.

The Canadian industry was fully exposed to the competitive forces of the international aerospace market. In some cases, its hourly labour rates were higher than those in the United States. The industry's export-market penetration was vulnerable to the economic forces associated with competitor's industrial-productivity improvements. The industry, like most world aerospace industries, was manufacturing high-cost and high-risk products. There were many hazards: a relatively long-term payback cycle, sporadic government purchasing decisions, tariff and nontariff barriers, monetary inflation, and rapid technological obsolescence.

Aerospace industries throughout the world generally received government support, particularly in the areas of research, development, and equipment modernization. For example, the U.S. aircraft industry benefitted from the annual $10 billion Department of Defense budget and the annual $6 billion NASA budget. By contrast, during the nine years ended March 31, 1976, the Government of Canada had provided $349 million to the Canadian aerospace industry through several programs. In short, the Canadian aircraft industry was not subsidized.

There were indications in 1976 that the Canadian aerospace industry was entering a growth cycle. The trend lines of Canadian sales and exports encouraged an optimistic outlook.

---

[5] Source: Chairman D. C. Lowe, *A Report by the Sector Task Force on the Canadian Aerospace Industry,* June 30, 1978.

The Business Jet Industry

Continued expansion of business-aircraft activities was expected to continue into the 1980s in what business aviation officials described as the "best growth climate in years."[6] Booming sales of business aircraft in Europe, the Middle East, and Africa were giving rise to a belief that the business aircraft was becoming a true business tool in these regions, much as it had in the United States about a decade earlier.

All forecasts pointed to an enormous upsurge in the sale of business jet aircraft. Exhibit 2 graphs the trends in the U.S. business jet industry from 1956 to an estimate of 1976 and beyond. Exhibit 3 illustrates the trends in world deliveries of all corporate aircraft from 1965 to 1975, with delivery estimates through 1981. Many factors were contributing to increase the desire for private business aircraft:

> Commercial airlines were reducing service drastically as they added the "jumbo" jets. In six years, the number of U.S. cities served by commercial airlines dropped from 525 to 395.

reasons to buy jet

EXHIBIT 2 Growth trends in U.S. business flying (semilog paper)

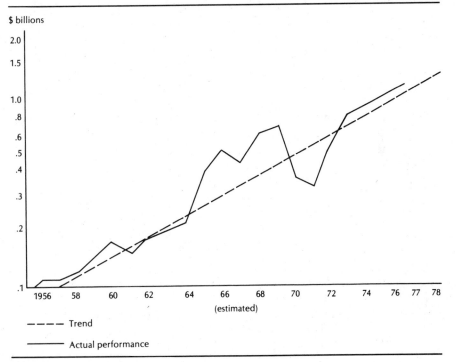

Source: *Aviation Week and Space Technology.*

---

[6] *Aviation Week and Space Technology*, September 11, 1978, pp. 46–56.

EXHIBIT 3 Unit worldwide corporate jet deliveries (all models)

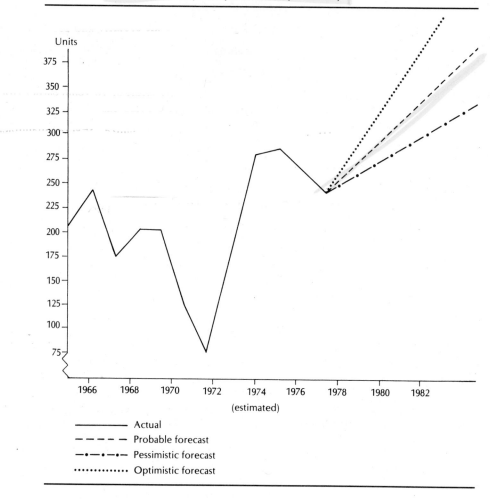

Units

————	Actual
— — — —	Probable forecast
—•—•—•—	Pessimistic forecast
············	Optimistic forecast

reasons to buy jet

Ninety-seven percent of all scheduled-air-carrier passengers in the United States flew out of only 150 airports.

Flights were packed with tourists and other occasional travelers. This made it difficult to obtain reservations and impossible to work en route. The amount of executive time spent traveling was increasing and most of this travel time was being wasted.

Corporate planes provided the management of many companies with new flexibility and shortened reaction time in special situations.

Cost savings could be achieved; for example, Xerox flew 15,000 employees per year on a company-owned shuttle plane between its Stamford headquarters and its Rochester (N.Y.) plant, saving $410,000 annually over commercial air fares.

There was growing concern for the security and protection of top executives from the growing incidence of airplane hijackings.

Finally many organizations were trading up to newer or larger aircraft to replace outdated, older equipment. Essentially, technology permitted such improvements over the aircraft of 10 years earlier (for example in fuel economy) that the buyers could easily justify the update.

To cash in on the business jet bonanza, several manufacturers were planning to introduce new models. The following business jets would be on the market in some fashion by 1979:

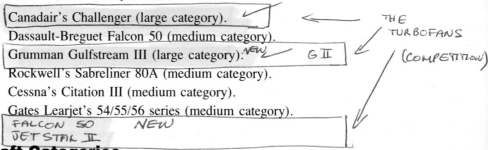

Canadair's Challenger (large category).

Dassault-Breguet Falcon 50 (medium category).

Grumman Gulfstream III (large category). *NEW* — *G II*

Rockwell's Sabreliner 80A (medium category).

Cessna's Citation III (medium category).

Gates Learjet's 54/55/56 series (medium category).

FALCON 50   NEW
JET STAR II

THE TURBOFANS (COMPETITION)

Corporate Aircraft Categories

More than 100 different aircraft models were offered to the business flyer.[7] Hence, the selection of the right aircraft for an individual company was a complex task. John Pope, Secretary of the National Business Aircraft Association emphasized this advice: "Any aircraft selected involves a compromise, because the worst error you can make is buying more aircraft than you need and underutilizing it."[8] The general categories in order of performance and price were: single-engine piston, multiengine piston, turboprop, turbojet and turbofan.

Single-engine piston aircraft, while not usually considered "corporate," did provide starting points for many smaller companies, as well as individuals who combined business and pleasure flying. . . . Multiengine piston aircraft were the next step up, offering the additional security and performance afforded by a second engine. . . . Piston-engine twins were considered excellent entry-level aircraft for smaller corporations, with a relatively high percentage owner-flown. . . . Turboprop aircraft were referred to by some as "turbojets with propellers attached.". . . Turboprops used significantly less fuel than pure jets but could easily cost more than $1 million.[9]

Turbojet and turbofan aircraft flew faster and, for the most part, farther

[7] "Corporate Aviation: The Competitive Edge," *Dun's Review,* January 1979, p. 89.
[8] Ibid.
[9] Ibid.

than the other aircraft. A turbojet was not usually a first-time purchase for a smaller company. Prices in this category ranged from $1 million to $7.5 million. The turbofans offered greater low-altitude efficiency than the turbojets. The Challenger, JetStar II, Falcon 50, GII and GIII were turbofans.

The following rules of thumb were often used to determine the suitability of different planes for different flying needs:

Average distance per flight	Appropriate type of aircraft for this distance
150– 200 miles	Single-engine piston
200– 500 miles	Multiengine piston and smaller turboprop
500– 750 miles	Turboprops and small turbojets
750–1,000 miles	Small turbojets
1,000–2,000 miles	Medium-size turbojets
2,000–4,000 miles	Large turbofans and large turbojets

Corporate Jet Competition

The Falcon 50, Gulfstream II and III, and JetStar II seemed to compete directly against the Challenger. Exhibit 4 summarizes sales by segment and model from 1965 to 1975. A schematic layout of each competitive plane is shown in

EXHIBIT 4 Worldwide corporate jet deliveries (units)

Model	1965	1966	1967	1968	1969	1970	1971	1972	1973	1974	1975	1976 prices (000s)
Small jet market												
Citation 1								52	81	85	69	$ 918
Falcon									1	21	26	1,905
Lear 23	80	18	1									—
Lear 24		24	26	28	33	20	10	16	21	22	18	—
Lear 25				18	25	18	10	23	45	40	14	1,315
Lear 35/36										4	47	1,679
Hansa			3	6	14	4	1	1	5			—
Sabre 40	26	31	5	5	1	6						—
Corvette										6	5	—
Westwind #1151/52/54	30	50	25	10	12	5	4	11	12	12	4	—
Total small jets	136	123	60	67	85	53	29	103	165	190	183	
Medium jet market												
Hawker Siddely 125	43	58	20	32	39	32	18	24	24	25	13	2,075
Sabre 60			11	20	14	6	9	4	4	20	9	2,200
Sabre 75								6	1	10	19	2,406
Falcon 20	14	43	63	38	25	18	7	24	46	17	29	3,005
Total medium jets	87	101	94	90	78	56	34	60	75	72	70	
Large jet market												
JetStar	18	22	18	18	11	2	4	10	6	1	0	5,035
Gulfstream			2	35	36	17	14	14	17	18	20	5,500
Total large jets	18	22	20	53	47	19	18	24	23	19	20	
Grand total	211	246	174	210	210	128	77	194	284	290	273	

.085 .089 .114 .252 .22 .148 .23 .124 .08 .066 .0073

75 58 84 98 91 90

Exhibits 5 and 6. Exhibit 7 compares the salient product differences for the Challenger and its competitors.

The new Dassault-Breguet Falcon 50, with its flight testing scheduled for completion by October 1978 and certification expected in December 1978, was slightly ahead of the Challenger program. The Challenger would probably not be certified until August 1979. Flight tests of the Falcon 50 had shown that its performance figures were better than expected in terms of landing strip required and rate of climb. The Falcon 50 was essentially a modification of the medium-sized Falcon 20, which had been introduced 14 years earlier.

The new Falcon 50 would be available or delivery by March 1979 and its performance in terms of projected operating cost per mile and range was second only to the Challenger. The print advertisement for the Falcon 50 claimed that it

EXHIBIT 5 Cabin floor outline

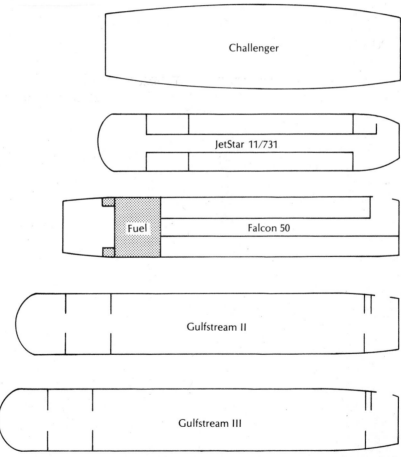

Note: Challenger data based on engineering statistical analysis. For performance guarantees see Technical Specification.

EXHIBIT 6

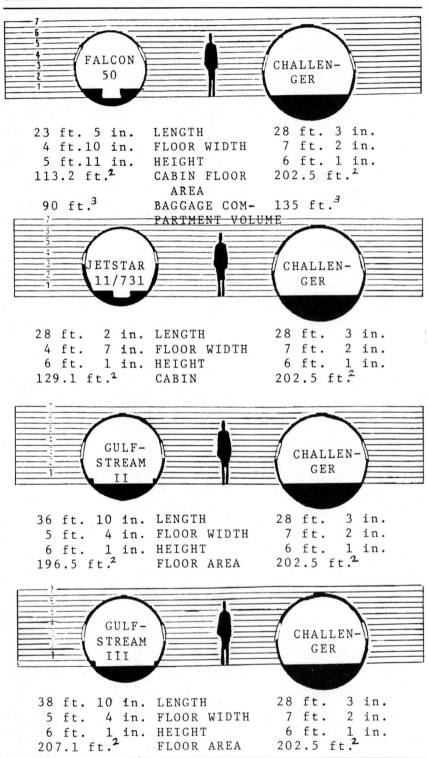

23 ft. 5 in.	LENGTH	28 ft. 3 in.
4 ft.10 in.	FLOOR WIDTH	7 ft. 2 in.
5 ft.11 in.	HEIGHT	6 ft. 1 in.
113.2 ft.^{2}	CABIN FLOOR AREA	202.5 ft.^{2}
90 ft.^{3}	BAGGAGE COMPARTMENT VOLUME	135 ft.^{3}

28 ft. 2 in.	LENGTH	28 ft. 3 in.
4 ft. 7 in.	FLOOR WIDTH	7 ft. 2 in.
6 ft. 1 in.	HEIGHT	6 ft. 1 in.
129.1 ft.^{2}	CABIN	202.5 ft.^{2}

36 ft. 10 in.	LENGTH	28 ft. 3 in.
5 ft. 4 in.	FLOOR WIDTH	7 ft. 2 in.
6 ft. 1 in.	HEIGHT	6 ft. 1 in.
196.5 ft.^{2}	FLOOR AREA	202.5 ft.^{2}

38 ft. 10 in.	LENGTH	28 ft. 3 in.
5 ft. 4 in.	FLOOR WIDTH	7 ft. 2 in.
6 ft. 1 in.	HEIGHT	6 ft. 1 in.
207.1 ft.^{2}	FLOOR AREA	202.5 ft.^{2}

EXHIBIT 7 Comparative specifications   2000-4000

	Operating cost per nautical mile	Maximum range	Cruising speed	Fuel consumption 100 nm at cruise speed	Noise decibles*		
					Take-off	Sideline	Approach
Challenger	$ .93	3,900 nm.	547 mph	4,160 lb.	78	87	90
JetStar II	$1.25	2,800 nm.	538 mph	7,250 lb.	n.a.	n.a.	n.a.
Gulfstream III	$1.16	3,600 nm.	534 mph	6,410 lb.	90	102	98
Gulfstream II	$1.26	3,187 nm.	541 mph	7,723 lb.	90	102	98
Falcon 50	$1.06	3,550 nm.	528 mph	6,200 lb.	87	94	97

* 1979 FAA 36 Regulation = Take-off: 89, Sideline: 94, and Approach: 98.

† Initial proposal for first 50 units.

Source: Canadair comparative advertising material (based on statistical analysis).

would be the fastest business jet in the world, although this statement was disputed by the calculations made by Canadair engineers. Messrs. Halton and Taylor believed that the Falcon 50 would be around for some time, although its fuel consumption would be a major competitive disadvantage.

Gulfstream II and III

The Gulfstream II first flew in October 1966 and represented the latest technology at the time of its certification. Its turbojet engines were powerful, but consumed considerably more fuel than used in the more recent high-bypass turbofans used by the Challenger. In addition, engine noise was high both inside and outside the cabin. Since 1966, 173 Gulfstream IIs had been sold around the world.

Grumman had accelerated developmental work on a new Gulfstream III to replace the Gulfstream II in response to new demands on the market and the news of the Challenger. The Gulfstream III would be an aerodynamically modified version of the Gulfstream II, but it would use the same engines. The first prototype of the Gulfstream III was scheduled for completion in August 1979 and the first production unit was scheduled for delivery in March 1980. A print advertisement showing the Gulfstream III is shown in Exhibit 8.

JetStar II

The JetStar II, available since January 1976, was a re-engineered version of the original JetStar which had been certificated in 1961. Although the new engines of the JetStar were turbofans, they were medium-bypass fans and not as efficient as high-bypass fans in minimizing fuel consumption. More than 112 JetStars had been sold since 1961.

According to a company spokesman, Lockheed-Georgia anticipated no new changes to its JetStar II in order to meet forthcoming competition from the Challenger, Falcon 50, and Gulfstream III. Lockheed was still attempting to determine its market share in the larger-cabin business fleet, with the performance and acceptance of the three new aircraft still unknown. JetStar IIs were being built at the rate of one per month and the earliest promised delivery date was June 1978.[10]

The Challenger Program

Early in 1976, much of Canadair's subcontract work was nearing completion and Canadair was not selling enough of its own CL-25 water bombers to fill the gap. Canadair executives needed an ambitious project if they were to meet government demands for eventual self-sufficiency. Mr. Halton commented:

---

[10] *Aviation Week and Space Technology,* September 11, 1978.

EXHIBIT 8 Gulfstream III ad

The faster the Gulfstream III flies, the farther behind it leaves every other executive jet.

If you drive any kind of vehicle, you know that speed impacts how far it's going to travel. Automobiles or airplanes, the law is the same: the higher the speed, the shorter the range.

For example, the long range cruise speed of the Gulfstream III is Mach .77, or about 510 mph. At that speed, the Gulfstream III has an NBAA IFR range of 4,205 statute miles.

That's more than enough range for the Gulfstream III to fly non-stop routinely between London and New York in about 8 hours with at least 8 passengers and baggage. (No other executive jet can do that.)

Boost the cruise speed of the Gulfstream III to its maximum—Mach .85, or over 560 mph—and its NBAA IFR range becomes 3,226 statute miles with the same payload.

That's still enough range to fly at least 8 people at *top speed* from Boston to London or between any two airports in the continental United States in less than 6 hours. (No other executive jet can do that, either. The fact is, the Gulfstream III can fly more people farther faster than any executive jet.)

But we're not advocating speed.

We're talking about *productivity*.

The Gulfstream III offers such unique flexibility in trade-offs between speed, range and payload that it can fly virtually any kind of mission—and do it with optimum productivity.

At a time when the world's businesses are placing increased emphasis on maximizing every investment, it is little wonder that the thoroughly proven Gulfstream III continues to dominate the market for long-range executive transports.

If you are planning for the acquisition of an aircraft that can help make your organization more effective and productive, now is the time to look into the Gulfstream III.

A full-scale demonstration of this remarkable airplane on one of your upcoming business trips at home or abroad could shape your thinking about business jets for years to come.

The man to talk to is Charles G. Vogeley, Senior Vice President of Gulfstream Marketing. Call him at (912) 964-3274; or write to him at Gulfstream American Corporation, P.O. Box 2206, Savannah, Georgia 31402 U.S.A.

He can show you why the Gulfstream III continues to leave its challengers farther and farther behind.

The Gulfstream III. The Ultimate.

Gulfstream American

Member GAMA

We knew that we needed to do something in the general-aviation business and a market-research study indicated that business aviation would be a growth market. In November 1975, Fred Kearns talked with Bill Lear about his concept of an advanced business aircraft based on two known pieces of technology, the supercritical wing used on military aircraft and the high-bypass fanjet engine. In January 1976, I met with Bill Lear and by March 1976 we were negotiating options on the Lear design. Jim Taylor was hired in April 1976 to head up the marketing for the new aircraft and by May he had arranged a selling seminar to which he invited 200 chief pilots and senior corporate officers to Canadair's plant to unveil the Challenger concept.

Bill Lear, who built the first business jet in 1961, had developed the original concept of the Challenger around an 88-inch diameter fuselage. Representatives of the business market for the jet responded to the design encouragingly. However, Canadair decided to change the rear design drastically for a number of reasons, one of them a fuel-tankage problem. Also, at the original meeting with 200 chief pilots and executive officers, potential customers expressed demands for roominess. Consequently, Canadair engineers redesigned the jet with a 106-inch fuselage. As it happened, the extra width made the plane capable of seating four abreast. Lear disassociated himself from the Challenger program in response to this change and dubbed the Canadair design ''Fat Albert.'' Canadair executives recognized the possibility of creating a ''stretch'' version of the Challenger that perhaps could carry up to 50 passengers.

It was clear at the beginning of 1976 that in order to finance the project, at least $70 million would have to be raised in addition to the company's own $70 million. Projects with this degree of leverage were not uncommon in the aerospace industry and the Canadian government agreed to *guarantee* a $70-million Eurobond for Canadair. A forecast schedule of investment outlays is shown in Exhibit 9.

The Challenger's most salient product benefits as conceived by Canadair's marketing and engineering staff were:

Large wide-body cabin: excellent size for executive, air taxi, third-level carriers, and cargo.

Fuel economy: lowest operating cost per nautical mile compared with direct competition.

Long range: long single-stage flight or numerous short-stage flights without refueling.

Competitive speeds: very competitive, high cruise speed in long-range configuration.

Low noise levels: most closely meets FAA standards for 1979.

Market forecast

Canadair was already building a test model for fatigue tests, a test model for static tests, and three preproduction models for the eventual production plan which would be as follows:

EXHIBIT 9

CL 600 CHALLENGER
Pro Forma* Cash Flow Profile as of June 1976
($000)

	Sep. 76–Dec. 79 not assignable	Dec. 77–Oct. 80 lot #1 aircraft 1–50	Apr. 79–Aug. 81 lot #2 aircraft 51–100	Feb. 80–Apr. 82 lot #3 aircraft 101–150	Oct. 80–Jan. 83 lot #4 aircraft 151–200	Jul. 81–Dec. 83 lot #5 aircraft 200–250	Total
Labor, overhead cost	$ 86,400	$ 72,460	$ 28,350	$ 26,350	$ 24,980	$ 25,315	$ 264,855
Material, equipment cost	20,925	81,148	94,970	107,450	113,045	126,100	543,638
Other costs (rentals, service)		17,550	925	713	760	750	42,298
Program support cost	21,600	18,936	10,440	11,100	12,784	14,475	73,810
Marketing	6,075	5,030	2,744	2,938	3,390	3,836	17,938
Finance		31,326	10,700	2,938	3,390	3,836	42,026
Total cost	$135,000	$226,450	$149,129	$148,551	$154,959	$170,476	$ 984,565
Revenue		$205,000	$225,500	$238,500	$253,000	$268,000	$1,190,000
Cumulative	$(135,000)	$(156,450)	$(80,079)	$ 9,870	$107,911	$205,435	$ 205,435
Date #1 aircraft ordered		Jul. 76					
Anticipated date last aircraft ordered		Nov. 76	Apr. 78	Oct. 79	Apr. 81	Oct. 82	
Delivery date #1 aircraft		Nov. 79					
Anticipated date last aircraft delivered		Sept. 80	Aug. 81	June 82	May 83	Apr. 84	
Assumed average price per aircraft		4,100	$4,510	$4,770	$5,060	$5,360	$4,750

* This data is presented for case study purposes only and does not purport to represent actual estimating data.

[Handwritten annotations: "50 units 50 50 50 50" below the per-aircraft row; "= 250" at bottom right]

1979— 6 units
1980—50 units
1981—80 units

The first test unit was expected to fly by April 1978 and the preproduction models were to be available for delivery by the end of 1979. This production plan was adopted in response to an analysis of the market trends for this category. Table 2 traces the market history of jet sales in the medium and large categories.

TABLE 2 Market history (units): Sales of medium and large size jets (Gulfstream II, JetStar, Falcon 20, HS 125)

1966:	123	1971:	43
1967:	103	1972:	72
1968:	123	1973:	93
1969:	111	1974:	62
1970:	69	1975:	51

10-year total: 850 units

The United States was the major market for corporate aircraft. Table 3 summarizes the geographic distribution of corporate-aircraft sales during 1966–1975:

TABLE 3 Distribution of sales, 1966–1975 (all corporate planes)

	Units	Percent
North America	565	66.5
Europe	189	22.2
Central and South America	25	2.9
Asia	24	2.8
Africa	37	4.4
Oceania	10	1.2
	850	100.0

On the basis of this history, Canadair's marketing staff first calculated pessimistic, probable, and optimistic worldwide-sales forecasts for the medium and large jet category from 1978 to 1988, judged to be the Challenger's sales life (Table 4).

Canadair executives then narrowed this down to a forecast for Challenger sales only (Table 5).

The most-probable-sales estimate for this period represented a 40 percent share of the probable world market during 1978–88. In the midterm, Canadair *large/med*

TABLE 4 Worldwide business-jet sales forecast, 1978–1988 (Challenger category, executive configuration only)

	Pessimistic	Probable	Optimistic
North America	600	625	675
Europe	200	225	275
Central and South America	25	40	65
Asia	25	40	65
Africa	50	75	95
Oceania	10	15	20
	910	1,020	1,195

TABLE 5 Challenger sales forecast, 1978–1988 (executive configuration only)

Sales 1978–1988 for Chall.

	Pessimistic	Probable	Optimistic
North America	150	250	300
Europe	55	80	105
Central and South America	15	20	25
Asia	15	25	35
Africa	20	30	50
Oceania	5	5	10
	260	410	525

executives could consider a stretched version of the Challenger for the commuter and freight market. Adding this version would raise the probable forecast to 560 units, the pessimistic to 333, and optimistic to 750 units. The average variable cost per unit for the first two hundred units was projected to be $4.1 million per jet but variable costs per unit were expected to show some improvement because of the experience curve effect after the first 200 jets. Exhibit 9 shows a pro forma cash flow for the first 250 Challengers that might be produced. No cost or investment data had been generated on the stretched Challenger model.

can't cover variable costs

Pricing

The marketing staff had prepared several pricing options for the Challenger. It was necessary to finalize pricing for the first 50 orders and work out a *general* pricing plan for the rest of the projected sales. Exhibit 10 contains data on the existing competitive prices and the marketing staff's best estimate of future pricing moves by the competition.

One pricing option for the first 50 orders was to undercut the competition by $1.2 million, setting the price at $4.1 million per Challenger. To some executives, a $1.2 million discount seemed large for such a superior product, even though the Challenger had flown only "on paper." They pointed out that all new aircraft faced this issue of confidence and that most buyers understood the

EXHIBIT 10 Expected pricing movement in the large-jet market ($000)

	1976 current price*	Expected BCA price†							
		1977	1978	1979	1980	1981	1982	1983	1984
Challenger‡	$4,100									8%
JetStar II	5,345	$5,195	$5,611	$6,057	$6,544	$7,068	$7,633	$8,244	$8,900
Gulfstream III	6,200	?	—	—	—	—	—	—	—
Gulfstream II	5,500	5,900	6,354	6,844	7,371	7,938	8,549	9,208	9,910	7½
Falcon 50	5,750	5,750	5,750	5,750	6,153	6,583	7,044	7,537	8,060

* Average BCA equipped prices.
† Smith and Taylor were less certain of pricing activity after 1980.
‡ Initial proposal for first 50 units.
Source: Company records.

process of designing an all-new aircraft and the process of gearing up a volume production system. Because the breakeven volume under the low-price option was larger than the probable-sales forecast, the price was expected to rise after the first 50 orders.

Alternatively, the Challenger could be priced at parity with the competition. In this case, the price would probably increase in step with inflation and the pricing of competitive products.

Some executives suggested that the Challenger's superior product characteristics required a premium price even in the short run. They believed that the Challenger could maintain a premium over competitive prices in the long run.

The purchase price for each Challenger would include training for captains, maintenance training for mechanics, programmed maintenance assistance from Montreal, and service and support from any of the three planned service facilities. Bill Lear, who had done the initial Challenger design, would receive 5 percent of the *sale* price of the first 50 units sold, 4 percent on the second 50, and 3 percent on all orders beyond the first hundred.

The following terms of purchase were proposed:

1. Each customer would be required to make a 5 percent deposit for each plane ordered. All deposits would be placed in escrow with accrued interest at the Canadian prime rate (10 percent in 1976).
2. One year before delivery, the customer would pay 30 percent of the purchase price.
3. Six months before delivery, the customer would pay 30 percent again.
4. The customer would pay the final 35 percent of the purchase price upon delivery.

Service

After-sale service was an important purchase criterion for the customer. Canadair executives tentatively had decided to build three factory-owned service centres which would service only Challengers. Their cost, $4.5 million each, was included in the planned $140 million investment. One centre would be located in Hartford, Connecticut, where Canadair's U.S. sales office was located, one in the southwestern United States, and one in Europe. The selection of these locations was based on the projection that these areas would provide the majority of Challenger sales. Only technical personnel would operate from these facilities.

The service facilities would have to be completed in time to service the first jets as they were sold at the end of 1979. Canadair would have to service early Challenger buyers very well to enhance its credibility and improve sales prospects. There was some concern at Canadair about whether factory-owned centres were the best way to provide service. Some corporate jet manufacturers such as Gulfstream and Hawker-Siddely utilized service distributors. Hence, the 200 Hawker-Siddely 125s in the United States were serviced by a distributor network of 14 outlets. This method of servicing, if chosen by Canadair, would eliminate the $4.5 million investment in each service facility, but because the Challenger was technically more advanced than its competition, special in-house expertise might offer certain advantages and would not require handing over technical information to distributors who serviced competitive aircraft.

Advertising and Promotion

The advertising and promotion budget for the Challenger program in 1976 was set at about $2.5 million. Because the Challenger was a new and unproven airplane, the marketing staff and its advertising agency had decided to mount a print-advertising campaign in the leading technical and business magazines to support the sales force's personal selling activities. Domestic and international advertising campaigns were planned for journals such as *Professional Pilot, Business Week, Business and Commercial Aviation, Interavia,* and *The Wall Street Journal.* All of the Challenger's competitors advertised in these journals, trying to reach the executive in charge of purchasing a business jet and the pilot who would be flying the jet.

To achieve high readability scores for their advertising, Canadair executives were prepared to use a bold, confident, and "challenging" theme. Examples of the proposed advertisements are shown as Exhibits 11, 12 and 13. This copy differed markedly from what the competition typically employed. Of the total advertising and promotion budget, $625,000 was to be allocated to print advertising.

Studying the competition's advertising copy, Mr. Taylor sensed that the competition had already begun to react to the Challenger program. This was particularly evident in the Gulfstream II and JetStar II advertisements. Still, the Canadair marketing group was worried that its own bold campaign could backfire and damage the credibility of the Challenger by taking pot shots at the competition, especially when the Challenger had no flight tests to back it up. If their theme proved inappropriate, they could quickly develop other themes and

EXHIBIT 11

This business jet design is so advanced, it's making the competition airsick.

Enter the Canadair Challenger. Not just another business jet, but the first new concept in business jets in about 20 years.

And we're not just saying that with empty words.

We're sending forth this solid challenge:

We challenge any business jet to fly as fast.

We challenge any business jet to offer as much range.

We challenge any business jet to fly as efficiently.

We challenge any business jet to match our wide-body comfort.

And now, we'd like to plunge into some specifics, demonstrating why our competition is feeling a bit queasy at the moment.

The Challenger challenges the JetStar II.

The Challenger is really much more of a star than the JetStar II. It will carry 17% less fuel, yet travel 1,400 statute miles further.

The Challenger will be faster, quieter, 40% less expensive to operate. As well as a sprawling 25 inches wider.

The Challenger challenges the Falcon 50.

Compared to the Challenger, the Falcon 50 is a bird of a different feather. The Challenger will fly up to 35 mph faster (New York to Los Angeles in 5 hours and 11 minutes).

The Challenger will also fly 1,000 miles further, be quieter, and burn 20% less fuel while doing so. And as for the inside story, the Challenger will have 42% more cabin volume than the Falcon 50, and 76% more baggage space.

The Challenger challenges the Gulfstream II.

The Challenger will carry 40% less fuel, yet travel 900 miles further.

The Challenger will be about ⅓ less expensive to operate.

And the Challenger will be easy to take in still another way. Noise. We'll be significantly quieter than the Gulfstream II. And because we'll be 10 inches wider, we'll even challenge their cabin for passenger comfort and room.

How we're meeting the challenge.

We're meeting the challenge of the Challenger by discarding the hand-me-down technology that the competition uses.

Our business jet will incorporate the most sophisticated and proven technology currently available.

That includes the Lycoming ALF-502 turbofan with a 5 to 1 high bypass ratio. Its power will provide us with the best thrust-to-weight relationship of any commercially obtainable plane.

We also bring you a new wing. An advanced, yet proven, airfoil concept that will delay the formation of shock waves.

So prepare yourself for this shock: we'll not be just faster than any business jet, we'll be faster than a DC-10.

The company that's behind all this is Canadair, makers of over 3,800 aircraft, 580 supersonic.

For more information on the Challenger, formerly known by the drawing board name LearStar, write to Jim Taylor at Canadair Inc., Dept. T, 274 Riverside Avenue, Westport, Conn. 06880. Or call him at (203) 226-1581.

You'll become convinced that the Challenger, the business jet that's making the competition airsick, can be a very healthy investment for your company.

canadair challenger
We challenge any business jet to match it.

*All performance figures in this advertisement for CHALLENGER are based upon wind tunnel tests and engineering statistical analysis with flight testing to begin in early 1978.

EXHIBIT 12

Our competition wastes a lot of energy.
And they'll be wasting a lot more when they try to explain these figures.

On a 1,000 nautical mile trip, the *challenger* will burn:

- **36% less fuel than a JetStar II.**
- **45% less fuel than a Gulfstream II.**
- **20% less fuel than a Falcon 50.**
- **11% less fuel than a Falcon 20F.**

These are the numbers that add up to trouble for the competition.

The numbers that prove the Challenger will be the business jet that not only outperforms all the rest, but outconserves all the rest of the full-cabin business jets.

The environment will save. You will save. And with fuel costs taking off even faster than a Challenger, we don't have to tell you what the savings will be.

Our economy isn't a con.

The same engine that will let us go so fast (Montreal to

London in 5 hours, 29 minutes) is also what will use up our fuel so slowly. It's the Lycoming ALF-502 turbofan with a 5 to 1 high bypass ratio. This design means exceptional fuel efficiency.

So does our new wing. An advanced configuration that will delay the formation of shock waves. So drag, which is such a drag, won't drag as much. And lift will be lifted. So the Challenger will fly faster, further, and more economically than any other business jet.*

Our economy will also apply to maintenance. The Challenger's engine is fully modular for on-airframe servicing. Meaning our engine is a snap to fix. You won't be paying $1,000 for labor to replace a $50 part.

Tomorrow's plane without yesterday's technology.

Scratch the twenty-year-old technology the competition embraces. The Challenger is being built from scratch.

Incorporating all the latest proven aspects of both design and technology.

Even our cabin is a big idea. The Challenger will be the first wide-body business jet. Almost a full foot wider than any other, and two spacious feet wider than most.

Now who's behind all this, you ask? Canadair. Canadair has built over 3,800 aircraft, 580 supersonic.

There's much more detailed information on the Challenger, formerly known by the drawing board name LearStar, and Jim Taylor has it. Write to him at Canadair, Dept. T, P.O. Box 6087, Montreal, Canada H3C3G9. Or call him at (514) 744-1511.

He'll spend all the time you need talking about the plane that will expend so little energy.

canadair challenger
We challenge any business jet to match it.

*All performance figures in this advertisement for CHALLENGER are based upon wind tunnel tests and engineering statistical analysis with flight testing to begin in early 1978.

EXHIBIT 13

Finally, the first new concept in business [jet] in twenty year[s]. The Cana[dair Challe]nger. We hereby ch[all]enge any business jet [to] match it.

The Canadair Challenger is the class business jet that's in a class by itself.

Respectfully dismissing twenty-year-old technology, it's being built from scratch.

In fact, the engineering of this aircraft is so brilliantly eclectic that it lets us hurl forth the Canadair Challenger Challenge.

We challenge any business jet to fly as fast.*

We challenge them to offer as much range.*

We challenge them to fly as efficiently.

We challenge them to match our wide-body comfort.

And now we'd like to tell you just how we've engineered the best business jet yet.

We bring you a new wing.

Our newly designed wing is why the Challenger will outperform all the rest. This advanced configuration delays shock waves. So drag, which is such a drag, doesn't drag as much. And lift is lifted. What's more, the wing weighs less. The result:

The Challenger can fly from Montreal to London in 5 hours and 29 minutes. Faster than a 747!
*Guaranteed speed and range.

Room to move while you're moving.

Stretch your legs and stoop no more — the Challenger is the first wide-body business jet. Almost a full foot wider than all the rest. With six feet of headroom and a flat floor.

The Lycoming ALF. It's the best engine going.

The Challenger's engine is the Lycoming ALF 502 Turbofan with a 5 to 1 high bypass ratio. (These fans make the Challenger efficient.) On a 1,000 nautical-mile trip it will burn 54% less fuel than the JetStar I and 20% less than the Falcon 50.

After you take off, we don't take off.

Our service and support is as disciplined as our engineering. There'll be Company Owned and Operated Service Centers. There'll be other Authorized Service Stations. And a year of computerized maintenance comes free.

But let us not forget the company that's behind all this. Canadair. Canadair has built over 3,800 aircraft, 580 of them supersonic.

For more information on the Challenger, formerly known by the drawing board name LearStar, write to Jim Taylor at Canadair Inc., P.O. Box 6087, Montreal, Canada H3C3G9. Or call him at (514) 744-1511.

canadair
Challenger

We challenge any business jet to match it.

COPYRIGHT CANADAIR

advertisements. In any case, the advertising agency would be paid 10 percent of the expenditures for media space.

To reinforce the print-advertising campaign, brochures and other sales literature were printed. An active direct mailing program could be used to solicit inquiries from potential prospects. The Challenger would also be promoted through press releases and press conferences, pilot seminars, photography, and newsletters, so that magazine articles would chronicle the progress of the Challenger engineering and marketing activities.

All competitors generally used this kind of promotion, but with varying degrees of intensity and success. The Falcon 50 marketers had used comparative advertising but had made no mention of the Challenger in their advertising. Canadair executives believed this obvious exclusion was an attempt by the Falcon 50 people to present the Challenger as unworthy of consideration. The JetStar II and Gulfstream II advertising did not use comparative approaches.

Exhibit 14 contains rate and reach data for full-page advertisements (the typical size in the large-jet business) in publications typically used by corporate-airplane advertisers. Media space could be purchased as early as the third week in July.

The Selling Task

Selling process should be tailored to customer.

President Kearns described the selling process this way:

> Each sale *is* different. It isn't like going to the military with a proposal and finding that you have just won a competition and the armed forces are going to buy 225 of your airplanes in the very first contract. It isn't like going to the airlines and selling batches of 10 or a dozen transports at once, all to the same specifications, with the same number of seats and the same colours inside and on the tail! It is, in fact, a matter of doing a complete presentation and proposal for every single prospect you approach. We start out with a prospect list made up of present business-aircraft operators plus other major corporations throughout the world who do not yet operate any aircraft. These organizations often have the need but we in the industry have yet to prove it to them. We gather data on the companies. We get an idea of their current needs by talking to their pilots, or we make some estimates if they have never operated an aircraft.
>
> We study the trips their people make, the points they routinely travel between, the longest and shortest flights, how many go on each trip, etc. Gradually a picture emerges to show us each prospect's specific requirement. And armed with that study, we approach the prospects with our sales proposals.

The first pitch was usually made to a firm's pilot. He generally had only veto power and not purchase power, but his acceptance was crucial. The salesman had to determine how much he would be able to use the pilot to make the sale. Mr. Taylor described three possibilities:

1. The pilot is strongly in your favour. He would act like an in-house salesman for you.
2. The pilot is unsure. The first task is to move him to neutral and then improve his and management's attitudes.

EXHIBIT 14 Print advertising rate data

Publication	Edition	Circulation (000s)	Distribution	Full page (1 time)	Half page	Frequency discount 7 times	Frequency discount 13 times
The Wall Street Journal	Eastern	606	Daily	$14,101	$ 7,050		
	Midwest	458		11,366	5,683		
	West	289		7,958	3,534		
	Southwest	168		4,049	2,024		
	North America	1500		36,265	18,132		
Business Week	International	59	Weekly	$ 2,450			
	European	31		1,710			
	Northeast	218		6,180			
	Midwest	182		5,120		10%	5%
	Pacific Coast	131		3,640			
	Southwest	51		1,480			
	Southeast	66		1,900			
	North America	738		9,000			
Fortune	North America	600	Biweekly	$13,710			
	Eastern	201		7,000		8%	4%
	Midwestern	159		5,130			
	Southeastern	60		2,610			
	Southwestern	48		2,210			
	Western	115		3,820			
	International	70		4,020			
	European	46		3,070			
Forbes	North America	665	Monthly	$10,990		7%	4%

Publication	Edition	Circulation (000s)	Distribution	Full page (1 time)	Frequency discount 3 times	Frequency discount 5 times	Frequency discount 7 times	Frequency discount 13 times
Dun's Review	Eastern	90	Monthly	$3,405				
	Central	86		2,665	7%	6%	5%	
	Southern	32		1,515				
	Western	40		1,160				
	All	248		5,405				
Aviation Week and Space Technology	All North America	97	Weekly	$4,343	2.5%	1.8%		4%
Business and Commercial Aviation	All North America	50	Monthly	$2,850		11%		6%
Flight International*	All	47	Weekly	$1,670		6%		6%
Interavia*	All	3	Monthly	$ 390	14%	22%		

Notes: * International circulation.
[1] All rates are noncontract rates.
[2] All rates are black and white ads.

Source: Standard Rate and Data Service.

3. The pilot is against the product right off, clearly the least-preferred situation. The first task here is to cool him off and try to get to the chief executive officer and sell him first.

The salesman had to be very perceptive in assessing to what degree the influencers on the selling decision would be involved, and finding out who exactly would make the final decision.

Prospects were identified with the assistance of a *Business and Commercial Aviation*[11] study that measured the impact of company aircraft in the U.S. top 1000 industrials as compiled by *Fortune* magazine.

This summary of the business performance of the Fortune 1,000 industrials showed that the aircraft operators, for whatever reason, were more efficient. The 514 aircraft-operating companies controlled 1,778 aircraft in 1975, an increase of 125 over 1974. This study concluded that:

> . . . nearly one half of the nation's biggest corporations are not operators even though their dollar volume of business indicates a cash flow that would support capital equipment such as an aircraft. In some cases, the nature of a firm's activities precludes the need for travel to locations not well served by public transportation; for others, the scheduling flexibility and effective utilization of personnel afforded by business aviation is not a strong incentive in the firm's type of business endeavors. But there are many corporations, we suspect, where the concept of business aircraft still is not appreciated or fully understood, and it is in this area that a greater knowledge of corporate aviation is needed.[12]

Hence, part of the selling task involved giving a potential customer an education in the advantages of corporate-owned aircraft in general before making a pitch for a particular model.

Another study identified companies owning the most expensive and largest fleets in the United States (Table 6).

TABLE 6 The most expensive corporate fleets

Company	Number of airplanes	Fleet value ($ millions)
Coca-Cola	5	$17.2
3M Co.	7	16.2
Rockwell International	21	15.6
Mobil	28	14.4
IBM	9	13.2
Atlantic Richfield	20	13.0
General Motors	14	12.8
United Technologies	14	12.3
Exxon	16	11.3
Tenneco	26	11.1
ITT	13	10.9
Shell	24	9.7

---

[11] Arnold Lewis, "Business Aviation and the Fortune 1,000," *Business and Commercial Aviation*, December 1978, pp. 1–4.

[12] Ibid.

TABLE 6 *(concluded)*

Company	Number of airplanes	Fleet value ($ millions)	
Diamond Shamrock	3	9.0	3
Gannett	4	8.9	2·2
General Dynamics	5	8.8	1·7
U.S. Steel	4	8.8	2·2
Conoco	19	8.7	
Texaco	8	8.3	
Time	9	8.2	
Johnson & Johnson	7	8.1	
Marathon Oil	14	8.0	

Data: Aviation Data Service Inc.

The People behind the Selling Task

Mr. James Taylor, 55, had been hired by Canadair in April 1976 to market the Challenger concept to the corporate market. Mr. Taylor's fascination with aircraft went back many years. His father had been a test pilot in both World War I and World War II. James Taylor had scored successes for the Cessna Aircraft Corp. and the French-based Dassault-Brequet Aircraft Corp. When Mr. Taylor joined Dassault in 1966, the "Fan Jet Falcon 20" soon became the industry sales leader in terms of both units and dollars. In 1966, Lear had sold 33 jets worldwide through 200 dealers, but in 1967, Mr. Taylor and his four salesmen sold 45 Falcon 20s in North America without the assistance of any dealers.

Mr. Taylor believed in direct sales rather than a dealer network because, as he put it: "It is a narrowly defined market. When I sell direct, I have better control over hiring, training, the territory, and the price. I like to bring prospects in for seminars, take a mock-up to key cities, and make extensive use of direct mail."

Joining Cessna in March 1969, he became the architect behind the highly successful "Citation" marketing and product-support programs which transformed the aircraft into the world's most successful business jet in its initial four years of production.

Mr. Taylor brought three key people with him to Canadair. Mr. Bill Juvonen had been with Mr. Taylor on three previous marketing programs including the Falcon 20 and the Citation. He became the vice president of sales responsible for Canada and the United States west of the Mississippi. Mr. Dave Hurley had spent five years with Cessna and had worked with Mr. Taylor on two programs. He became the vice president of sales responsible for the eastern half of the United States. Barry Smith had been the director of corporate marketing services for Atlantic Aviation, a company that serviced and distributed such corporate jets as the Gulfstream II, the Hawker-Siddely 125 and the Westwind. He had later worked for James Taylor in the same capacity on the successful Cessna Citation program. Mr. Taylor immediately hired him as vice president, marketing services. Mr. Smith would be responsible for advertising, direct mail, and all the "inside" marketing services. These four men made up the marketing team that would have to sell 50 Challengers before September 30th, 1976.

Final Question

The Challenger's design was undergoing constant modification. Mr. Taylor described the chief engineer, Mr. Halton, as "the most open-minded engineer I've ever met. For example, one of our customers suggested an APU (auxiliary power unit) system to assure power to the cabin electricals in flight. Harry designed in the APU system. Similarly, traditional aircraft use DC electricals but there are customer advantages in using AC. Harry put in AC. When Harry cannot accommodate one of our design suggestions, he always has good reasons and he takes the time to tell us. Normally, a chief pilot would not want you talking to his boss, but with the Challenger, some pilots not only are talking to their bosses, they are relaying information to us and to them." However, it was time to finalize the design and move ahead on a production system that would produce 80 aircraft per year.

Although Mr. Taylor had been very successful using a direct sales approach, other companies made extensive use of dealer networks, particularly in foreign countries. The "five percenters" (agents) in foreign countries also raised the issue of controlling their selling practices, especially in countries where mordida[13] was almost a standard practice.

The pricing strategy and promotion strategy would have to provide fairly rapid market penetration. Advertising and service expenditures already comprised $16 million of the investment budget; changes in these expenditures would have to promise compensating paybacks. There had to be a high probability that the proposed marketing plan would deliver the sales forecast for the Challenger. Mr. Taylor smiled and commented wryly to his aides: "This is going to have to be the biggest selling job in history. I think we can count on working 6 days a week, 14 hours a day, from now until September 30."

Two manufacturers were rumoured to be looking at the Challenger statistics to see how best to compete with this wide-body turbofan. Messrs. Taylor, Halton, and Kearns sat down on the morning of July 4, 1976, to review the Challenger strategy for the next three months and the longer term.

---

[13] Mordida represents payments to government officials in return for favors.

Index of Cases

This book has been set Linotron 202, in 10 and 9 point Times Roman, leaded 2 points. Part numbers are 33 point Helvetica Light and Part titles are 36 point Helvetica Medium. Chapter numbers are 30 point Helvetica Light and Chapter titles are 24 point Helvetica Medium. Case numbers are 24 point Helvetica Light and Case titles are 30 point Helvetica Medium. The size of the overall type page is 35 by 47½ picas.